A PERSONAL PERSPECTIVE

AUSTRALIA AND AUSTRALIANS

What we are and why

P.J.S. HASKER

Copyright © P.J.S. Hasker 2024

All rights reserved. This publication is copyright. Apart from fair dealing for the purposes of private study, research, criticism or review permitted under the Copyright Act, no part of this work may be stored or reproduced by any process without prior written permission. However, the author agrees to the citing of material in this document provided there is due acknowledgement of the source and that the contents are not used maliciously or out of context. Enquiries should be made to the publisher.

First published 2024

P.J.S. Hasker
36 Cosmic Street,
Robertson, Queensland, Australia 4109

 A catalogue record for this work is available from the National Library of Australia

ISBN: 978-0-646-89777-6

Typeset in Times New Roman 12pt

Cover design by Rachel Li

Back cover images, clockwise from top:
1. Vintage engraving of First Peoples of Australia, 19th Century. Source: duncan1890, iStockphoto.com
2. Tasmania Probation Station. Source: Mary Evans Picture Library, prints-online.com
3. Prospectors panning for gold. Source: benoit, iStockphoto.com
4. Australian cottage. Source: Rachel Li
5. Soldiers paying respect. Source: kanyakits, iStockphoto.com
6. Post-World War II immigration. Source: Rachel Li, 2024

Disclaimer: The author makes no representations or warranties about the accuracy, reliability, completeness or suitability for any particular purpose of any material in this publication.

The author does not consider or pretend that this document is an academic disquisition but rather an attempt to present a montage of facts and ideas to provoke serious reflection on who and what is an Australian. The author makes no claim to originality but hopes his approach to the topic is found interesting and some readers find his effort worthwhile.

The author has not referenced the document in the customary way except to include the source of material drawn upon in a list headed Readings; italics are used for quoted text. The source of many images is missing. Insufficient access to resources, time and drafting skills limited what the author could accomplish. Much of the information was sourced from the Internet. Referencing of this material was overlooked, especially with relation to websites interrogated. The author apologises for this lack of acknowledgement and any error of fact; deception was not on his agenda.

The author has made every effort to contact copyright holders for permission to reproduce material used in this book. Any person or organisation who may have been overlooked should contact the author.

Dedication
To Vernon
Amicus Certus In Re Incerta Cernitur

Vernon Hill is a true Australian though born an Englishman. He arrived in Australia on 9 June 1959 after driving a battered old 1952 VW Beetle from England to Mumbai (Bombay), where he boarded the SS Stratheden bound for Fremantle. Settling in Brisbane he completed studies in physiotherapy and later medicine. After several years of service in regional hospitals he joined the Spinal Unit at Princess Alexandra Hospital, where I first encountered him. In 1988, he assumed the role of Director, a position he held until his retirement in 2000.

Vernon is mentally and physically highly energetic and creative, which is evident in both his medical work and personal life. His diverse range of interests includes wheelchair sport, cricket, environmental restoration, woodturning, writing poetry and taxidermy. His generous spirit extends widely, as seen in his application of knowledge and skills to aid communities affected by devastating earthquakes in Armenia (1990), Pakistan (2005) and Nepal (2016). Although the term 'gentleman' may be considered old-fashioned or even obsolete, it is a fitting description for this generous and dedicated man.

The Bush

GIVE us from dawn to dark
Blue of Australian skies,
Let there be none to mark
Whither our pathway lies.

Give us when noontide comes
Rest in the woodland free—
Fragrant breath of the gums,
Cold, sweet scent of the sea.

Give us the wattle's gold
And the dew-laden air,
And the loveliness bold
Loneliest landscapes wear.

These are the haunts we love,
Glad with enchanted hours,
Bright as the heavens above,
Fresh as the wild bush flowers.

James Lister Cuthbertson (1851-1910)

Preface

Towards the end of the twentieth century an 11 year-old Chinese school girl ambushed me with a question: what is an Australian? I had no answer, not even a glib throw-away line, for the question is Gordian with no simple answer. After much thought and fruitless questioning of fellow Australians, I settled on a list of qualities that have evolved in those largely of European origin, who have inhabited this continent over the past 200 years. These qualities are as follows:

- To speak Australian English: perhaps one or more other languages as well.
- Direct: no-nonsense approach to life and people.
- Healthy disregard for (not intimidated by) those in authority.
- Friendly, mateship, helpful: readiness to help others.
- Willing to give anything 'a go'.
- Flexible: not put off by changes or things going wrong.
- Resourceful: able to use initiative and resources at hand.
- Practical: tough muddy boots; no-nonsense; laid back.
- Sense of a 'fair go'.
- Sympathy for the loser or underdog (dislike of 'tall poppies' – exception being sportsmen/women).
- Zany humour: used in friendship but also to prick swollen egos, pretentious behaviour, etc.
- Democratic attitude (welcomes the opposition).
- Egalitarian (not greatly stratified by caste, class, religion, employment).
- Doesn't stand on dignity.
- An affinity with 'the bush'.

There is nothing unique about any of these characteristics when taken individually. What is unique and sets the Australian apart is to find many or all of them in a population. What was it that instilled these characteristics in Australians, more specifically Australians born or arriving here up until the 1960s? In the course of answering this question I shall include answers to questions foreign students often ask about aspects of Australian life and culture. I shall also mention members of my family when relevant – for my forebears arrived in Australia 200 years ago. They were among the first European immigrants to come to Australia and my story is mainly the story of the European settler; non-European immigration began mainly in the 1970s.

I include information on my forebears not as a family history but to add authenticity to what I have written and to honour some of my ancestors. They provide real-life examples of how early immigrants (including convicts) coped with the challenges posed by this new land and rose to fill distinguished roles and become highly regarded by the communities in which they lived. Also, when discussing nationhood, I underscore the importance of narratives in fostering national unity. Each of us possesses our unique story, and the intertwining of these narratives shapes the tapestry of our national identity. By way of example, this is my story.

My thesis is that these characteristics evolved over time as challenges of all kinds were met and overcome. I seek to follow a common thread in answering the question this girl posed but, for reasons given above, wander off course at times. When considering the common thread, the reader should keep in mind the following assertions:

1. The vast landmass that is the continent of Australia has been a major factor in shaping who we Australians are. Consequently, I shall talk about both the land and its people for they are intertwined – how the land forged the people and how the people shaped the land.

2. When Europeans arrived here they found the land already occupied by a people who had lived on the continent for 60,000 years and had the oldest continuous culture of any people on earth. These unquestionably *authentic* Australians had a vastly different relationship with the land from the affinity Europeans had with the land of their fathers and which they would attempt to follow in their new country.

3. An important evolutionary factor was a willingness of the European Newcomers to cast off the cloak of tradition. They set about building a totally new life, a life unfettered by the baggage of the past; in other words, their willingness to become a new people.

Little mention is made in this document about the people for whom Australia had been home for millennia, and were *ipso facto* Australian; telling how this collection of characteristics evolved is very much the story of the European Newcomers. It must be said the story of those who were already here is largely untold and their contribution to building this nation is inestimable.

The who and what we are today as a people and a nation is open to debate as is where we are going, issues which are the focus of interest in the section titled *Quo vadimus*. The approach taken when considering nationhood draws upon the interpretation expounded by the French scholar Ernest Renan in his 1882 lecture *What is a Nation* – an interpretation that seems most fitting for today's Australia, given the diversity of its population.

Considerable, some may regard as excessive, attention is given to Australia's part in World War I (WWI) and World War II (WWII), mainly because of their defining nature and the emergence of the ANZAC Spirit and partly because of the inclusion of family history and the reality of war in my formative years. Being born in September 1938 in the central Queensland coastal town of Rockhampton, the wailing of air-raid sirens and reveille calls were sounds of my early childhood. Many of my teachers had not long returned from the battlefield as had the long columns of marchers on ANZAC Day. To disregard these wars would render any notion of evolving Australianness virtually incomprehensible.

History is multi-layered. We have personal history, family history, community history and so on until that referred to as national history. History is a story and, like any good story, the underlying themes are grounded in the human condition and the narrator is no mere bystander but one blinkered by beliefs, limited knowledge and personal experience – and therefore incomplete or even worse biased. The lens through which I look is shaped to some extent by my ancestral past but mainly by my personal past. When I was 24 years of age, fate, in the guise of a horse-riding accident, committed me to a radically new life in a wheelchair. My choice was to embrace that new life or wither on the vine. I chose the former; the latter I believed negated the very meaning of life itself. It is with this bias that I approach the Australian story: one of releasing the shackles of the past – the personal transformation of convict or free-settler, migrant or indigenous inhabitant – a willingness to become a new people.

Australia is a 'work in progress'. The above thesis is, thereby, somewhat conjectural. Little attention is given to the vast changes rendered by post-1970s migration. This is my interpretation. It may not fit a specific individual but, like a statistic, I hope it will give an understanding of the forces that have shaped us until recently and issues that currently confront us as a nation.

Preface

Australia is a very ancient land and so I begin far back in time, not mythological time but geological time; a time long before lands such as China existed. The land that became the island continent of Australia is large (7.6 million km^2) and geologically very old.

The work is divided into two sections. The first and notably larger, titled *Quemadmodum eramus*, considers influences at play until the mid-20th century. It initially touches upon features such as geology, flora and fauna contributing to the uniqueness of the continent and the events leading to the completion of the world map by cartographers. It provides context for the smaller second section titled *Quo vadimus* which considers the current situation and issues surrounding national identity. It should be read only after careful, insightful reading of the preceding section.

Acknowledgements

I thank the late Tom McEwan, Ian Robinson, Malcolm Jones, Warren Hoey and my sister Philippa Franks, for reading earlier drafts and providing suggestions for enhancement.

I thank Rachel Li for her imaginative book cover and background designs for the dedication and section pages. Rachel arrived in Australia from Shandong Province in China in 2008 as a student to study graphic design. She has worked in the design industry since graduating, focusing mainly on marketing promotions.

I thank Gail Strong and Sam Brown for their photography and all who generously permitted me to use images displayed on Flickr, Unsplash and Wikimedia.

I especially thank Jin-jin Lete for her invaluable assistance in researching sources of maps and photographs, both in libraries and on the Internet, her computer assistance and reading the manuscript aloud to me, which led to editorial changes.

I thank David MacDonald for his knowledge and advice on family history.

I greatly appreciate the encouragement received from John and Libby Earwaker, Sim Hasker, Jill Hawke and Roy Ames.

Last but certainly by no means least I acknowledge Peta McDonald-Smith, not only for her understanding of the task at hand and her creativity in producing the product you hold in your hands, but also for her initiative, tolerance and patience.

P.J.S. Hasker
November 2024

Table of Contents

Preface v
Acknowledgements viii

Section One: *Quemadmodum eramus* 1

1 An Ancient Land 2
    Gondwana 2
    A new super-continent 2
    Gondwana breaks up 2
    Australia emerges 3
    Geology 3
    A flat land 3
    Spectacular landscapes 4
    Minerals, gemstones and gold 6
    Climate 7
    Rivers 9
    Fauna and flora 10
    Unique land – unique people 15

2 *Terra Australis* Revealed 16
    Who discovered Australia? 16
    The European navigators 16
    Cook takes possession 21
    Cook's 'discovery' 22

3 The First Australians 23
    An ancient people 23
    Aboriginal society 23
    Hunter–gatherers 24
    Use of fire 24
    Guides, bushmen, stockmen and trackers 25
    Spirituality – Dreaming and the Dreamtime 27
    Ancient art 28
    Modern art 30
    Contemporary art 31
    Alien cultures collide 32
    This land is our land 33
    Military service 36
    First Australians' legacy on the new Australian character 39

4 Convict Beginning 41
    Britain's unwanted 41
    The First Fleet 41
    Near starvation in an alien land 44
    A nightmare voyage 45
    Early convict life in New South Wales 46

Emancipation – a better life 48
Emancipists *vs* exclusives – convict life gets harsher 49
Ancestral arrival 51
Convict imprints 54

5 Currency Lads and Lasses 56

6 Explorers 59
Ancestral explorers 65
Aboriginal guides 66

7 An Alien Land 67
An alien inhospitable land 67

8 Gold 73
Half a century of gold-rushes 73
The diggers 74
All men are equal! 76
The miner's licence – a catalyst for rebellion 76
The diggers rebel – Eureka Stockade 77
Eureka legacy somewhat problematic 79
A new society 81
Gold near home 83

9 Bushrangers – Ned Kelly 85

10 Australia a Name – Australia a Nation 90
Six self-governing colonies 90
Colonial borders finalised 93
A progressive new society 93
Federation 93
An independent nation 95
National anthem, symbols and emblems 95
Australia's system of government 96
Federal tensions 98

11 Carving Up the Land 99
Squatters, selectors and dispossession 99
In the beginning 100
The early years 1790-1830 101
Squatting – Occupation of Crown land without legal title 102
Squatting made legal 103
Squatter's life 104
Squattocracy 104
Unlocking the lands 105
Selectors 105
Post-Federation closer settlement 106
Currency squatter 107
MacDonald – the frontiersman 108
Agrarian dream or nightmare 109

12 Immigration Pre-Federation 110
British institutions 110
Enlightened administrators 111
Involuntary migrants 1788-1830 112
Convict demographics 113

  Early free-immigrants 1830-1850 113
  Gender imbalance 114
  Long, expensive, tough ship's journey 115
  Arrival in Australia 115
  Reasons for migrating 116
  1850-1860 – Gold-rushes 116
  Immigration 1860-1900 117
  Irish presence 117
  Non-British migrants 118

13 Some Thorny Issues 119
  Emancipists *vs* exclusives 119
  'Skeletons in the cupboard' 119
  Religious and ethnic conflict 120
  Boom, bust and unions 121
  Anti-Asian sentiment 121

14 Immigration Post-Federation 123
  Restricted immigration – White Australia Policy 123
  Immigration WWI-WWII 123
  Early Post-WWII migrant boom 124
  Snowy River Scheme 125
  End of the White Australia Policy 126
  1970s-today: Humanitarian (Asylum seekers) 126
  1970s-today: Skilled migrants 127
  Demographic changes post–WWII 128
  Urban society 129
  Why choose Australia? 130
  Impacts of and concerns about immigration 131
  Pause and take breath 132

15 World War I – A Baptism of Fire 133
  First World War 133

16 Gallipoli 138
  The landing 139
  Withdrawal from Gallipoli 146
  Mutual respect 147
  Back to Egypt 148

17 Middle East Campaigns 149
  Western desert – Senussi 149
  Sinai Peninsula 150
  The charge at Beersheba 153
  Jerusalem by Christmas 154
  Jordan Valley – Spring and summer 1918 155
  Damascus – 'The Wild Ride' 157

18 Australian Light Horse 160
  Light horsemen cum airmen 160
  The light horsemen 161
  The horses 162

19 Light Horse Field Ambulance 166
  The 3rd Light Horse Field Ambulance 168
  Friend and foe 176

20 The Western Front..179
    The Somme – Fromelles, Pozieres, Mouquet Farm, Bullecourt 179
    Flanders 1917 183
    The Somme 1918..185
    Armistice 187
    Casualties on the Western Front 187
    Chinese presence..189

21 The Aussie Soldier 190
    Fierce fighters 190
    Puzzling Aussies 191
    Enterprising larrikins enjoy life..192
    Troublesome Aussies..192
    Australians' view of discipline...195
    Aussie soldiers not donkeys 196
    Not angels...196
    Last word..197

22 Second World War 199
    Global conflict 199
    Australia at war...201
    Second AIF 202
    Militia 202

23 North Africa 204
    Overview 204
    Siege of Tobruk 205
    El Alamein..207

24 Pacific War 210
    Malaya and Singapore 212
    Prisoners of Japanese..213
    Attacks on the Australian mainland..216

25 Kokoda 219
    The Track..219
    The soldiers 220
    The battles – The 39th – Kumusi to Isurava..222
    Retreat to Imita Ridge 228
    Back to Kokoda and the Buna-Gona-Sanananda beachhead 229
    Some final words 232

26 Australia Turns from Britain to America 234
    Americans in Australia...235

27 ANZAC Day 238
    More than remembrance...240
    ANZAC Day evolving..241
    The commemoration of ANZAC Day 243

28 Aussie Women...246
    Convict women and early colonial years...246
    Who were these free-women? 248
    The fate of single women 248
    Life in the bush..250

       Julia MacDonald – wife of P.F. MacDonald 253
       New found freedom, new woman 254

29 Isolation and Innovation 259
       The ends of the earth 259
       The Outback 259
       Outback survivors 260
       The Mailman 261
       QANTAS 261
       Royal Flying Doctor Service 262
       School of the Air 263
       Artistic portrayal 264
       The real Australia 265

30 *Terra Australis* Revisited 266

Section Two: *Quo vadimus* 269

31 How ya goin' mate? 270
       Soothsayers 270
       Naysayers – a centennial assessment 272
       Inferiority – a transplanted society 273
       Millennium Australia 273
       A troubled psyche – Aboriginal dispossession 274
       Letting in the light 275
       Confluence of the waters 276

32 Identity 278
       The self and belonging – acceptance 278
       To feel Australian – doubts about identity 278
       An Australian character 280

33 Nationhood 282
       A spiritual entity 282
       Shared experience 282
       Remembering and forgetting 283

34 Weaving a Grand Narrative 285
       The past – having done great deeds together 286
       The present – harmony 286
       The present – the desire to live together 287
       The present – invest in the heritage jointly received 287
       Relationships with the land 288

35 Reflections 291
       Inheritance 291
       Freedom, honesty, trust and the law 291
       Spirit of ANZAC 292
       To thrive 292

36 Where Are We Going? 294
       A unifying agency 294
       Belonging 294
       A blank sheet 295

Appendix 1: Asian Immigration to USA and Canada 297

Appendix 2: Montesquieu 298

Appendix 3: Territorial Imperative 299

Appendix 4: A Matter of Geography 300

Appendix 5: Civilisation 301

Appendix 6: Racism 303

Appendix 7: Qualifiers of Australianness 306

Appendix 8: The Holy Grail of Permanent Residency 307

Appendix 9: A New Life 308

Readings 309

Image and Illustration Credits 320

Glossary 343

About the Author 345

Section One

Quemadmodum eramus

Chapter 1
An Ancient Land

Gondwana

Australia is a very ancient land. The landmass that became the island continent of Australia existed as early as 600 million years ago. Together with the landmasses that now make up the continents of South America, Africa, Antarctica and the subcontinent of India, it was part of a super-continent called Gondwana. At that time the landmass that is now Eurasia existed only in bits and pieces.

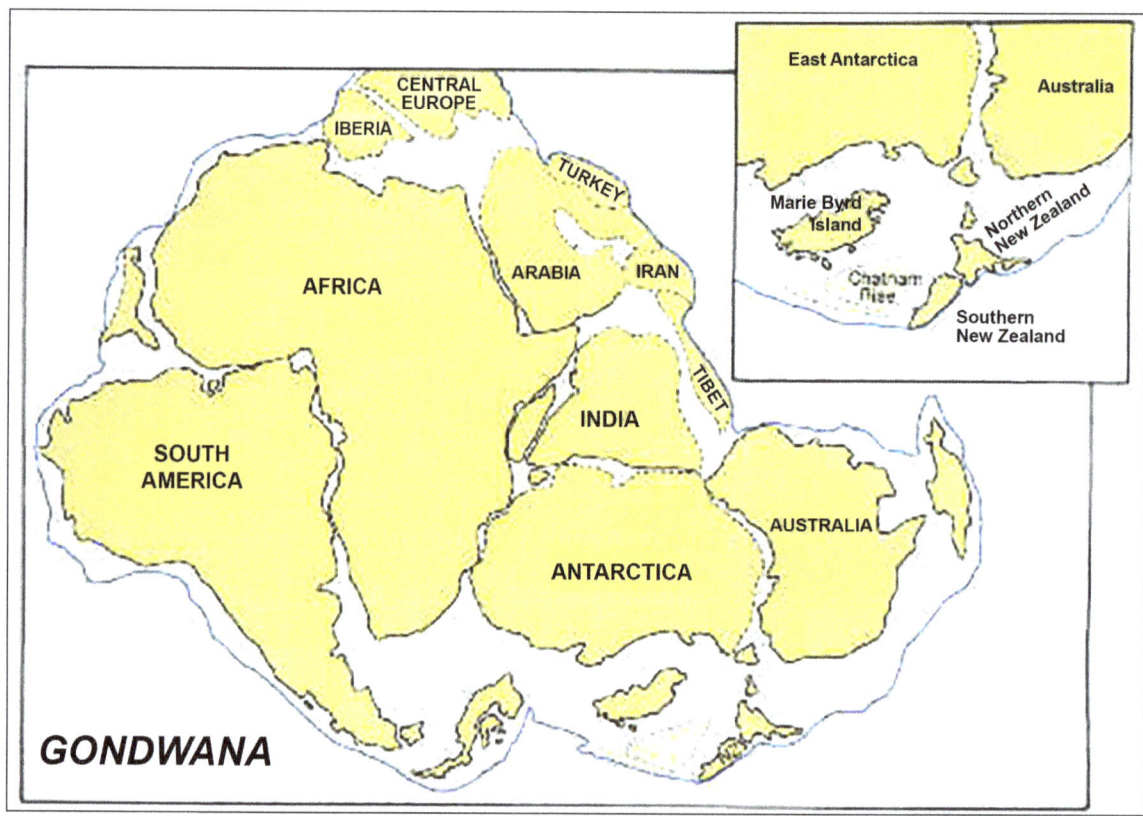

Gondwana. Source: Diseno creacion by Javier Diaz UNELLEZ-VPA 2014

A new super-continent

From 600 up to 280-225 million years ago Gondwana gradually merged with scattered blocks of continental crust to form a new super-continent called Pangea. At the end of this long period Pangea consisted of two principal land areas: Gondwana and another called Laurasia.

About 200-180 million years ago, when dinosaurs dominated the earth, Pangea began to break up into Laurasia in the north and Gondwana in the south.

Gondwana breaks up

Around 100 million years ago, Gondwana began to break up. What would become India and South America broke free and drifted northwards. Eventually, the Indian plate collided

Chapter 1: An Ancient Land

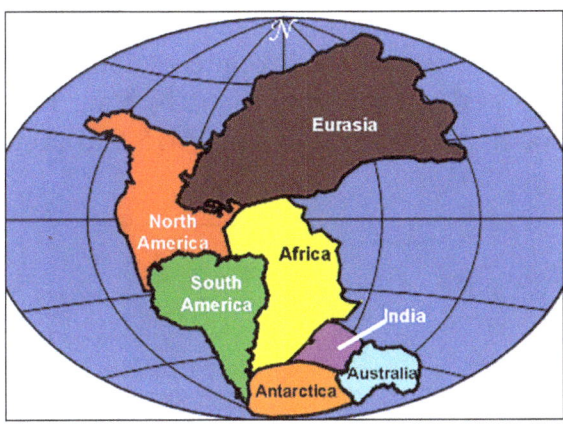

Pangea. Source: Daigle S (2022). *Puzzle Me Pangaea and the Seven Continents*

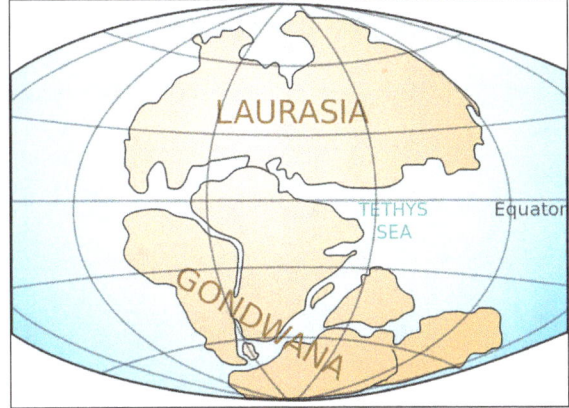

Laurasia-Gondwana 200 million years ago. Source: Kudling L, Wikimedia Commons

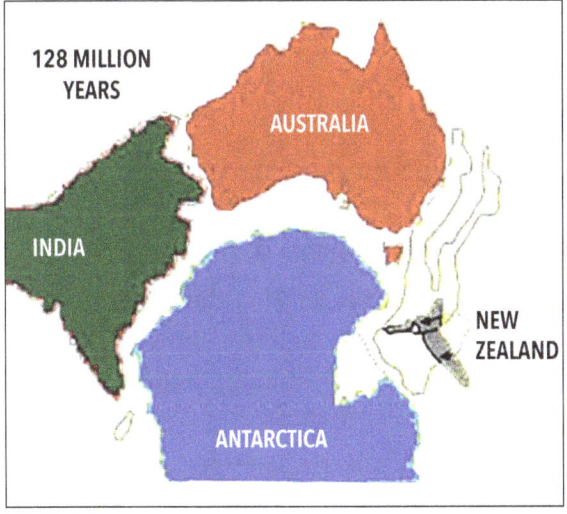

Gondwana splits. Source: Australian Antarctic Division

with Asia forming the Himalayas. The Indian plate continues to move northwards and is being shoved under the plate that supports Nepal and China. The result is the Himalayas are moving gently north-eastward and the mountain peaks are slowly getting higher.

Australia emerges

After the dinosaurs disappeared, about 85 million years ago, Australia broke away from Antarctica and began to drift northwards. Its journey from the cold polar regions towards the tropics was accompanied by dramatic changes in climatic conditions. During this journey the ocean levels rose and fell during periods of warmth and cold. Until recently, Australia has remained isolated from the rest of the world.

It is still moving northwards at around the rate fingernails grow and will collide with Southeast Asia within the next 30 million years.

Geology

Geologically, Australia has been very stable. There has been little buckling and folding of the earth's crust that has produced high mountain ranges or deep rifts elsewhere. This, together with the relative absence of glaciation and infrequent volcanic activity, has produced an older flatter landmass than for other continents, rich in mineral deposits but shallow in soil covering.

Australia's rocks are some of the earth's oldest, with some up to about five billion years old. The MacDonnell ranges in Central Australia are the oldest in the world.

This ancient continent has been more weathered and its soils more leached than any other area of comparable size anywhere in the world.

A flat land

Most of Australia's landscape consists of lowland plains that are flat or have low hills. About 87% of the total landmass is less than 500 m above sea level and 99.5% less than 1,000 m. The highest mountains are in the Great Dividing Range in the east of the continent. It runs from northern Queensland to southern Victoria. The Australian Alps are part of this larger range and contain Australia's highest mountain, Mt Kosciusko (2,228 m). Australia's lowest point, Lake Eyre, is 15 m below sea level and is close to the centre of the continent.

The flatness of the land had advantages when building the Trans-Australia railway, which runs east-west across southern Australia. On the 900 miles (1,440 km) centre section across the Nullabor Plain not one stream of water was crossed and no tunnel had to be built. This line contains the longest straight stretch of railway in the world: 297 miles (475 km) from near Ooldea to Loongana.

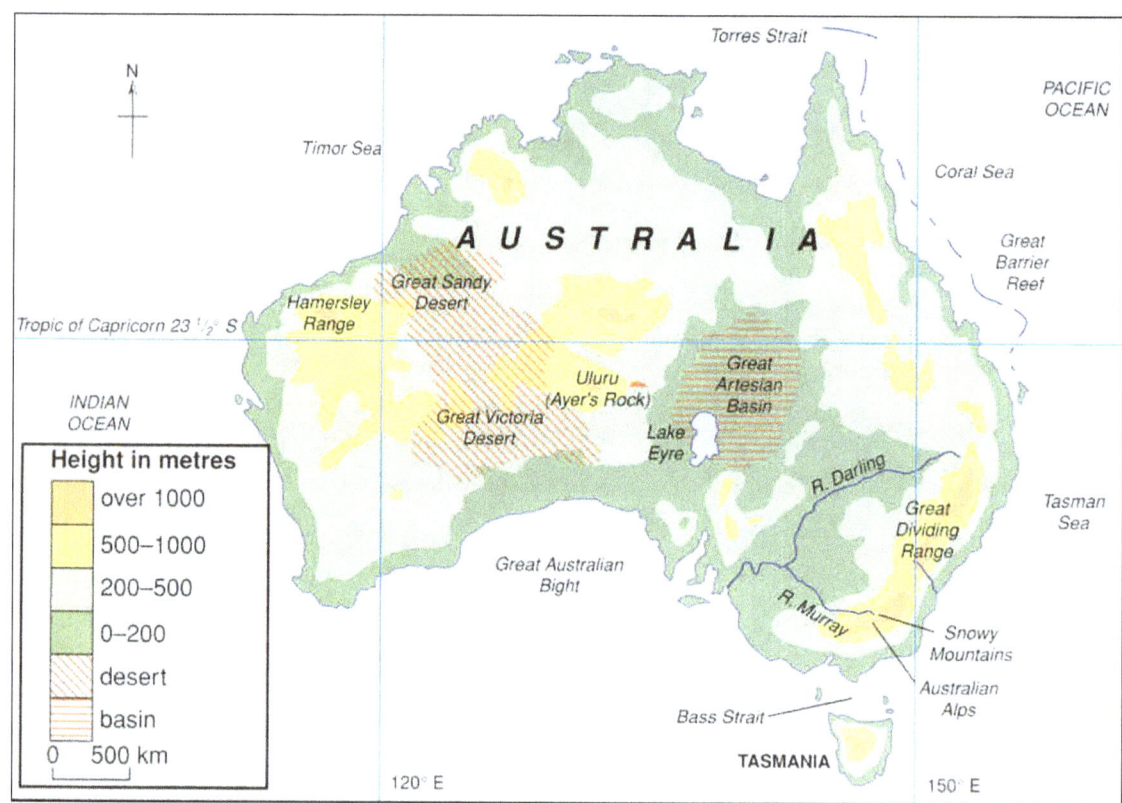

Elevation. Source: Bureau of Meteorology

Spectacular landscapes

Australia's comparative flatness does not mean it has no spectacular landscapes.

Uluru, the world's largest solitary rock, is one of Australia's most spectacular landforms. It is a huge 348 m high sandstone rock that rises almost vertically out of the surrounding flat desert plain. The sunlight gives it a different colour at different times of the day.

Wolfe Creek meteorite crater is the second biggest crater in the world. It is 880 m in diameter and the crater floor is 50 to 60 m below the rim, which rises 25 m above the surrounding flat desert land. Scientists consider it was formed when a 50,000 tonne meteorite crashed into the earth 300,000 years ago. The crater that was left was probably about 120 m deep.

Uluru, 2019. Source: Antoine Fabre, Unsplash

Wolfe Creek crater. Source: Tourism WA

Wilpena Pound is a huge natural amphitheatre in the southern Flinders Ranges of South Australia. This large basin-shaped structure ringed by cliffs covers an area of 83 km², and the interior measures 11 km x 8 km. Although it has a crater-like appearance, it is not a meteorite impact crater. The structure was originally a huge dome pushed up by earth movements about 650 million years ago. The floor of the Pound is about 200 m above the surrounding plain, and the outer ring of cliffs rising 500 m from the plain is all that remains of much taller mountains surrounding the Pound, since eroded by many thousands of metres. The highest prominence is St Marys Peak, at 1,170 m above sea level.

The Twelve Apostles are huge limestone rock formations that rise majestically from the Southern Ocean. They were separated from the cliff shore by the action of wind and waves over the past 10-20 million years.

The Three Sisters is a set of three closely-spaced, steep-sided rock pillars, on the edge of the Blue Mountains Plateau. Their name is derived from an Aboriginal legend about three sisters, Meeni, Wimlah and Gunedoo, who were turned to stone for their misdeeds.

Other spectacular landforms and landscapes that are popular tourist destinations include Kata Tjuta (The Olgas), Katherine Gorge, Sydney Harbour, Cradle Mountain, Jenolan Caves, Great Barrier Reef, Undara Lava Tubes and K'gari (Fraser Island), the largest sand island in the world.

Wilpena Pound. Source: Jayne Vaughton, Words on Wheels

Twelve Apostles, Great Ocean Road, Port Campbell National Park. Source: Trevor Kay, Unsplash

The Three Sisters. Source: Stefan Jürgensen, Flickr

Minerals, gemstones and gold

The geological processes that have taken place during the Australian continent's long history have made it rich in coal, minerals such as iron ore and bauxite, gemstones and gold.

The opal, Australia's national gemstone, is almost unique to Australia, which produces 95% of the world's precious opal. A very special series of geographical and climatic phenomena must coincide for opal to form. These special criteria occurred in what are now the great desert regions of Central Australia. Opals are often referred to as the *fire of the desert* because of a fiery display of all colours of the rainbow. An Aboriginal legend states the colours of the opal were created when the rainbow fell to earth.

Iron ore – haematite. Source: Learning Geology

Australian bauxite, Weipa. Source: The Australian Aluminium Council

Opals. Source: Brisbane Opal Museum

Newland Coal Mine dragline. Source: Leighton Holdings

Australian pink diamonds, sourced from Argyle mine. Source: Jewellery World Magazine

The Welcome Stranger replica, largest nugget found in Australia. Source: Dunolly Museum

Climate

Apart from Antarctica, Australia is the world's driest continent. Its most notable climatic feature is a high year-to-year (decade-to-decade) rainfall variability. More than any other landmass, Australia is marked by infrequency and unreliability of rainfall. About one-third of the continent is hot and dry, having a total annual rainfall less than 250 mm. Almost 20% of available land is some form of desert. The wettest areas are in the east, where there is a tropical monsoon climate.

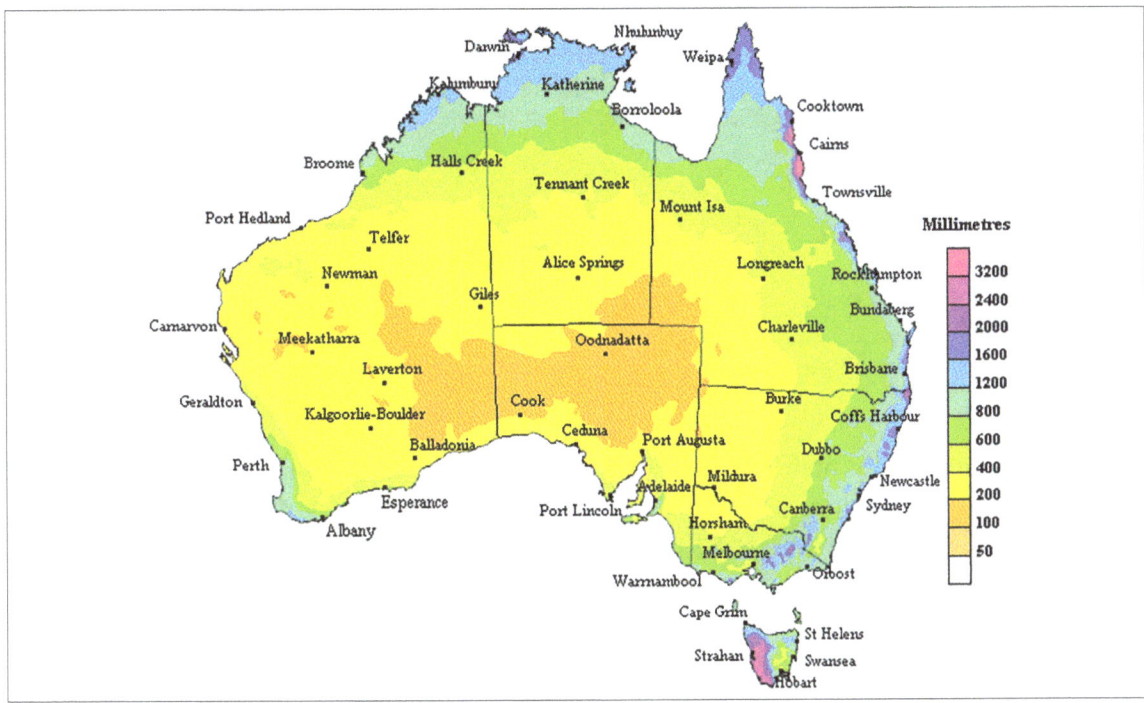

Average annual rainfall (1961 to 1990). Source: Bureau of Meteorology

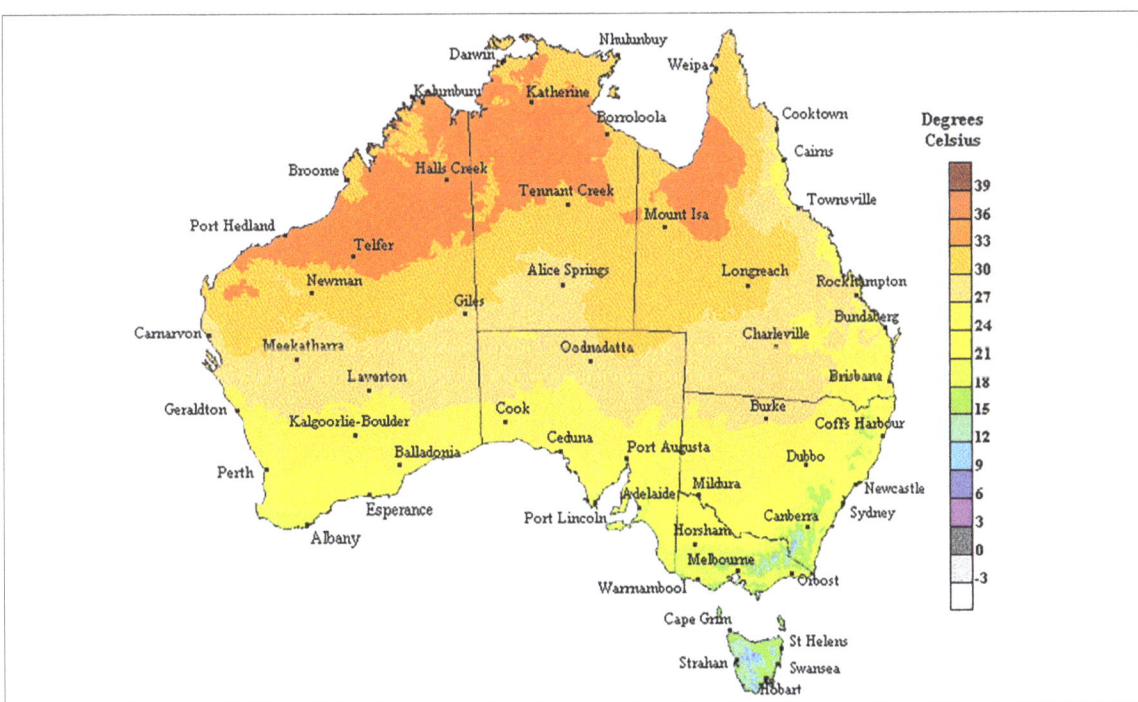

Average annual maximum temperature (1961 to 1990). Source: Bureau of Meteorology

The island continent of Australia features a wide range of climatic zones, from the tropical regions of the north, through the arid expanses of the interior, to the temperate regions of the south. The Tropic of Capricorn, which separates the Torrid Zone from the Temperate Zone, runs through Rockhampton on the east coast of Queensland.

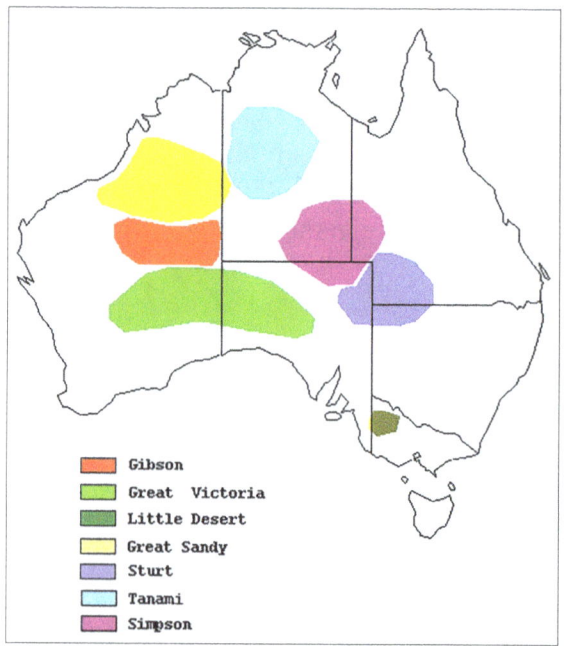 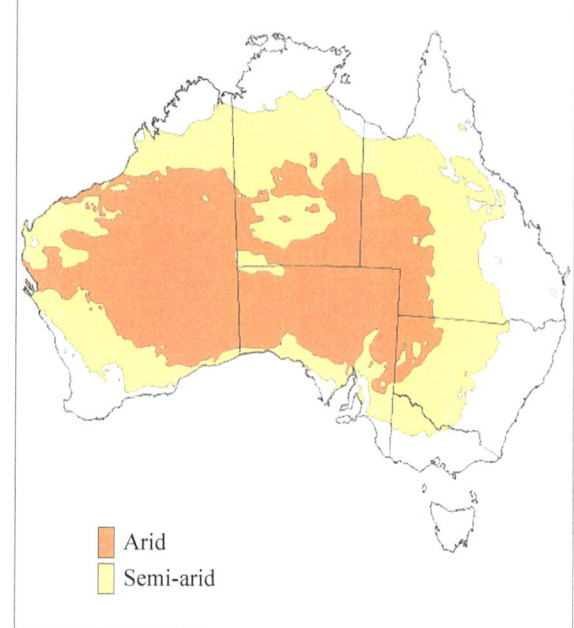

Deserts. Source: Bureau of Meteorology

Climate zones (arid and semi-arid). Source: Bureau of Meteorology

Seasonal fluctuations in both rainfall and temperature can be large in parts of the country. In northern Australia, temperatures are warm throughout the year, with a 'wet' season from approximately November to April (inclusive), when almost all the rainfall occurs, and a 'dry' season from May to October. Further south, temperature becomes more important in defining seasonal differences and rainfall is more evenly distributed throughout the year, reaching a marked winter peak in the south-west and along parts of the southern fringe.

Prolonged heat waves, with a number of successive days over 40°C, are relatively common in summer over much of inland Australia, as well as parts of the north-west coast.

It is not surprising that most Australians live in the south-east, where the climate is Mediterranean, i.e. hot and dry in summer and mild and wetter in winter.

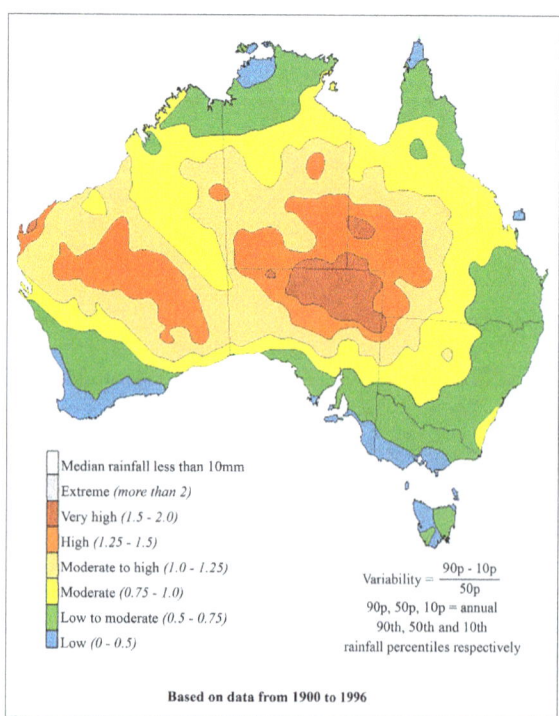 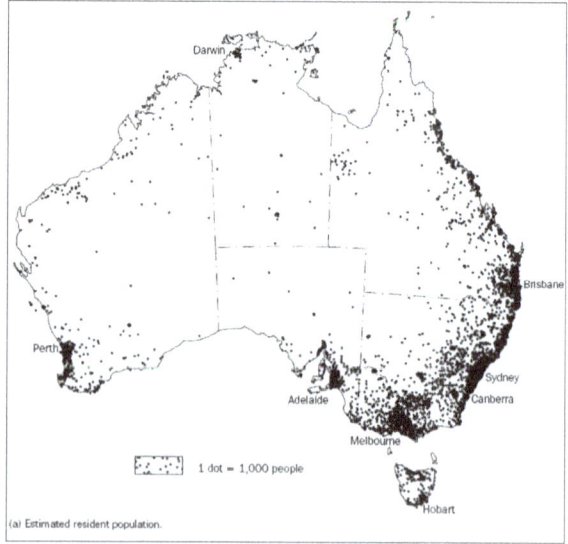

Climate variability (1900 to 1996). Source: Bureau of Meteorology

National, state and territory population, June 2023. Source: Australian Bureau of Statistics

Chapter 1: An Ancient Land

Rivers

The low mountain ranges and low erratic rainfall coupled with very high evaporation (particularly in inland Australia) lead to low surface water flows and seasonal river systems. The discharge of Australia's rivers into the sea is by far the lowest from all continents. Australia has no great rivers like the Yangtse, Ganges, Mekong, Amazon, Mississippi, Congo, Nile, Rhine and Danube. Most rivers rise in the Great Dividing Range and flow east a relatively short distance to the sea. There are few rivers in the central part of Australia because there is so little rain. Most rivers and small streams dry up for several months each year.

Coopers Creek in flood.
Source: Unknown

Australia's longest river, the Murray, rises in the Australian Alps and flows west. Its chief tributaries are the Murrumbidgee and Darling rivers. The length of the Murray together with the Darling River is 3,718 km. Except for northern Queensland, all rivers flowing west from the Great Dividing Range end up in the Murray. The Murray-Darling Basin comprises about one-seventh of the Australian continent, a huge catchment basin by any standards, but neither the Murray nor the Darling is a major river on a global scale. Water flows in the Murray have decreased to critical levels due to reduced rainfall and excessive use for irrigation.

Murray-Darling Basin. Source: Jack Crawford, July 2021. *How capitalism is killing the Murray-Darling Basin*

Increasing the flow of the Murray River was one of the objectives of the Snowy River Scheme that was begun in 1949 and completed in 1974. Water from the easterly-flowing Snowy River was diverted through tunnels to the western side of the Australian Alps to join the headwaters of the Murray. However, this has had a detrimental effect on the Snowy River. The New South Wales and Victorian governments agreed to restore 21% of the original flow to the Snowy River by the year 2010. Eventually, the river flows will be restored to 28%, which is the minimum amount that scientists suggest the river needs to return it to good health.

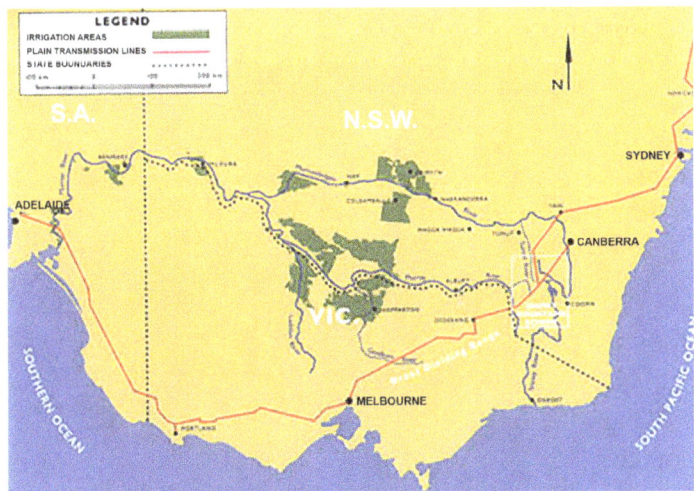

Snowy River Scheme – *Snowy! Power of a Nation*. Source: Snowy Mountains Hydro-electricity Authority, 1993, via Powerhouse Museum

Fauna and flora

The Australian continent's 75 million years of isolation from the rest of the world, its slowly drying climate and generally poor soils have created a unique fauna and flora. Two hundred and fifty of the 295 species of Australian mammals (including marsupials) are found only in Australia. About 710 of the 800 Australian reptiles are found nowhere else, and 80-90% of the insects and arachnids are unique to Australia. Of the 18,000 species of flowering plants found in Australia, 15,000 are found nowhere else in the world.

The increasing dryness and generally poor soils favoured plants and animals which could make the most of available food sources, survive poor seasons and breed up quickly when rain was received. Vegetation of the arid interior has adapted to dry conditions and responds quickly when rainfall is received. Very occasionally, favourable conditions can bring heavy rains to many parts of the normally arid to semi-arid region of inland Australia, with falls of up to 400 mm over a few days being recorded in the most extreme cases. Such heavy rainfalls often lead to widespread flooding and a subsequent short-lived 'blooming' of the desert regions.

However, despite the richness and diversity of Australia's animals and plants, none is suitable for domestication; the dingo is considered to have arrived in Australia about 4,000 years ago.

Dingo (*Canis lupus*). Source: David Clode, Unsplash

Mammals

When reflecting on the strangeness of Australian animals compared with fauna in the rest of the world, Charles Darwin considered it was almost as though two distinct Creators had been at work.

Mammals that reached Australia before its separation from Antarctica were all marsupials, i.e. animals that give birth to dependent young, which are kept in pouches on their mother's body for the early part of their lives. In other parts of the world marsupials were gradually replaced by placental mammals that give

Kangaroo (*Macropus* spp.). Source: James Wainscoat, Unsplash

Koala (*Phascolarctos cinereus*). Source: Di Weng, Unsplash

Wombat (*Vombatidae*). Source: Betty Chen, Unsplash

Marsupial lion (*Thylacoleo carnifex*). As big as an African lion, this ferocious marsupial predator was armed with sharp, slicing teeth and long thumb spikes. Source: Peter Schouten

Diprotodon optatum. The largest marsupial that ever lived. As big as a rhinoceros, it probably fed on grass and the leaves of bushes and small trees. Source: Australian Museum

birth to fully developed young. Well known marsupials include kangaroos, wallabies, koalas and wombats.

Up until about 40,000 years ago very large animals, or megafauna, roamed Australia. They included giant marsupials, birds, reptiles and monotremes. Why they became extinct is open to conjecture – both climate change and the arrival of humans have been suggested as causes.

Australia is home to one of the world's most unusual animals, the duckbilled platypus or ornithorhynchus. It lays eggs like a reptile but is classed as a mammal because it suckles its young.

Platypus (*Ornithorhynchus anatinus*). Source: Ronald Bradford, Unsplash

Giant kangaroo (*Procoptodon goliah*). This huge kangaroo stood up to 3 m tall. It fed by picking the leaves off bushes and small trees. Source: Australian Museum

Birds

Australia is renowned for its bird life such as the kookaburra (laughing jackass), cockatoos and parrots. The emu (Widji), Australia's largest native bird, is the second largest flightless bird in the world. It grows up to 2 m tall and can run at speeds up to 50 km/h on long, powerful legs. Prior to the arrival of Europeans emus were found throughout the Australian mainland but their range has been reduced by white settlement. Adult birds are usually found in pairs or small parties. The male does all the parenting. The cassowary, which inhabits rainforests in north Queensland, is also a large flightless bird.

Reptiles, insects, spiders and termites

Australia has a wide variety of reptiles, insects, spiders and termites.

Snakes

Australia is home to 28 dangerously venomous snakes, including taipans, death adders, tiger snakes, brown snakes and copperheads plus the less toxic black snakes. The Coastal Taipan grows to 2.9 m and has the third most toxic terrestrial snake venom known, while the Inland Taipan grows to 2.3 m and is regarded as the most toxic snake in the world.

Kookaburra (*Dacelo* spp.). Source: John Gould (1804-81), *The Birds of Australia*, 1840-48

Emu (*Dromaius novaehollandiae*). Source: Christian Bass, Unsplash

Carpet snake (*Morelia spilota*), Australia Zoo. Source: Yang Shuai (Nixie), 2009

Coastal taipan (*Oxyuranus scutellatus*). Source: David Clode, Unsplash

However, there are also non-venomous snakes of which the carpet snake, a python, grows up to 4 m long, though most do not exceed 2.5 m. They live almost everywhere in Australia, eating small animals such as rats, possums and birds. Smaller snakes prefer to eat lizards. Large pythons occur in northern Australia and can grow to much greater lengths.

Insects

Australia is also home to many types of spiders. Funnel web spiders are more common in southern Australia and can deliver toxic bites. Redbacks are one of the most dangerous spiders in Australia. Their venom is toxic to humans and bites cause severe pain.

Redback spider (*Latrodectus hasselti*). Source: Peter Firus, Wikimedia Commons

Witchetty grub (*Endoxyla leucomochla*), Alice Springs, Central Australia. Source: Michael J. Barritt, 2010

Witchetty grubs, the larvae of moths and beetles that bore into and eat the wood and sap of trees and shrubs, were an important part of the First Australians' diet. The grubs (up to 15 cm long) were eaten raw or cooked. They taste like scrambled eggs and peanut butter with a crispy chicken skin coating.

Termites

Huge termite mounds, like military tank traps, can be seen over much of the northern part of Australia. Termites can destroy wooden structures and usually Australians take great care to protect their houses via physical or chemical barriers. Some species of termites build 'magnetic' mounds that are aligned east-west to reduce the absorption of heat.

Cathedral termite mound, 2.5 m, Litchfield National Park, NT. Source: Geoff Whalan, Flickr

Magnetic termite mounds, Litchfield National Park, NT. Source: Australian 4 Wheel Drive Rentals

Plants

Australia has a wide diversity of plants of all kinds. Until 20 million years ago it was covered by tropical or subtropical rainforest. As the continent cooled and dried, rainforest areas shrank and now occupy only a very small percentage of the continent. Now two main plant groups dominate the landscape – eucalypts (*Eucalyptus* spp.) and wattles (*Acacia* spp.) which are adapted to harsh conditions with seasonal, erratic and variable rainfall. Tea trees (*Leptospermum* spp.), which belong to the same family as eucalypts, are also widespread. The Waratah (*Telopea speciosissima*) is found nowhere else, being unique to southern Australia.

Eucalypts occur mostly in open forests and woodland. One species of eucalypt, *Eucalyptus regnans* or Mountain Ash, is the tallest hardwood tree in the world with specimens reaching 80 m or more in height. Some trees felled during the 19th century were measured at up to 114 m tall. Only the softwood Californian redwoods (*Sequoiadendron giganteum*) are taller.

Wattles range from small shrubs to tall trees. They grow throughout Australia but particularly in arid and semi-arid regions, where they tend to replace eucalypts as the dominant woodland species. The boab, a strange-looking tree, is native to Australia.

Golden wattle (*Acacia pycnantha*). Source: Australian National Botanic Gardens

Double trunk boab tree (*Adansonia gregorii*). Source: Birgit Bradtke, Outback Australia Travel Secrets

Clockwise from left: Manna gum (*Eucalyptus viminalis*). Source: Alan Couch, Flickr; Waratah (*Telopea speciosissima*). Source: Australian National Botanic Gardens; Golden wattle flower (*Acacia pycnantha*). Source: Australian National Botanic Gardens

Unique land – unique people

The vast distances of this dry, hot continent, its infertile soils and absence of animals and plants that could be domesticated plus the vagaries of fire, flood and drought have profoundly affected the moulding of the life and characteristics of Australia's human inhabitants.

Australia's first inhabitants, the Aboriginals, arrived from the nearby north about 60,000 years ago. Over time they learnt to survive by becoming part of and relating closely with the land and were left undisturbed to carry on their unique way of life for tens of thousands of years and their way of life changed little.

In contrast, over the past 8,000 years, lives of the inhabitants of Europe and Asia became increasingly complex and sophisticated. When Europeans arrived in Australia they could survive only by trying to conquer the land, as they did not possess the understanding of the land held by the original inhabitants. This required great resourcefulness, determination and courage.

Both Australia's original and more recent inhabitants have altered the land but in vastly different ways.

The British naval ship *Beagle* visited Australia in 1836, just half a century after Europeans arrived in Australia. In his journal of the voyage the young Charles Darwin closed his entries on Australia prophetically:

> *After several tedious delays from clouded weather, on the 14 March we gladly stood out of King Georges Sound on our course to Keiling Island. Farewell Australia. You are a rising child and doubtless some day will reign a great princess in the south but you are too great and ambitious for affection yet not great enough for respect.*

Chapter 2
Terra Australis Revealed

Who discovered Australia?

Who discovered Australia? It was certainly not Captain Cook. An ancient people had inhabited it for 60 millennia and a fifth continent was a land known to the maritime civilisations of the ancient world under a variety of names:

- *Sinim* or Queen of the South to the Hebrews;
- The southern land of *Chui Hiao* to the Chinese; and
- *Uru* to the Sumerians and Peruvians.

The Greeks in Homer's time (800 BC) referred to a great southern continent as *Ausio*, the great south land of milk and honey. The Greeks would have obtained this knowledge of world geography from earlier civilisations.

The Roman historian Lucian (ca. 150 AD) described an animal with very short front legs and very long hind legs, and a pouch to carry its young. Most likely this was a description of a kangaroo.

Certainly Chinese and other Asian seafarers were frequent visitors to Australia for centuries before the earliest European voyages into the Pacific. However, it was the Europeans who finally sought out the great south land. By the end of the 1400s, European countries such as Portugal and Spain were developing new methods of building ships, navigating and charting. They wanted riches, spices, territory and Christian converts and their seafarers undertook voyages of exploration – or discovery from a European perspective.

The European navigators

Since the time of the Romans and Greeks many scholars in Europe believed the Earth was a sphere and there must be a land mass in the southern hemisphere to balance the three known continents in the north – Europe, Asia and Africa. A map portraying this view of the world (Ptolemy – about same time as Lucian) shows Africa and Asia linked in the south by a narrow strip of land running across the southern border and enclosing the Indian Ocean. This strip is marked *Terra Incognita* or Unknown Land. Opinions of people differed on whether or not this land was inhabited because many considered no human could survive the heat of the tropics and cross the equator.

The European view of the world changed in the 15th century when Portuguese navigators, seeking a sea route to Asia, showed the tropics could be crossed and Africa extended far into the southern hemisphere. In 1498 Vasco De Gama became the first European to sail around the Cape of Good Hope and eastwards to India. By 1516 the Portuguese had established a colonial outpost on Timor. Portuguese ships may have reached Australia in the early 1500s. In 1531, the name *Terra Australis* appeared for the first time on a map, the Oronce Fine map of the world. The voyages that would map *Terra Incognita*, the Unknown Land, had begun.

Chapter 2: *Terra Australis* Revealed

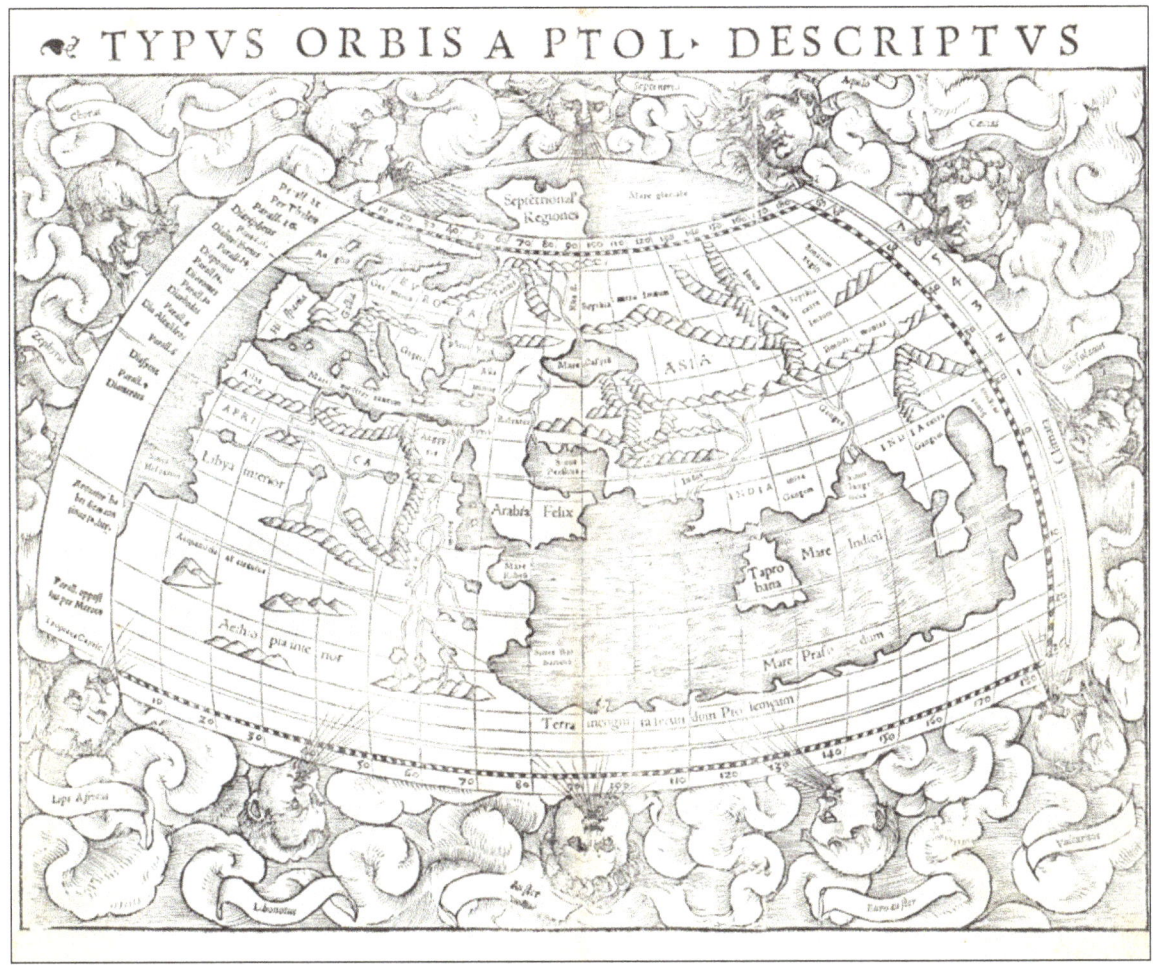

World map from Ptolemy, Geographia. Source: James Ford Bell Library, University of Minnesota

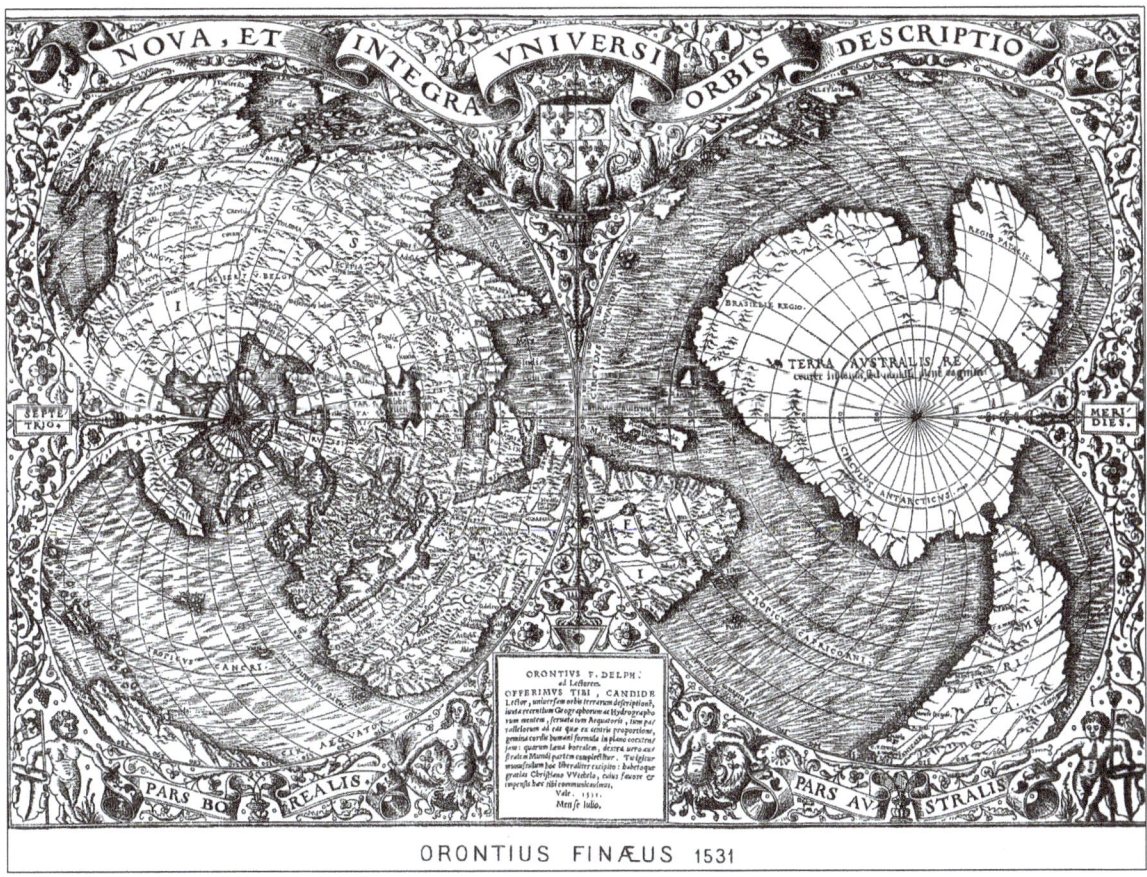

Map of the world showing the name *Terra Australis*. Source: Oronce Fine, 1531

The Portuguese were followed by the Spanish. In 1606 the Spanish navigator Luis de Torres sailed through Torres Strait, establishing that *Terra Australis* was cut off from New Guinea. This voyage ended Spanish exploration of the area.

The Dutch now became the most enterprising navigators of the age. Driven by the spice trade, Dutch navigators began sailing to what is now Indonesia just prior to 1600 and by 1610 were well established there. The Dutch East India Company was founded in 1602.

At first they used routes that were slow, the voyage from Holland to Java taking about a year. In 1611 they began using a route that took only 6 months. Instead of sailing northwards after rounding the Cape of Good Hope, they utilised the westerly winds of the southern Indian Ocean by sailing east from the Cape to the longitude of the Sunda Strait, where they turned north to the Strait of Java. The problem with this route was estimating longitude and so knowing when to turn north. Some sailed too far east and encountered the coast of *Terra Australis*.

During the first half of the 17th century, Dutch navigators charted most of northern, western and southern Australia:

In 1606, William Jansz in the *Duyfken* (20 m long) mapped 300 km of the east coast of the Gulf of Carpentaria.

In 1616, Dirk Hartog explored the coast near Shark Bay.

In 1622, the *Leeuwin* rounded the south-western corner.

In 1623, Jan Carstensz followed the route of the *Duyfken* and mapped the main features of the western side of Cape York.

In 1627, the *Gulden Zeepaard* mapped the Great Australian Bight as far as Eyre Peninsula.

In 1642, Tasman sailed by the southern part of what he called Van Dieman's Land.

In 1644, Tasman charted the northern coast from Cape York to the Ashburton River in Western Australia.

As these discoveries were incorporated into the maps of the world, the name *Terra Australis* began to be replaced by *New Holland*. The Tasman Bonaparte map included all

The Brouwer Route was discovered by Dutch explorer Hendrik Brouwer (ca. 1581-1643) in 1611. Source: Redgeographics, Wikimedia Commons

The 1999 replica of *Duyfken* under sail in ca. 2006. Source: Rupert Gerritsen, Wikimedia Commons

the Dutch discoveries prior to 1644. It linked them together and gave the whole the name *New Holland*. This map, however, showed the east coast of Van Dieman's land linked up with New Guinea. Tasman and other Dutch navigators before him did not know of the existence of Torres Strait, despite Luis de Torres having sailed through the strait many years before.

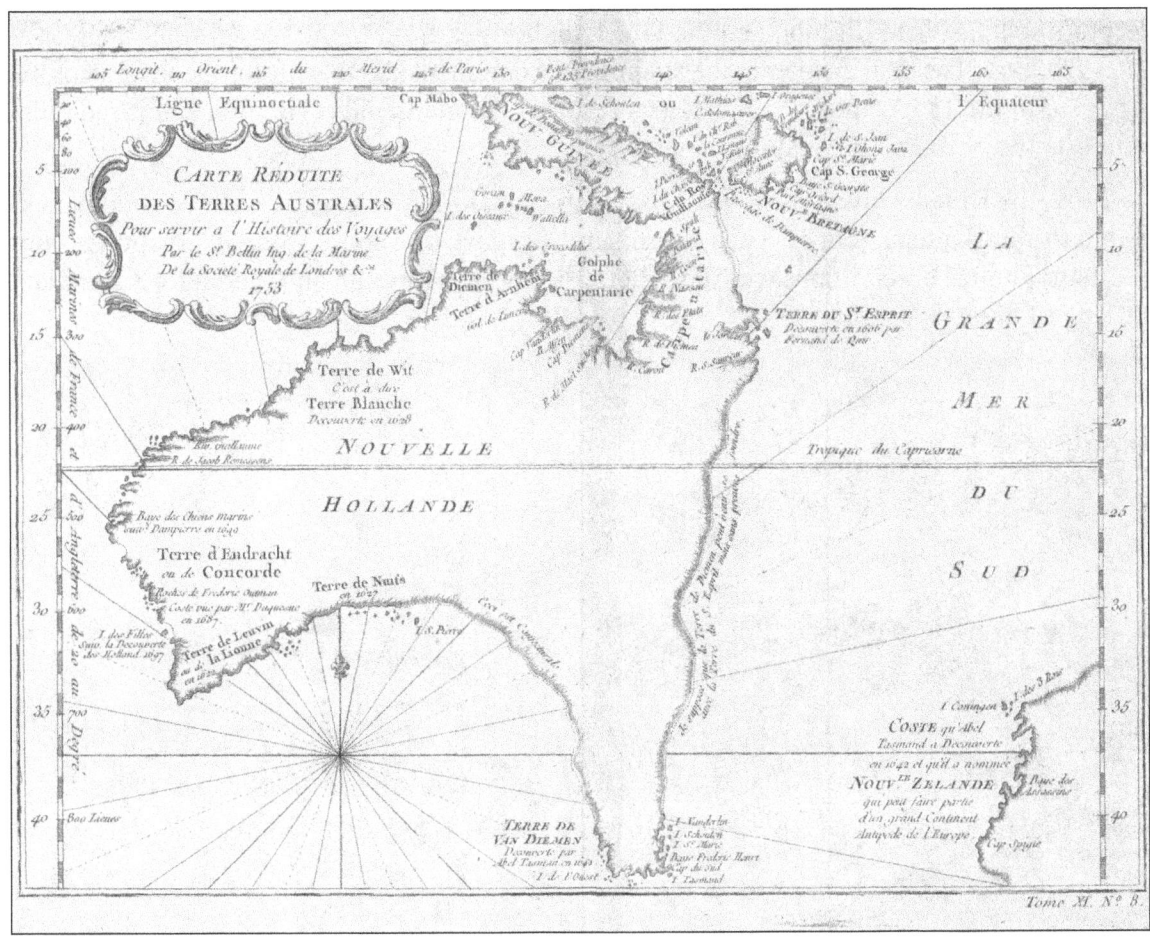

Tasman Bonaparte map. Source: National Library of Australia (NLA), No. 230625933

By 1650, cartographers were producing maps of the region (e.g. India, East Indies) that included New Holland, a land with all but its east coast and part of the eastern southern coast displayed. Obviously it was known but why did it languish for over 100 more years before that blank was largely completed? It was because the reports of these observations were unflattering.

Jan Carstensz (1623) wrote:

> *This is the most arid and barren region that could be found anywhere on earth. The inhabitants, too, are the most wretched and the poorest creatures that I have ever seen.*

In 1696-97, William de Vlamingh recharted the west coast from the Swan River to the Willems River near North West Cape. He reported:

> *Nothing has been discovered but a bare, barren, desolate land. Neither have they met with any signs of habitation, some fires excepted, and a few black naked men. Neither were any remarkable animals or birds observed, except principally in the Swan River, a species of swan ...*

Tasman reported there was nothing profitable in the land he named Van Dieman's Land:

> *... only poor, naked people walking along beaches without any rice nor many fruit, very poor and bad tempered.*

In 1699, the Englishman William Dampier explored a barren part of the north-west coast and then around the north to New Guinea. He did not consider the country very attractive and referred to the natives as:

the miserablest people in the world.

Reports such as these discouraged the Dutch authorities from taking any further interest in *New Holland*. The final chapter in the shaping of a continent had to wait for the interest of the English. In the 18th century England, as a result of the industrial revolution and its colonial interests, was becoming a major sea power.

In 1769, the British Government commissioned Captain James Cook to take astronomers to Tahiti to watch a solar eclipse. The government also gave him some secret instructions. After the astronomical observations were completed he was to sail south and search for a continent or land of great extent.

The Bark, *Earl of Pembroke*, later *Endeavour*, leaving Whitby Harbour in 1768. Oil painting by Thomas Luny, ca. 1790. The *Endeavour* overall length 33 m, extreme breadth 8.89 m, 397 gross tonnage. Source: NLA, No. 134301494

Chart of part of the South Sea showing the tracts and discoveries made by His Majesty's ships, 1773. Source: NLA, No. 230731491

After leaving Tahiti Cook sighted New Zealand. He then continued westward. On 18 April 1770 he encountered New Holland near Cape Everard and followed the coast north to Cape York then through Torres Strait and back to England via the Cape of Good Hope. His charting of the eastern coast of *Terra Australis* almost finalised the map.

The mapping of the coastline of *Terra Australis* was finally completed by Matthew Flinders. In 1797 he sailed around Van Dieman's Land proving it was an island and circumnavigated the mainland during 1801-02. In 1814 Flinders published a nearly complete map of the coastline and suggested the name *Australia* instead of *New Holland* in his book *A Voyage to Terra Australis*; he had produced the map in 1804 while a prisoner on Mauritius. The name *Australia* had been used in various books and maps for over 100 years.

General chart of *Terra Australis* or Australia, showing parts explored between 1798 and 1803 by M. Flinders, Commr. of HMS *Investigator*, 1814. Source: NLA, No. 232588549

Cook takes possession

Cook's secret instructions were to search for:

> *... a Continent or Land of Great extent ... and ... with the consent of the natives to take possession ... or if you find the country uninhabited take possession for His Majesty by setting up proper marks and inscriptions as first discoverers and possessors.*

He was not equipped to take territory by conquest, the other means by which territory could be lawfully acquired. From their observations along the east coast in 1770, Cook and Banks judged the inhabitants were few in number and merely nomadic rather than proprietors. Accordingly, they inscribed their marks on trees and, on Possession Island in Torres Strait, Cook raised the flag and took possession of the whole Eastern Coast in the name of King George III. He named it *New South Wales*. The portion west of 135°E was still regarded as *Dutch New Holland*.

Cook had proclaimed New South Wales a British possession on the basis of *Terra Nullius* (land belonging to no one), but he was wrong. At that time an estimated 750,000 people inhabited the continent, sparsely populated by European standards. For tens of thousands of years they had considered this land theirs.

Cook's 'discovery'

Cook first landed in a large bay he called Botany Bay because of the many kinds of new plants and flowers found by the ship's botanist, Joseph Banks. Botany Bay, which at first stood for wonder and bounty of nature, was believed to be a kind of paradise.

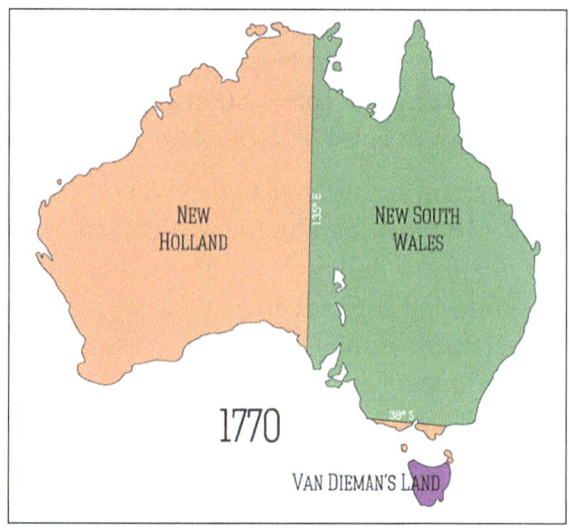

Cook takes possession. Source: Dutch Australia Cultural Centre (DACC)

While Cook did not discover Australia, he did locate the east coast which had not been known by the rest of the world prior to that time. What he came across was the far more fruitful part of the continent, the part where most people now live. Unlike the reports of the earlier navigators, Cook's reports and those of Joseph Banks were very favourable and so set the next stage of the Australian story.

Chapter 3
The First Australians

An ancient people

When Australia detached itself from Antarctica and began drifting northwards it carried no humans. Some 60,000 years ago the first humans arrived from South-east Asia, when the sea level was much lower than it is today and mainland Australia was joined to Tasmania and New Guinea. By 20,000 years ago people were living all over the continent. About then the climate of the earth began to get warmer and ocean levels rose as the ice melted; this continued on and off for about 12,000 years. With rising seas, Bass Strait became inundated, separating Tasmania from the mainland and isolating those living in Tasmania. About 8,000 years ago, Australia was separated from New Guinea by the flooding of the Gulf of Carpentaria, Torres Strait and the Arafura Sea.

Over the tens of thousands of years of living in Australia, the Aboriginal people, the First People of Australia, gradually adapted their way of life to the changing environment. They developed very egalitarian social and political structures and a culture in which their way of life was intrinsically connected to their environment. They walked the land not only to feed themselves but also to worship. Almost everything that lived in the land was revered in the eyes of some. In essence, the hallmark of their culture was 'oneness with nature'.

Aboriginals were not totally isolated from external contact. Traders from South-east Asia had visited the northern coast long before Europeans arrived. They brought pottery, cloth and metal tools. However, these external influences were far less significant in impacting the country than the internal processes of change wrought by these original inhabitants of Australia. Their use of fire altered the landscape and some academics suggest their arrival hastened the extinction of the mega fauna.

Aboriginal society

Aboriginals learned to live in remarkable harmony with the land. They have the longest continuous cultural history of all groups of people on earth. At least 30,000 years ago they were practising burial rites – ranging from cremating the dead to burying the corpse after decorating it with red ochre. They used grinding stones to shape the heads of their axes before anywhere else in the world. Unfortunately, only a fraction of the knowledge of their remarkable way of life has survived.

Traditional Australian Aboriginals largely lived the nomadic life of hunter-gatherers, following the seasons and moving systematically through their own lands in search of food. Moving regularly from place to place also had a positive impact on health by its effects on hygiene. They knew the land so well they usually collected food with ease. Knowing the seeding and fruiting times of scores of edible plants and the nesting and breeding times of hundreds of birds and animals, they specifically sought their particular foodstuffs according to the time of the year. Classical Aboriginal society was as sophisticated as traditional European farming methods.

Populations were denser in areas of abundant food, such as in many places on the coast and along rivers. In the desert numbers were low because one small group might have to travel over huge areas to harvest enough food and water for survival. They lived and travelled mostly in small family units of 15-30 individuals. A number of these family units could be linked by a common language, blood relationships, marriage ties, shared ceremonies and shared responsibility for sacred places and objects.

When at rest they lived in open camps, caves or simple structures made from bark, leaves or other vegetation. Their finest houses were simple shelters. In the dry inland they normally slept in the open with a low pile of brushwood and leafy branches to ward off the winter wind. In most parts of the country they were virtually naked. Painting the naked body for ceremonies was one of their fine arts.

In 1800, probably about 250 different languages were spoken. A typical Aboriginal probably knew several languages and several dialects. The languages were complex in grammar – being more like Latin and Sanskrit than modern English. A language once spoken in northern Queensland made a clear distinction between 'he', 'she' and 'it' and had a fourth gender to refer to edible plants. There was intense regionalism and so diversity not only in language but also in customs, rituals, food preferences and religion.

Courage and fear were strong strands in their daily lives. They were religious, believing that the world was the work of mythical creators who still held power long after they had created every valley, rocky outcrop and species of animals and birds. The performing of age-old rituals ensured these divine ancestors continued to provide benefits.

Hunter-gatherers

With just a few very simple tools Aboriginals learned to live in what we consider a harsh and inhospitable environment. The men hunted large animals such as kangaroos, emus and turtles and the women and children hunted smaller animals, e.g. lizards, goannas, snakes, echidnas, bandicoots and birds and collected fruits, berries and other plants plus bird and turtle eggs. Depending on location people caught fish and collected many types of shellfish including mussels and oysters. Every part of an animal or plant was eaten or used to make useful items such as clothing, baskets, tools and weapons.

To ensure animals and plants were never over-hunted or over-collected they took only enough to feed the number of people there at the time and wasted nothing. They would stay in an area only for a certain time, which helped ensure they did not hunt, fish or harvest in an area for too long. This ensured there would be food for the following seasons and the next time they or someone else needed it. Birth control was practised and in times of food scarcity, such as drought, even infanticide.

Use of fire

Fire was the core of Aboriginal technology and central to their life. Wherever a family camped, they used fire for cooking as well as for warmth. Fire was the only source of warmth at night for they mostly went naked, except in the south where possum skin rugs were made. They used fire as: protection against evil spirits; a focal point to gather around; a means of making weapons; and to sharpen the digging sticks which the women used to gather plant foods. In some regions they used fire to: cremate the dead; send messages to the living; and drive away mosquitoes.

As they moved between camp sites Aboriginals carried fire as lighted firesticks but had the ability to create fire by rotating a stick on a wooden plate to ignite dry grass from the heat generated. Fire was frequently used to drive out animals from long grass as well as to clear land for hunting and attract game to fresh shoots of vegetation. This is also known as 'fire-stick' farming because larger game such as wallabies were attracted by the fresh vegetation that grew after the burn-off. Fire was used regularly to manage the land and prevent more devastating blazes. The early Newcomers considered the grasslands resembled a gentleman's park or estate; hence the word 'park' appears in many place names. Surveyor-General Thomas Mitchell referred to the grasslands of western Victoria as Australia Felix.

Aboriginals using fire to hunt kangaroos, watercolour painting by Joseph Lycett, ca. 1775-1828. Source: NLA, No. 138501179

My recollections of the use of fire are from my childhood. When we were boys, my brothers and I spent many weekends and holidays on a cattle property on which an Aboriginal family was employed. In August, the driest month and last month of winter, we often rode horses about the paddocks with one of the men, who burnt patches of grass by throwing lighted matches into the dry, dead grass. When the warm weather and, with luck, some rain came in September, grass would produce green shoots and provide feed for the cattle. Another example involved a young Aboriginal man living on the property. He made spears for fishing by heating long sticks to straighten them before hardening the sharp end by charring the outside in a fire.

Guides, bushmen, stockmen and trackers

The oneness of the Aboriginals with the land resulted in their having the following unique skills when compared with other peoples: an extraordinary knowledge of the landscape; a heightened sense of direction; and great powers of observation and tracking ability. They were superb bushmen and overall played a significant part in the pioneering and development of Australia following the arrival of Europeans. The Aboriginal trade routes known as Dreaming Tracks were vital to early pastoralists for establishing the stock routes that served as the foundation of the pastoral industry.

European explorers often depended on the bushcraft of Aboriginal guides. The explorer Ludwig Leichhardt noted that his guides remembered the tiniest details about places, and likened their eyes to cameras, constantly recording images of the country about them. My ancestor John Warby developed into a good bushman. Governor Macquarie referred to him as *My Excellent Guide* but records report him being accompanied by Aboriginal guides. John Warby viewed the Aboriginals in a more humane way than most of his contemporaries. In his role as Superintendent of the famous wild cattle of the Cow Pastures he built a close friendship with the local Aboriginals, the Tharawals. When he was granted 260 acres (104 ha) on Bow Bowing Creek in 1816, Warby named his estate *Leumeah* after the Aboriginal phrase for 'Here I Rest'. The only recorded negative comment about him after his arrival in the colony was made by a Captain Wallis, who reported John refused to accompany him on a trip to massacre Aboriginals.

Given their bushcraft, it is not surprising that Aboriginals became great stockmen. I observed their skills in my time on cattle properties. They knew where the cattle were on the property and could track them with ease. In addition, they could identify animals individually and

Retrieving a runaway. *Stockmen rounding up cattle on horseback at Doomadgee in the 1960s.*
Source: John Oxley Library, State Library of Queensland

Hector Rutherford and Joyce Stuart, *The Oaks*, Glen Geddes, where the author spent much time during his youth, ca. 1951. Source: Mary Sheldon

Mary Sheldon and Alfie, *The Oaks,* ca. 1951. Source: Mary Sheldon

so knew which ones were missing. Owners of the vast unfenced cattle runs in northern Australia relied heavily on Aboriginal stockmen before the coming of fences, motorbikes, 4-wheel drive vehicles, fixed-wing aircraft and helicopters. This is acknowledged by Tom Cole, who worked in the north as a drover, station hand and buffalo hunter in the 1920s and 1930s. He ends the introduction in his autobiography about his experiences and those of other men with whom he worked and respected with the words:

> *This would not be complete without a tribute to the many aborigines with whom I worked and got to know so well. Their amazing endurance in that harsh and unforgiving environment, their bushmanship and incredible tracking and hunting abilities, their uncanny skill with their primitive spears and boomerangs, never ceased to amaze me.*

The tracking skills of the Aboriginals were used to find missing and wanted persons. Colonial police forces commonly employed a contingent of 'black trackers'. Two trackers from the Queensland Police Force assisted in the capture of Ned Kelly, one of Australia's most notorious bushrangers. Black trackers were employed well into the 20th century.

Spirituality – Dreaming and the Dreamtime

At the centre of Aboriginal culture is what is termed the Dreaming and the Dreamtime. The Dreaming relates to a time of creator ancestors and supernatural beings. These creator ancestors formed the features of the land and all living things and set down the laws for social and moral order. The Dreaming, as well as answering questions about origins, provides a harmonious framework for human experience in the universe and the place of all living things within it. This mystical period of 'time before time' is known as the Dreamtime.

In Aboriginal folklore, features of the landscape are the most visible signs of past activities of ancestral beings. Waterholes or entrances to caves were formed where these beings emerged from the earth. Where they held great battles, hills were formed from their bodies and lakes from pools of their blood. The ancestral beings also left a record of themselves and their actions in the form of a rich variety of art. During their epic journeys, the ancestral beings sang and performed ceremonies, made engravings or paintings on rock and in caves and left sacred objects.

The term Dreaming describes the relationships between the spiritual, natural and moral elements of the world. It is often used to refer to an individual's or group's set of beliefs or spirituality; for instance, an Aboriginal might say that he/she has Kangaroo Dreaming or Shark Dreaming. Through the Dreaming, Aboriginal people are bound to the land, law, spirit, art, family and each other.

The Dreamtime is not only an ancient time of creation, but also continues as the Dreaming in the spiritual lives of the Aboriginal people today. Present-day Aboriginal people are continuously reminded of the presence of the creator beings when they walk through their country. They are also reminded of the presence of the creator beings through songs, paintings and ceremonies. The journeys and events of the Dreamtime are re-enacted in the ceremonies, danced in mime form by living embodiments of Dreamtime creatures – human goannas, serpents or giant figures – each painted and elaborately decorated with traditional symbolic designs. Song-poetry chanted incessantly to the accompaniment of didgeridoos or clapsticks relates the stories of the events of these early times and brings the power of the Dreaming to bear on life today. Oodgeroo Nunukul (Kath Walker) wrote of the beginning of life:

> *In the Dreamtime all the earth lay sleeping. Nothing grew. Nothing moved. Everything was quiet and still. The animals, birds and reptiles lay sleeping under the earth's crust. Then one day the Rainbow Serpent awoke from her slumber and pushed her way through the earth's crust, moving the stones that lay in her*

way. When she emerged, she looked about her and then travelled over the land, going in all directions. She travelled far and wide, and when she grew tired she curled herself into a heap and slept. Upon the earth she left her winding tracks and the imprint of her sleeping body. When she had travelled all the earth, she returned to the place where she had first appeared and called to the frogs, Come out! *The frogs were very slow to come from below the earth's crust, for their bellies were heavy with water, which they stored in their sleep. The Rainbow Serpent tickled their stomachs, and when the frogs laughed, the water ran all over the earth to fill the tracks of the Rainbow Serpent's wanderings – and that is how the lakes and rivers were formed. Then the grass began to grow, and trees sprang up, and so life began on earth.*

All the animals, birds and reptiles awoke and followed the Rainbow Serpent, the Mother of Life, across the land. They were happy on earth, and each lived and hunted for food with his own tribe. The kangaroo, wallaby and emu tribes lived on the plains. The reptile tribes lived among the rocks and stones, and the bird tribes flew through the air and lived in the trees. The Rainbow Serpent made laws that all were asked to obey, but some grew quarrelsome and were troublemakers. The Rainbow Serpent scolded them, saying, Those who keep my laws I shall reward well. I shall give them a human form. They and their children and their children's children shall roam this earth forever. This shall be their land. Those who break my laws I shall punish. They shall be turned to stone, never to walk the earth again. *So the law-breakers were turned to stone, and became mountains and hills, to stand forever and watch over the tribes hunting for food at their feet. But those who kept her laws she turned into human form, and gave each of them his own totem of the animal, bird or reptile from whence he came. So the tribes knew themselves by their own totems: the kangaroo, the emu, the carpet snake, and many, many more. And in order that none should starve, she ruled that no man should eat of his own totem, but only of other totems. In this way there was food for all. So the tribes lived together in the land given to them by the Mother of Life, the Rainbow Serpent; and they knew that the land would always be theirs, and that no one should ever take it from them.*

As did many other ancient people, Australia's Aboriginal people studied the night sky, using it to survive as well as including their interpretation of what they saw into their Dreamtime stories. The best known constellation is the 'Emu in the Sky'. Its position in the sky signalled when to collect emu eggs. They were Australia's first astronomers.

The Aboriginal 'Emu in the Sky'. The Southern Cross is on the right. Source: Barnaby Norris and Ray Norris, 2007, Wikimedia Commons

Ancient art

Aboriginal art is the oldest ongoing tradition of art in the world. Initial forms of artistic Aboriginal expression were rock carvings, body painting and ground designs, which date back more than 30,000 years, plus fibre-craft, wooden sculptures and bark paintings. Art has always been an important part of Aboriginal life, connecting past and present, the people and the land, and the supernatural and reality.

Traditionally art was for purely cultural reasons and was able to be created or viewed only by people initiated to the proper level of knowledge. More recently, artwork has been made specifically for public viewing. Since the early 1970s, Aboriginal contemporary art has been practised more widely and with amazing diversity and vigour – to the extent that it has been described as the 'last great art movement of the 20th Century'. Regardless of whether the art is for private or public purposes, for many artists their work remains inspired by the traditional marks and symbols from the Dreaming and the artist's country.

At least 100,000 rock art sites thousands of years old occur throughout Australia – most of them in Western Australia, the Northern Territory and Queensland.

Wandjina figures are found in many rock art sites in caves and rock shelters throughout the Kimberley Region of Western Australia. The Worrorra, Wunambal and Ngarinyin people of the north-western and central Kimberley say that the Wandjina are the creator beings of the Dreaming, and that they made their world and all that it contains.

Wandjina figures, Mount Elizabeth Station, Kimberley, 2012. Source: Samantha Wood, Flickr

X-ray figure, Kakadu National Park, Australia. Source: Thomas Schoch, Wikimedia Commons

The X-ray style depicts animals or human figures in which the internal organs and bone structures are clearly visible. X-ray art includes sacred images of ancestral supernatural beings as well as secular works depicting fish and animals that were important food sources. The style is common to Arnhem Land in the Northern Territory and surrounding areas.

Gwion (Bradshaw) figures found on Wunambal Gaambera Country in the north Kimberley are reported to be more than 17,000 years old. If this is correct, they are the oldest known detailed pictures of human figures in the world. They are enigmatic human figures with elaborate headdresses, plus arm and waist decorations. Gwion look after the country and punish people who don't.

Gwion figures showing images of men and women. The women have 'garraggi', the bark bucket for carrying bush honey and sweet figs, and the men have 'gangan', which is a type of stick. Source: UQ News, 20-12-2012, courtesy of the Wunambal Gaambera Aboriginal Corporation

The Genyornis was a large flightless bird about three times the size of an emu. It was among the megafauna that became extinct after the arrival of the original human inhabitants.

Red ochre painting of the Genyornis (*Genyornis newtoni*) depicted on a rock in Arnhem Land. The allegedly 40,000-year-old painting could be the continent's, if not the world's, oldest work of art. Source: Brian Wolly, Smithsonian Magazine

Modern art

Albert Namatjira (1902-1959) is one of the best-known Aboriginal artists and the first to receive international recognition for his art. His water colours, painted in a western style, capture the vibrant colours of the landscapes, predominantly of areas in his tribal land in Central Australia. They depict iconic images of the Australian outback such as ghost gums and convey a spiritual connection with the land.

Namatjira's success encouraged a new generation of artists, whom he took on painting expeditions. He would explain the stories implicit in the landscape, schooling them both in painting and place. On each painting Namatjira would reveal important information about country and past ceremonies.

Portrait of Albert Namatjira, 1956. Artist William Dargie. Source: ©William Dargie/Copyright Agency, 2024

Glenn Helen country. Artist Albert Namatjira. Source: © Namatjira Legacy Trust/Copyright Agency, 2024

Ghost gum, Mt Sonder, McDonnell ranges, ca. 1957. Artist Albert Namatjira. Source: © Namatjira Legacy Trust/Copyright Agency, 2024

Contemporary art

Contemporary art takes many different forms and is difficult to categorise. Some work draws on traditional practices but often uses Western medium.

Kurdukadji (Emu). Artist Ezariah Kelly. Acrylic and Dry Pigments on Arches paper. Source: © Ezariah Kelly/Copyright Agency, 2024

Mayh Kuwarddewaken (Stone Country Animals). Artist Graham Badari. Ochre and Acrylic on Arches paper. Source: © Graham Badari/Copyright Agency, 2024

Artist Margaret Preston (1875-1963) promoted and appropriated Aboriginal art. She was convinced that a modern and necessary identity for Australia could emerge only from the inspiration of the art of the First Australians.

Aboriginal landscape, 1940. Artist Margaret Preston. Source: © Margaret Preston/Copyright Agency, 2024

Still life, 1941. Artist Margaret Preston. Source: © Margaret Preston/Copyright Agency, 2024

Alien cultures collide

Prior to about 8,000-10,000 years ago all people on all continents were predominantly hunter-gatherers. Subsequently, agriculture replaced hunter-gathering in Europe and much of Asia, Africa and the Americas. The cultivation of land and herding of animals made it possible to feed larger numbers of people and so allowed population increase and the establishment of towns and cities and along with it the growth of professions and cultural activities not directly related to food collection. From this start other factors, such as the development of writing and technology and the exchange of knowledge, set in train events that would end in the societies and nation states that littered the global map 200 years ago.

However, although they were not wholly cut off from external contact, the Aboriginals remained largely hunter-gatherers. They did not develop agriculture because there were no animals or plants suitable for domestication, soils were generally poor and infertile and overall rainfall was low and unreliable. This prevented the development of complex societies with their various specialisations that occurred on other continents. The Aboriginals were left vulnerable to being engulfed by the coming of the Europeans.

The anthropologist W.E.H. Stanner wrote:

> *If one tried to invent two styles of life as unlike each other as could be, while still following the rules which are necessary if people are to live together at all, one might end up with something like the Aboriginal and European traditions.*

Here was an utter contrast in peoples, for they spoke very different languages, had very different histories, customs, rituals and religions and contrasting attitudes to property, plants and livestock. Their cultures were totally incompatible. The collision of two such traditions had inevitable consequences. Consequences for Australia's first inhabitants were disastrous and far-reaching, particularly in relation to the issue of possessions and land ownership. They were dispossessed of their lands, which severely impacted on their way of life. In contrast, consequences for the Newcomers were benign but in no way insignificant, and it is their story I shall follow.

Our notion of possessions is alien to the traditional culture of the First Australians, who shared material things within groups. They did not 'own' land but saw themselves as part of it. The idea that an individual could 'own' land was foreign to their thinking. Inhabiting land was based on their custom and tradition, not a formal written system of land title. They did not use fences or barriers as in the traditional European way of marking land ownership. They divided the land up into traditional lands using geographic boundaries such as rivers, lakes and mountains. Knowledge about boundaries was passed down by the elders to the younger people through song, dance, art and storytelling. The lack of a system of land ownership in the European tradition of private land ownership was used to give credence to the idea of *Terra Nullius*, meaning 'land-belonging-to-no-one'. This legal concept prevailed until 1992, when the Mabo judgement regarding islands in the eastern Torres Strait rejected *Terra Nullius* by recognising a form of 'native title' to these islands by the Meriam people. In 1996 the Wik decision stated that native title rights could co-exist with statutory pastoral leases depending on the terms and nature of the particular leases.

The different attitudes of Aboriginals and the Europeans towards land had a moral tone. To the Aboriginals the land was part of this life and the future of the group and was not something to be bought and sold, i.e. not a commodity for exchange. On the other hand, the Newcomers believed that land could not only be bought and sold but also taken for exploitation by productive agriculture, and that those who carried out this action had some kind of 'moral right' to the land. They considered a people who were not Christians and who did not try to 'improve' the land of their birth by agriculture were inferior beings and deserved to have their country taken over.

This land is our land

The Europeans assumed their ways were superior to Aboriginal ways. They made few attempts to understand the people already here, their beliefs or their customs, or to understand how they had come to terms with an often-harsh environment. Few attempted to learn their languages. The early governors wished the Aboriginal Australians no harm and invited them to adopt 'civilised' ways and learn the advantages of cultivating the land, but Aboriginals did not want to change their way of life. Their reluctance to do so was considered further proof of their inferiority.

The Europeans found it difficult to understand a society organised around kinship and relationship to the land. There were no 'chiefs' to deal with. Except for John Batman's treaty with Aboriginals, no treaties were negotiated to regulate the movement of Europeans on to the land on which the First Australians lived. In 1835, Batman purportedly made a treaty with members of the Kulin tribes around Port Phillip Bay. This gave Batman 600,000 acres (240,000 ha) of land in exchange for assorted paraphernalia, including a mirror, flour etc., which was to be repeated on an annual basis; an extremely one-sided deal. In response to this arrangement, Governor Bourke issued a Colonial Office proclamation stating an individual person could acquire land only through distribution by the Crown, thereby implementing the concept of *Terra Nullius*.

In hindsight, the Newcomers' notion of 'improve' is questionable. They believed it was their role to bring 'benefits' of civilisation to Australia and to make the land productive; the natural resources were to be used in any conceivable way to achieve this. Mindless destruction began within weeks of their arrival; in March 1788, an order was issued forbidding the cutting down of trees within 15 metres of the Tank Stream. In their struggle to survive and prosper, the stewardship of the Newcomers has been more one of exploitation. The plants and animals, the agricultural, grazing and mining practices they introduced, in ignorance, arrogance or simply not caring, have not been kind to this great land.

As the settlers moved inland, the First Australians were forced from their hunting grounds, their watering holes and in fact their source of life. They speared cattle and sheep and on occasions raided homesteads and outstations killing many or all of those present. However, retaliation by the Europeans was harsh, as they had superior weaponry and often superior numbers. Resistance by the Aboriginals was not very effective because the small and semi-autonomous groupings of their society made the formation of significant fighting forces virtually impossible. Two celebrated resistance fighters were Pemulwuy (1790s around Port Jackson) and Jandamarra (1890s in Kimberley area). Also, the concerns that commonly provoke aggressive responses between different peoples, e.g. arguments over territory, ideology and rule by minorities, were simply not issues in Aboriginal society.

The most intense frontier conflict in Australia's history occurred in Van Dieman's Land (Tasmania) from 1824 to 1830. The hostilities, known as the 'Black War', culminated in the infamous 'Black Line'. In late 1830, an attempt was made to drive the First People from their homelands in eastern Tasmania to a specially designated reserve in the Tasman Peninsula. Several thousand settlers and soldiers formed a 'human chain' that moved south for many weeks across the settled districts of Tasmania. It was an embarrassing failure; only two Aboriginals were captured and two others were recorded killed. Over the next few years most were persuaded to resettle on Flinders Island. All Aboriginals in Van Dieman's Land were eventually killed or died.

For more than a century violence and conflict were a part of life on much of the frontier. Government and settlers carried out punitive expeditions, believing that creating terror was the only effective means for assuring security in the future. The settlers retaliated to any opposition from Aboriginals, sometimes massacring whole groups of people regardless of age or gender. The attackers justified the brutality of these attacks by using the argument that these 'savages' needed to be 'taught a lesson' to ensure future peace. This indiscriminate killing continued throughout the 19th century and into the 20th and was premised on the assumption that it was both necessary and legitimate to kill Aboriginal men, women and children without summons, trial or conviction. Total numbers killed on either side are unknown, as unsurprisingly, few records were kept. The destruction of evidence (burning of bodies) was the hallmark of the Native Police Forces. Historian Henry Reynolds estimates 20,000 Aboriginals and 2,000-2,500 Europeans were killed over the whole continent.

Native police units consisting of Aboriginal troopers under the command usually of a single white officer were raised in all mainland colonies as a cost-effective and very brutal paramilitary aid in the expansion and protection of the colonial frontier. Troopers were usually recruited from areas very distant from where they were deployed. The Queensland force was notorious for conducting widespread extrajudicial shooting of Aboriginal people under the official euphemism of 'dispersal'. In 1868 the Port Denison Times reported about activities in the Burketown district of the local native police detachment, led by a Sub-Inspector Uhr:

> *Success I hear was complete. One mob of 14 he rounded up, another mob of nine, and the last mob of eight, he succeeded with his troopers in shooting. In the latter lot there was one black who would not die after receiving 18 to 20 bullets, but a trooper speedily put an end to his existence by smashing his skull... Everybody in the district is delighted with the wholesale slaughter dealt out by the native police, and thank Mr Uhr for his energy in ridding the district of fifty-nine (59) myalls.*

Despite such atrocities being committed, the general population largely supported the activities of the native police. Those who criticised the violence employed by both Native Police and settlers attracted contempt.

John Stuart, a paternal uncle of my mother, served with the Queensland Native Mounted Police Force, which he joined in 1869 as a Cadet/Acting Sub-Inspector. In 1876 he was promoted to 2nd Class Sub-Inspector and in 1893 to Travelling Inspector. In 1896 he became the first Chief Inspector of Police. In his doctoral thesis, Johnathon Richards noted that in 1879 Stuart, reporting from Port Douglas, wrote: *I regret to say that I find half measures of no use and that there is but one way of putting a stop to these outrages and the sooner and more effectually it is done the better*. By whom the outrages were committed was not mentioned. Stuart was described by Rockhampton residents in 1888 as a 'very humane man'. He considered the *Native Police should be abolished and substituted with Police patrols* and *Sub-Inspectors in charge of detachments should be first humane and secondly firm*. I have not heard anyone mention him nor have I sighted any documents mentioning him, except for a bible in which were written locations of the various postings he had throughout Queensland. It appears he has erased a word, probably 'native', on two occasions on the left-hand page (see image on page 35).

Few murderers of Aboriginals ever stood trial and those, who did, were generally exonerated by prejudiced juries to the acclaim of a prejudiced general public. A rare exception was the retrial, conviction and hanging of seven of 12 ex-convict stockmen responsible for the Myall Creek Massacre near Inverell in 1838. Initially all 12 had been tried and acquitted of killing 28 defenceless Aboriginal men, women and children. One of the jurors later said he knew they were guilty but could not convict a white man of killing a 'black', a view the majority of the population held.

While the vast majority of Newcomers undoubtedly viewed the First Australians as inferior, some even looked upon them as sub-human, sadly, an attitude still present today. In 1883,

Britain's governor of New Zealand and the Western Pacific reported to British Prime Minister William Gladstone how Queenslanders treated indigenous Australians:

The habit of regarding natives as vermin, to be cleared off the face of the earth, has given to the average Queenslander a tone of brutality and cruelty in dealing with 'blacks'. ... ... I have heard men of culture and refinement, of the greatest humanity and kindness to their fellow whites ... talk, not only of the wholesale butchery ... but of the individual murder of natives, exactly as they would talk of a day's sport, or of having to kill some troublesome animals.

Two infamous incidents of retaliation by Aboriginals were the *Hornet Bank* Massacre and the *Cullin-la-ringo* Massacre. In 1857 the Jiman people killed 11 Europeans at Martha Fraser's *Hornet Bank* station on the Dawson River, Central Queensland; local squatters with the help of the Native Police retaliated by later shooting several Jiman men. In 1861 Aboriginals attacked a party of settlers led by Horatio Spencer Wills at the new *Cullin-la-ringo* station, near Emerald, Queensland. Wills and 18 Europeans were killed. On hearing the news, my great grandfather, P.F. MacDonald, who had sold the lease of *Cullin-la-ringo* to Horatio Wills the previous year, assembled a party and set off to provide what help he could. He described the massacre site in a letter to John Jardine, 23 November 1861:

We then dismounted in order to examine the ground more minutely and about 300 yards distant [from the sheep yards] we found some pieces of a tent which had been partly erected and also found some articles of clothing and then some blood-stained patches of grass which marked where their victims had evidently fallen. Upon further examination...we discovered where the main camp had been situated. The ground was strewn with broken boomerangs, nulla-nullas

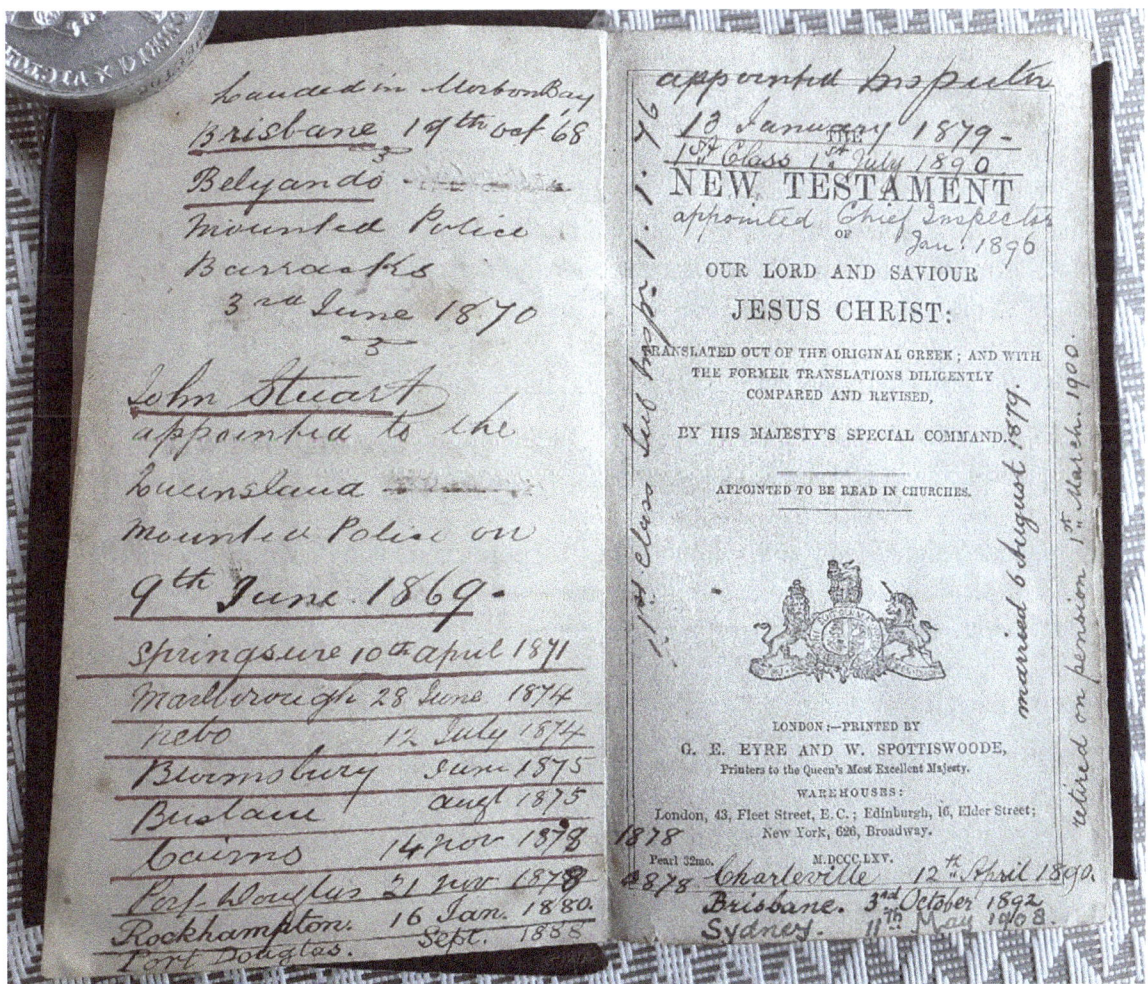

Page from J. Stuart's bible. Source: Tom Hasker

and spears, and here too the blood-stained grass and flannel pieces indicated many...marks of this [wicked?] atrocity. The bodies had been already buried close by and a good deal of property lay scattered around but otherwise the place appeared quite deserted – it was not easy to imagine a place so gifted by nature should have been the scene of such a cruel massacre...

I have been informed by the survivors of the Wills party that, although the men who felt the necessity of carrying firearms for their protection, though requested by Mr Wills [not to do so?]...got the young women from the Aboriginals on the stations around to entertain a few gentlemen...one of them when his brother was leaving the place a few days before the massacre expressed himself in the following words: 'Although it's quiet Jamie this is just...that I am afraid something will happen to us'...

A little over a week after the massacre, a large party of police, native police and civilians tracked down the suspected tribe and killed between 60 and 70 of them. The general belief was this murderous attack was induced by Horatio Wills neglecting to use *proper precaution and by allowing too great familiarity between his people and the Blacks*....

At that time the deadliest frontier wars raged in Central Queensland as Aboriginals retaliated aggressively to the confiscation and desecration of their lands. Most Europeans viewed them as savages and during my childhood I heard the words 'and the Aboriginals were very savage' many times.

The convict's scorn for Aboriginals was entrenched in many from emancipist society. P.F. MacDonald was very much a man of his times. However, he did not consider Aboriginals worthless. He had a high degree of trust in them and used them on his expeditions of exploration and as labourers on his properties. Despite his outward attitude towards them, he turned to them when alone. Aboriginals, who were not part of his workforce, camped for generations in the vicinity of *Yaamba*.

Although the original inhabitants were supposed to be protected by British law, this protection was difficult to enforce – almost impossible at the frontiers of settlement – because distance and the resulting delay in communication hindered the monitoring of conflict between squatters and Aboriginals, and the whereabouts and activities of the Native Police. Also, as happened so often in other parts of the world, diseases, against which they had no resistance, took their toll. Much of Australia is now in the hands of the Newcomers. This was inevitable. No treaty, agreement or pact of any kind would have guaranteed otherwise.

A technologically-advanced society has no scruples and will commit any sin when seeking resources. Nothing illustrates this more starkly than the fate of the Native Americans, whose social structure was far more advanced than that of their Australian counterparts. Treaty after treaty has been signed and often immediately dishonoured. The disregard technologically-superior societies have for more primitive people and their habitats continues, e.g. in New Guinea, Mexico and Brazil. Australia is not exempt.

Military service

Despite the discrimination they suffered, First Australians, like their Newcomer counterparts, rallied to Australia's flag in both WWI and WWII. Many were killed fighting or died as prisoners of war. Five First Australian servicemen are known to be buried at Gallipoli. From 500 to 800 Indigenous Australians served in WWI, mostly in the 2nd AIF and the militia. That people with field skills ideal for war were not actively recruited is simply bewildering.

Indigenous Australians served under the same conditions as European Australians and generally there was little racism between soldiers. Ethnicity was not recorded in the enlistment process. Sadly, on discharge they were subjected to the discrimination they had escaped while on active service. For example, only one Aboriginal Australian is known to have received land under a 'soldier-settlement' scheme, despite the fact that much of the best farming land in Aboriginal reserves was confiscated for soldier-settlement blocks.

Above: Non-commissioned Officers (NCOs) and Gunners who served at Gallipoli; France, ca. 1916. Front Centre is Indigenous soldier, 2141 Private Alfred Jackson Coombs. Source: Australian War Memorial (AWM), No. P01242.002

Left: Group portrait of the 'Special Platoon' of Aboriginal Australians, who volunteered for service during the Second World War, 1940. Source: AWM, No. P02140.002

Arthur Murdoch. Source: Brisbane John Oxley Library, State Library of Queensland

I met WWI indigenous veteran Arthur Murdoch in 1962, while working on *Elgin Downs* station in central Queensland. Arthur would have been about 64, was respected by all and highly regarded by the manager Jack Cooper for his horsemanship and knowledge of cattle and the country. In that year a population census was held by the Federal Government. Only Cooper and the cook had personal forms. All others on the station, married or single, were to be recorded on the one form, which Cooper assigned to me for completion. Arthur refused to discuss the matter when I approached him, which puzzled me. Someone said it would have been something to do with his war service pension. It was only after the 1967 referendum that I realised the reason for Arthur's refusal to cooperate. An Internet link to further information about Arthur is: https://onesearch.slq.qld.gov.au/permalink/61SLQ_INST/1dejkfd/alma99183928726802061

Two notable Aboriginal Australians who served in WWII were Reg Saunders and Len Waters. Saunders was the first Aboriginal Australian to be commissioned as an officer in the Australian Army. He served in the Middle East and later in Korea as a Company Commander. Both his father and uncle had fought in Europe in WWI. As a boy Len Waters developed a real interest in aeroplanes and flying and in WWII became Australia's only Aboriginal fighter pilot. He flew a P-40 Kittyhawk named *Black Magic* in the South-west Pacific theatre, where he completed 95 missions, mainly close air support. By the end of the war, he had risen to the rank of Warrant Officer. He also held the RAAF middleweight boxing title. Following his discharge in 1946, he attempted to start a regional airline serving South-west Queensland. However, he was unable to secure finance or bureaucratic agreement. He reportedly wrote four letters seeking government approval but none was answered. He went back to shearing sheep to earn a living and died in 1993 at the age of 69.

Lt Reginald Walter Saunders shaking hands with Lt Thomas Currie Derrick, 1944. Source: AWM, No. 083166

Reg Saunders, 1940. Source: AWM, No. 003967

Waters' P-40 N-15 Kittyhawk aircraft, *Black Magic*. Source: AWM, No. P02808.001

Sgt Leonard Victor (Len) Waters, ca. 1944-45. Source: Wikimedia Commons

First Australians formed a significant majority of NORFORCE, a unit within the Australian Defence Force's Regional Force Surveillance Group, whose responsibility was surveillance, reconnaissance and intelligence gathering in the remote areas and seas of northern Australia. Not only their bushcraft and survival skills were being utilised but also their instinctive connection to country and community.

Badge of the North-West Mobile Force. Source: Wikimedia Commons

Australian Defence Force soldiers from Regional Force Surveillance Unit on deployed Operation Resolute, on board the Zodiac boat to conduct a long-range patrol on Katers Island in remote Western Australia. Source: Department of Defence

First Australians' legacy on the new Australian character

It is likely that the meeting of the two cultures had a greater influence on the moulding of us Newcomers than simply to fill our vocabulary with mellifluous words such as Woolloomooloo, Yarrawonga, kangaroo and Dirranbandi. We share the same style of humour and love of the beach and surf, which reflects our image of being egalitarian, playful, relaxed and connected to nature. Our affinity with the water probably originated at the very beginning of European settlement. In the first 50 years swimming was very popular around Sydney and most people could swim. This was probably a result of watching the Aboriginals, who were very skilled in the water.

It is unlikely that the absence of 'chiefs' and the egalitarian nature of Aboriginal hunter-gatherer society would have contributed to the disregard Australians have for those in authority, as other factors probably brought about this aspect of our character. Something of the special connection of Aboriginals with the land and its deep spiritual significance for them must have been absorbed by some settlers, who came to Australia in the decades following the arrival of the Europeans. Thus there are some 'New Australians' for whom the bush is not an alien place, to be feared or avoided as much as possible, unlike today's visitors from Europe and Asia. It can even be a place to visit for relaxation and recharge. However, unlike the First Australians, few of us can claim to be part of this harsh, unforgiving land and feel completely at home in it.

Apart from the brutal dispossession of their land suffered by the First Australians, the most tragic aspect of this clash of people and cultures was the total failure of the New Australians to comprehend from the very beginning that they could learn so much from the nomadic people they held in such disdain. Their powers of observation and sense of locality were second to none. Their knowledge of the vagaries of the climate and land over which they had roamed for millennia would have been priceless. What other treasures in knowledge they possessed can be merely a matter of conjecture. Australians can only hope that all is not completely lost and that we may be wise enough to one day learn to look upon this great land through eyes akin to those who were here before us.

Fortunately, not all who set foot on Australia's shores had a poor regard for First Australians. As heirs to the Enlightenment there were some who viewed First Australians far more generously. They included governors, colonisers and others. An example of one with such a view was Nicolas Baudin, French navigator and cartographer. In a private letter to Governor King, with whom he had formed a friendship during his stay at Port Jackson in 1803, he wrote:

> *I now write to you as Mr King, my friend, for whom I shall always have a particular regard... To my way of thinking, I have never been able to conceive that there was justice or even fairness on the part of Europeans in seizing, in the name of their governments, a land seen for the first time, when it is inhabited by men who have not always deserved the title of savages or cannibals... it would be infinitely more glorious for your nation, as for mine, to mould for society the inhabitants of its own country over whom it has rights, rather than wishing to occupy itself with the improvement of those who are very far removed from it by beginning with seizing the soil which belongs to them and which saw their birth. These remarks are no doubt impolitic, but at least they are reasonable from the facts... not only have you to reproach yourself with an injustice in having seized their land, but also in having transported on to a soil where the crimes and diseases of Europeans were unknown...*

Unfortunately, such people were far too few in number. The First Australians, stripped of their land and heritage, were relegated to the scrap heap of history. But these people with the oldest continuous culture of any on planet earth and having survived for 60,000 years on this continent refused to simply fade away despite their ordeals over the past two centuries. Like the phoenix they are rising from near extinction; their languages, music, dance and art are already performed with acclaim throughout the world. In due course they will take their rightful place in this nation and, in doing so, add significantly to Australia and what makes an Australian.

Chapter 4
Convict Beginning

Britain's unwanted

The European Newcomers who came initially to Australia in the wake of reports by Cook and Banks did not come willingly. They were Britain's unwanted – convicts sentenced to transportation to the ends of the earth; to *Terra Australis* or that part of it Cook named New South Wales.

In the 1700s the enclosing of the 'common' lands in Britain forced the poorer rural people into the towns and cities. The aggregation of land was considered necessary to produce more food for a growing population. Generally this land was added to the large estates of the aristocracy, which increased the crime of poaching. The population explosion in the cities caused widespread poverty and the crime rate increased dramatically. In their efforts to survive the poor thought little of stealing and very strict laws were passed in an attempt to prevent it. People were convicted for very minor offences by present day standards and very harsh punishments were handed out.

Simple stealing merited transportation for seven years. Stealing goods worth more than one shilling (about A$50 in today's money), stealing with violence, stealing from a dwelling or highway robbery merited death by hanging. In general judges and juries tended to commute death sentences to transportation.

As a result of the harsh laws the gaols were overflowing and so rotting hulks (old troop transports and naval ships at anchor but still floating) that dotted the ports of southern England were used to hold prisoners. The filthy overcrowded conditions in the hulks made typhus endemic. Transportation was seen as the solution to the problem of overflowing gaols.

By the early 1770s, the British were transporting about 1,000 convicts annually to the colonies in America. This ended in 1776 when the colonies rebelled. In 1770 Cook had sailed up the east coast of Australia and reported favourably about it. The British Government, relying very much on the advice of botanist Joseph Banks, who had accompanied Cook, decided to establish a penal colony at Botany Bay in New South Wales.

The First Fleet

In 1787 a fleet of 11 ships under the command of Captain Phillip set sail for Australia. On board were 568 male convicts, 191 female convicts and 13 convict children, along with 700 seamen and soldiers (marines) plus their wives and children. Cattle, pigs, goats, sheep and poultry were acquired at stops on the voyage. They had no draught animals. The trip of 15,063 nautical miles to the 'end of the earth' took eight months. Even in this age of jet transport, Europeans are reluctant to visit Australia as they consider it to be too far away.

On 18 January 1788 this 'First Fleet' arrived in Botany Bay. Phillip considered it was an unsuitable site and so the fleet sailed on to Port Jackson (Sydney Harbour) one of the world's best natural harbours. Phillip wrote of his first entry into the harbour:

> *We got into Port Jackson early in the afternoon and had the satisfaction of finding the finest harbour in the world, in which a thousand sail of line may ride in the most perfect safety.*

On 26 January the men landed at Sydney Cove, which is now Circular Quay. They hoisted the British flag, drank the King's health and began work. Land was cleared for sowing crops, trees were cut down for the building of wooden huts, stores were landed from the ships and labour was organised for shaping a 'disciplined' community. While the work progressed, Phillip lived in a small canvas house and the officers, marines and convicts camped in tents made principally from old sail-cloth.

Within a few years the convicts toasted each 26 January, the anniversary of their arrival, with: *the land, boys, we live in*. This day is now celebrated as Australia Day.

Captain Arthur Phillip. Source: NLA, No. 136096089

HMSS *Sirius*. Source: First Fleet Fellowship Victoria Incorporated

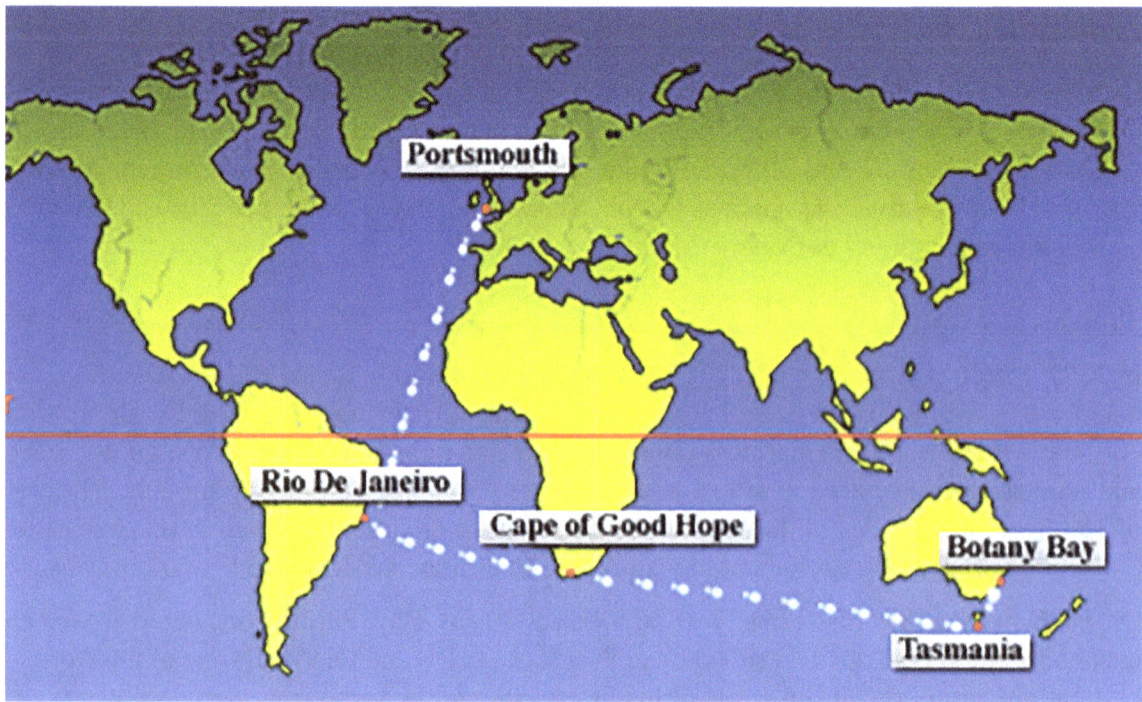
Route of the First Fleet. Source: First Fleet Online, University of Wollongong

On arrival, the women remained on board while sufficient tents and huts to accommodate them were erected. They disembarked some 10 days later. Despite a raging thunderstorm, the first bush party in Australia was held that evening. There was much dancing, singing, drinking and fornicating. The next day, 7 February, the Governor's commission was read, and Phillip took the oaths required by law in the presence of the whole population (civil, military and convicts) assembled before him. The settlement, named after Lord Sydney, Britain's home secretary responsible for the colony, is now Australia's largest city.

The First Fleet was followed by the Second Fleet in 1790 and the Third Fleet in 1792. After this transport by individually dispatched ships began. In 1793 three convict transports arrived: the *Pitt* in February, the *Royal Admiral* in October and the *Kitty* in November. My great, great, great grandfather, John Warby, was on the *Pitt* – by the time it arrived population of the colony numbered in excess of 4,000. Convict transports continued to arrive thereafter for three-quarters of a century when finally, in 1868, transportation to the Australian colonies finally ceased.

The Europeans had a disastrous impact on the local Aboriginal people, who suffered the same fate as the indigenous people of the Americas when Europeans arrived, i.e. high mortality rates from introduced diseases to which they had no genetic immunity. In 1789, thousands died in an epidemic of smallpox or possibly chicken-pox. By the early 1800s the Aboriginal population of the Sydney basin was reduced to 10% of the 1788 estimate.

The First Fleet in Sydney Cove, 27 January 1788, painting by John Allcot, 1937. Source: NLA, No. 135776002

View of the settlement on Sydney Cove, Port Jackson, 20 August 1788. Source: Rare Book Collection, State Library of Victoria

Circular Quay (Sydney Cove), 1994. Source: J. Helyar, Wikimedia Commons

Phillip's policy towards the Aboriginal people was enlightened for that era. He ordered that they be well treated and anyone killing them be hanged. King George III had instructed him to:

> *... endeavour, by every possible means to open an intercourse with the natives, and to conciliate their affections, enjoining all our subjects to live in amity and kindness with them.*

Phillip developed a close relationship with Bennelong of the local Eora people. Bennelong was one of the first Aboriginals to adopt European dress and ways, and learn English. In 1790 Phillip built him a hut on what is now called Bennelong Point, the site of the Sydney Opera House.

Bennelong taught the Europeans about his people's language and customs. He accompanied Phillip on his return to England in 1792, where he was presented to King George III. When he returned to Sydney in 1795, he was shunned by both the colonists and his own people. He began drinking alcohol to excess and was killed in a tribal fight in 1813.

Bennelong, native interpreter (copy of etching), 1937. Source: Mitchell Library, State Library of NSW, No. 9628743

Sydney Opera House, Bennelong Point. Source: Peter Read, University of Sydney, *A history of Aboriginal Sydney*

Near starvation in an alien land

The Newcomers found a land, climate, plants and animals that were totally alien to their experience. There was nothing that was like 'home' in Europe. There was nothing a traveller to China would have found even 3,500 years ago. The Aboriginal people lived largely as hunter-gatherers and had little to barter. The First Fleet had brought enough food to last the colony for only two years. This was supplemented with an occasional kangaroo and fish but starvation was ever present during the first couple of years.

The colonists struggled to establish European agricultural practices in a climate and environment that was unfamiliar to them. The seasons seemed upside down, the soil around Port Jackson was infertile and few knew anything about farming. No draught animals were available before 1803, so all cultivation was performed by hand.

When Phillip spoke to all assembled the day after the women came ashore, he told them work would not be as hard as that of a farmer in England with a wife and family to provide for. While people would not be worked beyond their abilities, he expected every individual to contribute his or her share. However, the convicts were unwilling workers and their marine guards refused to supervise them. Livestock either died or wandered away and Aboriginals became increasingly hostile as their lands were occupied and cleared.

Rationing was commonplace and Phillip was evenhanded but strict. Convicts received the same rations as their guards and Phillip shared in the meagre rations and other austerity measures himself. Convicts and marine officers alike were hanged for stealing food. All uniforms were threadbare or ragged and the signs of status were vanishing. Most of the marines were barefoot and drill, rituals and spit-and-polish were gone. Because clothes and rations no longer symbolised rank, marines expressed their superiority in actions, with every curse, kick and blow showered on convicts to prod them to work carrying a tinge of superiority.

By April 1790 weekly rations had been reduced to 2 ½ lb (1.14 kg) flour, 2 lb (0.91 kg) salted pork and 2 lb (0.91 kg) rice. The flour and rice were crawling with weevils and on boiling the pork shrank to half its weight. The settlers were close to starving when the Second Fleet arrived in June 1790 and rations were immediately increased.

In 1789, Phillip granted a convict, James Ruse, 12 ha of land near Parramatta, which he cultivated and established the colony's first farm, growing grain and vegetables. Further grants of land were given to ex-convicts and soldiers and by 1792 there were 600 acres (240 ha) under crop and thriving vegetable and fruit gardens. The Newcomers were beginning to come to terms with a new life in the strange, new land.

When Phillip left in 1792, the worst was over. There were no further famines in New South Wales. He left behind a viable settlement with a European population of 4,221, of whom 3,099 were convicts; a settlement that had a sense of community and feeling for the supremacy of law, authority and equality and perhaps a grudging cooperative endeavour into which circumstances had forced the convicts. As the Newcomers battled with droughts, floods and fires over the following century, this grudging cooperative endeavour became the part of the Australian character that would bind the Australian soldiers so solidly together in WWI.

Regrettably, this emerging society did not embrace the Original Australians. Few colonists adopted an enlightened attitude towards them. Most considered them little better than a hindrance, despite the fact that for millennia they had endured in the land the Newcomers found so harsh and destructive. Some explorers employed their knowledge of the terrain and the police took advantage of their tracking skills but ignorance, greed and cultural bigotry curbed any possibility of creating a harmonic, productive, synergistic relationship. This has had tragic consequences for the Original Australians and left incomplete the formation of the 'New' Australian. One can only hope that he will not be stillborn.

A nightmare voyage

Transportation was a terrifying prospect. The convicts knew there was little chance they would see their homeland or their loved ones again. They did not really know what fate awaited them in the land 'beyond the seas' but to reach it they had to suffer a long, cruel journey.

Those in the First Fleet were lucky having Captain Phillip, a naval officer, in command. He ensured the fleet and those it carried arrived in as good condition as possible. Subsequently, transporting the convicts was contracted out to private operators and, although voyages were one to two months faster, conditions onboard the ships were appalling.

The ships leaked in both calm and rough seas, making it impossible to keep dry. For the first 20 years, the convicts were chained up for the entire time at sea. The cells were divided into compartments by wooden or iron bars. No fresh air reached the holds and convicts suffered from both cold and overheating. On some ships as many as 50 convicts were crammed into a single compartment and on the *Neptune*, a ship in the infamous Second Fleet, more than 500 convicts were confined in a space 21 m by 9 m by 1.7 m.

Their rations were meagre and in addition to cold and heat stress they suffered from hunger and thirst. Someone chained next to a dead person would not mention the death for as long as possible so as to get the dead person's rations. There was no escape from the lice or human excrement and always there was seasickness.

Female convicts were subjected to varying degrees of degradation and the ships transporting them inevitably became floating brothels. In 1817 a British judge acknowledged that it was acceptable for younger women to be taken to the cabins of officers each night, or thrown in with the crew.

Brutal ships' masters, harsh discipline and scurvy, dysentery and typhoid resulted in a huge loss of life. Rarely did convicts arrive in good condition. The *Sydney Cove Chronicle*, 30 June 1790, reported the arrival of the Second Fleet, the contract for which was with a shipping company engaging in the transport of slaves:

> *At last the transports are here... 278 died on the fearsome journey to Sydney Cove. . . . The landing of those who remained alive despite their misuse upon the recent voyage, could not fail to horrify those who watched. As they came on shore, these wretched people were hardly able to move hand or foot. Such as could not carry themselves upon their legs, crawled upon all fours. Those, who, through their afflictions, were not able to move, were thrown over the side of the ships; as sacks of flour would be thrown, into the small boats. Some expired in the boats; others as they reached the shore. Some fainted and were carried by those who fared better. More had not the opportunity even to leave their ocean prisons for as they came upon the decks, the fresh air only hastened their demise. A sight most outrageous to our eyes were the marks of leg irons upon the convicts, some so deep that one could nigh on see the bones.*

One-quarter of the convicts in the Second Fleet died during the voyage and more soon after its arrival. Death rates of this magnitude were common until about 1820, when improved conditions of transportation were introduced. On the *Pitt* conditions for the 410 convicts were little better than those of the Second Fleet. Fifteen convicts died during a smallpox outbreak soon after it left England. When off Africa convicts broke out in ulcers from lack of Vitamin B and showed symptoms of scurvy. Then 27 non-convicts died from fever and later 29 convicts died. On arrival 120 were sick but male convicts were put to work immediately and continued to die throughout the hot, humid summer and the winter.

No doubt those convicts who survived the voyage were glad when it was over but a hard life awaited them.

Early convict life in New South Wales

Life was harsh for all in the initial years of the colony, but especially so for the convicts, whose labour was required to establish the settlement. Most convicts transported to Australia had worked previously as labourers, farm workers or domestic servants. While few could read or write, some had received a professional, trade or artistic education.

As mentioned earlier the colony, especially the convicts, was fortunate in having Phillip as its first Governor; he was a leader of men who carried out his task in a practical and visionary manner. He recognised the colony could not be run simply as a prison camp to be successful. Before leaving England he said:

> *In a new country there will be no slavery and hence no slaves.*

Phillip encouraged the convicts and gave them hope for the future. For example, when two convicts on arrival sought to sue the captain of their transport ship for stealing their possessions during the voyage, Phillip not only allowed this but also found in their favour and ordered the captain to make restitution. This was in stark contrast to the situation in Britain, where convicts had no right to sue.

When the marines refused to supervise the convicts, he appointed overseers from the convict ranks to ensure the others worked. He also began the practice of utilising the knowledge and skills of convicts, whatever their crime. In addition he introduced a process of convict emancipation that culminated with Governor Lachlan Macquarie (1810-1821), a military officer who, like Phillip, had progressive ideas.

Phillip set working hours of 5.00 am to 7.00 pm with 2.5 hrs for meal breaks. The most hardened male convicts were assigned to hard labour in chain-gangs and set to work making roads and breaking stones needed for building. The vital task of cultivating crops was undertaken by women as well as men. As a naval officer he enforced strict discipline and punishment for convicts found guilty of crime included hard labour, flogging and hanging.

Until the end of transportation convict labour was used to construct public facilities such as roads, bridges, courthouses and hospitals. Most convicts were assigned to military officers, emancipated convicts and free-settlers. They were classed as 'assigned convicts' with some working as labourers and others as domestics. The person receiving these assigned convicts was responsible for providing them with food, clothing and shelter.

Flogging prisoners, Tasmania, drawing by James Reid Scott, 1859. Source: NLA, No. 135505322

Female convicts not assigned to domestic service were sent to the 'Female Factory', where they were set to work washing and making clothes. The system of selection of servants often meant that the gentry and officers could choose the pretty young convicts. Accommodation at the Female Factory was limited and women had to find lodgings as best they could. Few opportunities to earn money to pay for this forced many women to take up prostitution to survive.

For the majority of white women, 'making do' in the colony involved living with a man, sometimes married but usually not. Officials of the colony, even at the highest levels, lived openly with convict women or the daughters of convicts. The governors condemned these de facto relationships and promoted marriage but there were a number of barriers to marriage. Some new arrivals had husbands and wives back in Britain. Convicts needed the permission of their masters to marry and this was granted only reluctantly as the masters had to support any offspring. For many years there were no Catholic priests. Also, de facto relationships were acceptable in the environment from which most convicts had come.

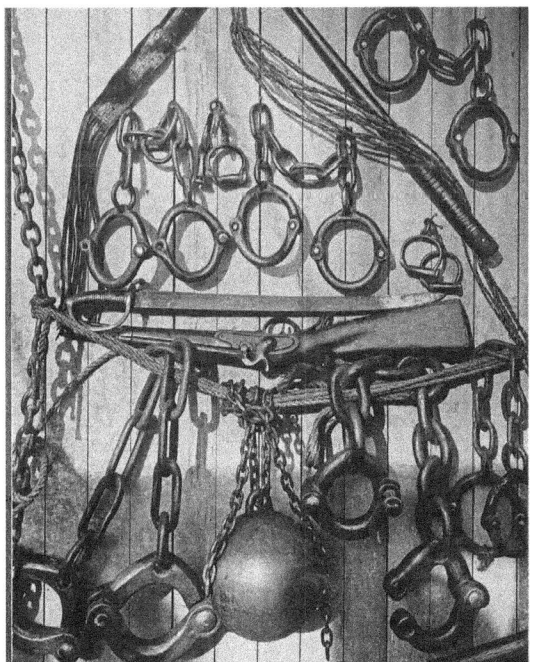

Relics of convict discipline, Beattie Museum, Hobart. Source: NLA, No. 142164079

There was nothing genteel about this colonial society. In the struggle for survival there was little opportunity for fun. Life was raw and behaviour coarse. Whoring, brawling and drinking were commonplace and drunkenness was widespread as it relieved the harshness and monotony of life. When in the early 1800s time finally became available for leisure activities, it was outdoor sports that flourished. Cricket, fishing and bush-walking were popular. A strong interest in horse racing developed along with gambling in its various forms. On 15 October 1810 a 3-day racing carnival, Australia's first recorded sporting event, was held in Hyde Park. The preference of Australians for outdoor activity rather than the indoors was possibly largely a result of the more favourable climatic conditions than in Britain.

What was considered as the low moral tone of the colony was blamed upon the shortage of women. There were three times as many men as women on the First Fleet and in 1800, there were 971 European women and 4,733 men in New South Wales. Even by 1822, the ratio had improved only marginally with 5,977 women and 20,600 men, while the difference was even greater in Van Dieman's Land. It was not until the 1850s that numbers became more even, while disparity in numbers continued well into the 20th century in the Northern Territory and other outback areas. The clergy tried hard to change it but few had time for religion. The chaplain of the First Fleet considered Phillip was indifferent to religion, except for it being a form of social regulation. The foundations for a church were laid at Parramatta in 1792 but before it was finished it was converted into a gaol and then a granary. Australia developed into a secular society. Unlike Americans, Australians generally give little more than lip service to religion.

Emancipation – a better life

If a prisoner was uncooperative or committed further crimes there was an equally well defined scale of punishments he would receive: first working on a road gang; then being sent to a penal colony; and finally capital punishment. There were also a number of incidental punishments a prisoner could receive: flogging; solitary confinement; treadmill; the stocks; food deprivation; and thumbscrews.

Convicts who had served their sentences were called 'expirees'; they could set up a business or a farm. Those placed on a good behaviour bond could be granted a 'ticket-of-leave'. This exempted them from public labour and allowed them to work for themselves but they could not return to Britain. Tickets-of-leave were normally granted after four years for those with a seven-year sentence, six years for a 14-year sentence and eight years for life. After this convicts could be given conditional or absolute pardons; those given an absolute pardon were allowed to return to Britain. They were called 'emancipists' and had the same rights as the 'expiree' or those with a 'ticket-of-leave'. Expirees also preferred the term 'emancipist' as it implied that they had attained liberty and strove for the liberty of others.

Australia's first Postmaster, Isaac Nichols, 1809. Source: National Museum of Australia

Isaac Nicholas, transported to Sydney in 1791 for stealing, was appointed the colony's first Postmaster in 1809, a position he held until his death in 1819. He had the sole authority to board ships to collect all incoming mail and his house served as the colony's first post office. The design depicts him boarding the *Experiment*, a 142 ton brig in Sydney Harbour.

Governor Lachlan Macquarie (1810-1821), the 5th Governor of the colony of New South Wales, insisted convicts, whose sentences had expired or who had been given conditional or absolute pardons, be treated as social equals. He appointed educated and successful emancipists to official positions; examples were Francis Greenway as Government Architect, William Redfern as Government Surgeon and Andrew Thompson as a Magistrate. He befriended many of them; Greenway became one of Macquarie's best-known emancipist friends. Greenway, an architect, had been convicted for forgery and his death sentence commuted to transportation. Macquarie played a leading role in the social, economic and architectural development of the colony. His influence on the transition of New South Wales from a penal colony to a free-settlement was crucial to the shaping of Australian society.

After the period of food shortages in the first few years of the colony, the convicts were better fed than they had been in Britain. Ex-convicts, as well as free-settlers, received free grants of land for sheep. Many became farmers or set up their own businesses. Many emancipists became extremely wealthy and in turn formed an emancipist class of high social and economic standing. The emancipists were concerned with equality of human rights and considered themselves the true Australians, because the colony had been established specifically for them. Transportation ceased to be seen as a dreadful punishment. Not all were happy with this.

Emancipists *vs* exclusives – convict life gets harsher

Macquarie's liberal policy, especially of inviting ex-convicts to dinner at Government House, upset many of the free-settler community. These free-settlers, who tended to be among the wealthy landowners, considered themselves colonial gentry. They sought to exclude the emancipists and their offspring from positions of influence, arguing that it rewarded criminality. They were known as 'exclusives'. Also, they were discontented with Macquarie's authoritarian rule as he attempted to enforce his progressive ideas. Their complaints to the British Government resulted in a judge (J.T. Bigge) being sent to New South Wales to report on Macquarie's administration. Bigge's report recommended the appointment of a legislative council to assist the Governor in making laws and raising revenue, and transportation be re-established as a deterrent to crime in Britain. Bigge's siding with the exclusives led Macquarie to resign.

After Macquarie left in 1821, the lives of the convicts became much harsher. Flogging was more frequent and confinement in isolation increased. Free time was abolished and tickets-of-leave and pardons became harder to obtain. No free land grants were given to convicts when they had served their sentences. Centres of 'secondary punishment' were established at Moreton Bay or Brisbane Town as it was known (1824), Norfolk Island (1825) and Port Arthur (1830) for convicts who misbehaved while serving sentences. Order at Moreton Bay was maintained by flogging, head-shaving women, applying leg-irons, neck-chains and treadmill and solitary confinement. Port Arthur and Norfolk Island were infamous for cruelty. The following statements give an indication of the horrendous treatment inflicted upon the convicts on Norfolk Island:

Judge Sir Roger Therry wrote:

> *Their sunken glazed eyes, deadly pale faces, hollow fleshless cheeks and once manly limbs shriveled and withered up as if by premature old age, created horror among those in court. There was not one of the six who had not undergone from time to time a thousand lashes each and more. They looked less like human beings than the shadows of gnomes who had risen from their sepulchral abode. What man was or ever could be reclaimed under such a system as this?*

Bishop Ullathorne wrote:

> *I have to record the most heart-rending scene that I ever witnessed. The turnkey unlocked the cell door and then came forth a yellow exhalation, the produce of the bodies of the men confined therein. I announced to them who were reprieved from death and which of them were to die. It is a literal fact that each man who heard of his reprieve wept bitterly, and each man who heard his condemnation of death went down on his knees, and with dry eyes, thanked God they were to be delivered from this horrid place. The morning came, they received on their knees the sentence as the will of God. Loosened from their chains, they fell down in the dust, and, in the warmth of their gratitude, kissed the very feet that had brought them peace.*

Flogging a prisoner at Port Arthur. Source: Victorian Collections

No free-settlers were allowed into the Moreton Bay district until 1842. Norfolk Island ceased to be a penal colony in 1855 and Port Arthur in 1877.

The governors who succeeded Macquarie associated more closely with the exclusives, and the emancipists lost many of the rights Macquarie had granted them. Tired of discrimination, many emancipists left New South Wales for other Australian colonies, where they believed their children would be given a better opportunity in life. At some locations they were accepted, while at others they were not. For example, in North-east Victoria, wealthy landowners organised meetings to keep Australians of convict origin out of the region.

During 1788-1822 the majority of Europeans arriving in Australia were either convicts or ex-convicts. Although free-settlers began to arrive in the 1790s, their numbers were small until the mass immigration schemes of the 1830s took effect. Thus convicts formed the majority of the colony's population for the first few decades, and by 1821 there was a growing number of freed convicts who had been granted land or appointed to positions of trust and responsibility. It was these convicts, most of whom were guilty of petty crimes committed in trying to survive the conditions of England at the time, who built up the colony from nothing at the beginning. They were the pioneers who, through hard work and perseverance, enabled the colony to survive and expand to the stage of self-sufficiency.

In the 1820s and 1830s, the period when most convicts were sent to the colonies, the policy of assigning convicts to private employers was expanded. By the mid-1830s only around six per cent of the convict population was 'locked up'. In a new system introduced in 1842, on arrival all convicts would be allocated to Probation Gangs, which were engaged in building public works. After two years well-behaved convicts were issued a Probation Pass, which 'permitted' them to work for private employers for wages. Part of their wages was withheld as a form of compulsory saving. Whether the Government found them a job is unclear, as is whether or not their accommodation, food and medical care were also provided. Thus the majority were working for free-settlers and the authorities. Even so, convicts were often subject to cruelties such as leg-irons and the lash. However, such punishment was not arbitrary, as no convict could be punished except by due process of the law. Furthermore, convicts had more legal rights than if they had remained in Britain.

Transportation of convicts to New South Wales, Queensland and Tasmania continued until 1840, 1842 and 1853, respectively. Transportation to Western Australia, which began in 1850 to supply labour, ceased in 1868; Perth, like Melbourne and Adelaide, had been established as a free-settlement. By the time transportation ended the convicts had served their purpose. The population of the colonies had grown from 30,000 in 1821 to around one million in the mid-1800s. There were enough people to do the necessary work so the colonies could sustain themselves and continue to grow. It was well into the 1880s or early 1890s before the last convicts completed serving their sentences. Overall, a total of about 160,500 convicts were transported, of whom only 4,700 were women. The vast majority were English (70%), Irish (24%) and Scottish (5%); some were Maoris, Chinese and slaves from the Caribbean.

Australia's convict beginning is unique and had a significant part in shaping the Australian character. Certainly it would be largely responsible for the Australian sense of freedom, equality and a 'fair go for all'.

Ancestral arrival

My ancestors were among those early convict arrivals and their lives would be typical of those who helped to develop the Australia of today. On 14 February 1792, my great, great, great grandfather John Warby arrived at Port Jackson after a 7-month voyage in the convict transport ship *Pitt*. In 1791 when 24 (or perhaps 18) years old, he and another man, William Deards, had been sentenced to transportation for the term of seven years for stealing two donkeys.

The *Pitt* off Dover, 1787. Source: National Maritime Museum, Greenwich

John Warby had worked on a farm in Hertfordshire as a farm labourer and his farming skills were a real asset in the colony. At the end of 1792 Phillip granted him 50 acres (20 ha) at Prospect Creek, eight kilometres from Parramatta, to grow crops. Taking full advantage of this opportunity he worked hard and by 1801 had eight acres (3.2 ha) sown to wheat, 13 acres (5.2 ha) under maize, 25 bushels of maize in stock and 10 pigs, as well as two workmen, one an assigned convict and the other already free, in his employ.

During Governor Bligh's administration he was appointed to the position of Superintendent of the wild cattle in the Cow Pastures region, with responsibility for the protection and culling of the herd. By the time of Governor Macquarie's arrival in the colony he had an extensive knowledge of the Camden/Appin area.

In 1816 Macquarie granted Warby 260 acres (104 ha) of fertile land in the district of Airds, on the site of present day Campbelltown, which he named *Leumeah*. Among Warby's neighbours at Airds was his fellow accomplice William Deards, who had a 30 acre (12 ha) grant.

By 1826 Warby had built a house, granary, barn, stables, storeroom and a hut for assigned labourers and had acquired extensive land holdings. In October 1826, he applied for an additional grant of land without purchase, stating that he currently held 400 acres (160 ha) of land by grant and 400 acres by purchase (300 of which were cleared or under tillage), owned 120 head of cattle and 100 pigs, and employed and maintained eight convict servants. By 1829 he was also squatting at Gundagai.

John Warby's cottage, later known as *Leumeah House*, built between 1816 and 1826. Source: Michelle Vale

John Warby's barn, later known as *Leumeah Barn*, built between 1816 and 1828. Source: Michelle Vale

He gained increasing respect within the colony as a guide and assistant to exploration parties in the south-western region of Sydney. Governor Macquarie referred to him as *my excellent guide*. This opportunity to explore must have given him a great sense of freedom. Warby also had another skill – the knack of being able to communicate with a broad cross-section of the community from governors to black trackers. He remained a prominent member of the community in predominantly emancipist Campbelltown until his death in 1851. Hard work and a willingness to grasp opportunity when it came his way brought him land and good living conditions he could never have dreamt of in England.

In September 1796 Warby married 16 years-old Sarah Bentley, who had arrived the previous April on the *Indispensible*. Of the 133 convict women transported, two had died. Sarah had worked as a housemaid in England and had been sentenced to seven-years transportation for attempting to pawn clothes – 2 cotton gowns, a checked linen apron, a muslin checked handkerchief, a scarlet cloth cloak and a shawl handkerchief – stolen from her employer. Petty theft of clothes was a crime commonly committed by convict girls and women. As was the case for most convicts, neither John nor Sarah could read or write. John and Sarah produced 14 children (9 boys and 5 girls) of whom 11 survived to adulthood.

Most of the daughters of convicts married young, and had no hesitation in marrying an ex-convict if he had money. Nine of John Warby's children married convicts or children of convicts. In 1822, one of his daughters, Sarah, aged 16, married emancipist Alexander MacDonald at the recently completed St Luke's Church of England, Liverpool. They made their mark on the marriage certificate – neither could read or write – but Sarah signed the marriage register with a firm hand, when she remarried six years after Alexander's death in 1847. We can only guess how Sarah and Alexander met. It could well have been at church because they lived in the same district and late in life Sarah wished to give something towards a new Presbyterian manse.

Chapter 4: Convict Beginning

Alexander came from the slums of Edinburgh, where he had worked as a brass founder's labourer. In March 1812, when 14 years old, he and a Robert Gunn were charged that, whilst in the company of others, they had robbed a number of men. Both Alexander and Robert were convicted for robbery with violence and sentenced to transportation beyond the seas for life. The Solicitor General stated it appeared that Alexander MacDonald and Robert Gunn were among those who were led and were not leaders of a gang and they were less guilty than some who had fled, and others who had already received sentence. The leaders were hanged. Many felons were hanged for crimes that were minor by comparison with those of Alexander. On 3 December 1812 he and Robert departed England on the *Fortune II* and arrived at Port Jackson on 12 June 1813. The ship's indent described him as being 5 feet 4 inches (163 cm) tall with brown hair, hazel eyes and a fair complexion. On arrival Alexander was assigned as an unskilled labourer to an emancipist with a small holding in the Airds district; Alexander was his only servant.

In 1818 he was given a ticket-of-leave in which he was described as being a labourer, 5 feet 6 inches (168 cm) tall. The extra height was quite likely due to reasonable food and a healthy outdoor life. He received a conditional pardon in 1836, which described him as being 5 feet 7 inches (170 cm) tall. Perhaps the added height was a sign of self-respect, which enabled him to walk tall.

Alexander was a hard worker and John Warby gave him 20 acres (8 ha) of land as a marriage gift for the nominal price of five shillings. Four years later Warby assigned him a further 10 acres (4 ha) for 40 pounds six shillings and eight pence. His landholdings were at least 57 acres (22.8 ha) when he died at 50 years of age in his residence *Campbelltown View*. He had lived in the Campbelltown District for the last 30 years of his life.

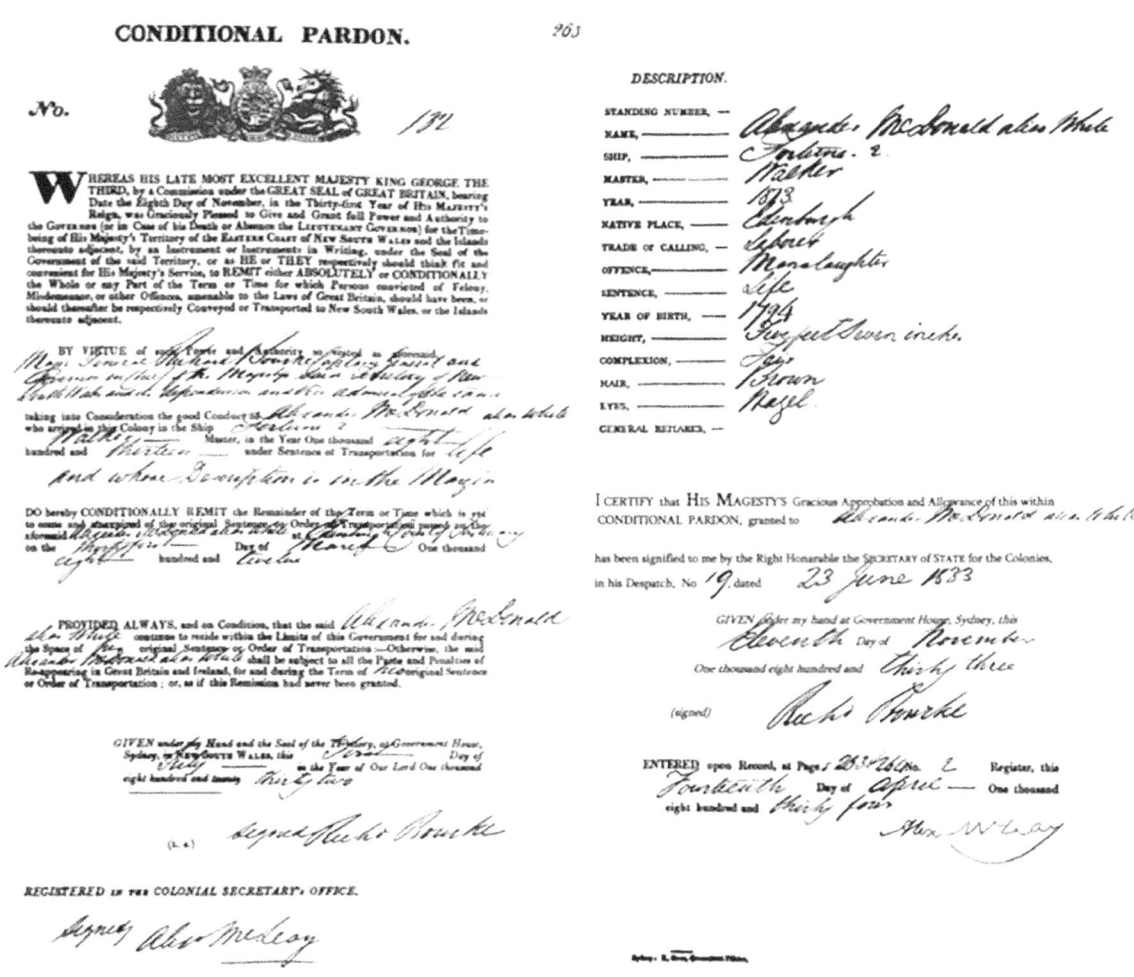

Conditional Pardon paperwork for Alexander MacDonald. Source: David MacDonald

It appears that Alexander and Sarah's children received a good education. These children ventured forth to become pioneers in rural Victoria, NSW and Queensland. They accepted a challenge where they saw it and used their energy and intelligence to further their own careers and the development of their own country. The fifth son, P.F. MacDonald, was my great grandfather. He was the only ancestor my family spoke about but not about his early life. At no stage did he ever mention his life and it was not until the 1970s that we knew anything about who came before him.

St Luke's Anglican Church, Liverpool, NSW. Source: Maggie To, St Luke's Parish, Liverpool

Designed by emancipist Francis Greenway and built by convict labour, it is reputed to be the oldest standing Anglican Church in Australia.

In November 1810 Governor Macquarie directed the emancipist Acting Surveyor James Meehan to mark out the ground for the town of Liverpool with a square at the centre for the building of a church. The church, completed in 1822, was constructed from locally produced sandstock bricks and mainly cedar timber. Since then a number of additions and changes have been made.

The persistent endeavour of John and Sarah Warby to make the most of their lives in spite of their social and physical environment was typical of a great many who were transported. When John Warby died in 1851, his family covered all levels of colonial society, whether emancipist, free, colonial-born, English, Irish, Scottish, Catholic or Protestant.

Convict imprints

The convicts would have loathed those in authority who assigned them to backbreaking toil and maintained discipline by brutal means. They would have observed the lawless and corrupt activities of members of the New South Wales Corps, who replaced the remaining marines who returned to England with Phillip in 1792. Corps officers gained power and with a few rich colonists virtually managed the colony for almost two decades. This was a period of unruly behaviour and lawlessness, during which Corps officers occupied land and built up a trade in rum that finally became 'the currency' of the colony; hence the Corps became known as the 'Rum Corps'. In 1808, the Corps, urged on by most of Sydney's wealthy men deposed the Governor, William Bligh. John Warby was one of a group of settlers who signed a letter of support sent to Bligh in the lead up to this. Law and order was restored in 1809 when Governor Macquarie arrived with his own regiment of soldiers. The convicts would have had at best little respect and a strong dislike for those exercising power and authority. Thus it is not surprising that Australians have scant regard for those in authority today and any who would control their lives.

However, despite having little respect for those in authority, Australians generally have respect for the institutions of authority. Australians expect public services and government provision far more, for instance, than Americans. This expectation and our sense of egalitarianism probably began in January 1788. In those early years the 'government' was the main provider of the necessities of life for both individuals and the community; in other words the provider of food, shelter, clothes and work.

Macquarie did not believe that convicts, who had paid their debt to society, should carry the stigma of emancipation to the grave. But within a decade of his departure a reluctance by many to acknowledge the removal of the convict stain was evident. Even those who did not bear scars on their backs still carried an indelible stigma in the eyes of the 'respectable'. The reluctance to acknowledge the convict stain within families has persisted until very recently. The secret of my convict ancestry was so well kept that my mother expressed disbelief when told of it in the 1970s. Without doubt, the fear that a life and social position so carefully and painstakingly built could be destroyed, should the echoes of 'rattling chains' be heard, would be deeply etched into the Australian psyche. Thus Australians, however friendly they appear to be, are very sensitive to questions that probe into who and what they are. We are accused of being superficial although friendly.

Traditions can be the very cement of a society but can also shackle the human spirit and therefore stifle all aspects of human endeavour just as surely as irons and chains. Those transported would have had little love for the country that had banished them forever. They would have had no love for the poverty and social divisions that denied them the opportunities of life and caused them to end up on the other side of the world. They must have been more than ready to turn their back on the old ways. Whatever this place was they found themselves in, it had been built by their sweat and their toil, by their brains, ingenuity and resourcefulness, and by their unflagging spirit in the face of adversity. For them this place would be where all were free, were as good as one another and all would get a 'fair go'.

The characteristics that sprouted from the soil of convict beginnings would grow stronger and be added to over the next century as their sons and daughters, and like-minded unfettered Newcomers set about exploring and settling a vast and, to them, alien and often inhospitable continent, while they continued to battle with those in authority and those who would lord it over them.

Chapter 5
Currency Lads and Lasses

By 1813 most of the population of the colony were under 12 years of age and native-born of convict parents. These native-born sons and daughters of convicts were considered slightly inferior and became known as 'Currency Lads and Lasses'. 'Currency' was the name given to the mix of coins and notes from many countries used in the colony and contrasted sharply with English gold pieces called 'sterling' and considered the genuine article. Wealthy free-settlers and religious leaders in Old Sydney Town had feared these children would take after their parents, but by the 1820s observers reported the native-born were becoming good citizens. They did not drink heavily and were honest. The girls were modest and mild-tempered but liked to use tortoise shell combs to display their curly hair with a bit of style. Also, the terms 'sterling' and 'currency' were being used to describe two groups of people in the colony: sterling referred to non-convict, British-born residents, whereas currency applied to those who were colonial-born, a name they began to bear with pride. The native-born were observed to be forming a unique group within the colony.

Compared with industrial England family life of early New South Wales children was stable. Former convicts actively sought apprenticeships for their sons, often with government bodies; here teachers were generally convicts or ex-convicts. Currency Lads did not want jobs as farm labourers, which was what convicts did.

The land, that the newcomers found strange and at times frightening, smiled upon their children. As a result of the mild winters and a healthy environment and diet, they were taller, more slender and healthier than English immigrants of the same age. Some observers considered the native-born aged prematurely, reporting the girls were often pretty and delicate looking when young but by 25 or 30 years of age looked about 50. Visitors today make similar remarks about Australian women. The harshness of the climate takes a heavy toll on one's complexion.

The currencies differed in speech from others. They spoke with a distinctive accent – a nasal twang. Some of their words came from Aboriginal languages and some were their own creation. Many of their words and expressions contemptuously categorised as 'colonial' were underworld terms or from British dialects; such language was not sterling English, not the language of respectable London society. Swearing coloured their conversations. Shifts in the meaning of standard English words, for example 'mate', reflected social ideals that differed from the British. The Australian accent was established in the first 60 years. The distinctive Australian vocabulary was stabilised during the second half of the 19th century.

The currencies had a healthy self-respect and showed a strong independence of disposition and a quality of being bluntly direct. They were free-hearted, generous, shrewd and good-natured; every one of them seemed equal with the rest. They had a certain lack of automatic deference to their obvious betters. They considered 'Jack was as good as his master', unlike the Englishman 'who dearly loves a lord'. They despised 'crawlers' or to use a current expression 'brown nosers'.

The Currency Lads and Lasses were the first non-Aboriginal Australians and pride in their colonial birth was growing. They and the emancipists regarded the country as their own and amongst them the first signs of nationalism emerged. They looked down on the wealthy and voluntary newcomers from England as 'self-imported devils'. This dislike intensified when, after the Bigge Report, transportation was re-established to act as a deterrent to crime. As well as harsher prison conditions, distribution of land to ex-convicts (emancipists) became more restrictive and biased against their children in favour of the wealthy and socially accepted English immigrants.

This animosity was given voice by prominent, wealthy, colonial-born William Charles Wentworth, when he was snubbed by Sydney's 'socially respectable' class, the exclusives; his parents had not married and his mother had been a convict. He became head of the emancipist party, which sought equal rights and status for ex-convicts and their descendants; and in 1822 founded a newspaper, *The Australian*, the colony's first privately-owned paper, to champion his causes. He also became Vice-President of the Australian Patriotic Association. Later he became very conservative and he and the exclusives were reconciled. He eventually settled in England, where he died. However, Wentworth probably did not feel England was his real home because, at his request, his body was returned to Sydney for burial.

The interest of Australians in sport began with the native-born in those early years of the colony. They saw it as another means of setting themselves apart. They thought it essential to excel in all types of sport, especially in games played against the English. In 1832, Horatio Wills, whose father was transported in 1797 for highway robbery, founded what was mainly a sporting paper, *The Currency Lad*. It appeared as 'published by Horatio Wills, an Australian'. Horatio believed a man should be rewarded for ability and effort. He resented the way those born overseas looked down on the native-born. As far as he was concerned there were no divisions between men.

In 1859 at the age of 24 Horatio's son Thomas, a first-class cricketer and all-round sportsman, persuaded the Melbourne Cricket Club that cricketers needed a game to keep themselves fit during the winter season. He founded the game of Australian Rules football and formed the Melbourne Football Club. Thomas had attended the famous Rugby School in England but, when deciding about a code of football declared: *We shall have a game of our own*. This was a radical proclamation because at the time all models and patterns of behaviour were being imported. The sporting and cultural elite in Melbourne at that time were basically English and English-educated. The new colony of Victoria saw itself as containing the seeds of a 'New' Australia, one free from the convict stain. Wills was probably the only native-born among them, and he got access because he had been to Rugby.

Some believe Australian Rules was an adaptation of an Aboriginal game – marngrook – which was played without the European idea of goals – the greatest honour went to the man who kicked the possum skin stuffed with charcoal highest in the air or leapt highest to catch it. In 1839 Thomas's father, Horatio Wills, 'squatted' in the Western District of Victoria at Mount William on Djabwurrung land. He learnt to speak their language but may have been involved in their harassment and even murder. Thomas grew up having Aboriginal playmates and playing Aboriginal games.

His father's political ambitions were frustrated because he was the son of a convict. Dissatisfied with his own life and disappointed with Tom, Horatio moved to Queensland, the new frontier, in 1859. In Central Queensland he purchased a property, *Cull-in-laringo,* where two years later he and 18 others at the homestead were killed in the biggest massacre of whites by Original Australians in Australian history. Thomas, who was away getting supplies, survived but began to drink heavily and eventually committed suicide at the age of 44.

Wills bought *Cull-in-laringo* (sought and found) from Peter Fitzallen MacDonald, my great grandfather, who had moved north in 1857. The fourth child of Alexander and Sarah MacDonald, he was born at Campbelltown, NSW in 1830. Physically he was a typical Currency Lad, standing well over six feet (183 cm) compared with his emancipist father's five feet seven inches (170 cm). At 17, after working for his father for a while, he left Campbelltown to join the rush to the Turon River gold-field. By 1850 he was overlanding livestock down the Murray River as far as South Australia. He had some luck later at the gold-fields at Bendigo but abandoned his claim because of an outbreak of typhoid fever, which was prevalent on the gold-fields. From 1851 to 1854 he was an overseer on a sheep and cattle property near Geelong. He remained there as manager until 1857, when he went to Queensland. MacDonald, an ambitious young man, probably ventured north to seek fortune and influence, and perhaps also the hope that distance and frontier challenges would muffle the 'rattle of convict bones'.

Wentworth, Wills and MacDonald were resourceful, practical, willing to 'have a go' (attempt anything), flexible and not thwarted by things going wrong, characteristics that became part of the Australian character. MacDonald reflected his generation in a credo for life that was not based on ancestral background or family stability, but on individual hard work and the will to persevere. In a native-born's need to prove his superiority, his singular aim was to grasp any opportunity that might bring rapid financial rewards and, perhaps, social status.

Wentworth and Wills were strong nationalists. I am not aware that MacDonald held any nationalist sentiments but at no stage did I hear his side of the family refer to England as 'home', which still occurred in the first half of the 20th century. Wentworth and Wills were schooled in England, while MacDonald's schooling was much more humble, although he did spend two of his primary school years at The King School. Like Wentworth, MacDonald's early-held liberal views became conservative with time.

Wentworth and Wills and probably MacDonald would not have identified with the Currency Lad lounging at Macquarie's Chair. Their speech and manner would have resembled the 'respectable' society they desired to be part of. They sought to be gentlemen and accepted by the very people our Currency Lads wanted nothing to do with. Currency Lads rejected the Englishness of this class and those in authority as a source of personal identity and instead adopted more informal manners and social customs and a distinctive way of dressing considered slovenly and uncaring – a style of dressing more suited to the climate.

It was amongst the Currency Lads and Lasses or native-born Australians, a term they began to use because New South Welshmen was difficult to say, that the first signs of nationalist sentiment emerged. They appeared to identify more with being from the colonies than sons and daughters of Great Britain. An editorial from a Sydney newspaper said:

They have lost their English spirit and have degenerated into Australians.

They regarded this land as their own. A gap was growing between the ruled and those meant to rule.

A relaxed Currency Lad and stiff-backed English couple at Lady Macquarie's Chair, Sydney, 1830.

Lithograph print *Mrs Macquarie's seat Government Domain, Sydney, N.S. Wales* by Augustus Earle (1793-1838). Source: Australian Prints and Printmaking

Chapter 6
Explorers

Almost from the day the First Fleet landed Phillip began exploring the Port Jackson area in search of suitable farming land on which to grow food for the colony. Exploration of the region continued over the next two decades before the Blue Mountains were finally crossed and the rich pasture lands of the western plains discovered. Until then there was no need to construct physical barriers to prevent the convicts escaping. The Blue Mountains in the west, the ocean to the east, the rivers, the thick, strange bushland and the Aboriginals served as prison walls.

In 1795 ex-convict, John Wilson, reported cattle grazing in the Nepean River area. They were descendants of four cows and two bulls that had escaped from the fledgling Sydney Cove settlement in 1788. Governor Hunter proclaimed the district west of the Nepean River a sanctuary for the wild cattle and named it the *Cow Pastures*. He declared no person was to cross the Nepean or disturb the cattle without written authority, making it the south-western boundary of the colony. Wilson had gained extensive knowledge of much of the country within 161 km of Sydney while living with the Aboriginals after gaining his freedom in 1792.

In 1798 Wilson by-passed the Blue Mountains, when, on Hunter's instruction, he made two journeys to the south-west of Sydney. These two journeys revealed the nature of much of the

Mount Hay, Blue Mountains National Park. Source: Bob Mendelsohn, Flickr

Looking north along the Nepean River, 2006. Source: Brian Voon Yee Yap, Wikimedia Commons

Kanangra Walls and Valley. Source: Chris Couvret, Flickr

Mount Banks, Blue Mountains, NSW. Source: Adam JWC, Wikimedia Commons

rich southern tablelands of New South Wales. He reached Mount Towrang near the present city of Goulburn on the second trip.

In 1802 when travelling along the Nattai and Kowmung Rivers and Christy's Creek, Francis Barrallier, engineer, surveyor and an ensign in the NSW Corps, advanced as far west as the Kanangra Plateau before his provisions were consumed, while trying to find a route over the Blue Mountains. In 1804 botanist George Caley travelled as far as Mount Banks (King George) in an attempt to cross the mountains.

John Warby, who had settled at Prospect in 1793, developed an extensive knowledge of the Cow Pastures region. In 1803 Governor Bligh appointed him Superintendent of the wild cattle grazing there. Warby blazed the track that was laid out on the Cow Pastures Road in 1805 by ex-convict James Mehen, who became Deputy Surveyor-General. Most of the route is now known as the Camden Valley Way.

Warby gained increasing respect within the colony as a guide and assistant to exploration parties in the south-western region of Sydney. He accompanied Barrallier on one of his expeditions and the botanist George Caley in 1806 in his attempt to retrace Barrallier's route along the Nattai River.

In 1810 he accompanied Macquarie, Blaxland and their party on their tour of investigation from Prospect Hill to Cow Pastures. Macquarie was impressed with the country and called it *Airds*. Macquarie met Warby's family at their hut and promised an additional grant of land to 'our excellent guide'. In 1815 Macquarie once again engaged Warby as guide for a revisit to Cow Pastures and an expedition into the rough scrub country of the Nallia River. Macquarie referred to him as 'my excellent guide'.

It was not until May 1813 that a route over the mountains was found by Blaxland, Lawson and W.C. Wentworth along with four convicts, four pack horses and five dogs. This was a tremendous struggle. Deep precipices continually blocked their way, and their horses stumbled on the stony hillsides. The scrub was so thick that they had to cut their way through it. After 10 days some of their horses collapsed with fatigue. A week later some of the party became ill but they continued on until they saw expansive green plains lying to the west. They realized they had found a route across the mountains. Exhaustion and shortages of water, provisions and fodder for the horses forced them to return to base. In November 1813, surveyor George Evans followed their route, crossed the Great Dividing Range and reached the plains on the far side. He reported their rich grazing and farming potential. A year later a 162 km road across the Blue Mountains was completed in six months by 30 convicts who were pardoned and given a small grant of land each.

Convicts building a road over the Blue Mountains, NSW, 1833 by Charles Rodius (1802-1860).
Source: NLA, No. 135505644

The crossing of the Blue Mountains was the forerunner of many expeditions of exploration undertaken over the next six decades. The explorers travelled into unknown country, giving names to mountains, valleys, plains, lakes, rivers and deserts. Like Barrallier, some were soldiers and surveyors under orders. Some like Blaxland, Lawson and Wentworth hoped to find pastoral land, minerals or routes for roads, railways or telegraph lines. Some searched for lost expeditions or hoped to gain fame and then fortune, while others like Caley were scientists or simply adventurers. They suffered danger, hunger and thirst, and overcame hardships such as extreme heat, boggy soil and rugged terrain. Many died or, like Leichhardt, disappeared into the desert, never to be seen again.

A major motive for exploration in the three decades following the crossing of the Blue Mountains was to find out what happened to the rivers flowing west from the Great Dividing Range. Expeditions led by Oxley, Mitchell, Sturt and others revealed they did not flow into an inland sea, the existence of which was a popular belief at the time. They found Australia's inland rivers formed two large drainage systems: the Murray-Darling and Lake Eyre Basins. The rivers of the former finally become the Murray that enters the sea 83 km south of Adelaide at Lake Alexandria. Those of the latter such as the Georgina, Coopers Creek and Diamantina, which flow only after periods of rain, drain into Lake Eyre – a gigantic salt pan most of the time.

The Murray-Darling Basin (green), Lake Eyre Basin (grey) and Great Artesian Basin (hatched). Source: Department of the Environment and Heritage, 2006

Later expeditions, many of which were epic desert treks and transcontinental journeys, put an end to speculation about what was in the centre of Australia.

In 1841 Eyre crossed southern Australia from east to west, travelling from Fowlers Bay, 912 km north-west of Adelaide, across the Nullabor Plain to Albany. He set out with one white man, Baxter, and three Aboriginal men. When water and supplies ran low two

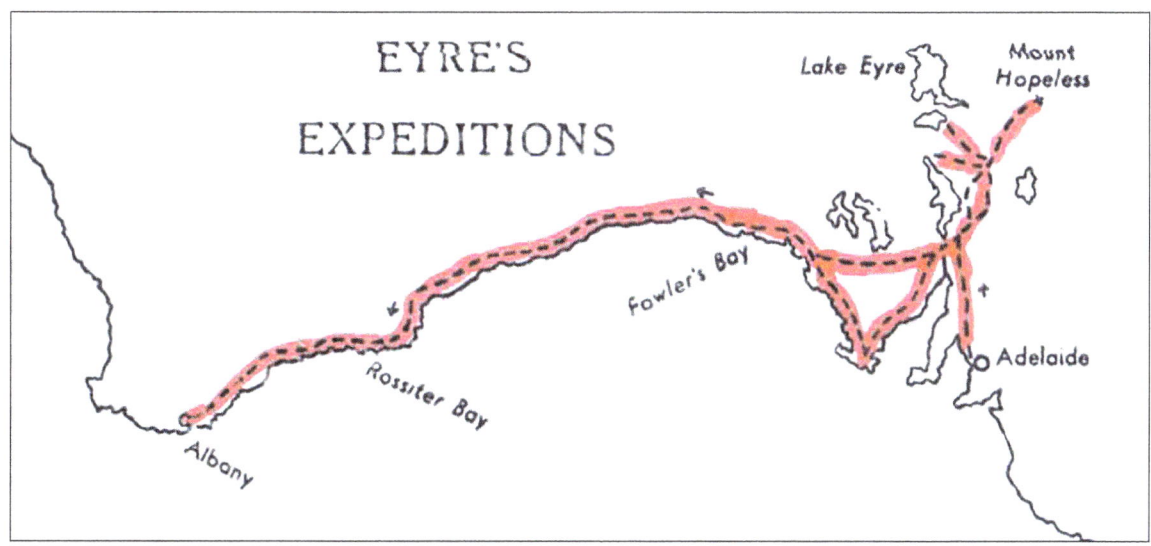

Eyre's expeditions. Source: Wikimedia Commons

of the Aboriginals killed Baxter and ran off with what remained. Eyre and Wylie struggled on, finally reaching Albany.

In 1844-1846 Sturt, who still believed there must be an inland sea, led another expedition to locate it by travelling into the centre of Australia. He left Adelaide with a large party and dragging a whaleboat. They travelled through extremely difficult country, enduring scorching heat; there was a severe drought at the time. On reaching the Simpson Desert he turned back, reluctantly realising there was no inland sea. He reported:

> *The stillness of death reigned around us. No living creature was to be heard. Nothing visible inhabited that dreary desert but the ant.*

In 1844-45 Leichhardt led an expedition to find a new route to Port Essington – the site of an early attempt at settlement 300 km north of Darwin. Lacking government funding, his party was lightly manned, provisioned and equipped. After a trek of 4,800 km, during which he used his experience in living off the land and one of his party being killed by Aboriginals, he returned to Sydney by boat to a hero's welcome. However, some after whom he named noteworthy features were concerned with their names appearing on the map along-side ex-convict members of his expedition he also honoured in this manner.

The name Leichhardt appears in a variety of ways throughout Queensland. My Uncle Peter rowed for the Leichhardt Rowing Club. One of the state primary school teams against which I played rugby league came from The Leichhardt Ward School, a boys-only school. Rockhampton had a Leichhardt Hotel which, at some stage, my great grandfather, P.F. MacDonald, had acquired. It had passed down to my mother's family and in my youth my family invariably had a midday Sunday dinner there and many Christmas dinners as well. Like in all hotels in those days, tables were laid with silverware on white linen tablecloths. Occasionally a table or two would be occupied by teenagers from Victoria on a school tour. They were easily distinguished by complexions unravaged by the Queensland sun, a fact my parents always remarked upon.

Leichhardt had no delusions about the Australian bush and his undertakings:

> *Life in the bush without that scientific understanding which enables one to sense the deep warmth of nature like the heart of a friend is very exhausting.*

Leichhardt was a keen observer, assiduous record keeper and prolific collector. He ensured the originals of specimens sent to Europe for identification were returned to Sydney. The aim was to form a collection here because he believed that those who took an interest in the new land and considered it their home were the beginnings of a mighty nation that would forget old Europe.

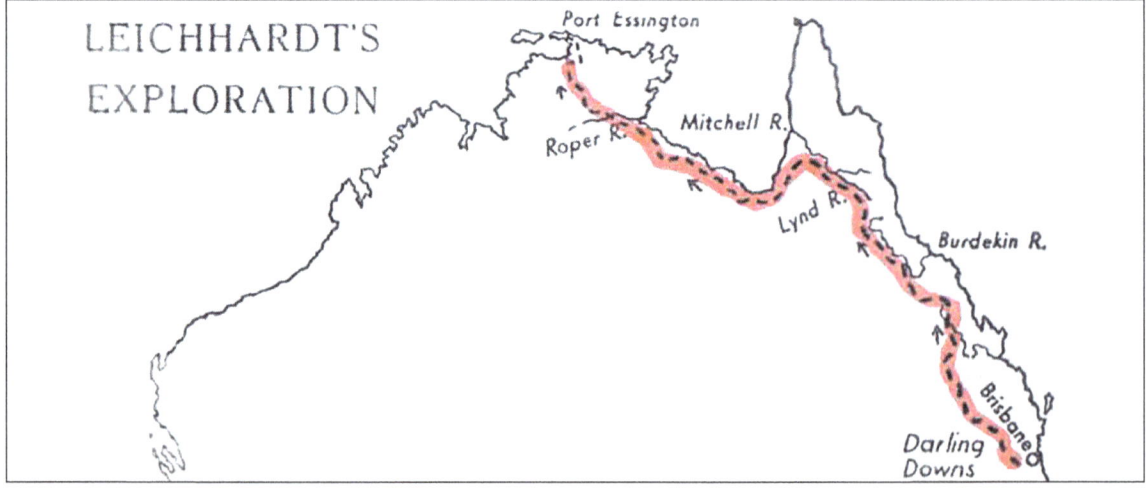

The first expedition of Leichhardt. Source: Wikimedia Commons

In 1848 he and his party of seven including two Aboriginals vanished without trace when trying to pioneer a route from Brisbane to Perth. This remains one of Australia's greatest mysteries. It was Leichhardt from whom Patrick White, Australian Nobel Laureate, drew inspiration for his great novel *Voss*.

In the mid-1850s, Gregory led a party of six east from the Victoria River across the north of Australia to Cape York and then south to Brisbane, in all covering 3,000 km by sea and 8,000 km overland. They lost horses from crocodiles and drowning, their sheep died in the intense heat and their rations were destroyed by the heat, ants and rats. They were compelled to eat bats and slaughter their pack animals to survive. However, Gregory was a careful leader and lost none of his men.

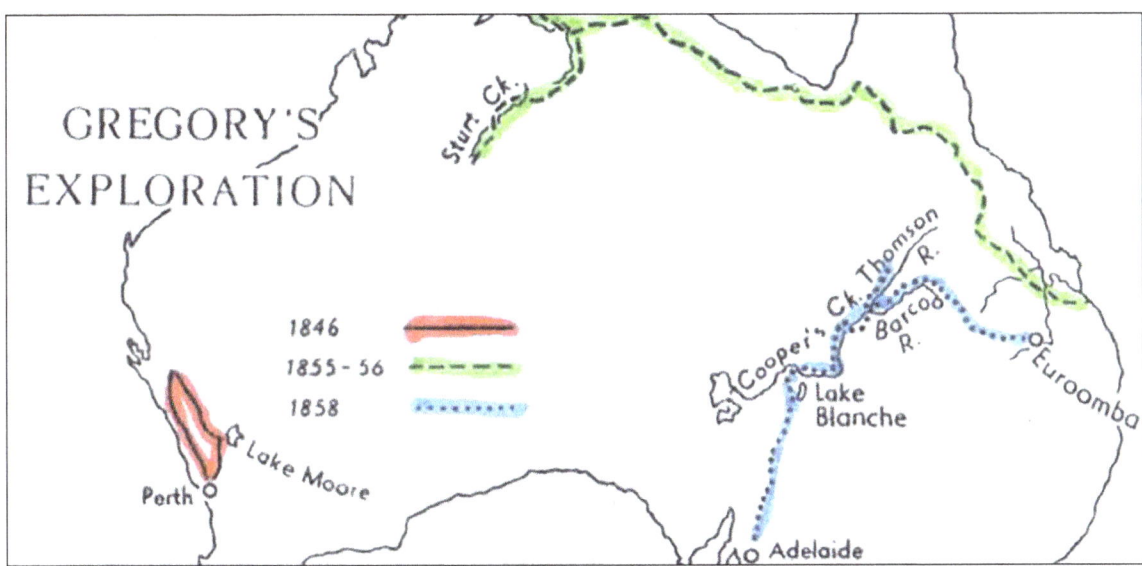

Map of the explorer Augustus Charles Gregory's route in Australia. Source: Wikimedia Commons

In 1860-61 Burke and Wills died of starvation in tragic circumstances on their return after crossing Australia from Melbourne in the south to the Gulf of Carpentaria in the north. Altogether seven of the 18 who set out lost their lives and only one completed the entire journey and returned to Melbourne. They could have survived had they befriended the local Aboriginals.

Possibly the greatest explorer was Scottish-born John McDowell Stuart who, in 1862, was the first to cross Australia from south to north and back again; he led six expeditions to the centre of Australia without losing a single man. At ease in this 'inhospitable' environment he could read its signs in the on-going quest for water. The overland telegraph line, which

Return of Burke and Wills to Coopers Creek, 1873-1876, Nicholas Chevalier (1828-1902). Source: National Gallery of Australia

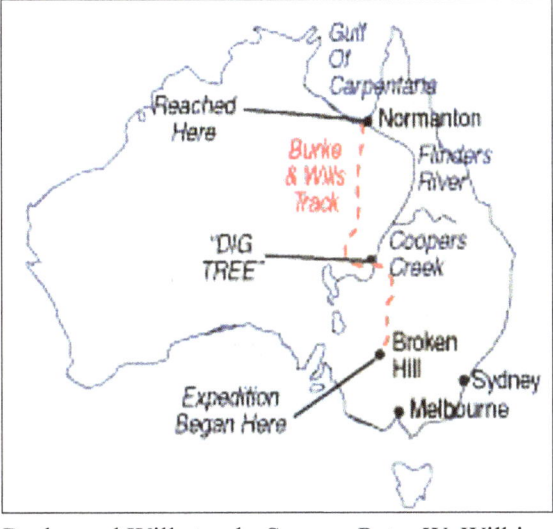

Burke and Wills track. Source: Peter W. Wilkins

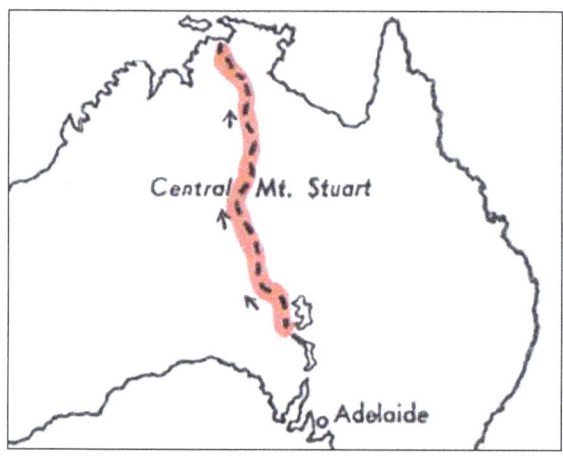 

John McDowell Stuart's route, 1862. Source: Wikimedia Commons

Central Mount Stuart, 2003. Source: Tannin, Wikimedia Commons

was completed in 1872, followed very closely the route he took. One of Australia's great construction projects, it provided a link between the continent and England.

The courage, determination, endurance, generosity, fortitude and professional skills of Ernest Giles were probably superior to those of most other explorers. Between 1872 and 1876 he explored Australia's unknown western interior, crossing more 'undiscovered' country than any other European-Australian explorer. He was the first European to see Uluru and Kata Tjuta (The Olgas as he named it) and named the Gibson Desert after his companion Gibson who, on one expedition, after riding off on their only horse to seek water, was never heard of again. Giles struggled 100 km on foot back to the camp. When crossing the Gibson Desert on his last expedition, the starving Giles, virtually blinded with scurvy, devoured a small dying wallaby – fur, skin, bones, skull and all. Giles achieved little more than confirming a large part of the inland was dry, sun-baked and almost uninhabitable for whites.

Any lingering belief in the existence of a great inland river or sea was finally dispelled. To the Newcomers inland Australia was an arid unforgiving world with a 'dead heart' at its centre. For the First Australians, however, it meant life – with just about every feature in the landscape full of meaning.

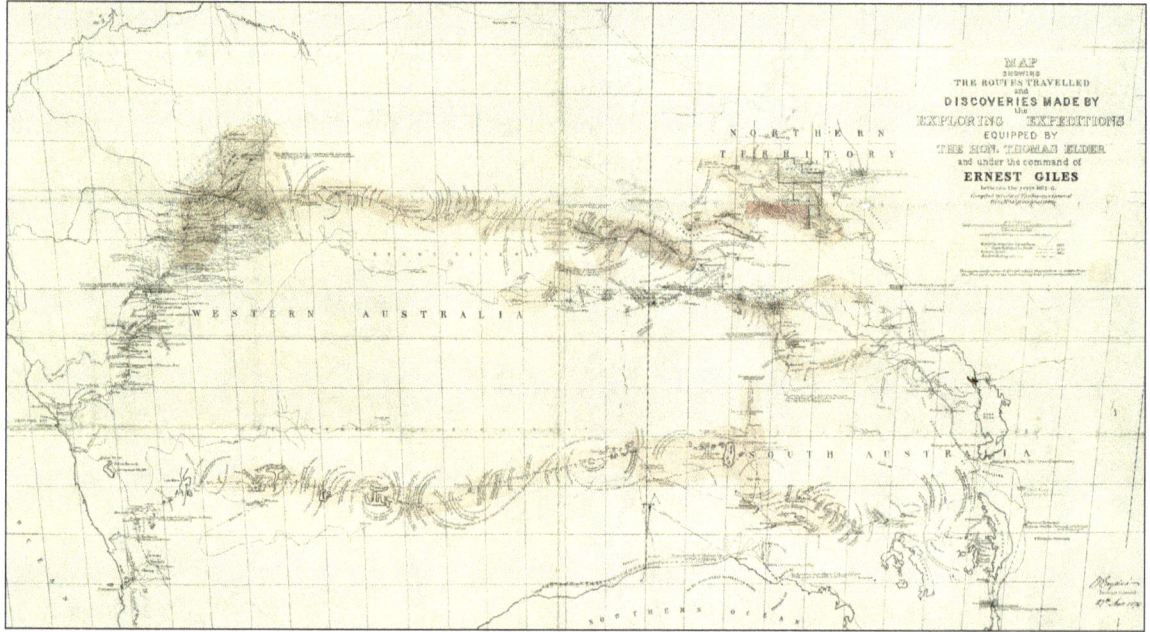

Map showing the routes travelled and discoveries made by the exploring expeditions equipped by Thomas Elder and under the command of Ernest Giles, during the period 1872-76. Source: NLA, map RM 2902/1

Ancestral explorers

P.F. MacDonald, a grandson of John Warby, undertook much of the exploration of the unsettled country west of Port Curtis in Central Queensland. In 1857 he left Victoria to make his fortune on the Canoona gold diggings. There was little gold to be found so he changed his focus to land. By then in Victoria there was no longer land for the taking. MacDonald and associates set about discovering land suitable for sheep grazing, taking up country which they favoured and disposing of it for profit. In four expeditions from 1858 to 1860 he opened up the lands of the Mackenzie, Nogoa, Comet and Isaacs Rivers in the areas that became Peak Downs and Springsure.

Though these were not trips of epic proportions, he suffered the same risks, dangers and privations common to the explorer. During these trips he and his party had many narrow escapes from encounters with hostile Aboriginals, who as elsewhere did not take kindly to this invasion of their land. His progress would have been severely hampered by the brigalow (*Acacia aneura*) scrub that covered much of the country he traversed. In 1858 on his first expedition, he almost perished when his exploring party was cut off by floodwaters, 350 km west of Keppel Bay. In a letter to his brother from Canoona, dated 8 March 1859, he wrote:

> *I have only just returned from an expedition which I shall never forget. We left Marlborough the last week in November 1858, with five-weeks rations, and travelled westward in view of Lake Salvator, and the beautiful peaks eastward, a distance of 200 miles in a direct line from Keppel Bay.*
>
> *When we arrived at the junction of the Comet and Mackenzie Rivers [on the return journey], the rain commenced and continued without one hour's intermission for twenty-one days. During nineteen days we never saw either sun, moon or stars. We had only about seven-days provisions. It was impossible for our horses to travel, as they floundered at every step, and became as poor as old working bullocks – literally nothing but skin and bone, having lost every hair except their manes and tails.*
>
> *After many ineffectual attempts to make a few miles towards home, we were compelled to encamp on a clear patch of about half an acre, in the midst of thick scrub, surrounded by water, for nineteen days, during which time we scarcely saw a living thing – birds and animals had evidently gone to seek a higher spot on firmer ground.*
>
> *I spent many a weary day hunting for food. Had it not been for small berries, roots of briars, and the bottle tree, I doubt very much if we should have been able to exist. If we had commenced killing our horses in the first instance, we had no way of preserving the flesh, our salt and sugar having been melted with the rain, and in the absence of both fire and sun it would have been impossible to dry it or keep it from decomposition. For eleven days three of our party dined off an emu*, without tasting either flour, tea, or sugar, and it was the only bird or animal above the size of a crow that we were fortunate enough to shoot during that time; by the way I ate more of the latter (crows) than all other birds put together, although I was much prejudiced against them, for from the day we started we were followed by as many crows as there were men in the party, and strange, if we were separated at any time, the crows would also separate according to our numbers.*
>
> *When I reached the farthest out station yesterday week, I met with the party that had been organised to go in search of us, equipped by public subscription. I started from Marlborough the following day, and reached Canoona late last*

night. I am reduced in weight from 15 stone to 11 stone 4 pounds. This will give you some idea of the kind of animal hunger has transformed me into.

* He subsequently engraved an emu on his silverware.

MacDonald, an imposing man standing 186 cm (6 feet 2½ inches), had grit and determination and organised a second trip within weeks of his return. As a bushman he was adaptable and confident in his own judgement and optimistic despite the hardship and danger of bush travel. He appreciated its ruggedness and on occasions its unexpected beauty, but primarily the grazing potential of the area. As expected of explorers, he recorded with care the physical features of the terrain across which he moved. He was at ease in the bush, which retained a compelling attraction for him.

Aboriginal guides

Explorers invariably included Aboriginals in their parties as guides and go-betweens with the people whose country they passed through. A famous case is the surveyor Kennedy who met his death at the hands of hostile Aboriginals, while trying to open up a route to the tip of Cape York Peninsula. Because of the sheer exhaustion and sickness his party was suffering, Kennedy decided to make a fast dash to the Cape with the Aboriginal Jacky Jacky as his only companion. At one time Kennedy became bogged up to his shoulders and had to be rescued by Jacky Jacky. Kennedy's feet were very swollen and he became ill. Jacky Jacky carried Kennedy on his back for a kilometre at a time. When hostile Aboriginals speared Kennedy just 20 kilometres from the Cape, Jacky Jacky cut the spear out of his back and carried him to the creek to bathe his wounds. Finally Kennedy died in Jacky Jacky's arms. On his return, Jacky Jacky (Galmahra) was widely honoured with a government gratuity. He returned to his tribe and later wandered aimlessly, finally burning to death when he fell drunkenly into a campfire. Today many of Aboriginal descent look on Jacky Jacky as a collaborator, an 'Uncle Tom'.

John Warby and P.F. MacDonald were not exceptions. Warby took members of the local Dharawal Aboriginals with him in his role as guide. On his expeditions into the bush, MacDonald always included at least one of his Aboriginal servants.

The fact that explorers had Aboriginals in their parties or were often on the verge of dying from starvation or thirst in country inhabited by the First Australians does not detract from the enormity of their suffering and achievements. For the Newcomer explorers it was an alien land. For their mere survival, let alone success, this land required of them endurance, determination and perseverance, qualities that the squatters and settlers who followed them would also need.

Chapter 7
An Alien Land

An alien inhospitable land

The characteristics conceived in our convict beginnings strengthened and extended during the next century as the explorers, squatters, small settlers and miners, who followed them, confronted an environment unlike any they had ever experienced. Nothing was familiar. It was as though the world had been turned upside down.

The climate was different. Storms were violent. Rainfall was erratic; often there was too much or too little. There were no seasons as they knew them. Instead of summer-green deciduous trees that coloured autumn with their turning leaves, they saw the cold olive green of trees that retained their leaves in winter; trees that gave them little protection from the rain or from the sun that beat relentlessly down upon them. The native animals were weird. Some such as egg-laying mammals and animals with pouches aroused their curiosity and interest; others such as spiders and snakes terrified them. Mountains were often rounded and rivers disappeared into swamps.

Unlike the First Australians whose connection with the land was spiritual, where every part of it was familiar and told a story, the Newcomers found it vast and empty, lonely and threatening. They had great difficulty coming to terms with their new environment. Our Asian and European visitors will understand this for they feel uncomfortable and lonely when out of the city in the country. They are frightened by animals such as insects, spiders and snakes. Screams from Asian students lodging at my home are regularly heard when a blue-tongued lizard (a skink) or even a cockroach appears. Moths and flying ants attracted into their rooms by lights almost cause panic. Wealthy squatters endeavoured to feel more 'at home' by living in grand houses surrounded by replicas of English gardens. John Glover,

Hobart Town, taken from the garden where I lived, 1832 by John Glover. Source: Dixson Galleries, State Library of New South Wales, No FL1632633

an artist and man of considerable wealth, is an example. He arrived in Van Dieman's Land in 1831 and acquired a large rural holding, where he built a two-storey Georgian house.

Through the European eyes of the Newcomers the natural landscape appeared dull and monotonous. They saw no beauty in it. The first Australian oil painting was a view of Sydney Cove by convict artist, Thomas Watling, who had been sentenced to 14 years in Australia in 1792 for forging a bank note. Watling had left England on the *Pitt*, the ship that brought my ancestor John Warby to Australia. Watling escaped in Cape Town but was recaptured and placed aboard the *Royal Admiral*. In trying to paint, Watling complained he could not find the sorts of things in the Australian landscape that a landscape painter could conventionally make pictures from.

Artists struggled for almost a century before painters such as Arthur Streeton and Frederick McCubbin finally reflected the distinctive Australian landscape through Australian eyes.

A direct north general view of Sydney Cove, ... 1794 by T. Watling. Source: Dixson Galleries, State Library of New South Wales, No FL1026578

From left:

Near Heidelberg by Arthur Streeton, 1890. Source: National Gallery of Victoria

Sunlight Sweet, Coogee by Arthur Streeton, 1890. Source: Wikimedia Commons

Chapter 7: An Alien Land

At about the same time when Streeton and other artists were depicting the landscape through new eyes, writers and poets also began writing about the variety and beauty to be seen in it. In her poem *My Country* Dorothea Mackellar expressed her feelings very poignantly.

The love of field and coppice
Of green and shaded lanes,
Of ordered woods and gardens
Is running in your veins.
Strong love of grey-blue distance,
Brown streams and soft, dim skies
I know, but cannot share it,
My love is otherwise.

I love a sunburnt country,
A land of sweeping plains,
Of ragged mountain ranges,
Of droughts and flooding rains.
I love her far horizons,
I love her jewel-sea,
Her beauty and her terror –
The wide brown land for me!

The stark white ring-barked forests,
All tragic to the moon,
The sapphire-misted mountains,
The hot gold hush of noon,
Green tangle of the brushes
Where lithe lianas coil,
The orchids deck the tree-tops
And ferns the warm dark soil.

Core of my heart, my country!
Her pitiless blue sky,
When, sick at heart, around us
We see the cattle die –
But then the grey clouds gather
And we can bless again
The drumming of an army,
The steady, soaking rain.

Core of my heart, my country!
Land of the rainbow gold,
For flood and fire and famine
She pays us back threefold.
Over the thirsty paddocks,
Watch, after many days,
The filmy veil of greenness
That thickens as we gaze ...

An opal-hearted country,
A wilful, lavish land –
All you who have not loved her,
You will not understand –
Though Earth holds many splendours,
Wherever I may die,
I know to what brown country
My homing thoughts will fly.

Lost by Frederick McCubbin, 1886. Source: National Gallery of Victoria

The land had begun to imprint a sense of identity upon the Newcomers. Miles Franklin closed her novel *My Brilliant Career* (1901) with:

I am proud that I am an Australian, a daughter of the Southern Cross, a child of the mighty bush.

Dame Nellie Melba (1861-1931), the first native-born Australian diva, did not live permanently in exile. She said:

If you wish to understand me at all you must understand first and foremost that I am an Australian.

It was a new country; she was its first star on the world stage.

Despite this new perspective there remained a disquiet about the bush as reflected by Frederick McCubbin in his *Lost* paintings; and the centre of the continent in particular. This was the 'dead heart' of the continent –

dead because it was seen as being devoid of life; nothing, they thought, survived there. This was starkly, and morbidly, expressed by native-born Barcroft Boake (1866-1892) in his poem *Where Dead Men Lie*, the first three verses being:

> *Out on the wastes of the Never Never*
> *That's where the dead men lie!*
> *There where the heat-waves dance forever –*
> *That's where the dead men lie!*
> *That's where the Earth's loved sons are keeping*
> *Endless tryst: not the west wind sweeping*
> *Feverish pinions can wake their sleeping –*
> *Out where the dead men lie!*
>
> *Where brown Summer and Death have mated –*
> *That's where the dead men lie!*
> *Loving with fiery lust unsated –*
> *That's where the dead men lie!*
> *Out where the grinning skulls bleach whitely*
> *Under the saltbush sparkling brightly;*
> *Out where the wild dogs chorus nightly –*
> *That's where the dead men lie!*
>
> *Deep in the yellow, flowing river –*
> *That's where the dead men lie!*
> *Under the banks where the shadows quiver –*
> *That's where the dead men lie!*
> *Where the platypus twists and doubles,*
> *Leaving a train of tiny bubbles.*
> *Rid at last of their earthly troubles –*
> *That's where the dead men lie!*

Half-a-century later Sidney Nolan experienced a landscape totally new to him when he travelled throughout the remote areas of the continent hoping to experience the 'real' Australia that lay beyond the settled coastal fringes. In the Alice Springs region he saw the country from the air when he flew several times on a mail delivery run.

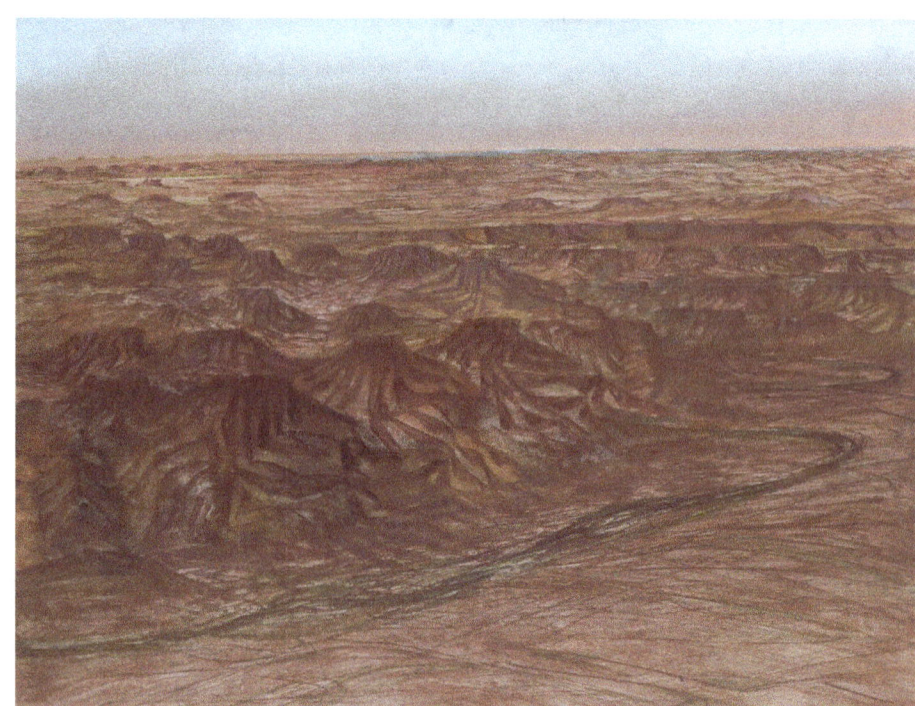

Central Australia by Sir Sidney Nolan, 1949. Source: © The Sidney Nolan Trust. All rights reserved. DACS/Copyright Agency, 2024

During the previous decade (1940s) water colours of the central Australian landscape by First Australian artist, Albert Namatjira (1902-1959), had opened our eyes and our senses to new ways of seeing the centre of Australia – a region of extremes and far from being a 'dead heart'.

North ranges looking south, ca. 1950s. Artist Albert Namatjira. Source: © Namatjira Legacy Trust/ Copyright Agency, 2024

From the moment the First Fleet landed in this strange, and in many respects terrifying, land, the Newcomers quickly set about changing the environment, not only because of their desperate need for food and shelter but also to make it more familiar and tolerable. Such was their haste to cut down trees that in March 1788 an order was issued forbidding cutting down trees within 15 metres of the Tank Stream.

They believed it was their mission to bring the benefits of civilisation to this place and to make the land productive –'to improve it'. So the First Fleeters and those who followed them set about trying to 'tame and control' this land, forcing it to give up its wealth; and there was great wealth to be had. But the land demanded a price. It demanded a 'new' man – resourceful individuals who could endure hardship and loneliness. However, even today, despite their camping weekends and 4-wheel drive treks, the Newcomers have not yet 'come to terms' with this vast land as the First Australians have. Most of us prefer to huddle together in cities near to or along the coast. The inland remains an 'alien' land.

Blythewood Grange, Ballarat, built by a successful goldminer in 1878. Source: Club Wyndham, Ballarat

In general the architectural styles adopted were solidly grounded in Europe. There was little acknowledgement of the environment and way of life in the design of the grand houses wealthy squatters and city dwellers built and lived in. The public buildings erected when States' coffers permitted were neo-classic or neo-gothic in design with little concession, apart from some minor twists to give some Australian significance, to the new land and people they were built to serve. A possible exception is the so-called 'Queenslander'. These airy wooden houses with verandahs are set high on wooden posts allowing an underneath that provides for semi-outdoor living protected from the sun and rain. The Sydney Opera House, sitting proudly on Bennelong Point, melds in with the harbour and boating life but how much it reflects things Australian is debatable.

Highset Queenslander with front verandah, 2016. Source: Michael Coghlan, Flickr

The new Parliament House in Canberra broke from the classical styles used in the past – styles that served the expression of authority and power. Its Australian-born designer had 'who we are' very much in mind. He considered Australia has a landscape or natural attitude, that we think of ourselves as an outdoor people, and Parliament House should express this in the simplest of terms. The chosen site, Capital Hill, was a natural hill upon which an Australian flag had flown for decades. He embedded the building into the hill and surmounted it with a giant flagstaff and flag. The architects sought to have the flag as the emblem on the hill. Our Parliament House tries to avoid a statement of power and authority – with which Australians have so often been at odds. It represents democracy. Australians are a very democratic people. Being able to walk on top of the parliament, the idea that the people are above parliament, is part of the symbolism and what being 'Australian' represents.

Sydney Opera House. Source: Alexander Bickhov, Unsplash

Despite this, the evolution of a truly and unashamedly confident style of private and public architecture that fits our ways and landscape has yet to evolve.

Australian Parliament House, Canberra. Source: Christopher Biggs, Flickr

Chapter 8
Gold

Half a century of gold-rushes

Unlike the early rush for land, which favoured the accumulation of wealth by relatively few, the early gold-rushes distributed wealth into many hands. People from all walks of life became rich. Just as they had discouraged efforts to find a way across the Blue Mountains – the mountains kept the convicts in – the early colonial administrators discouraged prospecting for gold and suppressed any reports of gold-finds. They feared the largely convict population would descend into lawlessness and an upset in the social order in general. The squatters supported this policy because they feared losing their workers. However, the exodus of people from Australia to the Californian gold-diggings put an end to this and the government actually offered a reward for finding gold. In the second half of the 1800s, gold became a major factor in shaping Australia and the 'Australian'.

When Hargraves reported finding gold near Bathurst on the Turon River in early 1851 – the area reminded him of California from which he had recently returned – it was well publicised and he was well rewarded. He called the area *Ophir*. Soon after, other alluvial finds were made in New South Wales.

Later that same year gold was discovered in Victoria. Melbourne businessmen, worried about the loss of labour to NSW, had offered a reward for its discovery. For almost a decade these diggings yielded up gold on a massive scale; Victoria produced a third of the gold extracted in the world during this period. Of all the gold-rushes in our history, none played so significant a role in the development of Australia and the 'Australian' as the Victorian gold-rushes of the 1850s.

Gold-discoveries continued to be made throughout Australia during the rest of the century. Droves of miners, commonly known as diggers, moved around the country, mostly 'on foot', as reports of new discoveries spread. Broadly, they moved in an anti-clockwise direction: Queensland, Northern Territory and finally to Western Australia. In Queensland, discovery of gold at Gympie in 1867 saved the fledgling State from insolvency and social disruption.

In 1892-93 major gold-strikes occurred around present-day Coolgardie and Kalgoorlie in the red desert region about 550 km east of Perth. The gold-bearing land between them became known as the Golden Mile. At the time, eastern Australia was in the grip of a deep economic depression. Vast numbers of miners sailed west to seek salvation on the gold-fields. Few had any money and so most trudged, often pushing miners' barrows, across hundreds of kilometres of desert wasteland from the ports of Perth or Albany to get there. Some even crossed the continent on foot.

Life on the Western Australian diggings was very hard. Food and essential supplies were very expensive and water was almost as precious as gold. In 1896 the Gold-fields Water Supply Scheme – a dam and 530 km 760 mm steel pipeline, eight pumping stations and two small holding dams – was undertaken to supply water to the gold-fields. The project, the most ambitious ever carried out on the continent at that time, was completed in 1903 and still operates today.

The wealth flowing from the Western Australian gold-fields ended the depression. Also, the money flowing backwards and forwards between east and west integrated the economies. Miners repatriated money back home to the east and purchased supplies brought in from the east.

Miners and others from the east also contributed to the political union of the country. By 1900 about a third of Western Australia's population was located in the gold-fields region and its political influence was largely responsible for that State belatedly joining the Federation. A reluctant Government finally held a referendum in which the large majority voted in favour of union with the eastern colonies.

Australian gold diggings, ca. 1855, by Edwin Stocqueler (1829-1895). Source: NLA, No. Pic T273 NK10

By then, however, the age of the digger was coming to an end because the rich alluvial deposits he could work were largely exhausted. Discovery of deep gold-reefs nearby ushered in the highly capitalised operations of the modern mining industry. Mining companies sourced cheap, acquiescent labour from southern Europe. Over the century-and-a-half following the first gold discoveries, mining of gold and silver, base metals and coal continued to play a major part in the economy of the nation and the miners, united by their unions, confronted company bosses and occasionally governments with a fervour far more radical than their barrow-pushing predecessors.

The diggers

Those infected with gold-fever came from all over the continent and from all walks of life. Doctors and lawyers, teachers and clergymen, businessmen and shopkeepers, clerks, tradesmen and labourers, artisans, police, magistrates and other government officials, adventurers, layabouts and ne'er-do-wells, all these and more left the urban areas; farmers left their farms, pastoralists left their properties as did farm hands, shepherds and bush workers; crews deserted their ships; and men abandoned lovers, wives and families. They left everything and rushed to the gold-fields with the hope of striking gold. They were joined by immigrants, most of whom were from the British Isles, although significant numbers also came from Southern China, Chile, continental Europe, North America, the Pacific Islands and New Zealand. These immigrants brought with them new ideas and ways of doing things.

The Roaring Days

The night too quickly passes
And we are growing old,
So let us fill our glasses
And toast the Days of Gold;
When finds of wond'rous treasure,
Set all the South ablaze-
And you and I were faithful mates,
All through the roaring days!

Henry Lawson

The digger's life was hard, unhealthy and far from genteel. Most diggers lived in tents. Their diet was poor and they had little time to cook. Lack of sanitation resulted in dysentery and typhoid; and eye infections were common. Exposure to heat and cold, working in damp conditions and sleeping in wet blankets took their toll. Flies, ants and mosquitoes made life miserable. Men greatly out-numbered women, who generally had a civilising effect.

Men from all walks of life shared the hard, heavy and sometimes dangerous task of working a claim. Often two or three people worked a claim, sharing costs and any gold found. The

The Gold Diggers by Emil Todt, 1854. Source: National Gallery of Victoria

teamwork required for underground mining increased miners' solidarity, at least within their partnerships. The social background of a partner mattered little in the drive to get rich.

The diggers mixed into a uniformity forced by necessity. They dressed similarly and abandoned previous habits, customs and manners. A highly educated Oxford 'gentleman' could be associated with an illiterate labourer. Those inappropriately dressed were quickly put in their place with language used against officious officials, such as the cry of *Joe, Joe*; Australians do not like people appearing to put on airs and are suspicious of 'tall poppies'.

The diggers took an active part in maintaining order on the diggings. Despite their hatred of the police they still assisted police in capturing thieves and other criminals. It was the custom to call public meetings, known as 'roll-ups', for political and other purposes, by sending men to all the various camps each carrying a tin dish. These heralds would beat their tin dishes and yell, *Roll-up, roll-up*. Rollups were called to organise parties to hunt down felons who, when caught, were sometimes cuffed and beaten and ordered off the diggings on pain of death, but, as a rule, were handed over to the police for trial.

It was probably because of this attitude of the diggers that the Victorian diggings avoided the violence and lawlessness that plagued the Californian gold-fields. There were occasions when some suggested murderers should be summarily dealt with by their captors, but such resolutions were not endorsed at the roll-ups, although, on more than one occasion, it was said that, if the Government could not provide protection from bushrangers, the diggers would have to protect themselves.

The rough and tumble of life on the diggings exposed them to new ideas, attitudes and expectations. Many immigrants, more particularly those who rushed to the gold-fields, were influenced by the attitudes of the native-born of convict descent. Furthermore, because striking gold depended little on who or what you were, those with new-found wealth often had different ideas of how society should be ordered from the old class structures of Britain. Life on the diggings strengthened the belief that all men were equal.

Some who rushed to the gold-fields were lucky and won small fortunes, which they invested in businesses and farms or spent quickly and recklessly. However, most received little or no reward for their efforts and sought work wherever they could find it. Some continued to chase the elusive gold from digging to digging. The attraction of the diggings was not simply a lust for gold. Many were attracted to the free, roving digger lifestyle with its blurred social distinctions and a sense of 'mateship'. They spread the digger ethos throughout the continent.

The diggers, it can be seen, shared much in common with their convict predecessors, i.e. the emancipists and ticket-of-leave men and women plus their children and the nativeborn, the Currency Lads and Lasses. Both groups were a diverse lot brought together either by gold or justice in circumstances that mixed them together in a uniformity of clothing and living. Both had disdain for the authorities that controlled or regulated their lives and class structures that locked them into a way of life. Both cherished freedom and the right to participate fully in society.

All men are equal!

While the belief that all men were equal might have been nurtured on the gold-fields, not everyone was included. The First Australians were not; neither were the Chinese, the largest foreign contingent who had flocked to the gold-fields. In 1858 there were 40,000 in Victoria, representing one-tenth of the population; they made up the greatest number of 'foreigners' on the gold-fields and in the whole of Australia for the rest of the century. Despite the multinational mix on the diggings, Chinese were not welcomed by most diggers. They were too different in looks, customs and behaviour and lived apart as a community. Significantly, by working hard in large organised groups, they generally found gold if any was to be found. Their apparent success was resented by the other diggers, most of whom found nothing, and violence erupted on a number of diggings. In all instances, the European attackers were a minority of their community. This violence resulted in the Victorian and New South Wales Governments passing laws to restrict Chinese immigration (see Appendix 1).

The worst instance of violence was the Lambing Flat riot – a drawn-out series of incidents on the Burragong gold-field in New South Wales in 1860-61 – the most notorious being on 30 June 1861 when 3,000 miners drove the Chinese off the Lambing Flat diggings. The armed attack on police in a reaction to their arrest of the 'ringleaders' was possibly the most serious civil disorder to have occurred in Australia involving more people and lasting longer than the Eureka incident. The Colonies' response to this unrest of restricting the entry of Chinese into Australia was the beginning of the so-called 'White Australia Policy' adopted at Federation and not revoked until after the Second World War.

The miner's licence – a catalyst for rebellion

In Australia the state owns and controls the minerals and water in the earth and their exploitation. When gold was found in quantity near Bathurst, the government introduced the miner's licence in an attempt to ensure order on the gold diggings and to prevent erosion of the functioning of society that a mass exodus to the gold-fields would bring about. Anyone arriving at the gold-field had to buy a monthly licence. This allowed the holder to peg out a 'claim' – a surface area about four metres square – and keep any gold found. A licence gave everyone a chance to dig for gold but was quite expensive. The idea was that a miner who didn't find gold wouldn't be able to renew his licence and so would most likely go back to his original job.

This system of mining regulation was adopted when gold was found in Victoria. However, it did not suit the underground mining required when the easily mined alluvial gold ran out. The diggers had to seek gold-bearing reefs by sinking shafts as deep as 50 metres. This required considerable effort and expenditure and they had no income until finding gold. Also, they had to spend a lot of money before finally finding any gold, which meant they really needed to work larger areas of ground.

The miners accepted the need by the Government to raise revenue to meet the cost of policing, administration and infrastructure. However, they resented the high cost of the licence and the way it was administered and policed, particularly the introduction of mounted troopers to enforce the law. Miners had to carry the licence at all times and present it on request. Those who did not have it on their person could be arrested – even if their licence was nearby in a shirt pocket. Unlicensed miners were fined.

The searches for licences were known as 'digger hunts'. When the miners were working underground they had to stop and come to the top. The troopers summoned a miner to come up with the words: *Show me your licence, you digger dog*. Miners warned each other of the approach of digger hunts by yelling *Joe* (after Governor Joseph Latrobe; 'Joe' became a term of mockery). Sometimes a digger would be asked for his licence several times a day, which exacerbated his hostility towards the authorities. Digger hunts came to symbolise the Government's oppression of the diggers and led to major protests on gold-fields.

The diggers rebel – Eureka Stockade

The miners' grievances extended beyond their resentment of the cost and enforcement of the miner's licence, incompetent and corrupt police and lack of services. Many overseas gold-rush immigrants had spread radical ideas about social and political rights, which had been enflaming Europe at the time. Thus miners came to view the licence fee as nothing less than a tax – a tax without representation, so they wanted 'the vote'. They also wanted the vast areas of land held by relatively few squatters to be opened up for selection by small settlers. Furthermore, the monthly renewal fee of 30 shillings for a mining licence seemed very unfair when compared with an annual rental of only 10 pounds for 3,000 acres (1,200 ha) paid by squatters. The underlying issue was political power – squatters had it, miners did not.

An increase in frequency of digger hunts in September 1854 brought these simmering grievances to the surface. Violence finally erupted in mid-October. At Ballarat, the Eureka hotel was torched following a nearby meeting of 10,000 miners protesting about police failing to charge the publican and two accomplices, who miners believed had murdered a digger. On two more occasions over the following eight days, 10,000 or more assembled on Bakery Hill to vent their grievances. Bakery Hill, which lay directly across open ground from the Government Camp, had become a gathering point for protest. However, despite the murder case being reopened, the rage of the diggers was fanned by the arrest and charging of three diggers with arson.

On 11 November a crowd of 10,000 gathered again on Bakery Hill and formally established the Ballarat Reform League to give voice to their demands. Its leadership was moderate, although there was clearly a division between those who wanted to achieve their goals with

Swearing Allegiance to the Southern Cross by Charles A. Doudiet, 1854. Source: National Museum of Australia

moral force and those who favoured a more direct approach. Two weeks later three of its leaders went to Melbourne to demand political rights and pardoning of the three miners. Their use of the word 'demand' incensed the Governor, who responded by strengthening the Ballarat forces with extra military and police.

On the afternoon of 29 November 1854 12,000 diggers, the biggest crowd yet assembled, gathered at Bakery Hill in front of a newly erected podium to hear the delegation's report. Above the stage atop a 60-foot (18 m) pole flew the Southern Cross, the 'rebel' flag, hastily designed and stitched together the previous night – a unifying symbol clearly visible from all over the diggings. When told their demands had been rejected, the diggers could no longer be placated by those advocating compromise and moderation. They agreed to burn their licences and resist the arrest of unlicensed miners. Soon fires blazed and smoke billowed as dozens threw the hated licences into the flames.

The Eureka flag. Source: Wikimedia Commons

Next morning a major digger hunt was launched. Its aim was to bring matters to a head by isolating the belligerent diggers and getting the support of the majority. However, this seriously misjudged the situation. Animosity was universal. Abuse and rocks were hurled at police and soldiers, the Riot Act was read and the sound of gunshots that followed stirred miners' anger even more.

That afternoon 500 determined diggers assembled spontaneously at Bakery Hill. For the second time the Southern Cross flew high above them. Leaders advocating moderation were absent. The time for those who believed in physical force had come. An Irishman, Peter Lalor, was one of them. Until then he had played more a backroom role. On the previous day he had spoken briefly and the diggers liked his style and what he said. Now, with his 'belly filled with fire', he responded to the urging of the crowd.

He mounted the podium, looked all around, proclaimed *liberty* and called for volunteers for a militia. Soon six companies of men from 19 nations formed up in front of the podium. He ordered those who did not intend to take the oath to be faithful to the Southern Cross to leave – none did – and all companies to fall-in around the flag staff. He removed his hat, knelt and raised his right palm towards the flag and in a forceful tone and measured pace administered the oath. With heads bowed and right hands raised towards the flag the miners repeated after him:

> *We swear by the Southern Cross to stand truly by each other and fight to defend our rights and liberties.*

Raffaello Carboni, Lalor's second-in-command, later wrote that those who took the Eureka oath were of all nations and colours, and had come together irrespective of nationality, religion or colour to salute the Southern Cross as a refuge for all the oppressed from all countries on earth.

In what could be a flash of prescience Governor Hotham reported the incident to the Secretary of State, Sir George Grey, in London in the following words:

> *... they dispatched emissaries to the other diggings to excite the miners, and held a meeting whereas the Australian flag of independence was solemnly consecrated and vows proffered for its defence ...*

The rebels, for that is what they now were, retrieved their flag, attached it to a long staff, and marching behind it, moved to an area called the 'Eureka lead'. Here they raised the flag and erected a stockade in readiness for an attack by the troopers. Riders had left earlier to other gold-fields to seek reinforcements.

The troopers attacked at dawn a couple of days later. Because it was a Sunday only 150 miners were in the stockade; believing there would be no attack on the Sabbath, the others had left. It was carried out to pre-empt a meeting Lalor had called for later that day. The battle lasted for only 30 minutes. Five soldiers and 30 miners lost their lives. The stockade was destroyed and 120 miners were arrested and 13 were charged with treason. A third of those killed and a quarter of those arrested were Irish-born. The latter included Peter Lalor, the leader of the rebellion.

The rebellion was quickly put down but the Government lost the political battle because public sympathy strongly favoured the miners. All 13 miners arrested on treason charges were acquitted. The Miner's Licence was replaced by a Miner's Right, which had a fee of one pound a year and included the right to vote in parliamentary elections.

Eureka legacy somewhat problematic

Eureka has not become part of the Australian folk psyche. It is not on the lips of the man in the street. Its legacy has been somewhat problematic. On its second anniversary 200 gathered at the site of the stockade in remembrance; a larger crowd observed its 50th anniversary but only a small group were present at its centenary. Dissension clouded its 150th anniversary.

Why is this so? Unlike Gallipoli and Kokoda, where Australians faced a common enemy with a common purpose, the Eureka story is more complex and nuanced; one where, as in a family, pitting like against seemingly like can blur the vision.

The diggers were heirs to the emancipist tradition and although the blanket of the convict stain had by then descended upon the colonies, the Currency Lads and Lasses had not been suffocated. They had simply disappeared and remained there for over 100 years. The exclusivists, however, were still very much in evidence in the form of the squattocracy and those who did not call this land 'home' – those more comfortable with the status quo. For them diggers were nothing more than rebels and Eureka seemed tainted. They failed to see the miners, who were from all walks of life, were, in reality, like average citizens; not simply a few agitators who wallowed in pools of political heat. As a result, in 1891 striking shearers opportunistically appropriated its spirit and its symbol, the Southern Cross. Tainted it must be!

I first heard the Eureka story, not from my family, but when at Allenstown State Primary School, on Dawson Road, Rockhampton. It was part of our Social Studies (history and geography) course. I remember going with my class to see the movie *Eureka Stockade* starring Chips Rafferty as Peter Lalor. It was probably around 1950. I cannot remember whether other classes or schools went, or whether it was on instruction by the Education Department or its Minister. At the time Queensland had a Labor Government; Labor Governments had been in power in Queensland for more than 20 years. I recall nothing of the Eureka centenary in 1954. I was then at Geelong Grammar School, whose honour boards are littered with names of the former squattocracy. The school, of Anglican persuasion, was not aloof from attending a historical movie for we were bussed into Geelong to see a movie about Martin Luther.

Eureka's 150th anniversary was observed in a variety of ways. Australia Post issued a 50c stamp depicting the Southern Cross and the Perth Mint produced a dollar coin. About 700 people, many of them unionists, attended a ceremony at the stockade site. John Howard, then Prime Minister of the Liberal-National Coalition Government, did not attend any celebration ceremonies or allow the Eureka flag to be flown above Parliament House in Canberra. However, it flew above all State Parliaments – Labor Governments were in power in all States.

Tainted it surely is but to relegate it to the garbage bin of history would be a grave mistake. Few will deny Eureka is relevant to all Australians no matter what their political bias or social leanings. It embodies much of what we are and believe in. What the story of Eureka and its tattered symbol need is a good wash and repair. But it will take courage and understanding to acknowledge the Eureka legend, and like ANZAC, accept it for all of us.

In no way were the miners violent revolutionaries wanting to turn the world upside down. Eureka was relatively peaceful. Even those who had sworn the oath believed in an orderly, civilised society. Few were in the stockade at the time of the attack because it was a Sunday. They wanted changes but fighting was a last resort, to be engaged in only if pushed too far. There is no hint of fanaticism here. All charged with treason were acquitted because the sentiments of the general public were in support of them. The diggers represented far more than a small, disgruntled section of the general population. Even conservative Prime Ministers, Robert Menzies and John Howard, acknowledge its significance.

Menzies stated:

> *Freedom of speech, the right to vote and political equality are hallmarks of the historic uprising. The Eureka revolution was an attempt at democratic government.*

When pressured into making a short statement, Howard said:

> *The events of Eureka 150 years ago were central to the development of Australia as an independent country.*

Howard, a monarchist but unquestionably a true democrat, possibly had more sympathy for Eureka than he was prepared to admit. After ten years as Prime Minister he suffered a crushing defeat. The ABC subsequently produced a program called *The Howard Years*. I sent the following letter (unpublished) to the *The Courier Mail* newspaper:

> *No matter what one thinks about the documentary "The Howard Years", John Howard's stewardship or John Howard the man, his remark about his catastrophic electoral loss does him great credit and Australia proud. Howard, who stubbornly refused "to go" said,* It wasn't a night I couldn't handle. If you play the democracy game you must accept that at some point you will lose. *Howard accepted it; his party accepted it; we accepted it. Few nations are as fortunate as we are. The democracy game is more than a concept or fine words. It is a mind-set – a mind-set embedded in the psyche of the people. For us to lose such a precious characteristic would be tragic. We should never risk losing it.*

Eureka and the gold-fields played a key role in the democracy we enjoy today. Sentiments to this effect were expressed by noted Eureka author, John Molony, in a paper prepared for Federal Parliamentarians for the 150th anniversary:

> *Democracy is much more than a system. It is an ideal and spirit born day by day in those who believe in it. Eureka had its brief and bloody moment 150 years ago. Eureka lives on in the heart and will of every Australian who understands, believes in and acts on the principle that the people are "the only legitimate source of all political power".*

I have since discovered that John Molony's *ideal and spirit* and my *mind-set embedded in the psyche of the people* is what the 18th century French philosopher Montesquieu referred to as 'a spirit of government that is infused among the population and those that govern'. It is the shared sentiments, the shared beliefs, the shared sense of legitimacy of institutions: when whole political systems destroy that spirit, that legitimacy, they very easily crumble or collapse outright. I am sure that no matter where you come from – be it from lands of tyrants, or despots, or ravaged by war, or engulfed in poverty – it takes time, possibly a good deal of time to absorb this spirit.

Any remaining doubts about who these Eureka rebels were, what they stood for and what they were prepared to fight for, are surely dispelled by the obituary of Alexander Cameron MacDonald, an older brother of my great grandfather, P.F. MacDonald, published in *The Rockhampton Morning Bulletin*, 21 June 1917:

> *... with his brother, Mr. P.F. MacDonald, he fought for freedom at the historic Eureka stockade under the commander-in-chiefship of Mr. Peter Lalor... .*

Details about P.F. MacDonald, by virtue of him being my great grandfather, are given throughout this treatise. The following extracts about his brother Alexander Cameron are from the Australian Dictionary of Biography:

> *Australian by birth, he wanted his country to know its origins and history. ... recognised as an authority on Aboriginal place names and customs and had compiled a vocabulary of their words and meanings. In October 1851 MacDonald made a sketch map of the Ballarat goldfield, ... He also compiled a large Map of the Colony of New South Wales ... . His wide travels took him sometimes far into central Australia. In 1886-98 he was active in promoting committees for exploring Antarctica ... . Probably his most important accomplishment was with the Victorian branch of the Royal Geographical Society of Australasia (which he helped form). ... He read many papers on geographical science to the Australasian Association for the Advancement of Science. ... elected a fellow of the Royal Geographical Society, London, in 1885. ... His many other memberships included scientific and historical societies, the Victorian Institute of Accountants and the Australasian Institute of Bankers. He was also a magistrate for Queensland.*

Sons and daughters of currency went to great lengths to blot out the convict stain. The obituary incorrectly states Alexander was educated at King's School, Parramatta and his father was a highland MacDonald of the historic Glencoe and Cameron clans. The veracity of Alexander's Eureka claim is also highly questionable but, true or false, its very presence is evidence that Eureka was not tainted.

The MacDonald brothers were no radical miscreants. Quite the contrary; they were 'fair dinkum' Australians who served their country with distinction in the community, business, science and politics. These sons of currency felt so strongly about Eureka they wanted posterity to believe they did their bit by being there.

The Eureka Stockade was more than a tantrum thrown by a group of miners over mining conditions. Under the Southern Cross they had sworn to defend their rights and liberty and were prepared to confront authority in the process. It symbolised their ideals, values and hopes for a new kind of society – a society to which we are grateful heirs.

A new society

The colonial administrators and others of like mind were not mistaken in fearing gold would transform society. The gold-rushes of the 1850s turned society upside down. As a consequence, the decade forms a watershed between a convict past and a free-person future; a watershed between the rigid hierarchical class structure of traditional society that had thwarted the emancipists and a more liberal, progressive society that emerged; a watershed between a struggling economy relying largely on convict labour and wool and one that eventually provided one of the highest living standards in the world: an economy based on free-persons, wool and gold.

This advance in the Australian story was largely driven by the Victorian gold-rush experience of the 1850s, which carried over to all the other colonies. Appearance of cracks in the edifice of the old society began with the mass exodus to the gold-fields. When servants left, their masters and mistresses had to do menial tasks themselves. Labour shortages in the cities drove wages and conditions well above those in the rest of the world; for instance, in 1856 the '8-hour day' was granted to the building trades in Melbourne.

Those returning from the gold-fields laden with gold had no intention of going back to their previous jobs or place in society. The gold-rushes made many rich – some very rich – unlike the early land-rushes, when relatively few became wealthy. Many could 'buy and sell' their former masters and employers; wealth brought them status whatever their background. With gold in their pockets they broke free from their assigned place in traditional society. To the dismay of those 'at the top', its rigid hierarchical class structure collapsed – without a drop of blood being spilt. A 'coarser', more egalitarian, informal society echoing life on the diggings took its place. Gold created the first truly 'middle class' in the world with economic and political influence.

In due course unlucky diggers had to find work. Most middle-class immigrants returned to the cities after the initial rush, where many became prominent in business, politics and law. The supply of free labour ended the need for convicts and transportation finally ceased.

In 1855 a Westminster system of responsible government was established in Victoria – probably partly the result of the democratic winds blowing from the gold-fields. In 1856 the first Parliament was elected. Election of this parliament was the first time in the world the secret ballot was used. The parliament consisted of an upper house elected by larger property owners and a lower house elected by a wider section of the male population, including minor landowners, rent payers and gold-diggers. Peter Lalor, the leader of the miners' rebellion, was among those elected to this first parliament. All British males of sound mind and record, and 21 years old or older, were granted the right to vote in 1857 regardless of their income or property, so long as they could read and write. Other states adopted this policy over the ensuing decades. South Australia had preceded Victoria in these reforms by a year.

In less than a decade, the gold-rush transformed Melbourne from a small colonial town into a bustling metropolis. The influx of money funded a huge construction program, resulting in the building of many impressive civic structures including the Post Office, Treasury and Parliament House. Gold also led to the construction of schools, churches, galleries, the State Library and Flinders Street Station, which was the first railway station in Australia.

The impact of the gold-rush extended far beyond Melbourne, benefiting regional centres and beyond. It brought about profound changes in architecture, and advancements in transportation and communication—such as railways, Cobb & Co coaches, and the telegraph. Moreover, it spurred lifestyle transformations and fostered the growth of the arts. Victoria's population surged from 80,000 in 1850 to over half a million by 1861, contributing to Australia's overall population nearly tripling from just over 400,000 to more than 1,100,000. The gold-rush firmly established Australia on a robust economic footing.

The gold-rushes also played a significant role in the evolution of our language. A vast terminology blossomed on the gold-fields; some was brought from California but much of it was Australian; for example, the meaning of 'nugget' changed from a 'lump of anything' to a 'lump of gold'. The language that emerged from the social mixing bowl of the gold-fields marked the Australian-born (currency) from the British-born (sterling); it was clearly identifiable as Australian English. The language of the gold-fields spread from there to all parts of society.

The gold-rushes had little effect on the Australian accent. It had evolved some decades earlier and a population continually on the move did not give regional accents a chance to develop. Those seeking gold around the continent carried gold-terminology with them and the accent in which it was spoken. The gold-rushes were, therefore, important in enforcing the homogeneity of the Australian accent across the continent.

Many terms disappeared at the end of the gold-rushes but some survived. Of those that have, none is more loaded with meaning than 'digger', to describe that free spirit of those who sought gold on the diggings. In a sense, it was the diggers – these men of diverse backgrounds with a distain for authority and yearning for a new life – who came together on the gold-fields pursuing a common purpose and took over the baton from their emancipist predecessors.

Sixty years after Eureka the name 'digger' was bestowed upon another group of men from all walks of life brought together by a common purpose. Fighting in trenches on the battle-fields of war they displayed all the qualities of their digger forebears. Their humour, courage and a fighting ability second-to-none added further meaning to the term 'digger' – a term that embodies so much of what it means to be 'Australian' and proudly borne by all their successors.

Gold near home

One of those to leave the land and seek a fortune in gold was my great grandfather P.F. MacDonald. He joined the rush to the Turon gold-field and soon after headed off to Bendigo, where he had some luck but was forced to abandon his claim by an outbreak of typhoid fever, a common disease of the colonies, especially on the gold-fields. He then worked near Geelong on a sheep and cattle property, first as overseer then as manager. Once again, however, like the song of Sirens or the Rhine Maidens, he found the lure of gold irresistible.

In 1858 MacDonald joined the throng who rushed north on the news of the discovery of gold at Canoona – the catalyst responsible for my hometown of Rockhampton. The Canoona gold-field was 50 km north of Rockhampton, which at the time consisted of three primitive buildings and about a dozen men. Within three months an estimated 15,000 people landed in Rockhampton expecting instant riches but the gold was soon exhausted. Penniless diggers were helped to return to Victoria or to the inland NSW gold-fields. Once again, wealth from gold eluded MacDonald but he did not return south. He grasped the opportunity the frontier offered and became wealthy from squatting and real estate.

Yang Shuai (Nixie), 2011 at Monument to Canoona gold discovery, Pacific Highway, just south of *Glen Geddes*. Source: Peter Hasker

A quarter of a century after the Canoona rush, gold was found at Mt Morgan, 38 km west of Rockhampton. Mining this mountain was a task for big business not thousands of independent miners or small groups of diggers. For reasons unknown the now wealthy MacDonald was not part of this venture that required money rather than sweat and toil. However, in the 1900s his investments included shares in the fabled Mt Morgan.

A syndicate of six, three Morgan brothers and three Rockhampton businessmen, who mined the mountain until 1886 when the Mount Morgan Gold Mining Company Limited was formed, made large fortunes. The mine finally closed in 1981. At one stage it was the largest and richest gold mine in the world. As well as gold it produced considerable quantities of silver and copper. What was once a large mountain is now a hole over 2.5 km long and over 300 m deep – one of the largest artificial holes on earth.

One of the syndicate, William Knox D'Arcy, later made another fortune when he financed oil drilling in Persia (now Iran) – a venture that led to formation of the British Petroleum Company (BP). Money made by another member endowed the Walter and Eliza Hall Institute. Yet another member, John Ferguson, built *Kenmore* – one of the finest homes not only in Queensland but also in any of the Australian colonies. It is said he intended it to be the future government house for the proposed new state of Central Queensland. At the time (1894), he was President of the Central Queensland Separation League. After his death in 1906 the house was sold to pastoralist Stuart MacDonald, a son of P.F. MacDonald.

On visits to *Kenmore* my mother often played with a younger male cousin Charlie. A favourite playing spot was amongst some banana plants at the back of the house. These were sustained by the outflow from a septic tank and both children contracted diphtheria – she was probably about seven years old and he a year younger. In the early 1900s, diphtheria caused more deaths in Australia than any other infectious disease. Fortunately her oldest brother, 'Gem' Stuart, was studying medicine at Melbourne University and obtained some antitoxin.

The MacDonald family lived at *Kenmore* until 1915, when the home was sold to the Sisters of Mercy for use as a hospital. On 14 November 1915, the Mater Misericordiae Hospital was officially opened. Over the next half century my mother's family continued its association with *Kenmore* cum hospital both as medical professionals and patients. Her brother 'Gem' and sister Adah and my father, who succeeded 'Gem' in the practice, admitted patients and operated there. All of us spent time there as patients – my last being the first two weeks after suffering a C6 injury to the spinal cord in a horse-riding accident.

Mater Hospital, Rockhampton in 1919. Source: Rockhampton Historical Society

Mining also lured my mother's father, Simson Stuart, a medical immigrant from Northern Ireland, who arrived in Rockhampton on the migrant ship *Scottish Hero* on 28 January 1884 and married P.F. MacDonald's daughter Annie Adah in 1886. Although he viewed his fellow Catholic Irish compatriots through the eyes of an Orangeman he was nonetheless an Irishman – a great story-teller, good company, a philanderer and 'hopeless with money'. It fell to my grandmother's lot to collect money from those with unpaid bills, while her husband dissipated much of what money they had on hair-brained schemes, including mines – none of which ever paid a return. P.F. MacDonald made sure there was no way his profligate son-in-law could ever get access to any of his wealth. Some dark blue sapphires did come into his possession, possibly in return for medical services rendered. One stone graced my mother's engagement ring; others my sister's engagement ring and cuff links, which my mother gave to me and which I have passed on to my nephew Peter.

Chapter 9
Bushrangers – Ned Kelly

I do not understand Australians' attitude towards Ned Kelly! exclaimed an English friend of mine now settled in Australia. Her bewilderment is not surprising for the way we view Ned Kelly is bound up with who he was and what he represented. When we think of Ned Kelly it resonates with those characteristics in our makeup we have met before: the latent anti-authoritarianism that lurks within us, the empathy with those who have battled against great odds and lost and a love of freedom. Ned Kelly was among the last of those outlaws of society, the 'bushranger'.

The forerunners of the bushranger were convicts who fled into the bush to escape the harsh, or for some, boring penal life. Some of these 'bolters', as they were called at first, mistakenly thought they could get to China or find their way back to England. Escape was relatively easy but survival was not. They were not 'at home' in the bush, and mountains and the ocean were akin to prison walls; Aboriginals were also a threat. Early on in NSW most escapees died or, after becoming demoralised, wandered back to the settlement. Bushranging began to flourish around 1825 when the colony 'broke out of its narrow coastal plains'. Convicts escaped from chained road gangs and found good hiding spots close to new trunk roads. In Van Dieman's Land bolters were a problem from the early days because of the need to send out armed convicts to hunt kangaroos to feed the fledging colony. They simply disappeared into the rugged landscape. By 1821, 53% of the population were convicts under sentence and many roamed free in the bush.

Over time these bolters began to be referred to as 'bushrangers'. Their crimes ranged from petty theft to murder and if caught, often with the aid of Aboriginal trackers, they were flogged or hanged. Most of them survived by robbing travellers and farmers to obtain food, money, guns and horses; a few joined up with Aboriginal people. They often received help from assigned convicts, ex-convicts and occasionally even free-settlers out for profit.

While free-settlers had no love for the bushrangers, they also disliked the mounted police who hunted them. The rebellious nature of the bushrangers, as displayed in their hostility towards police and authority, and their willingness to fight to keep their freedom, struck a chord with the ordinary man. By the late 1820s these sympathies had crystallised into folk ballads, the most notable to survive being *Bold Jack Donahue*, which became the seminal convict hero ballad.

Up until this time ballads were cautionary songs with a repentance message and stressed convicts were victims of a harsh fate they could not change; for instance, the chorus of *Van Dieman's Land*:

> *Come all you gallant poachers, give ear unto me song.*
> *It is a bit of good advice although it is not long.*
> *Lay by your dog and snare, to you I do speak plain.*
> *If you knew the hardships, you'd never poach again.*

Jack Donahue, an Irish rebel, was transported to NSW in the 1820s, escaped and spent two years bushranging before being killed in a gun battle with the police. The ballad reveals a big change in attitude. Repentance and acceptance of the status quo are not exhorted; rather the song lauds opposition to a rigid society and its enforcers, the hated mounted police. It extolls freedom and the willingness to fight and die for it rather than lose it. It appeals to mateship; we will do this together. Its chorus is the antithesis of that of *Van Dieman's Land*:

> *O come along me hearties, and we'll roam the mountains high;*
> *Together we will plunder, together we will die.*
> *We'll wander over valleys and we'll gallop over plains,*
> *And we'll scorn to live in slavery, bound down by iron chains.*

The *Ballad of Bold Jack Donahue* and similar ballads were popular and sung with passion in the pubs and wherever men gathered in the countryside. They were heady stuff; so heady the authorities referred to them as treason songs. In 1830 Governor Darling banned the song. Anyone caught singing it risked going to jail for inciting rebellion. Owners of public houses (pubs) could even lose their licenses to operate.

A second difference between earlier ballads such as *Van Dieman's Land* and *Bold Jack Donahue* was in their attitude towards the bush. *Van Dieman's Land* presents the bush as sterile and hostile; it imprisons:

> *Our cos were fenced with wire, we slumber when we can*
> *To drive away the wolves upon Van Dieman's Land.*

Not so for Jack Donahue. For him the bush was freedom and the animals the early settlers thought so weird were his friends:

> *As Donahue made his escape, to the bush he went straightway*
> *The squatters they were all afraid to travel by night and by day*
> *And every day in the newspapers, they brought out something new,*
> *Concerning that bold bushranger they called Jack Donahue.*

> *Resign to you – you cowardly dogs! a thing I ne'er will do,*
> *For I'll fight this night with all my might, cried bold Jack Donahue.*
> *I'd rather roam these hills and dales, like wolf or kangaroo*
> *Than work an hour for Government! cried bold Jack Donahue.*

Bailed up by Tom Roberts, 1895, Inverell district where Captain Thunderbolt had operated. Source: Wikimedia Commons

Bushranging gained momentum after the discovery of gold in the 1850s brought an influx of immigrants and wealth to the bush. In addition to travellers on lonely roads, station homesteads and country stores, coaches transporting gold became prime targets for many bushrangers. There was a lot of stock theft as well. The law enforcement authorities, depleted by police joining the gold-rush, had little chance and few resources to restrain them.

This new wave of bushrangers came from various backgrounds: ex-convicts from Tasmania lured by gold, unsuccessful gold-diggers and those who thought it was an easy or exciting way of life. Among the latter was a new breed – native-born Australians. They were mainly the sons of small selectors, often of Irish background, struggling to survive on blocks of land too small and soil too poor to make a living. Faced with poverty, they often stole horses and cattle from the wealthy squatters. Consequently, they were often in conflict with nearby squatters and loathed the authorities who they considered sided with the squatters.

These bush-bred youths and young men had expert knowledge of horses, firearms and the bush. Inspired by tales of the likes of *Bold Jack Donahue*, they roamed the countryside in search of fortune and adventure. They had little regard for authority and hated the police. They believed their antisocial behaviour was justified, maintaining the wealthy squatters became prosperous by unfair means.

Like their escaped convict predecessors they were often sheltered by the rural poor, many of whom were Irish immigrants or the descendants of political transportees. But they were more fortunate in having family and relatives who sympathised with them and so would help them and inform them of the movements of the police. As a result, it was difficult for the police to catch them.

Well-armed and mounted on fine horses, often stolen race horses, they conducted audacious raids. These men often became folk heroes as many other citizens shared their views, admired their daring deeds and the way they defied authority and at times made the police look stupid. Two well-known examples who operated during the 1860s were Captain Thunderbolt, the gentleman bushranger, and Ben Hall.

Captain Thunderbolt is memorialised by a statue at the intersection of the New England Highway and Thunderbolts Way, Uralla, NSW.

Statue of Captain Thunderbolt, Uralla, NSW. Source: McGoodwin, Wikimedia Commons

Ben Hall is commemorated by several bush ballads, the first verse of *The Ballad of Ben Hall* being:

> *Come all Australian sons to me: a hero has been slain,*
> *And cowardly butchered in his sleep upon the Lachlan plain.*
> *Oh, do not stay your seemly grief but let a teardrop fall,*
> *Oh, so many hearts will always mourn the fate of bold Ben Hall.*

Not all bushrangers were heroes; most were nothing more than thieves and murderers. Not all outside the law were bushrangers; many were stock thieves (duffers). The most famous cattle duffer was Harry Redford, sometimes referred to as Captain Starlight.

In 1870 Redford secretly assembled a mob of 1,000 head of cattle on a property on which he was working. Knowing they would be recognised by their brands if he tried to sell them in Queensland he headed for South Australia. After travelling a bit more than three months and 1,500 km through country that had defeated explorers Sturt and Burke and Wills, he sold them to a property owner near Marree. He did not lose one beast. It was a remarkable feat. On the way he sold a white bull that was recognised. In 1872 he was arrested and put on trial in Roma, Queensland. However, the locals considered him a hero and had been put on trial by men who had accumulated wealth through the laws they had made to promote their own interests. When the jury declared him 'not guilty' the crowded courtroom burst into applause. The forebears of many cattle operations in Queensland today, including those of well-known families, made their starts by duffing. It is still a rare occasion that a jury will bring down a guilty verdict in stock theft trials.

The most celebrated and last outlaw to join the pantheon of Australian folklore heroes was Ned Kelly. There is no greater praise than to be described as being 'as game as Ned Kelly'. Born in 1854, the eldest of eight children, his life spanned that period noted for its wild colonial boys. His Irish parents brought their children up to resent wealth and a law that was unfair.

When Ned was aged twelve his father died and his mother took up a small selection in wild rugged country near Glenrowan. Ned and his brother Dan became infamous horse and cattle thieves; when sixteen he was imprisoned for three years for receiving a stolen horse. After his mother was imprisoned in 1878 for attacking a policeman, Ned, Dan and two friends took to the bush.

Later that year they ambushed four policemen sent to arrest them. Ned shot and killed three of them. The newspapers denounced what had become known as 'The Kelly Gang' and the Government offered a reward. But Ned had many supporters and for almost two years they helped the gang dodge police. The gang fitted the popular image of brave and bold bushrangers. Songs at the time portrayed Ned as a people's hero, brave man, daring horseman, champion rifle shot and friend of the poor. The *Ballad of the Wombat Ranges*, which extolled Ned's killing of the policemen and was so popular attempts were made to suppress it, ends:

> *But brave Kelly muttered sadly,*
> *As he loaded up his gun,*
> *Oh, what a bloody pity*
> *The bugger tried to run!*

The gang's most daring deed took place in early 1879. They bailed up the entire town of Jerilderie for two days, robbed the bank and Ned handed over his 8,300 word manifesto now known as the *Jerilderie Letter*. In it he pleads his innocence and desire for justice for both his family and the poor Irish settlers of Victoria's north-east. While the bush people were amused and delighted, the supporters of law and order, the respectable in cities and towns, were appalled at this. Newspapers accused the police of weakness and being poorly led.

In 1880 Ned made his last stand against the

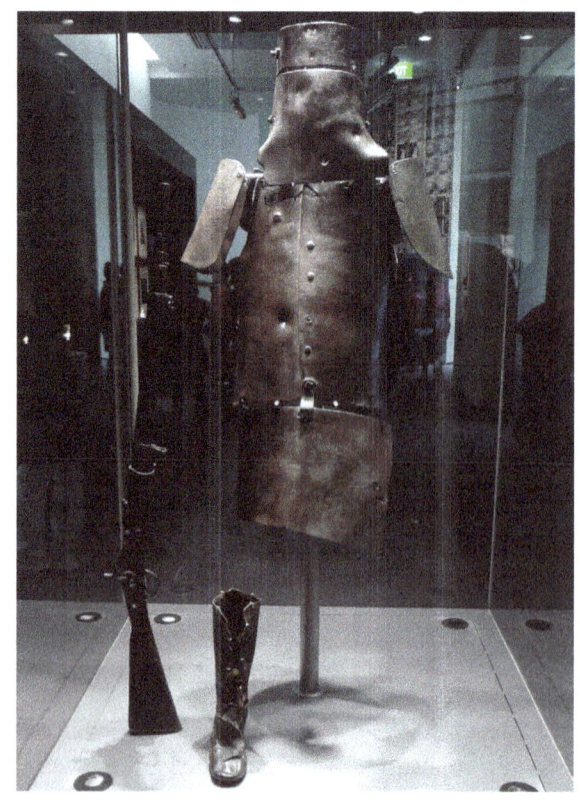

Ned Kelly's armour at State Library of Victoria.
Source: Wikimedia Commons

police wearing his famous suit of armour. On the night of 27 June the police surrounded the Glenrowan Inn, where the four bushrangers held 62 hostages. Ned began the gunfight, leaving and returning to the inn several times. Finally he was brought down by shots to his legs when trying to return to the inn to rescue his brother and friends. Only Ned survived the siege; the others were shot or burnt to death when the police set fire to the inn.

Ned was put on trial in Melbourne, found guilty of murder and sentenced to death, despite protests by thousands of supporters. On 11 November 1880 Ned Kelly, aged 24 years, was hanged at Pentridge Gaol. His body was placed in a wooden axe-box and denied a burial in consecrated ground. Finally, in January 2013, his remains minus his skull (stolen in 1978) were given a dignified funeral and buried in an unmarked grave close to his mother and brother in Greta Cemetery near Wangaratta.

Despite efforts to brand him a common criminal, thief and murderer his name lives on in Australian mythology as someone who would not kowtow to the aristocracy and arrogant authorities who tried to dictate how he should behave. He is remembered in songs like *Poor Ned* by Redgum. The town of Glenrowan capitalises on his story for the tourist trade.

Sidney Nolan immortalised the Kelly legend through a renowned series of paintings that captured Kelly as a hero of the people. In one of these paintings, a defiant Kelly, rifle at the ready, sits astride his horse with an air of perfect authority. It implies that gunning down police and robbing banks of loathed landlords is what a brave man does. Throughout the series, Nolan employs an abstract representation of Kelly's head covered in armour which conveys a sense of invincibility and could be interpreted as a symbol of freedom.

The Story of the Kelly Gang, an Australian film made in 1906, was more than an hour long. This was the longest narrative yet seen in Australia and the world and is regarded as the first full-length feature film ever made.

Ned Kelly, taken day before execution 1880.
Source: NLA, No. SR 364.15520922 L722

The death of Ned Kelly and the expansion of railways brought an end to the bushranger era in Australian history. Of course, the Kelly legend is not shared by all Australians but the myth will endure. It has joined those found in most countries: that of the rebel, who resists tyranny with a passion for freedom.

We rob their banks
We thin their ranks
And ask no thanks
For what we do.

Chapter 10
Australia a Name – Australia a Nation

The continent of *Terra Australis Incognita* was not referred to as 'Australia' until the 18th century, when the name Australia was used in various books and maps. Flinders popularised its use and around 1814 the colonists began using the name. In 1817 Governor Macquarie began using it in his official correspondence. It was more than 80 years later that the political entity, the nation we call 'Australia', came into being. Australia is the only nation to occupy a whole continent, an island continent. How did this happen?

Six self-governing colonies

It began when Cook proclaimed the whole of eastern Australia from Bass Strait to Cape York a British possession, which he named New South Wales.

The penal colony Captain Arthur Phillip established in 1788 at Port Jackson, what is now Sydney, was the British Crown Colony of New South Wales. As Governor of New South Wales Phillip exercised nominal authority over all of Australia east of the 135th meridian; in 1825 this boundary was reset to the 129th meridian. Over the next half century the separate colonies of Western Australia, South Australia, Victoria and Queensland were created from parts of New South Wales and the remainder of the continent. New Zealand was administered from New South Wales until 1841.

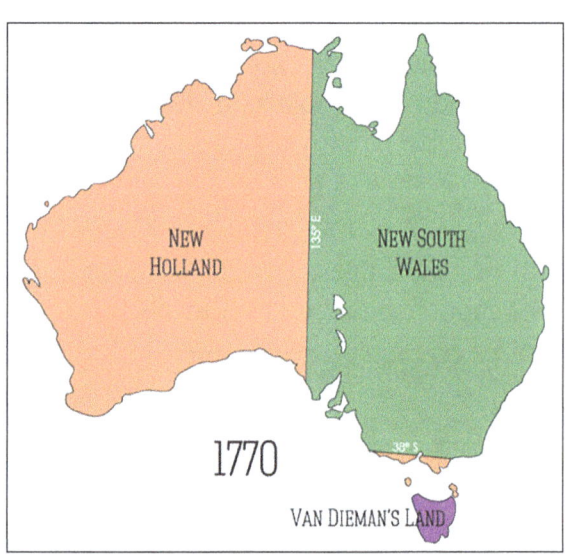

New South Wales as proclaimed by Cook.
Source: Dutch Australia Cultural Centre (DACC)

Tasmania

Hobart was established as a penal settlement in 1804. The early settlements in Van Dieman's Land were dependencies of New South Wales, but Van Dieman's Land became a separate colony in 1825. In 1856 it was renamed Tasmania in order to remove the unsavoury connotations with crime associated with its name. In total, some 75,000 convicts were transported to Van Dieman's Land, or about 40% of all convicts sent to Australia. Although transportation stopped in 1853, Port Arthur, the last penal settlement in Tasmania, did not close until 1877.

Western Australia

Perth, the first full-scale settlement in the western third of the continent, was established in 1829 as the capital of the Swan River Colony, a 'free-settler' colony. The border between it and New South Wales was set at the 129th meridian. In 1850, as Western Australia, it became

Chapter 10: Australia a Name – Australia a Nation

Perth, established in 1829 as capital of the Swan River Colony. Source: Unknown

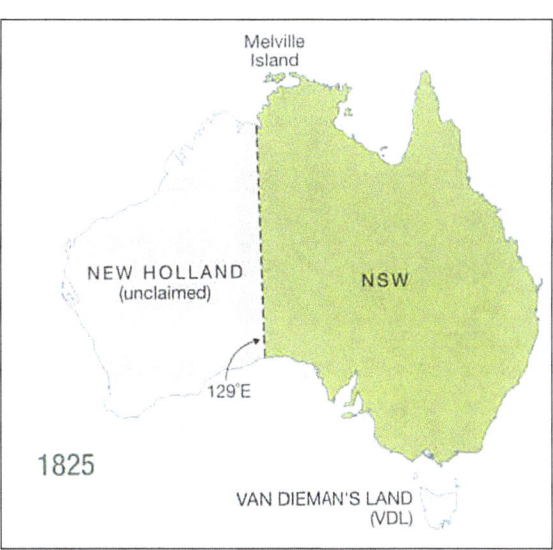

Van Dieman's Land became a separate colony in 1825; renamed Tasmania in 1856. Source: Unknown

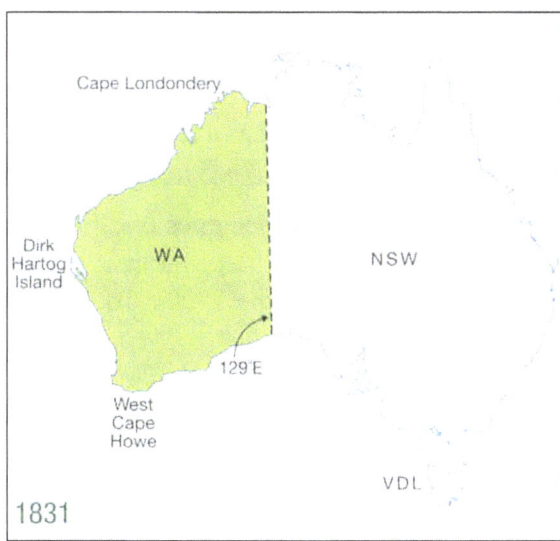

In 1831 the colony of Western Australia was commissioned. The entire continent was finally encompassed by the two colonies of New South Wales and Western Australia. Source: Unknown

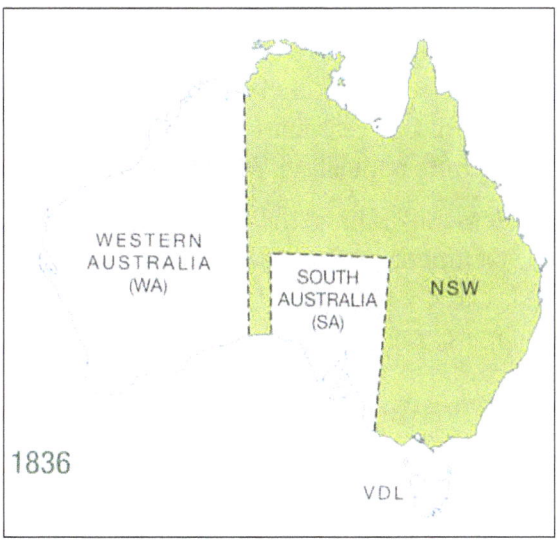

In 1836 the colony of South Australia separated from New South Wales for administrative purposes with Adelaide it's capital. Source: Unknown

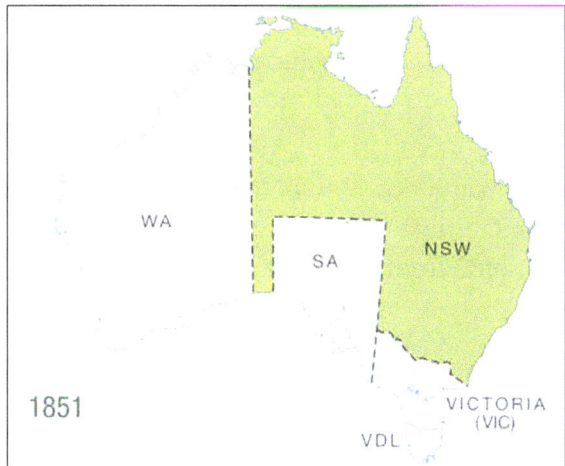

In 1851 the colony of Victoria established as the part of New South Wales south of the Murray River. Source: Unknown

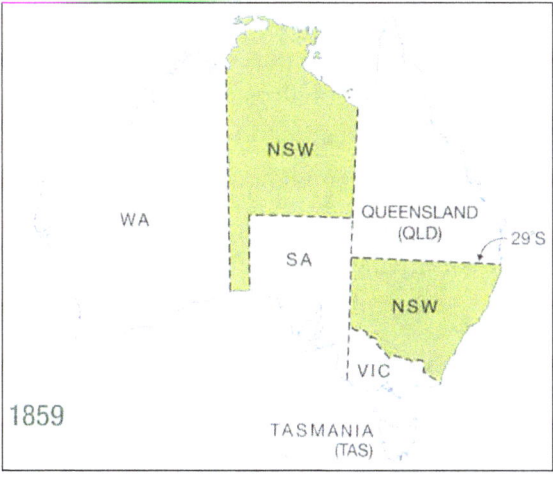

In 1859 the colony of Queensland separated for administrative purposes from New South Wales. Source: Unknown

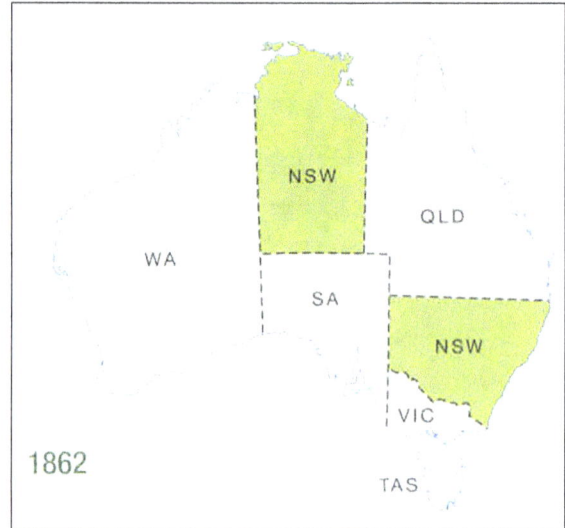 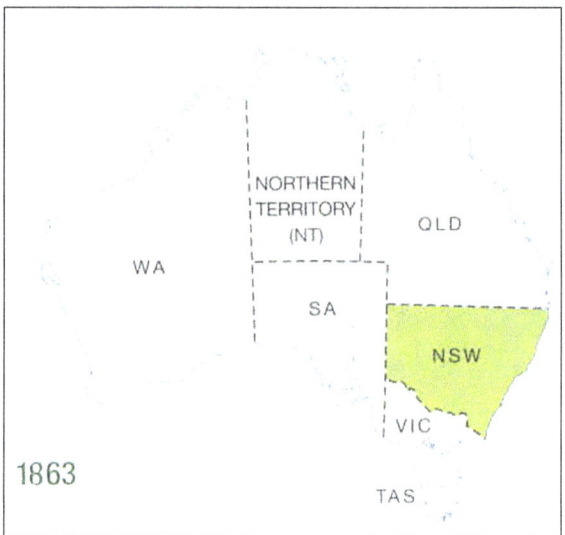

In 1862 the land that is now the Northern Territory remained part of New South Wales for administrative purposes. In 1860 South Australia changed border with Western Australia from 132° to 129° E. Source: Unknown

In 1863 the part of New South Wales north of South Australia was handed over to South Australia to administer as the Northern Territory. In 1911 Northern Territory transferred to Commonwealth control. Source: Unknown

a convict colony at the request of farming and business people who wanted cheap labour. Transportation ceased in 1868. Great Britain granted it a full constitution as a separate colony in 1890; its population was 48,000.

Western Australia is the largest state of the Commonwealth. While it occupies one-third of the continent, only its south-west corner is fertile and substantially settled; the rest is arid and scarcely habitable. Its economy stagnated until the gold-rushes in the 1890s. Today it is a major exporter of iron ore and other minerals.

South Australia

In 1836 the colony of South Australia was established, when its territory was separated for governance purposes from New South Wales. Adelaide was established as the centre of a planned colony of free-immigrants, promising civil liberties and freedom from religious persecution and as such does not share the convict history of Sydney, Hobart, Brisbane and Perth. The site for Adelaide was surveyed and laid-out in 1836.

Victoria

Melbourne was founded in 1835 as a free-settlement. In 1851 the colony of Victoria was established from the part of New South Wales lying south of the Murray River and east of South Australia. As a result of the gold-rush in the 1850s, Melbourne became the financial centre of Australia.

From 1901 to 1927, while Canberra was under construction, Melbourne was the capital of Australia. It was the largest city in Australia at the time. While Melbourne remains an important financial centre, its importance slowly waned from the 1970s onwards as Sydney increased in population and business importance.

Queensland

Brisbane was established in 1824 as a penal settlement for the more troublesome convicts. The penal settlement was closed in 1839 and free-settlement permitted in 1842. In 1859 the colony of Queensland separated for governance purposes from New South Wales.

From the time early explorers returned with news of vast grazing lands, successive governors and then governments had struggled to maintain administrative control of land and its orderly possession and marketing. Land disputes between governments and squatters were common. My great grandfather, P.F. MacDonald, was no exception. In 1869 he sued the Crown for damages resulting from its resumption of leaseholds and river frontages that he had taken up. The case, known as the Great Northern Run case, dragged on until 1880 when it was settled for £22,700 in his favour.

P.F. MacDonald took a keen interest in current affairs of the state and region. He served as the member for Blackall in the Queensland House of Assembly from 1873 to 1878. During his time in parliament he was strongly attacked for using it to further his own interests rather than those of his constituents. He did not recontest the seat in November 1878, saying he was tired of parliamentary affairs. He claimed he was so involved with the district he could not serve its interests or those of the electors without serving his own. He stood unsuccessfully for the seat of North Rockhampton in 1888. He was a progressive squatter, supporting secular education and liberal land legislation for viable selectors.

Colonial borders finalised

When the colony of Queensland was created, New South Wales was reduced in size to its present borders, although what is now the Northern Territory remained part of New South Wales until 1863, when it was handed over to South Australia. In 1911 the Northern Territory was separated from South Australia and transferred to Commonwealth control. In 1978 the Territory was granted responsible government, with a Legislative Assembly headed by a Chief Minister.

A progressive new society

A progressive new society was emerging in Britain's Australian colonies. The people who constituted it were keen to look forward, not back. They were innovative. They readily adopted new technology and pioneered many reforms that underpin the electoral practices of modern democracies and industrial relations.

In 1856 Victoria and South Australia introduced the secret ballot, which became known throughout the world as 'the Australian ballot'. In 1856, South Australia eliminated professional and property qualifications, which determined a man's eligibility to vote, allowing all adult men to vote, and in 1892 allowed all women to vote. In the 1890s the colonies adopted the principle of one vote per person, stopping the practice of plural voting.

A movement for an 8-hour working day began in Victoria and New South Wales in 1856, and following strike action the stonemasons were granted it in the same year. The world's first Labor government was appointed in 1899 in Queensland. It lasted just seven days. In 1904, a Federal Labor Government was sworn in as the first National Labor Government in the World.

By the end of the 19th century the six colonies were firmly established, and their people were probably more prosperous and better off than any elsewhere in the world. The colonists were using exciting innovations such as electric telegraphs, telephones, cable and electric trams, and gas and electric light soon after they were invented. All shared the same continent but they were not a nation. In their youth my mother's parents and siblings were Queenslanders and my father's parents were Victorians. They were not 'Australians'.

Federation

Why had the colonies not united? There had been some discussion of a federal assembly and a Governor-General in 1850, when the British government formalised the division of Australia into six separate colonies and granted them limited self-government. Eight inter-colonial conferences were held between 1863 and 1880, at which common areas of concern were discussed such as the lack of a standard schedule of tariffs, trade, customs duties, defence and communications by post and telegraph. However, no impetus for unification resulted from any of these discussions.

Local loyalty was strong; there was no broad feeling of Australian nationality. State loyalties are still evident today. You need only attend an inter-state sporting event, for example a State of Origin Rugby League match, to learn a Queenslander feels very much a Queenslander. More significantly, any serious consideration of unification was prevented by inter-colonial rivalries and fears by the smaller colonies about the dominance of the larger colonies.

There was intense rivalry between New South Wales and Victoria; they had developed in radically different directions throughout the second half of the 19th century. Once the easily-obtained gold had been mined by about 1860, Victoria absorbed the surplus labour force from the gold-fields in manufacturing, protected by high tariff walls. Victoria became a stronghold of protectionism, liberalism and radicalism. New South Wales, which was less radically affected demographically by the gold-rushes, remained more conservative and was still dominated politically by the squatter class and its allies in the Sydney business community. New South Wales, as a trading and exporting colony, remained an adherent of free trade. It would never agree to surrender its free trade principles to a national government dominated by Victorians so long as Victoria was more populous and economically stronger.

By the 1890s, several factors began to change this situation:

- A prolonged depression in Victoria, which began in the 1880s, allowed New South Wales to recover the economic and demographic superiority it had lost in the 1850s.
- A steady rise in imperial sentiment in the 1880s and 1890s made the creation of a united Australian dominion seem an important imperial project.
- The intrusion of other colonial powers such as France and Germany into the south-west Pacific area made colonial defence an urgent question, which became more urgent with the rise of Japan as an expansionist power.
- The issue of Chinese and other non-European immigration made federation of the colonies an important issue, with advocates of a White Australia Policy arguing the necessity of a national immigration policy.

The first attempt at federation in 1891 failed. It was revived some years later and by 1899 all eastern colonies had voted in favour of federation. In Western Australia, sharp divisions about federating delayed the holding of a referendum in that colony. Finally, on 31 July 1900, three weeks after the British Parliament had voted the Australian Constitution into law, an overwhelming majority in Western Australia voted in favour of union with the eastern colonies. Western Australia was not specifically mentioned in the preamble, which begins with the simple words 'Whereas the people… have agreed to unite', as its support was given too late for the document to be redrafted. Absent from not only the preamble but also the body of the constitution was any reference to the indigenous people of Australia – laws for them were to be made by the States. Neither did they feature in the so-called race clause, which enabled the Federal Parliament to pass laws that discriminated negatively against any race other than the Aboriginal race.

There was no compelling need to federate. National sentiment was the precondition of union. Those committed to federalism were pursuing a sacred ideal of nationhood. Australia was to federate to meet its destiny to be a great nation, proud and independent, respected around the world – a nation with a strong, independent identity, inferior to no other, and capable of attracting the allegiance of all its citizens. It was indeed a nation consisting of a single geographical unit, a whole continent with only natural boundaries, and a relatively homogeneous people.

On 1 January 1901 the Commonwealth of Australia came into being as a dominion of the British Empire. It was agreed that the capital of the new nation would be in New South Wales but at least 100 miles (160 km) from Sydney, initially. Melbourne was the seat of government. In 1911 the Australian Capital Territory (ACT) was annexed from New South Wales to provide a location for the proposed new federal capital. This was on Ngunnawal land. An international competition to determine the most appropriate design for the new capital was held. An American architect Walter Burley Griffin and his partner and wife, Marion Mahony Griffin, submitted the winning entry. Construction and establishment of the new national capital took until 1927, when the seat of government moved from Melbourne to Canberra. Griffin designed the city for a population of 75,000 people but the population has now grown to almost 500,000.

At present the Commonwealth of Australia consists of five mainland states (New South Wales, Victoria, Queensland, South Australia and Western Australia), Tasmania and three territories (Australian Capital Territory, Northern Territory and Norfolk Island).

Australia is most fortunate as a nation in having been forged from negotiation, not as most nations were from conflict and aggression. Apart from overcoming any resistance by the original inhabitants, the nearest to armed struggle in the colonies was the Eureka Stockade incident. It was the new nation's participation in the 1914-1918 war that developed a real sense of nationhood.

An independent nation

When the Commonwealth of Australia was created in 1901, it was as a Dominion of the British Empire and its citizens were British subjects and held British passports. The legal status of Australian nationality or Australian citizenship was not created until passing of the Nationality and Citizenship Act 1948 allowed Australians to travel under Australian passports. Aboriginals also became Australian citizens, although they were not counted in the Australian population until after a 1967 referendum.

Australia, like the other Dominions, became in practice independent from the United Kingdom following the passage of the Statute of Westminster in 1931, which severed all legislative links between the United Kingdom and Australia, leaving the Crown as the only remaining connection. Australian law was made unequivocally sovereign by the passage of the Australia Act 1986 and associated legislation in the United Kingdom. This act confirmed the High Court of Australia as its highest court of appeal. Until then, some Australian cases could be referred to the Judicial Committee of the Privy Council for final appeal.

National anthem, symbols and emblems

National anthem

Australians all let us rejoice, For we are one and free;
We've golden soil and wealth for toil, Our home is girt by sea;
Our land abounds in nature's gifts, Of beauty rich and rare;
In history's page, let every stage,
Advance Australia Fair.
In joyful strains then let us sing, Advance Australia Fair.

Beneath our radiant Southern Cross, We'll toil with hearts and hands,
To make this Commonwealth of ours Renowned of all the lands;
For those who've come across the seas, We've boundless plains to share;
With courage let us all combine To Advance Australia Fair.
In joyful strains then let us sing, Advance Australia Fair.

The following symbols and emblems are used to represent Australia: the national flag, the national flower (the wattle) and national gemstone (the opal). The Commonwealth Coat of Arms is not used to represent the entirety of Australia but represents the Australian Government departments and agencies, statutory and non-statutory authorities, the Parliament and Commonwealth courts and tribunal.

Australian flag and the Commonwealth Coat of Arms. Source: Permission to reproduce the Commonwealth Coat of Arms granted by the Department of the Prime Minister and Cabinet

The Australian flag consists of three main elements: the *Union Jack* in the upper left sector, denoting Australia's historical links with Great Britain; the *Southern Cross,* which strongly places Australia geographically; and the seven-pointed *Commonwealth Star* or *Star of Federation,* denoting the six states and the combined territories of the Commonwealth.

The Coat of Arms consists of a shield composed of two rows of devices representing the six States of the Commonwealth enclosed by an ermine border signifying the federation of the States into the Commonwealth. The Crest of the Arms is a seven-pointed gold star symbolic of national unity. The shield is supported by the kangaroo and the emu, further identifying the Arms as being exclusively Australian.

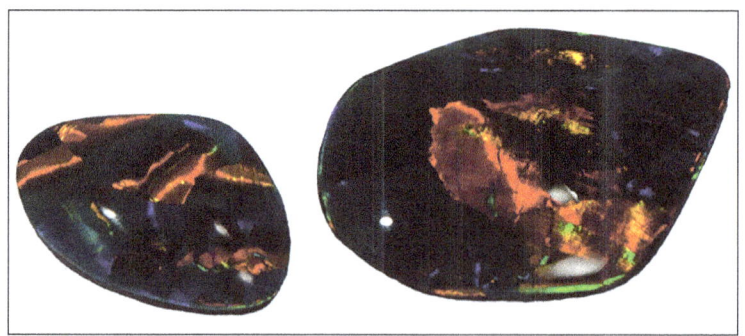

From left:
The golden wattle, (*Acacia pycnantha*). Source: Australian National Botanic Gardens; Black opal from Lightning Ridge, NSW. Source: Geoscience Australia

Australia's system of government

Overseas students and friends, particularly those from Asia, have difficulty understanding our system of government. A few think England has some sort of jurisdiction over Australia. Some wonder at the presence of the English monarch. Most have no interest at all, believing it has nothing to do with them. Unsurprisingly, those accustomed to autocratic regimes have little or no idea or understanding of having a parliamentary representative, whom constituents may approach on all manner of matters.

Australia is a constitutional monarchy, a federation and a parliamentary democracy. Its system of government is based on the liberal democratic tradition, which includes religious tolerance and freedom of speech and association. Its institutions and practices reflect British and North American models but are uniquely Australian.

Australia's head of state is the ruling monarch of Great Britain, who is currently King Charles III of Great Britain. His title is King of Australia. He is represented by the Governor-General, who carries out virtually all the functions of a head-of-state, without reference to the monarch. The monarch appoints a Governor-General (on the advice of the elected Australian Government) to represent him. The Governor-General has wide powers, but by convention acts only on the advice of ministers of the Government of the day in virtually all matters. Like much about Australia, the role of the monarchy is odd; for all practical purposes, the monarch could reside on Mars and probably, using Montesquieu's terminology (see Appendix 2), the spirit of government permeating the population and those who govern them is virtue rather than honour, upon which a monarchy relies.

There are three levels of government: the Federal Government, State and Territory Governments and below these Local Governments. At the federal and state levels, the three inter-connected arms of government (legislative, executive and judicial) undertake their activities separate from each other according to the principle of the Separation of Powers.

The Parliament of Australia is the legislative branch of Australia. Parliament consists of the monarch of Australia, the House of Representatives (the 'lower house') and the Senate (the 'upper house' or 'house of review'). The House of Representatives consists of 151 members, who represent districts known as electoral divisions (commonly referred to as 'electorates' or 'seats'). Each division elects one member every three years using preferential voting. The Senate, on the other hand, consists of 76 members: twelve for each state elected for six-year terms, and two for each territory elected for three-year terms. Senators are elected using a form of proportional voting with half elected every three years. Voting in Australia is compulsory.

The Commonwealth Parliament operates within the conventions of the Westminster System, as do all the State and Territory Parliaments. The head of the Commonwealth Government (executive or administrative arm of government) is the Prime Minister. This person is the leader of the political party or coalition of parties that wins a majority of the seats in the House of Representatives or, in a minority situation, can guarantee supply (the passage of important financial bills). He/she appoints Ministers from the House of Representatives and the Senate to conduct executive government. Policy decisions are made in Cabinet meetings, which involve the Prime Minister and Senior Government Ministers. Apart from the announcement of decisions, Cabinet discussions are not disclosed and Ministers are bound by the principle of Cabinet solidarity. The leader of the largest party outside the government becomes the Leader of the Opposition, a recognised part of the Westminster form of government. He/she appoints a Shadow Cabinet of Opposition members who 'shadow' each member of the Ministry, asking questions on matters within the Minister's portfolio.

General elections are held at least once every three years. The Prime Minister has discretion to advise the Governor-General to call an election for the House of Representatives at any time, but Senate elections can be held only within certain periods prescribed in the Constitution.

The judicial arm of government consists of the High Court of Australia and subsidiary Federal Courts. The courts hear cases arising from the administration of the law, using both Statute law and Common law. The other two arms (legislative and executive) are not permitted to influence the judiciary. The High Court of Australia arbitrates on any disputes that arise between the Commonwealth and the States, or among the States, concerning their respective functions; in other words, it interprets the Constitution. Being the ultimate court of appeal, it ensures some uniformity of legal interpretation throughout Australia.

Federal tensions

The federation is not without its tensions. The states feel disadvantaged by too much power residing in Canberra. The Constitution gives the Commonwealth powers to legislate in specific areas. Where Commonwealth and State laws conflict, the Commonwealth has precedence. For reasons of uniformity and finance, there has been a growing trend for States to cede their legislative powers in certain areas to the Commonwealth. The Commonwealth, however, had no power to compel the States to unlock their borders during the COVID-19 pandemic. When selecting his ministry, the Prime Minister endeavours to have all states represented to allay concerns by State Premiers of being disadvantaged or overlooked.

The tension between the states and central government is starkly illustrated by the experience with Western Australia, which entered into the Federation reluctantly. Dissatisfaction with what they perceived as centralist policies, distribution of their state's resource wealth and increased power of central government and the feeling the Federal Government was pandering to the business and power interests in the eastern states grew in the decades following federation. Western Australians felt cut off and ignored by the East. Many blamed physical separation as Western Australia is a long way from Canberra. Also, they sensed their interests were genuinely different from those of the rest of Australia. Many considered secession the only solution. In a 1933 State referendum, 68% voted in favour of secession from the Federation but the British Parliament rejected Western Australia's petition for separation. However, the failure of the secession movement in the 1930s did not destroy its secessionist sentiments. During the 1970s a Westralian Secession Movement was formed and, in the lead up to the 1999 referendum on Australia becoming a republic, secessionist sentiments surfaced again. In 2017 a non-partisan Western Australian Secessionist Movement was formed in response to disproportionate returns on GST (Goods and Services Tax) payments.

Despite these tensions the Federation has held fast. The young nation has been an exemplar of stable government and Australians have distinguished themselves on the battlefield and in science, the arts and sport. The population has grown from under four million to about 27 million in 2024 and a way of life has evolved that few other nations can emulate.

Given the uncertainties of a rapidly changing world, the greatest test awaiting the young nation is whether the constitution and form of government chosen when it eventually decides to become a republic will usher in a further century of untrammelled progress.

Chapter 11
Carving Up The Land

Squatters, selectors and dispossession

Since time immemorial land has been the source of wealth, power and security. Land may also provide a sense of identity or a feeling of belonging. Land is of finite quantity and so not surprisingly a source of conflict.

English philosopher John Locke argued that individual freedom depends on the liberty to use and dispose of one's possessions as wished according to the extant law and not be subject to the arbitrary will of another. The type and security of land tenure strongly influence the human society that evolves. Under English law at the time of early settlement, ownership of land gave one the right to: vote; participate in parliament; and occupy certain offices of the land. Those without land had none of these rights.

Various systems of land ownership have developed throughout the world under the influence of historical, cultural and economic factors and are exposed to a continual process of change.

The system of land ownership regulates the relationship of the people to the land, specifically the power of disposition over land and the right to use the land. The owner has the right of disposition (sell, lease, bequeath, give away or lend, etc. a parcel of land), whereas the occupier has only the right to use the land.

Private ownership of land is a Western concept that was first introduced into many developing countries by Europeans. It arose under a specific legal order by original acquisitioning of land (occupying and making the land arable) or changes in ownership (conquest, contract or inheritance). With collective and communal ownership, the right of disposition is in the hands of kinship or political groups, which are larger than a single family.

Some societies have not developed any forms of personal or private rights to land that would grant a right of disposition. Instead, the individual is allotted land for his/her own usage that reverts to the hands of the group (tribe) as soon as it is no longer used. The Aboriginal people of Australia are an extreme example.

It is not unusual that laws governing the land exist at different levels, e.g. government laws and traditional tribal laws. If conflict arises between these two levels, it leads to considerable breakdowns and obstructions in the legal guarantees and, thus, the usage of the land.

Ironically, the time-tested English law that underpinned the possession and management of land failed completely to acknowledge Australia's Aboriginal people had any right of possession of the land they had lived on for thousands of years. English law or those interpreting it believed that cultivating (clearing, tilling) the land legitimised its expropriation. This anomaly was finally acknowledged in the High Court Mabo Case, which quashed the concept of *Terra Nullius* and granted Native Title Rights to Australia's First People. However, claims for Native Title can be made only on Crown land. The court ruled that Native Title had already been extinguished on private property held under freehold title.

Australia gave an opportunity for all who made the effort to acquire land and thereby wealth. Their occupying of land over the first hundred years was far from orderly or methodical.

Ongoing friction between the governments and settlers plus the resistance of the First Australians to the callous appropriation of their land dogged the colonies for decades. The colonial governments had neither administrative resources to carry out due process nor law enforcement resources to enforce the law. Initially large areas of land were occupied by relatively few settlers; however, the final outcome was not a small minority of wealthy, politically powerful landholders with large holdings as in South America but a multitude of land holdings, the area of which largely depended on the nature of the country. Thus Australia's egalitarian ethos remained intact.

In the beginning

Modern Australia could be said to have begun at sunset on Wednesday 22 August 1770, when on Possession Island and without permission from the local inhabitants and inhabitants of the land, Captain James Cook declared the entire east coast of New Holland a British possession.

In doing so Cook was not actually following his secret instructions to the letter. They read:

> *You are ... to observe the Genius, Temper, Disposition and Number of the Natives, if there be any and endeavour by all proper means to cultivate a Friendship and Alliance with them... You are also with the Consent of the Natives to take Possession of Convenient Situations in the Country in the Name of the King of Great Britain: Or: if you find the Country uninhabited take Possession for his Majesty by setting up Proper Marks and Inscriptions, as first discoverers and possessors.*

Cook also carried a letter from James Douglas, the 14th Earl of Morton, and president of the Royal Society in London, counselling him to treat with kindness and understanding any indigenous people encountered. Earl Douglas urged Cook and his scientists to show the utmost patience and forebearance with respect to the Natives of the several Lands where the Ship may touch and proceed with an understanding that asserted, unambiguously, the indigenous ownership of the land. Douglas urged them:

> *To check the petulance of the Sailors and restrain the wanton use of Fire Arms. They are the natural, and in the strictest sense of the word, the legal possessors of the several Regions they inhabit.*
> *No European nation has a right to occupy any part of their country or settle among them without their voluntary consent.*
> *Conquest over such people can give no just title; because they could never be the Aggressors.*

On 7 February 1788, the ceremonial reading of the Royal Commission to all present at Sydney Cove, formally claimed for the Crown:

> *... all territories (land) called New South Wales extending from the Northern Cape or Extremity of the Coast, called Cape York in the Latitude of Ten Degrees thirty-seven Minutes south, to the Southern Extremity of the said Territory of New South Wales, or South Cape, in the Latitude of Forty-three Degrees thirty-nine Minutes south, and of all the Country Inland to the Westward as far as the One-hundred and Thirty-fifth Degree of East Longitude, ... and that it is your Majesty's pleasure we should grant him such powers as have usually been granted to the Governors of your Majesty's Colonies in America.*

Unlike the colonies in America, all beneath the surface (resources such as water, oil and minerals) belonged to the Crown and not to the owner or occupier of the land. The claim over Aboriginal lands and the administration of them without acknowledgement of prior ownership or use established the concept of *Terra Nullius*.

The *Proclamation* of Governor Bourke in 1835 in response to Batman's land use agreement with Australia's First People was the final 'nail in the coffin' of this cavalier expropriation of another's land. Bourke implemented the doctrine of *Terra Nullius* upon which British settlement was based, reinforcing the notion that the land belonged to no one prior to the British Crown taking possession of it; in other words, ownerless land ripe for development. Not that Australia's indigenous people were strictly hunter-gatherers; journals and letters of early surveyors, explorers and settlers describe rudimentary forms of agriculture and settlement. Aboriginal people therefore could not sell or assign the land, nor could an individual person acquire it, other than through distribution by the Crown. Its publication in the colony meant that, from then, *all* people found occupying land without the authority of the government would be considered illegal trespassers. Just what rights this allowed Australia's First People is unclear to this day.

Land administration was one of the most important tasks overseen by colonial governments. Australia was an enormous parcel of real estate about which practically nothing was known by the rest of the world. The land had to be mapped and described so orderly settlement and commerce could take place; for instance, legal creation of properties and title deeds of ownership. This monumental task was carried out by government surveyors, a tough breed of human being with a great work ethic, endurance and sheer will-power to succeed, and intrepid early explorers (see Explorers, page 59). Their expeditions consisted of a few men, frequently including indigenous Australians. Often they received help and assistance from the indigenous people whose land they passed through; people who referenced their land without the need for detailed written descriptions and maps, without which the Newcomers' society was virtually moribund.

As the interior was explored and mapped, settlers followed, eager to take up land. The first great pastoral expansion into the interior from the eastern and south-eastern seaboard in the late 1820s initiated the Australian frontier. The frontier regions were often fraught with violence as the Aboriginal people were forced off their homelands, which were their source of livelihood; many were murdered in the process. Naturally many resisted and an ensuing guerrilla-like conflict lasting almost a century took its toll on both sides.

The early years 1790-1830

Food production was paramount for the new colony. Phillip's instructions were to begin cultivating the land immediately on landing but the land around Farm Cove (Circular Quay, Sydney) was unsuitable for farming and by late 1791 had been abandoned. More suitable farming land had been found at Rose Hill (now known as Parramatta), where a second settlement was established. By 1794 the rich farming land along the Hawkesbury River was also being settled.

Governors of New South Wales had the authority to make free grants of land of up to 12 ha to male ex-convicts (emancipists and expirees), officers and free-settlers. The first ex-convict to receive a grant was James Ruse but Governor Phillip withheld the title until 1791, by which time Ruse's capacity as a farmer and his right to freedom had been proven. Ex-convicts granted land were encouraged to cultivate it by being provided with tools, provisions, grain, cattle, sheep and pigs; this was another difference between Australia and North America, where immigrants received little or no government assistance.

The first free-settlers to receive land grants (at Liberty Plains, now Strathfield and Homebush) arrived on 16 January 1793. The early governors tended to be prudent with these grants; by the end of Macquarie's term (1821) less than 3,000 km^2 of land had been granted. During the 1820s land grants were phased out and by 1831 the granting of free land had ceased. In 1791 an auspicious early grant of 41 ha of land at Parramatta was made to Lieutenant James

McArthur, who with his wife Elizabeth crossbred sheep to produce the Australian Merino (see page 248, paragraph 2). The opportunity to become wealthy from the production of wool, and to a lesser degree meat, drove the rapid occupation of seemingly unlimited land.

Squatting – Occupation of Crown land without legal title

The governors sought to have an orderly occupation of land, which proved difficult given their limited resources. They tried to limit it to the already settled districts of New South Wales. The difficulty in doing so increased when the Blue Mountains were crossed in 1813, revealing the lightly-timbered fertile plains to the west. In 1826 the boundaries of the settlement were set. In 1829 these were extended to an area defined as the Nineteen Counties. Only land within the Nineteen Counties was made available for sale but preventing illegal occupation of land beyond these boundaries was impossible; it was too far away from main settlements, surveyors and police.

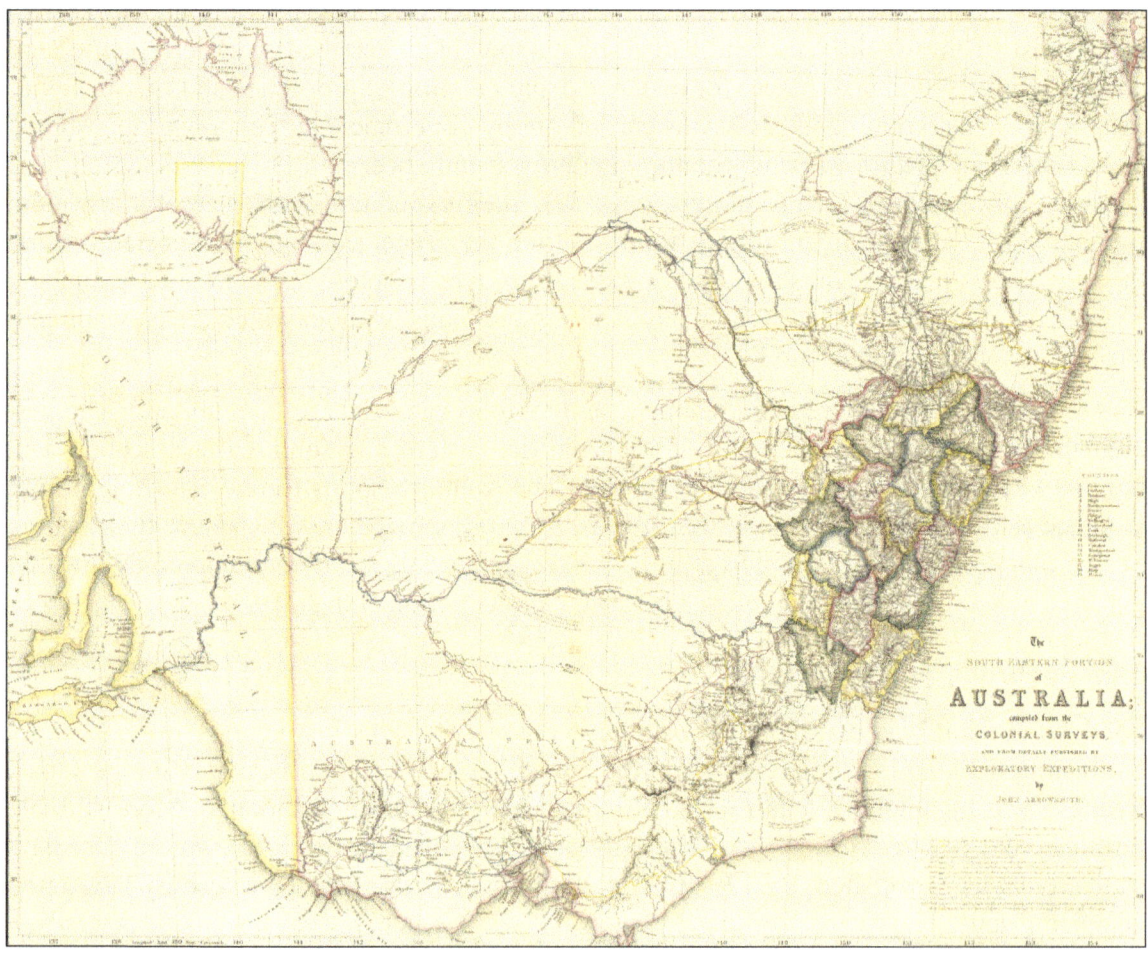

The south-eastern portion of Australia; compiled from the Colonial Surveys, and from details furnished by Exploratory Expeditions. Detailed map of New South Wales, issued in the *London Atlas* by John Arrowsmith. The 'newly formed' counties are marked, as are the inland expeditions made during 1817–1840. The Squatters' Map – Nineteen Counties – map produced in 1837.
Source: Wikimedia Commons

When the boundaries were set (Nineteen Counties) there were already settlers in some places beyond the proclaimed boundaries. They were mainly ticket-of-leave convicts or ex-convicts (emancipists) who, having obtained a small grant under the old system, or without any grant at all, set themselves down in remote situations. They were said to be 'squatting' – an American term of contempt for a person who occupied land illegally – and were referred to as 'squatters'. Their acquisition of livestock was also suspect. Governor George Arthur, who is credited with first using the word 'squatter' officially, issued an order in 1828 stating

... the practice of squatting has been followed for the most part by freed convicts possessing sheep, probably acquired by the most exceptional means.

Arthur implied that the sheep were stolen and said that, with these thefts, the freed convicts started their own sheep runs (stretches of unfenced land used to graze livestock). For a century the forebears of many well-known pastoralists stocked their newly acquired runs with stolen sheep and cattle. Up until today few juries have been prepared to convict fellow graziers charged with cattle and sheep duffing (theft).

The ex-convicts were not alone in occupying land illegally. From the mid-1820s squatting became more widespread, often by wealthy, and usually socially important, landowners within the Nineteen Counties wanting more land and better pastures for their growing flocks and herds. They rode until they found good grass and, if possible, permanent water, and there they would squat. The practice of squatting cost little; squatters occupied as much land as they wished and paid nothing. Despite the uncertainty of land tenure, they established huge runs on the best land, where they grazed large numbers of sheep and cattle.

Squatting made legal

Squatting activity increased during the 1830s, driven by the demand for grazing land to meet the needs of the expanding sheep industry. The land as far north as what is now Queensland and Victoria in the south was rapidly occupied. The more recently established colonies of South Australia and Western Australia did not experience the squatting practice of the eastern colonies, although lack of survey and unfair allocation of land hindered orderly occupation of the land.

In 1836 squatting was given legal recognition by the introduction of a 10-pound annual licence that permitted squatters to graze stock on the land they occupied. The term 'squatter' was adopted for referring to all such landholders. There was no guarantee of longer tenure and fines were levied for unauthorised occupation. This both discouraged unauthorised occupants, and encouraged men of capital to take up land as tenants of the Crown.

In 1839 the legal position of the squatters was strengthened further by the introduction of levies charged on all stock depastured outside the settled districts. In 1844 regulations were proposed to restrict the area of individual runs and to make extension of leases conditional on periodic purchases of land within them. This suggestion was thwarted by squatters with big runs and who had significant financial and political standing. They wanted ownership and not merely a lease of the land they occupied.

In 1847 the concept of areas within and without the Nineteen Counties was discontinued. New South Wales was divided into three areas: settled (the former Nineteen Counties), intermediate and unsettled. Squatters in unsettled districts could stay on their land if they paid a 10-pound annual licence fee for a 14-year lease. At the end of a lease they had the pre-emptive right to purchase 1 square mile (256 ha) in every 25 square miles of the run. The Government retained the power not to renew a licence but the squatters were quick to apply for the new leases. They felt more secure, which encouraged them to improve their properties, e.g. build homesteads with a range of outbuildings, construct dams or tanks and erect fencing and to invest in equipment to improve the efficiency of their operations. When the British Government agreed that squatters could have leases over their land, it insisted that the Aboriginals should retain the right of access to the land.

By the 1850s the south-eastern corner of Australia was largely comprised of extensive pastoral leases held by a relatively few squatters. During the late 1850s, pastoralists in New South Wales were extending the boundaries of settlement ever northward throughout what would become the new colony of Queensland.

Squatter's life

Initially pioneer squatters led a hard life. Their belongings and provisions were stacked high on bullock wagons, dragged along rough bush tracks and often over virgin ground. They took the basic provisions needed for the first year: tea, sugar, flour and salt. A campfire oven, pans and knives were all they had for cooking. Their flocks could consist of four to five thousand sheep along with horses and dogs.

Where they chose to squat they built crude huts. As they became wealthier and tenure became more secure they built more substantial houses; in some cases these were rather grand residences. Other buildings were constructed around the homestead.

Squatters House, post 1847, Delegate, NSW. Source: New South Wales Government

Purrumbete House, Weerite, Vic. Source: Purrumbete Homestead

The wealthy squatters normally brought overseers and shepherds from the United Kingdom and utilised assigned convicts. Squatters who did not occupy land within the Nineteen Counties were not eligible for assigned convicts. Those who succeeded in finding suitable country and managed to obtain a loan had to pay a high rate of interest. They used the money to buy necessary equipment. If their funds were adequate, they hired one or two helpers.

Managing the early Australian run relied on the use of shepherds, who at various locations on the run looked after a flock of sheep. By day the sheep were allowed to roam, followed closely by the shepherd and his dog. At night the sheep were placed in portable yards formed by moveable rails. To avoid the ground in yards being fouled, they were moved frequently. Many Chinese worked as shepherds. Shepherding was lonely and often dangerous, with shepherds and sheep being prone to attack by Aboriginals defending their land.

Squattocracy

As a group, the squatters were among the wealthiest, most socially significant and politically powerful colonists. Whether they held the land as a proprietor or lessee, the term 'squatter' came to be used to refer to a person of high social prestige, who grazed livestock on a large scale. Many built imposing homesteads and their life-styles hinted at pretensions to the life of the English country gentry, although some continued to lead an unnecessarily rough and frugal life. By 1846 squatters were being referred to generically as the 'squattocracy', a play on the word 'aristocracy'. By 1850 much of the land was occupied in pastoral leases held by the squatters.

The 'ordinary' colonists resented the privileges enjoyed by the squatters. However, many squatters were nothing more than *kings in grass castles* as Mary Durack titled the first of her books about her squatter family. Squatters, especially those beyond the south-eastern part of Australia, faced insecurities not only regarding land tenure but also those inflicted by nature: flood, fire, drought and also the market. The nature of the land and the economics of its exploitation required large holdings and considerable capital investment. Many succumbed to the ravages of drought and economic depressions.

Unlocking the lands

Because of their privileges and huge grazing properties, squatters were looked upon resentfully by the less fortunate miners and city dwellers, who also wanted land. Radical ideas about social and political rights, that were inflaming Europe, were a legacy of the gold-rush. By the late 1850s colonists were demanding not only the right to vote but also opening up the lands of the squattocracy for selection by settlers with small or no holdings. They regularly elected state governments committed to resuming large holdings and reallocating smaller portions.

The squatters' domination of land was challenged in the 1860s, when the 14-year leases expired. Selection acts were passed in various colonies giving those with limited means free-selection before survey of Crown land. In New South Wales the *limits of location* of the Nineteen Counties became redundant. The intention of the acts was to encourage closer settlement, based on intensive agriculture, such as wheat-growing, rather than extensive agriculture, such as wool production. Generally, the acts provided for the sale of land at auction, forcing squatters to bid against prospective farmers for land that they already controlled by leasehold. The wealthy squatters were able to purchase the choicest land and much of the land taken up by selectors was unsuited to farming.

Passage of the 1861 Crown Lands Acts resulted in landed squatters in New South Wales taking any opportunity they could to protect their runs from selection, wherever it was seen as a threat, and at the same time acquire significant freehold estate. This they did by turning provisions of the Acts to their own advantage, while occasionally bending the truth at the same time. Subsequent legislation sought to overcome short-comings of these Acts.

Nowhere in Australia was the demise of the squattocracy more stark than in the Western District of Victoria, Thomas Mitchell's 'Australia Felix'. In the late 1850s, just 240 families held all the pastoral licences issued in Victoria. Wool made them enormously wealthy. The houses they built were grand as was their lifestyle. Few of them remain today and little remains of their grand enterprises. Purrumbete is an example. By 1963 only 991 acres (396 ha) remained of the 100,000 acres (40,000 ha) taken up in 1839. I savoured the Western District and life of the squattocracy in the wool boom days of the 1950s when, as a teenager, I spent many happy holidays on my uncle's sheep property outside Coleraine.

Selectors

A potential settler had the right to 'select' between 40 and 640 acres (16 and 256 ha) provided he had the funds to improve the land acquired, guarantee he intended to live on it and show that he intended to farm it for crops. Few selectors succeeded. Growing crops was difficult in the harsh Australian climate and most of the land was poor. Many returned to city life.

Selector's hut in Camp Mountain, Samford Valley. Source: Wikimedia Commons

Selectors seldom had much money and to survive the father of the family often worked on a squatter's run, in a sawmill or at another job, while mother and children looked after the farm. A settler could be deeply in debt to the bank. They were nicknamed 'cockies' (cockatoo) because they could only scratch a living from the poor soil. Some managed to successfully grow crops and stayed on, and in doing so helped contribute to the growth of small towns all around the country. The difficulties of colonial farming life of the small landholder are depicted by author Steel Rudd in his humorous stories about Dad and Dave.

Selectors often came into conflict with squatters who already occupied the land. The squatters regarded selectors as locusts making holes in their land. They would clash over straying stock, water rights, weed control or fences. In New South Wales a new act in 1884 sought to compromise between the integrity of the large pastoral leaseholds and the political requirements of equality of land availability and closer settlement patterns. The Act divided pastoral runs into Leasehold Areas (held under short-term leases) and Resumed Areas (available for settlement as smaller homestead leases).

A famous case of the animosity of squatters and selectors is the saga of Ned Kelly, the son of a transported convict. The Kellys were a poor selector family, who saw themselves as downtrodden by the squattocracy and as victims of police persecution. In his poem *The Death of Ned Kelly*, renegade son of squattocracy and poet, John Manifold, wrote:

> *Come out of that, Ned Kelly, you done a lawless thing;*
> *You robbed and fought the squatters, Ned Kelly, you must swing.*
> *If those who rob, says Kelly, are all condemned to die,*
> *You had better hang the squatters, for they've stolen more than I.*

Post-Federation closer settlement

Closer settlement remained the corner-stone of rural development well into the 20th century, the most well-known examples being the soldier settlement schemes after WWI and WWII. These schemes were undertaken in all States to help repatriate servicemen, who had fought overseas. Crown land was used where possible, but large pastoral leases were also split into small farms. The resumption of land had significant or even fatal outcomes for those whose land was taken, for example, land resumption in Victoria's Western District for WWII veterans. Landholders lost large portions of land and even an entire property, if they could not reach agreement with the War Veterans Commission (which mostly targeted properties with no active owner-residents). This loss of land and falling wool prices brought about the demise of the grandee squattocracy of the Western District.

The post-WWI schemes were largely failures. Soldiers were given small parcels of land potentially suited to farming. Many learned they were unsuited to be farmers and the land they received would not sustain them and their families. Many of them, like their selector forebears, simply walked off the land back to the large towns and cities from whence they

Soldier-settlers clearing land at Beerburrum, north of Brisbane, to make way for pineapples.
Source: Margaret Wood, ABC Rural

came. An investigation in 1929 found the main causes of settler failure were a lack of capital and land, settler unsuitability and falling prices for agricultural produce.

Taking note of the mistakes of the past, post-WWII schemes were more successful. In order to buy or lease a block, applicants were required to be certified as qualified and to remain in residence on that land for five years. In this way remote rural areas set aside for such settlement were guaranteed a population expansion which remained to increase infrastructure in the area. However, as Jill Ker Conway details in her celebrated autobiography *The Road from Coorain*, life was hard and nature cruel.

Other closer-settlement schemes have been undertaken. The Fitzroy Basin Brigalow Development Scheme 1962-1978, one of the largest land development schemes by a Queensland government, is a successful example. Crown land resumed from existing lessees was sold or balloted; portions were returned to those from whom it was resumed, and for reserves and roads. By the 1970s, most of the brigalow scrub had been cleared and sucker regrowth was under control. The battle to clear the brigalow was won. The gain was vast new productive agricultural lands. The loss was a legacy of unforeseen environmental problems including the decline of rich biodiversity. Its success was partially due to the fertile, high-nitrogen soil of the brigalow scrubland. In addition, it was the first closer-settlement scheme that provided a combination of infrastructure, adequate financial assistance and large enough blocks to provide a decent living.

Currency squatter

Like many with convict parentage my great grandfather, P.F. MacDonald, made a fortune out of land and joined the ranks of the squattocracy, although with a diffidence unlike his untainted compatriots, those free-settlers of Australia Felix, the Western District of Victoria, who set about a life of an English country gentleman. In 1858 he travelled north from Victoria to seek a fortune on the Canoona gold-fields but became more interested in land. He would have known that most of the desirable land of the western half of Victoria and the lands extending to the north had been occupied and stocked and so became more interested in land than gold. He remained in the Capricornia region of Queensland, where he established successful grazing and business enterprises.

In association with several others, MacDonald undertook hazardous exploring expeditions in the north and west, taking up country which he favoured and disposing of it advantageously. In four journeys of investigation during 1858 to 1860, he reported on the lands of the Mackenzie, Nogoa, Comet and Isaacs Rivers in the areas that became Springsure and Peak Downs. In 1858 he almost perished when his exploring party was isolated by floodwaters, 350 km west of Keppel Bay. He took up a number of leasehold areas as a result of this trip.

The explorer Leichhardt had written glowing reports on the fertility of the rich black clay soils in the Central Highlands. MacDonald was the first to take up the land in what is now Emerald Shire. In 1860 he was so impressed with the lush greenness of the district after rain, he named a property *Emerald Downs*. Between 1861 and 1865 he took up a number of properties, which he combined to form a huge holding covering an area of 143 square miles (36,600 ha), which he then sold.

On one occasion MacDonald set out to inspect a lease but the vendor could not find it. During their search MacDonald was impressed with some land they covered and took up a lease, naming it *Cullin-la-ringo*. He also took up the lease of *Fernlees*, which joined it on the east. As he had also taken a lease on *Yaamba Station* near Rockhampton, he sold the lease of *Cullin-la-ringo* to Horatio Wills in July 1860.

In 1860, he settled down at *Yaamba* to develop his various lease holdings. Unlike southern squattocracy with northern leases run by managers, *Yaamba* would be his home. His was not the 'Visitor' mentality of many immigrant settlers, whose intention was to return to Britain after a few years, having profited from land speculation, investment or the sale of runs they licensed and stocked. He was a 'Currency Lad' free of inherent traditions that prevented them from adopting the new land as their home, or colonial society as their own. By comparison, MacDonald, critical and assertive, exhibited the belligerent pride of the native-born in superior strength, stamina and understanding of the land.

Administrative control of the land in the new colony of Queensland was inadequate, despite the extensive detail and conditions in a succession of land acts. Inadequate or lack of survey resulted in constant disputes regarding boundaries of land under tender. MacDonald, like so many of his land-hungry compatriots throughout the colonies, argued with neighbours and governments over rightful possession of the land. By 1866 he became involved in land disputes between government and squatters. In 1867 he sued the Government when it resumed and leased to others licensed but unsurveyed land at Springsure, which he had taken possession of. The case, known as the 'Great Northern Run Case', dragged on for 15 years when it was settled for a large sum in his favour. There had been firm support for him initially but the magnitude of the compensation figure alienated him from squatters, politicians and legal representatives as it did from the community and the press.

In order to establish and remain on the land he used his experiences in sheep farming and lessons in economy dating back to childhood. Given this background he probably had a particular advantage over immigrant settlers of his generation. Many came with money to invest and, although greedy to possess land, did not have the experience of the bush or of a country with a harsh physical geography like Australia. They were confronted by an environment hostile to the uninitiated and a frontier society of an aggressively independent character.

MacDonald – the frontiersman

MacDonald's undertakings, both as explorer and squatter, immersed him in the frontier war that raged for over two decades in the mid-1800s. He was not fearful of the bush but knew the danger of confrontation reaching flashpoint at any time. He took extreme care in any encounter and avoided them if possible. Clashes between settlers and Aboriginals were intrinsic to his youth at Campbelltown, where he was a product of emancipist society in which, for many, the convict's scorn of Aboriginals was entrenched. On learning of the *Cullin-la-Ringo* massacre he raised and led a reprisal party to the Nogoa area. Sixty to seventy Aboriginal deaths occurred in the subsequent retribution. He would have been aware that his grandfather, John Warby, had enlisted the aid of friendly Aboriginals as trackers and had refused to participate in punitive raids against their clansmen.

Unlike many squatters MacDonald did not 'keep the blacks out' in an attempt to ensure safety or leave his holdings because of fear of attacks. He preferred to keep unknown Aboriginal clans off his runs if possible, but used local Aboriginals as an unpaid labour source. He provided them with some rations of flour and sugar and at times tobacco. At *Yaamba*, Aboriginals, other than those who worked for him, camped in the vicinity of the homestead for generations.

MacDonald's attitude to Aboriginals remained two-fold. Wary of groups he might encounter in the bush, he nevertheless acknowledged that others who were guides, guards and horsemen aided European survival. On his expeditions into the bush, he always included at least one of his Aboriginal servants. He trusted his 'own' Aboriginals, who were integral to his enterprise. In his old age he displayed an outwardly derisive attitude but continued to trust and depend upon them. He turned to his station Aboriginals when he was alone.

In a situation common to squatters whose stations were in the region of bloody conflict, he was compelled to pay wages at almost double the general rate in order to persuade his servants and shepherds to remain.

Agrarian dream or nightmare

From the earliest days colonial legislators and administrators had a monumental task: a fair, efficient carve up of the land. Their vision was, and to an extent still is, that the empty lands of the coast and interior would be densely populated by families working their own farms and serviced by prosperous towns. They did not quite achieve this and still have not.

Australia, unlike the USA, has no vast expanse of fertile plains and networks of flowing rivers. Its rainfall is capricious, and drought is the norm. The family farmer battles with the elements and the vibrant inland towns envisaged have not eventuated; they remain stagnant or in decline, some awaiting the fate of those that once blossomed north of the Goyder Line. Much of the land itself lies desecrated. It appears we have been over-optimistic in the pastoral and agricultural expectations of our land. While no one would advocate the return of a squattocracy, there is a need for rural development in the form of land amalgamation with caveats to provide agricultural and pastoral blocks of sufficiently generous size to make a good living despite the market and drought.

However, their efforts have not been in vain. Unlike many countries with colonial histories, Australia has not become a land of landed barons but one with middle class values and institutions; a robust, economically prosperous, contented, free society; a successfully functioning constitutional democracy. This is no mean achievement but ever lurking in the background is the issue of indigenous dispossession.

In the carve-up of the land, the legislators and administrators were never able to ensure its orderly occupation. The frontier moved inexorably throughout the great land grab of the squatters, cutting a swathe through Aboriginal lands, virtually annihilating all who stood in the way. The alienation of Crown land accompanying closer settlement in the 1860s accelerated the dispossession of indigenous Australians. The enormity of this dispossession is capped by the fact that, despite Aboriginal Australians fighting alongside other Australian troops in both World Wars, no land was ever granted to these returning servicemen. A heinous case is that of the Lovetts from Lake Condoh in the Western District of Victoria. While five sons went to WWI and four of them later enlisted for WWII, not one of them was allocated a single square inch of land as a returned soldier.

As mentioned in the Introduction, land and how we view and deal with it underpins our society. How we have carved up the land has not been simply the responsibility of legislators and administrators – squatters, selectors, townsfolk, city folk, in fact all of us from Phillip and the convicts to immigrants (Chinese, Indian, European, Asian, New Zealanders, etc....) arriving today are complicit in this dispossession. Making amends is the responsibility of all who consider themselves Australian. An attempt to do this has been made through the 'Acknowledgement of Country', which is often made at the commencement of an event, such as a meeting, speech or formal occasion and supposedly reminds us from whom the land was taken. It, however, has become little more than perfunctory words gabbled by a priest; a litany falling on deaf ears; a recitation having little or no meaning. Something substantial is needed. Something that adds substantially to the Australian story.

Chapter 12
Immigration Pre-Federation

One can but wonder what went through the minds of members of the First Fleet as they stepped on to the shore of Sydney Cove. One can be certain that they did not view themselves as migrants. They did not fall on to their knees kissing the ground of a promised land, although in due course this is what it would become. In a twisted way they were more like flotsam and jetsam washed up on its shores. One can only speculate about the thoughts of the Aboriginal people witnessing a sight never seen before in their 60,000 years of existence. It certainly would not have been invaders although they would soon consider them such. Nor would they have grasped that their lives, like those of the unexpected arrivals and all who would come after them, would change forever. However, no paradise awaited them, only purgatory.

British institutions

These outcasts from the English penal system consisted almost entirely of English, Scots and Irish; most were English. They could well have been French – the French navigator, known to us as La Perouse, sailed into Botany Bay only several days after the arrival of the First Fleet. France had seceded Quebec to the British only twenty-five years previously. They could also have been Spanish. Nearly three centuries earlier, the Spanish Conquistadors, aided by superior technology and Old World disease, had subjugated the formidable Aztec and Inca empires. By the mid-16th century Spain controlled much of western South America and southern North America. The indigenous population of the Americas declined dramatically between 1492 and 1650. The Spanish were no outcasts with enlightened leaders. Their mission was clear: to plunder gold and silver and convert souls. Today, Central and South America are a motley collection of semi-failed states from which immigrants strive to enter North America.

That the outcasts were British was not insignificant because, more than any other people, the British had been engaged in an important experiment: seeking a form of government that best served its people. This had largely begun with the signing of Magna Carta, which established the principle that everyone is subject to the law, even the king, and guaranteed the rights of individuals, the right to justice and the right to a fair trial. The evolution over subsequent centuries of democratic government in England had been very much bound up with curbing the arbitrary rule of the monarch. Today it refers to the powers of executive government.

So British institutions and ways were the foundation of Australia and the 'Australian', i.e. the Westminster parliamentary system of government, the British legal system, a sound working bureaucracy, the rule of law, freedom of speech and general acceptance of representative constitutional democracy. But there was nothing democratic about Australia's beginning. After all, it was a penal settlement ruled by governors, who acted on behalf of the British Parliament.

Enlightened administrators

To start a settlement in New South Wales literally from the ground up was an enormous undertaking; in some ways even more so than settling the moon would be today. It would require a prodigious amount of physical effort (labour) as well as knowledge and skills.

The colony was fortunate in the quality of the early governors. Because of the distance from and poor communications with England, the early colonial administrators were virtual autocrats; the first five totally so, but in no way were they self-serving despots. In practice they ruled by consent, with the advice of military officers, officials and leading settlers, among whom were men of the Enlightenment who believed in reason and progress. The great indictment that can be levelled against them is their failure to establish and nurture a sound ongoing relationship with Australia's First People or at least have them treated humanely as urged by their overlords, the British Colonial Secretaries. Whether a harmonious relationship was ever a possibility is a matter of conjecture.

They were naval or army officers, knowledgeable sons of the Enlightenment, who took their jobs seriously and, within the mores of the time, carried out their tasks with the best interests of the colonists in mind. Like all such men they made enemies, often for their positive emancipist policies. Within forty years they guided New South Wales from a penal colony to a free settlement. In 1823 a 5-member appointed Legislative Council was established to advise the Governor on legislative matters. By 1860 all colonies had partial self-government, except Western Australia, which became self-governing in 1890.

The colony's first governor, Captain Arthur Phillip, was aided by a handful of other officers and a contingent of marines. Soon after arriving at Sydney Cove, 7 February 1788, reading aloud the Proclamation of New South Wales established Phillip's authority and the extent of the colony's jurisdiction and its first courts. Amongst other matters, Phillip was instructed to implement the common and statute laws of England as far as the circumstances of the colony would allow. The colonists had brought their law with them and the political and social structures that would form the institutions and culture of modern Australia. The colony was not envisaged simply as a remote dumping ground for convicts but one that should be self-respecting and adult in its public life.

Phillip's messages to the convicts that day made clear that a functioning society would need to foster a sense of mutual responsibility. He pointed out that he knew many of them would grasp the opportunities their new life offered. Those who committed crimes would be severely punished and theft of property and livestock would carry the heaviest punishment. He urged them to be honest amongst themselves, to forget habits of wrongdoing and indolence, and to contribute to the building of a community and of a new British colony.

Combining discipline and order with leniency and intellectual authority with a deep personal commitment, he offered both a vision and a sense of opportunity and shared humanity to the banished people, who had inherited the role of pioneers. By the time Phillip sailed home in December 1792, the colony was taking shape, with official land grants, systematic farming and water supply.

Unfortunately Phillip was far less successful in laying the ground work for good relations with Australia's First People. His attitude towards them was friendly as shown by his interaction with Bennelong. He made great attempts to bridge the cultural gap but was unable to develop and assert a clear, consistent policy regarding them. This eliminated all chance of winning their confidence. With the resulting fall in confidence in them combined with a rising fear of them, problems arose that await a solution over two centuries later.

Governor Macquarie (1810-1821), the fifth and last of the autocratic governors, played a major role in shaping Australian society in the early 19th century. He promoted the cause of the emancipists and undertook wide-ranging public works programs. Many consider him to be the 'father of the nation'. In 1819 John Bigge was commissioned to report on Macqaurie's administration and the situation in New South Wales.

Sir Thomas Brisbane (1821-1825), another learned Scotsman, succeeded Macquarie. He was instructed to carry out Bigge's recommendations, i.e. to tighten security, discipline and punishment in the colony, so once more felons saw it as a place of dread rather than a land of opportunity. Brisbane was a consummate astronomer and like Macquarie he encouraged capable ex-convicts.

Sir Ralph Darling (1825-1831) succeeded Governor Brisbane. His treatment of convicts was brutal. While he was a competent administrator, he lacked experience in dealing with civilian society. As a result, he came into conflict with the liberal emancipists, who wished to introduce greater social and political freedom. However, he did endeavour to improve the treatment of female convicts and made sincere efforts to give the nation's First People the protection of British justice.

Sir Richard Bourke (1831-1837), the eighth and most popular of the early governors of the colony, created controversy within the colony by combatting the inhumane treatment handed out to convicts. He limited the sentence a magistrate could pass to 50 lashes and the number of convicts a man could employ to 70, which upset the magistrates and employers, as did the granting of rights to emancipists, such as allowing the acquisition of property and service on juries. Bourke was responsible for implementing the concept of *Terra Nullius* upon which British settlement was based, when in 1835 he issued a proclamation stating an individual person could acquire land only through distribution by the Crown.

Bourke set religious denominations on an equal footing before the law by abolishing the Anglican Church's authority as the State Church of New South Wales. He also increased spending on education and attempted to set up a system of public non-denominational schools. The forerunner of the current state system was established by Governor Fitzroy in 1848. Free, secular, compulsory education was first introduced by Victoria in 1872.

Involuntary migrants 1788-1830

Australia's first European migrants were convicts transported mainly for petty theft; about 3,546 males and 766 females arrived between 1788 and 1792. Transportation of convicts had several advantages over free-men to establish a settlement from scratch. It would reduce the over-crowding of English gaols and prisoners could be selected for gender, age and health, and most importantly, could be assigned to work of any kind and at any location for the lengths of their sentences if need be. To ensure convicts were productive they were assigned according to any skills they might have. Transportation of convicts continued to supply much needed labour until the flow of free-immigrants could fill these needs.

Males were assigned to work on government projects or on farms for free-settlers, who were responsible for their food, clothing and housing. Females worked in government factories or were assigned to free-settlers as domestic workers. In the 1820s the assignment of convicts to private employers expanded and by the mid-1830s most convicts were assigned to private employment.

Before the 1820s, immigration was almost wholly a matter of convict transportation. Convict arrivals increased greatly after 1815 and were highest from the mid-1820s to 1840, when transportation to New South Wales ceased. Transportation to Tasmania continued until 1852 and between 1850 and 1868 to Western Australia to alleviate a labour shortage. The last transported convict died in Western Australia in 1938.

The system was organised to keep them in Australia, where their labour was needed. For the first 30 years of the colony, after finishing their sentence or being pardoned, convicts either worked for wages or took up a grant of land. By the 1820s, emancipists held considerable wealth but looked with jealousy on the free-settlers who made up only one-fifth of the population but held much of the land. The free-settlers viewed the emancipists and convicts as labourers for their benefit and resented them having access to their own land. Each group eyed the other as intruders. Their dislike for each other intensified after the implementation of Bigge's recommendations, when privileges of ticket-of-leave holders were restricted, appointment of emancipists to positions of responsibility ceased and land grants to emancipists were abolished.

Convict demographics

When transportation ceased, about 164,000 convicts had arrived, the majority (85%) being males of whom most (80%) were of productive working age (16-35). Three-quarters of convicts were transported for non-violent property crimes, with more than half exiled for their first offence. The proportion of first offenders decreased over time with alterations in English law that increasingly punished recidivism. They were made up of English and Welsh (70%), Irish (24%), Scottish (5%) and the remaining 1% from the British outposts. While the majority of convicts were common offenders, social and political rebels accounted for up to 10% of the Irish population. Nearly 40% of convicts transported had left the place of their birth long before in the course of their work, so migration was a part of everyday life but few would have thought of going to the other side of the world. Fewer than 5% ever saw their homeland again.

Only 15% of convicts transported were women. Of these, just over 6% were from England, whereas 20% were Irish-born. Most female convicts were single and were transported mainly for theft, most often for stealing items such as clothing, fabric, money and jewellery. These were objects they would come across in their jobs, as the vast majority were domestic servants. Convict women were under-employed, had few employment options and were always in excess supply. They were considered no substitute for men in physical occupations such as land clearing, construction of roads, bridges and buildings, ploughing, sawing, stone cutting and hauling.

Before 1830 the majority of convicts from England were from urban areas and knew little about farming, while most of the Irish came from the countryside. Subsequently the typical convict had been born in or exposed to a rural environment and consequently was a more appropriate worker in agriculture.

In 1820 convicts made up 80% of the population. By 1828 when the first census was taken, the white population was 36,598 of whom 20,870 were free and 15,728 were convicts. A quarter of the population were born in the colony and a quarter were women. There were 25,248 Protestants and 11,236 Catholics. A decade later the convict component had fallen to 23% owing to the ongoing arrival of free-born immigrants. Convicts and their descendants outnumbered the free-settlers until the gold-rushes in the 1850s.

Early free-immigrants 1830-1850

The first free-colonists arrived in 1793 but their numbers, along with convict numbers, grew slowly until 1820, after which they rose significantly; free-immigrants averaged a little under one-third of the total inflow between 1820 and the early 1830s. Because of a chronic shortage of labour that persisted throughout the 1820s, British authorities began to encourage the immigration of free-settlers. Initially access to land grants was restricted to those with adequate resources to develop the land and employ convict labour. Despite the increasing number of immigrants and convicts the labour shortage had worsened by the 1830s. People on farms needed labourers to clear the land, plant crops and take care of animals.

Convict labour was not sufficient for the expanding settlement. Employers were forced to increase the wages they offered to workers in order to compete for their labour. The solution to this labour problem was not more convicts but more free-settlers. Convicts were seen as a bad moral influence and many people wanted transportation to stop. Furthermore, free-migrants were vital for a sustained population that could aspire to representative government. However, British migrants lacked any real incentive to go to New South Wales. They continued to go to North America; the journey took only a quarter of the time and the fares were a quarter to a third as expensive. North America was also free of convicts.

The colonial administration realised that, if it wanted immigrants, it had to subsidise migration. In 1831 land grants ceased and a systematic program of assisted migration began, whereby revenue from the sale of land was used to pay or partially pay the ship fare of eligible applicants from Britain. Thereafter, the ratio of free-immigrants to convict arrivals rose rapidly. In the second half of the 1830s, free-immigrants outnumbered convict arrivals by two-to-one. About one-third of migrants who came to Australia between 1830 and 1850 paid their own fares. By 1850, government- and employer-assisted immigrants had effectively replaced convict labour. Some even came as indentured workers, for example Scottish crofters, the victims of Highland Clearances.

Initially, financial assistance was limited to productive workers only; age and health restrictions were imposed and families without young children were specified. Skilled tradesmen had preference over labourers, and to correct the gender disparity, often females over males, and British over non-British. The assisted migration included paupers from the poor houses. Only rarely were attempts made to pay for Europeans to come as migrants. Recruiting agents in the British Isles tended to place expediency above instruction, often resulting in immigrants failing to meet the expectations of colonial officials. Despite this, by 1850 free-workers had effectively replaced convict labour. In 1851 almost 98% of the adult population of New South Wales indicated in the census that they were 'free'.

Free-migrants, whether they paid their own fares or came with help from the government or employer, had profound effects on convict colonies. Free-settlers on average were more independent, more radical in many of their political views and more attached to family. While convicts were overwhelmingly male, free-settlers included a greater proportion of women. More so than the convicts, free-migrants were a challenge to law and order. They demanded liberties and privileges, which a convict society could not easily concede. Slowly, however, the civil liberties of free-migrants and emancipated convicts were expanded.

Gender imbalance

A significant repercussion of the high percentage of males in convicts transported, and earlier free-migrants also, was a gender imbalance that persisted for many decades. Any alleviation of this by native-born females was counteracted by on-going arrival of males. While the masculinity of the emerging society may have been an efficient means for undertaking the physical effort of establishing the colony, officials worried about the moral tone it created. Gender imbalance limited the opportunity for heterosexuality and increased the probability of sexual alternatives, e.g. homosexuality and bestiality, and ill-treatment of women, especially Aboriginal women.

In 1821, before many free-immigrants had arrived and consequently natural increase had not exerted much equalising effect on the relative numbers of men and women, there were an estimated 388 adult males per 100 adult females in mainland Australia. Schemes were established to encourage young women to emigrate. Groups of women from cities, towns and villages responded. Those who were skilled in agricultural work, sewing and specific domestic tasks as well as general household work were preferred.

The first assisted migrants arrived in 1832 and included a majority of single women. Natural increase as well as explicit attempts to encourage female immigration helped reduce this disparity between the genders; Caroline Chisholm promoted the immigration of single Irish girls. Nonetheless, a substantial male dominance persisted. In 1840 the white population on the continent contained three males for every female and in 1861 there were still 166 adult males for each 100 adult females.

From 1860 the gender ratio of the Australian population became much more 'normal'. Following the gold-rushes of the 1850s, a decline in immigration (with its preponderance of males) and hence its importance as a source of population growth relative to natural increase largely reduced this structural peculiarity by the end of the century. By 1901 the number of adult males per hundred adult females had fallen to 112. While some imbalance in gender numbers remained, it was no longer so marked as to dominate the Australian way of life.

A masculine (blokey) society emanated from the gender imbalance of the transportation system with reliance on one's workmates, pair bonding of shepherds tending flocks of sheep and the absence of white women in the bush. Even today at social functions, particularly in the 'bush', males tend to gather together in one part of the room and females at another.

Long, expensive, tough ship's journey

By 1842 every embarkation port had a depot to house people and care for their health until their ship left and so protect them from rogues. The voyage to Australia was not for the fainthearted. In the 1840s a concerted effort was made to make the journey and Australia seem more appealing but still most British migrants went to America.

Ships sailed through the Southern Ocean to take advantage of the roaring forties. Passengers and crew faced mountainous seas, freezing temperatures and the possibility of striking icebergs, which were drifting northwards. Simply arriving was an achievement.

Ships were overcrowded. Passengers with sufficient money travelled in cabins on the upper deck in relative comfort. Accommodation for those with little money was hardly better than that for convicts. They suffered below in steerage, where conditions were cramped and filthy. The air was stale and usually foul with the smells from children not toilet-trained and those who were seasick or suffering from diarrhoea and other diseases. There were many deaths on board, especially of children, due to unhygienic conditions. These people were not used to living, cooking and cleaning under such cramped conditions, while being tossed about by storms or baked in the heat of the tropics.

For the free-migrant, the distance enforced feelings of separation and permanency. Authorities adopted a high degree of state regulation and intervention to help alleviate the disruption to passengers' lives. For the migrant, the result of a more disciplined and ordered journey allowed them to disembark in a far healthier condition, both mentally and physically, than even those travelling the shorter journey across the Atlantic.

Arrival in Australia

On arrival in Australia migrants were often disappointed when they saw what their new 'home' was like. They were allowed to stay on board ship for 10 days, while they attempted to find work. Some could stay in government barracks for another month, after which they were left to their own devices. Often unscrupulous people took advantage of them, robbing them or taking their money on pretence of getting them accommodation or employment; the situation was especially bad during the depression of the 1840s.

There was no government employment agency. Unless they had been brought out by a particular employer, they had to find their own work. They usually went to a depot, where employers came to find servants, labourers or tradesmen. If they did not find work with board and lodgings, they had to find accommodation of some kind. Some migrants went to work on the land, which they found both boring and lonely.

In the 1840s it was very difficult for married men and women with children to find work, because employers did not want to pay for food and lodgings of children, who did not work. In Sydney, single women also discovered it was hard to get jobs and found themselves homeless and friendless in a strange new land. These were the women whose plight so horrified Caroline Chisolm (see Aussie Women – The fate of single women; page 248).

Reasons for migrating

There were many reasons why people migrated to the new colonies:

- Migrants in the 1830s and 1840s left because of poverty and unemployment.
- Irish potato blight in the 1840s forced many to leave to survive.
- Small farmers lost farms and farm workers' jobs due to changes in land use.
- Cities were overcrowded and work difficult to find.
- Inadequate housing and rent and taxes were very high.
- People left for political and religious reasons, particularly Europeans.
- After 1831 most of a migrant's fare was paid by the government.
- Wages in Australia were high and there was plenty of work for tradesmen.
- Australia was viewed as a peaceful, easy-going country with plenty of land.
- It seemed easy to become a wealthy farmer.
- Single women came to find husbands or work as servants.
- The wool industry was booming and squatters needed shepherds plus other farm-workers.

Despite attempts by the elite to supplant the English class system into Australia, people were valued for what they could achieve with their own hands. Newcomers were astonished to find that even the Irish, regarded in England as the lowest form of humanity, could become respected members of the community. A democracy of 'honest sweat' had begun to build the tradition of the 'fair go' in 19th century Australia.

1850-1860 – Gold-rushes

Immigration to Australia in the nineteenth century peaked in the 1850s, when migration increased rapidly as a result of the discovery of gold in New South Wales and Victoria. Immigrants poured into the country and on to the gold-fields. People arrived in far greater numbers and from more varied backgrounds than ever before. Most immigrants were from the United Kingdom, although significant numbers also came from Continental Europe, China, Chile, North America, the Pacific Islands and New Zealand. Gold attracted migrants in such numbers that in less than a decade more people arrived in Australia than had been living in the colonies in 1851. From 1851 to 1861 the population of Victoria rose from 80,000 to 500,000 and that of Australia almost trebled from just over 400,000 to more than 1,100,000. Never again was immigration to be so large relative to the size of the existing population. Interestingly, despite the lure of gold, substantially fewer British migrants emigrated to Australia than to America.

The gold-rushes added to the labour scarcity. Men from all over the continent and all walks of life left their jobs to seek their fortune, which caused a labour shortage in both the city and the bush. Consequently, the level of immigration to Australia in the 1850s was still bolstered by various schemes of assisted passage. However, during the 1850s 80% of the migrants coming to Australia paid their own way.

The gold-rush decade of the 1850s divided a colonial past, whose economy relied largely on convict labour and sale of wool, from an economy based on free-men, wool and gold; an economy that eventually provided one of the highest living standards in the world. (see Gold – a new society for economic, social and political changes brought about by the rush for gold; page 81.) It did not, however, wash away the convict stain which, along with the desire to maintain the newly gained standard of living, would affect migration dramatically when the colonies federated.

Immigration 1860-1900

The gold-rush decade was also a watershed in the impact of immigration on population growth. Between 1790 and 1860 about 75% of total population increase was the direct result of immigration, whereas from 1860 until 1890 a significant decline in immigration resulted in natural increase making up about 60% of population growth. By 1890 the population had reached 3 million. In the depression of the 1890s the flow of migrants to Australia virtually ceased and remained low until the outbreak of WWI. The vast majority of people leaving Britain and Europe, over a million each year, continued to prefer North America.

By 1901, after a little over a century of convict transportation and free-settler migration, the non-indigenous population of Australia had reached 3.8 million, of whom 77% were Australian-born. Unsurprisingly, given the focus of migrant assistance, the major ethnic groups were the English, Irish and Scots. Germans, numbering about 100,000, made up the fourth-largest European ethnic group on the continent (see Non-British migrants; page 118). The next main group were the Chinese (around 29,000), who made up the largest Asian group.

Immigration was a significant issue leading up to Federation. Australians desired to maintain a predominantly white population adhering to British customs. They were not alone in this view (see Appendix 1). Trade unions were keen to prevent labour competition from Chinese and Pacific Islander migrants, fearing they would undercut wages and living standards. The colonies needed to federate and establish a unified immigration policy to address these concerns effectively.

Irish presence

The Irish, more than any other group, effectively utilised Australian immigration schemes. They were largely rural people, who helped supply the two immigrant categories most in demand: domestic servants and agricultural workers. Numbers were small during the first 40 years compared with the numbers who left Irish shores during the Great Famine (1845-1850) and its aftermath (1860s and 1870s), when the bulk of Irish immigrants arrived in Australia. The number of Ireland-born in Australia peaked in 1891 at 228,000 or about 27% of immigrants from the British Isles.

Between 1848 and 1870 about 80% of assisted immigrants were Irish, including extremely high percentages of females, which served to correct the gender imbalance of the colonial populations. Irish women were willing to marry non-Irish husbands. The Irish contained high proportions of Catholics.

Despite the animosity between the Irish and English, they experienced little sense of segregation, with few geographical or occupational concentrations of any significance. In addition, unlike the Irish in North America, they did not occupy ghettoes. Though 'on the whole' less literate and skilled than contemporaneous immigrants, Irish immigrants continued to move upwards into many spheres of colonial society, especially the public service, the police force and the professions.

Non-British migrants

While the overwhelming majority of arrivals in Australia were from the British Isles, small groups of non-British citizens also arrived in Australia during the 19th century, especially during the gold-rush and also under various contract arrangements. Small numbers from Asia also found their way here.

Small numbers of Germans, Italians and Swiss were admitted to Australia under a contract scheme that had failed to attract much interest from the British. Germans began immigrating to Australia in the late 1830s and became prominent in settling South Australia and Queensland. During the second half of the 19th century several colonies funded the immigration of skilled immigrants from Europe, starting with the assistance of German vintners to South Australia. The Germans maintained strong cultural ties with their German heritage and were a well-established and popular community.

In the 1860s, the pearling industry began using Aboriginal divers in Western Australia; men, women and children were forced or tricked into working, virtually as slaves. In the 1880s they were largely replaced by Asians using breathing apparatus. Most of the Asian divers were Javanese, Timorese and Japanese. While all contributed to the development of the pearling industry, Japanese divers probably contributed most.

From 1870 to 1900, more than 2,000 cameleers, known as 'Afghans', were brought in, mainly from Baluchistan, Afghanistan and the north-west of British India (now Pakistan). They were the 'backbone' of transportation in the outback and helped 'open up' the Australian outback. They were integral in transporting supplies, equipment and tools for construction of the Overland Telegraph Line and Trans-Australian Railway.

Prior to 1850, an estimated 3,000 Chinese had arrived in Australia as indentured labourers. After the discovery of gold Chinese arrivals increased substantially; a heavy poll tax levied on every arrival by the Victorian government had little effect on quelling numbers. They avoided the tax by disembarking ship in South Australia and New South Wales and walking to the gold-fields. They came from Southern China, where enterprising agents offering loans and assistance found no shortage of takers for a journey to Australia. By 1861, Chinese were the third-largest migrant group in Australia after the British and Germans and made up around 3.3% of the total Australian population. On the gold-fields intolerance and prejudice against them exploded into violence and finally lead to the colonies passing anti-Chinese immigration laws. (see Gold – All men are equal!, page 76).

Chapter 13
Some Thorny Issues

Despite the large majority of immigrants, both convicts and free-settlers, coming from the British Isles, colonial Australia was not free of social, political and ethnic tensions. Its penal beginning, Irish-English enmity, Asian (Chinese) immigrants and native-born *vs* new-settler differences were the sources of conflict and tensions that smouldered and occasionally flared up throughout the 19th century. Australia's First People were being dispossessed of their land and removed from their country to reserves or missions as the land was opened up for the settlers.

Emancipists *vs* exclusives

The earliest rift in Australian society was that between free-settlers (exclusives) and ex-convicts (emancipists). The exclusives tended to be among the wealthy landowners and thus saw themselves as a superior class. They looked down on the emancipists, who resented being excluded from land grants.

During early decades emancipists far outnumbered free-settlers and there was considerable intermingling between ex-convicts and free-settlers, for example marriage. The society that emerged was relatively open and fluid with new political possibilities, and had formed some of the hallmarks we prize today: a cheeky humour for 'pricking the pompous' and a sense of equality (a convict lawyer was no better or worse than a convict 'navvy').

With the end of the transportation era and finalisation of sentences, large numbers of emancipists entered the mainstream of settlement. Immigrant settlers had little recourse but to assimilate with emancipists and the native-born. Many immigrants, more particularly those who rushed to the gold-fields, were influenced by the attitudes of the native-born of convict descent.

'Skeletons in the cupboard'

Any prejudice of free-settlers against their transported countrymen morphed into the convict stain in the late 1840s, when the anti-transportation movement began a 'shaming campaign' to end transportation. It was not the inhumanity of the system that disturbed them but the hated convict stain they believed tainted the colony. According to historian John Hirst, the major effect of transportation was the trauma of the nation that had to come to terms with its shameful origins.

Families went into denial about their forebears; our past was hidden and in many instances forgotten. My mother's family was a case in point. It was so hidden and secret that she expressed disbelief when confronted with the fact in the mid-1970s. Her great grandfather was an illiterate 'government man'. Her grandfather, P.F. MacDonald, reflected the emancipist vulnerability in his silence about his roots. Egalitarian attitudes were developing in society by the 1850s, but MacDonald was typical of the native-born, who tended to 'block out' their origins because of this colonial shame that became deep-seated late in the 19th century. MacDonald was a prolific letter writer and the absence of comment relating to his father and his grandparents, whether in Australia or Britain, suggests his rejection of a dark heritage. He did not acknowledge family links with Britain, and none of his family travelled there. The irony is the ancestral stories my mother told were of being descended from kings.

The threat of social rebuff was ever present. MacDonald, aged 30, wrote of the sting of social rejection, when his bride's guardian frowned upon the marriage match and refused later to engage in business dealings with MacDonald, whom he termed a 'stranger'. A further social rebuff was meted to MacDonald, when his friendship and close working relationship with a member of a highly respected, English immigrant family ended suddenly in public verbal abuse by the man he had claimed as a friend. A further example may be the engagement of my uncle 'Gem' Stuart to Miss Isabel Lucas, younger daughter of the Agent-General for South Australia, which was announced in The Daily News (Perth, WA, 16 August 1923). This marriage did not eventuate nor did my mother ever mention it, which was odd because she 'adored' him and spoke much about him.

Thus self-doubt about their worthiness and a sense of inferiority or cultural cringe pervaded the collective psyche of a people, who were world leaders in arts, science, innovation, sport and more. One hundred years would pass before the convict stain turned from shame to pride.

Religious and ethnic conflict

Ethnic and religious conflicts were prevalent in colonial Australia. English-Irish relations were bitter and hateful. The Irish in Australia were potentially an out-group; they were mostly Catholic, generally poor and less educated than the rest of the population. Relations between the two groups were always uneasy and were tested on two particular occasions; the first was in 1868, when an Irishman attempted to assassinate Prince Alfred, Australia's first royal visitor; and the second was in 1883, when non-Catholics protested against a tour by John Redmond for fund-raising and advocating Irish Home Rule.

In the former case large public meetings were held in every town and district to reaffirm loyalty to the Queen, at which the speakers were representative of the chief ethnic groups: English, Irish, Scots and native-born. Speakers each proclaimed not only their loyalty to their own group but also to the other groups as well. In addition they went to great lengths to dissociate the assassin from the local Irish. No clergyman was allowed to speak. The largest of these demonstrations was in Sydney on the day after the terrible event, where an estimated 20,000 people assembled in Hyde Park.

In the latter case Sir Henry Parkes, Premier of New South Wales, appealed to the Irish community not to transplant the animosities of the old world into the new. He told a crowd of 8,000 he was not there to speak against the Irish but rather to protect the purity of Australian public life. He said the Irish should cherish the memory of the bright and heroic passages in their history and maintain the burning indignation of the wrongs they had endured, but they had come to Australia for a different reason. When the Irish came to Australia, like the English, the Scottish and German settlers, they had no right to revive the animosities of their old country, Parkes warned. He counselled restraint and told the crowd the colony of New South Wales was there for one grand purpose, to found an Australian state in which they wanted none of the strife, contention, hot blood and bitter words of any country whatsoever.

At this time there was no firm Australian identity. The speakers at public meetings did not present themselves as Australians. They were declaring that English, Irish, Scots and native-born people all agreed that ethnic and religious passions should not be allowed to run riot. No savage outburst of sectarian warfare ever broke out. Historian John Hirst suggests the following reason:

> *The Irish were poorer than the rest of the population but were far from being outcasts. There was no residential segregation of the Irish. In every community*

there were prosperous respectable Irish citizens. They had been among the founding population of this society and were scattered throughout it. They enjoyed equal civil and political rights and their church was accorded a status equal to that of the Church of England and the Church of Scotland. The mixture of Protestant and Catholic worthies in every locality willing to join each other on the platform composed a society that could not be readily polarised from the top.

The Catholic-Protestant division, still largely due to the Catholic-Irish nexus, was still palpably obvious during the decade after WWII. Subsequently it rapidly lost significance, possibly because of the influx of migrants of Catholic allegiance from Europe and weakening of religious sentiment. By the turn of the 21st century it had evaporated, only to be replaced by a far greater religious dichotomy, that of Christianity and Islam.

Boom, bust and unions

The economic boom fuelled by gold and wool lasted through the 1860s and 1870s. By the 1880s children of gold-rush migrants were starting families of their own. Their dream of owning their own home created a land boom that spilled over into massive financial speculation. Investment returns, profits and wages became higher and higher. Labour shortages persisted despite the steady inflow of migrants.

In the 1880s unions grew in number and strength. They demanded and got an 8-hour working day and other benefits unheard of in Europe and forced up wages until they were the highest in the world. Australia gained a reputation as 'the working-man's paradise'. Some employers attempted to 'undercut' the unions by importing Chinese labour. Race subsequently became a point of difference in values between employers and unionists.

In 1891 a decade-long depression, which set in when the turbo-charged economy collapsed, created high unemployment and ruined many businesses. Employers responded by reducing wages. Unions responded with a wave of strikes, resulting in a series of bloody confrontations, particularly in the pastoral areas of Queensland. An especially violent instance was the Shearers' Strike of 1891, when pastoralists endeavoured to reduce wages and erode unionism by employing non-union labour, who were often Chinese labourers. As a consequence of the strike, many unionists were arrested and 12 were jailed. Property was destroyed and gun-fights took place as the police and army were 'called in'. A major drought, the 'Federation Drought', which affected the eastern states from 1895 to 1903, exacerbated the economic situation. The vision of Australia as a 'working-man's paradise' faded.

The unions reacted to these defeats by forming their own political parties within their respective colonies. These were the forerunners of the Australian Labor Party. The industrial struggles of the 1890s also produced a new strain of Australian radicalism and nationalism, which promoted socialism, republicanism and independence. This new-found Australian consciousness also gave birth to a profound antipathy towards Chinese, Japanese and Indians.

Anti-Asian sentiment

The Chinese were seen initially as oddities, later as rivals and then as a threat to white Australia. During a period of more than 20 years, 40,000 Chinese men and 9,000 Chinese women flocked to the gold-fields. By 1861, they comprised the third-largest group in Australia following the British (including the Irish) and the Germans. Ideas of the rights of the individual, democracy and egalitarianism, imported from Europe and America during the gold-rush, were not extended to the Chinese (nor to Australia's First People). Any admiration of their work ethic was offset by envy and resentment when times 'got hard'. Antipathy towards them occasionally erupted into violence: Turon 1853, Meroo 1854, Rocky River 1856, Tambaroora 1858, Lambing Flat, Kiandra and Nundle in 1860 and 1861. This led to Victoria followed by New South Wales restricting Chinese immigration and levying residency taxes on them, despite protests from pastoralists, who believed the Chinese were peaceful, valuable colonists.

Between 1863 and 1904 some 60,000 South Pacific Islanders were trafficked under the guise of indentured labourers. Known as 'blackbirding', most were recruited by deception or kidnapping to work as unpaid or poorly paid labourers on Queensland sugarcane farms. Legislation intended to prevent their exploitation was badly administered, which resulted in giving legitimacy to a form of slavery.

In the 1870s and 1880s, the growing Trade Union Movement began a series of protests against 'foreign labour'. The earliest union work codes excluded Chinese, Japanese, Afghans and Pacific Islanders but accepted Afro-Americans, New Zealand Maoris and mixed-race born in Australia. Their arguments were that Asians took jobs away from white men, worked for 'substandard' wages, lowered working conditions and refused unionisation. Objections to these arguments came largely from wealthy landowners who argued that, without Asian workers, tropical regions would have to be abandoned. Despite these objections to restricting immigration, between 1875 and 1888 all Australian colonies enacted legislation, which excluded all further Chinese and other Asian immigration. The pursuit of a uniform immigration policy became a driving factor in the federation of the colonies.

Chapter 14
Immigration Post-Federation

Restricted immigration – White Australia Policy

Immigration was a major factor in causing the Australian colonies to come together in a Federation. Consequently, one of the first pieces of legislation passed in the new Federal Parliament was the *Immigration Restriction Act,* which along with several other acts embodied the so-called White Australia Policy. This was a strengthening and unification of disparate colonial policies designed to restrict non-white settlement. It aimed to exclude people of non-European origin and effectively gave British migrants preference over all others through the first four decades of the 20th century. Exclusion was achieved by applicants sitting a 'dictation test' that was impossible to pass. The legislation had strong bipartisan support in the new parliament with arguments ranging from economic protection to outright racism. Between 1949 and 1973, governments progressively dismantled the legislation under-pinning the policy.

Immigration WWI – WWII

After federation immigration continued much as it had during the 1890s but virtually ceased during WWI. The 1914-1918 war, which affected virtually every family in Australia, had major repercussions for Australians of German and Austro-Hungarian, Bulgarian and Turkish heritage. With the rising tension between the British and German Empires, German-Australian communities often found themselves the subject of suspicion and animosity. This changed to outright hostility, when war broke out in 1914.

In 1915, Germans (and Austrians), who were old enough to join the army (7,000), were interned in concentration camps across the continent or faced restrictions to their daily lives, that included the closure of German schools, the banning of the German language in government schools, the banning of German music and the renaming of foodstuffs and many places with German place names. To avoid persecution and/or to demonstrate that they were committed to their new home, many, as did the British Royal Family, changed their names into Anglicised or Francophone variants. Many sons and grandsons of German migrants joined the AIF and went to fight for Australia on the Western Front. Most distinguished was John Monash, who later was knighted on the battlefield for his brilliant generalship that changed the course of warfare. Early on, even he was looked upon with suspicion because of his German parentage.

Following the signing of the Armistice in 1918 a revival of assisted migration schemes ensued. The British Government offered ex-servicemen free passage to one of the dominions or colonies and 17,000 arrived in Australia between 1919 and 1922. Church and community organisations such as the YMCA and the Salvation Army sponsored migrants. Small numbers also arrived independently. As the United States sought to limit migration of Southern Europeans, increasing numbers of young men from Greece and Italy paid their own way to Australia. By the 1930s, Jewish settlers began arriving in greater numbers, many of them refugees from Hitler's Europe. During the 1920s more than 340,000 immigrants arrived. Two-thirds of them were assisted migrants from Britain, plus small numbers of Greeks, Italians and Yugoslavs.

The 1929 stock market crash and the Great Depression 'put an end' to sponsored migration and immigration declined sharply through the 1930s. Unemployment rates skyrocketed during the Great Depression and attitudes towards immigrants turned hostile.

Prior to WWII, as the political climate for Jews in Germany and Austria darkened, Australia agreed to accept 15,000 Jewish refugees from Europe. Just 5,000 arrived in 1939 before Jews in Europe could no longer escape. Approved groups such as these were assured of entry by being issued with a Certificate of Exemption from the Dictation Test.

Immigration ceased for the duration of WWII, 1939-1945. As in WWI, when WWII broke out, internment camps were set up to incarcerate civilians considered to be a threat on the home front. By September 1942, the total number of internees in Australia was 6,780. They included 3,651 Italians, 1,036 Japanese and 1,029 Germans. Among the internees were women and children. A striking story of internment is that of the Dunera Boys. They were about 2,000 male German Jewish refugees aged between 16 and 45 who had escaped from Nazi-occupied territories. In 1940 they were expelled in a blanket deportation from Britain on HMT *Dunera* along with Italian Prisoners of War and a couple of hundred Nazi sympathisers and interned at Hay and Orange and later Tatura. They included musicians, artists, philosophers, scientists and writers. Following their release in 1941 many chose to remain in Australia, making a significant contribution to the nation's economic, social and cultural life; examples were artist Ludwig Hirshfield Mack, who contributed to the renewal of Australian art and Franz Stampfl, who coached Roger Bannister for the 4-minute mile. Hirshfield Mack was my art teacher at Geelong Grammar School and I often saw Franz Stampfl in his navy blue reefer jacket at the side of the Melbourne University athletics track. He continued coaching after becoming a quadriplegic in 1980 in a car accident.

After the war Australia received a large influx of ethnic German displaced persons, who were a significant proportion of Australia's post-war immigrants. German immigration continued under assisted migration programs promoted by the Australian government. In 1991, there were 112,000 German-born persons in Australia. By July 2000, Germany was the fifth most common birthplace for settler arrivals in Australia after the UK, Ireland, Italy and New Zealand.

Early Post-WWII migrant boom

Immigration since WWII has transformed the size and makeup of Australia's population. During the war the government decided that the future defence of Australia required a larger population, the slogan being 'populate or perish'. This was to be achieved by both a higher birth rate and a planned immigration program with an annual target of 70,000 migrants (1% of the population).

In 1945 an Assisted Passage Migration Scheme, known as the 'Ten Pound Pom' (the price of the ticket), was established to encourage British migrants. Only about half the target number took this opportunity, so it was gradually extended to other countries. When Southern Europeans began to outnumber British arrivals in the mid-1950s the Australian government restricted their sponsorship. Increased financial assistance to British migrants during the 1960s returned the British component to the top position.

The selection qualifications were straightforward: migrants needed to be in sound health and under the age of 45 years. There were no skill requirements at first, although under the White Australia Policy people from mixed-race backgrounds found it very difficult to take advantage of the scheme.

In 1947, Australia began taking refugees from the war in Europe under the international Displaced Persons Resettlement Scheme. During the seven years this operated, in excess of 170,000 Europeans, more than 17,000 of them Jewish, were admitted. When this source of migrants was exhausted, the Government signed formal agreements to sponsor migrants from a number of European countries including Germany, Italy, Greece and Malta. Under these 'assisted passage' schemes, migrants were given temporary accommodation in exchange for guaranteeing to provide two-years labour on government projects such as the Snowy River Scheme.

Immediately on arrival migrants were taken to migrant hostels, which often were former military barracks. Migrants were frequently shocked at the primitive conditions. With men and women separated into single gender barracks, shared bathrooms and kitchens and a communal dining room serving unfamiliar, and often unpalatable food, migrant hostels were neither comfortable nor welcoming. Sometimes families were separated; husbands lived in barracks close to their work and women and children stayed behind in the migrant accommodation. Conditions were, at best, basic. The intention was that migrants stay for only four-six weeks until they could be resettled near their workplace. At times, however, work was difficult to find and some stayed for months if not years.

Other migrants arrived unassisted and lived – some in comfort, others not – with family and friends, and found work independently of the Government. All migrants, especially those who did not speak English well, had to put up with prejudice (see Appendix 3). They were referred to officially as 'New Australians' in an attempt to replace terms such as 'pom, balt, wog and reffo'. Australians and their way of life at that time from an Italian perspective were satirised by John O'Grady in *They're a Weird Mob* using the pseudonym *Nino Culotta*.

By 1960, the population was 10 million and around nine per cent of the population were of non-British origin, mostly Italians, Germans, Dutch, Greeks and Poles. By 1971, one-in-three people living in Australia was either a migrant or child of migrants. Between 1945 and 1975 Australia's population almost doubled (7.39 to 13.89 million). Almost three million migrants arrived, half from Britain and half from other European countries. In 1976 the top six birthplace groups were from European countries and accounted for 70% of all people born overseas. By then the White Australia Policy had been scrapped. This brought about major changes to immigration and consequently the population make-up of Australia.

Between 1951 and 1985 some 20,000 students from South and South-east Asia were sponsored in Australian training and degree programs under the Colombo Plan launched in 1951. While students were compelled to return home after their studies were complete, a number later migrated permanently to Australia under skilled migration programs.

Snowy River Scheme

More than 100,000 migrants from 30 different countries worked on the Snowy River Scheme in south-east Australia. Work began in 1949 on the construction of a network of dams, tunnels and power stations. The scale of the project was without precedent in Australia and saw a number of pioneering engineering techniques tested in the mountains. It took 25 years to complete.

There were numerous accidents as conditions inside the tunnels were damp, dirty and dangerous – ultimately claiming 121 lives. Everybody who worked in the tunnels suffered hearing loss because of the air pressure from the underground rock-blasting.

Living conditions in the towns and camps that popped up around the project were not much better. Biting cold winters and scorching summers made life inside the often poorly equipped dwellings difficult for wives and families, who had followed their husbands to the other side of the world. The new communities served as incubators for modern (multicultural) Australia. Post-war migrants from Europe, where they had been enemies, were suddenly living and working at close quarters.

Ordinary Australians assimilated with Europeans more quickly and gently than most critics of ordinary Australians had allowed for. There were no closed areas of settlement and separate schools, with strong political groupings extending into the general community or separate church groupings.

End of the White Australia Policy

After the conclusion of WWII successive governments dismantled the White Australia Policy in stages. In 1948, Australian citizenship was established – before that, all Australians were British subjects. The Policy was effectively dismantled between 1949 and 1966. The dictation test was abolished in 1958. Other restrictions on non-European migration were relaxed from 1966 and the number of arrivals started to increase accordingly. By the 1960s mixed-race migration was becoming easier and in 1967 Australia entered into its first migration agreement with a non-European country, in this case Turkey.

In 1973, the quota system based on country of origin was replaced by 'structured selection', whereby migrants were to be chosen according to personal and social attributes and occupational group. Furthermore, all migrants regardless of race or ethnicity could apply for Australian citizenship after three years of residence. In 1975, racial discrimination was made illegal, which led to a significant increase in non-European immigration, mostly from Asia. The ethnic makeup of Australia began to change rapidly.

These laws so displeased the British Government in London that it allowed them only with reluctance. It certainly showed a fledging nation prepared to take an independent stance on what it considered a matter of self-interest. Importantly, the zeitgeist of today is a far cry from that of a century-and-a-half ago when European nations and Japan scrambled for colonies in Africa and Asia and around the world purity of race increasingly mattered. At that time almost every race of people in the world, probably Chinese even more than Australians, shunned alien cultures to some degree; even until recently, Chinese referred to non-Chinese as 'foreigners' or 'red devils'.

Furthermore, it was a commitment from the nation to the dignity of labour and its proper reward. The labour movement in Australia (trade unions) was determined to avoid forfeiting hard-won working conditions and a standard of living unequalled anywhere else in the world. Workers would have suffered most directly if 'cheap labour' became prevalent, as has happened in the global economy of today.

Importantly, it gave the new nation (institutions and citizens), inflicted with the convict stain, time to be 'bedded down' in such a way that a hundred years later has enabled it to run a multi-ethnic immigration program envied by the rest of the world. In no way was this a foregone outcome; take Argentina for example. At the time of Federation the Argentine and Australia were among the richest countries in the world per head of population. Both were high food producers, rich in natural resources and with free education, so had a great number of highly educated people. Melbourne and Buenos Aires were the cities one went to. They remained very wealthy nations (in top 10) until the 1930s, when they diverged as a result of poor functioning of Argentinian institutions. Argentina started to suffer from authoritarian regimes and corruption, which brought it down from its halcyon days. On the other hand Australia has become known for its very powerful, strong institutions, the rule of law, transparency in government relations and enforcement of the law and controls, a country to which people from all parts of the world wish to migrate.

1970s-today: Humanitarian (Asylum seekers)

Humanitarian intakes of Lebanese and Cypriot people during the early 1970s were followed by a significant wave of Indochinese arrivals, displaced by the Vietnamese and Cambodian conflicts. Over 2,000 Indochinese refugees landed in boats on Australian shores in the late 1970s, but the majority of the 80,000 Indochinese permanent migrants came by air after they were formally processed by Australian officials at refugee camps in Malaysia and Thailand. In 1989 more than 42,000 Chinese students were permitted to remain in Australia after the Tiananmen Square massacre.

From the late 1990s, increasing numbers of asylum seekers fleeing conflict in the Middle East and Sri Lanka began arriving in Australia by boat, mostly organised by people smugglers. Other sources of boat people included Afghanistan, Sudan and Iran. Australia does not accept arrivals seeking asylum in this way and detains them in offshore internment centres for processing.

Australia has maintained a fairly consistent annual humanitarian migrant intake of about 13-14,000 for many years. In 2015 an additional resettlement of 12,000 refugees from Syria and Iraq was accepted.

1970s-today: Skilled migrants

The assisted passage scheme ended in 1981 and only refugees are now given any level of support on their arrival in Australia. In 1988 migration moved away from 'family reunion' towards an emphasis on skilled and business categories, who are eligible for limited support services: English tuition (AMEP) and a 24-hour interpreting service. Many other services are provided for refugees and humanitarian visa holders. From the beginning, Australia has taken a more deliberate and active approach to encouraging immigration than have comparable countries, e.g. assisted passages to North America for free-settlers were unknown.

Australia's current migration program allows people from any country to apply to migrate here, regardless of their nationality, ethnicity, culture, religion or language, provided they meet the criteria set out in law. Permanent migrants enter Australia via one of two distinct programs – the Migration Program for skilled and family stream migrants or the Humanitarian Program for refugees and those in refugee-like situations. Each year, places or quotas are allocated for people wanting to migrate permanently to Australia under these two programs. Since the late 1990s there has been a growth in temporary migration including international students. Unlike the permanent Migration Program, the level of temporary migration to Australia is not determined or subject to quotas but is demand-driven.

Components of annual population growth ('000s), Australia, 1982-2015

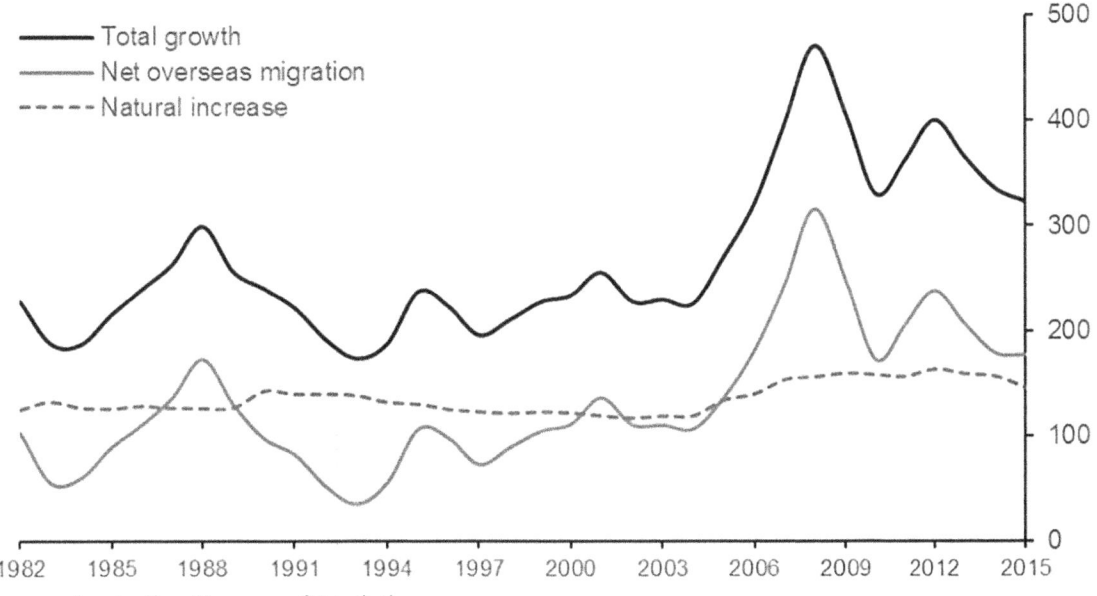

Source: Australian Bureau of Statistics

Current permanent immigration levels in Australia are exceptionally high. Migrant numbers began to rise significantly in the 1990s. Net overseas migration has increased from 30,042 in 1992–1993 to 178,582 persons in 2015–2016. Numbers of temporary immigrants (students and business subclass 457) have risen considerably in that time: 113,000 and 25,786 in 1996 to 310,845 and 85,611 in 2016, respectively. In August 2018 the population reached 25 million, 33 years ahead of schedule.

A further indication of the recent high rate of immigration is the 2016 Census, which revealed that nearly one in five (18%) of the overseas-born population had arrived since the start of 2012. Furthermore, the proportion of the Australian population born overseas (26%) is the highest in the world; this compares with the 22.6, 14.3 and 21.7% reported for 1901, 1954 and 2001, respectively.

Demographic changes post-WWII

For two centuries the United Kingdom was the primary source country for permanent migration to Australia but, as outlined above, major changes began with arrivals from Europe at the end of WWII and arrivals from Asia beginning in the 1970s. This change in source of immigrants is reflected in the following pie-charts showing the five most commonly reported countries of birth of Australians born overseas according to the 1901, 1954, 2001 and 2016 censuses. Notable features are the decline in numbers from the UK (teal) and the increase in Other (orange), which consists of small numbers from many countries.

China surpassed the UK as Australia's primary source of permanent migrants in 2010-2011. Since then, China and India have continued to provide the highest numbers of permanent migrants. New Zealand citizens also feature highly in the number of settler arrivals, but they are not counted under Australia's Migration Program unless they apply for (and are granted) a permanent visa.

Change in ethnic makeup of Australian population born overseas.

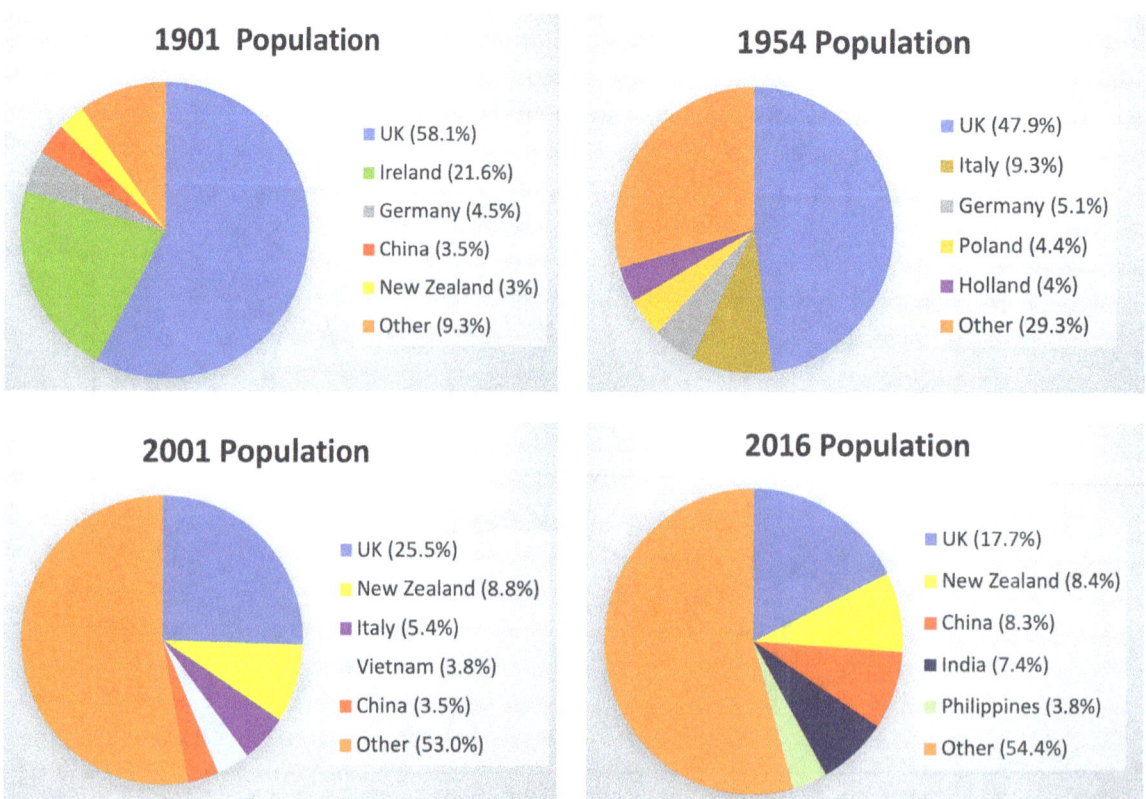

Source: Compiled from Parliamentary Library Research Papers 2018-19. Population and migration statistics in Australia, 7 December 2018. Joanne Davies, Statistics and Mapping Section

In 1901, most of our immigrants came from just a few countries. By 2016 Australia had become a nation of people from over 190 different countries and 300 different ancestries. The top ten of the most commonly nominated ancestries in the 2016 Australian census are given in the table below.

Ten most-commonly-nominated ancestries in the 2016 census

Nominated ancestry	Percent
English	36.1
Australian	33.5
Irish	11.0
Scottish	9.3
Chinese	5.6
Italian	4.6
German	4.5
Indian	2.8
Greek	1.8
Dutch	1.6

Source: Australian Bureau of Statistics

The number of people identifying as being of Aboriginal or Torres Strait Islander origin is on the rise, increasing from 2.5% of the Australian population in 2011 to 3.3% (or almost 798,365 people) in 2016.

The 2016 Census also showed:

- Over 300 separately identified languages were spoken in Australian homes.
- English is the only language spoken in the home for close to 72.7% of the population.
- More than one-fifth (21%) of Australians spoke a language other than English at home, the most common being Mandarin, Arabic, Cantonese and Vietnamese.
- Over 40% of the overseas-born population spoke only English at home, with Mandarin the second-most commonly spoken language at 8.3%.
- Nearly half (49%) of all Australians were either born overseas (first generation) or have at least one parent born overseas (second generation). The remaining 51% were at least third generation – born in Australia to Australian-born parents.
- Nearly half (47.3%) of people had both parents born in Australia and 34.4% of people had both parents born overseas.
- For the first time, most people born overseas were from Asia, not Europe.
- Most overseas-born Australians (61%) live in New South Wales and Victoria.
- Of the overseas-born population, nearly one in five (18%) had arrived since the start of 2012.
- Even within second-generation Australians, demographic splits are beginning to emerge, with those aged 40 and under more likely to be of Asian ethnicity and those over 40 more likely to have both parents born in a European country.

Urban society

The society that convicts and emancipists created was highly urban. Very few would ever have ventured into the bush but for the power of the colonial government to assign them to rural employment. Towns offered work, housing and pleasures – amusements, gambling – and access to sex, with or without marriage. The shepherds and cow-herders were assigned to the bush frontier. They may have disliked and feared the isolation but could do little about it until their sentences expired.

Not only was the proportion of the Australian population in towns high in 1841, but also it continued to increase during the rest of the nineteenth century. By 1850, 40% lived in towns. In 1836, Charles Darwin visited Sydney, and was so impressed with its growth that he described it as *the most magnificent testimony to the power of the English nation*. He had just spent much time in Spanish America, where poverty and slavery were evident everywhere. By 1870, 37% of Australia's population lived in the cities. It was a time when Australia became one of the most urbanised countries in the world. In 1901 the urban share had increased to 52% of the total population. No other region of recent settlement was so heavily urbanised as Australia at the end of the 19th century. A number of reasons are given for this, namely:

- The urban origin of convicts and early free-settlers.
- Free-settlers returning to the cities looking for work after failing to make a success of their small settler blocks.
- Land policies that made Australia less attractive to farming migrants than the USA and other new countries. After 1860 the United States gave land free to settlers. In Australia, on the other hand, land could be obtained only at a price.
- The high labour productivity of the rural workforce in Australia in the 19th century.
- The dominant primary industry, wool growing, had unusually low labour needs per unit of output.
- The isolation of pastoral stations in the outback made them particularly uncongenial to women and children. Hence there was a strong tendency for the dependent population to congregate in the towns and cities.
- The Australian population growth depended heavily upon immigration. Immigrants arrived by ship at one of the major ports and, so it was argued, a combination of inertia and the harshness of the interior deterred many from proceeding further.

A century later Australia is even more urbanised. In 2016, 89% of its population lived in urban areas and 71% in major cities (populations of 100,000 or more).

Melbourne and Sydney are the top choice for arrivals, with more than 90% of recent skilled migrants flocking to the east-coast capitals. Sydney and Melbourne account for about 40% of the country's population.

Source: Twitter @NaytaData using data from Australian Bureau of Statistics

Why choose Australia?

With few exceptions, such as our transported forebears, immigrants have chosen Australia to make a new life, one where they would be better off financially and have greater opportunities for their children. My understanding of why people want to settle here is based on many years of teaching English as a second language to immigrants (TAFE AMEP), where a class of about 16 often contained 12 different nationalities; also from having had for many years overseas students, mostly from Asia, living in my home.

Not surprisingly they like our clear blue skies, our beaches, Medicare, unemployment benefits and other government services; but what really matters is what and who we are.

They say we are friendly. They like our openness, honesty, relaxed ways, lack of corruption and nepotism, safety on the streets, approach to politics and absence of conflict and fear. Some come from countries where not being liked can be a matter of life and death. A more nebulous comment made is *I feel free here*. What they are saying is that, in general, they like Australia, Australians and the Australian approach to life.

Australia, being a migrant nation and a young one at that, does not rest firmly on centuries, or more, of life and tradition, but over two centuries of migration has evolved so favourably as a people, society and nation that it is a prime destination for migrants.

Impacts of and concerns about immigration

Just as it was a century ago, immigration is now a hot issue for debate, probably even more so. There is a range of views in the Australian community regarding the composition and level of immigration. A 2002 study outlined potential dilemmas associated with immigration-driven population growth: the environment, housing, infrastructure, employment, economic growth and aging population. Also, some research suggests current immigration has a negative effect on social cohesion by creating social divisions and risking long-term national unity, or by creating 'ethnic stratification' in Australian society. The problems that occurred in South-western Sydney suburbs with regard to compliance with restrictions during the COVID-19 pandemic give some credence to these concerns about the need for an integrated society.

As outlined, migration has been a strategy of governments since the early colonial era to meet labour shortages and other collective needs. A continent that supported an indigenous population of under a million at the time the First Fleet arrived now supports 27 million. Labour shortages, particularly skilled labour, still stalk the economy but the economic argument for immigration seems to be little more than a giant ponzi scheme. So far as population numbers go, it is highly unlikely that *homo sapiens* is exempt from the same laws that control the population of any living creature. In other words population numbers should be kept at a level that is in balance with the sustainable use of resources.

The pre-federation concern of unions that employer support for 'cheap' migrant labour was simply to drive down wages is no longer a valid immigration issue. Much of Australia's manufacturing industry has taken advantage of the modern global economy by relocating to countries where labour is cheaper. Highly skilled labour is now the target of Australia's immigration program. Even so, unions remain concerned about the number of temporary low-skilled migrants on work-related visas.

What cannot be denied is the form an immigration program takes is important because it affects the nature of a nation significantly. Who we are as Australians, our language, typical characteristics, behaviour, looks and general demeanour will stem from those who came and currently come here as immigrants. For instance, Australian anti-authoritarianism is said to come from convicts and the working class and lower middle-class immigrants, who followed them. The shortage of labour removed the workers' fear of the boss; working class and lower middle-class free-immigrants asserted their freedom after being held in more restraints in their homeland.

Both Australia and America began as British colonies but are vastly different today in many ways. Australia's immigration program has largely been selective with assisted passage and often some form of help by the colonial administration on arrival. Convicts, as would be expected, were catered for in various ways. Convicts and subsequently immigrants being conditioned to 'government' assistance has resulted in Australians having a welfare mentality. Americans, on the other hand, who largely selected themselves, have an attitude of self-help.

Trust is important for a cohesive well-functioning society. Australians, an Indian student told me some years ago, are very trusting. Surprised, I asked what he meant. His wife had been applying for jobs and in no instance were any of her documents queried. This was not the case in India, where fake documents are common he told me. From my experience the same can be said about China. Truthfulness is not an Asian characteristic. What matters is 'face'. Trust goes hand in hand with truth and honesty. Turkish migrants considered Australians very honest – that few of them would lie. Paradoxically, could our convict heritage be responsible for any propensity Australians have for telling the truth and respecting other's property? On their arrival Phillip urged them to be honest among themselves and meted out the severest punishment for stealing.

Pause and take breath

Australia, in just over two centuries of migration, has evolved as a people, society and nation to become a prime destination for migrants. Can it continue to do so and maintain social cohesion and the qualities and characteristics that make its citizenship so sought after?

In many ways the Australia of today is not what it was at federation or immediately post-WWII, when the population was homogenous and largely of British ancestry, while its core characteristics, values and institutions were those mentioned in the Preface to and throughout this opus. Factors influencing their evolution included convict settlement, the gold-rushes, two world wars and the Great Depression; the war and depression years consumed much of that half century and immigration, in terms of number of arrivals, played only a minor role. However, I suggest relatively low numbers and restrictive immigration policies were significant in giving the new nation time to establish itself on a sound footing.

By the end of WWII Australia had a sufficiently well-developed sense of self or identity to seek out a new destiny. The convict beginning, which cast its shadow of shame for over a century, was confronted and the so-called convict stain is now a mark of pride. Special ties with Britain began to weaken and those with America strengthened. Significantly, the nation embarked on an ambitious immigration program. Initially migrants were from Europe and two decades later they began arriving from Asia and elsewhere around the world with the result being the diverse population (see above) of today.

Since the early 1800s, meeting the need for labour has been the driving force behind much of the immigration to Australia. Current immigration rates are historically high and the 2016 census statistics (see above) indicate a very diluted local absorption pool compared with that of the 1950s and 1970s when arrival rates were much lower. The alleged success of the post-WWII immigration program may be partly attributed to the staged nature of the source of immigrants (British, then European, then the world). If this is the case and if Australia is to maintain the institutions, qualities, characteristics and values that have served it so well, thought should be given to implementing an 'absorption period' to allow more recent arrivals time to settle in; in other words, the immigration rate be reduced with the original goals in mind.

Strangely, or perhaps unsurprisingly, any comment or debate about immigration makes no reference to Australia's First People nor their participation. Many immigrants and overseas students I meet do not realise Australia has an indigenous people or would know one if they saw one. It may be that First Australian leaders have more urgent issues to deal with but to ignore immigration would be a serious mistake.

Chapter 15
World War I – A Baptism of Fire

The notion of being Australian was fused and tempered in the furnace of war. The federation of the six colonies (New South Wales, Victoria, Tasmania, South Australia, Western Australia and Queensland) to become States of the Commonwealth of Australia did little to heighten a sense of being part of a community transcending State boundaries – of being Australian. This sense of togetherness was forged just over a decade later, when volunteers from all States of the fledging nation fought side by side in that very bloody conflict, the First World War. The soldiers who survived brought home a new word to identify their country and its people. That word was 'Aussie'.

The Aussie soldiers were proud to find they fought as well as or better than their English and French counterparts, i.e. the 'Pommies' and 'Frogs'. In doing what they did, the way they did, they defined what it is to be Australian. They embodied the qualities required by explorers, squatters and settlers in their battle with a harsh, vast and unpredictable land, e.g. the ability of bush communities to cope with drought, floods, bushfires, loneliness and defeat; the nonchalance and disregard of conventions of the Currency Lad; and qualities such as resourcefulness, initiative, give-it-a-go, a fair go, disrespect for authority, mateship and equality.

The Aussie soldier came from all parts of the country, from the city and the bush, and from all walks of life and so these qualities became universal. Few families were not touched by loss and suffering, none more so than the humble rural couple Frederick and Maggie Smith. Of their seven sons who marched off to war, only one returned. On the bloody battlefields culminated the expression of the Australian character that had been evolving since convicts and their guards of the First Fleet first set foot on this land.

Barely a generation later the Australian character was again tested in the furnace of WWII and was not found wanting.

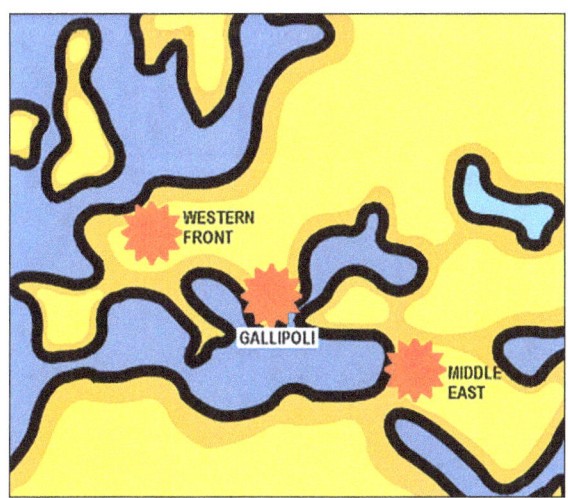

Main geographical regions in World War I. Source: ANZAC Day Commemoration Committee

First World War

When Britain entered the war against Germany and its allies Austria-Hungary and Turkey on 4 August 1914, Australia automatically followed and immediately organised a force to send to Europe. At the time Australia's population was about 5 million. Of the 416,809 who enlisted, 330,000 embarked for overseas, 226,073 were wounded and 59,258 were killed or died of wounds. Australians made their mark in each of the main theatres of the war: (1) on the Western Front in France and Belgium; (2) on the Gallipoli Peninsula; and (3) in the Middle East in Sinai-Palestine.

All were volunteers, as Australia and South Africa were the only countries in the war that did not resort to conscription. A higher proportion of the population enlisted than from any other country.

All around Australia men rushed to enlist and there were various reasons for doing so. Many believed they had no choice but to protect England from invasion. Others thought it was a once-in-a-lifetime opportunity to travel, and many just didn't want to miss out on something so exciting. *Don't worry*, they told their mothers, wives and girlfriends, *it will all be over by Christmas.* Little did they realise the horrors that awaited them and made them the stuff of legends. This force was called the Australian Imperial Force (AIF) and consisted of an Infantry Division and a Light Horse Brigade. Of five more divisions subsequently raised, only one, the Third Division, was raised in Australia.

The First Division was formed in August 1914. Among the first infantry units raised were those that formed the 3rd Brigade, sometimes known as the 'All-Australian Brigade'. It was comprised of the 9th Battalion raised in Queensland, 10th Battalion raised in South Australia, 11th Battalion raised in Western Australia and 12th Battalion – one half of which was made up of Tasmanians, while the other half was made up of Western Australians and South Australians.

The 9th Battalion was the first battalion recruited in Queensland. Some had not visited a town in their life until they passed through Cairns, Townsville or Charleville on their way to Brisbane to enlist. Among the large variety of occupations stated by 129 members of the original battalion that embarked were: miner, carpenter, schoolteacher, blacksmith, motor driver, plumber, sailor, seaman, horse-breaker, law clerk, watchmaker, jeweller, drover, reporter, university lecturer, medical student and clergyman; a few even stated their occupation as gentleman. Peter Fitzallan MacDonald Stuart, aged 20, was among the first to enlist in the 9th Battalion, doing so on 1 September 1914.

A grandson of P.F. MacDonald and an elder brother of my mother, he had attended the Rockhampton Boys Grammar School, where he became Senior Prefect and in this role presented the retiring headmaster F.W. Wheatley with a large marble clock on behalf of the boys. He was of a short, stocky build and an all-round athlete, who was a favourite with all. He played senior football with the Eureka Rugby Union Club and was in a Central Queensland team that beat New South Wales. He rowed for the Leichhardt Rowing Club and was a strong swimmer. My mother said he would swim across the Fitzroy River and back, where the Criterion Hotel now stands.

A younger friend and admirer of Peter, Roy Jardine, who rowed in the same crew and played in the same rugby team, later became headmaster of the Rockhampton Boys Grammar School – a school he had also attended. In a letter to me, his wife Kath wrote:

> *Roy once said to me of his boyhood friend he loved so much ... that he reminded him of Coriolanus,*

P.F. Stuart. Source: Peter Hasker

Chapter 15: World War I – A Baptism of Fire

Rockhampton Grammar School Tennis Fours, 1913. Standing (l-r): John Fryer, Charles Paterson. Seated: P. Stuart, H.A. Kellow, Leonard White. Source: Peter Hasker

Shakespeare's tragic figure. ... not that there was any hint of the negative aspect of the Shakespearian tragic figure in Roy's assessment of his character. It was simply his proud arrogance that his younger friend admired. Roy came from a more humble background than Peter, his father being a stationmaster in the Queensland Railways.

The other activity the boys shared was the exploration of the local countryside. ... It was on an expedition to reach Double Heads accompanied by Harold Charlton ... that an exciting incident occurred. During their attempt to reach the 'blow hole' Harold Charlton fell and broke his leg. Peter ... put the leg in splints crudely manufactured while Roy went to get a rowing boat ... and brought him back to Yeppoon.

Eureka Football Club – Premiers 1912-13, Charity Cup winners 1912-13-14. P.F. Stuart (3/4) back row, 5th from right. Source: Peter Hasker

My mother told me about the incident, adding that Peter did a faultless job with the splint. From the little my mother said about him I think Kath's choice of arrogance may be misplaced. Like his older brother 'Gem', he had the confidence and demeanour of the 'patrician' and had no time for fools or personal failings. It was he who kept a younger brother, Simson, in line, even resorting to an occasional thrashing; and from this aspect was sorely missed when he went off to war. In a letter to his father dated 29 April 1916, he wrote:

> *Sim is over 18 now and it is not much etc. his lolling about – perhaps I should not speak but I would like to see Sim come away ... then I could look after him – I know it is asking a horrible lot for our Muviar to let us all get into this show – but at the same time I think it is worth it for the best in Sim is not being developed but the worst at present. ... I don't mean this from any silly patriot standpoint but to the making of Sim. Sorry Dad if I have gone a bit over the line but I can't express exactly what I mean but think you understand.*

Peter Stuart was a Colour Sergeant in the contingent of 14 cadets who represented Queensland at the Imperial Cadet Competition at the Canadian National Exhibition, Toronto, September 1912. On this occasion he won the silver medal for swimming against all other cadets from the British Empire. Peter intended making a military career. On his return he received a postcard from his former headmaster, F.W. Wheatley, who was at Balliol College, Oxford, inquiring about how he had got on, on his return from Canada and whether he had been accepted by the Military College (Duntroon). As well as being Head Master of the Rockhampton Boys Grammar School, Wheatley had been Battalion Commander No. 3 Battalion C.C.C. and had provided written support for Peter's ambition:

> *Peter F.M. Stuart has been a pupil at the Boys' Grammar School Rockhampton under me for the last five and a half years. He is a boy of enormous strength of character, fitted to lead, with a good influence over his fellows. He will make an ideal soldier, and will I trust be admitted to the Military College.*

Silver medal won by Peter Stuart in the Imperial Cadet competition at the Canadian National Exhibition, Toronto, 1912. Source: Peter Hasker

When war broke out he was working in the Clermont district on an uncle's cattle property, while waiting to enter Duntroon Military College. However, going to College and thereby gaining a commission would have delayed his joining the war effort. He enlisted immediately as a private soldier giving his occupation as 'jackeroo'. I believe he did this out of a sense of duty rather than seeking excitement and adventure. Peter Stuart joined Section 15, Platoon 4,

A Company, 9th Battalion (Qld) and boarded the troop ship *Omrah* in Brisbane. By the time they reached Egypt he had gained his corporal stripes.

The First Division arrived in Egypt in December 1914, where it underwent training in sight of the great pyramids prior to being sent to the Western Front in France. The intensity of this training, mostly by their own officers, was exceptional. British and French officers remarked that the Australians threw themselves into the *toiling and slogging in the desert ... as though it was real war*. A British officer on the Division commander's staff said *a better division than the First Australian had never gone to war.* By then the generals had decided to call these soldiers and their New Zealand comrades the Australian and New Zealand Army Corps or ANZACs. However, they did not go on to Europe. Their baptism of fire was at Gallipoli, a name now etched into the Australian psyche.

Chapter 16
Gallipoli

The Gallipoli campaign was an attempt to crush Germany's ally Turkey by seizing control of the Dardanelles Straits and taking Constantinople (now Istanbul). The British thought Turkey was weak and, if attacked, would need German help, which could help break the stalemate of the trench warfare on the Western Front. Also, taking control of this area would open a supply route to Russia. Given their huge tactical and strategic value the Straits were heavily defended, chiefly by natural geography. To the north they were protected by the Gallipoli Peninsula and to the south by the shore of Ottoman Asia. In addition, fortresses were well positioned on cliff-tops overlooking shipping lanes.

When in March 1915 a massive Anglo-French naval force failed in an attempt to take the Dardanelles, the Allies decided to use land forces to take the Gallipoli Peninsula. They believed this would give them control of the Dardanelles and enable them to capture Istanbul. Preparations for this, although too hasty, gave the Turks time to boost defences around the Straits with ground forces. The Australian First Division, which had been training in Egypt, now joined a larger British Empire contingent assembled to undertake this task.

The plan was for the Australians to land on a broad front centred about a mile north of Gaba Tepe on the Aegean coast. They were to advance across the peninsula to prevent Turkish retreat from or reinforcement of Kilitbahir, which the British landing at Cape Helles would attack. The French were to make a diversionary landing at Kum Kale on the Asian shore.

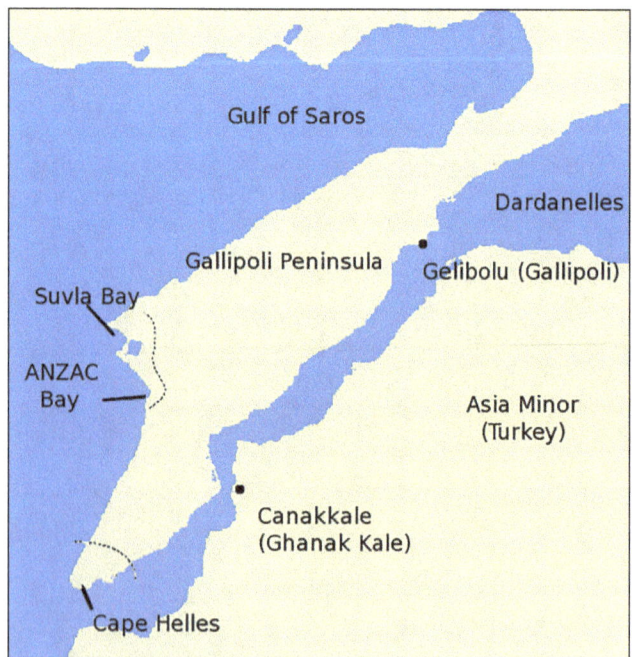

An overview of the Gallipoli Peninsula. The dotted lines approximately mark the furthest advance of Allied Forces. Source: Scott Simeon, Wikimedia Commons

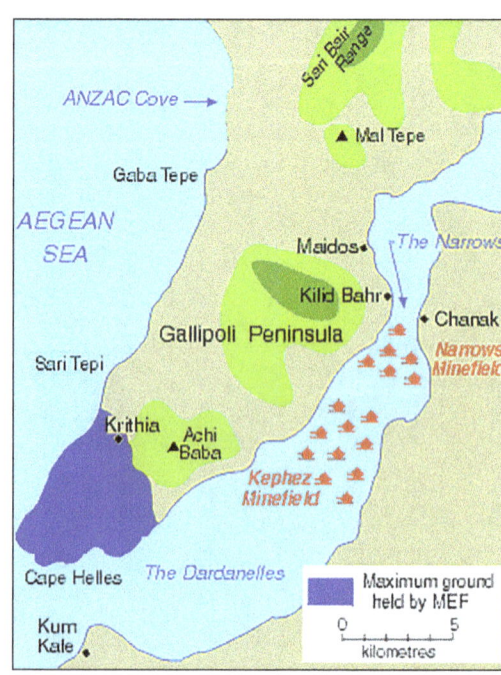

The Gallipoli Peninsula Map. Source: ANZAC Day Commemoration Committee

The landing

On 25 April 1915, the First Division made an amphibious assault at what is now known as Anzac Cove, on the Gallipoli Peninsula. On ANZAC Day the division was unable to capture its objectives but secured a toehold on the peninsula. It served throughout the campaign until the evacuation in December 1915.

The men of the 3rd Brigade were considered exceptionally tough and so it was chosen to be the covering force for the ANZAC landing. It was the first ashore at around 4.30 am and its 9th Battalion was heavily involved in establishing and defending the front line of the ANZAC beachhead.

The Brigade was divided into two groups, the first of which was A and B Companies of the 9th battalion, B and C Companies of the 10th Battalion and A and C Companies of the 11th Battalion. The second group comprised the remaining companies of these battalions plus the 12th Battalion. The first group was taken on three battleships to a rendezvous opposite the landing beach, while the second group went on seven destroyers.

Around 2.00 am (with the moon slowly moving below the horizon) the troops were transferred to row boats, each taking 30-40 troops, that had been placed on either side of the troop-carrying battleships. In tows of three, these were towed by small steam-boats closer to the landing beach, released and then rowed to the beach. However, a strong current carried the tows off course; attempts by some of the boats to remedy this resulted in some mixing of the battalions. The boats concentrated about a mile and a half further north than intended in a shallow, nameless cove (now known as Anzac Cove) between Ari Burnu to the north and Hell Spit to the south. The terrain was the most wild and difficult on the entire Gallipoli Peninsula, an area that had been deliberately ruled out by general staff reconnoitring the coastline. The troops were confronted with a 100 m rugged hill that they set about climbing under intense machine gun and rifle fire from the Turks above.

Anzac Cove. Source: Google images

Australia and Australians: What we are and why – A personal perspective

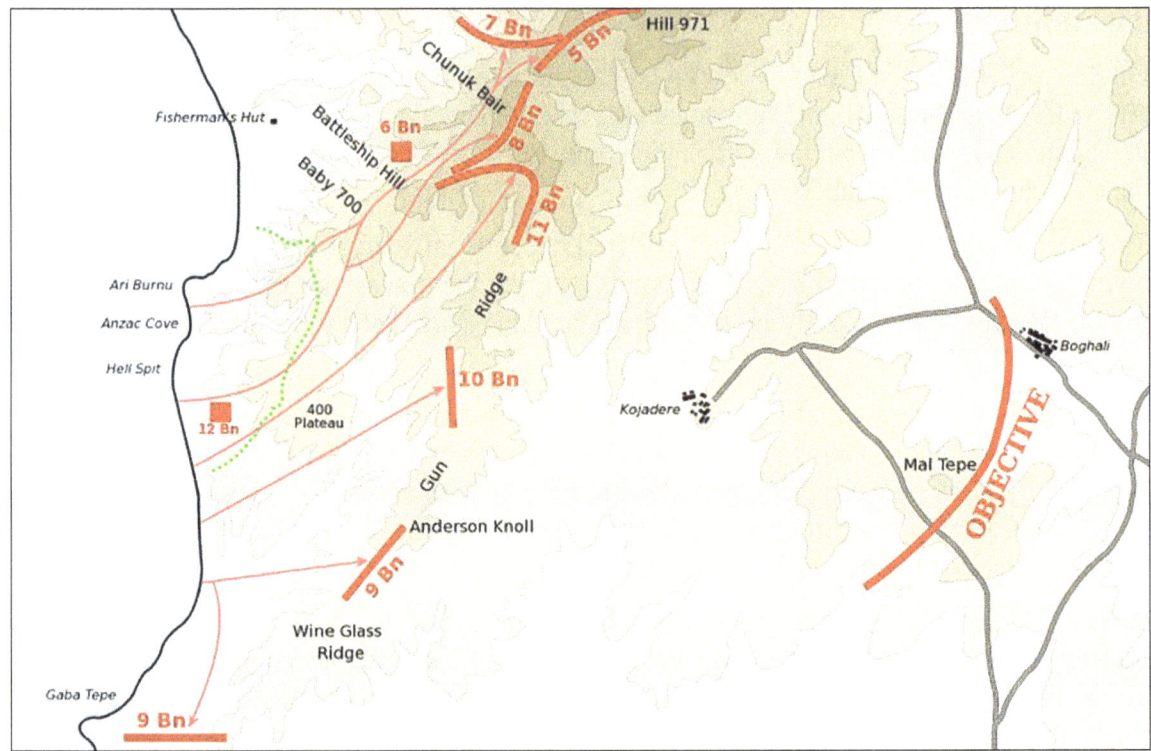

Map of the planned landing of the 2nd and 3rd Brigades of the Australian 1st Division. The red lines mark the first day's objectives, the green dotted line marks the actual advance achieved on the first day. Contours are at 50 metre intervals. Source: Wikimedia Commons

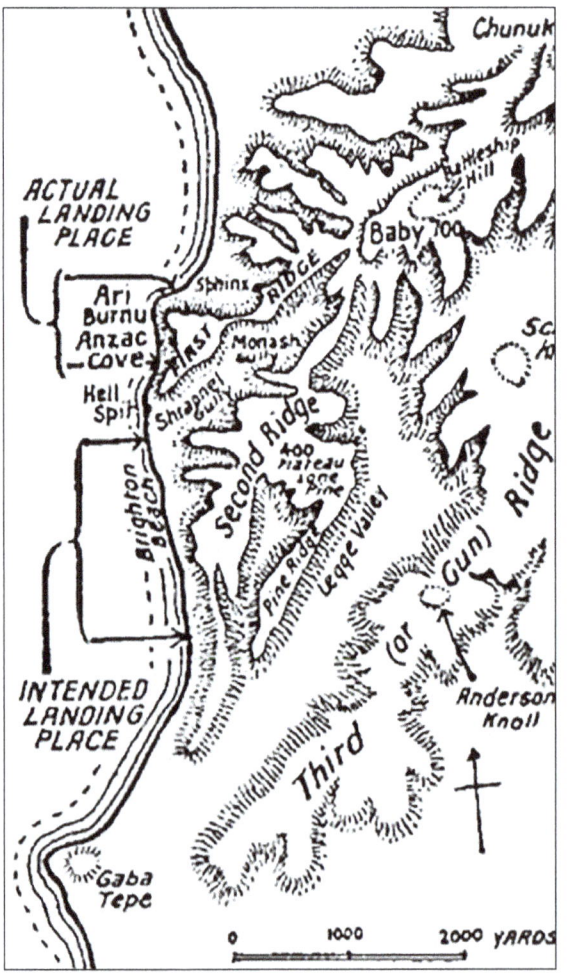

The Landing at ANZAC, 25 April 1915. Source: ANZAC Day Commemoration Committee, *The Courier-Mail*

Sergeant H.R. Gower of the 9th Battalion, and from Rockhampton, wrote to his parents about the landing from Victoria Hospital, Alexandria. He referred to the effective use of the bayonet by the Australians, which was a hallmark of their fighting in this war and the next, and mentions sighting a wounded Peter Stuart:

> *We effected a landing and fixed bayonets and awaited orders. ... We were then ordered to take the hill in front of us which we did at the point of the bayonet, the Turks running like rabbits.*
>
> *I was then ordered to take a party and take a hut and search it. We rushed it with the bayonet and drove about ten Turks out and these were either bayoneted or shot. ... The whole force then continued to advance under heavy fire. ... Talk about a Chinese New Year, it was like a million of them put together. ... I never saw anything like it; we lay in our position for about two hours not daring to move with shrapnel killing and wounding men all around you. ...*

There were about forty men, one officer, two non-commissioned officers, myself and someone of the sixth Battalion. We prepared to make our last stand. We formed an open square, fixed bayonets and continued firing until there were about twenty of us left unkilled or unwounded. I noticed Peter Stuart with blood all over his face, hit through the head or something. It was the last I expected to see of him. ... There were about ten of us left then. We then prepared to cut our way out and yelling we made for their left flank which when we reached it opened out and let us through. They will not stand the bayonet. Just as we got through about five of us went down, myself with one through the thigh.

Australian troops charge a Turkish trench at The Nek, 7 August 1915. Source: Wikimedia Commons

Being a member of Section 15, Platoon 4, A Company of the 9th Battalion, Peter Stuart was among the first ashore; Lieutenant Duncan Chapman, Section 13, Platoon 3, is credited with being the first ashore. He was in one of the first boats that landed and described the event in a letter to his parents, written from a hospital in Valetta, Malta, of which the following are excerpts:

At about 2 o'clock we were all ordered to put on our gear then soon afterwards we fell in on deck. I think the engines had stopped but I'm not quite sure. The moon showed us the land of the Turk in the distance and one wondered how long it would be before the peaceful looking night or rather morning would be broken by the booming of the guns, cracking of rifles. Everything was done quietly; but I think the feeling of suppressed excitement was felt by most for at last we were to tackle the real thing.

Then we – that is the 15th and 16th Sections, for the 2 companies had previously gone through disembarkation and so knew exactly where to fall in and to what boat to go – fell in. Each boat held about two and a half sections. Being one of the rowers for our boat, I was one of the first to climb down the ladder into the lifeboat. ... Very quietly all the boats of our lot got fastened to each other and then to the Pinnace which was to tow us in a distance of 2-and-a-half to 3 miles.

Mudros Harbour, Lemnos Island, April 1915. A line of towed boats loaded with AIF troops preparing for the Gallipoli landing. Source: AWM, No. H16825 (Donor Major F.J. McAdam)

We went for a little cruise about at first to see if we were all secure or wait for the moon to set for there she was a bright orange gold colour to the right of our landing direction. I said to Jack 'Have a look at the moon it looks very peaceful'. Somehow I wanted to see exactly how the moon and everything looked so that if I got through I would know precisely how it looked. Funny or rather mad idea. Well soon we were silently gliding over the water. I think there were either six or eight boats in our tow. The boats being towed were in pairs. We were all pretty quiet but the occasional bits of conversation here and there as to how many rows of boats there were. At last the moon had sunk and it was fairly light and you could distinguish the different lines of parallel to us. It was getting lighter and lighter; the day was breaking.

Half past four someone said. I know I was waiting – in fact we all were – for the bang of shots but still we were getting closer and still not a sound. Someone said 'there cannot be any Turks there' for we were silently gliding towards a hill covered with bushes and thick foliage. It was quite daylight now. Again someone said 'There is no one there' but someone else 'Just wait until we strike the shore'. The boats unhitched from the Pinnace ... There we were about fifty yards or so to row before we struck the beach with a crunching sound. This was the time I expected to hear the bullets.

They put the ladder down from the bow and two or three climbed down onto the shore and still not a sound. The rest of us were sitting quietly waiting our turns when suddenly there was the crack of the rifle and then crack, crack outside of the boat and cracking in the air for they were using explosive bullets too. They all took it very coolly, hardly a word being said. The naval officer had to tell them to slip along and jump off from the sides into the water up at the bow for they all seemed content to wait their turn to go down the gangway although it was raining lead. Well they skipped along a bit and then my turn came for I was sitting aft rowing stroke with another chap. I put my oar down, went forward jumping as they were all doing by now into the water got wet up to my hips only.

Then as soon as I got out of the water down on the sand I went. Off came the pack (previous order) and then we started to crawl for the hill about thirty or forty yards away. Half way across I stopped to fix my bayonet; meanwhile the air was thick with bullets hitting and ploughing up the sand all about you and yet I was not hit. Lord knows why. Well I reached the bottom of the hill and there I put a clip off (of five cartridges into the magazine of my rifle) crawled up a bit further up the incline of the hill and lay there for about ten minutes wondering when I was going to be hit for I thought it impossible for these bullets to go on 'ping pong' just over me then 'smack' in the front of me and 'smack' just to the other side without striking me. Funny though you did not feel so awfully frightened.

I heard chaps just by me shouting to each other to 'Come here' *then* 'I say, Jack, here we are come and join us, come on Ned' *and so on. I said to a chap near me* 'pretty warm place', 'Yes, it is a bit'. *You talk just ordinarily but you hope and pray that you will not be hit. It was a queer sight to see these black looking objects on the beach.*

Most of us had started to scale the hills then it was properly daylight we all charged up the hill but the Turks went like the wind and did not wait for the bayonet. A German officer and a few Turks were wounded in the trenches. Then we cut over the hill and down the valley after them; but the bush was far too thick. ... You cannot see anything in it.

There were a few of us sniped off but not many. Smoke though, they are terrible shots. They cannot shoot for tarts. Anyway we chase the black devils. Mind you we did not fire a shot before we took the first line of trenches on the brow of the hill but we got ones and twos now. They started to straighten things up now. We were made to get into firing line, supports, reserves and so on. Made it a bit shipshape. We were ordered to entrench on the second hill but afterwards a higher order came to push on for the counter attack was now in full swing.

It was a great sight to see all the war boats as they stood out booming away at a fort about three miles from our right. One forgot that it was real warfare watching the shells from the Queen, Prince of Wales, the Triumph and four more coming screeching along in the air. Then dust and you would see a cloud of smoke where the shells burst. It was masterly the way they got on to those forts. ... And all this while the noise of the rifles and machine guns were going on. It was a glorious sight.

It would be great one for the pictures especially the way the boats full of troops would come along then swing right out and swerve in again with shrapnel from all parts breaking about them. ... You have no idea what it was like, these boats getting tugged calmly along to the shore with shells bursting all roads. Most of them used to be missed but some boats had bad luck and were hit. They were tugged along to the shore just the same. In one boat only three got out alive but they bounded off straight up the bank to have a cut at what – well I cannot say what they called it. ...

I was out on the right flank mixed up with all battalions and owing to the top of the hill being swept with machine guns, we had to back down a bit for the bullets were humming like a swarm of bees overhead getting one or two of us who did not keep their heads flat on the ground. We gradually crawled down the slope of the hill and we were right then. Then they started to sweep the whole of the valley with shrapnel. It was not too nice. You could not move one way for the shrapnel or the other from machine gun fire. There I lay for two hours but could not fire. They had the range to a T for all the places – regular traps. I have been in nicer places in my life however, the fire slackened a bit after a time so we went to the left a bit and charged over the ridge down the gully up the next and so on lying down a few seconds in each rush forward.

Well, a party of about 40 of us away on the right in the firing line gradually got cut right off. The devils came to within 80 yards all round, but were frightened of cold steel. At any rate we were dropping all roads. That is when I was hit. ...

... I merely received a glancing bullet over the left eye. It went in one part of the eyebrow and came out on the other an inch further on, so there is nothing serious about it. It dinted my thick skull a bit. There's nothing wrong with me, for the wound is absolutely closed up. I can see pretty well now, this is, I can see absolutely square before owing to shock the left eye brought things to a focus at different distances to the right eye, the images crossed at an angle 15% but today that has worn off. ...

... I think the enemy must have thought we were in far superior numbers to what we were for with a hot fire from the others and our bit of fire on those point blank against us a lot of us got through. The devils near us got right up on all sides firing at about 50 yards but they were awfully bad shots. Why we were dropping so quickly was because the atmosphere was thick with bullets especially explosive ones that burst in the air if they did not hit you. They also used dum dums.

How I got back I really do not know. Some chaps gave me a hand up and down the hills and valleys. I suppose it was the terrible thick foliage bush or whatever you call it. All the way to the beach there was popping pop all about you with shrapnel bursting here and there. I surprised the chap helping me over the last green patch to the water which was a shrapnel bed. I looked a long time at the shrapnel falling on it, watched where it fell. Gathered all my strength for I had lost a fair amount of blood, saw the shrapnel did not go to the left side and got up and sprinted. I left the other chaps hundreds of yards behind. I was around the corner and sitting down when they got up. The chap that had been helping me did not say anything, just looked at me, don't know what he thought. I've never run so hard in all my life but I did it in even time though it was in boots but of course I did not have my gear on. I would have beaten Postle [famous pre-war professional runner from Pittsworth and the fastest man in Australia].

Shells and bullets make one do things that at other times he is quite incapable of doing. You know those fellows were sniping at our men all roads right in amongst us. They hid under the thick bushes and you could not see them. Of course you get them here and there. Oh, but the place must have been thick with them. It was rather hard on us as we had only rifles to their artillery and hundreds of machine guns. It is a German idea those machine guns. We had our machine guns but that in only one machine gun section to the battalion. Then again they had the ranges of every bush pretty nearly ranged off to the inch. Not many of their mines went off though.

New Zealanders and a battalion of Indians came up in the afternoon but we had to retire that evening to the trenches we dug on the first hill for the night. During the night we got up our artillery. Next morning from the boat I could see that our chaps were pretty right and the casualties on Sunday compared with Monday proved it. Down at the dressing station at about 6 pm ...

We went to Alexandria. I wired or got someone to cable you from there. Most of the serious cases were taken off there – we had a thousand wounded on our boat – and then I came with the rest to Malta as they had no more room and here I am at Valetta hospital. ...

> *... I do not think they got much of a muster; they called the roll for the Third Brigade, especially for the Ninth Battalion for it was the Queenslanders who landed first. But they took the hill as they were intended to do. The Australians can fight if they cannot do anything else. ...*

The Morning Bulletin, Rockhampton (16 August 1915) reported Trooper Lyons' letter home:

> *... they all say that Peter Stuart was a mad reckless beggar on that Sunday they landed and he was a frightful source of trouble to the Turks and they soon lost track of him. Then I met Harold Fairweather who told me how he happened to meet Peter wandering around on a hill and though he looked as if he had lost an eye and must have had a rough time; the amazing vitality which he was always noted for still stuck to him. He recognised Fairweather first and stopped with their party until they got down to the beach. I hope he got away without any trouble.*

By June the two bullet holes over Peter Stuart's left eye had healed but it was not quite as good as it used to be. A bit of explosive bullet remained in his right eyebrow. He returned to Gallipoli via Alexandria and Lemnos. He had not suffered from malaria or any other illness since his previous stay in Lemnos and felt very fit again.

The Gallipoli campaign, which had been planned as a swift operation, became a protracted and bloody eight-month struggle. In that period the frontline of the ANZAC battlefield remained little changed from the ground captured on the first day of the landing. A space less than three-quarters of a square mile (2 km²) in size became home to over 20,000 men; but home only in terms of a place where one lives. Here they fought to survive bullets and hand-to-hand fighting, the dysentery and disease brought by the flies that came with the summer heat, and the winter cold. The stench of death, disease and unhygienic conditions were everywhere. In August 1915 as he rode away from Anzac Cove over to the ridges above Suvla Bay, Mustafa Kemal noted in his diary that:

> *For the first time in four months I was breathing air which was more or less pure and clear, because in the Ariburnu district and its neighbourhood, the air we breathed was polluted by the corruption of human corpses.*

Soon the air above Suvla Bay was also putrid with the smell of the dead. As they battled the odds, those qualities that had been growing in the Australian character for a hundred years took firm root. But not for one minute did they consider themselves heroes. What sustained them were the values they took with them from home. What carried them through were the thoughts and hopes about home and those they had left at home. This shows clearly in Peter Stuart's diary.

15.6.1915
... Sometimes I wish to be back straight away to the front ... I think by the time it is safe here – but am afraid the front a lot of these chaps that are always talking about that they long to get back to is the front of a beer keg. ... – for I am totally wrong for we are off too – we are right out to sea already. Ho Ho through the submarines back to the shock and shells. In a way I am not sorry; this is I am not one of your heroes. I am scared of it – scared ... but one could not keep one's self respect and stay behind even though you know well what it is.

16.6.1915
... Funny how cheerful one feels after tea at night. ... One would not think that all these lads were going back to the land where it rains lead and shrapnel but to a picnic. ...

18.6.1915

... Say we are off to Gallipoli at 2 pm so ought to get there this evening – I don't seem to worry – but suppose I will very much when I just start to get into it again. Wonder how the dear old Dad, Murrar, and family are – it must be a horrible strain for them all with Gem and I both at the front – it makes it hard yet I suppose really easier taking all these risks when there is such a loving family at home waiting in suspense for every little bit of news from you – but such is this life – but one must endure it and with God's help come out more fit to cherish and love your family – love one does not realise how utterly unmeasurably, how boundless it is till you find the chances against you so great – but words are paltry. One must also prove worthy of his family's affections. ...

We are to leave for Gaba Tepe in about an hour in minesweepers so ought to be there at 10 pm – that means trenches tonight for us – so it's once more back to the music.

I'm afraid I am a funny fellow for I don't know whether I am glad, sorry, happy, frightened or what; I seem to hate the idea of it sometimes yet I would not for anything stop out of it – rather like a rowing race you don't like it _____ it too hard yet in a way you do. Well, Peter, you don't understand yourself – no more does anyone else exactly – except perhaps your Dad who reckons he does yet I don't know if he does altogether. Hope the deuce Gem looks after himself up there – hope I see the dear lad bird up there. Funny how casual one is for instance the question going _____ answer 'Oh yes'. So today is the anniversary of Waterloo – wonder did they have to go _____ Archie Bat. Hope they don't greet us too warmly at Gaba Tepe. It will be good to get back with all the boys again. I'll turn in and have a good sleep _____ be ready. Hope this eye stops _____

Withdrawal from Gallipoli

The Gallipoli campaign was a heroic but costly failure. In December 1915, it was decided to evacuate the entire force from Gallipoli. Over the 11 nights from 8 to 20 December 1915, 90,000 troops were evacuated from Anzac Cove and Suvla Bay. The entire operation evacuated 142,000 men with negligible casualties and was regarded as the most successful of the war.

The well-planned withdrawal was done in stages. Lots of things were done to disguise what was happening. Cricket matches were staged in full view of the Turks, self-firing rifles were designed and made, tunnels were dug with the intention of blowing 'mines' after the evacuation. 'Silent days' were staged where no noise was made at all. No firing, nothing. This was to get the Turks used to silence from the trenches. Men were taken off at night but during the day a few would be returned as though they were reinforcements arriving to make things look as normal as possible. Delayed action charges were left in trenches and barbed wire entanglements were made to block trenches as the men withdrew. When considering the success of this operation the following should be kept in mind. The Turks were willing to see them go and were not inclined to attack, the Turkish High Command having ruled against attacking a withdrawing enemy.

'Gem' Stuart, an older brother of Peter Stuart, was attached to the 3rd Light Horse Field Ambulance. He had volunteered when doing his Medical Internship at the Melbourne Hospital, and when accepted was involved with its formation. It was the last field ambulance on the peninsula at the time of the evacuation. The following extract is taken from his account, which he wrote in 1919, of the Ambulance's war service:

The weather was now becoming decidedly cold. Snow fell and everything moist became frozen. ... The transport of provisions became very difficult and we had a foretaste of what winter life on the peninsula would be like.

On November 29th we received orders to be ready to move at 2 hours notice. We packed up and after 'standing by' for 8 days we were ordered to re-open the hospital. Three days later we once more received orders to be ready to move. ... Guns were being moved from their positions to the beach, jetties were being erected, troops were leaving and there was general talk of evacuation from the peninsula.

On 16th December ours was the last ambulance at ANZAC. At roll call in the afternoon we were informed that the unit was expected to leave at the shortest notice and volunteers were called for among the unmarried men to remain behind in the trenches with the men of the brigade who were to be the last to leave. ... Every man volunteered, and a Corporal and five men were detailed for the honoured post.

Mutual respect

A mutual respect developed between the Australians and their Turkish foes. Following the landing at Suvla Bay, casualties among the opposing armies were particularly high, and the hot and humid weather made the stench of bodies particularly nauseating. A days truce was arranged to facilitate the removal of the dead and wounded; this momentary contact led to a strange camaraderie between the armies, and courtesies not observed elsewhere in the war. It is recorded that one old Turkish batman was regularly permitted to hang his platoons washing on the barbed wire without attacking fire; and that there was a 'constant traffic' of gifts being thrown across 'no-man's land', dates and sweets from the Turkish side, and cans of beef and cigarettes from the ANZAC side. Thus the Australians fought fiercely but not bitterly, despite the horror and carnage they suffered. They saw the Turkish soldier as an honourable enemy. Words from C.E.W. Bean's poem *Abdul* express this sentiment:

*Yes, we've seen him dying there in front —
Our own boys died there, too —
With his poor dark eyes a-rolling,
Staring at the hopeless blue;
With his poor maimed arms a-stretching
To the God we both can name ...
And it fairly tore our hearts out;
But it's in the beastly game.*

*So though your name be black as ink
For murder and rapine,
Carried out in happy concert
With your Christians from the Rhine,
We will judge you, Mr Abdul,
By the test by which we can —
That with all your breath, in life, and death,
You've played the gentleman.*

On ANZAC Day 2006 the Turks joined in the Melbourne ANZAC Day March.

The Gallipoli campaign cost an enormous number of lives. Many thousands of Australian, New Zealand and other Allied soldiers died. Australian casualties were more than 26,000 with more than 8,000 deaths, while New Zealand lost 2,700. More than 21,000 British soldiers were killed along with 10,000 French, 1,300 Indians and 50 from Newfoundland. Some 85,000 of the defending Turkish troops were killed and 164,000 wounded. Soldiers in Australian units won 9 Victoria Crosses.

Although it was a failure as a military campaign, Gallipoli was where the legend of the ANZACs was born. Some suggest it was where Australia became of age as a nation. Gallipoli united our forces at the front as well as uniting Australians in grief. It showed that our soldiers could stand up to the horrors of modern warfare and display courage, friendship, humour and ingenuity under fire; they washed away the convict stain and thereby any self-doubt Australia was a proper nation. While the soldiers at Gallipoli were only ordinary men, through a quirk of fate they were elevated to the level of heroes and are seen by many as the ideal of what it is to be 'Australian'.

Back to Egypt

After evacuating Gallipoli, the Australians returned to Egypt, encamping at Tel el Kebir. In February-March 1916 they were re-organised to form the 1st, 2nd, 4th and 5th Divisions. At this time a 3rd Division was being raised in Australia; its commander for most of its war service was Major General John Monash. In March 1916, the 1st and 2nd Divisions moved to France and the 4th and 5th Divisions undertook the defence of the Suez Canal until moving to France in June. The 3rd Division moved to France in December 1916 after spending three months training in England.

This reorganisation led to the creation of the 49th Australian Infantry Battalion as part of the 13th Brigade of the 4th Division. The new battalion comprised 14 officers and 500 other ranks (all of whom were veterans of the 9th Battalion), plus 3 officers and 470 other ranks as reinforcements. Thus, like the 9th, the 49th Battalion was basically a Queensland unit. The 13th Brigade (which comprised the 49th, 50th, 51st and 52nd Australian Infantry Battalions) was commanded by Brigadier General T.W. Glasgow and the 49th Battalion was commanded by Lieutenant Colonel F.M. de Lorenzo.

Peter Stuart was one of the veterans of the 9th Battalion who went into the 49th Battalion. By April he had gained his 2nd Lieutenant's commission. He met up with his brother 'Gem' Stuart of the 3rd Light Horse Field Ambulance about a month later. In a letter home to his brother Les dated 19 June 1916, 'Gem' wrote:

> *Pete left me about a fortnight ago and I hope that it won't be as long a spell as before that I see him again. He looks a burly ruffian for although he hasn't grown much taller he's very thick set and he'd be exceedingly nasty to meet in a brawl.*

Chapter 17
Middle East Campaigns

After Gallipoli, the 1st, 2nd and 3rd Light Horse Brigades, which had fought there unmounted, were reunited with their horses. After a year in Egypt the horses of the Light Horse had become used to the diet, sand, water and climate and so were well conditioned for desert warfare. Except for two regiments, the 13th Light Horse and part of the 4th Light Horse, the Australian Light Horse Brigades remained in the Middle East, where they fought against the Senussi in Libya and in the Sinai and Palestine campaigns. They played a major role in the fall of Damascus and defeat of the Turks.

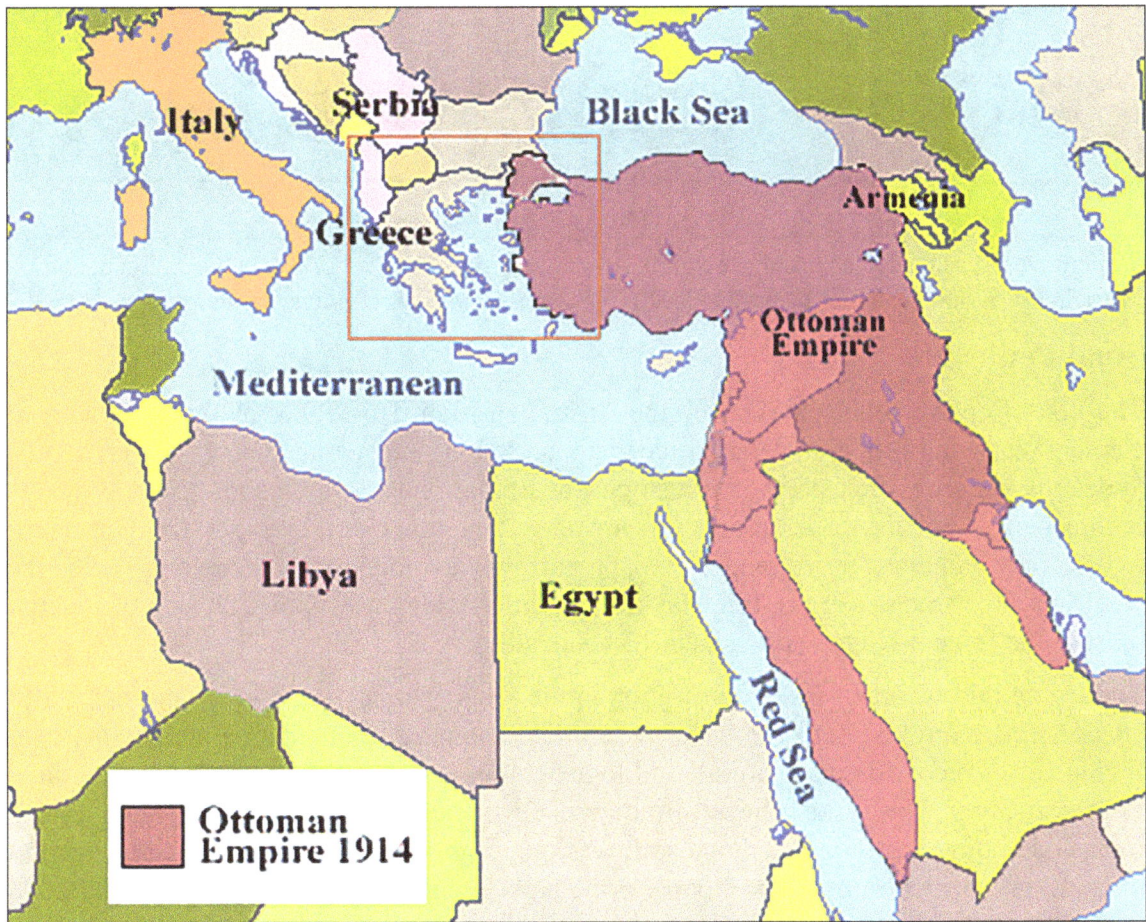

Map showing the Ottoman Empire in 1914. Source: The National Archives, UK

Western Desert – Senussi

Australian Light Horsemen first saw action as part of a multi-national force formed hurriedly in November 1915 to fight in the Western Desert against the Senussi, Arab tribesmen based in Libya, whom the Turks had persuaded to attack the British. For some years the Senussi had been waging a guerilla campaign against the Italians. The Australian unit, known as the First Light Horse Composite Regiment, was made up of all the Australian Light Horse Reinforcements under training and waiting deployment to Gallipoli and also those who, because of wounds or illness, had yet to return or those that had been left behind to watch the stores and equipment in Egypt. Despite being outnumbered, the Western Frontier Force was able to defeat the Senussi at Wadi Senba (11-13 December 1915), Wadi Majid (25 December 1915) and Halazin (23 January 1916), which reduced the threat the Senussi presented. The Australians then joined in the Sinai campaign.

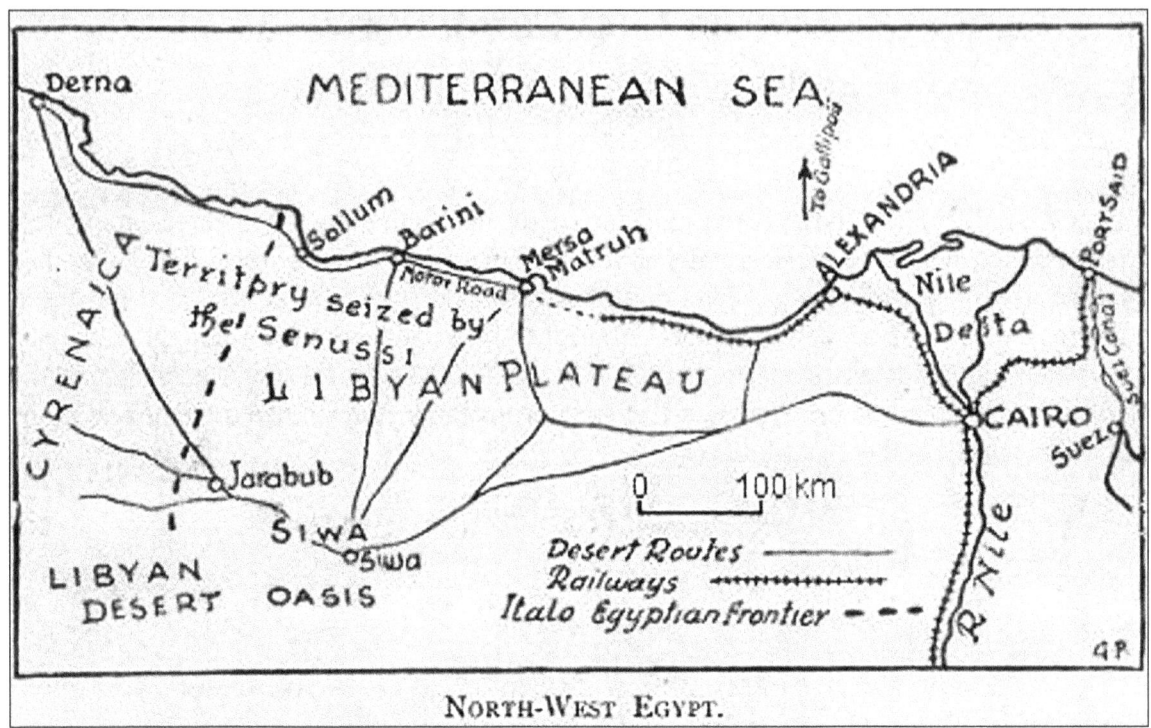

Western Desert campaign against the Senussi. An old map showing the borders between Egypt and Libya in 1915. Source: Serag Yehya M (2018), *Impact of politics on Urbanism - lessons from Egypt*

Sinai Peninsula

The first offensive action in Sinai by the Australian Light Horse was as the main combat element of a small British Imperial Force that made a long-range raid from 11-14 April 1916 to destroy water resources at the Turkish post at Jifjafa. They covered some 260 kilometres in three–and-a-half days over largely unknown territory, much of it by night. On their return to base they endured a fierce sand-storm and narrowly avoided a mass drowning, when the wadi in which troops were resting was flooded in a sudden downpour. During this action most of the force managed on less than 12 hours sleep.

The Jifjafa raid was the first demonstration in the Sinai campaign of a swift and successful attack across many kilometres of waterless desert by mounted troops, cooperating with Royal Flying Corps reconnaissance aircraft and logistically supported by the newly raised Camel Transport Corps. The Turks believed Jifjafa was beyond the striking range of British ground forces defending the Suez Canal and so it was only lightly garrisoned. From early April to mid-July 1916, British mounted troops, principally Australian Light Horse, conducted 16 of these operations with the strike force varying in size from one squadron to two brigades.

In August 1916 the Australian Light Horse went into combat as part of the British forces that defeated the Turks at Romani, a crucial group of oases in a great waste of sand dunes, and forced them back to the Gaza-Beersheba line. The Turks had been preparing a massive force for a second attack on the Suez Canal; their first one had failed.

On 22 December 1916 the ANZAC Mounted Division made a long, night ride and at dawn attacked the big Turkish post at Magdhaba. Unless it fell in one day they would be without water. Almost at sunset a retreat to water was ordered but they made a dismounted bayonet charge and took Magdhaba. Lack of water forced some to return to El Arish. During the long ride back, their third night in the saddle, guided by luminous compasses and the stars, the men slept with the reins thrown over the necks of the horses. Staggering into the camp, the horses showed their excellent memory of places by taking their riders back to the wells they already knew.

Two weeks later the same thing occurred in an almost identical attack at Rafa. Again almost at sunset, as a retreat to water was ordered, a final bayonet charge won the battle. Observers noted a remarkable thing. As the final charge of fiercely yelling troopers was almost on top of the trenches, the Turks dropped their guns and surrendered, but the Light Horsemen jumped down into the trenches and shook hands with the startled Turks. They were delighted not to have to kill the enemy they had learned to respect at Gallipoli. Their field ambulances treated friend and foe alike. In a letter home to his brother Les (June 1916), 'Gem' Stuart of the 3rd Light Horse Field Ambulance wrote:

The Turks are not altogether bad chaps and they fight very cleanly ...

The 1st Australian Light Horse Brigade passing over the steep sandhills at Esdud, January 1918. Source: AWM, No. B01510

Belah. An Australian Light Horse camp in the desert. Note rows of tents in the foreground. Source: AWM, No. B01615

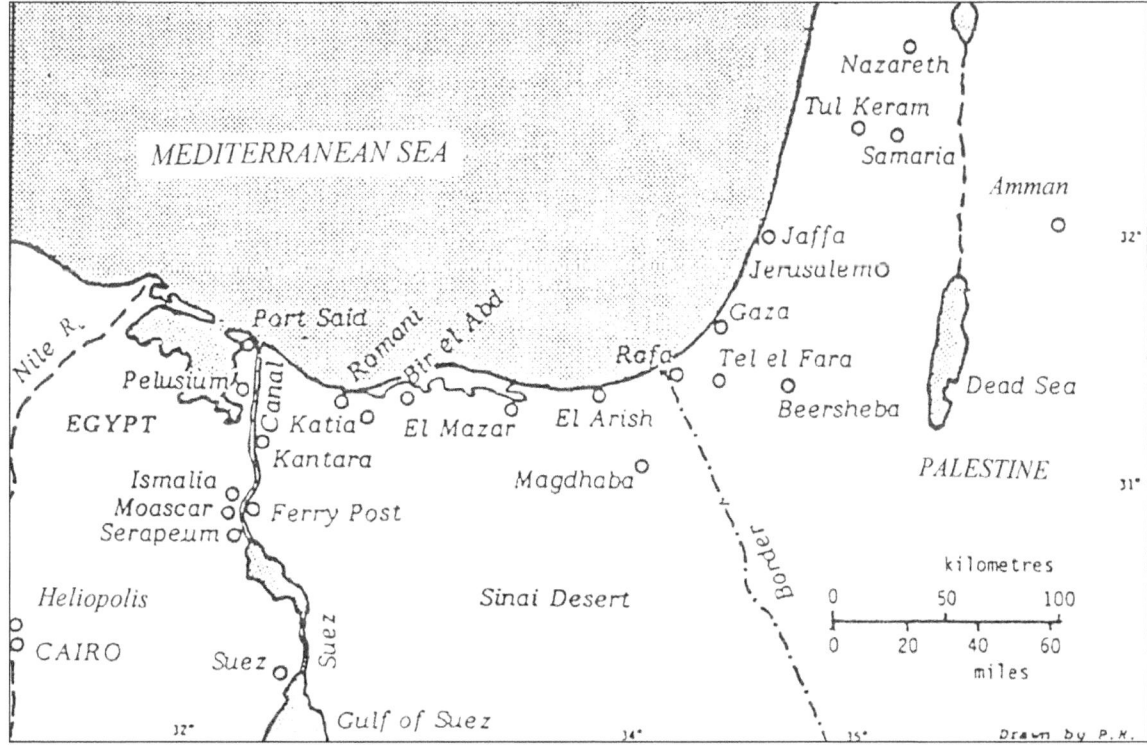

Egypt and Palestine. Source: Patrick M. Hamilton, *Riders of Destiny: the 4th Australian Lighthorse Field Ambulance 1917-1918 – an autobiography and history*, page 8

Gaza-Beersheba line. Source: Patrick M. Hamilton, *Riders of Destiny: the 4th Australian Lighthorse Field Ambulance 1917-1918 – an autobiography and history*, page 87, map 5

By early 1917 Sinai was cleared of all organised Turkish forces and the campaign to take Palestine began. The stronghold of Gaza dominated the southern coastal route into Palestine. A strong defensive line ran from Gaza on the coast to Beersheba. After two frontal attempts to take Gaza had failed (the First and Second Battles of Gaza), allied forces took it on the third attempt in early November 1917 after first attacking and taking Beersheba. It was on 31 October 1917 during the Third Battle of Gaza, that the 4th Light Horse Brigade made its famous mounted bayonet charge, the last great mounted charge in history.

The charge at Beersheba

Beersheba lay in a waterless area. The battle plan required a long over-night approach over waterless desert and capturing the town quickly with its wells intact or perish from thirst. It had to be taken in one day. The attack by British and ANZAC troops began at dawn and after a day of fierce fighting the battle was at a stalemate – the heavily manned trenches protecting the town remained intact. Time was running out. The Australian 4th Light Horse Brigade were ordered to make a desperate do-or-die frontal mounted attack. By then many of the horses had been without water for nearly 48 hours. General Grant said to his men: *Come on. We're going into Beersheba to water tonight.*

The 4th and 12th Regiments formed up behind a ridge from whose crest Beersheba was in full view. Their course lay down a long, slight slope that was bare of cover. The 800 Australian Light Horsemen moved off in a classic, three-line charge formation, going from walk-march, to trot then canter. They could see very little in the dust and the setting sun and were guided by the minaret of the mosque that still stands today.

The Turks held their fire, expecting the advancing 'infantrymen on horses' to dismount 600-700 metres from their trenches but the horsemen changed their tactics. To the Turks' surprise, about two kilometres from the trenches the troopers spurred their horses to a gallop. Shrouded in a cloud of dust and with wild yells and brandishing long bayonets drawn like swords flashing in the setting sun, the three thundering lines of Light Horsemen charged against the Turkish artillery, machine guns and armed trenches.

This photograph possibly represents a re-enactment of a charge for a cinematographer when a brigade was staged near Belah in February 1918. Source: AWM, No. P12049.007

Beersheba, Palestine, November 1917. Ambulances waiting in front of the town mosque to collect battle casualties from the local Turkish hospital which is out of sight. Source: AWM, No. P01668.004

Trooper Elliot, who had crept to a hillock within two miles (3.2 km) of Beersheba to act as range-finder for artillery, wrote:

> *It was the bravest, most awe-inspiring sight I've ever witnessed, and they were .. yelling, swearing and shouting. There were more than 500 Aussie horsemen ... As they thundered past my hair stood on end. The boys were wild-eyed and yelling their heads off.*

The Turkish artillery opened fire and shrapnel exploded above the plummeting lines of horsemen. Some were hit. However, the huge mass of horsemen thundering towards them unnerved the Turks, who failed to adjust their sights. Soon the shells were bursting behind the charge and the bullets were whistling harmlessly over the horsemen's heads. They jumped the trenches. As they did so the Turks thrust their bayonets up at the horses disemboweling some of them. Some horsemen leapt off their horses and fought with bayonet and pistol in ugly hand-to-hand fighting, while others rode on into the town.

After some bitter fighting Turkish resistance collapsed. Few casualties were incurred and most importantly 15 of the 17 wells, which had been prepared with explosives to be detonated if the town was captured, were still intact. The charge was incredibly successful. They were not fearless heroes. Trooper Vic Smith said:

> *Of course we were scared, wishing to hell we weren't there, but out of it. But you couldn't drop out and leave your mates to it; you had to keep going on.*

Although there was enough water at Beersheba to support the Allied mounted forces, they could mount only one-day operations until water supplies to the north were captured. They struck north-west from Beersheba through the villages of Jemmameh (al-Jammama) and Huj to the coast and finally, over-ran the Gaza-Beersheba line taking 12,000 Turkish prisoners. However, stubborn rear-guard action by the Turks delayed the Allied pursuit and saved their retreating army from encirclement and destruction.

Jerusalem by Christmas

After capturing Gaza they pursued the enemy northwards along the plains lying between a narrow coastal sandy belt and the Judean Hills. The objective was to take Jerusalem by Christmas. Cantering, trotting and walking, they travelled light. They found the going rough and were dogged by supply problems, particularly water; on one occasion horses went for 72 hours without water. Where possible, enemy positions were taken by manoeuvre. For example, at Latron on 18 November the 3rd Light Horse Brigade enveloped a strong enemy position, forcing the Turks to withdraw. They continued on up barren hills and across trackless rocky uplands of mountain country broken by steep ravines and stony valleys. Reaching Jaffa on 15 November they advanced inland to Jerusalem over hazardous rocky hills just as torrential rains began to fall. Mud hindered not only the animals but also vehicles as the only proper road turned to mud.

Only the 10th Light Horse Regiment took part in the final attack on Jerusalem, which was taken on 9 December 1917. The Desert Mounted Corps then rested and refitted. The horses of the Australian Mounted Division needed 10-days rest to recover their vigour after the exertions of the campaign; in addition boots and clothing were in a state of disrepair and guns needed overhauling. The men had been clothed and equipped for summer and found Jerusalem and the Judean hills in December and January bitterly cold. The ANZAC Mounted Division was re-equipped in January 1918 and the Australian Mounted Division in the following month.

Jordan Valley – Spring and summer 1918

In March and again in April 1918, two major raids were carried out across the Jordan River in attempts to destroy the railway at Amman. These tested both men and horses. The terrain was a maze of rocky mountains, where wheeled vehicles could not be used and horses and camels were restricted to goat tracks skirting precipices. In both instances they faced bitter rains, icy winds and slippery rocks and gorges raked by rifle and machine gun fire. In the first attempt in late March the town of Es Salt was captured but the garrison at Amman proved much too strong and troops were withdrawn. Another attempt was launched on 30 April 1918. The 3rd Australian Light Horse Brigade took Es Salt on 1 May but the Turks, who had been planning an attack, quickly reversed the situation. The Desert Mounted Corps withdrew across the Jordan two days later. Although both operations were tactical failures they helped to convince the Turks that the next major offensive would be launched across the Jordan.

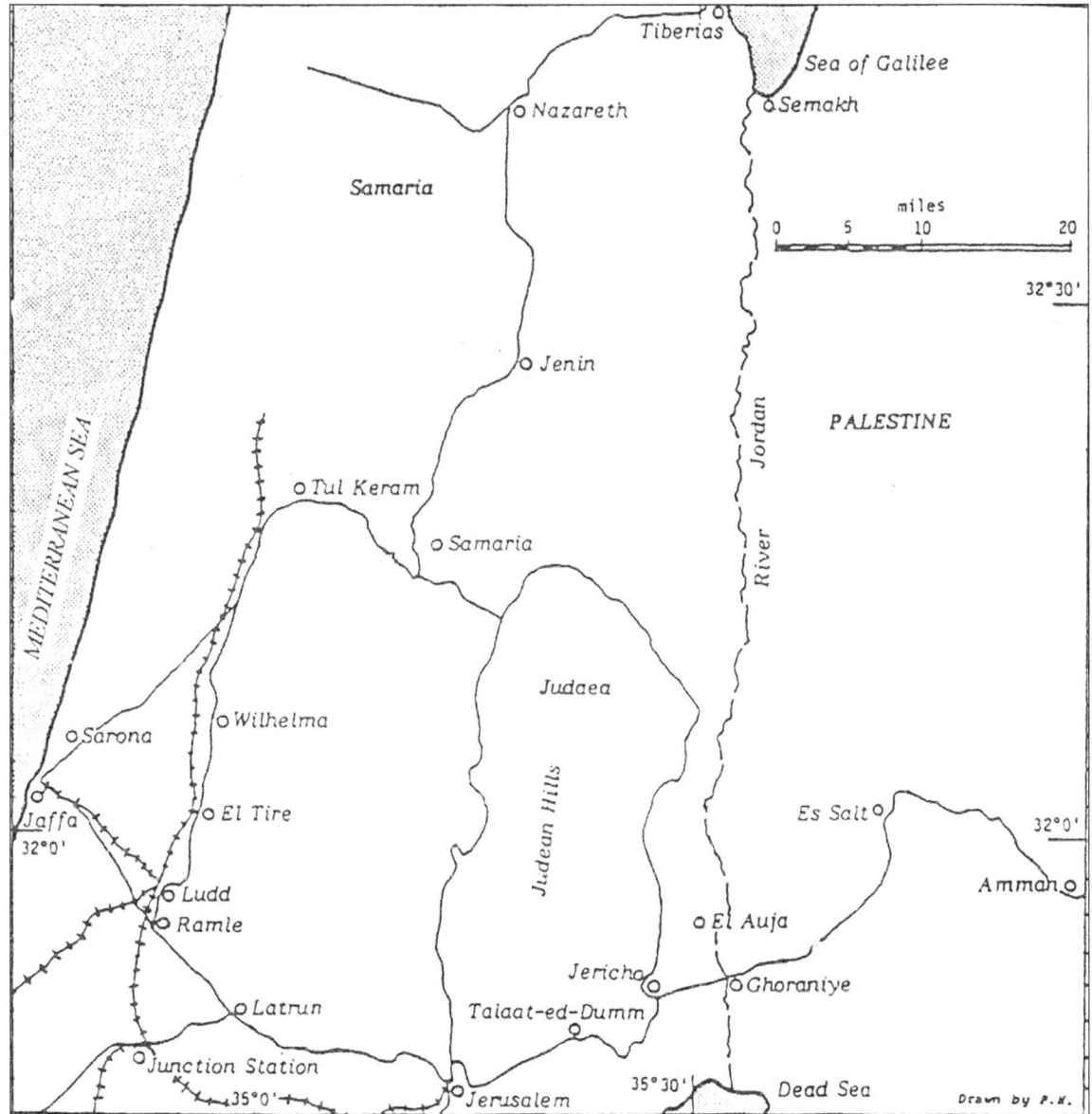

Palestine. Source: Patrick M. Hamilton, *Riders of Destiny: the 4th Australian Lighthorse Field Ambulance 1917-1918 – an autobiography and history*, page 116, map 7

The Light Horse spent the summer in the Jordan Valley, which now had turned into a humid, dust-laden oven crawling with snakes, spiders, scorpions and malaria-carrying mosquitoes. In mid-July the Desert Mounted Corps repulsed a strong attack spearheaded by the German Asia Corps. Like the Australians in France, the Light Horsemen did not give up their positions simply because they were surrounded. This was the first and only time German troops were employed as storm-troops in the Palestine campaign.

Camp at the foot of the Judaean Hills in the Jordan Valley, near Jericho. Source: Frank Hurley (1917-1918), State Library of NSW

Jordan Valley, Palestine, ca. 1917. An Australian Light Horse unit raising dust on the move. Source: AWM, No. H02984 (Donor J. Campbell)

Damascus – 'The Wild Ride'

The final Palestine campaign to take Damascus and drive the Turks from Palestine and Syria was launched in September 1918. The plan was to surprise the Turks by attacking along the coast, while all the time making it appear the main attack would be from the east. The infantry was to open a gap in Turkish lines through which the Desert Mounted Corps would pass and ride north along the Plain of Sharon before turning inland, cross the Judean Hills and on to the Plain of Esdraelon, capture El Afule and Beisan and block the Turks' retreat. To achieve maximum surprise, preparations were made in great secrecy and much effort put into deceiving the enemy. The bulk of their forces were kept in the east as long as possible. Without control of the air this deception would not have been possible.

In great secrecy, three cavalry divisions including the Australian Mounted Division, now armed with swords, were moved to the coastal flank. They did so at night, leaving their tents standing and dummy horses made from wooden frames and sticks in their old lines. Horses and men were hidden in olive and citrus groves north of Jaffa near Ludd. Only the ANZAC Mounted Division remained on the Jordan. They had the job of making it appear that the big push would come eastwards from the Jordan Valley.

Supplies for each man consisted of two-days rations, one emergency quota and two-days rations per horse. Everything was done to spare the horses any extra weight. Speed was important. Damascus had to be reached before rains expected in early November turned dust into mud and before malaria took its toll.

At dawn on 19 September 1918 the main attack in the west began. It was a complete success. The two cavalry divisions and the Australian Mounted Division rode through the gap opened in the enemy's line and continued northwards up the coastal plain before turning inland. By next morning Beisen, Nazareth and El Afule were occupied. By noon the 3rd Australian Light Horse Brigade had captured Jenin. After a sharp fight at Semakh on 24 September, the 4th Australian Light Horse Brigade advanced to Tiberias. During 25 and 26 September the Australian Mounted Division and 5th Cavalry Division concentrated at Tiberias in preparation for the advance on Damascus. The Australians took the opportunity to freshen up both themselves and their horses by swimming in the Sea of Gallilee (Lake Tiberias).

From Tiberias the final dash to Damascus was made in two converging lines. One was direct from Beisen to Deraa, towards which the remains of a Turkish Army were approaching with the Arabs in pursuit. The relentless bombing by the Australian-piloted planes allowed the Arab irregulars to keep on the track to Deraa. When they arrived there, the Arabs started an orgy of killing unarmed and wounded Turks.

The other was direct to Damascus. The 3rd Australian Light Horse Brigade led this advance. North of Lake Gallilee it forded the Jordan River where the water came only up to the horses' bellies and set out on its task of getting there ahead of the sick and starving remains of the Turkish armies, that were fighting a bitter rear-guard action. Sore feet and the terrain on the road to Damascus slowed the horses down, giving the Turks an advantage. Then the dreaded malaria began to affect troops, earlier than expected. Some men, delirious with fever, began falling from their saddles.

On the evening of 30 September the 3rd Light Horse Brigade reached Damascus. At 5.00 am next morning they entered the city ahead of any other allied troops. Soon after 7.00 am they had left and were in vigorous pursuit of the enemy. Colonel Lawrence (of Arabia), to whom history has accorded the honour, with an Arab escort did not enter until a few minutes before 8.00 am. The official historian wrote:

> *The Australians on this wonderful morning were the only calm, purposeful men in the clamorous city. Years of campaigning had moulded them into reserved*

men of the world, and the streets of old Damascus were but a stage in the long path of war. They rode with drawn swords, dusty and unshaven, their big hats battered and drooping, through the excited people of the ancient city, with the same easy casual bearing, and the same quiet self-confidence, which mark their bearing on their country tracks at home. They ate their grapes, and smoked their cigars, and missed no dark smiling eyes at the windows; but they showed no excitement or elation. And their lean, long-tailed horses, at home now like their riders on any road in the world, found nothing in the shouting mob or banging rifles of the Arabs, or in the narrow ways and vivid hues of the bazaars, to cause them once to shy or even cock an ear.

Between 19 September 1918 and 2 October 1918 the Australian Light Horse Division captured 31,335 prisoners.

On 5 October an epidemic of malaria and influenza suddenly broke out. Soldiers, who had gone through battles unscathed, collapsed into makeshift hospitals and then into graves. While the casualty rate during the advance was low, effects of disease were horrific. The wave of Spanish flu accompanied by malaria put nearly half the Desert Mounted Corps out of action. Almost four times as many horsemen died in the cramped unhealthy dormitories of Damascus as had been killed on the advance.

On 27 October the Australian Mounted Division left Damascus. It reached Homs on 1 November, the day after the granting of an armistice with Turkey. After a few days at Homs it moved to Tripoli, where it remained until the final move to Egypt.

Damascus Incident, Power H. Septimus. Depicts the 3rd Australian Light Horse Brigade advancing on Damascus.

With drawn swords they rushed forward towards Damascus. More terrifying than the speed was the noise. It could be heard in the city as it rolled ahead of them. … Not only their speed but also the sight of the great Australian horses coming at a gallop, the flashing swords and the ring of shoes upon the metal, was impressive and helped subject the populace.

Source: AWM, No. ART03647

The Capture of Damascus. The advance guard of the 3rd Australian Light Horse Brigade swept into Damascus on the morning of 1 October 1918. Majors Olden and Timberly of the 10th A.L.H. Regiment demanded to see the Civil Governor and formerly accepted the surrender of the city. They then continued their gallop straight through in pursuit of the fleeing Turks and Germans. Lawrence with Sherifan (Arab) troops arrived some hours later – by that time the 3rd A.L.H. Brigade had come and gone. Source: New South Wales Lancers Memorial Museum Incorporated, lancers.org.au

The Desert Mounted Corps Memorial stands near the summit of Mt Clarence, Albany, Western Australia.

The memorial originally stood in Port Said, Egypt, until it was damaged in anti-British riots during the Suez Crisis of 1956. Albany is also linked with the corps by the fact that the ANZAC mounted units left Australia from there in November 1914.

The memorial is a 9-metre bronze statue of an Australian mounted soldier assisting a New Zealand soldier, whose horse has been wounded. In 1916, Brigadier General J.R. Royston, commander of the 3rd Australian Light Horse Brigade, suggested that a memorial be erected at Port Said in honour of Australian and New Zealand mounted soldiers killed in the Sinai-Palestine Campaign.

Source: Grant65, Wikimedia Commons

Chapter 18
Australian Light Horse

Light horsemen cum airmen

Some Light Horsemen exchanged horses for aircraft and played an important part in enabling the ground forces to operate practically unmolested by hostile aircraft, especially in the lead-up to the thrust to take Damascus. This included considerable support for Lawrence and the Arabs.

The Australian Flying Corps recruited heavily from the Light Horse. It was felt their horse-riding abilities gave them a natural advantage in flying and with their knowledge of the desert they could also recognise the difference between a retreating and advancing force. It was also felt that recruiting Light Horse officers as observers would increase the operational efficiency of both the Australian Flying Corps and the Australian Light Horse. The most distinguished of the recruits was Ross Smith, a member of No. 1 Squadron, which carried out a lot of Lawrence's requested bombing raids, helping bolster the tenuous support of the Arabs.

Paddy McGuiness and Hudson Fysh, who founded QANTAS, were Light Horsemen, who became pilots after Gallipoli.

General Sir Harry Chevaulle [i.e. Chauvel] inspecting the 1st Squadron A.F.C. at the Medjdel aerodrome, January 1918. Photographer Frank Hurley (1885-1962). Source: Mitchell Library, State Library of New South Wales

In Palestine flying operations were not straight-forward and specialised like they were on the Western Front. The Australian Squadron was required to do many missions that were unthought of in France, such as landing behind enemy lines and blowing up a water channel or cutting telegraph wires. The airmen of 1 Squadron also had to be an escort, undertake reconnaissance and be a bomber in the one mission, and often a ferry plane as well. The mechanics kept the planes in the air through their skill and ingenuity, despite the lack of parts, equipment and harsh conditions on the plane and engine, such as the ever-present sand.

The light horsemen

They were called 'Light Horse' to distinguish them from the 'Heavy Horse' that was still in favour in some circles of the British Army. The Australian Light Horse soldiers were actually mounted infantry. They differed from cavalry in that they usually fought dismounted, using their horses as transport to the battlefield and as a means of swift disengagement when retreating or retiring.

The Light Horsemen were not armed with swords because it was considered the weight of the weapon was not worth the remote prospects of its use. The sword and scabbard weighed some 2 kg and the rifle bucket on the other side, needed to balance the load on the horse, another 1.4 kg not normally needed by the Light Horsemen, who slung their rifles on their backs. Encouraging outcomes of mounted actions by British cavalry after Beersheba resulted in re-equipping the Australian Mounted Division with swords in July 1918. However, the ANZAC Mounted Division remained mounted infantry to the end.

Apart from his imposing mount, the Light Horseman's uniform differed only slightly from that of the common soldier's drab khaki, namely, by the addition of polished leather accoutrements and spurs. The slouch hat was often adorned with a most distinctive embellishment – the emu feather plume. This plume became the symbol of the Light Horse.

Men of the original (1st) Light Horse Regiment at Roseberry Park Camp, NSW, before departure from Australia. Source: AWM, No. J00450

Studio portrait of 2436 Private (Pte) Harry C. Murray, 11th Light Horse Regiment. Source: AWM, No. P00889.004

The image of the Light Horsemen differed somewhat from their fellow diggers. Official historian, H.S. Gullet, described them as:

> ... in body and spirit the true product of the Australian countryside ... the very flower of their race.

He considered the Light Horsemen had been bestowed with a certain 'native' quality, forged from Australia's pioneering heritage. David Barker, a Light Horseman and well-known WWII illustrator, often portrayed his fellow troopers appearing 'very sure of themselves', at times almost cocky, or verging on the larrikin, their hats at a jaunty angle and appearing nothing less than the epitome of their hardened 'colonial' background.

Australian troopers seemed almost as much at home in the desert as the Bedouin, the Arab nomads. Survival in the bush brought out 'making the best of it' skills such as resourcefulness, independence and 'mateship' – sticking with your mates through thick and thin. It also gave them field craft: a good eye, together with the ability to judge distance, time and space, an appreciation of how the land as a whole lies, etc. It gave them a practical bent. So in the desert they tied corks to hats with string to keep off the flies and were indifferent to snakes, spiders, huge centipedes and scorpions. When water was short, instead of washing knives, forks etc. in soap and water, they cleaned them with dirt or sand.

Spear pump at Zilzie. Source: Peter Hasker

The shortage of water was a continual problem for both men and horses. Introduction of the spear-point pump to tap water in the desert partly overcame this problem. It was a 2.5-inch (6.35 cm) steel tube with a solid point at one end and a section with holes covered by wire gauze to keep out the sand that was driven into the ground with a sledgehammer or a makeshift pile driver. Water flowed within the few minutes it took to set up canvas troughs. It could be retrieved and reused. A single horse could carry the whole apparatus easily. The pump saved time and work and greatly increased flexibility of movement. It enabled Light Horse patrols to operate deep into the desert in the region just east of the Suez Canal. However, it was impractical to try to water the entire force in Egyptian Sinai in this manner. Lieutenant Colonel L.C. Wilson of the 5th Light Horse Regiment, who had seen spear-point pumps used in Queensland before the war, was responsible for this example of Australian resourcefulness and initiative. In my childhood, a spear pump and windmill only about 50 metres from the high water mark of Zilzie beach supplied our beach house with fresh water.

The horses

The majority of horses and mules used over the three-year campaign passed under the control of Major A.B. 'Banjo' Patterson. Patterson's prose and poetry had brought the ethos of the Australian bush to a wide and varied audience. His poems became national symbols of the bush, idealizing it for the town dweller. Except for *The Army Mules*, he wrote little during this period that became well known. The gruesome reality of being with an advancing army did not give him the inspiration his beloved bush had.

Patterson, born in 1864 and the son of a station owner, falsified his birth date by two years to be accepted for military service. He had been working as a solicitor in Sydney and spent most of his leisure time with horses. His passion for horses was supported by sound theoretical and practical knowledge. His mastery in the training and care of horses enhanced the performance of the British forces in the Middle East. Patterson arrived in Suez in December 1915 and he and his unit took charge of the horses of the Light Horsemen, who were away fighting at Gallipoli. When the battered remnants of that army returned to Egypt after the evacuation, Paterson followed them through Palestine and Syria.

The horses were constantly on the move, carrying loads of 120 kg or more. Water was always brackish and scarce and rations often insufficient. At the end of a hot day's march, tied to a picket rope, they were exposed to the sun and wind and the dreaded sandstorm. The

Chapter 18: Australian Light Horse

The 1st Australian Light Horse Brigade horses at water. Source: AWM, No. B01490

charge at Beersheba was made over rough ground and across 20 enemy trenches; many of the horses had been without water for 52 hours before they drank at the wells.

The common mount for the Light Horseman was the Waler, an Australian working horse breed. Originally known as *New South Walers,* they combined a variety of breeds brought to the Australian colonies in the 1800s. Bred in the Australian outback, the Waler was a hardy animal with great endurance, even when wasted from lack of food and water. It was used as a stockman's horse and prized as a military remount. Walers had also been used by exploration expeditions that had traversed inland Australia.

The Waler was especially suited to working in the harsh climate of the Sinai Peninsula and Palestine, where it proved superior to the camel as a means of transporting large bodies of troops. The gait of the Waler was considered ideal for a cavalry mount. It could maintain a fast walk and could progress directly to a steady, level canter without resorting to a trot, which was noisy, liable to dislodge gear and resulted in soreness in the horse's back.

Of the tens of thousands of horses used by the allies, the ones ridden by the Australians had the lowest rate of sore backs. In contrast to the British, who usually rode at a trot through the desert sands, the Australians preferred a fast walk. This is not a natural step; it has to be patiently taught and requires sensitive hands.

The soldiers developed very close relationships with their horses. A soldier's horse was much more than something to carry him into battle. It was a 'mate'. Through suffering and deprivation, a bond developed between man and beast, a feeling of affection and trust, a real partnership. Once mounted on a good horse a trooper did everything to keep it. The trooper soon found that to have a good horse evacuated sick behind the lines meant that someone else would acquire it. Thus he went to great lengths to prevent his charger being declared unfit for duty. On the other hand a trooper, who found himself landed with a bad one, made sure that something happened to it as soon as possible. My mother told the story about a very recalcitrant horse remount that was to be destroyed. It was a very large and particularly fine looking animal. When 'Gem' Stuart heard about its intended fate, he attempted to master it. He galloped it out into the desert sands and finally returned successful. This horse, admired by all, served him faithfully for the rest of the war.

During rests away from lines and also after the Armistice, race meetings were held and the pick of these battle-trained horses competed favourably with local Egyptian horses and with other thoroughbred horses. At the Victory Meeting at Heliopolis in May 1919, horses from the ANZAC Mounted Division won five of the six events. At one such horse show and sports 'Gem' Stuart won the officers' jumping competition.

Some men and horses were together all through the war; others, who had shipped their own horses from Australia, for longer. During the many months of fighting many men dreamt of going home with their horses and being cheered while riding them in a triumphal march in Sydney or Melbourne, but that was not to be. Reasons given were not enough ships, the price of transport and Australia's strict quarantine regulations. Most of the horses were sold to the British Army as remounts for Egypt and India. Horses that had escaped slaughter by war were also auctioned to the highest bidder. An estimated 22,000 English, Indian and Australian horses were sold to Egyptians.

Australian Mounted Division, Horse Show and Sports, Palestine. Officers' Jumping Competition, won by Lt. Col. 'Gem' Stuart, 3rd A.L.H.F.A. Presented by General W. Grant D.S.O. Pine cone presumably from the Middle East. Source: Bill Hasker

In his account of the 3rd Light Horse Field Ambulance 'Gem' Stuart wrote:

> *... before leaving Tripoli, we had to get rid of our horses; These according to classification were either handed over to Imperial Units or destroyed & the destruction will be passed over with only this remark, that many of the men found it impossible to lead their own horses up to be shot, and got outsiders, as it were, to do it for them.*

When Dorothy Brooke, the wife of a former commander of cavalry in Egypt, visited Cairo in 1930, she saw broken down old horses with the arrow-shaped British brands still visible on their mangy flanks being forced by the lash to haul heavy loads, slowly being worked to death. She began an Old War Horse Fund and raised enough money to buy 56,000 horses 'sold into bondage in a foreign land'.

Parting with their Walers was one of the hardest events the Light Horsemen had to endure. A poem by 'Trooper Bluegum' sums up the men's sentiment:

> *I don't think I could stand the thought of my old fancy hack*
> *Just crawling round old Cairo with a 'Gyppo on his back.*
> *Perhaps some English tourist out in Palestine may find*
> *My broken-hearted Waler with a wooden plough behind.*

> *No: I think I'd better shoot him and tell a little lie:--*
> *'He floundered in a wombat hole and then lay down to die.'*
> *Maybe I'll get court-martialled; but I'm damned if I'm inclined*
> *To go back to Australia and leave my horse behind.*

Only one Waler is known to have been returned to Australia, Sandy, the mount of Major General W.T. Bridges, who died at Gallipoli in May 1915. In 1950, a memorial to the approximately

140,000 horses that served in the Desert Campaign in WWII was erected outside the Royal Botanic Gardens in Sydney. It consists of a long bronze relief of three horses, ammunition pouches around their necks, being led over the sand dunes by an Australian Light Horse Trooper.

The inscriptions on the left and right read:

> *Erected by members of The Desert Mounted Corps and friends to the Gallant Horses who carried them over Sinai Desert into Palestine 1915 – 1918. They suffered wounds, thirst, hunger and weariness. Almost beyond endurance but never failed.*
>
> *They did not come home. We will never forget them.*

Desert Mounted Corps memorial, Sydney. Source: Gail Strong

Chapter 19
Light Horse Field Ambulance

An important element in the success of the Light Horse was the efficient, highly mobile medical support of its three field ambulances, whose purpose was to provide medical transport and aid to the wounded and sick soldiers of a Light Horse Brigade. Unlike mounted units in the British and other Dominion armies, the primary medical personnel of the Light Horse Field Ambulances were fully mounted. Stretcher-bearers were able to keep up with the Light Horse. They ensured the removal of the wounded from the front line or regimental aid posts to an advanced dressing station, at which there were surgical and resting tents.

Typically an ambulance was commanded by a Lieutenant Colonel. All officers of the ambulance were medical doctors or surgeons. Dental units were often attached to the ambulance as well. The ambulance was divided into two sections, referred to as the Mobile Section and the Immobile Section. The role of the Mobile Section was to travel with the brigade into combat, establish a Dressing Station, retrieve the wounded by stretcher or cart and transport them to the Dressing Station. The role of the Immobile Section was to establish and operate a Receiving Station, to which wounded were dispatched from the Dressing Station. The ambulance's surgeons would operate on the wounded at the Receiving Station. From the Receiving Station, sick and wounded were evacuated firstly to the Casualty Clearing Station and ultimately to a Base Hospital.

A number of different methods were used for transporting the wounded. 'Sand carts', which could carry two or three stretchers, were two-wheeled vehicles with wide metal treads drawn by four horses. They proved very effective in the Sinai, despite numerous defects in early models, resulting in broken wheels and axles. A second method of carrying the wounded was by camel, in devices known as 'cacolets', horizontal platforms suspended from either side

Middle East, ca. 1917. A camel fitted with a cacolet designed to carry wounded in a prone position. Source: AWM, No. H02808 (Donor J. Hunter)

Chapter 19: Light Horse Field Ambulance

A horse-drawn sand sledge designed for use in the desert during the Sinai campaign, ca. 1917.
Source: AWM, No. H00789

Walk (An incident at Romani), 1919-1922 by George W. Lambert.

At the Battle of Romani on 4 August 1916, two sand carts of the 2nd Light Horse Field Ambulance were sent to bring in severely wounded men from an exposed part of the line. On the return journey a Turkish battery fired at them, whereupon the horses immediately tried to break into a gallop. The corporal, remembering the wounded, signalled 'walk' and, galloping to the head of the party, helped to steady the team. The horses resumed the regulation pace, and the enemy gunners, apparently recognising their mission, turned their fire elsewhere. The corporal and drivers were awarded the Military Medal for their gallant behaviour.

Lambert portrayed the moment when the four horses pulling the two-wheeled ambulance cart break into a gallop, with dust flying up behind them and a rider galloping up beside the cart to pull them up.

Source: National Gallery of Australia

of the camel's saddle, to which the wounded were strapped facing forward. Unfortunately, as the camel moved, the cacolet would bounce about, sometimes sufficiently to cause the passenger to vomit. Camels were slow, moving on average only two-and-a-half miles an hour. They also attracted flies that could spread bacteria from the camel's digestive tract to hastily dressed wounds. A better solution was the 'sand sledge'. Drawn by two horses, these provided a comfortable means of transport for the seriously wounded.

The 3rd Light Horse Field Ambulance

My mother's oldest brother, 'Gem' Stuart, a medical graduate from Melbourne University, was attached to the Third Light Horse Field Ambulance with the rank of Captain, when it was formed in Victoria in 1914. At the time he had been acting as a medical officer at Broadmeadows. In 1917 he took over command of the Ambulance. The quotations that follow in this section about the Field Ambulance are from his account of the Ambulance.

On its formation the Ambulance's commanding officer was Lieutenant Colonel R.M. Downes. Downes was a demonstrator in anatomy at the University and a tutor at Ormond, and worked as a clinical surgical assistant at the Melbourne and Children's hospitals. He led it on Gallipoli and, when the ANZAC Mounted Division was formed in March 1916, became its Assistant Director of Medical Services (senior medical officer). When the Desert Mounted Corps was organised in August 1917, he was appointed its Deputy Director of Medical Services.

Downes was an innovator. He introduced the sand sledge and the concept of having mobile sections of the Ambulance, which could move close to the battle, while the immobile tented sections, some distance back, provided more extensive treatment in safer conditions. He also created a mobile surgical unit. During the battle for Es Salt in May 1918, he delivered medical supplies by dropping them from aircraft.

In the advance to Damascus in September 1918 Downes' medical arrangements were stretched to the limit. Then in Damascus, malaria struck the weary troops by the thousand. Downes and his medical units also had to cope with the great influenza epidemic and with thousands of sick and wounded prisoners. Almost all of the medical officers, including Downes, were stricken with malaria but with immense determination he stayed at his post.

On arrival in Egypt the Ambulance went to Mena, where its time was taken up with drill and sightseeing and then moved to Heliopolis. At Mena they got their first taste of the discomforts caused by sand and the 'Khamseen', a vicious hot south-westerly wind.

The whole desert appeared to be lifted up bodily and hurled forward at an enormous velocity and the feelings and tempers of all were sorely tried. Eyes, throats, ears and every other organ of the body seemed to be full of sand and life at Mena during a Khamseen was far from pleasant.

The Ambulance, less its transport section which remained in Heliopolis, accompanied the unmounted 3rd Light Horse Brigade to Gallipoli in May 1915. The Ambulance was carried on the final leg of its journey to ANZAC Cove by the motor torpedo destroyer *Wolverdine*.

The crew of the Wolverdine *were kindness itself to all of us, and one of the officers remarked that it was their duty to do everything for us as we were regarded as food for guns.*

However, it did not begin serving the 3rd Light Horse Brigade until late August and so was not with it during its suicidal attack at The Nek. The Ambulance spent July in Lemnos and was the last ambulance to leave the Peninsula, being evacuated on 16 December.

Chapter 19: Light Horse Field Ambulance

In November 1915 a unit, the First Light Horse Composite Regiment, was formed to operate against hostile Senussi tribesmen in Western Egypt, with operations based at Matruh. 'Gem' Stuart was appointed as the regiment's medical officer. All medical personnel were drawn from the 3rd Light Horse Field Ambulance members remaining at Heliopolis.

At the end of January 1916 the Ambulance moved with the Brigade to Serapeun on the Suez Canal. By then the scattered sections of the Ambulance had been reunited and reorganised. While there it accompanied the Brigade in three expeditions or 'stunts' across the Sinai desert during the first half of 1916, the second of which was the Jifjafa raid.

After the Jifjafa raid 'Gem' Stuart met up with his brother Peter, who left shortly after for the Western Front with the 4th AIF Division. This was the last time 'Gem' saw him.

Sand, flies and lack of water were big factors to be overcome on operations in the Sinai Peninsula.

There one could never get away from it, sand appeared on all sides as far as the eye could reach and the rays of a merciless sun forever beat down. Water more often than not was at a premium and it was here that one learnt to the full how necessary it was to control one's thirst. Very often a single water bottle had to suffice for a period sometimes extending to 48 hours and only those who have experienced this can fully understand what it means.

After spending all night in the saddle it was no pleasant matter in the morning to be greeted by the intense heat of the sun coupled with heavy sand blowing in all directions. At this time and right through the desert campaigning, eye trouble was very prevalent and it was almost an impossibility to ride at day without goggles. Further the flies were an intolerable nuisance and fly veils were almost next door to a necessity ...

Finding one's way in the desert was a challenge. The sandhills in this region were extremely steep and difficult to negotiate and a large body of troops could easily pass by unnoticed.

It is great credit to the drivers and bearers of the Ambulance that they soon adapted themselves to the desert, travelling over new tracts of it during both day and night, and not one instance of them losing their way is recorded. It is the same common sense that played such a large part in the success of the Australians in the Sinai campaign.

In August 1916 the Ambulance accompanied the Brigade during its Romani operations.

Throughout the Romani fighting your saddle constituted your home, as when not using it for its specific purpose, you always slept by it at night in order to be close handy in the event of a quick move out.

On 15 August 1916 Major W.A. Fraser took over command of the Ambulance. Coincidence knows no bounds. On moving to Brisbane to live after my discharge from hospital following my horse accident the general practitioner we attended, John Fraser, turned out to be W.A. Fraser's son. John Fraser became a good friend of the family but unfortunately none of us ever engaged in any discussion with him about Light Horse matters.

'Gem' Stuart notes that in September 1916 the Brigade conducted a number of small operations which he refers to as the 'Mazar stunts'. They involved treks of 48 km to and from the site of action and taxed the provision of supplies, particularly water, to the limit. It was also on these operations that Downes' sledges were first used by the Ambulance. Stuart noted that Downes had begun building and experimenting with a sled during the previous April and considered they were unsurpassed for the transport of cases such as fractures of the thigh, until they moved completely off sandy country.

At El Arish they encountered a new torment – dust. All sides were unanimous in that it was infinitely better to be on sand than firmer country, where dust was prevalent in good weather and mud in bad weather. On the morning of the battle after the night ride to Magdhaba it was very difficult to recognise anyone, as all were smothered in dust from head to foot.

> *From El Arish on, it was a regular thing to find yourself at dawn absolutely covered in dust after a night ride.*

At Shellal the dust nuisance was extremely bad and all-day-long clouds of dust passed through the camps. Throughout the Gaza-Beersheba operations dust caused great inconvenience when on the move and at times parties found it difficult to keep in touch. When the dust combined with the darkness of the nights:

> *... it was essential to keep the nose of your horse right up against the tail of the horse immediately in your front otherwise it was an impossibility to keep in touch with your unit.*

> *But the climax occurred when the Jordan Valley was reached and to fully appreciate the dust there one has only to live with horses in the valley a few days. Most of the tracks leading through were inches well nigh feet deep in dust and to travel in a column along any of them was nothing short of hell.*

> *The dust was of a very fine nature, similar to powdered chalk, and seemed to hang in the air and one felt a feeling akin to suffocation when passing through it. This also affected the horses and, though you might groom for hours, the dust could never be quite got out of them.*

> *In some of our camps large distances had to be traversed taking the horses to water and as this occurred twice a day, the dust made the ride most unpleasant and very hard on the personnel which, at this time, was at a very low ebb due to sickness.*

> *... no one will ever forget the trials and tribulations suffered through these causes and of all the places we have been in, Jordan Valley and Shellal stand on their own and one would almost prefer paying a visit to hell than return, under similar conditions as prevailed in the past, to either of these spots.*

Stuart gives an indication of the hard riding undertaken by the Light Horsemen in the Sinai-Palestine campaigns in remarks about the third night of the Magdhaba action and the subsequent Rafa operation.

> *Owing to the loss of sleep the two previous nights all found it very hard to remain awake and, almost without exception, everyone at some time or other that night found themselves dozing in the saddle. Repeatedly, men would shoot out in front of the unit and wake up with a start to find themselves among strangers. Only those who have experienced this can fully realize what a mighty unpleasant thing it is to fight against sleep on a night ride. To add to the discomfort, we were being initiated into our first experience of dust which arose in dense clouds the whole night through.*

> *About 100 wounded, some seriously, had to be recovered and treated and it wasn't until the morning of 25 December that the last patient arrived back at the Receiving Station established at El Arish. Over the five nights of the operation, 20-25 December 1916, the unit had practically no sleep.*

Regarding the Rafa action he wrote:

> *The whole stunt, from leaving Masaid until our return there, was most trying and strenuous both for man and horse. Some of the personnel were without sleep for*

periods up to 66 hours and a considerable portion of this time was spent in the saddle. One team alone covered a distance of over 100 miles in 56 hours and most of this was through sandy desert country.

After the First Battle of Gaza the Ambulance lost its way in the night-time withdrawal, resulting in it being the last unit to cross recently occupied enemy territory. The 3rd Light Horse Brigade, which had withdrawn sometime previously, was surprised to see them, presuming they had reached their destination a long time previously.

Transporting the sick and wounded was an ongoing challenge for the ambulances. Not only were resources limited but also the terrain hampered movement. The rough hilly country and wadis took their toll of wheeled transport. Camels were slow and unsuited to harder country.

The Second Battle of Gaza (19 April 1917) resulted in high numbers of casualties and all available transport was required to convey the wounded from the firing line to the temporary dressing station. Because the dressing station was continually under very heavy shell fire and bombing, sand carts had to be requisitioned to send patients on to the collecting station as quickly as possible. This overtaxed the remaining transport working from the firing line. In some instances, as many as nine patients were brought in on one cart whereas three constituted a normal load. They were continually under rifle and shell fire in addition to bombing. The average distance from the regimental aid posts to the temporary dressing station was about a kilometre and a similar distance existed between the dressing station and the collecting station. This problem of insufficient transport was partly overcome subsequently with the introduction of motor vehicles.

Several days after the fall of Beersheba the Brigade and the Ambulance retired to Karm. This occurred at night across unknown country intersected with numerous wadis. The loose nature of the soil and the close atmospheric conditions caused a heavy cloud of dust to hang over the Brigade. This, plus the darkness of the night, made it impossible for the rear section of horsemen to see the section in their immediate front. The transport became separated owing to the impassable crossings of the wadi but, except for the water cart, managed to rejoin the column. A man accompanying the camels and a donkey he was riding fell down a 'cistern'; both were rescued without injury. A little further on a sick camel, which was being led, had to be dug out, when it fell into a Turkish dugout. Then a water cart tipped over in a wadi and had to be emptied of its valuable contents and considerable trouble experienced before the party could continue the journey.

These challenges had to be overcome. It was an ambulance's job to keep up with the fighting force, the wheeled transport swaying and bumping along, and deal with the casualties. In other words,

> : *... where there is action the carts must go ...*

During December (winter) the Ambulance accompanied the Brigade, less the 10th Light Horse Regiment, in operations in the Judaean Hills on the slow push forward from Burj to Khurbetha El Harith. The 10th had joined the British force advancing on Jerusalem. Cold, wet weather made conditions trying for man and beast.

Living conditions during this period were severe. Supplies were erratic. Tents were rotten or worn and bivouac sheets were unavailable and there was no change of clothing:

> *... the Brigade and Ambulance resembled tramps in extremis. ... Xmas day spent in the Judean Hills will be remembered ...; a dinner of bully beef and biscuits (nothing hot not even tea) much rain and no shelter ....*

Horses developed foot rot from standing in the rain and mud. Because of the inability at times of getting wheeled transport sufficiently forward, camels were relied on for front-line

Officers of the 3rd Australian Light Horse Brigade Field Ambulance.

Left to right: Lieutenant Colonel G.E.M. Stuart DSO CO, 3rd Australian Light Horse Field Ambulance; Captain (Capt) Nelson; Capt Farrowridge; Capt Trembath; Capt Quinlan; Capt Molesworth; Major Clarke, second in command. Source: AWM, No. B00801

Deir-El-Belah, Palestine, ca. 1917. Group portrait of officers of the 3rd Australian Light Horse Field Ambulance (ALHFA) sitting in front of a tree.

Left to right: back row: Captain (Capt) William George Tregear, Capt Andrew Bernard Morris and Capt James Eustace Shelly.
Middle row: Capt Henry George Leahy, a doctor, Capt Sydney Ernest Holder (?), Colonel Stuart and Capt Robert (Bert) Grieve Woods.
Front: Lieutenant Francis Aloysius Comins, a dentist with the Australian Dental Corps was attached to the 3rd ALHFA. Source: AWM, No. P02171.002

work despite hills not being camel country. Five cacolet camels died on Xmas day; by then both camels and cacolets were worn out.

Moving in this region involved great difficulties. Rain made the roads almost impassable – on some days they were:

> ... by the time the new site had been reconnoitered, the 'road' (a compliment) had become impossible for any vehicle with less than six horses in it. After one or two vain attempts to move as a whole the Ambulance had to remain in status quo for that night with the exception of one Amb. wagon with 6 horses and mounted messenger. The C.O. travelled in the wagon and after going about one and a half miles, pitch blackness, rain and mud put a stop to moving ahead any further, so it was a case of just sitting down for the night; on the first gleams of light it was found that the wagon was situated practically under the muzzles of a Battery of 13 pounders, in fact the wagon held up the firing of one gun of the battery which had found a target and it was not until the other guns opened up fire that the horses developed sufficient energy to pull the wagon out of the mud bed in which it had settled.

In early January 1918 the Brigade and Ambulance returned to Belah for a spell of two months, most of this trek being put in during heavy rain and over roads feet deep in mud and water.

Further examples of the difficulties faced by the Ambulance are drawn from its part in the failed Es Salt operation. The town was taken by the 3rd Light Horse Brigade on 1 May 1918 but two days later was relinquished to fervent Turkish opposition.

> At 20.30, 29/4/18 we mounted and moved off, the night being pitch dark. The road all the way to the pontoon crossing the River Jordan was without exaggeration 12" to 2 feet deep in dust. It was absolutely awful and unless we kept well blocked up it was a matter of impossibility to know where we were heading for.

> As soon as the ambulance wagons left for Ghoranieh the mobile column proceeded to get on to the Damieh Es Salt track, ... As we could not follow the Ghoranieh Damieh road in order to reach the Es Salt track on account of shell fire, we hugged and climbed the foot hills taking all the cover we could. It was simply one continuous climb all the way, extremely arduous and slow. The track was only a goat track and not even that in places and hardly wide enough to allow two horses to pass. One only had to slip and he would be over the almost precipices along the edges of which the track led. Some had very narrow escapes. The track was not only nearly perpendicular in places but was as smooth as glass and very slippery, in places it was covered with loose boulders. Previously it would have been thought impossible to have got camels over certain parts, but this experience has still to reveal what sort of country the camel will not negotiate. It was like a spell to travel for as short a distance as 100 yards on level going. The track zig-zagged and wound round and round all the way. We all walked and led our horses, occasionally mounting when we came to the level part of the track but on the ascending and descending parts it was too dangerous and again we were saving the horses as much as possible. The camels and pack-horses soon showed signs of fatigue. The tent sub-division was compelled to walk the whole way helping the natives to lead the camels for it was too great a task for one native in places. The same applied to the pack-horses, these had to be led singly over many parts.

> Capt. Shelley and his party pushed on at 07.00 to catch the Brigade again and then proceeded to the town, which by this time was in our hands. The packs

> *proceeded soon after with orders to halt on the hill where B.H.Q. were established, overlooking the town of Es Salt. The wounded were placed on camels and taken here also. The road was very slippery and camels were sliding down the inclines. In places it was very steep and the camels found it very hard to ascend. One camel came down a steep part of the road on its rump which was not too pleasant for the patients it was carrying. We had to barrack the camels at B.H.Q. and have the wounded carried down to the hospital on stretchers, a distance of over one mile. It was considered far too much for the wounded to be jolted about by the motion of the camel descending, which seems to be the worst motion of all to experience when riding these animals.*

This part of the track was really good compared with that along which the Ambulance transported the wounded, when Es Salt was evacuated on 3 May. The order to withdraw immediately was received at 5:30 pm. Most of the medical and surgical equipment had to be abandoned because of the hurried departure from the Dressing Station.

> *... As soon as the camels arrived the patients were speedily loaded ... each patient was given a drink of hot tea before moving off. Yeomanry horses which had lost their riders in action were sent to us to convey patients able to ride ... . They had a long and perilous ride in front of them across the rugged, precipitous mountains of Moab to the Jordan Valley, some twenty miles before they could receive further attention. ...*

> *It was bitterly cold all night and the moanings of the patients were awful. Some patients begged to be dismounted and left behind, their sufferings were so severe; not only did they have to contend with the cold but in addition to their wounds all were feeling the effects of hunger. ... We were trying to reach the valley of the Jordan before dawn on account of the enemy's artillery seeing us. They had a full view of the track and commanded its entrance.*

> *... We had great difficulty in bringing the camels down; it was a case of leading one at a time over places where previously it would have been thought impossible for camels to go. One burden camel fell over a precipice and was killed, the native leading it escaping miraculously. Great difficulty was experienced with a camel that jibbed all the way. This camel at last lost its footing on a smooth surfaced rock inclining outwards from the side of the hill and fell over a precipice taking two wounded men with it. They, however, were rescued shortly after.*

After this arduous, all-night trek they arrived at the Jordan Valley just as dawn was breaking. Some of the bearers dismounted and went back to help get the camels down a very steep slope. Then the camels were barracked and spelled for a short time. Two men were found dead in the cacolets.

The Brigade and Ambulance spent much of May, June, July and August in the Jordan Valley. The conditions experienced during this period were considered the worst of the whole campaign. They were plagued by sandflies and mosquitoes and in places by flies and scorpions also, as well as dust.

> *The most trying ordeal ... in fact practically in every camp in the Jordan Valley, was the watering of horses, three miles twice a day in terrific heat and through clouds of dust.*

Nor did the Ambulance have an easy time during the five weeks in July-August, when it camped at Madbeh, where it did more than merely collect and evacuate patients.

> *... in fact the work was exceptionally severe. Only to look after horses under such conditions (9 miles daily in clouds of dust merely to water) was damnable*

to say the least, but when on top of that is added nightly (a case of being the safest policy owing to hostile command of view) collections of sick, sometimes by camels, sometimes by wagons, always accompanied by bearers, on odd occasions drawing shell fire from a hostile battery, then words fail.

At the end of August 1918, the Brigade and Ambulance left the Jordan Valley to re-organise for the big offensive. They encamped at Ludd amongst numerous olive trees that provided shade and shelter from the winds. Swords were issued to the regiments for the first time and the Ambulance overhauled its equipment.

Special attention was paid to pack-saddle equipment as experience on previous operations had shown that our wheeled transport might have to be dispensed with at any time and at very short notice. This was of course due to the exceptionally hilly nature of the country. Additional pack-saddles were issued for this purpose.

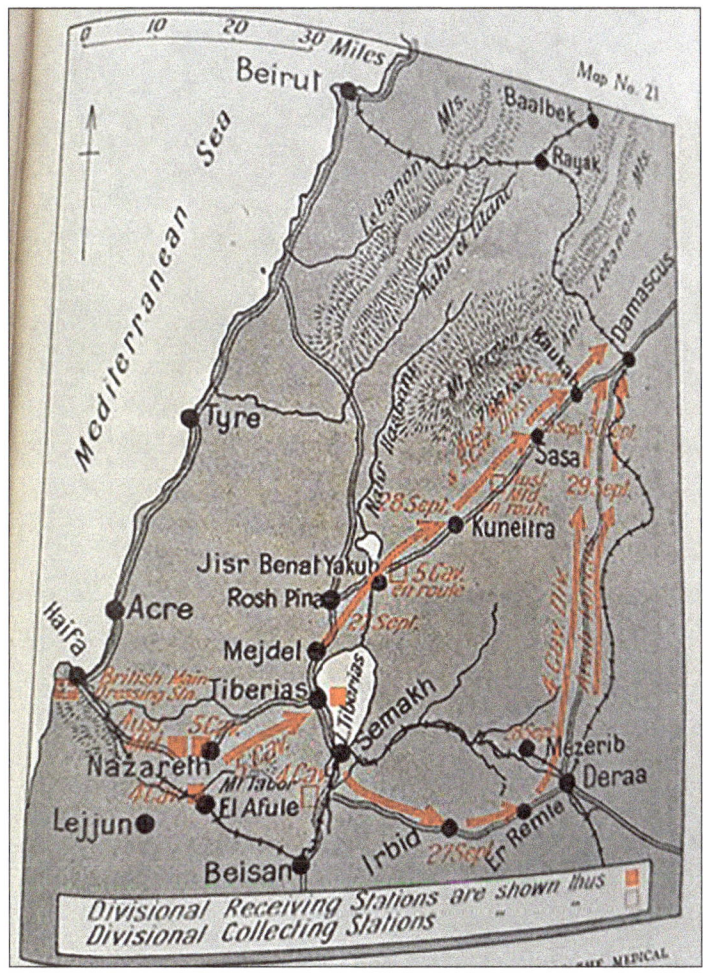

The push to Damascus. Source: Butler AG (1930). *Official History of the Australian Army Medical Services 1914-1918.* Volume 1, page 726, map 21

On 19 September the Brigade and Ambulance left Ludd and concentrated at Jaffa from where they began the drive to Damascus. At Jenin an ill 'Gem' Stuart could not proceed and rejoined the Ambulance four days later at Mejdel on the shore of Lake Tiberias.

The men lost no time in getting into the lake, taking horses with them. It is difficult to say whether men or horses enjoyed the water most, for the horses did not want to come out ... .

On 1 October the Ambulance halted for two days 1.6 km south of Damascus, where a dressing station was set up for the sick and wounded. By then abnormally large numbers were reporting sick from recurrent malaria and influenza. From 5 to 27 October the Ambulance camped at Kaukab, where the 3rd Australian Light Horse Brigade was in charge of a POW camp, in which there were about 15,000 prisoners. On 27 October the Brigade, less the 10th Regiment to look after the POW compound, left Kaukab for Homs and from there travelled in easy stages to Tripoli, which was reached on 9 November 1918.

The Brigade and Ambulance camped in the midst of young mulberry and olive trees at Mejdelaya about 6 km south-east of the town. In the wet weather the country turned into a quagmire. In the morning after a wet night the Unit's horses could be recognised only by their shape. Every horse was over its hocks in slush. This brought about a move to a beach site at the beginning of December.

A group comprising all ranks and transport of the 3rd Australian Light Horse Field Ambulance, ca. 1918. Source: AWM, No. B00800

Friend and foe

The Ambulances were not immune to attack. For example, while preparing for the Second Battle of Gaza, Casualty Clearing Stations (CCSs) had been bombed and straffed at Belah, where the Brigade was camped:

> *... one beautiful evening at about 10 o'clock the sky seemed to be suddenly full of enemy planes, which bombed and machine-gunned the CCSs particularly, but one plane came across the CCS almost due south and dropped bombs as it came. One bomb fell immediately between our lines and the CCS, the second on the immediate outskirts of the 3rd LHFA, the third in the centre of the 3rd LHFA between the Officers' and the Sergeants' Messes ...*

> *Patients were crawling out of the tents with ghastly wounds, while some were killed outright. No lights could be lit for the enemy planes were still flying overhead at what appeared to be roughly 300 feet (90 m); they had evidently dropped all their bombs but were machine-gunning the tents. The difficulties of dressing the dreadful wounds under the circumstances can be imagined. However, something had to be done and Major Whitford decided to operate where necessary. Accordingly an operating theatre was improvised in the E.P. tent used as a mess by the men ... . During all this time enemy planes were about, and were machine-gunning the tents of the CCSs & the Ambulance, so that all lights had to be out until the immediate danger passed over ... . Eventually, after many exciting spells of waiting in the darkness, whilst the anaesthetist continued his task under the greatest difficulties, all cases were dealt with.*

Chapter 19: Light Horse Field Ambulance

3rd Light Horse Field Ambulance Casualty Clearing Station at Gamil on the Wady Ghuzze during the operation of blowing up the Turkish Railway from Beersheba to El Aiya. Source: AWM, No. J00459

The Ambulance treated friend and foe alike. Stuart's report frequently refers to transporting and treating wounded and sick Turks. Regarding the aftermath of the Turks' retreat from Jemmameh (al-Jammama):

> *The condition of the Turkish wounded was pitiful, some of them being wounded 48 hours previously by bombs from our aircraft and had lain unable to do anything for themselves until picked up by our troops. Their wounds in many instances were fly-blown and their general condition, owing to the movement of their bowels, was terrible. One Turkish officer had had a tourniquet applied too tightly to a shattered leg and, when the bandage was removed, the leg was found to be quite black and the smell so offensive that it was only with difficulty that attention could be given to the unfortunate man. Several cases of sickness were brought in and many were delirious and made the night hideous with their incessant cries for water.*

> *As soon as all patients had received breakfast on the morning of the 10th the worst cases were sent by motor ambulances and the balance (except 4 Turks) were sent by cacolet camels to Tel El Sheria. It was found that there was not sufficient transport for all the patients. Consequently, 4 Turkish sick, who were past all hope of recovery and quite unable to stand a long camel journey, were placed in the shade of a screen and given a supply of water. Two of these died before the party left the place.*

On reaching Damascus orders were given that no medical units were to enter it. This was due to the disturbed state of the city and confused political situation; Damascus and everything in it were considered the possession of the Arab army of the Sherif of Mecca. It was not until the following day that the first medical unit did so, which was unfortunate because of the very large numbers of Turkish sick and wounded. However, nowhere had the concern for and treatment of Turkish sick and wounded been clearer. Commander of the Desert Mounted Corps, General Chauvel, laid down at the outset that the care of Turkish sick and wounded was a responsibility of the Corps and the first duty of the medical service. The Corps' medical services now comprised only the mobile portions of the field units with the cavalry divisions and all were below strength with sickness. The immobile sections did not arrive until considerably later.

On 1 October the 3rd Light Horse Field Ambulance set up a dressing station outside Damascus. A great number of prisoner patients were admitted and continued to pour in on the following day:

> *The Turks were in a pitiful condition and looked ill-clad, ill-fed and exhausted but it was as much as, in fact more than, the ambulance could do to look after the seriously ill. Some considerable difficulty was experienced in feeding patients as medical comforts were not available. The weather was fairly hot and owing to lack of shelters our Turkish patients suffered considerably. They were on the continual cry out for water and our men worked hard to satisfy their ravenous thirsts. They fought like animals to get around the water supplies. However, all that was possible was done for them.*

The Light Horse Brigades were admirably served by their Field Ambulances who stuck by their sides under fire in trying conditions of sand, dust and rough terrain. 'Gem' Stuart was twice mentioned in dispatches for ensuring the 3rd Light Horse Field Ambulance kept up with its Brigade equipped and ready to receive sick and wounded:

> *This officer has commanded the Brigade Field Ambulance during the recent operations. Notwithstanding the serious transport difficulties, both in the (plains) during the month of November and in the hills during December, his ambulance was always at hand ready equipped to cope with the casualties. His organization and enterprise were such that the evacuations of wounded and sick during this strenuous period were carried out in an efficient and most satisfactory manner. (1-3-1918)*

> *This officer is the CO of the Brigade Field Ambulance. During the recent operations, Sept 1918, he kept his Ambulance well up with the Brigade and energetically and promptly satisfied all calls of sick and wounded. During the epidemic of Influenza and Malaria at Damascus in October this officer was through sickness and other causes the only MO left with the Ambulance and though sick himself carried on the work of his Unit, while same was largely over-crowded with patients that the hospitals were unable to accept.*

45th memorial plaque located in the grounds of Shrine of Remembrance, St Kilda Road, Birdwood Avenue and Domain Road, Melbourne, Victoria. Jessica Bowman and Bill pictured. Source: Bill Hasker

Chapter 20
The Western Front

The Western Front extended for almost 800 km from the Swiss border to the North Sea. When the Australians arrived it was a virtual stalemate. Both sides had suffered severe casualties since the onset of hostilities but all attempts to break through had failed. After arriving in France, the Australian Divisions went to a quiet part of the front known as the 'Nursery'. This was their training ground for the harsher experiences to come. Losses on the Western Front were greater than at Gallipoli.

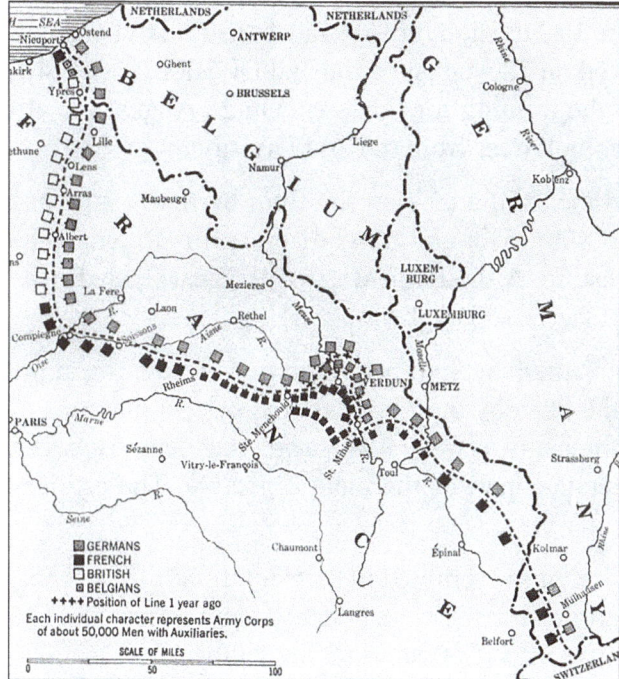

The Western Front – early summer 1916. Source: Weintraub Stanley (2014). *Silent Night: The Story of the World War I Christmas Truce*

The Somme sector. Source: Craig Renard, diggerhistory.info

Trench warfare for the Gallipoli veterans was a new experience, and tragically the Australians learnt the hard way about such dangers as exposing themselves to the enemy. Where the country was of a marshy nature, their trenches were not dug in the soil but comprised sandbag breastworks above ground level. This explains something I heard my aunt say several times in my youth – that it was no good to be tall.

The Somme – Fromelles, Pozieres, Mouquet Farm, Bullecourt

In July 1916, the 1st, 2nd and 5th Divisions joined the Somme Offensive. This began on 1 July 1916 and lasted until 18 November 1916. It was an attempt to break through the German lines along a 40 km front north and south of the River Somme. These lines contained some of the heaviest German fortifications on the entire Western Front. It was one of the largest battles and the bloodiest of the war with more than one million casualties.

179

Fromelles

The 5th Division was involved in a disastrous attack at Fromelles, suffering 5,533 casualties in 24 hours and was effectively incapacitated for many months afterwards. The commander of the 15th Brigade, Brigadier General 'Pompey' Elliott, concluded it would fail and tried to have it cancelled – unsuccessfully. Jimmy Downing, in Pompey Elliott's brigade, wrote what it was like:

> *Stammering scores of German machine-guns spluttered violently ... The air was thick with bullets, swishing in a flat criss-crossed lattice of death ... Hundreds were mown down in the flicker of an eyelid, like great rows of teeth knocked from a comb.*

Pozieres and Mouquet Farm

At huge cost the 1st and 2nd Divisions captured the French village of Pozieres and the ridge on which it stood. On 6 August, the 4th Division relieved the 2nd Division and after repulsing a major German counterattack pushed north along the ridge towards Mouquet Farm, a major German strongpoint with the aim of capturing it. The Germans had turned the farm into a fortress with deep dugouts and tunnels connected to distant fortifications. Fighting was intense and by the time it was replaced by the 1st Division on 15 August the 4th Division had suffered 4,649 casualties. The 1st was relieved on 22 August by the 2nd Division, which still had not fully recovered from the effects of the fighting for Pozieres. On 28 August the 4th Division, reinforced by a Canadian Brigade, took over from the 2nd Division.

On 3 September, the 4th Division launched the final attack on the farm by the Australians using the strongest battalions available, the 49th, 51st and 52nd of the 13th Brigade. The 49th had spent the last 10 days of August resting. Although it was the freshest Brigade, the 13th Brigade was also the least battle-experienced.

The 49th was deployed in four waves to attack the fabeckgraben (high trench) running at the back and right of the farm. The assault on the farm by the 51st, assisted by two platoons of the 52nd attacking diagonally from the south-east, was to be both strong and deep. Between the 49th and 51st, the 52nd would attack another part of the main objective. The artillery support for this action was considerable.

Prior to the first phase of the attack, the Australians assembled in their jumping-off trenches, where they were to remain in very cold conditions for some six hours without overcoats. The troops moved off under the cover of smoke just after 5.00 am on 3 September.

On the right, the first wave of the 49th easily took its objective, and the second wave moved through these men into the shell holes to act as a screen. The barrage had been timed to remain on the fabeckgraben for only three minutes, but because the enemy trench was some 100 yards ahead, the time for its capture by the third wave was very short. As soon as the barrage lifted, these troops advanced but ran into heavy fire from the Germans who were deeply entrenched and whose machine guns and rifles inflicted severe casualties. The left flank of the 49th's attack was repulsed, and although some men entered the trench, they were driven out into shell holes; however, the 49th rallied and eventually took part of the fabeckgraben. In addition, the pits on the right were cleared with bombs, two machine guns and a number of prisoners were captured and barricades were erected on both flanks.

After meeting with apparent success initially, the 51st and 52nd Battalions suffered huge casualties. The 52nd found no dugouts for sheltering from artillery bombardment; men saw others near them literally blown to pieces. The Germans quickly infiltrated back into the shell holes and the 52nd retired leaving the 51st Battalion to fend for itself. Artillery bombardment forced the rear elements of the 51st to withdraw and its two advanced companies were completely surrounded and all their members were either killed, wounded or captured.

The Australian thrust had been defeated except on the crest of the ridge, where the 49th, supported by a company of the 50th Battalion, dug in deeply and held firm. Remnants of the 52nd Battalion struggled to safeguard the flank of the 49th. When reinforced about 11.00 am by a bombing party, the 52nd consisted of about 90 men, i.e. all that remained of three companies. But the battle was not yet over and shortly thereafter the enemy broke through on the left but were driven back. They next appeared 90 m to the front but the 49th did not attack as it was already defending 180 m of trench. By this time, the men were desperately tired. Around mid-afternoon (3.30 pm) the Australians handed over control to the Canadians, suspended all operations and implemented safeguards to hold the high ground already captured.

The Canadians began relieving the Australians, and by dawn on 4 September, the position was still secure. However, the handover had not been completed when the Germans again massed in front and started to advance, but their advance was halted and they began vigorous sniping.

The 49th's forward elements were quickly organised for an attack by the now (promoted on 29 July) Lieutenant Stuart and a Lance Corporal Scott. Before this was initiated, Stuart saw a white handkerchief being waved from the German position and jumped on the parapet to beckon the enemy, only to be instantly shot. His death was a tragedy, but the German who shot him might not have seen the white flag or it might not have been raised or answered in the proper manner. Lieutenant P.F.M. Stuart was buried 180 m west-south-west of Courcelette. Private G.A. Ball wrote to Dr Stuart, Peter's father:

> *Being a member of the bombing platoon of which your late son Lieutenant Stuart was in charge I have been requested by the remainder of the boys to offer you our sincere sympathy in your recent bereavement. Previous to our friend's death we had been training for a period of three months and we found him every inch a thorough sport and gentleman. I know that it will please you to hear that some of the members of the bombing platoon including myself served with your son in Gallipoli. We are all proud to say, Sir, that we served under such a brave and gallant officer, and more than pleased to say that his death was duly revenged.*

On occasions the Australians butchered Germans following breaches of accepted behaviour after surrender. When a beloved officer or sergeant was the victim of 'white flag treachery' the Diggers' anger was almost impossible to check. Raising a white flag, men shamming death and machine guns concealed on stretchers were common ruses Germans resorted to.

The 49th Battalion had disembarked at Marseilles on 12 June 1916 and arrived at the front line on 21 June. Later that month Peter attended a six-day 'school of instruction' in the field, learning the techniques required to become a bombing officer. The bomb was in reality a grenade, which was armed by striking it against a pad taped to the wrist, to light the fuse, similar to striking a match. It was the job of the bombing officer to deliver the armed grenade to the enemy. The means of delivery were varied and included hurling the grenade across 'no-man's-land' into the German trenches, using a catapult or alternatively running to the German trench and throwing the grenade in. 'Bombing' was particularly dangerous as Peter's older brother, Lieutenant Colonel 'Gem' Stuart of the Third Light Horse Field Ambulance pointed out in a letter to his sister Adah:

> *... remember always that your little brother is in the best company, for the worst part of this war is that it seems to demand as sacrifices the best and bravest. You know the business they put Pete on to was battalion bombing officer .... It is absolutely suicidal and Petey fully realised it when writing to me about it. However, as he said, he did not have any whippersnipper ordering him about and that was a comfort. As bombing officer one is either being killed or maimed for life. I might say when he wrote and told me I was too scared to pass it on in my letters; I don't know whether Pete himself did. ... the esteem that they had*

of him as a man and a soldier made a man proud to be his brother ... but again it made you absolutely mad to see the men in command didn't take it into their hand to see that he got some official recognition. However, I ask nothing better than to go out as he did.

Exterior view of Mouquet Farm, before its destruction by shellfire. Source: AWM, No. J00181

Looking south towards Pozieres, this position was the scene of severe trench warfare, Mouquet Farm, October 1916. Source: AWM, No. E00005

AIF Memorial, Mouquet Farm, France, 2012. Source: Dianne Diprose, Flickr

Mouquet Farm, Pozières – watercolour over pencil on cardboard by Fred Leist (1878–1945), Australian official war artist. Source: AWM, No. ART02875

The very weary men of the 49th Battalion, the last Australian unit in the battle, were finally relieved at dawn on 5 September. Mouquet Farm eventually fell to the Canadians on 27 September. The Battle of Mouquet Farm cost the Australians dearly, casualties being: the 1st Australian Division 2,650 officers and men; 2nd Australian Division (6th Brigade only) 896 officers and men; 4th Australian Division 7,158 officers and men.

The fighting at Pozières and Mouquet Farm is primarily remembered as Australian battles. The three Australian Divisions suffered over 23,000 casualties. The Australian Official Historian Charles Bean wrote that the Pozières ridge is:

> *more densely sown with Australian sacrifice than any other place on earth.*

If the losses from Fromelles on 19 July are included, the Australians sustained more casualties in six weeks in France than they had in the eight months at Gallipoli. In a letter written at this time, Melbourne journalist Lieutenant J.A. Raws, who was killed in the Somme battle, vividly described the battle scene:

> *... we lay down terror-stricken along a bank. The shelling was awful ... we eventually found our way to the right spot out in no-man's-land. Our leader was shot before we arrived and the strain had sent two other officers mad. I and another new officer took charge and dug the trench. We were shot at all the time... the wounded and killed had to be thrown to one side ... I refused to let any sound man help a wounded man; the sound had to dig ... we dug on and finished amid a tornado of bursting shells ... I was buried once and thrown down several times ... buried with dead and dying. The ground was covered with bodies in all stages of decay and mutilation and I would, after struggling from the earth, pick up a body by me to try and lift him out with me and find him a decayed corpse ... I went up again that night and stayed up there. We were shelled to hell ceaselessly. X– went mad and disappeared... there remained nothing but a charred mass of debris with bricks, stones, girders and bodies pounded to nothing ... we are lousy, stinking, unshaven, sleepless ... I have one puttee, a man's helmet, another dead man's gas protector, dead man's bayonet. My tunic rotten with other men's blood and partly spattered with a comrade's brains.*

By December 1916 all five Australian Divisions were on the Somme. In the following April and May, all but the 3rd Division fought at Bullecourt. More than any other battle of the war Bullecourt probably aroused the greatest disgust in Australian troops for their British commanders. The 4th Division was virtually wiped out. However, casualties, though high, were not on the scale of those at Pozières or later that year in Flanders.

Flanders 1917

After Bullecourt the Australians saw action in Flanders at Messines and Passchendaele, which further enhanced their reputation for courage and military skill.

Messines

The first major action by Australian troops in Flanders took place in June 1917 at Messines in the Ypres area of Belgium. Along with a New Zealand Division and a British Division, the Australian 3rd Division spearheaded an attack, which gained its objectives within three hours of the battle commencing. It gave the Allied forces strategic high ground and a significant morale boost. It was also the first large-scale battle of the war for the 3rd Division and the men were keen to maintain the reputation won by the other divisions at Gallipoli and the Somme.

The attack was launched immediately after the simultaneous detonation of 19 mines placed in tunnels dug underneath the German lines along the Messines Ridge, one of the most strongly held German positions on the Western Front. Probably about 10,000 Germans were killed.

This was then the largest man-made explosion in history and reportedly felt in London. For more than a year Australians specifically recruited from the coal- and gold-fields for the purpose, along with others from Britain, Canada and New Zealand, had been tunnelling under the German trenches and laying explosives. The attack at Messines was a precursor to the much larger offensive at Passchendaele.

Passchendaele (Third Battle of Ypres)

All five AIF Divisions fought in the Battle of Passchendaele, which was really a series of battles between July and November 1917. All were part of an offensive to push the Germans off the Passchendaele-Messines ridge and achieve a break-through. The most significant for the Australians were the victories of Menin Road (20 September 1917), Polygon Wood (26-28 September 1917) and Broodseinde (October 1917). It was at Broadseinde that all the Australian Divisions fought side by side for the first time. The Australians were withdrawn in October. The battle ended in mid-November, when the village of Passchendaele, or what was left of it, was eventually taken by the Canadians.

Stretcher bearers of the 57th Battalion, passing through the cemetery near the mound in Polygon Wood in the Ypres Sector. Source: AWM, No. E01912

Five Australians, members of a field artillery brigade, passing along a duckboard track over mud and water among gaunt bare tree trunks in the devastated Chateau Wood, a portion of one of the battlegrounds in the Ypres salient. Hurley James Francis (Frank), 1917. Source: AWM, No. E01220

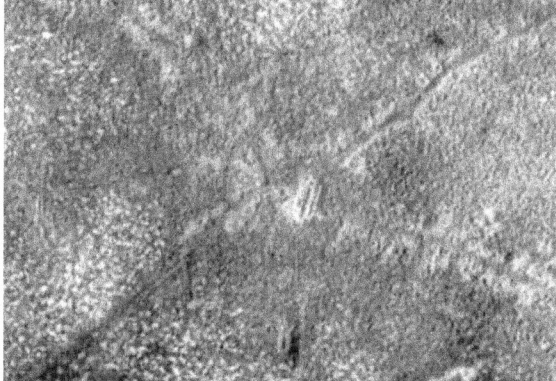

Aerial view of the village of Passchendaele before (left) and after (right) the Third Battle of Ypres, 1917. Source: Wikimedia Commons

The Battle of Passchendaele became synonymous with all that is loathsome in war; it certainly represents the futility and stupidity of warfare. It cost more than half-a-million lives over its three months. The Germans lost about 250,000 lives and the British 300,000 of whom 36,500 were Australian. Ninety-thousand British or Australian bodies were never identified, 42,000 were never recovered; these had been blown to bits or had drowned in the dreadful morass. Much of the fighting took place in mud so deep that men drowned in it. Many of the drowned were exhausted or wounded men, who had slipped or fallen off the duckboards and were unable to escape the filthy, foul-smelling glutinous mud, sinking deeper to their death as they struggled.

The Somme 1918

Back on the Somme in 1918 the Australians continued to make their mark in actions at Villers-Bretonneux, Dermacourt, Hamel, Amiens, Mont St Quentin and Peronne. The battles at Villers-Bretonneux and Hamel have a special significance for the Australians and are further examples of their resolve and resourcefulness, which proved distinctive and influential.

Villers-Bretonneux

On 24 April 1918 the Germans took the village of Villers-Bretonneux, defended at the time by the British. This was part of the massive spring offensive launched in a desperate gamble to win the war in the west before the Americans arrived. The Americans had come into the war when the Germans began sinking their ships that were supplying the Allies. That day, the British and Germans engaged in the first ever tank duel — one of the German tanks, Mephisto, was later captured and is now on display at the old Queensland Museum. British commanders planned an immediate counter-attack as they needed to recapture the village before the Germans could complete their defensive works.

The two Australian Brigades given the task were ordered to attack the village frontally in daylight. Their commanders, Brigadier Generals William Glasgow and Harold 'Pompey' Elliott, refused, Glasgow declaring: *If God Almighty gave the order, we couldn't do it by daylight*. The assault began at 10.00 pm, still earlier than Glasgow had wanted, the plan being for the Brigades to encircle the village in a classic pincer movement. This wasn't quite achieved and some Germans escaped through the gap before it was closed after daylight the following day, ANZAC Day, and the village recaptured. This ended the German advance towards Amiens.

The people of the village of Villers-Bretonneux maintain a strong feeling for Australians because of their part in liberating the village. They have designed a logo for their internet site in which the letters VB form a kangaroo. The main Australian war memorial is outside the village and it is here that the French and Australians commemorate ANZAC Day each year.

Australians were involved in the fighting around Villers-Bretonneux in the heavy attack by the Germans that began on 23 April, during which they engaged in house-to-house and cellar-to-cellar fighting. One German wrote:

> *We have the Australians opposite us and they are very quick and cunning. They glide about in the night like cats and come right up to our trenches without our seeing them.*

A little over 20 years later in North Africa the Germans would once again experience these cats in the night.

The Battle of Hamel

The Australians had nothing but distrust and contempt for their British commanders. They were old-fashioned generals with old-fashioned ideas, if they had any at all. Despite reforms, the British army generally remained a class-structured entity, where aristocratic traditions, wealth, social distinction and well-cut uniforms still counted. With few exceptions, status conferred by birth and school remained the prerequisite for choosing the upper ranks of the military. It was an Australian general who pioneered a new way of fighting battles.

Soon after being put in command of the Australian Corps, Lieutenant General John Monash was given the task of recapturing Hamel, a village north-east of Villers-Bretonneux. This was the first time in the war Australians were commanded by an Australian. Compared with other battles, the Battle of Hamel was not a large battle. However, Monash believed in the extensive use of machines, meticulous planning and coordination, and low casualties. He took all his objectives within 93 minutes of the battle starting with fewer than 1,000 Australian casualties.

The Battle took place in the early hours of 4 July 1918. Infantry, artillery, tanks and planes worked together for over 2 km, with relatively few losses. It was the first time that tanks were used to supply the front troops with food, water, ammunition and medical supplies, and transport the wounded.

Monash knew he needed better information about the progress of the battle than any general had ever had to co-ordinate the massive firepower, infantry, tanks and aircraft. To get this he used a range of

Portrait of Sir John Monash taken outside the General's headquarters near Villers-Bretonneux in May 1918. Source: Mitchell Library, State Library of New South Wales, Reference code 897276

The Australian Corps Memorial Park at Le Hamel, France. Source: *The Courier Mail*, 6 November 2008

methods, including the pioneering of wireless in battle. He used aircraft to gather information and also to attack the enemy and drop supplies to his advancing troops.

Monash knew complex plans required careful explanation and communication. He combined openness in discussing tactics with junior officers with rigid insistence that once a course of action had been decided, it was followed through to the letter. He ensured all ranks down to non-commissioned officers were aware of relevant plans.

Monash believed a battle could be won only after a great deal of preparation. He wrote:

> *A perfect modern battle plan is like nothing so much as a score for an orchestral composition, where the various arms and units are the instruments, and the tasks they perform are their respective musical phrases.*

The Battle of Hamel was the most well-prepared battle of the First World War; Monash's battle plan became the blueprint for future battles. On 12 August Monash was knighted, KCB on the battlefield by King George V, the first time a British monarch had honoured a commander in such a way in 200 years.

Armistice

The Allies eventually breached the Hindenburg line by 5 October and the war was essentially over. The German Government asked for an immediate armistice on land and water and in the air.

In the most successful period of the Australian campaign, 27 March-5 October 1918, the AIF made up less than 10% of the entire British forces. It captured 23% of the prisoners, 23.5% of the enemy guns and 21.5% of the ground wrested from the Germans.

Casualties on the Western Front

Of the 313,814 soldiers who embarked from Australia, 53,000 died in France and Belgium. About 18,000 have no known graves. There were 152,171 Australians wounded – many being wounded more than once.

The Australian soldiers who fought in France and Belgium, their dead and especially those buried in unknown graves, are commemorated by the Villers-Bretonneux Memorial, the Australian National Memorial, which stands within the Villers-Bretonneux Military Cemetery.

Above: Villers-Bretonneux Military Cemetery. Right: The Australian War Memorial – Villers-Bretonneux. Names recorded of almost 11,000 soldiers whose bodies were never recovered. Source: Commonwealth War Graves Commission, cwgc.org

The 10,700 Australian servicemen actually named on the memorial died in the battlefields of the Somme, Arras, the German Advance of 1918 and the Advance to Victory. One of them is Lieutenant Peter Stuart, memorial panel 149. The Australian Defence Force is actively involved in the recovery and, using DNA technology, identification of the remains of missing Australian servicemen, which will be returned to their families, enabling appropriate reburial and commemoration. I have given them a sample of my DNA.

The largest Commonwealth war cemetery in France is at Etaples. Within a six hectare enclosure, bordered on either side by the pine forest and in front by Canche Bay, are the graves of 11,658 soldiers, mostly British, who fell between 1914 and 1918. There also lie 461 Australians.

Etaples Military Cemetery. Source: Commonwealth War Graves Commission, cwgc.org

The sacrifice on such a scale of young people, most in their prime of life, is beyond comprehension. Students from the North Mackay High School visited the cemetery in October 2004. The diary entry of one of them, Claire Pailthorpe, puts poignantly what she made of it:

> .... we all ended up sitting on top of the memorial, which overlooked the entire cemetery. ... sitting there feeling warm, safe and somewhat contented – I couldn't help but feel the emptiness. It was the emptiness inside – the gap left by millions of lives taken, lost souls, heartbroken mothers, wives, children.
>
> My final thoughts as I watched the silent headstones, was that we have to live the life these soldiers gave us – we have to live our lives to the fullest, love our friends & family to the utmost – it's the least we can do – live the life these men never got.

Cobbers, bronze statue depicting the rescue of a wounded soldier – Australian Memorial Park, Fromelles. Source: www.anzacsinfrance.com

Cheng Ling kneels along with her husband and daughter at her grandfather's grave in France, 2009. Source: *South China Morning Post*, China's WWI SCMP Chronicles

Chinese presence

There are many Chinese names on tombstones in the cemeteries of Europe. Roughly 140,000 Chinese worked on the Western Front in non-combatant roles such as cleaning up the battlefields and burying the dead, digging tunnels and trenches, repairing tanks, assembling shells for artillery, transporting munitions and unloading supplies and war materials.

China, wanting to earn a seat at the negotiating table at the war's end, offered soldiers, which Europe declined. However, the offer of labourers was finally accepted. Winston Churchill said:

> *I would not even shrink from the word 'Chinese' for the purpose of carrying out the war. These are not times when people ought in the least to be afraid of prejudices.*

Chapter 21
The Aussie Soldier

The Aussie soldier was quite different from his British counterpart and probably all other soldiers. Australian soldiers earned a reputation as outstanding fighters. They were volunteers and took to soldiering their carefree disregard for officialdom and had scant time for the dictates of bureaucracy. They despised the swagger of officers, especially the English.

An officer had to win the respect of his troops. It was not issued automatically with his badge of rank. When it came time to fight, the Australians were always ready. The rest of the time they regarded as their own. Their behaviour was rough-house, cheeky and even loutish on occasion, but it was also caring and loyal.

Many British officers treated the aggressively familiar Australians with disdain, denigrating them as crude and ill-mannered, but the brash colonials were unimpressed by any superior airs. The Australians were often surprised at the deference shown by the 'subservient' British Tommy to his superiors and could not believe he was willing to obey orders without question.

In *The History of the British Cavalry* the Marquess of Anglesey praised the closeness of Australian officers and soldiers in the Middle East:

> *so long as they gave themselves no airs and were truly efficient, a close association with their men developed... The material differences between officers and men in camp and field were not very great ...*

The Australian soldiers impressed Field Marshall Douglas Haig from the start and his admiration for them grew as the war continued, though they never ceased to puzzle him, as they did most British officers and ordinary soldiers.

Fierce fighters

After inspecting the Australian 2nd Division on its arrival in France in March 1916, Haig wrote in his diary:

> *The men were looking splendid, fine physique, very hard and determined-looking. The Australians are mad keen to kill Germans and to start doing it at once!*

Warfare on the Western Front was different from Gallipoli. The Australians learned the art of war the hard way but they learned very fast. They maintained a very high level of morale in their first battle experience, the Battle of the Somme. More than once Haig intervened personally, when he thought the Aussies were advancing too rapidly because of ignorance.

The Germans learned to fear Australians because they were reckless, ruthless and vengeful. During the Third Battle of Ypres in autumn 1917, the Australians met the Germans on high ground, in front of Polygon Wood. That evening the official communique read:

> *One ANZAC Corps obtained all its objectives and took 3,900 prisoners. The other ANZAC Corps took all its objectives and met the Prussian Guards whom they had met before at Pozières on the Somme. This Corps took no prisoners.*

Possibly the most feared combatant in WWI was sniper Billy Sing, who chalked up 150 confirmed kills at Gallipoli but is said to have killed about 300 men. Although referred to as 'The Assassin' and 'The Murderer' by his fellow ANZACs it is reported he never fired at a stretcher-bearer or any soldiers, who were trying to rescue wounded Turks.

Sing was born in Clermont, Queensland. His mother was English and his father a Chinese farmer from Shanghai. He developed into a deadly marksman as a boy and it was because of his reputation that the recruiting office accepted him. Racial prejudice even discriminated against those offering to fight for their country. A failed marriage, poor health from wounds and being gassed plus post-traumatic stress disorder dogged him after the war and he died penniless and alone in Brisbane in 1943.

A less-well-known veteran of WWI of Chinese heritage was Caleb Shang, who twice won the Distinguish Conduct Medal as well as the Military Medal.

A WWII veteran of Chinese heritage was Wellington Lee. He joined the RAAF, aged 15, and served through the war. He was later Victorian State Secretary of the Returned Services League (RSL), a Melbourne City Councillor and Labor candidate for Kooyong in 1974.

Private William Edward (Billy) Sing DCM, ca. 1918. Source: AWM, No. P03633.006

Private Caleb James Shang DCM and Bar, MM. Source: AWM

Wellington Lee, P00899 SH030 DJG20. Source: Museum of Chinese Australian History

Puzzling Aussies

The casual ways of the Australians puzzled not only most British officers but also ordinary soldiers. An amusing illustration of this occurred during the Third Ypres offensive when a British officer, Lieutenant King, was stuck with a small left-over of his company in the mud near Poelcapelle. The men were exhausted, having been under constant fire for two days, and were desperate to be relieved. They thought they had been forgotten. King later wrote:

> *Suddenly, to my great surprise, I heard voices behind me and I looked back and there were three very tall figures, and one was actually smoking. I could hardly speak for astonishment. I said, 'Who the hell are you? And put that cigarette out, you'll draw fire!'*
>
> *He just looked back at me. 'Well, come to that, who are you?'*
>
> *I said, 'I'm lieutenant King of the 2/5th East Lancashire Regiment.'*
>
> *At which he said: 'Well, we're the Aussies, chum, and we've come to relieve you.' And they jumped down into the shell-hole.*

Well, naturally, we were delighted, but of course there are certain formalities you've always got to carry out when you hand over, and I was a bit worried about that. So I explained, 'There are no trenches to hand over, no rations, no ammunition, but I have got a map. Do you need any map references?'

He said, 'Never mind about that, chum. Just fuck off.'

They didn't seem to be a bit bothered. The last I saw of them they were squatting down, rifles over their shoulders, and they were smoking, all three of them. Just didn't care!

Enterprising larrikins enjoy life

An Egyptian assessment of the Diggers was:

Not since pre-historic stone ages has such a naked army been seen in civilised warfare as the Australian army corps fighting on the Gallipoli Peninsula. They display an utter abhorrence for superfluous clothing. They are famous throughout Europe for their hard-fighting, hard-swearing and nakedness, even to a sense of indecency.

Men bathing, enjoying a swim in the sea after returning from the trenches. Gallipoli Peninsula, Turkey, ca. 1915. Source: AWM, No. G00269

Aussie enterprise and their readiness to ignore authority was displayed by some men of the 49th Battalion while it was temporarily manning the defences of the Suez Canal prior to going to France. They were camped near Cairo. The men soon became bored with camp life and nearby attractions were too much for some. Each morning one enterprising fellow began collecting a picket of six to eight men and marched them into the town and back again in the evening. It took about a week before their ruse was discovered.

Troublesome Aussies

Right from the beginning British officers complained about the undisciplined behaviour of the Australians and their disregard for stiff military protocol. Officers and soldiers did not keep the necessary distance, they were indifferent to dress regulations, dressing even with nonchalance – some didn't even shave every day. A noteworthy example is Brigadier General Pompey Elliott, who liked to look dishevelled, particularly if 'foppish' English staff officers were around.

Some soldiers even dared to object, if they had to carry out a task they did not like. They were slow to salute or use the word 'Sir'; some even addressed their commanding officer by his first name. Lieutenant General Sir Philip Cherwode, who became General Officer Commanding of the Desert Column, once complained to General Chauvel:

> ... not only do your men fail to salute me when I ride through your camps, but they also laugh at my orderlies.

The British War Cabinet believed they could not win the war with dirty, slovenly troops. At the start of the Gallipoli campaign its Secretary, Sir Maurice Hankey, looked into what was going on. He visited every corner of the peninsula and spent a good deal of time in the Australian trenches. He was impressed with what he saw and wrote to the Prime Minister:

> I do hope that we shall hear no more of the 'indiscipline' of these extraordinary Corps, for I don't believe that for military qualities of every kind their equal exists. Their physique is wonderful and their intelligence of a high order.

A group of the 46th Australian Infantry Battalion just after coming out of the line in front of Monument Wood, May 1918. Source: AWM, No. E02307

Brigadier General H.E. 'Pompey' Elliott, standing at the door of a captured German Divisional Headquarters near Harbonnieres. Source: AWM, No. E02855

The Prince of Wales, the future Edward VIII, also countered the tales of indisciplined Australians when in Egypt in 1916 reporting on the defences of the Suez Canal. Edward was often impatient with ceremony, convention and 'Society' and wrote:

> They have fought so d-d hard and are so keen, that it is hard to deal severely with them.

Behind the lines the behaviour of the Australians clashed totally with the conduct of the British Army. In February 1918 Haig told his wife that they had to put the Australians into separate convalescent camps. This was because they were giving so much trouble, when mixed with the British, as well as putting revolutionary ideas into their heads. An example of the contaminating Aussies is a story told by a British soldier:

> His Colonel decided to have a full dress parade for the mounting of the guard. Every morning all smartened up and the band playing we marched up and down. The Aussies who were camped nearby used to look on in amazement. When off duty we used to talk to them and they kept asking whether we liked doing it. Naturally we said 'of course not'. We were supposed to be off duty resting but all our time was taken polishing and cleaning as well as turning out on parade. The Australians did not approve of it because they never polished or did anything. They had a band and their brass instruments were all filthy but they knew how to play them. One day they said they would soon fix it for us.

> *The next day our Sergeant Major, who was a stickler for discipline, was just getting ready to call us all out when the Australians started with their band. They marched up and down the road outside the field, playing any old thing. There was no tune you could recognise. They were just blowing as loudly as they could on their instruments. It sounded like a million cat-calls. The Sergeant couldn't make his voice heard. They never tried to mount another parade, because they could see the Aussies watching us from across the road, just ready to step in and sabotage the whole thing. They just posted the guards in the ordinary way as if we were in the line.*

Haig believed that a great deal of the problem was caused by the relaxed disciplinary methods of General Birdwood, the English officer who commanded the 1st ANZAC Corps and later the Australian Corps. Birdwood, however, was one of very few senior British officers who had the touch to command Australians and extract their best qualities.

Australian officers were also of an independent spirit. British army officers were not supposed to argue with their superiors. Banjo Paterson, like many of the Australians, had a defiant independence, especially when standing up to the demands of his seniors, ensuring the best horses went to the fighting men. He explained with sarcasm:

> *No officer, not even a staff popinjay or a brigadier, should be allowed to select a horse for himself.*

Paterson was particularly scornful of the puffed-up generals booked into the grand hotels in Cairo, many doing such jobs as reporting on waste of jam tins. Allenby was also unimpressed. When he took command, he ordered them to move out of Cairo nearer to the action.

Brigadier General Glasgow shocked his commanding officer when he refused to attack the French village of Villers-Bretonneux from Cachy, because it would cost too many lives. He also wanted the time of the attack changed. He famously said:

> *Tell us what you want us to do, Sir, but you must let us do it our own way.*

After some arguing Glasgow got his way. The attack, on 25 April 1918, was a resounding success and considered by General Monash, the Australian senior commander in France, to be the turning point of the war.

The official war historian (C.E.W. Bean) described Glasgow as:

> *... the most forcible of the three strong brigadiers of the 4th Division. With keen blue eyes looking from under puckered humorous brows as shaggy as a deer-hound's; with the bushman's difficulty of verbal expression but sure sense of character and situations; with a fiery temper, but cool understanding and a firm control of men; with an entire absence of vanity, but translucent honesty and a standard of rectitude which gave confidence both to superiors and subordinates, he could—by a frown, a shrewd shake of the head, or a twinkle in [the eye] ... awaken in others more energy than would have been evoked by any amount of exhortation. According to Monash, 'Glasgow succeeded not so much by exceptional mental gifts, or by tactical skill of any very high order, as by his personal driving force and determination'. Australian Prime Minister, Robert Menzies, later described Glasgow as 'the complete personal embodiment of the AIF'.*

Glasgow grew up in the small town of Tiaro. Just prior to the war he bought a cattle property in Central Queensland. After the war he returned to raising cattle as well as serving his country as a politician and diplomat. I first heard the name Sir William Glasgow after leaving university, when I went to work on *Elgin Downs*. The manager, Jack Cooper, had previously managed Glasgow's cattle property and held him in high regard. Cooper related a story about Glasgow's manager, whom he succeeded, failing to put the bulls out with the breeding females one year.

Australians' view of discipline

The Australians considered the British were obsessed with discipline and would never have put up with it. On several occasions they took action, when they saw British soldiers being punished for breaches of discipline such as being drunk or wearing dirty clothes when off duty. One form of punishment, termed 'First Field Punishment', required the soldier to parade in full pack, after which the pack was taken off and Military Policemen (MPs) strapped him up against a wooden cross, often one in a wagon wheel. It looked like he was crucified. This happened twice a day, an hour in the morning and an hour at night, for as many days as the sentence demanded. On one occasion Australian troops, incensed by the sight of a man undergoing Field Punishment, cut him loose again and again, threatening the MPs with loaded rifles, daring them to truss the soldier up again. On another, a member of the 49th Battalion freed a British soldier from a timber frame, where he had been tied and flogged. Colonel Lorenzo, commander of the 49th Battalion, approved of his soldier's action.

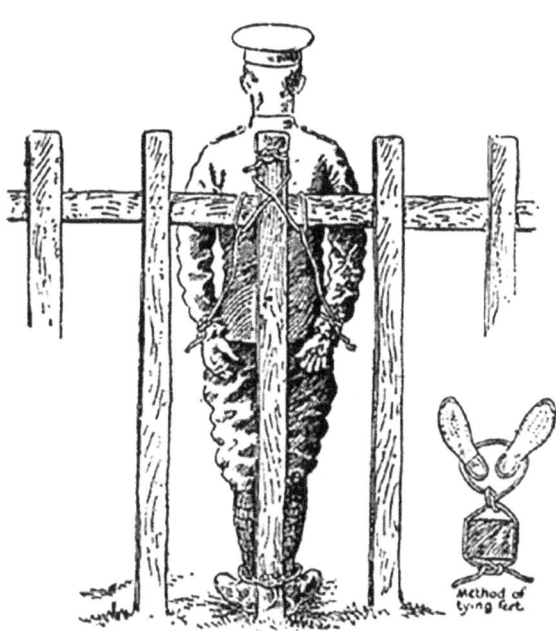

Illustration of method of attachment to fixed object as required in Field Punishment no 1.
Source: AWM

The Australians demonstrated that discipline has nothing to do with dedication and very little with training. The keywords are collective discipline and individualism. Monash, the Australian general who succeeded Birdwood, wrote:

> *Very much and very stupid comment has been made upon the discipline of the Australian soldier. That was because the very conception and purpose of discipline have been misunderstood. It is, after all, only a means to an end, and that end is the power to secure co-ordinated action among a large number of individuals for the achievement of a definite purpose. It does not mean lip service, nor obsequious homage to superiors, nor servile observance of forms and customs, nor a suppression of individuality... the Australian Army is a proof that individualism is the best and not the worst foundation upon which to build up collective discipline.*

The official historian, C.E.W. Bean, put it more dramatically, when he wrote about the gallantry and audacity of the 1st Division at the landing on Gallipoli and the endurance displayed during the testing period that followed:

> *He (the Australian soldier) had scattered to the winds once and for all the notion often reiterated that an Australian force would be ineffective through lacking discipline. In flame of the whitest heat was tested the discipline of the new force, raised suddenly by a people unaccustomed to restraint, naturally haters of the system of cast and subordination on which most armies are trained. It was not the discipline of habit which made either the Australians or New Zealanders endure.*

Aussie soldiers not donkeys

Unlike their British colleagues, common Australian soldiers were not treated like ignorant donkeys, but like individuals, who will function better in a team when they know their collective goal. The Aussie officers explained extensively to their men the objectives of the battle they were about to engage in. Even ordinary soldiers then knew the strategy that was behind it. When they became cut-off they still knew what to do, what the goal was.

Not angels

The Australians were no angels as the following examples show. Australian troopers were almost as much at home in the desert as the Bedouin. Many of these desert Arabs had the reputation of being great thieves – ready to take what they could from those who invaded their lands. However, they soon found these horsemen with feathers in their hats very adept at stealing their food, firewood, poultry and livestock. Much as the Australians scorned the deference shown by the British soldier to his superiors, they were more than ready to discriminate against the local population.

Australian troops resting during World War I, ca. 1918, by Frank Hurley (1885-1962). Source: NLA, No. 147393480

At times their conduct on and off the battlefield was reprehensible. A rather high number of Aussie soldiers were put behind bars for some time. In the winter of 1918 the average of 9 per 1,000 Australian soldiers in prison was much higher than the 1.6 per 1,000 for the Canadians, New Zealanders and South Africans. Field Marshall Douglas Haig was convinced this was due to the low standard of discipline among the Australian divisions.

There are accounts of downright cruelty – even war crimes – committed by Australians against the enemy. Robert Graves in *Goodbye to All That* quotes an anonymous Australian, who told him the biggest lark he had was at Morlancourt, when the Australians took it the first time:

> *There were a lot of Jerries in a cellar, and I said to 'em: 'Come out, you Camarades!' So out they came, a dozen of 'em, with their hands up. 'Turn out your pockets,' I told 'em. They turned 'em out. Watches and gold and stuff, all dinkum. Then I said: 'Now back to your cellar, you sons of bitches!' For I couldn't be bothered with 'em. When they were all safely down, I threw half a dozen Mills bombs in after 'em. I'd got the stuff all right, and we weren't taking prisoners that day.*

Some engaged in 'ratting'. Angered and frustrated by sniper fire small groups combed cellars and dugouts for Germans, generally without the leadership of officers or NCOs. They drove them out with phosphorus bombs and then shot or bayoneted them. Sometimes they allowed them to run before shooting them. Sometimes they would put a grenade in the German's pocket and pull the pin out and let him run towards the German line.

In his diaries Bean records incidents of cowardice, brutality, ill treatment of prisoners, shameful treatment of the wounded and the dread many felt about returning to the front line.

Some Australian soldiers (129 including 119 deserters) were sentenced to death for mutiny, desertion to the enemy or treachery. The punishment for these crimes was death but none was executed. The Governor-General had to confirm all sentences passed by courts-martial. He failed to endorse any death sentences despite strong demands by the British Army for the authority to carry it out on Australian soldiers. Brigadier General Glasgow believed strongly that deserters be executed and argued strongly for a change in rules without success.

Neither were Australians blemish-free of what we refer to as 'war crimes'. In December 1918 a black event took place at the village of Serafin. Throughout the desert campaign the Allied forces, many Australians and New Zealanders in particular, had experienced run-ins with the Bedouins, the native desert people. Some Australians and other troops were encamped near Serafin preparing to return home, when a Bedouin came into the camp and stole from a New Zealander, who chased him. The Bedouin shot him dead. The Australians and New Zealanders and some Scottish troops surrounded the town and asked the chief to give up the murderer. When that didn't happen they went back the next night and massacred, it is said, every able-bodied man in the village, then burnt it to the ground. General Allenby, the Commander-in-Chief, brought them to parade, called them a bunch of cowards and murderers and withdrew recommendations for awards and citations.

Last word

The last word is best left to eminent British war correspondent Philip Gibbs:

> *The Australians slouched up the Street of the Three Pebbles with a grim look under their wide-brimmed hats, having come down from Pozieres, where it was always hell in the days of the Somme fighting. I liked the look of them, dusty up to the eyes in summer, muddy up to their eyes in winter—these gipsy fellows, scornful of discipline for discipline's sake, but desperate fighters, as simple as children in their ways of thought and speech (except for the frightful others) and looking at life, this life of war and this life in Amiens, with frank, curious eyes, and a kind of humourous contempt for death and disease, and English Tommies and French girls and 'the whole damned show', as they called it. They were lawless except for the laws to which their souls gave allegiance. They behaved as equals of all men, giving no respect for generals or staff officers or the devils of hell. There was a primitive spirit of manhood in them, and they took what they wanted, and were ready to pay for it in coin or disease or wounds. They had no conceit of themselves in a little, vain way, but they reckoned themselves the only fighting-men, simply, and without boasting. They were hard as steel, and finely*

tempered. Some of them were ruffians, but most of them were, I imagine, like those English yeomen who came into France with the Black Prince, men who lived 'rough', close to nature, of sturdy independence, good-humoured, though fierce in a fight and ruthless. They had money to spend beyond the dreams of our poor Tommy. Six shillings and sixpence a day and remittances from home. So they pushed open the doors of any restaurant in Amiens and sat down to table next to English officers, not abashed, and ordered anything that pleased their taste, and wine in plenty.

Chapter 22
Second World War

The ANZAC spirit was clearly evident in Australia's later participation in wars, campaigns and peacekeeping operations. Mateship was important in seeing the ANZACs through the Gallipoli campaign and the ordeal of the trenches of France. The spirit was there at Tobruk, El Alamein, Kokoda, Changi and the Burma Railway.

Global conflict

World War II was a world-wide conflict fought between the Allied Powers and the Axis Powers from 1939 until 1945. The Big Four Allied Powers were USSR, USA, UK and China; France, before its surrender in 1940 and after its liberation in 1944, was a major ally. The major Axis Powers were Germany, Italy and Japan, with Germany and Japan being the major military powers. The war was more global than WWI both in nations involved and theatres of combat. Armed forces from more than 70 nations were engaged in aerial, naval and ground-based combat throughout much of the world.

A number of causes underlie WWII, such as the terms and conditions forced on Germany by the Treaty of Versailles. However, the Axis Powers had militaristic Governments with imperial ambitions, particularly Japan, who wanted access to resources for its economic expansion. Nazi Germany, led by Adolf Hitler, annexed Austria and Czechoslovakia and began its persecution of the Jews. Fascist Italy, led by Mussolini, occupied Ethiopia in 1936; it had already colonised Libya during the previous two decades. Imperial Japan had annexed Taiwan in 1895, Korea by force in 1910 and, having occupied Manchuria in 1931, began a full-scale war with China in 1937. The Japanese committed major atrocities in China, the most notorious being the Nanking Massacre, in which about 300,000 Chinese were slaughtered. Japan's militarist Prime Minister Tojo ruled virtually as a dictator; Japan's goal was to build a great empire in Asia. In the end, war was inevitable if nations were to maintain their sovereignty and freedom.

WWII officially began on 3 September 1939, when Britain and France declared war on Germany after it had attacked Poland. German forces quickly overran much of Europe and by mid-1940 Britain was the only European nation still fighting against Germany. Britain was saved from invasion, when it defeated Germany's attempt to gain air superiority in the Battle of Britain, fought during July-October 1940. Australian volunteers, along with those from other nations, took part in the Battle of Britain and later more than 10,000 Australians served in Bomber Command, which took the war to the heart of Germany.

The RAAF 460 squadron flew more Lancaster missions and dropped a greater tonnage of bombs over Germany than any other squadron in Bomber Command.

Encouraged by Germany's victories, Mussolini took Italy into the war on the German side in June 1940. However, doubts expressed by the German Ambassador to Italy about the Italians' stomach for war 'Italians not in a state to fight war militarily, materially, morally' proved correct. Italy invaded Greece and British-held Egypt later that year but failed and brought German forces into these theatres of the war in 1941.

Laverton, Vic, 14 November 1944. Avro Lancaster bomber aircraft 'G for George' on the airfield at RAAF Station Laverton. Source: AWM, No. VIC1747A

By June 1941 the Germans had defeated the Greeks and the British forces sent to defend Greece and strategically important Crete. German forces remained there until 1944. Though this was a disastrous campaign for the Allies, German losses were also crippling.

In North Africa the Italians invaded British-held Egypt, where UK and British Commonwealth forces guarded the strategically important Suez Canal and Arabian oil-fields. In their counter-attack the greatly out-numbered UK Commonwealth forces forced the surrender of the entire invasion army and advanced well into Libya. In early 1941 German land and air forces arrived to bolster the Italians and the Desert War began in earnest. The turning point in the Desert War and consequently the War in Europe was the Second Battle of El Alamein, which began in October 1942. German forces were finally caught between the British forces in the east and British-US forces in the west; US forces had landed in North Africa in November 1942. In mid-1943 the Allies invaded Italy.

In June 1941, the USSR, which had signed a non-aggression pact with Germany in August 1939, entered the war, when attacked by Germany. By the beginning of 1943 the Russians had halted the German advance east, the turning point being the Battle of Stalingrad.

In September 1940 Japan signed a peace treaty with Germany and Italy. Japan had decided to become a member of the Axis Powers. It believed the war in Europe gave it the opportunity to pursue its ambitions for securing resources in South-east Asia through the conquest of European colonies that the colonial powers were unable to defend. In September 1941 Japanese troops occupied French Indochina with the acquiescence of the Vichy French.

The Pacific War began on 7 December 1941, when Japan attacked the US Pacific Fleet in Pearl Harbour; the United States was the only country with sufficient naval forces to oppose Japan in the Pacific. Fortunately, the Japanese missed the most vital targets, the American aircraft carriers. The Japanese also destroyed the US air force in the Philippines and landed troops in northern Malaya. Both the USA and Britain declared war on Japan as did Australia.

The USA entered the European conflict several days later, when Germany and Italy declared war on USA.

The Japanese eliminated the British navy as a force in that part of the world, when its bombers sank the battleship *Prince of Wales* and the battle cruiser *Repulse* off the coast of Malaya on 10 December 1941. They fought their way down the Malayan Peninsula and at the end of February forced the surrender of the supposedly mighty fortress of Singapore. As a result 80,000 Allied troops became prisoners of war. Within six months Japan controlled most of South-east Asia. The first major setback to the Japanese advance was inflicted by the USA in naval battles in the Coral Sea (May) and at Midway (July), which removed any immediate threat of Japanese invasion of Australia. By the beginning of 1943 Allied victories had stopped the Japanese advance south and east and US forces began an 'island hopping' strategy to retake the Philippines and defeat Japan.

After the overthrow of Mussolini in July 1943, Italy joined the Allies in October. Towards the end of the war, many countries declared war on Germany and the Axis Powers. Some of these countries had been barely involved in WWII. The USSR did not declare war on Japan until 8 August 1945; a state of war still exists between Russia and Japan, the obstacle to their signing a peace treaty being a dispute over the Kuril Islands.

The European war ended in March 1945, when Germany surrendered unconditionally after Hitler committed suicide. The war in the Pacific ended in August 1945, after the USA dropped nuclear bombs on Hiroshima and Nagasaki. WWII resulted in the deaths of more than 60 million people, making it the deadliest conflict in human history.

As in the previous world war Australia played a significant part in many theatres of the war, not simply measured by numbers of personnel involved but those numbers in relationship to its small population of 7 million and the performance of its soldiers, who reinforced the ANZAC legend. Of the 993,000 who served, 27,073 died or were killed in action, 23,477 were wounded, 23,376 were Japanese POWs (8,031 of whom died) and 8,184 were German POWs (265 of whom died). About 560,000 members of the Australian Imperial Force (AIF) served overseas. On D-Day, the invasion force included up to about 3,000 Australians.

More than 18,000 Italian prisoners of war captured in the Middle East were shipped to Australia. Many of them chose to work as cheap labour on Australian farms, where their lifestyle was so good that an estimated one-in-five prisoners returned to Australia after they were repatriated at the end of the war.

The war had brought about further consolidation of Australia as a nation, particularly geo-politically. Paul Hasluck, historian and Governor-General, observed:

> *The war meant that during six years, to an increasing extent, the people were called on to think and act as one nation and they were virtually under the leadership and control of one Australian government, with the state governments being used as its agents on most of the big matters and carrying on the local routine on other matters with reduced resources.*

Australia at war

Just as it did in WWI, Australia participated in WWII from the very beginning. Like the previous war, WWII began as a European war. It was a war all hoped would not take place. My mother, who was in hospital after my birth, said she felt a great sense of relief when Neville Chamberlain returned from meeting Adolf Hitler, declaring 'peace in our time'. Like all other Australians, our family had suffered from WWI. Her reading *Gone with the Wind* while in hospital would have reinforced these sentiments. Australians knew that, if Britain went to war, Australia would go to its aid, which it did just one year later.

In September 1939, immediately on learning that Britain and France had declared war against Germany, the Australian Prime Minister, Robert Menzies, informed the Australian people in a radio broadcast:

> *It is my melancholy duty to inform you officially that, in consequence of a persistence by Germany in her invasion of Poland, Great Britain has declared war upon her, and that, as a result, Australia is also at war.*

At the end of 1941, when Japan attacked Pearl Harbour and entered the war on the Axis side, John Curtin, Prime Minister for only two months, told the Australian people:

> *... we are at war with Japan ... because our vital interests are imperilled and because the rights of free people in the whole Pacific are assailed.*

This was the first time Australia had made an independent declaration of war against a hostile power. Only a couple of weeks later Curtin stated that Australia now looked to America as a partner in fighting the war, that had come to its front door.

Australia was not prepared for war. It had a small navy and air force, and a very small permanent army (Permanent Military Force or PMF) and a large under-trained part-time Militia (Citizen Military Force or CMF) unprepared for war. Training of the CMF increased and numbers were boosted with further volunteers. Members of the Militia tended to come from inner-city working-class backgrounds during a time of extreme economic hardship. Groups of mates enlisted. The Militia units were restricted by law to serving only in Australia and its territories, so a volunteer expeditionary force, the Second AIF, was formed for overseas service. When Japan entered the war, conscription was introduced to expand the Militia.

Second AIF

Four volunteer infantry divisions, the 6th, 7th, 8th and 9th, were raised and formed the Second AIF. They included men who had transferred from the PMF and CMF. Unlike in WWI few who volunteered were seeking adventure. Some joined up out of a sense of duty and others because whatever the army was offering would have to be better than their current jobs and lives. Many joined to escape the poverty of the Great Depression of the 1930s. At that time one-in-three was unemployed and vast numbers of jobless men tramped from town to town looking for work or, at the very least, a handout of food and tea. Some volunteered, hoping to be allocated a 'soldier-settler' block if they survived. They came from all walks of life: teachers, timber workers, taxi drivers, carpenters, con men, lawyers, labourers, illiterates, butchers, bakers, etc.

The 6th, 7th and 9th Divisions were transported to the Middle East, where they fought against the Italians and Germans in campaigns in North Africa and against the Germans in Greece and Crete and the Vichy French in Syria. Most of the 8th Division were sent to Malaya to fight the Japanese and became POWs at the fall of Singapore. An Armoured Division was also formed but remained in Australia.

The 6th, 7th and 9th Divisions distinguished themselves with their fighting prowess in North Africa and the Middle East, returning home in 1942 and early 1943 to join in the Pacific War in New Guinea and elsewhere.

Militia

Considerable ill-feeling between the AIF and the Militia developed, because of attitudes produced by the differences between them. With the restriction on the Militia to fighting only on Australian territory, many in the AIF considered the Militia wore the uniforms of soldiers but there was no chance they would ever be involved in combat. They branded members of the Militia 'chocolate soldiers' or 'chocos', implying the young, mostly 18-20 year-old recruits were only imitation soldiers and would 'melt' in battle. Naturally, the Militia bitterly resented the name. They were also known as 'Koalas' because, like koalas, they were protected by the Government and were not to be 'shot at or exported'. The Militia recruits were denied adequate training and equipment, and were regrettably poorly treated by the authorities with scant regard for their welfare and feelings. This tended to ratify their 'second-class' status in the eyes of many senior AIF commanders.

As there was an increasing likelihood that Japan would enter the war, three Militia Battalions were sent to garrison Port Moresby in 1941. They were poorly equipped, with very little training and no combat experience. Within a month dengue fever, malaria, dysentery and tropical ulcers had reduced numbers by 25%. Another brigade joined them in May 1942. The fate of New Guinea was in their hands from late July, when the Japanese began their advance on Port Moresby along the Kokoda Track, until the end of August, when AIF reinforcements arrived.

Contrary to expectations, most of the Militia, the so-called 'chocolate' soldiers did not melt. When they did, it was largely the result of their inadequate training and poor leadership. The Militia and Second AIF troops served side-by-side in Papua New Guinea in some of the most bitterly fought campaigns of the war, the most notable being that along the Kokoda Track, where the 39th Militia Battalion upheld the spirit of ANZAC at the very highest level. Sadly, the 53rd Militia Battalion did not, largely as a result of lack of training, incompetent leadership and a splinter group of malcontents that compromised the remainder. It was made up of 'cast offs' and misfits. They were virtually shanghaied and many nursed a grudge against Australian authorities. Most had never seen or handled a rifle when they left Australia. Unchecked by the morale-building influence of good leadership this festered in their minds and had tragic consequences on the Kokoda Track.

Chapter 23
North Africa

Overview

As had been intended for the First AIF in WWI, the plan for the 6th and 7th Second AIF Divisions was to complete their training in the Middle East (Palestine) before joining the British Expeditionary Force in France. The conduct of their WWI counterparts had not been forgotten. Wavell, the British general who met the first units of the 6th Division that arrived in the Middle East, implored them to disprove the reputation that Australian soldiers were 'rough, wild and undisciplined, given to strong drink'. However, the surrender of France intervened. They remained in the Middle East, where the 9th Division joined them. More than any other human endeavour, war never goes according to plan.

The 6th Division went to train in Palestine. On their way up to Gaza they travelled on the railway Australians had built in WWI. After a years training they helped retake East Libya from the Italians. At Christmas 1940 those still training in Palestine were served dinner by their officers. Drinking, brawling and visiting brothels were common in their free time.

The 7th Division underwent a number of changes. The bulk of these troops went to Syria, where they fought a hard-won victory in the campaign against the Vichy French. One of its brigades excelled itself in the siege of Tobruk and another was transferred to the newly created Australian 9th Division, which played a significant role in the siege of Tobruk and at El Alamein.

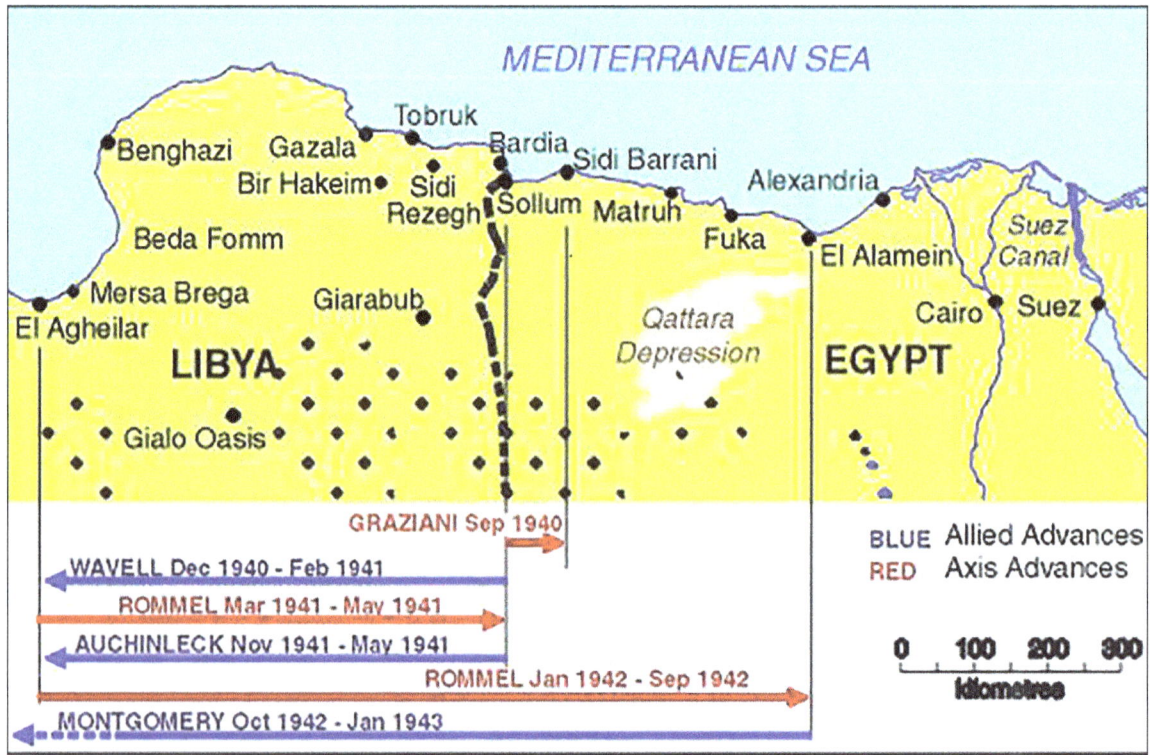

North African campaigns. Source: ANZAC Day Commemoration Committee

In September 1940 Italy invaded British-held Egypt, where British and British Commonwealth forces were guarding the strategically important Suez Canal and Arabian oil-fields. In their counter-attack, the greatly out-numbered British forces, which included the Australian 6th Division, forced the Italians back to Tripoli in Libya taking major fortresses at Bardia and Tobruk on the way and capturing 130,000 prisoners.

In early 1941 German land and air forces arrived to bolster the Italians and forced the British to retreat almost to their original positions in Egypt. However, they failed to take control of the strategically important port of Tobruk, which was relieved the following November by the British offensive that regained most of the ground previously lost to the Germans.

In mid-1942 the Germans launched another major offensive, retaking Tobruk and forcing the British to retreat almost to Alexandria before being stopped in the First Battle of El Alamein. The turning point in the Desert War and consequently the War in Europe was the Second Battle of El Alamein, which began in October 1942. The German forces were finally caught between the British forces in the east and British-US forces in the west; US forces had landed in North Africa in November 1942. In mid-1943 the Allies invaded Italy.

Siege of Tobruk

Tobruk was an excellent place to supply the desert campaign. It had a deep, natural harbour with many natural, defensive features that had been heavily fortified by the Italians. From April 1941 to December 1941 when the siege was finally lifted, Allied troops in Tobruk held out against repeated and determined attacks by vastly larger and better-equipped German forces. Denying General Erwin Rommel a safe port through which to resupply his forces slowed the Axis advance across North Africa, thereby giving the Allies time to build up forces and prepare for the defence of Egypt. Rommel subsequently captured Tobruk in a new offensive in 1942.

For most of the siege, 14,000 Australians made up the bulk of the defending forces of 23,000 (the 9th Division backed up by a brigade of the 7th Division and four regiments of British artillery) commanded by Australian Major General Leslie Morshead. His instructions were to hold the fortress for eight weeks, but the Australians held it for more than five months when, totally exhausted, they were gradually replaced by British, Polish and Czech troops.

Unlike in WWI, the Australian Government insisted that Australians be led by Australians. Morshead insisted on discipline and routine and meticulous personal hygiene, including troops shaving daily. He fostered a culture where nothing was more highly valued than resolution, initiative and refusal to budge, even when against superior forces. Regardless of the dust, heat, vermin, unpalatable food, brackish water, boredom and fear, they emulated their ANZAC forebears in tenacity, courage and doing things differently. Constant air raids and straffing, artillery fire and attacks by tanks did not cower them. A German POW said:

> *I cannot understand you Australians. In Poland, France and Belgium, once the tanks got through the soldiers took it for granted that they were beaten. But you are like demons. The tanks break through and your infantry still keeps fighting.*

A strong perimeter was established around Tobruk – an outer defence circle and an inner defence circle. In one part Australians and Germans were only 200 m apart. The Australians dug extensive tunnel networks and shelters to supplement their trenches and weren't afraid to use them when bombarded. Instead of attacking the tanks head on, they attacked the follow-up infantry. The tanks were easy targets once their ground support had been eliminated.

After proving their ability to repel enemy attacks, they went on the offensive with daring nightly patrolling, in which they crawled on their stomachs under barbed wire and through mine-fields for great distances. Using all their bush-craft to avoid detection, reconnaissance patrols gathered information and, if possible, secured prisoners for identification. Armed with this information, fighting patrols went out to do as much damage and to kill as many of the enemy as possible. They would creep up on an enemy post, surround it and then, at a given signal, rush in with the bayonet and kill soundlessly – not firing a shot. The perpetual shadow of a silent, stealthy death unnerved the enemy, who would put down artillery and mortar barrages on little or no provocation.

The Germans misjudged the Allied forces when they attempted to demoralise the garrison with propaganda broadcasts. Early on in the siege the British traitor known as 'Lord Haw Haw' contemptuously referred to them as 'rats' in their holes, because they sheltered underground during the bombing raids. The Germans overlooked the self-deprecating nature of Australians, who identify with the underdog and never give in when challenged. This only increased the resolve of the Australians. They embraced the description, calling themselves the 'Rats of Tobruk'. Chester Wilmot, pre-eminent Australian war correspondent, wrote:

> *Berlin Radio made a fatal mistake in trying to jibe and scare the Australian soldier into surrender. The longer the odds Lord Haw Haw offered against the Diggers' chance of getting out, the more heavily the digger backed himself.*

The bulk of the 9th Division was withdrawn from Tobruk in September and October 1941 with only the 2/13th Battalion remaining in the fortress at the time the garrison was finally relieved in December. The defence of Tobruk cost the 9th Division 3,164 casualties (650 killed, 1,597 wounded and 917 captured).

While the 6th and 7th Divisions returned to Australia in early 1942, the 9th Division remained in the Middle East carrying out various duties and training in Palestine and Syria. In July, eight months after their withdrawal from Tobruk, they returned to North Africa, where they played a prominent role in defeating the Germans at El Alamein.

VX47906 Corporal Frank Joseph Littlejohn (left) and another member of 2/32nd Battalion with a painted bren gun carrier. On the side is a painting of a rat holding a cigarette and the words "rats to you", symbolising the rats of Tobruk, painted by TX12 Private R.E. (Rufus) Webster. Source: AWM, No. P02522.002

El Alamein

In early 1942 the Axis forces launched another offensive. They retook Tobruk and by the end of June had forced the Allies back deep into Egypt. The capture of Cairo and the Suez Canal seemed a very real possibility. The Allies established a defensive position near the tiny railway siding of El Alamein, just over 100 km west of Alexandria, where the battlefield narrowed to 60 km between the Mediterranean coast and impassable steep slopes of the Qattara Depression. It was here in July 1942 that the Axis advance was stopped (First Battle of El Alamein) and from here in October 1942 that the Second Battle of El Alamein was launched. The Australian 9th Division played an important part in the former and was pivotal in the success of the latter, thereby enhancing the reputation earned defending Tobruk.

On 1 July, the Germans launched a major attack during the first week of which the 9th Division returned from Syria. It was assigned the most northerly section of the defensive line and soon after captured the strategic high ground around Tel el Eisa. The Australians spent the next few days fighting off heavy counter-attacks when the German forces, which had been focused on the southern flank of the battlefield, were redirected against them. Their tenacity in the north prevented Rommel from creating a chance to outflank the British forces in the south. Later that month one Australian Battalion, the 2/28th, was virtually wiped out. By the end of July both sides had suffered great losses and had fought each other to a standstill. The tremendous resolve of the Australians and their heavy sacrifice put Rommel on the defensive and helped destroy the myth of his invincibility. The Allies now held the important high ground near the coast. This provided good observation of the enemy and an excellent position from which to launch further offensives.

2/32nd Australian Infantry Battalion holding German counter-attack at El Alamein, Western Desert, Egypt, on 31 October 1942. William Dargie, 1943. Source: AWM, No. ART22251

25-pounder guns of the 2/8th Field Regiment at Royal Australian Artillery in action on the coastal sector near El Alamein. Second battle of El Alamein. The Allied Forces attack: 10:00 pm, 23 October 1942. Source: AWM, No. 024515

From August until the end of October, the Allied forces steadily increased in strength, whereas the Axis forces weakened, their supply lines strangled by Allied air and naval attacks. The Axis forces went on the defensive and prepared for the Allied offensive. This included laying thousands of mines in an eight km belt, referred to as the Devil's Gardens, along the entire 55 km El Alamein line. Finally, an Allied army of 220,000 men, 1,100 tanks and 900 guns faced 180,000 men, 600 tanks and 500 guns of the Axis powers. The Allied plan was for infantry to push forward and clear paths through the enemy's defensive mine-fields to allow armoured forces to get into the enemy's rear areas. The main assault was to be made in the north along the coastal plain by forces (30 Corps) that included the Australian 9th Division. This attack was designed as a feint to draw Axis forces northward away from the planned main breakthrough point further south in the desert proper.

The Allied offensive (Second Battle of El Alamein) began on 23 October with a massive artillery bombardment that lit up the night sky. As usual in war, things did not go as planned. The initial attack further south failed to break the Axis line. However, the initial advances by the Australians went well and they seized high ground around a point known as Trig 29. After beating off a fierce German counter-attack they were turned north, a move that threatened to cut off a German Division trapped against the Mediterranean Sea. Because of this threat, Rommel threw the whole Axis armoured force against the Australian positions. For five days fighting raged around Trig 29. It involved some of the fiercest fighting the Australians had experienced. However, by drawing the weight of Axis forces, the 9th Division enabled the Allied armoured spearhead to attack the weakened Axis positions further south, eventually forcing a way through. Faced with encirclement by early November, Rommel withdrew and began a headlong retreat to Tunisia.

During the five-month campaign, the 9th Division suffered 5,829 casualties, or virtually half of its normal fighting strength. The overall campaign from July to November 1942 cost 1,225 Australian lives. During the final 12 days the 9th Division lost 620 men. In this final battle, it suffered 20% of the Allied army's casualties of 13,500 killed, wounded or missing, though it formed only 7% of the total force of 220,000 men.

Montgomery's first act after the battle was seen to be won, was to travel to 9th Division HQ and thank them for their redemption of the initially-failed 10th Armoured Corps attack in the south.

The commander of 30 Corps stated that the El Alamein breakthrough was:

> ... *only made possible by the 9th Division's Homeric fighting.*

General Alexander, Commander-in-Chief Middle East, when reviewing a divisional parade at Gaza in Palestine on 22 December, told them:

> ... *The battle of El Alamein will make history and you are in the proud position of having taken a major part in that great victory. ...There is one thought I shall cherish above all others – under my command fought the Nineth Australian Division.*

When the Allies landed in Normandy Major General Francis de Guingaund, Chief of Staff of Field Marshal Montgomery's Land-force Headquarters, said:

> *My God, I wish we had 9th Australian Division with us this morning.*

As at Tobruk the Australians were a thorn in Rommel's side. Aggressive patrolling allowed them to dominate no-man's land, which was important for gathering information. They would charge the German infantry and tanks with screaming war cries that completely unnerved both the tank crews and infantry. At night there was much hand-to-hand combat. Once again the Germans, though resolute fighters, would baulk at the prospect of bayonet fighting and instead surrender. In the war of attrition, as key officers and brave men fell, other men stood up to take on their roles and responsibilities. After the battle Rommel, the German commander, said:

> *I could have won North Africa with a division of Australians under my command.*

The desert war was a long and weary fight not only against the Axis forces but also against the desolate forces of nature. During the day the heat was exhausting – some days exceeding 50 °C. The nights were freezing. Fleas, flies, dust and sand penetrated everything, every mouthful of food. Food supplies were meagre and boring. Malnutrition, dysentery and skin disorders took their toll on many soldiers after three months in the desert. Survival, amongst other things, depended on sustaining a sense of humour and learning to rely on and support your mates.

At a fearfully high price the Australians had played a crucial role in ensuring the Allied victory in North Africa. They returned to Australia in 1943 to fight in the Pacific War.

Chapter 24
Pacific War

The war in Europe, Africa and the Middle East was far from Australia. The Pacific War brought war on to Australia's doorstep. In 1941, when armed conflict with Japan seemed inevitable, most of the Australian 8th Division was sent to Malaya. The rest of the Division was deployed on the strategic islands of Timor, Ambon and New Britain. The Pacific conflict began in December 1941, when the Japanese bombed Pearl Harbour and invaded Malaya. The 6th and 7th Divisions were recalled from the Middle East, returning in early 1942. The 9th Division stayed on in North Africa for a further year, returning in early 1943.

Map of Imperial Japanese advances in the South-west Pacific and South-east Asia areas during the first five months of the Pacific Campaign of the Second World War. Source: United States Army Center of Military History. *The Campaigns of MacArthur in the Pacific*. Volume I

The Japanese gained control of the sea and air almost immediately and advanced rapidly down the Malayan Peninsula and by mid-February Singapore had fallen. By the end of March the Netherlands East Indies, most of the islands to the north and east and much of the northern part of the mainland of Papua New Guinea were under their control. Apart from Portuguese East Timor, where the Australian Independent Company fought a guerrilla campaign until the end of 1942, the war for Australia shifted to Papua New Guinea, which the Japanese wished to secure to consolidate their position in the South Pacific.

When their plan to seize Port Moresby, the major Allied base, by amphibious invasion was thwarted by the Battles of the Coral Sea (May 1942) and Midway (June 1942), the Japanese made a two-pronged attempt to take it by land. In late July troops landed in Buna-Gona area on the Papuan north coast and began a full-scale offensive across the Owen Stanley Range. A supporting offensive in late August failed, when a largely Australian force repulsed an elite force of Japanese marines in two weeks of fighting around Milne Bay. This was the first defeat suffered by Japanese land forces.

The Japanese advanced to within 50 km of Port Moresby before being forced back to Kokoda and finally to their heavily defended coastal bases at Buna, Gona and Sanananda. In November, Australian and American forces began an assault on these positions and slowly overcame them in bitter, close-quarters fighting. Their strongpoint at Sanananda fell on 22 January 1943. Conditions in the Japanese base were horrific, as their supplies had been exhausted and many had resorted to cannibalism.

This victory saved Australia not only from invasion but also from isolation and guaranteed the viability of the only American base in the Western Pacific.

Heavy brutal fighting continued until September, when Lae fell. While fighting by the Australians continued in New Guinea and other spots in South-east Asia for the rest of the war, it was very much a secondary theatre to the American advance to the Philippines and defeat of Japan.

Except for the mistakes which were made, plus disease, suffering and horror common to all wars, and, sadly like the previous war, ignorance and failure to grasp the situation in the field by those in high command, the Pacific War bore little resemblance to that fought in the Middle East and North Africa, or Gallipoli, Palestine and the Western Front in the previous world war. The latter were fought in temperate climates, in deserts and, except for the rain and mud of Flanders, solid land, where periods of dry weather occurred. Supplies, hospitals and reserves were not far behind you and by-and-large your foe was in front of you and readily seen. On the other hand, the Pacific War was fought in the tropics, in the heat and incessant rain of the jungle, where tropical diseases caused far more casualties than the fierce, bitter fighting; a jungle that not only hindered movement but also in which the enemy was invisible

Map of New Guinea showing Kokoda track position. Source: ANZAC Day Commemoration Committee

– only the throw of a hand grenade away. Fighting was at such close quarters that, on one occasion during the Kokoda Campaign, a Japanese climbing a tree in the dark grabbed hold of an Australian bayonet mistaking it for a branch. Supply lines were lengthy and maintained with difficulty. Evacuation of the wounded was no mean feat. The Australians sent to fight in these conditions were ill-equipped and unprepared. They had to improvise and learn, in many cases from their foe, as they fought. The Japanese were brutal and barbaric; the Germans, by comparison, were gentlemen. The Japanese gave no quarter and expected none; it was a disgrace to be taken prisoner – the only outcome of battle being victory or death.

The casualties suffered by both the Allies and the Japanese in Papua and New Guinea highlight the nature of this conflict in stark relief. The following data given to illustrate this are suspect. A total of 5,770 Australian soldiers are known to have died in Papua and New Guinea, the Bismarck Archipelago and Bougainville. Roughly 5,000 American soldiers, marines, sailors and airmen died in the New Guinea campaign. Only five percent of the 200,000 Japanese troops sent to Papua and east and central New Guinea returned home.

If there is a high point in the coalescing of those qualities that make the Australian – endurance, mateship, initiative, resourcefulness, larrikanism … – it must be in the fighting in New Guinea, in particular that during the Kokoda Track Campaign.

Malaya and Singapore

During WWI Australia based its defence on the 'Singapore Strategy'. Britain would build a large naval base at Singapore to defend its imperial interests and also Australia. In return Australia would provide forces to help defend Britain and its Empire in the event of a European war. Australia considered Japan to be the only likely enemy in the Asia-Pacific region. The idea was that a strong British fleet based at Singapore could defeat a Japanese invasion fleet, thereby making Australia safe.

British naval vessels, however, would not be permanently based at Singapore. The whole 'Singapore Strategy' was dependent on vessels being dispatched from European waters in time of crisis. The flaw in this was there was no guarantee that Britain could spare a fleet if there was a war in Europe. When the Japanese threat loomed in late 1941, Britain could spare few vessels for Singapore. What arrived early in December was not a great fleet but a small squadron based around just two large battle ships, *Prince of Wales* and *Repulse*. Japanese bombers sank them a few days later in the opening hours of their invasion of Malaya. With the loss of the ships, the Singapore Strategy crumbled and with it the rationale for defending Singapore. When British Commonwealth forces withdrew on to Singapore Island in January 1942 they prepared for a defence that was now to be conducted for mainly political reasons, perhaps the foremost being to maintain American support.

The Japanese fought with an ingenuity, initiative and ability to outflank their opponents that constantly surprised the Allied forces. They moved swiftly on bicycles down the dirt roads that connected the rubber plantations. Despite the clash-and-withdrawal nature of the campaign, the Australians were always ready to make a stand and wherever possible take the fight to the enemy. That is undoubtedly why they were almost the only defenders to earn Japanese respect for their fighting qualities. The 8th Division troops sent to Malaya earlier that year were deployed in the southern State of Johore waiting for the enemy to advance that far. They went into action on 14 January and achieved the few allied successes of the campaign. In the week of heavy fighting that followed, they were unable to halt the Japanese advance. The Australian and British forces retreated across the causeway to Singapore, where they made a final stand.

Within two weeks their position was untenable. More than one million civilian residents and refugees remained in the city, the Japanese had captured its main water supply, and their aircraft were free to bomb at will. At 8.30 pm on 15 February 1942 all resistance ceased, when Lieutenant General Arthur Percival, the GOC of British forces in Malaya, surrendered his force of over 130,000 troops. At least 1,800 Australians died in the Malayan campaign, nearly three-quarters of all the battle-deaths suffered by British forces. About 15,000 others became prisoners of war (POWs).

Prisoners of Japanese

The majority of more than 22,000 Australian prisoners of war were captured by the Japanese during the first few weeks of 1942. Most of them (14,972) were captured in Singapore; other principal Australian prisoner-of-war groups were captured in Java (2,736) – on its way back to Australia, elements of the 7th Division had been diverted to Java; Timor (1,137); Ambon (1,075); and New Britain (1,049). Those captured when Singapore fell were imprisoned at Changi. Many of them and those captured elsewhere were sent off to work camps in Burma, Thailand, Borneo and Japan. In captivity, Australian prisoners fared better than other nationalities because of core values such as their sense of mateship and egalitarianism.

By the war's end about 8,000 (36%) of these prisoners had died, mostly as a result of their captors' indifference and brutality. In comparison, only three percent of the 8,000-odd taken prisoner by the Germans died. Unlike the Germans, the Japanese neither signed nor adhered to the Third Geneva Convention. Throughout the war, Changi was the main transit camp for prisoners being sent to work camps. Bad though it was, Changi was heaven compared with the Thai-Burma Railway. The Sandakan to Ranau 'death march' in 1944 remains the greatest single atrocity committed against Australians in war. Of the 1,000 who set out, only six survived the war.

Changi

The Australians' ingenuity and resourcefulness were displayed at Changi, where entertainment was an essential part of maintaining morale and fighting boredom. There was no lack of talent on which to call, and a great deal of skill and ingenuity went into producing scripts, sets and costumes. Surprisingly the Japanese allowed a permanent concert party to be set up. It performed a new show every two weeks and over the years these included variety shows, musical dramas, pantomime and serious drama. Another group, formed to act as teachers and

Artworks by Murray Griffin, official war artist Second World War.
Left: *Working party returning to Changi camp*, 1944. Source: AWM, No. ART25108 Above: *Changi prison camp, early days*, 1942. Source: AWM, No. ART24480

lecturers, also established a library. David Griffin, who subsequently became Lord Mayor of Sydney, wrote a children's fable about happiness, *The Happiness Box*.

Survival depended upon a variety of factors. Strong emotions – the hate of their oppressors, love of family and will to live and get home – were important. When asked how and why they survived, some stressed military discipline, others individual initiative. The Australians quickly earned a reputation for being master smugglers. Some stole and scrounged from guards and even from each other. Compared with the Dutch and the British, characteristics which stood out were their tendency to look after each other, to lie and steal for each other and to help a mate out of a scrape. Most helped their mates and relied on them, when things got tough. Rarely did an Australian die alone. All needed luck.

Thai-Burma Railway

The notorious Thai-Burma Death Railway is a prime example of Japanese brutality and disregard for the lives of those they had conquered or taken as prisoners of war. Built to supply its campaign against the Allies in Burma, it ran 415 km from Ban Pong in Thailand to Thanbyuzayat in Burma through some of the most inhospitable disease-ridden terrain in the world. The maximum of human effort and an absolute minimum of mechanical equipment were used in its construction, which began in October 1942 and was finally completed in December 1943.

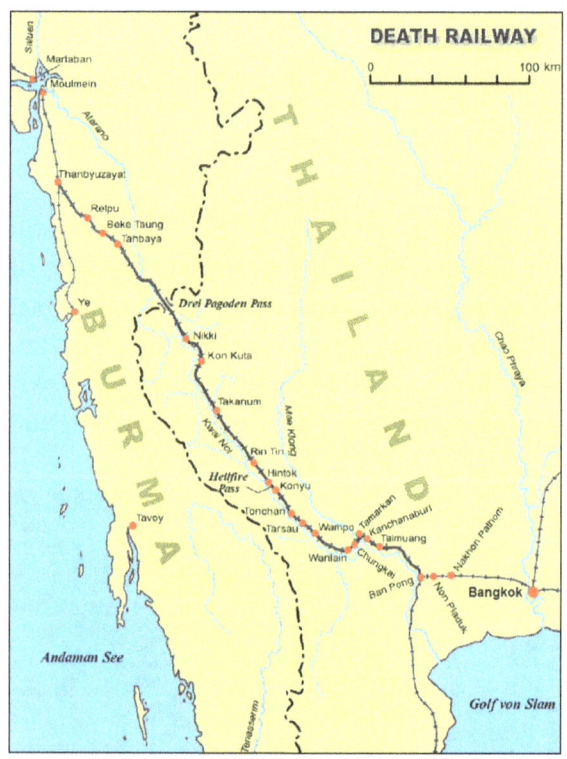

Above: Hellfire Pass. Source: David Iliff, Wikimedia Commons

Left: Thai-Burma Railway, Death Railway. Source: W. Wolny, Wikimedia Commons

Roughly every one of the 120,000 sleepers laid cost a human life. An estimated 30,000 British, 13,000 Australian, 18,000 Dutch and 700 Americans worked on its construction, during which about 6,000 British, 2,710 Australians, 2,600 Dutch and 400 Americans died. About half of the 200,000 Malay, Tamil, Burmese, Chinese and other forced labourers also perished.

Malnutrition was the biggest killer. Men were forced to work up to 18 hours a day at strenuous jobs on a totally inadequate diet. Food supplies were irregular and inadequate. Because of climate and transport problems food was also of poor quality. Those who were fortunate got a cup of boiled rice or millet three times a day. The prisoners supplemented this by scrounging, stealing and scavenging for herbs, eating fungus off trees and trapping lizards, snakes and rats.

Chapter 24: Pacific War

Japanese brutality, exhaustion from the relentless labour and disease – malaria, tropical ulcers, cholera, dysentery – also contributed to the huge losses. Unless bed-ridden and unable to stand, the sick still had to work. Japanese camp commandants insisted on men totally unfit for work being driven out and sometimes carried out of the camps. Those who stayed behind were accommodated in camp 'hospitals', which were simply one or more crude jungle huts.

The Australians nicknamed an infamous section of the railway on which they worked *Hellfire Pass*. Four hundred Australian prisoners began work at Hellfire Pass on ANZAC Day in 1943. It and adjacent cuttings were excavated by labour gangs working around-the-clock shifts. Forced to work up to eighteen hours a day and exhausted beyond belief, the men would look down into the cutting at night and think that the torches and lamps resembled the Fires of Hell. This work was done without the aid of reliable mechanical equipment. The most primitive of hand tools were used to drill holes for the explosives used in blasting the rock and for removing the waste rock. Of the 1,000 Australian and British soldiers who took 12 weeks to excavate it and a series of nearby smaller cuttings, 700 died.

Allied medical officers scattered along the 'Death Railway' did what they could to limit the suffering and death caused by disease and injuries. Neither drugs nor surgical equipment were supplied by the Japanese. The 'Free Thai' resistance risked their lives to get medical supplies into POW camps on the railway. The medical officers and orderlies improvised a great deal of equipment such as administering blood transfusions through bamboo pieces and stethoscope tubes. Their devotion, skill and enterprise saved the lives of thousands. The most renowned of these medicos was Edward 'Weary' Dunlop.

While attending university in Victoria in 1957 I joined the Rugby Union club and played in the second team. The standard of play was below that in New South Wales and Queensland, the Rugby States. Football in Victoria at that time meant Australian Rules.

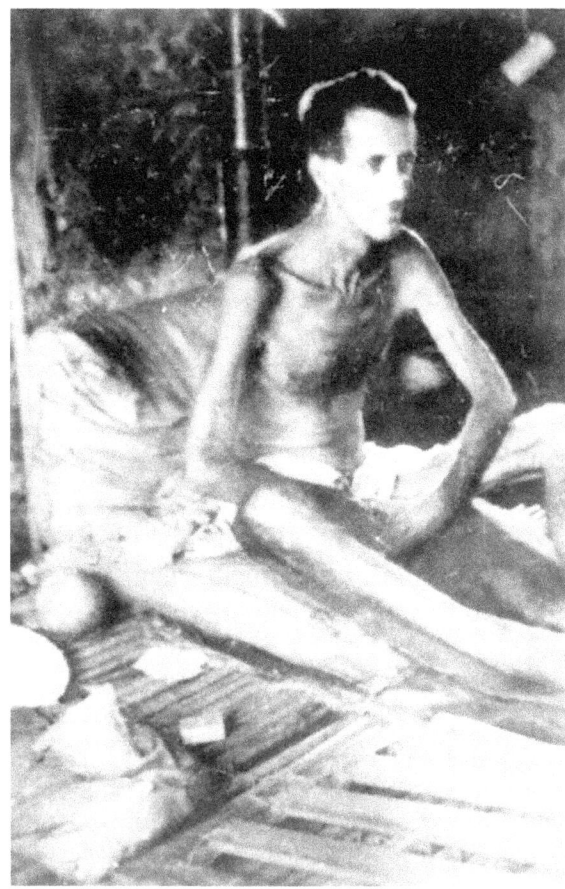

Burma or Thailand, 1945. An emaciated Australian prisoner of war (POW) showing the effects of beriberi, typical of the condition of many of the Allied prisoners of the Japanese at the end of the war. Source: AWM, No. P01433.020 (Donor B. Theobald)

Three 'fit' workers at Shimo Songkurai No 1 Camp, standing outside the camp hospital. Burma Thailand Railway: Songkurai, ca. 1943. Photo by NX37745 Private (Pte) George Aspinall. Despite a strict ban against photography by POWs, Pte Aspinall took photographs at great risk to himself and other prisoners. Source: AWM, No. P01433.020

After our game we would stay on to support the first team before getting together for a few beers. A regular supporter on the sideline watching our first team had, I learnt, once played for the Wallabies, the Australian representative Rugby Union Team, and was called 'Weary' Dunlop. Sometimes he would issue an invitation to spend the evening at his place. At no stage did I accept the invitation, mainly because I was not fond of late nights. Also, public transport was a problem and getting back to the residential college meant waiting for a lift with someone who had a car. The 'Seaweed' (naval cadets) players and supporters always went. I sometimes wondered why they did but was never sufficiently interested to ask why. Such is the ego-centric nature of youth. It was only many years later that I became aware of who 'Weary' Dunlop was and the important part he played in tending to the troops who toiled on the Thai-Burma Railway.

The prisoners' sufferings on the railway have come to epitomise the ordeal of Australians in captivity. The railway camps produced not only many victims, but also heroes who helped others to endure, to survive or to die with dignity. Through those qualities that can be bundled up in the term 'mateship', Australian prisoners fared better than those of other nationalities. Former prisoner and subsequently Federal Parliamentarian Tom Uren expressed it in these terms:

> *We were living by the principle of the fit looking after the sick, the young looking after the old and the rich looking after the poor. A few months after we arrived at Hintok mountain camp, a British force arrived. They were about 400 strong. As a temporary arrangement they had tents. The officers selected the best, the non-commissioned officers the next best and the men got the dregs. Soon after they arrived the wet season set in, bringing with it cholera and dysentery. Six weeks later only about 50 men marched out of that camp and of that number fewer than half survived.*

Sandakan

Australian prisoners were sent to Sandakan in 1942 to build an airstrip. While initially they were treated reasonably well, gradually rations were reduced and beatings increased. By late 1944, with Allied forces advancing towards Borneo, the Japanese decided to send about 2,000 Australian and British prisoners westward to Ranau, in Borneo's rugged interior. Weak and sick prisoners staggered for about 260 km along jungle tracks. Many died on the way, their bodies never recovered. Those too weak to march were left behind in Sandakan, where all died or were killed and those unable to continue marching were killed on the way. Only six – all Australians – out of those sent to Ranau survived the war.

Attacks on the Australian mainland

In the beginning WWII was remote from Australia but at the onset of the Pacific War, war came to Australia. In 1942 the Australian mainland came under direct attack for the first time. Towns in northern Australia were bombed and Japanese midget submarines entered Sydney Harbour.

Darwin bombed

On 19 February 1942 the Japanese began bombing Darwin. More than 260 Japanese fighter aircraft and bombers attacked the port and shipping in the harbour twice during the day, killing 252 Allied service personnel and civilians, sinking 21 ships and destroying 23 aircraft. Subsequent raids in April, June, July and November 1942 and March 1943 were carried out with forces of 30-40 fighters and bombers. Between these large operations groups of fewer than a dozen Japanese aircraft performed smaller raids. While most raids occurred in daylight, there were some small-scale night attacks. The 64th, and last, air raid on Darwin occurred on 12 November 1943. Despite popular fears these raids were not the precursor to an invasion but they did interrupt the use of Darwin's port facilities.

Darwin, NT, 19 February 1942. Scene during the first Japanese air raid on the harbour. The *Neptunia*, loaded with ammunition, has blown up at the wharf. In front of the explosion the tiny HMAS *Vigilant* carries out rescue work, whilst in the centre background a floating dock holds *Katoomba* which escaped damage. In the right foreground is *Zealandia*, another ammunition ship, which set afire and subsequently sank. Source: AWM, No. 134955

Darwin, NT, 19 February 1942. Bomb damage to the Darwin Post Office and surrounding buildings as a result of the first Japanese air raid. Source: AWM, No. P00480.001 (Donor W. Harvey)

Corrugated iron from air-raid shelter used as a cubby-house in our backyard. Source: Peter Hasker

On 3 March Broome, in Western Australia, was straffed. In succeeding months air attacks were made on other towns in northern Australia and a total of 97 air attacks on northern Australia and enemy air reconnaissance over the region occurred throughout much of 1944.

Rockhampton was prepared for air raids. Blackout conditions prevailed, e.g. car headlights were hooded much as traffic lights are today. I recall the wail of air-raid sirens being tested each Monday morning, probably around 11.00 am, because I remember hiding by my mother while she hung out washing. To this day I find the sound of sirens disturbing. There was an air-raid shelter at one end of the lawn at the front of our house. I cannot recall any details of the shelter but was told it was a simple underground construction, which became a garden bed after the war. I understand there was an alert one night so my mother marshalled all in the house to enter the shelter but overlooked my baby sister. Later in the War, a corrugated steel structure was erected at the other end of the lawn. This ended its life in the back-yard as a cubby-house, where we kids played all sorts of games including mothers and fathers – without doubt, like the garden, a much better fate than their war-time role.

Midget submarines enter Sydney Harbour

In May 1943, three Japanese 2-man midget submarines entered Sydney harbour. One was sunk by depth-charges and its crew committed suicide. A second became entangled in an anti-torpedo net, following which the crew destroyed it and also killed themselves The bodies of these four crewmen were cremated with full naval honours, in the forlorn hope that this show of respect for the dead men might help to improve the treatment of the many Australian POWs.

Several men watch as a Japanese midget two-man submarine is raised from the harbour bed. The Japanese submarine, which attempted a raid on shipping in Sydney Harbour on 31 May 1942 was rammed and sunk by gunfire before it could fire its torpedoes. Ronald N. Keam, 1 June 1942.
Source: AWM, No. 060696

The third submarine fired two torpedoes, one of which exploded beneath a small RAN depot ship HMAS *Kuttabul* killing 21 sailors. It evaded efforts to locate it and exited the harbour. In 2006 the submarine was finally located resting several kilometres off Sydney's northern beaches, where it and its two crewmen will remain protected by a 500 m exclusion zone.

Chapter 25
Kokoda

The Kokoda Track Campaign in Papua New Guinea continued from the end of July 1942, when Japanese troops landed in the Buna-Gona area, until the final surviving Japanese at Sanananda surrendered in January 1943. Along with Milne Bay, the Kokoda Campaign remains the most important ever fought by Australians to ensure the direct security of Australia.

It was a campaign where the high commands of both sides, especially the Allied side, failed to support their commanders and soldiers in the field. The Allies had deciphered the Japanese codes and so were warned of the Japanese intent to capture Port Moresby. Allied Supreme Commander Douglas MacArthur considered the Japanese would not attempt to cross the Owen Stanley Range. However, they did exactly this, launching their invasion before checking the practicality of such a route.

Neither the Allied nor the Japanese high command appreciated the nature of the environment in which their armies were fighting. For the Australians this contributed to what could be euphemistically called the misunderstanding of Allied Command in Australia of what was actually happening along the Track – in particular their failure to appreciate or acknowledge that the steady withdrawal of Australian troops in front of the advancing Japanese was no abject retreat but a tenacious, uncompromising and measured withdrawal. Fortunately, the Japanese miscalculated how long it would take to cross the range and reach Port Moresby. The debilitating effect of terrain, vegetation, heat, humidity, cold (at higher altitudes) and disease, while operating in the Owen Stanley Range, caused immense suffering and death of both Australian and Japanese forces.

The qualities that carried the Australians through Gallipoli and Tobruk shone again in the series of battles Militia and AIF units fought against the Japanese along the Kokoda Track. None exemplified this better than the 1,000-strong 39th Militia Battalion, which played a major part in creating the Kokoda legend. These troops displayed extraordinary courage, tenacity and devotion to duty in resisting the well-equipped, battle-experienced Japanese under deplorable odds and conditions on the Kokoda Track.

The Track

The Kokoda Track was the 60 km section of track between Port Moresby and Kokoda that connected the north coast of Papua with Port Moresby on the south coast. On the southern side of the Owen Stanley Range it began about 40 km from Port Moresby at a height of 610 m (2,000 feet) above sea level. After crossing a succession of high mountain ridges, it wound through thick jungle, clung precariously to steep mountain sides, plunged into deep, densely forested ravines between ridges, forded fast-flowing mountain streams and climbed peaks as high as 2,100 m (6,800 feet) above sea level before reaching the last towering ridge on which lay the village of Isurava at a height of 1,372 m (4,500 feet) above sea level. From Isurava, the track fell sharply over rough terrain to the village of Deniki, after which it was a relatively easy three-hour march to Kokoda Village situated on a small plateau about 366 m (1,200 feet) above sea level on the northern foothills of the Owen Stanleys.

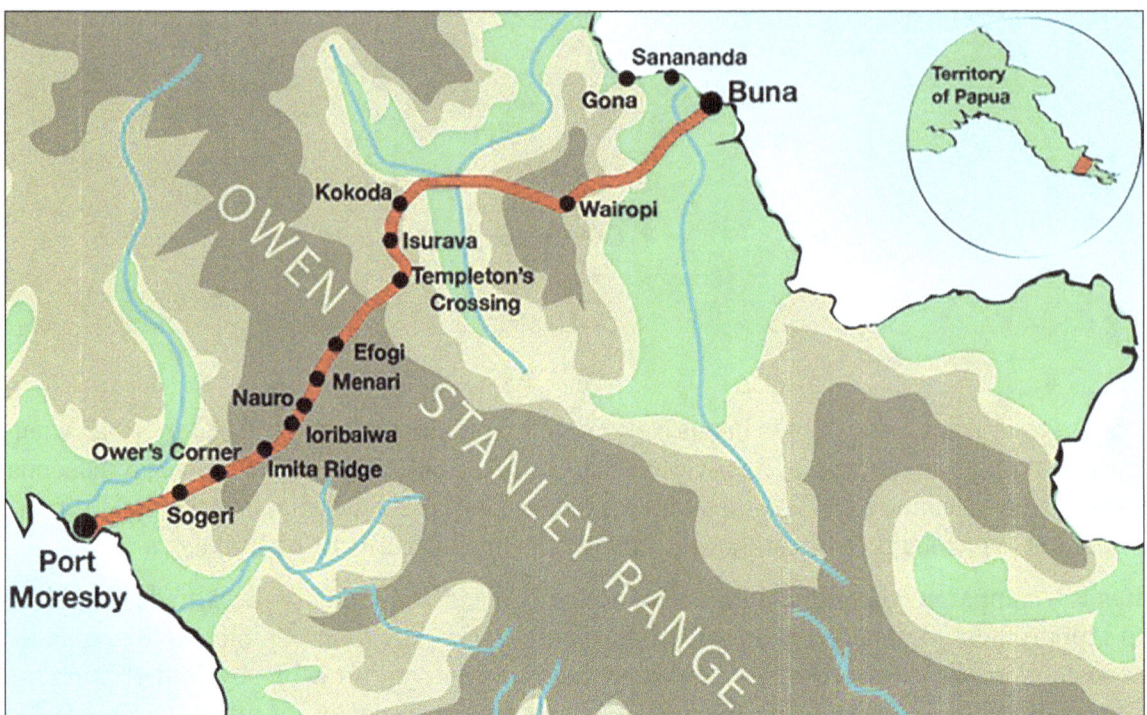

Map of Kokoda track, Territory of Papua. Source: National Museum Australia

From the adjacent villages of Gona and Buna on the northern coast of Papua, where the Japanese landed, narrow dirt tracks traversed coastal jungle and swamp before meeting at Igora and continuing as one track to the small village of Awala situated 56 km (35 miles) inland. From Awala, the track rose gradually as it traversed the foothills of the massive Owen Stanley Range. It crossed the wide, fast-flowing Kumusi River at Wairopi by means of a flimsy wire suspension bridge, and then passed through the small villages of Gorari and Oivi to reach Kokoda. In the oppressive coastal heat, it was a 3-day march from Gona-Buna to Kokoda for heavily-laden troops.

The Track is hard enough to walk in peacetime let alone during a war. As well as the steepness of the track, the soldiers had to contend with rainforests dripping with moss plus blood-sucking leeches as well as mosquito-infested swamps. In some places the jungle was so dense that it seemed like an eternal twilight, or even night. Frequent falls of rain kept troops constantly wet and turned dirt tracks into slippery quagmires of calf-deep mud, which exhausted them after they had struggled through several hundred metres of it. At higher elevations hot humid days alternated with intensely-cold nights. Malaria, dengue fever, scrub typhus and dysentery added to the misery of the exhausted Australians and finally the Japanese. Wet clothes and boots were a frequent source of unpleasant skin diseases.

The soldiers

From late July, when the Japanese landed on the north-east coast of Papua in the Buna-Gona area and began to press inland towards Kokoda, until late August when seasoned AIF reinforcements relieved them, all that stood between Port Moresby and the Japanese force equipped with heavy machine-guns, mortars and mountain guns were the poorly-trained and ill-equipped 'Chocolate Soldiers' of the 39th Battalion.

As well as the hostile terrain, climate and endemic tropical diseases, they faced an elite force of battle-hardened veterans of jungle warfare in South-east Asia equipped and trained to live and fight in the jungle and to move quietly and efficiently forward without need for roads or tracks. Wearing jungle greens and camouflaged with green paint, bushes and vines they blended in with the surroundings. On the other hand until well into the campaign the Australians were kitted out with heavy boots and khaki summer uniforms more suited to desert warfare than the jungle. These khaki uniforms stood out against the green of the jungle, while bare arms and legs exposed them to Japanese eyes as well as leeches, mosquitoes and the cold.

Using tactics they found very effective in the jungles of Malaya, the Japanese crawled along beneath the undergrowth and climbed trees to snipe. Having the advantage of overwhelming numbers, they made apparently suicidal frontal attacks. While the Australians fought desperately to contain this frontal attack, other Japanese troops would attempt to work their way around the flanks of the Australian position and encircle them. However, Frank Sublet noted the Japanese seemed unable to take advantage of their greater numbers, equipment and experience, whereas:

> *The free-thinking Australians, never bound by precedent, and with the initiative that stamped them, had quickly learned means of exploiting a hide-bound enemy, and in their withdrawals, never failed to find volunteers to ambush a pursuing enemy well out in front of their own defensive positions.*

The Japanese invasion force, the Nankai Shitai (South Seas Detachment) was typical of the 20th century Japanese Imperial Army, the vast majority consisting of conscript peasant farmers and public servants. They were trained to be totally obedient, ruthless and willing to die for the Emperor. They were expected to win or not come home, the latter being shameful. Their army instruction manual made it clear, whether wounded or otherwise, it was a disgrace to be taken prisoner or cling to life by accepting defeat. The Japanese officers sent to New Guinea had come through special schools of toughness and brutality, and were more severe on their own than the enemy. The lower-ranking officers, especially, treated their men badly. In Papua New Guinea Japanese troops did not desert because they feared fighting but to escape excessive cruelty and severe hunger.

The wounded Australians helped each other as they limped back along the Track. They were cheerful, refusing to give up the fight or admit defeat and rarely complained and never asked for help. Nobody was able-bodied as dysentery racked all of them; many cut slits in their trousers to avoid waste being contained.

Native bearers (popularly known as 'Fuzzy Wuzzy Angels') carry a wounded Australian soldier on a stretcher. They are moving up a steep hill track through thick tropical jungle. Damien P. Parer, Papua New Guinea, Owen Stanley Range, Kokoda Track, 30 August 1942. Source: AWM, No. 013286

An indication of the primitive lines of communication and of the difficulties encountered in the movement of troops is shown here. Native porters are carrying wounded Australian soldiers on stretchers from the jungle battlefield through a mountain stream to the hospital behind the lines, following a sharp clash with Japanese forces. All Australians in New Guinea pay a high tribute to the courage, endurance and comradeship of the New Guinea natives who played a very important part in the allied efforts to drive the Japanese from the country. Damien P. Parer, New Guinea, 2 September 1942. Source: AWM, No. 013256

Taking prisoners was out of the question for both sides. Prisoners had to be guarded and fed. Both forces were as much as 10 days march from their supply bases through the extremely difficult terrain. Lack of food and ammunition was a constant concern. Every item of food, ammunition and equipment had to be man-handled along the track or dropped by air.

Unlike the Japanese, the Australians received support from the Papuans. Although many of the Papuan Infantry Battalion deserted, some loyal members continued to patrol, collecting information and killing Japanese or the natives who sided with them. Others toiled under immense difficulties to supply the forward troops, and to carry out some of their wounded. The track was thick with stretcher traffic carried by the 'Fuzzy Wuzzy Angels'. Many Australians owed their lives to the efforts and care of these Papuans, who were faced with a gruelling 8-12-day march in terrible conditions. At the beginning of the campaign the Australians were fortunate to have the services of a successful plantation owner of German background, who knew the country and people very well. He knew how to organise and lead the Papuans and arranged the supply of food and munitions along the Track.

The battles – The 39th – Kumusi to Isurava

In early July 1942 100-strong (the three platoons) B Company – the best available – of the 39th Battalion, plus some platoons (300 men) from the Papuan Infantry Battalion (PIB), designated the Maroubra Force, were sent from Port Moresby to hold the airfields at Kokoda and Buna and collect supplies being sent around the coast by boat. The rest of the Battalion followed a couple of weeks later. B Company took the initial brunt of the Japanese advance from Buna, back to the Kumusi River then to Oivi, and finally to Deniki. After linking up with the rest of the Battalion, it took part in fierce battles at Kokoda and Isurava, where they were finally relieved by the 21st AIF Battalions.

Chapter 25: Kokoda

Papua, 14 July 1942. Kokoda Village and airfield. Source: AWM, No. 128400

After a gruelling 8-day march B Company arrived at Kokoda. They were exhausted despite being accompanied by native porters and heavy rains not having yet set in – luxuries those who followed them would not experience. They recuperated and practised some patrolling, while the supplies at Buna were collected.

On 21 July 1942 an advance force of 1,500-2,000 Japanese landed in the Buna-Gona area. Originally, their mission was to determine whether an attack on Port Moresby over the mountains was possible but by then it had changed from reconnaissance to invasion. Immediately on learning this, two of B Company's three platoons moved forward down the Track; one to reinforce a 40-odd PIB force positioned at Alawa and the other to provide them with a fall-back position at Gorari, a village half-way between Kokoda and Alawa.

First contact occurred on 23 July 1942, when the force at Alawa ambushed the advancing Japanese but were in danger of being surrounded so they took their wounded and withdrew to the Kumusi River. Here they were joined by a handful of PIB troops, their NCOs and officers. After crossing the river and destroying the wire rope bridge they set up another ambush. Their orders were to withdraw to Kokoda with any action being contact and rearguard only, since the size of the Japanese force was known. They moved back to join the Platoon at Gorari and together with the PIB troops halted the Japanese advance for 4 hours before having to withdraw. With at least 500 of Japan's best troops pursuing them aggressively, the Australian force staged a fighting rearguard withdrawal down the track to the village of Oivi, where they made another stand.

On the day the Japanese attacked, the Australians were boosted by a platoon of D Company flown in to Kokoda. About 75 Australian militia troops and a handful of local PIB troops faced several hundred Japanese. By late afternoon they were surrounded and faced annihilation. Under cover of darkness, a resourceful PIB Lance Corporal led them to safety across rugged terrain to the village of Deniki, south of Kokoda; the track to Kokoda had been cut off by the Japanese. Colonel Owen, commander of the 39th Battalion, and the remaining 50 men at Kokoda also withdrew to Deniki.

However, the Japanese did not occupy Kokoda, so Colonel Owen reoccupied it with his 77 exhausted men. That night about 400 Japanese launched an attack, which developed into a melee of hand-to-hand combat. In the bloody chaos men were bayoneted in the dark and Colonel Owen received a fatal bullet. Under cover of a heavy pre-dawn mist the Australians managed to extricate themselves and with their wounded withdraw to Deniki. There they were soon joined by Colonel Owen's successor and, exhausted by their 6-day trek, the remaining Companies of the 39th Battalion. This brought their number to 460 (433 men plus officers) and with about 35 Papuans of the PIB and a few others of Maroubra Force to 500. Toughened by their recent fighting, the exhausted, debilitated members of B Company were now driven by the desire to avenge their fallen mates. *Your mate beside you became your father, your mother and God, all rolled into one,* said a dying sergeant.

By this time the men were adapting to their surroundings and maximising their chances of survival. They had abandoned everything in their haversacks that was not essential. Underwear was abandoned. Many shared mess tins with their mates. They had learnt how to light a fire in the pouring rain and use their helmets as cooking pots.

The Australians had learnt as they fought, many of their lessons in jungle fighting coming from the enemy. The Japanese were using tactics tried and proved in Malaya – when they met opposition, they immediately attempted to outflank it and cut it off. They used their artillery and mortars, of which the Australians had none, to good effect and crawled along beneath the undergrowth to attack and climbed trees to snipe. They forced the Australians to adopt a pattern of conducting fighting withdrawals – fight, stop the enemy, then withdraw before being annihilated. However, this hit-and-run tactic proved effective for it unbalanced the Japanese, who were never certain of how many they were up against. In their attack on Kokoda the Japanese reported they had been up against a force of 1,000 to 1,200.

The new Battalion Commander was not pleased with the performance of B Company. He was unimpressed by their continuous withdrawals and on his way there he had run into a couple who had 'shot through' during the battle at Kokoda. Against the better judgement of the commanding officers who had served with the AIF in the Middle East, he ordered three of the newly arrived companies to retake Kokoda. After fierce fighting, much of it hand-to-hand with the bayonet doing as much damage as bullets, two companies withdrew back to Deniki. The third managed to occupy Kokoda and hold it for 2 1/2 days against successive waves of 400 Japanese but finally lack of supplies and reinforcements forced them to withdraw. For almost a week they repulsed a number of enemy attacks but, with food and ammunition running low, finally withdrew to Isurava and 'dug in' in readiness for the next onslaught.

Once Kokoda was in their hands, Major General Horii with his Nankai Shitai, the invasion force waiting in Rabaul, was ordered to invade Papua and capture Port Moresby. It was considered they could get to Port Moresby in eight days including fighting. The first units began landing at Buna-Gona on 18 August 1942. By 22 August 6,000 of the total of 10,000 had landed or were advancing to Kokoda. These did not include the 2,000 already at Kokoda-Deniki. Later reinforcements would bring the total to over 13,000. Horii, however, had his doubts. They had just two-weeks rations for there had been little time to prepare supplies. He had to be in Port Moresby in little more than a week.

Isurava

Isurava had a strong geographical advantage and Australians intended to hold out there until reinforcements arrived. A forward patrol mounted about 45-minutes walk down the track enabled them to take action against any Japanese movements that would give any idea of how few in number and poorly equipped they were. Maroubra Force awaited the arrival of reinforcements – the 53rd Militia Battalion and two AIF Battalions (2/14th and 2/16th of 550 each) that were on their way up the Track to relieve them. High command in Australia expected them to begin an offensive to push the Japanese back to the sea.

By now the Japanese had great respect for the fighting qualities of the Australians. The resistance put up by the 39th thus far was so strong they thought there were at least five times that number dug in. They would have attacked immediately had they known there were no more than about 400 weakened and exhausted men. Instead they took time assembling and deploying the 6,000 invasion force that had been struggling along the Track. The 10,000-strong Nankai Shitai had landed at Buna-Gona on 18 August.

A few days after withdrawing to Isurava, Maroubra Force got another commander – Lieutenant Colonel Ralph Honner took over from Major Cameron. He impressed the troops but was appalled by what he saw. B Company had been in continuous action since 23 July. They had been shot at, bombed, starved and suffered from boiling days and freezing nights, drenching rains, biting insects and disease. They had hollow eyes, rotting boots and foul, ragged uniforms and had not washed for 40 days, when last in Port Moresby. They seemed physically small compared with the men he had commanded in the Middle East. However one thing did impress him – they did not have a beaten-dog look and were still keen to 'have a go'.

Honner set about establishing his defences, ensuring they were dug in well and knew what to do. B Company got the toughest position – one that had to be held at all cost. The 53rd Militia Battalion was also deployed. It had arrived ahead of the two AIF Battalions, which were held back because requested supplies had not been delivered. The AIF were glad of a rest after a 5-day walk carrying 30 kg (65 lb) or more in some cases along the Track. Unlike the 39th, no porters accompanied them. Also, on their way they attempted to dye their uniforms jungle green by boiling them in a concoction of leaves and grass.

Down below, the 430 Australians could see the Japanese, like ants, preparing their offensive. For over a week they carried out aggressive patrolling in an attempt to hold out until the AIF reinforcements arrived to relieve them. Finally, on the morning of 26 August the battle began in earnest with shells from the mountain guns raining down on them. Throughout the day they held firm. That evening their spirits rose as the AIF units began to arrive and jump into the dugouts beside them. Oozing confidence and experience, the AIF men handled their weapons with ease. They knew what fighting meant and were ready to fight. To the exhausted militiamen, these tall, fit, muscular, well-equipped newcomers in clothes not torn to shreds seemed like gods. For more than a week these survivors of the 39th Battalion had been awaiting relief by the 2/27th, the third 21st Brigade Battalion. However, they stayed on to assist their AIF 'mates' because the Japanese were attacking in such great numbers. On the other hand the newcomers were shocked at the gaunt spectres who greeted them – faces without expression, eyes sunk back into their sockets, gaping boots and rotten, tattered uniforms – their bodies racked by dysentery and fatigue, many recently wounded, and all smelling like latrines. They were amazed these scarecrows of men were still fighting, let alone capable of fighting any longer. The division between them – any animosity and contempt for militiamen – evaporated. They were all Australians fighting for Australia.

The battle raged over four days, during which much of the fighting was almost within arms length. As platoon after platoon of AIF battalions arrived on the second day, they took over from the battered platoons of the 39th who were able to fall back, rest and take up the position of battalion reserve. On the third day the 39th, though scheduled to be relieved by the AIF arrivals, remained to fight. The next day the enemy threw in reserves and launched wave after wave of full frontal suicidal attacks. For eight hours the Australians resisted fiercely without withdrawal, resorting to hand-to-hand combat when they burst from their trenches to engage the Japanese with their bayonets.

All but three of the 30 wounded men of the 39th waiting to return to Port Moresby got up and stumbled back into action. Of the three who didn't one was minus a foot, one had a bullet in the throat, and the other a forearm blown off. They knew their battalion was in trouble. They did not do it for 'God, King and Country' but 'because the 39th expected it of us'.

Three platoons of the 39th that had been cut off by the Japanese advance staggered in that day and went into action. These walking scarecrows had been forcing their way through the jungle for three days and nights. They had scarcely eaten during this time, their uniforms were ripped to pieces and bloody feet protruded through boots almost falling apart. Disappointingly, most of the men of the 53rd Militia Battalion were not of this ilk. Their lack of training and discipline and poor leadership showed up in the battle and so they were taken out of action.

The Australians had neither the numbers nor ammunition to withstand the continual assaults. About 1,800 Australians [600 militia (39th, 53rd) and 1,200 AIF] had confronted about 6,000 Japanese. At the height of the battle there were probably four Japanese to one Australian. Under the cover of darkness on the fourth night they withdrew to make another stand. The Australians had lost about 250 with many hundreds wounded. The 2/14th, the most depleted unit, had its initial force reduced by half. However, the Japanese lost 550 killed and over 1,000 wounded. Also, these four days had wrecked their timetable to reach Port Moresby – they were running low in food and ammunition and had no re-supply system.

In the midst of this conflagration, during which the hail of bullets was so thick it literally defoliated the surrounding jungle, there was a brief ceasefire, when the priest Father Nobby Earl carrying a shovel suddenly walked on to no-man's land towards an Australian soldier who had just been shot. The Australians stopped firing. So did the Japanese. Both sides waited while he dug a shallow grave, put the body in it, covered it, said his prayers and left. The moment he was out of harm's way the Japanese unleashed a hail of lead.

Above: Courage, Endurance, Mateship and Sacrifice are the words placed on the pillars at a memorial in Isurava.
Source: Melocco Stone

Right: The Isurava Memorial honours the Australians and Papua New Guineans who fought and died on the Kokoda Track in World War II.
Source: ABC News, 2017

Fighting withdrawals – a tactic of withdrawing, setting up an ambush and withdrawing over and over again with fresh troops – continued through Alola, Eora Creek, Templeton's Crossing, Myola and Effogi. At Eora Creek on 4 September, the 39th Battalion, now down to about 150 troops – the rest were dead, missing, wounded or evacuated sick – took their turn to dig in and defend. They prevented the Japanese breaking the lines and allowed the AIF Battalions to fall back and regroup.

The next day the arrival of the 2/27th, the third of the 21st Brigade's Battalions, enabled the 39th to withdraw from battle. By then all were feverish, suffering from scrub typhus, hookworm and malaria; their boots and uniforms had rotted through. They had suffered 54 killed in action, while four died of wounds and 125 were wounded during their fight along the Kokoda Track. They regrouped at the tiny village of Menari, where Lieutenant Colonel Ralph Honner called a full parade to pass on the Maroubra Force Commander's commendation:

All of the Australian Army is proud of you.

Members of the 39th Battalion, AMF, parade after weeks of fighting in dense jungle during the Kokoda campaign. Their bedraggled dress reflects the hard fighting of past weeks. Damien P. Parer, Kokoda Track, 22 September 1942. Source: AWM, No. 013289

The 50 remaining men, wearing what was left of their uniforms and kit, stood proudly erect holding the sticks used for support on their trek back instead of rifles, which they had passed on to the newly arrived troops. Honner added:

For the rest of your days you'll be able to recall these in the warmth of knowledge that, when the heat was on, you did not buckle, did not take a backward step. None of us will forget our fallen comrades, but your own efforts have ensured they will not have died in vain…

He later recorded:

As I glanced along the lines of pallid and emaciated men with sunken eyes and shrunken frames, that testified to the hardships they had long endured, I saw no hang-dog look – only the proud bearing of tired veterans, who had looked death and disaster in the face and had not failed.

Honner summed up their achievement in the Battle of Isurava as Australia's Thermopylae for it was here these couple of hundred men retreating from Kokoda Village made a stand and hung on against a far greater enemy force until battle-trained reinforcements, mainly from the 2/14th Battalion, joined them. Honner said of his men:

> *In the testing crucible of conflict ... they were transformed by some strong catalyst of the spirit into a devoted band wherein every man's failing strength was fortified and magnified by a burning resolve to stick by his mates.*

> *On 9 September 200-odd hungry, dirty, unshaven emaciated survivors of the 39th walked into Ilolo near the start of Kokoda Track. They had been fighting in the mountains since July. They were dressed in rags – some without shirts or trousers. Many were wounded and all had dysentery. One, Smokey Joe Dawson, who began at 12st 7lb (80 kg) was down to 7st 5lb (47 kg). After recuperating at Koitaki Rest Camp at the foot of the Owen Stanleys, reinforcement and re-equipping, the 39th went back into action in the bloody battles at Gona and Sanananda.*

Retreat to Imita Ridge

Maroubra Force, which now consisted of the three 21st Brigade Battalions, continued the bitter fighting at Brigade Hill (Butchers Hill) before withdrawing to Ioribaiwa Ridge, during which the recently arrived 2/27th was cut off from the rest of the brigade and spent a week lost in the jungle. At Ioribaiwa Ridge the other two battalions were relieved by fresh battalions, including those of the 25th AIF Brigade and the 3rd Militia Battalion. After a four-day battle they withdrew to Imita Ridge, which had strong geographical advantages, and from which there was to be no further withdrawal.

The Japanese climbed on to Ioribaiwa Ridge, from where they could see the lights of Port Moresby. But the long fighting withdrawal of Maroubra Force, begun by the 39th and PIB and continued by the 21st AIF Brigade had gradually lengthened their supply lines and cost them dearly. Of the 6,000 combat troops, who had landed in Papua just over three weeks before, only 1,500 remained. Starving and riddled with disease they were showing signs of physical and mental collapse. They could do little more than send out a few exploratory patrols to test the strength of the Australian defences. So near yet so far.

In the last week of September the gaunt, exhausted and starving survivors of the 21st Brigade entered Koitaki Rest Camp. Of the 265 survivors of the 2/14th and 2/16th, the medical report said 189 would be fit in one week and 62 were permanently unfit for operations in mountainous country. Brigadier John Rogers, Blamey's director of military intelligence, observed:

> *Never in my life, in the worst part of Gallipoli, or anywhere, had I seen soldiers who looked so shocked and so tired and so utterly weary as those men.*

Along with the 39th they had taken the initial brunt of the Japanese invader. They did not recapture Kokoda or hold the track between Isurava and Ioribaiwa, but they delayed a far bigger army, inflicted far more casualties and fatally thwarted its advance.

High command back in Australia was ignorant of the horrific conditions of the Kokoda Track. MacArthur could not understand why the Australians kept withdrawing but the Japanese did not. He reckoned they must lack fighting spirit. He felt Americans could do a better job and after the Battle of Brigade Hill dispatched the 126th Division to New Guinea. Blamey considered it an ignominious defeat. He had gone back when he was told to go forward.

At Koitaki in early (9th) November Blamey spoke to the 21st Brigade, who were now thought to be ready to go again; only 73 remained of the initial 550 of the 2/14th. Some of them were expecting congratulations for their strenuous efforts in holding back the Japanese. Instead he told them there would be no more retreats. They were to advance and attack at all costs. *Remember*, he was reported to say, *it's the running rabbit that gets shot, not the man holding the gun!* The troops were outraged. Some dared to protest. Only the discipline of their officers and senior NCOs managed to settle them down. Many disobeyed the 'eyes-right' order later that day during the march-past parade. Subsequently, when Blamey visited a Port Moresby hospital, the men nibbled on lettuce leaves and whispered *run, rabbit, run!*, a popular song at that time. The Australians were not going to take such an insult lying down. The punishing they had been through had not extinguished the larrikin in them. In an effort to redeem their reputation they displayed extraordinary courage and murderous fighting when they relieved the 25th Brigade at Gona later that month.

Australians do not blindly bow to authority, nor is respect given gratuitously. The men of the 21st Brigade had none for Blamey. Earlier that year he had ordered an inscription to commemorate the capture of Damour, mainly by the 7th Division of whom they were part, to be cut into the stone above Nahr al-Kalb (Dog River), 20 km north of Beirut. The Australians had played a major role in the liberation of Lebanon and Syria from the Vichy French in 1941. Conquerors as far back as Ramses the Great and Alexander the Great had followed this tradition. In the cliff above Napoleon III's tablet is one celebrating the capture of Damascus in 1918 by the Australian Light Horse forces led by General Harry Chauvel.

The Australian journalist, war correspondent and poet, Kenneth Slessor, witnessed the ceremony and, so filled with contempt for Blamey, wrote the poem *An inscription for Dog River* on behalf of the soldiers:

> *Our general was the greatest and bravest of generals.*
> *For his deeds, look around you on this coast—*
> *Here is his name cut next to Ashur-Bani-Pal's,*
> *Nebuchadnezzar's and the Roman host;*
> *And we, though our identities have been lost,*
> *Lacking the validity of stone or metal,*
> *We, too, are part of his memorial,*
> *Having been put in for the cost,*
> *Having bestowed on him all we had to give*
> *In battles few can recollect,*
> *Our strength, obedience and endurance,*
> *Our wits, our bodies, our existence,*
> *Even our descendants' right to live—*
> *Having given him everything, in fact,*
> *Except respect.*

Back to Kokoda and the Buna-Gona-Sanananda beachhead

The Australians, now numbering 2,500 plus 25-pounders manhandled up the 'Golden Stairs' and into position, went on the offensive. On 24 September the Japanese were ordered to withdraw; their resources were being diverted to Guadalcanal. As they retreated the Australians came across stragglers – many of whom had been reduced to eating grass, wood, weeds, roots and poison fruit. There was evidence that some had even resorted to cannibalism. The sight of bodies stripped of flesh and other atrocities such as bound bayoneted corpses revolted the Australians, who took very few prisoners.

The Allied plan was for the Australians to pursue the Japanese along the Kokoda Track along with 'crack' American troops of the 126th US Infantry Regiment, which had arrived in New Guinea, to take Kapa Kapa trail, a shorter route across the Owen Stanleys and come out at Wairopi in front of the retreating Japanese, thereby cutting them off and wiping them out.

In early October the 25th Brigade was joined in the pursuit of the Japanese by the highly trained and experienced, well-armed and equipped 16th Brigade of the 6th Division. Over 10-days fighting at Eora Creek the 16th lost 300 killed or wounded. Kokoda was retaken on 2 November. In a large-scale attack at Oivi-Gorari, 4,000 (25th and 16th Brigades, 3rd Militia Battalion) entrapped the Japanese and inflicted huge casualties in savage often hand-to-hand fighting; no prisoners were taken. On 11 November the Australians reached Wairopi Bridge, where they came across fresh Japanese reinforcements, who stiffened the Japanese resistance considerably. The 126th US Regiment had not arrived as planned as they became lost in the jungle, emerging after 42 days in a deplorable state near the Buna–Gona beachheads.

By mid-November the campaign was back where it began. On 19-20 November the 'battle of the beachheads' began with bombing and an artillery barrage to soften up the Japanese. The battlefield was a rough semi-circle about 16 km wide and 8 km deep. It stretched from Gona in the west to Buna in the east. At the

The 'Golden Stairs' on the Kokoda Track between Uberi and Imita Ridge. These stairs marked the beginning of the steepest parts of the track. For those Australian troops moving along it for the first time these stairs gave them the first real indication of the degree of physical hardship they were about to undergo. Thomas Fisher, Nauro, Papua New Guinea, October 1942. Source: AWM, No. 026821

Allies retake Kokoda. Australian flag is raised as troops enter Kokoda, watched by a group of Australian troops. John Earl (Earl) McNeil, Kokoda Track, 14 November 1942. Source: AWM, No. 013572

centre on the coast was Sanananda/Giruwa, site of the Japanese headquarters. The terrain was no longer jungle but a mix of swamps, coarse grassland, coconut groves and beaches.

This was the first time American and Australian troops fought along-side each other in a joint operation. In the east the US 32nd Division attacked the Japanese forces in Buna. They were mainly young, inexperienced National Guardsmen from mid-west farming States. Very few were appropriately trained; only one regiment had performed a single night patrol. They arrived on the north coast fresh, looked rugged and were keen to show the Australians how to do it. Like MacArthur they expected a quick victory. Gona and Sanananda were largely left to the Australians – the weary 16th and 25th Brigades – who had pursued the Japanese along the Kokoda Track. They wondered about their optimistic American comrades in arms.

The Allies expected a quick victory. Their intelligence believed there were about 1,500 debilitated and sick Japanese troops across the whole Gona-Sanananda-Buna beachhead. However, at that stage the Japanese were not starving, reinforcements were arriving and they were well dug in behind strong, well-prepared defensives. There were 9,000 of them. Their orders were to fight to the last man; even the sick and wounded were to join in. Although outnumbered and finally reduced to starvation the Japanese held out for three months. This was partly due to ineffectual American troops but mainly to the extraordinary determination and courage of the Japanese.

At Buna the first battalions of the US 32nd Division went into battle on 19 November wading through swampland towards Japanese bunkers. They lived for three days and nights in the swamp. Day after day the Americans were cut down by the well-placed Japanese. By the end of the month 492 had been killed or wounded, while many were sick with malaria or dysentery. This was not what they had expected. Despite MacArthur's orders for action, they were reluctant to fight. Blamey considered them quite inferior to the Australian Militia and with great satisfaction told MacArthur that he did not consider them attack troops, adding:

From the moment they met opposition they sat down and have hardly gone forward a yard.

On 29 November General Ned Herring, Blamey's deputy, reflected this, when he wrote that the US 32nd Division:

had still not realised that ... while bombing, straffing, mortars and artillery may soften his resistance ... the men who are left will ... have to be taken out & killed in hard fighting. This I was at pains to explain to Harding this morning ... The organisation of [Harding's] HQ is worse than primitive.

The next day MacArthur replaced Harding with Eichelberger, telling him to take Buna or not come back alive.

Eichelberger found the American troops in a 'deplorable' state. They were hungry and sick, wore long dirty beards; their clothing was in rags and their boots worn out. They displayed little discipline or military courtesy. He ordered a cease-fire for a couple of days to reorganise the companies and platoons that were all mixed up. They still wouldn't fight so he led several units in an attack against the bunkers, which achieved its aim of raising their fighting spirit. However, MacArthur finally had to request the help of battle-hardened Australian troops. On 17 December the 18th Australian Brigade, veterans of Tobruk and Milne Bay, returned to action. After a little more than two-weeks savage fighting the Allies took Buna. Their forces had outnumbered the Japanese by three-to-one.

Total allied casualties at Buna were 2,817 (excluding sick) of whom 620 were killed, 2,065 wounded and 132 missing. The US 32nd Division sustained 1,954 casualties – 353 killed, 1,508 wounded and 93 missing. The 18th Brigade lost 267 dead and 557 wounded. Some

1,400 Japanese were buried at Buna; 1,000s of sick and wounded died. Only a couple of prisoners were taken.

Over the first couple of weeks at Gona the Australians made little progress and casualties mounted from frontal attacks similar to those on the Western Front in WWI. Fresh reinforcements were needed but Blamey declined MacArthur's offer of American troops. He told MacArthur they were not attack troops and he would prefer Australians, for he knew they would fight. Thus the 21st Brigade was flown in and on 28 November, still smarting from Blamey's rabbit remarks, went into battle in an almost suicidal fashion. By 3 December they had lost 340 out of 874 without much result. By then the 25th, which had been first in at Gona, during which time it had lost 200, had been relieved. Fresh troops were needed. The 39th Battalion, boosted with 100 of the best from the 53rd Battalion, flew in to join their 21st AIF mates. On 8 December, after taking part in disastrous attacks a couple of days earlier, the 39th went on the attack again. By next day the long, brutal fight for Gona was practically over. On 18 December the last Japanese position fell and the Australians went on to help the Americans at Sanananda.

The battle for Sananandara-Giruwa began in early November and lasted until the last week of January. Sick, exhausted men fought each other in hellish conditions in what was probably the most savage, bitter fighting of the campaign. After their fragile supply line broke down totally in January, many Japanese resorted to cannibalism – of both Japanese and Australian corpses. In December alone Australia lost 1,932 dead, wounded or sick from a combined force of about 2,500. The Americans fared no better. Of 1,400 sent to Sanananda in November fewer than 200 remained 'effective' by mid-December. Of the 7,000 or so Japanese troops who had participated at some stage, 1,600 were buried by the Allies, 2,200 escaped and 3,200 were unaccounted for and most probably died of wounds or disease in the jungle or in a later battle.

In the six-month campaign Australia had mortally lost 2,165 troops, with another 3,533 wounded. The US, who had come in late, lost 671 troops killed and 2,172 wounded. Out of a force of about 20,000 the Japanese lost 13,000 killed, with practically all the rest wounded or debilitated to some degree. Tropical diseases, as much as the fighting, took their toll on both armies.

When the 39th Battalion was flown to Port Moresby on 25 January 1943, battle casualties and medical evacuations had reduced it to seven officers and 25 malaria-ridden men. Much to its bitter dismay, the battalion was disbanded the following July. Only 650 of the 13,000 Nanki Shitai survived the campaign.

Some final words

I spent some years teaching English as a second language at a small English language college run by a Japanese person. The students came from various countries around the world but the majority were Japanese and Korean. They were mostly university students or not long out of university. I was quite surprised at the ignorance of these educated Japanese about the Pacific War, which they refer to as the American War. Furthermore, students from Asia generally express surprise when I tell them of the extent to which Australia was involved and so could empathise with those who suffered from the brutality of the Japanese – for example those from China who remind me of the 300,000 slaughtered at Nanjing.

The gross atrocities committed by the Japanese against soldiers and civilians cannot be excused. Probably more than anything else, the boiling hatred of their Japanese enemy, the thirst to avenge their butchered mates, is what kept the exhausted, sick and too-often-hungry Aussie soldier going. It is time that Japan acknowledged this tragic (in the Shakespearean sense) episode in their history and so get an answer to the question put by a middle-aged

Japanese woman to a middle-aged married Korean woman in one of my classes: *Why do you hate us so much?* It would allow the Japanese, who know nothing of Kokoda, to acknowledge the deprivation, starvation and exhaustion its troops suffered in the Kokoda Campaign – that 95% of the 200,000 sent to Papua and East and Central New Guinea did not return home – and reflect on what it was all about.

In the mosquito-infested disease-ridden swamps around Sanananda and Giruwa amidst hunger and slaughter, Rinzo Kanemoto wrote:

> *When you look around ... there is no agriculture. No towns ... What possible plus can our occupation of such a place offer to our national strength? Yet even given that, here we are, two large groups of white and yellow fighting over the Giruwa area, flinging the fires of war at each other ... What on earth is all this for? That soldiers ... had to die so horribly to secure such a completely worthless piece of land! What is the bloody sense of that?*

Was it nothing more than 'gyokuscai' – a glorious sacrifice for the Emperor? The Australians and the Japanese soldiers had much in common but blind obedience to authority was not a quality they shared. The Australians had no doubt about why they were there or what they were fighting for.

In 1992 Paul Keating visited Kokoda itself, the first Australian Prime Minister to do so. When he alighted from the helicopter he fell on his knees and kissed the ground. Here, he said, Australians were not fighting for empire, they were not fighting for the defence of the old world but the new world. Their world. Their values. Which is why, he considered, for Australians the battles in Papua New Guinea were the most important ever fought. Some challenge this but none questions the qualities displayed by those Australians.

Through the heroic efforts of Maroubra Force the Australian soldiers earned great respect from their Samurai foes who considered them superior to the English, Americans and Filipinos. Their respect for the fighting ability of the 39th was expressed verbally in 1972, when eight of the 39th Battalion survivors joined their Japanese counterparts in a reunion, the only instance of this happening among the Australian armies. An Australian journalist reported that the Japanese, led by two generals, sang their battle hymn and then joined the Australians in singing Waltzing Matilda. Afterwards an old Japanese general, a son-in-law of Tojo, bowed neatly from the waist and told him:

> *Never could we find a time and place to outwit and out-manoeuvre the 39th. And now we have waited 30 years to meet them here and tell them so. To tell them that, when our men of the great Nankai Division landed in New Guinea in 1942, they thought they were facing an Australian army of 10,000 strong on the Kokoda Track. Not for the first two months of battle just one battalion of young untested men – the 39th Battalion – only 600 strong.*

Chapter 26
Australia turns from Britain to America

The European war, a war on the other side of the world, posed no immediate threat to Australia. However, Japan's entry on the Axis side brought war to Australia's doorstep and an immediate shift in Australia's foreign relationships. Several weeks after declaring Australia was at war with Japan, Prime Minister Curtin, in his New Year message to the nation, signalled that Australia would cut its ties with Britain and ally itself with the United States of America, an alliance that persists to this day:

> *Without any inhibitions of any kind, I make it quite clear that Australia looks to America, free of any pangs as to our traditional links or kinship with the United Kingdom.*
>
> *We know the problems that the United Kingdom faces. We know the constant threat of invasion. We know the dangers of dispersal of strength, but we know, too, that Australia can go and Britain can still hold on.*
>
> *We are, therefore, determined that Australia shall not go, and we shall devote all our energies towards the shaping of a plan, with the United States as its keystone, which will give to our country some confidence of being able to hold out until the tide of battle swings against our enemy.*

The New Year of 1942 brought war to Australia's front door. In February the British Naval Base at Singapore was captured by the Japanese forces and Japanese planes bombed Darwin. Britain was locked in mortal combat with Germany and so was in no position to come to Australia's aid. The British and Americans had a 'Hitler first' strategy; Australia felt very vulnerable.

Against the wishes of British Prime Minister Churchill, Prime Minister Curtin recalled the 6th and 7th Divisions of the AIF from the Middle East to defend Australia. On their way back Churchill unilaterally ordered the diversion of the Australian 7th Division to Burma. Churchill, supported by US President Roosevelt, wanted at least one of the divisions to be diverted to Burma to help keep China in the war and provide a base for future operations against Japan itself. Curtin countermanded the order, telling Churchill Australia would not permit it but he allowed part (16th and 17th Brigades) of the 6th Division to land in Sri Lanka and spend several months as part of the island's defences. The 7th Division was engaged in the fighting on the Kokoda Track. The 9th Division returned from North Africa at the end of the year after participating in the Battle of El Alamein.

The entire country feared invasion but especially Queenslanders. Some families, who could afford it, moved. My aunt told my mother that for us this was not to be considered. We would stay and see it out along with everyone else. They agreed, however, that if the Japanese were to come, we should be taken west to a cousin's cattle property on the Central Highlands, a property originally taken up by P.F. MacDonald.

The coming of the Americans was, therefore, more than welcome. The American naval victories of the Coral Sea and Midway Island in May and June effectively removed the immediate threat of invasion. The Australian armed forces worked closely with those of the

Chapter 26: Australia turns from Britain to America

MacArthur Chambers Apartment Hotel (2004) formerly AMP Insurance built in early 1930s and headquarters of General Douglas MacArthur, Supreme Commander of Allied Forces in the South-west Pacific Area (SWPA). Source: Kgbo, Wikimedia Commons

USA under the leadership of General Douglas MacArthur, Supreme Commander of the South-west Pacific Area, who established his headquarters in Brisbane.

By the end of the war Australia no longer relied on Britain for security. It had a new great and powerful friend, the USA. Australia's special relationship with the USA in security matters has continued till this day.

Americans in Australia

Australia was a staging, training and supply base, which was part of the strategy to re-take the Philippines as a major step to defeating Japan. An estimated one million American servicemen and some female nurses passed through Australia between 22 December 1941 and the end of the war in 1945. Most Americans spent a very short time in Australia. Given Australia's fear of invasion by the Japanese, the American presence was greatly welcomed by the Government and general population.

The first troops arrived in Brisbane in December 1941, when their convoy en route to the Philippines was diverted. By early 1942 large numbers were arriving constantly, the majority of whom were based in or visited Queensland. By August 1942 two-thirds of American land forces were based around Brisbane, with about half of the remainder located in other parts of Queensland. Most had left by 1944.

One of the many sites of American camps was Rockhampton, where I was born and grew up. At the time Rockhampton had a population of 30,000 people. At its peak more than 70,000 American soldiers were stationed there. From late 1942 to early 1944 more than 300,000 Americans spent some time bivouacked in the Rockhampton area. These included part of One Army Corps or 'I Corps' commanded by Major General Robert Eichelberger – a small number of Corps troops and the 41st Division led by Major General Horace H. Fuller arrived in Rockhampton in November 1942. Another part of I Corps, the 32nd Division, led by General Edwin F. Harding encamped south-east of Brisbane near Logan Village. The 32nd Division and the 163rd Regiment of the 41st Division joined the Australians in New Guinea in the battles at Gona and Buna, which marked the turn of the tide in the ground war against Japan. After this campaign the Corps returned to Rockhampton, Australia, where it was engaged in training the forces beginning to arrive in that area for the coming campaigns that were to terminate with the surrender of Japan.

From the little my mother mentioned, I was aware that a General Eichelberger commanded 'I Corps' but until writing this I had thought 'I' stood for 'Intelligence'. My mother, her relations and friends became acquainted with many of the American top brass. The Americans requisitioned many buildings including residences – some belonging to family members and friends. I believe 'Clancolla' in Ward Street, the Rockhampton residence of one of P.F. MacDonald's sons, was taken over by the commanding officer of the 41st Division for a few months. The Americans regularly played tennis, often inviting my mother and other local women and men to join them; the women would provide drinks and eats. I have a very hazy memory of watching a game on the Rudd residence's court in Jessie Street, a court where we children would later play many games.

Other vague memories of the American presence include tents and igloos lining the roads north as far as The Caves and east to the coast at Yeppoon 40 km away and having my eyes checked by a US army doctor somewhere near where Central Queensland University now is located. I recall the early morning bugle calls from a small camp in Park Reserve by the Botanical Gardens that were a couple of hundred metres from our house. I can picture a small American aeroplane landing and taking off on the 400 metre stretch of road from the House Paddock gate to the homestead of a family property, *The Oaks*, 60 km from Rockhampton. Also, we children would fashion brown paper bags into soldiers' caps.

US Army volunteers built a chapel, St Christopher's Chapel, beside one of the camps several km from town. After the war army structures were balloted off to interested parties. My parents drew a Sergeants' Mess which was re-assembled on a block of land at Zilzie Beach, its khaki exterior being replaced with white and the two big roller doors to the large rooms at either end with red and white stripes. One large room served as a kitchen-living room and the other a dormitory with about eight beds where all the family and friends slept. A small room in between served as a dressing room.

The friendly invasion of Rockhampton by such a large number of American troops gave the residents of the city the opportunity to experience a different culture up close. My mother said that, despite the large American presence, relations with the locals were harmonious. Not only were the Americans most welcome but also military discipline was strict, with any breaches being punished immediately and severely, even by death. Any shops and hotels that tried to take advantage of the troops, such as overcharging, were listed and boycotted. The Americans could not get by without their daily ration of ice cream nor could their pilots find their way without a bevy of instruments she said. The Americans accused us of provincialism and having an inferiority complex.

Letter from one of the tennis players. Source: Hasker family

Buna, Papua New Guinea. General Sir Thomas Blamey and Lieutenant General R. L. Eichelberger at the entrance to a Japanese pillbox near the Buna airstrip, 1943. Source: AWM, No. 014091

Rockhampton, Queensland, Australia, April 1943. General Douglas MacArthur and Lieutenant General Eichelberger inspect the 542nd Regimental Area. Colonel Fowlkes and Lieutenant Colonel Simpson escort our distinguished visitors. Source: Australia @ War

The Sergeants' Mess, Zilzie Beach. Source: Peter Hasker

The Aussie bushman was amused by the Americans' lack of bush sense and naive trust in technology. The Inland Defence Road between Clermont and Charters Towers bisects *Elgin Downs* and *New Twin Hills*, properties run as one and where I worked in 1961-62. In my time it was a formed gravelled construction and still referred to as the Defence Road. At *Twin Hills* the road originally ran a bit west of the route taken when it was upgraded, which began when the Americans arrived in 1942. The original road followed the phone line through the bullock paddock in country that was heavy dark clay. Whenever we were in a certain part of the paddock the overseer would gleefully relate how convoys of large American trucks roared by, their drivers so engaged in waving and shouting greetings such as 'howday Aussie', they failed to see trucks bogged a little way ahead. With a roar their trucks would grind to a sudden halt joining those already bogged up to their axles.

The Americans were also amused by us. For instance Francis Catanzaro wrote:

> *I enjoyed listening to the Aussies: it seemed everything was either 'bloomin'' or 'bloody'. Everyone was a 'mate' to the Australians. 'Styke' and 'eyegs' (steak and eggs) was a favourite meal. If you were 'knocked up' it meant you were worn out or just tired.*

The Americans left their mark on us children. We picked up words from them; for example I still mix 'hood' and 'bonnet' and 'trunk' and 'boot', when referring to a car, and at times use 'gotten' as the past participle of 'got'. The songs we sang were mainly American.

Chapter 27
ANZAC Day

ANZAC Day puzzles foreigners. It is a holiday but shops are not open and some sort of service takes place at dawn. Later on that morning an odd collection of young and old men and women, and boys and girls, some in uniform, march in a parade with a military connotation to the music of numerous pipe and brass bands – a parade totally devoid of any display of military might and overt nationalism. The afternoon is dedicated to drinking and sport. To really know and understand Australians, one must understand what ANZAC Day is and what it is about. For Australians it is a sacred day. It is, de facto, Australia's real national day.

Gallipoli gave us ANZAC Day. The date, 25 April, was officially named ANZAC Day in 1916. On that anniversary of the landing at Gallipoli, commemorative ceremonies, services and marches were held all over Australia. Wounded soldiers from Gallipoli attended the Sydney march in convoys of cars, attended by nurses. Over 2,000 Australian and New Zealand troops marched through London, one London newspaper headline dubbing them 'The knights of Gallipoli'.

A sports day was held in the Australian camp in Egypt. This is not surprising given the place sporting activity had played in the lives of Australians. How can one be truly free if the body is not free to run, jump, climb, swim or try to come to be at one with the vast land that is Australia – to go forth into the vast spaces that beckon?

Peter Stuart competed with some success in the battalion sports, telling his father (letter from Serapeum dated 29.4.16):

> *Well, Dadrus, I have still a kick in me for I managed to win the hundred and twenty and four forty yards (servicing) officers race in the battalion sports – then when representing the battalion in the To…….. Sports again managed to pull them both off, but when representing the Tode in the Divisional Sports the _____ _____ was licked got a second and a third or two thirds am not sure but still it was not bad for a broken down crock.*

In its report of Peter Stuart's death, the Morning Bulletin reports he won four first prizes in swimming that day.

That evening he was one of a group of officers, probably from the 13th Brigade, who attended an ANZAC Day commemoration dinner, the menu and seating arrangements for which are shown on the opposite page.

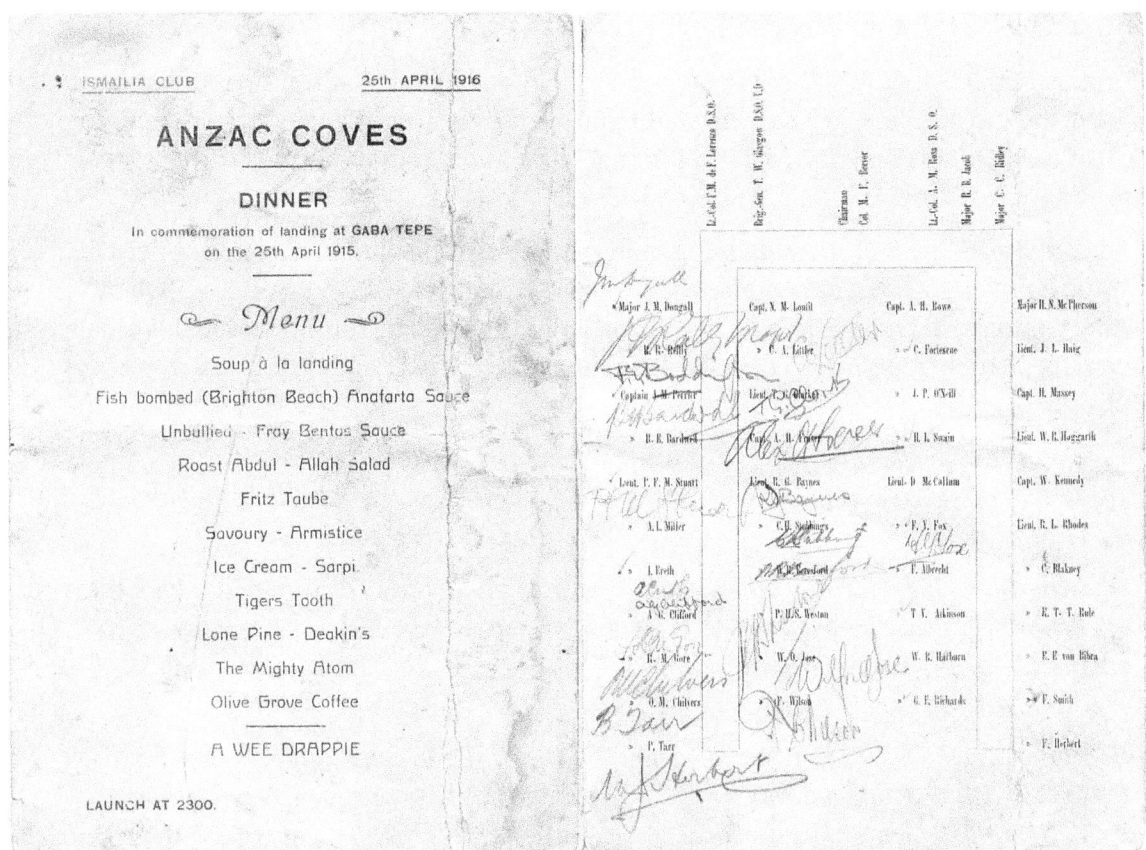

ANZAC Day 1916 dinner menu (above) and seating arrangements (below). Source: Peter Hasker

Table seating

Lt Colonel F.M. de F. Lorenzo DSO	Brig. General T.W. Glasgow DSO VD	Chairman Colonel M.F. Beevor	Lt Colonel A.M. Ross DSO	Major R.N. Jacob	Major C.C. Ridley

Major J.M. Dougall	Cpl N.M. Loutit	Cpl A.H. Rowe	Major H.N. McPherson
K.R. Reilly	C.A. Littler	C. Fortescue	Lt J.I. Haig
Cpl J.M. Parker	Lt T.G. Clarke	J.P. O'Neill	Cpl H. Massey
B.R. Bardwell	Cpl A.H. Fraser	H.I. Swain	Lt W.R. Hoggarth
Lt P.J.M. Stuart	Lt R.G. Baynes	Lt D. McCallum	Cpl W. Kennedy
A.I. Miller	C.H. Stubbings	F.Y. Fox	Lt R.I. Rhodes
I. Ereth	W.R. Beresford	F. Albrecht	C. Blakney
A.G. Clifford	P.H.S. Weston	T.V. Atkinson	R.T.T. Rule
R.M. Gore	W.O. Jose	W.R. Harburn	E.E. von Bibra
O.M. Chilvers	F. Wilson	G.E. Richards	F. Smith
P. Tarr			F. Herbert

In the 1920s, ANZAC Day became a day to commemorate all those who had died in the war and became entrenched as a national day of remembrance. It became a national public holiday in 1927. With the coming of WWII, it became a day to honour Australians who served and died in that war and subsequently all Australians who served, especially those who were killed in all the military operations in which Australia has been involved. In doing so Australians are reminded that the life and freedoms with which they are blessed did not come without sacrifice. They are reminded they owe it to those who made these sacrifices not to take for granted or to squander these blessings. In what they are doing and what they aspire to, young Australians in particular are challenged whether they are worthy successors of those to whom they give homage. ANZAC Day has become more than merely a day of remembrance.

More than Remembrance

For Australians, ANZAC Day is much more than a solemn occasion of remembrance and honouring the gallantry and sacrifices of their soldiers in war. It is much more than a day to reflect on the waste and loss, the grief and horror of war. It embodies who we are, what we are and what we aspire to.

The Gallipoli campaign was a defining moment for Australia as a new nation. After Gallipoli we were no longer Queenslanders or Victorians – whatever we were and from wherever we came, we were Australians and we were proud of it. Banjo Paterson expressed this eloquently in an open letter to the troops in 1915, a poem he titled *We're All Australians Now*:

Australia takes her pen in hand,
To write a line to you,
To let you fellows understand,
How proud we are of you.

From shearing shed and cattle run,
From Broome to Hobson's Bay,
Each native-born Australian son,
Stands straighter up today.

The man who used to 'hump his drum',
On far-out Queensland runs,
Is fighting side by side with some
Tasmanian farmer's sons.

The fisher-boys dropped sail and oar
To grimly stand the test,
Along that storm-swept Turkish shore,
With miners from the west.

The old state jealousies of yore
Are dead as Pharaoh's sow,
We're not State children any more
We're all Australians now!

Our six-starred flag that used to fly,
Half-shyly to the breeze,
Unknown where older nations ply
Their trade on foreign seas,

Flies out to meet the morning blue
With Vict'ry at the prow;
For that's the flag the Sydney flew,
The wide seas know it now!

The mettle that a race can show
Is proved with shot and steel,
And now we know what nations know
And feel what nations feel.

The honoured graves beneath the crest
Of Gaba Tepe hill,
May hold our bravest and our best,
But we have brave men still.

With all our petty quarrels done,
Dissensions overthrown,
We have, through what you boys have done,
A history of our own.

Our old world diff'rences are dead,
Like weeds beneath the plough,
For English, Scotch and Irish-bred,
They're all Australians now!

So now we'll toast the Third Brigade*,
That led Australia's van,
For never shall their glory fade
In minds Australian.

Fight on, fight on, unflinchingly,
Till right and justice reign.
Fight on, fight on, till Victory
Shall send you home again.

And with Australia's flag shall fly
A spray of wattle bough,
To symbolise our unity,
We're all Australians now.

* 3rd Australian Brigade that landed first at Gallipoli.

ANZAC Day does not celebrate heroic military victories or glorify war. The Gallipoli Campaign was a military disaster – the most successful 'military' action being the evacuation of the Gallipoli Peninsula – rather strange grounds for a commemoration. However, the ANZAC story is about triumphs against the odds, of courage and ingenuity in adversity. In commemorating a defeat, ANZAC Day exposes that part of the Australian psyche that sympathises with the underdog, that empathises with the battler; that characteristic of the 'Australian' rooted in our convict beginning and the challenges that confronted the explorers, early settlers and miners.

I remember listening to radio broadcasts of Davis Cup matches in the 1950s. As always we wanted the Australians to win but very often when they were winning, the crowd would almost barrack for the losing players if our players were strongly on top. I was made very aware of how very Australian this characteristic is on the evening of the 1996 federal election. At the time Christian, a university Ph.D. student from Friesing University, Germany, was staying with me. We were enjoying a bottle of wine after dinner. At about 09.00 pm I told him I would check the election results and he joined me. As soon as I turned on the TV I learnt the Liberal-National Coalition had won. Almost immediately the program shifted to Labor headquarters showing the crowd giving defeated Prime Minister Paul Keating a standing ovation. Our conversation went like this:

> Christian: *He's won.*
> Peter: *No, he's lost.*
> Christian: *He's won.*
> Peter: *No, he's lost.*
> Christian: *No. He's won. Look at them cheering him.*
> Peter: *No, he's lost.*
> Christian (bewildered): *It wouldn't happen in Germany.*

ANZAC Day focuses Australians on the ANZAC legend – the story that embodies the deeds and qualities displayed by the Australians at Gallipoli and other theatres of that war to end all wars. It is a story of free and independent spirits, whose discipline was derived less from military formalities, customs and tradition than from the bonds of mateship and the demands of necessity, of unity through common purpose. The qualities they displayed – endurance, courage, ingenuity, good humour and mateship – constitute what is described as the ANZAC spirit and have been the hallmark of Australians who have fought in all wars subsequently.

ANZAC Day parade, Brisbane 2007. Source: *Courier Mail*

These qualities did not suddenly appear out of the blue on landing at Gallipoli. The Gallipoli Campaign was simply the culminating event of all those moulding 'the Australian' from the moment the convicts and their guards first set foot on land in January 1788. At Gallipoli the characteristics that define the 'Australian' – resourceful, flexible, will have a go, their sense of humour and attitude towards authority plus equality – were demonstrated unequivocally. So the word 'ANZAC' embodies the essence of what it means to be Australian. On ANZAC Day our thoughts go beyond those who gave their lives. The motley collection of marchers from all walks of life who pass by with simple dignity remind us of who we are and light within us a flame of quiet but immense pride.

ANZAC Day evolving

Since that first anniversary of the landing at Gallipoli, ANZAC Day has been evolving. For instance, not only do we now remember Australians who served, especially those who were killed, in all wars in which Australia has been involved – the Australian descendants of Turkish soldiers who fought at Gallipoli now may join in the march. However, the Returned Services League, the organisation representing Australian veterans, says it is unlikely it will give approval to descendants of other former foes. It points out that Australia and Turkey have a special relationship.

Gallipoli has iconic significance to Turkey as well as Australia. Kemal Ataturk, who very ably defended Gallipoli, afterwards founded modern Turkey and became its first president. Turkey really accepted the bodies of the Australians that remained in Turkey after the war. This shows in Ataturk's eloquent tribute to those soldiers who did not return from Gallipoli:

> *Those heroes that shed their blood*
> *and lost their lives...*
> *You are now lying in the soil of a friendly country.*
> *Therefore rest in peace.*
> *There is no difference between the johnnies*
> *and mehmets to us where they lie side by side*
> *here in this country of ours...*
> *You, the mothers,*
> *who sent their sons from far away countries,*
> *wipe away your tears;*
> *your sons are now lying in our bosom*
> *and are in peace,*
> *after having lost their lives on this land*
> *they have become our sons as well.*

An officer of the Turkish armed forces reads this tribute in both Turkish and English at the joint Australian and New Zealand Dawn Service held at Gallipoli each year on ANZAC Day.

Above: Lone Pine Memorial, Gallipoli, 2012. Source: Jorge Lascar, Flickr

Right: Mustafa Kemal Ataturk Memorial, Canberra unveiled in 1985 honours the heroism and sacrifice of both the ANZAC and Turkish troops who took part in the Gallipoli campaign. Source: Peter Ellis, Wikimedia Commons

ANZAC Day has been developing and its broader meaning and significance have been evolving. It will continue to evolve or else lose its deep meaning and significance. However, at its core has been and I hope will always be, the Spirit of ANZAC (or simply ANZAC), which the official war historian C.E. Bean said stood for: *reckless valour in a good cause, for enterprise, resourcefulness, fidelity, comradeship and endurance that will never own defeat*, qualities that burst into full flower at Gallipoli and which go to the heart of what it is to be Australian.

The commemoration of ANZAC Day

ANZAC Day is marked in some way in just about every town in the country. Commemoration of ANZAC Day consists of services held at dawn, the time of the original landing, marches through the major cities and many smaller centres, followed by commemorative ceremonies where wreaths are laid at war memorials around the country. In my home town of Rockhampton the ANZAC Day marchers proceeded along the street in front of our house on their way to the Cenotaph at the Botanical Gardens nearby. It is the tallest First World War monument in Queensland. On its west, south, east and north faces are the words: In Remembrance, Freedom, Unity and Sacrifice.

Rockhampton cenotaph, Diggers Park, Botanical Gardens. Source: Ricki Palmer

The Dawn Service. This Service had its origin in an operational routine still practised by the Australian army. The half-light of dawn plays tricks with soldiers' eyes and, from earliest times, the half-hour or so before dawn has been a favourite time to attack. Soldiers in defensive positions were woken before dawn so they were alert and manning their weapons. This is known as 'stand-to' and is repeated at sunset. After WWI, returned soldiers sought the comradeship they felt in those quiet peaceful moments before dawn. With symbolic links to the dawn landing at Gallipoli at 4.28 am on 25 April, a dawn stand-to or dawn ceremony became a common form of ANZAC Day remembrance during the 1920s.

The ANZAC Day March. Those taking part in the marches are current serving members of the Australian Defence Forces and ex-servicemen and women, the veterans from all past wars. The veterans, wearing their full service medals, march proudly under the banners of the units they fought and served in. Most are in civilian dress, which varies, because life does not deal out an even hand, even to gallant men and women. Those too old to march ride in cars. The original ANZACS have all passed away and few WWII veterans remain. Their grandchildren, their grandparents' medals pinned to their chests (but on the right-hand side), sometimes march in their place.

A typical ANZAC Day Service. After an Internet search of a number of sites, including the Australian War Memorial and Parliament of Australia, the following was compiled. A typical Service contains the following features: introduction, hymn, prayer, commemorative address, laying of wreaths, recitation, The 'Last Post', a period of silence, The 'Rouse' or 'Reveille', and the National Anthem(s). Their meaning is as follows:

Laying of wreaths. Flowers have traditionally been laid on graves and memorials in memory of the dead. Laurel, rosemary and red poppy are used in wreaths on ANZAC Day. Laurel is a symbol of honour; the ancient Romans crowned victors and the brave with a laurel wreath. Rosemary, a herb said to improve memory, is commonly associated with remembrance. Rosemary has particular significance for Australians because it grows wild on the Gallipoli Peninsula. The poppy symbolises the sacrifice of shed blood. During WWI, red poppies were among the first living plants that sprouted from the devastation of the battlefields of northern France and Belgium. Soldiers reckoned the poppies were vivid red from having been nurtured in ground drenched with the blood of their comrades.

Recitation of an appropriate poem. The Ode, the fourth stanza of the poem *For the Fallen* by Englishman Laurence Binyon (1869-1943) is commonly read:

> *They shall grow not old, as we that are left grow old;*
> *Age shall not weary them, nor the years condemn.*
> *At the going down of the sun and in the morning*
> *We will remember them.*
> *Lest we forget.*

The 'Last Post'. The Last Post marks the end of the day. In military tradition it signalled the night sentries were alert at their posts and gave one last warning to any soldiers still at large that it was time to retire for the evening. In funeral and memorial services it is a final farewell and symbolises the dead have done their duty and can rest in peace. A period of silence for one or two minutes follows the Last Post. It is a sign of respect and gives time to reflect on the significance of the whole ceremony.

The 'Rouse' or 'Reveille'. These sounds originated from the bugle call used to wake soldiers in the morning. After the period of silence the Rouse is sounded as flags that have been at half-mast as a sign of respect and remembrance are raised to the masthead. This symbolises an awakening in a better world for the dead and rouses the living, their respects paid to the memory of their comrades, back to duty. Reveille is played only at Dawn Services on ANZAC Day, while The Rouse is played at all other Services.

For the first time since its inception in April 1916 commemorations were curtailed by the restrictions required to counter the Covid-19 pandemic. However, its spirit remained present when residents throughout Australia gathered on their driveways to commemorate this very Australian day. At 11.00 am at 36 Cosmic Street, Robertson, The Ode was read and a two-minute silence was observed.

ANZAC Day 2020 outside the author's home. L to R: Gavin Lawrence, Perbel Arsenal, Tim Yuan, Vivian Wang, Peter Hasker, Sheree McGee, Kim Xuan, Laura Liu. Source: Peter Hasker

Chapter 28
Aussie Women

Special mention must be made about the Australian woman. The female Australian, so visitors tell me, is a special species. In comparison with most other women they dress in a very casual but practical way and are viewed as rather rough and independent. The Aussie woman is capable of stepping into a man's boots and doing a man's work. This is not surprising. Women played a significant role in forming this nation.

Following the arrival of the First Fleet from the beginning women were involved with building the colony. No matter what part of society they came from, they had to perform all sorts of tasks. Women were, very largely, the civilising influence on what until recently was a man's world, especially so in the bush. As with Australians generally, it was the environment and break with traditions that played a significant part in moulding the Aussie woman.

Convict women and early colonial years

Life in the fledgling colony was especially harsh for convict women. From the day they disembarked from the First Fleet men took advantage of them and they suffered at the hands of authority and men. On arrival at Port Jackson, female convicts of the First Fleet were kept aboard for five days, while the ships were unloaded and simple shelters were erected. When finally brought ashore women were cleanly dressed, some even well dressed. Within an hour of their landing a violent storm struck but this did not deter the male convicts, who, soon after the women landed, embarked on two days of riotous behaviour and debauchery. This would be the lot of female convicts in the following decades.

Convict women were sexually vulnerable and officials did little to protect them or provide work for them. On arrival female convicts were usually assigned to domestic service or sent to the Female Factory, where they made clothes for convicts or household utensils such as brooms. When demanded by free settlers and convicts, many women were assigned indiscriminately not only to perform domestic duties but also to satisfy the sexual desires of those who demanded them. In contrast, an applicant seeking the services of a convict man had to show he owned a specific quantity of land, was of good character and habits and had adequate means of support for maintaining servants.

Lack of government accommodation forced some convict women to form attachments with men or to find lodgings. Because they had no money and there was little paid work for women, they were forced into prostitution to earn money. Those allocated to domestic service were generally thought of more as prostitutes than servants. Convict women were damned because they did not behave like ladies, who did not smoke, sing, smile, look men in the eye, drink alcohol, use bad language, dress in men's clothes, dance or fight. Women were blamed for the low moral tone of the colony, where life was raw and behaviour coarse with brawling, whoring and drinking commonplace. The outcome was female convicts were universally condemned and stereotyped as 'whores'.

Nothing could overcome the stigma of immorality that tainted most women. Those convict women, who formed attachments with governors or other prominent men and bore them children, were unable to shake off their 'common' status and assume anything matching the social standing of either these men or wives and daughters of men of similar rank. Marriage did not automatically ensure that women could flee from the 'whore' stereotype. For the majority of white women, 'making do' in the colony involved living with a man, sometimes married but usually not.

The government encouraged marriage between convicts and it was in the best interests of women to marry; it brought material comforts and afforded some protection against the advances of other men; but there were a number of barriers to marriage. Some new arrivals had husbands and wives back in Britain. Convicts needed the permission of their masters to marry and this was granted only reluctantly as their masters had to support any offspring. Prior to 1834 a marriage was invalid unless an Anglican clergyman officiated and a costly licence from the Governor was necessary; for many years there were no Catholic priests. Also, de facto relationships were acceptable in the environment from which most convicts came. Officials were outwardly scandalised and described women in de facto relationships as prostitutes.

Marriage between female convicts and native-born youths was very rare. This was mainly attributed to a sense of pride in native-born youths, who had what approached contempt for the vices and depravity of convicts, even when manifested in the persons of their own parents. The taint borne by female convicts was more permanent than it was for men.

Thus convict women were doomed as being members of the 'criminal class', the lowest order of society, who brought with them little in the way of work experience or traditional family values. In the colony they were expected to fail as workers, wives and mothers. However, convict women did not establish a cold and barren criminal subculture but one based on families, intimacy and warmth; they made good mothers giving birth and successfully nurturing the first generation of native-born white children.

I know nothing of the relationship between my convict ancestors John and Sarah Warby. Like so many who were transported, they were illiterate. Thirty-year-old John married 16-year-old Sarah within five months of her arrival on the *Indispensible*. The ceremony was conducted by the Reverend Samuel Marsden, the 'Flogging Parson', in a temporary church made from two old huts at Parramatta. A permanent structure was opened as Saint John's Anglican Church in 1803 and was the only church in the colony until 1809. It is now a Cathedral. Sarah had worked as a housemaid in London and had been convicted of stealing cotton and linen goods from her employer and sentenced to transportation to New South Wales for seven years. We can be fairly certain this was not a love match – not that many marriages at that time were. Very likely she did not have to suffer the indignities that many female convicts suffered. She was certainly fortunate in that a marriage occurred, for it would have gained her a degree of respectability. She was also fortunate that, despite what would have been a hard life, the marriage was successful.

St John's Anglican Church, Parramatta. Source: Hope Media Ltd

The couple had 14 children, of whom 11 survived to adulthood. At the age of 26 she had to care for six children under the age of six years. For much of this time she was alone, because John spent a considerable time away from home. Although John employed many male convicts, there is no record of him employing women to help Sarah with the children or domestic chores.

Whatever judgement we may pass on female convicts as a whole, we cannot deny their part in formation of the Aussie woman. From the arrival of the First Fleet until the end of the 1820s, when nearly half the population was still convict, transported women, like army shock troops, would have broken the shackles of tradition. Transportation in a brutal way had a greater effect on women than men in releasing them from the bonds placed on them by contemporary English society. They were transported equally with the men, enchained equally with the men, punished equally with the men and abandoned into an alien environment equally with the men.

For early colonial women, whatever course their life took, it was difficult and to survive required an independence of spirit and willingness to engage in a life, that elsewhere was not the realm of a woman. Except for the absence of the convict stain, life for free-women would differ from that of their convict sisters generally only by a matter of degree. While free-women married to men of high rank lived in comfort, in big houses with servants, their life was not necessarily easy. They were often lonely with their husband away on business and their children at school in England. To escape the feeling of loneliness these women would sometimes move into fields outside the management of the home. Many were vigorous women, who developed their own interests and took an active part both in their husbands' businesses and in public affairs of the colony. Elizabeth, wife of John MacArthur, is an example; for it was she, rather than John, who established the Merino breed of sheep and is rightly entitled to being referred to as the 'mother of the Australian wool industry'. In 1828-1830 Scottish woman, Eliza Furlong, walked 2,400 km through villages in Saxony selecting fine-wool Saxon sheep with which she subsequently established the fine-wool industry in Tasmania.

Convict women remained the dominant white female presence in New South Wales until well into the 1830s, when free-women, who began arriving in the 1820s, became the major female influence in pioneering and settling the new land.

Who were these free-women?

Some of the free-women were wives of wealthy adventurers. Some came with husbands, and some with families. Many were single women who, like convict women, were mainly domestic and farm workers; they sought husbands as soon as possible on arrival. Many had been thrust into the poor houses of England by the industrial revolution. As a group they were more literate than convict women and had a distinct advantage over convict women, i.e. their virtuous character, compared with the 'damned whore' image of the latter. They were selected for assisted passage on the basis of their home-making ability and their morality. However, free-immigrant women suffered the stigma of single women 'without male protection' and were subjected to the same disparaging terms used to demean convict women.

From whatever social class these free-women came, most came expecting a better life. However, the life that awaited them was harsh; the harshness for the wife attached to wealth or the young single girl from the poor-house was more a matter of degree than a substantial difference in lifestyle. For many at first it was nothing more than a matter of survival. For all it meant discarding old ways and traditions and establishing a totally new approach to living.

The fate of single women

By 1838 men still out-numbered women four-to-one in Sydney and 20-to-one in the surrounding country areas. To increase the female population, the British Government introduced a bounty system to encourage young British women to emigrate to NSW. The Government paid their fares out to the colony but did nothing to help them when they arrived. Most were poor and uneducated and many had to beg or become prostitutes to survive.

The resemblance between free-immigrant women and convict women did not end when they arrived in Australia. Although the government had paid for their passages, no assistance was provided on their arrival, either for accommodation or employment. The authorities, however, were well aware of the demand for workers and announced the arrival of immigrant ships and that women workers were available for distribution. Those women, who did not find work or take up immediately with a man, resorted to sleeping in the streets or caves or turned to prostitution to earn money for food and accommodation. On her arrival in Sydney in 1839, Caroline Chisholm, the wife of an army officer, was so shocked by the sight of these destitute women that she established 'homes' and sought jobs for them.

Lodging and food in Chisholm's emigrant houses was free but barely sufficient to keep a human being alive and so the women grasped at every opportunity to get out of them. Consequently, there was no difficulty in obtaining women from these emigrant houses; whoever wanted a female picked one to his liking and took her away. The women agreed to go with a sailor, ex-convict or any male, despite not having met the man previously and knowing nothing about him.

They followed these unknown men to unknown places and an unknown future. Some began their new lives in the fledgling cities and towns springing up in their new land. This new life was not easy and demanded a willingness, flexibility and ingenuity to adapt that would become characteristics of the Aussie woman. However the major driving forces in the evolution of the Aussie female were those women who began new lives far from the noise, smells and bustle of towns and cities. These were the women who followed their men into the bush, to mines, farms and pastoral enterprises. The story of the Aussie woman is surely their story.

Not surprisingly, among the men who sought partners at the emigrant houses were those who were hewing out a new life on selections in the bush. Thus, in the bush ballad *The Old Bullock Dray*, the balladeer sings:

> *Oh! the shearing is all over,*
> *And the wool is coming down,*
> *And I mean to get a wife, boys,*
> *When I go up to town.*
> *Everything that has two legs*
> *Represents itself in view,*
> *From the little paddy-melon*
> *To the bucking kangaroo.*
>
> *Now I've stood up a good cheque,*
> *I mean to buy a team,*
> *And when I get a wife, boys,*
> *I'll be all-serene.*
> *For, calling at the depot*,*
> *They say there's no delay*
> *To get an offsider*
> *For the old bullock dray.*
>
> *CHORUS*
> *So it's roll up your blankets*
> *And let's make a push;*
> *I'll take you up the country*
> *And show you the bush.*
> *I'll be bound you won't get*
> *Such a chance another day,*
> *So come and take possession*
> *Of my old bullock dray.*
>
> ** female emigrant house*

The balladeer expects little delay in a woman accepting him because no woman, in his mind, would get a better offer than his. But he wants more than the comforts a woman gives a man, more than a traditional homemaker and children. He wants an offsider for the old bullock dray; someone who will work with him as he battles to establish himself in an 'inhospitable' land.

Of course, not all women who ventured into the bush were from the female emigrant houses. At first these women consisted of the wives of selectors, and small and large landholders. Also there were the house-keepers and domestic workers in the homes of the better off. Later they were joined by teachers, nurses and wives of those men who did not go into the bush to dig for gold or to farm or graze cattle and sheep, but to set up businesses serving the needs of land-holders.

Life in the bush

Life in the bush was harsh for women in the early years of settlement. A woman faced the heat, dust and flies of summer and extreme cold in winter. She was usually alone all day, except for a convict servant if she had one. She could be constantly in fear of reprisals by Aboriginal people in her district. She usually had to live in a crude timber hut with a mud floor and no running water. She would have to slave from dawn to dusk washing, baking, churning butter, making cheese, tending a vegetable garden and looking after her children. For some women life became easier as their farms and sheep stations prospered. Wealth brought them large, well-furnished houses, many servants, fine clothes, good food and horse-drawn carriages, but for the majority of women daily life was a grind.

No matter what their social status was, no matter whether their husbands had considerable land-holdings or they lived in shanties and shacks, the women who went into the bush experienced the same physical environment, i.e. isolation and lack of facilities that had been taken for granted for hundreds, even thousands of years in civilised societies such as China. This required courage, stamina and initiative to brave conditions, then unfamiliar to any but the Aboriginals, in an isolated wilderness subject to drought and flood, bushfires, dust storms and invasions by insect life. Even the journey into the bush, whether by bullock dray or a more comfortable horse-drawn means, was generally difficult and sometimes dangerous when Aboriginals were hostile. The life of women who went into the bush was far different from that of their sisters on the other side of the world, both physically and emotionally. It was hard; it was raw; it was lonely. They learnt to cope with primitive conditions. Survival required an independence of spirit and willingness to engage in a life that elsewhere was not the realm of a woman.

Many went to live in houses constructed mostly of 'wattle and daub' with roofs of slabbed bark, shelters which they often helped construct, because as well as performing child-rearing and domestic duties, many women helped their menfolk build yards, fences and living quarters. On farms that grew wheat they assisted with tasks such as reaping, sewing sacks and winnowing.

Left: Woman in front of a wattle and daub hut with bark roof, Hill End, New South Wales, ca.1872. Source: NLA, No. 4735117 Right: Standing woman outside a selector's bark hut, Australia, ca. 1895. Source: NLA, No. 4313016

Isolation, something unknown to their sisters in the cities and towns, impacted heavily on women in the bush. In his short story *The Drover's Wife*, Henry Lawson tells of a woman's all-night vigil to protect her children, knowing that there is a snake in the wall of their slab hut. Isolation made their lives more difficult and more challenging in a number of ways; for instance the woman of the house could not go to a nearby store for food or other house-hold essentials. Horse transport and long distances to the city or country town centres meant shopping trips were very infrequent – sometimes only once a year. Essential supplies such as flour, tea and sugar were purchased in bulk. This meant that for much of the year daily meals were made from flour, sugar, meat and tea. If sufficient water was available for her to maintain a garden, the woman could include home-grown vegetables in the diet. Women coped with ingenuity to ensure the family had basic needs by making their own soap and tallow candles.

The impact of distance on shopping in those days is well illustrated by a story about my grandmother, the youngest daughter of P.F. MacDonald. Except for four years spent at boarding school in Victoria, during which time she did not return home, she had spent her life at *Yaamba Station* about 35 km north of Rockhampton. My grandmother married an enterprising young Irish doctor, Simson Stuart, who had travelled to Central Queensland on an immigrant sailing ship as ship's doctor. Like at least one First Fleet surgeon he was a graduate of Trinity College, Dublin. Although typically Irish in being a great raconteur but poor provider for his family, he was an Orangeman and did not harbour the anti-British feelings of his Catholic brethren. This is not surprising given his father, John Simson Stuart, was ex-Chief Inspector of the Royal Irish Constabulary. On arrival Simson inquired about eligible daughters of wealthy men and was told P.F. MacDonald at *Yaamba Station* had one. The daughter, Annie, was an excellent horsewoman, having ridden from an early age and to her father's delight 'went through the bush like a streak of sunshine'.

Annie tired of reading Hansard to her father and so accepted Simson's hand in marriage. They were married on 15 July 1886 at ages of 30 and 20, respectively, and set up house in Rockhampton. The grocer called on my grandfather to query the large quantities on my grandmother's first grocery order. She had ordered quantities she was used to seeing ordered for *Yaamba Station*. One of my childhood memories of my grandmother's house was a large container of fat and caustic soda bubbling on a wood stove. The caustic-smelling bars of soap were stacked in a verandah cupboard. I remember the plucking of fowls and ducks and the feathers saved for stuffing pillows and cushions, some of which I still possess.

Few doctors were available in the outback. Childbirth was solely managed by women, supported by midwives and district nurses who played critical roles in assisting with births and addressing community healthcare needs. Isolation posed ongoing health challenges for women until the founding of the Royal Flying Doctor Service in 1928, which significantly enhanced healthcare delivery for women and the entire community. Many regional towns and remote communities still lack resident doctors and adequate medical facilities. District nurses, versatile in their practice, continue to provide essential clinical care across all stages of life. The dedication of these nurses was vividly portrayed in the TV series "Remote Area Nurse," where Helen Tremain navigates the daily complexities of delivering healthcare to the remote Torres Strait Islander community.

Women played a significant role in the education of children. When home-based education was chosen over long-distance travel to school, wealthier people employed governesses who also carried out various household duties as well. Otherwise the mother or an older sibling or family relative would tutor the children at home. The majority of outback women had to undertake the education of their children alone.

Women in the bush lacked the company of other women. When a family prospered, the wife and children often moved to a distant but comfortable rural town, where she found companionship and there were schools for the children.

Loneliness caused many women to take solace in alcohol, an occurrence I came across when I went to work in the bush. The advent of the Pedal Radio in the late 1920s not only provided help in emergency medical situations but also helped reduce the isolation and loneliness by enabling women, who lived hundreds of kilometres apart, to speak with each other. They quickly developed a bush community over the air for it was the women who learnt Morse code and took on the role of Radio Operator.

The drover's wife, ca. 1945. Artist Russell Drysdale. Source: NGA, © Estate of Russell Drysdale

Women were initiated into work and other responsibilities at a young age. On smaller properties and settler blocks where families struggled financially, older girls looked after younger children. This freed their mothers for work in the home or assisting outside in the paddocks or yards. Young girls helped their mothers with arduous work and chores such as butter-making. Quite often girls from struggling families went into domestic service with a neighbouring family either on a payback system or for a wage. Even on larger properties where children's labour was not essential, both boys and girls helped with chores outside the house. In larger families older girls were trained to gradually take over supervision and care of their younger siblings. In prosperous families the need for girls to help diminished. However, the more typical outback girl in the 20th century was conversant with the ways of the bush and was often a competent horsewoman, i.e. riding well along with making essential items for her 'glory box'.

Except in large country homes of the squatter gentry and city houses, the genteel life and comforts of Britain and Europe were nothing but memories. However, women from middle-class backgrounds did try to maintain some semblance of genteel standards. They educated their children in what they considered was appropriate behaviour, manners and skills. They sustained the rituals of meals and dress and fitted out their homes as best they could. Stations graced by their presence would have a pleasant and prosperous atmosphere and very often even tents would have the homely touch of sheets, as well as blankets, on the beds and a dry sack or piece of carpet on the ground. Even women from working-class backgrounds would know how to make a house presentable, because many worked as servants before coming to Australia. It was the presence of women that had a civilising influence on what, for over a hundred years, was very much a man's world, i.e. a tough, rough world. Both in theory and in practice the home was usually the sanctuary. An Australian woman composed the words and music for the song *Bless this house* and Dame Nellie Melba, Australia's operatic star, lauded home life when she sang *Home Sweet Home*.

Survival in this new land, Australia, required that women became 'jills' of all occupations. As a result, that which every woman holds dear – her beauty – was at risk. Whatever her situation, no woman with a complexion evolved in higher, cooler latitudes could escape the ravages of the Australian climate, the heat of the Australian sun. My great grandmother Julia was an example. Because of her flawless white skin, she was known in her younger years as the 'White Rose'. My great grandfather brought her to Queensland, where the harsh subtropical climate of Central Queensland took its toll. My mother said that, as a little girl, she had to 'steel' herself to give her grandmother the obligatory kiss.

The silent sacrifice and dignity of these women, who helped build Australia, is lauded by George Essex Evans in her poem *The Women of the West*.

> *The roar and rush and fever of the city died away,*
> *And the old-time joys and faces – they were gone for many a day;*
> *In their place the lurching coach-wheel, or the creaking bullock-chains,*
> *O'er the everlasting sameness of the never-ending plains.*

> *In the slab-built, zinc-roofed homestead of some lately taken run,*
> *In the tent beside the bankment of a railway just begun,*
> *In the huts on new selections, in the camps of man's unrest,*
> *On the frontiers of the Nation, live the Women of the West.*

> *The red sun robs their beauty and, in weariness and pain,*
> *As slow years steal the nameless grace, that never comes again;*
> *And there are hours men cannot soothe, and words men cannot say –*
> *The nearest woman's face may be a hundred miles away.*

> *The wide bush holds the secrets of their longing and desires,*
> *When the white stars in reverence light their holy altar fires,*
> *And silence, like the touch of God, sinks deep into the breast*
> *Perchance He hears and understands the Women of the West.*

> *For them no trumpet sounds the call, no poet plies his arts,*
> *They only hear the beating of their gallant, loving hearts.*
> *But they have sung with silent lives the song all songs above –*
> *The holiness of sacrifice, the dignity of love.*

> *Well have we held our fathers' creed. No call has passed us by.*
> *We faced and fought the wilderness, we sent our sons to die.*
> *And we have hearts to do and dare, and yet o'er all the rest,*
> *The hearts that made the Nation were the Women of the West.*

Julia MacDonald – wife of P.F. MacDonald

My great grandmother, Julia Ayrey, is an example of a woman of a privileged background and good education who was taken to the bush. Her family were wealthy free-settlers, who had taken up land at Mt Gellibrand on the eastern edge of the Western District plains of

Victoria in 1841. On 1 January 1861 at the age of 21 Julia married P.F. MacDonald, the son of a convict. MacDonald had done well given the sharp contrast between his circumstances and the experience of her family during the 1840s and 1850s. The wedding was held in Geelong at the Corio Terrace residence of his brother Alexander MacDonald. Her uncle cum guardian (Julia was orphaned at 12 years of age) considered MacDonald an unsuitable match and did not attend the wedding ceremony. The banns were not read but MacDonald, in the manner typical of the native-born, secured a licence for the marriage. In February MacDonald took his newly acquired wife back to his base at *Yaamba*.

Yaamba was well located on the main track north from Rockhampton. However, the surrounding scrubby bush and swampy river flats were a far cry from the lush bush pastures at Mt Gellibrand. Crocodiles may have inhabited the nearby Fitzroy River and low-lying areas would be covered by up to two metres of water in flood times. It would have teemed with mosquitoes and sand-flies in the summer months.

MacDonald was a hard man. Hard work epitomised life at *Yaamba*. The MacDonalds had difficulty keeping female servants, so Julia did the cooking, laundering and housework and also cared for a daughter, who suffered from epilepsy. Although Aboriginals camped there, Julia did not have the contact with Aboriginal women that some bush women did. Station servants and female Aboriginals helped establish a flower and vegetable garden. MacDonald had intended *Yaamba* to be a temporary residence and to settle permanently on the coast. However, its location was convenient for managing his properties and in 1861 extensions to the homestead were carried out. Fortunately for Julia, her husband considered a woman should be expected to go to an outpost only if a home was available and so he did not take her to his more remote cattle stations occupied by station managers and station hands, who lived in tents.

Julia's activities in Queensland were confined to *Yaamba*, Canoona and Rockhampton, which contrasted with the comparative sophistication of life at and around Geelong. She was a competent horse-woman and often rode or drove a buggy into Rockhampton with her husband; the drive to Rockhampton by buggy took five hours. Since *Yaamba* was a distance from town, her husband's absence for extended periods probably deepened feelings of isolation. Rare visits to the colony of her youth might have heightened a sense of exile. Finally, in 1888, after spending 25 years within an environment in which she seemed an alien, she moved to Rockhampton to live.

New found freedom, new woman

A massive shift in attitudes and labour relations was required by the completely different physical and social environment into which women were thrust. There were no gadgets to lighten the burden of domestic tasks. Most of those living in towns and cities had some kind of domestic help, even if it were merely the girl from next door who helped out. But the wives of selectors or smaller land-holders seldom could afford domestic help. Even those who could did not necessarily get help because of a shortage of domestic workers and they had to perform domestic duties themselves. The undertaking of unaccustomed tasks required a loosening of the bonds of social convention.

Their hard life was balanced by a new-found freedom and social mobility. Fashionable clothes were unsuitable for the environment and physical work and, therefore, a necessarily relaxed style of dress was an index of practicality and greater freedom for women, not one of insularity. There was no demand to keep up a sort of appearance, or care who might visit and how rich they may be. If the visitors were rich, they had probably been poor when they arrived in the country and one might expect to be as well off in a few years. Furthermore, *wealth was insecure, for even those with vast holdings were nothing more than Kings in Grass Castles that could be swept away by flood, fire or drought.*

Chapter 28: Aussie Women

Annette Kellerman in her famous custom swimsuit, ca. 1900. Source: Library of Congress, Wikimedia Commons

It was an Australian swimmer and diver, Annette Kellerman, who first shed the figure-hiding full-length swimming outfit that was standard at the end of the 19th century. In those days women's swim-wear was not much different from street clothes. Kellerman considered it a ridiculous and impractical situation. When Edward VII invited glamorous Annette to give a special exhibition of her diving and swimming skills at London's exclusive Bath Club, she wore a much more daring skin-tight one-piece costume she had designed herself. The king did not disapprove. Never again would Western women be forced to conceal the contours of their bodies, when they went to the beach. Within a few years women all over the world were throwing away their traditional swim-wear and appearing on beaches in much less restrictive costumes. It took another four decades before they had advanced to wearing bikinis. Annette later took up offers from Hollywood to make silent movies, invariably showing her swimming and diving skills. She was the first major Hollywood star to do a nude scene.

The metamorphosis of the Aussie woman continued until well into the 20th century in the women who followed their men on to the soldier-settler blocks after both world wars and other closer settlement schemes, such as the Brigalow Development Scheme. The life on a soldier-settler block in western New South Wales is vividly described by Jill Kerr Conway in her autobiography *The Road from Coorain*. In particular it describes the life of a little girl doing a man's job helping her father. The migrant women, who joined their husbands working on the Snowy River Scheme, faced similar hardships to their settler forebears in the camps and towns built in the mountains to house the workers and their families. They had to work hard to overcome the hardships and establish communities in the strange, new, wilderness environment.

Although modern technology had lessened the impact of isolation and the hardship of physical work, women struggled and suffered very much as those who preceded them did. The ideal woman was a good manager, who

Palm Beach police measuring swimsuit length, 1925. Source: Etsy

coped under primitive conditions. She knew how to fix things that broke in the house. She could care for the sick, help fight a bushfire, aid a mare or cow in difficult labour when reproducing as well as laugh and joke about life's absurdities and reverses. She and her daughters looked a 'bit rough', behaved a bit 'unladylike' and had an independence of spirit. She bore little resemblance to her genteel forebears, who came from over the seas. She was an Aussie woman.

My mother's elder sister, Adah Stuart (1892-1963), exemplifies many characteristics of the Aussie woman. To help assuage her grief after her brother Peter (see page 181) and a close admirer were killed in action on the battlefields of Europe, her father encouraged her to embark upon a medical course. Her father was a great enthusiast for education and one of the people he most admired was his sister Geraldine who had trained as a medical doctor in the days when few women had entered the profession. Adah graduated from Sydney University in January 1922 and undertook her internship in Sydney.

Women's College, Sydney University; Adah Stuart, front row, second from left. Source: Peter Hasker

Adah Stuart. Source: Peter Hasker

In 1923, she set up a practice with a colleague, Doris Swanwick, at Wowan, 70 km southwest of Rockhampton in Central Queensland; Doris left the practice in September 1924 and Adah carried on alone. She also acted in an official way as medical officer. It was no genteel occupation. Housing was primitive, being little more than hessian coated with slaked lime, and the medical cases presented were varied and challenging. They included cases not generally associated with the medical profession such as pulling teeth; she even treated a dog for snakebite. The nature of the cases the recently graduated doctors encountered is illustrated by an incident reported in the *Morning Bulletin*, Monday, 6 August 1923: *Serious Accident at Castle Creek*. Irrigation works were being undertaken at Castle Creek. One morning a workman, Mr. Outhwaite, was badly injured by the collapse of heavy machinery. A messenger was despatched to the nearest telegraph station to arrange for a doctor and ambulance officer to be brought from Wowan.

> *Mr. Achilles, of the Wowan Ambulance Brigade, arrived at the camp about ten o'clock at night. He brought with him Drs. Adah Stuart and Doris Swanwick. ... the road between Banana and Castle Creek [was] almost impassable owing to the recent rain. The party had a very rough trip. Several times it became necessary to 'get out and push,' the doctors assisting. The doctors diagnosed the injury to Mr. Outhwaite as a fracture of the spine and decided to have him removed immediately. At eleven o'clock the party started out on its journey of over a hundred miles. Mr. Lord placed two motor drivers and a car at the disposal of the doctors in order that no unnecessary delay should occur.*

In 1927 Adah sold the practice, resigned as medical officer and returned to Rockhampton to join her brother 'Gem' Stuart in the family practice. He died in 1936 and soon after my father joined the practice. A year later he married my mother, Adah's younger sister.

The surgery was part of the old family home, *Kooltandra*, a large two-storied house in the middle of Rockhampton. In the early years, several staff had been employed. In her later years Adah did much of the housework herself. She would arise around 5.30 am daily, when she would dust the furniture and get down on her hands and knees to brush the staircase.

Kooltandra sketch by Ben Wickham, 1973. Source: Peter Hasker

After the death of her brother Simson in 1945, she also successfully ran a small beef property of 10,000 ha with the help of an Aboriginal overseer Hector Rutherford and his family. She would don her riding gear and help with the mustering. She also worked the sliding gate at the entrance to the cattle dip that contained a chemical to kill cattle ticks. She would be continually splattered with a foul-smelling mixture of dip chemical and cattle excrement kicked up by reluctant beasts jumping into it. She continued with this style of life until her death in 1963, aged 71 years. I was in hospital in Brisbane at the time. In a letter to me my mother wrote:

> *I asked Graham Ascough [the John Knox Presbyterian minister] to conduct the service for me at* Kooltandra *and then over at the crematorium, so he came up to the house to see me in the morning. When I said to him "of course you didn't know my sister" he said "well I did really, I knew her through her patients and her patients were her friends" and that's the way it goes in all the letters. They haven't only lost a doctor but a friend. That is something that the specialist misses entirely. Perhaps I had better keep a few of them just to prove that such a state of affairs ever existed.*

A powerful portrayal of the archetypal modern Aussie woman appears in the movie *Japanese Story,* in which Sandy Edwards, a geologist, uses her toughness, bush skills and independence of mind to survive the harsh environment of the Pilbara in Western Australia. Some may consider the characters of Sandy and the young Japanese businessman she is showing around, a little too stereotyped. Whether or not this is justified, it suggests the Aussie woman is strong and well. No one can be sure what path she will take from here, but what is sure is that the land on which she treads will have its say and she will have to adapt just as those who preceded her did.

Chapter 29
Isolation and Innovation

The ends of the earth

Open a map of the world or rotate a globe. Look for Australia. Look into its heartland. Australia could very well be a synonym for isolation. Though not the largest land mass, the island continent of *Terra Australis* maintains an absolute integrity like no other. Oceans stretch forever to the east, west and south. If we ignore the scattering of islands to its immediate north, flights to the rest of the world are lengthy even in modern airliners flying at almost the speed of sound.

Two centuries ago, however, the hours spent in today's airliners translated into weeks or months on sailing ships. The long voyage from Europe took four months in the 1830s and two to three months in the 1860s. Most who came never returned to the land of their birth. The Great South Land was indeed at the ends of the earth and remains so today despite modern transport and communications. Direct flights from Frankfurt to Beijing take two hours less than from Sydney to Beijing. Mumbai and Delhi are seven hours closer to Frankfurt than to Sydney. Thus a young, well-travelled German in a Munich bar said to me: *Australia! No I haven't been to Australia. That's a long way to go. You need a lot of time and money. In Europe it doesn't take much time to go anywhere.*

Some claim Australia's national obsession with winning results from a feeling of isolation from the rest of the world; from a sense of being remote from where all the action takes place. But has being at the ends of the earth produced the implied inferiority complex? Perhaps it emanates partly from our convict origins but more significantly from that ever-present isolation that cloaks Australia: the solitary brooding of the very vastness of the continent itself – a land of loneliness and unrelenting challenges of nature, where one either wins or 'goes under' and therefore demands a new and different character.

The Outback

Flinders' map of 1814 was little more than a coastline. What lay inland was a mystery. Some believed in an inland sea. For almost a century explorers and intrepid men seeking pastures for their herds and flocks added detail to the map. At its heart they found no inland sea but a harsh, inhospitable land – a desert. Except for the First Australians, who have lived there for millennia, it has swallowed men who ventured there all too easily.

When referring to inland Australia with its emptiness, huge distances and remoteness, Australians talk about the *Outback*. Like the end of the rainbow, wherever you are the *Outback* lies somewhere further on. It's out there somewhere, wherever you are going. Likewise, we also talk about it's *Back of Bourke*, or *Beyond the Black Stump*, meaning it's somewhere very far away in the heart of Australia. Only by going there and experiencing it can one really grasp the enormity of the *Outback*.

Outback survivors

When they finally reached the distant shores of the vast land that greeted them, most Newcomers remained close to the coast. But some did not and survived, not only economically and physically but also psychologically. They survived the stresses of a lonely life, where neighbours were few and far between. For them the comforts of city life were little more than dreams. There was no doctor at hand for those who suffered sickness or injury, no mechanic to call when machinery broke down, no shop nearby for spare parts or replacements. There was no library, theatre or place of entertainment. The pastoral industry they established was the mainstay of the Australian economy for more than a century and still makes a significant contribution to Australian exports, despite the expansion in mining since WWII. The lives of pastoralists were and still are the stuff of legends.

To survive and prosper in the outback they had to become self-reliant and to 'make do' with what was available. It required of them initiative, ingenuity, resourcefulness, innovation, toughness and resilience in adversity plus an independence of spirit. In that vast landscape there could be no strangers; any passer-by was a welcome link to life 'beyond the horizon'. And so their independent spirit was tempered by an acceptance that 'no man is an island'. They learned to support and help one another no matter who they were. Mateship was important for their survival. They came together in times of disaster and to play. They thought little or nothing of travelling as much as 100 miles (160 km) by horse to picnic races, dances and other social events.

Even in the 21st Century, the outback is not to be taken lightly and mateship remains important for survival. In November 2012 it claimed the life of a 25-year-old experienced bushman. He and his 30-year-old work-mate, who was near death when found, had broken the outback rule: 'never leave your vehicle if it breaks down'. When their 2-way radio fell silent a 'nearby' station manager set out to look for them. Six hours and 210 km later he found them lying in the red sands of the Simpson Desert. *I'm no hero*, he said. *You just do what you do for your mates. Out here you've got to look after each other*. He said he had seen crows fall dead from the sky and kangaroos die under the shade of gum trees as the temperature soared above 52 °C.

Simpson Desert, aerial view of parallel dunes. Source: Charlie Atherton

The Mailman

The only regular contact with the outside world for outback dwellers was the Mailman. He carried not only mail but also stores and supplies and those 'hitching a ride to somewhere', such as stockmen and other bush itinerants. The Mailman brought news and gossip so essential for binding the people of the outback into communities of sorts.

I experienced the bush mailman during the two years I spent at *Elgin Downs*, a cattle station that straddled the Clermont – Charters Towers road about halfway between these towns. His mail-run headed west at Elgin, the road passing within a hundred metres of the homestead. No one could say Elgin was in the outback but stations in the region were relatively large and so we were relatively isolated. It was a weekly service. Late each Saturday afternoon everyone would congregate by the homestead for the mailman's visit.

Tom Kruse on the Birdsville Track. Photo is a still from the film *The Back of Beyond*, John Heyer, 1954. Source: *The Daily Telegraph*, September 2016

Camel train on its way from Oodnadatta in South Australia to Alice Springs in the Northern Territory in 1872, a distance of over 500 km. The overland telegraph, which replaced the camel mail, came into operation in August 1872. Source: The National Archive of Australia, J2879, QTH 153/1

Probably the best-known mailman of the outback was Tom Kruse, who regularly drove the fortnightly Birdsville – Marree mail-run from 1936 for nearly twenty years in a worn-out truck. He had to contend with sand-hills, dust storms, flies and floods, swollen creeks and rivers along the 517 km Birdsville Track. Round trips normally took seven days but, when Coopers Creek flooded, could extend to as long as six weeks. Camels were used to transport mail and supplies from Oodnadatta to Alice Springs until around 1929, when the railway superseded them. The 520 km journey took the Afghan cameleers about four weeks. Between 1860 and 1920 about 20,000 camels and between 2,000 and 4,000 cameleers arrived in Australia to support a vast network of camel train routes across the inland of the country.

QANTAS

Mail contracts became a crucial element in the survival of Australia's iconic airline QANTAS. Queensland and Northern Territory Aerial Service was formally established in November 1920, when two WWI pilots decided aircraft must be better than horses and camels for long-distance travel in the outback and delivering mail. Operations servicing western Queensland began out of Longreach in February 1921.

As QANTAS' domestic routes expanded across Queensland and the Northern Territory, the QANTAS aircraft and pilots brought with them social changes. On outback stations, fresh fruit and fish were added to diets of canned foods; station women's drab, functional clothing could be shelved for modern fashions on special occasions; beer droughts were broken; yesterday's newspapers were available; and new movies were shown in tin-shed cinemas.

QANTAS moved its headquarters to Brisbane in 1931 and in 1934 began overseas services with a route to Singapore. Headquarters were moved to Sydney in 1938 with the introduction of flying boats. In 1944 QANTAS began using the 'kangaroo' in the design of its logo. After WWII it pioneered round-the-world services, and became the first non-USA operator of the Boeing 707 jet airliner. In 1979, it became the world's first all-Boeing 747 airline.

QANTAS is the oldest airline in the English-speaking world, and has the second oldest surviving airline name in the world, KLM Royal Dutch Airlines being a year older. Its greatest claim to fame is an enviable safety record, which was highlighted in the Oscar-winning 1988 film *Rain Man,* when the autistic, savant Raymond refused to fly with any other airline.

Refuelling at QANTAS hangar, Longreach. Source: SmarterTravel Media. Image credit QANTAS Founders Museum

Early premises of QANTAS, in Longreach, Queensland. Source: State Library of Queensland

QANTAS hangar, Cloncurry. Source: State Library of Queensland

Royal Flying Doctor Service

The Royal Flying Doctor Service (RFDS) was established in 1928 at Cloncurry in north-west Queensland. QANTAS provided a pilot, an aircraft and servicing. Its story is one of combining medicine, aviation and radio to bring health care to the people who live, work and travel in the remote outback areas of Australia. It was largely the result of the vision, resourcefulness, innovative, practical mind and persistence of the Reverend John Flynn. He believed strongly in the equality of all and the potential of inland Australia. At the beginning of the 20th century he established the Inland Mission – now Frontier Services – to serve the people of inland Australia.

Flynn began establishing bush hospitals and hostels that alleviated much of the dread associated with the great loneliness of the inland. However, while these provided an important service, the problems of distance and absence of a radio network or telephones remained, with many people dying from the lack of appropriate medical treatment. Flynn saw the potential in the aeroplane and the radio for overcoming the inability to make a distress call by encouraging the development of the pedal radio.

At that time, flying was still in its infancy. The first Flying Doctor pilot had no navigational aids other than a compass and inadequate maps, if any, and no radio. He navigated by landmarks such as fences, rivers, river beds, dirt roads or just wheel tracks and telegraph lines. He also flew in an open cockpit, fully exposed to the weather, behind the doctor's cabin. Airstrips were, at best, claypans or, at worst, hastily cleared paddocks. Flights were normally made during daylight hours, although night flights were attempted in cases of extreme urgency. Even today, although the aircraft are guided by satellite navigation systems, landings must often be made in difficult circumstances on remote dirt airstrips or roads, lit at night by kerosene flares or car headlights. As occurred when the service first began, the pilot is still responsible for determining if a flight can be undertaken safely in the prevailing weather conditions.

When an emergency call is received, a Flying Doctor Communications Officer can be in contact with a doctor, nurse and pilot within 30 seconds and an aircraft can be airborne within 45 minutes. While people are still isolated today, the RFDS network of bases across Australia ensures no one is more than two hours from medical help.

The Flying Surgeon

In 1959, the Royal Flying Doctor Service was expanded to include the Flying Surgeon Service to provide specialised medical attention to hospitals in remote communities throughout Queensland.

I am one of those who have the Flying Surgeon Service to thank – perhaps for even being alive. One night in May 1962 when working on *Elgin Downs*, I woke suffering from an excruciating pain in my abdomen. All I was able to do was fall from the bed on to the floor and crawl to another room, wake the sleeper and say I had to get to a doctor. I was placed on the back seat of the station manager's Ford Fairlane and taken to the Clermont Hospital, a two-hour drive away. The Flying Surgeon accompanied by his anaesthetist and nurse were called up, duly arrived and removed my appendix.

My next meeting with the Flying Surgeon was 14 years later. This time it was for social reasons rather than professional ones. My sister and mother and I had made a 14-hour driving trip to Longreach to spend a few days with my brother Bill, the Flying Surgeon. During our stay there we had a vivid demonstration of the weather he could have to fly in when called out to an emergency. One summer evening we were dining on a sheep station about an hour's drive away when a storm blew up. The rain poured down and lightning lit up the night sky, with accompanying mighty claps of thunder. In the middle of this storm my brother received a phone call informing him of a very bad car accident near Hughenden; a swaying caravan under tow had side-swiped a passing car. Surely, I thought to myself, no one would take a small plane up in weather like this, but fly they did. Bill returned next day with the sad news that they had arrived too late to save the injured, who had died.

School of the Air

The tyranny of distance meant children in the outback could not attend normal schools. Until recently the famous 'School of the Air', which began in 1951 in Alice Springs, has utilised the Flying Doctor Radio network to link children and their teachers and conduct a program of education, which includes all the usual subjects taught in primary schools. With improved technology there is now no need to use the RFDS radio network; telephones and the internet have become the current methods of communication. The organisation was also re-named in the mid-1990s to become 'The School of Distance Education'. They are still permitted, however, to use the more romantic name of 'School of the Air'.

Artistic portrayal

The struggle and isolation of people in the outback were portrayed by artists and writers, who finally viewed this vast land with Australian eyes. In *The Selector's Hut*, Arthur Streeton depicts a hardy pioneer busy clearing the land, while Frederick McCubbin portrays a young couple making a new start in a harsh land. Actually, they were not far from the urban life of Melbourne, which appears in the background of the right panel of McCubbin's triptych. A greater feeling of the isolation and loneliness of outback life is rendered by McCubbin in *The bush burial* and Russel Drysdale's *The drover's wife* (see Aussie Women).

Clockwise from above:

The bush burial, Frederick McCubbin, 1890. Source: Geelong Gallery

The pioneer, Frederick McCubbin, 1904. Source: Wikimedia Commons

The selector's hut (Whelan on the log), Arthur Streeton, 1890. Source: National Gallery of Australia

The real Australia

Advances in technology have put little more than a dint in the isolation of Australia from the rest of the world. The outback remains very much as it always was – remote. In 1872 the overseas telegraph brought us 'closer' to the rest of the world but it was too costly for most individuals. Railways 'shrank' the nation but mainly in coastal regions. Formed and sealed roads built to service the mining and pastoral industries have filled the empty space but only slightly. Aircraft were better suited to traversing the vast sparsely-inhabited outback but plane travel remains expensive. Only in the later decades of the 20th century have aircraft travel and telephone communications become affordable for the majority of Australians but it is still cheaper to fly to many overseas destinations than within Australia. However, the outback remains just that – that place further on, wrapped in isolation – a place where few choose to live out their lives.

Like those who came before them, newcomers setting foot on Australia's shores cling to the luxury and safety of the coast. Some test their 4-wheel drives (4WDs) on outback treks, while parking-lot speed-bumps are a sufficient challenge for the rest. Those who work on great mining projects scattered over inland Australia simply by-pass the outback – they 'fly-in and fly-out'. The few who venture inland wait in vain, as their predecessors waited, for medical and other services their city cousins take for granted. Outback dwellers remain almost as isolated and lonely as they ever were.

However, even though Australians are predominantly an urban people, the outback is firmly embedded in the national consciousness. For many it is the 'real' Australia, that part of the country that makes the continent and its people different from any other.

Highways, roads and rail lines. Source: Sieuwert Oost, IA Connections

Chapter 30
Terra Australis Revisited

From the breakup of Gondwana and onwards the continent Australia floated on its tectonic plate nestling beneath the southern stars midst the southern seas. In due course it cradled the genesis of a fauna and flora so different, so unique that Darwin mused it might well have been the creation of another god. It lay recondite to the world at large save for unknown nameless wanderers who, in the mist of bygone time, came across its shores and stayed on. Over millennia, generation after generation, they lived out their lives untrammelled by and unaware of the world beyond until that world happened upon them.

The continent's existence was little more than the figment of the imagination of philosophers and dreamers of the known world until eventually being recorded on the maps of the early cartographers as the mysterious *Terra Australis Incognita*. And it remained thus until, like a Daguerreotype image emerging from a silver plate through a mercurial mist, the coastline took shape in the wake of dauntless European seafarers, who set forth to plumb the world beyond during the Age of Exploration. Finally, the master mariners, James Cook and Matthew Flinders, lifted the veil from the face we all know so well as Australia.

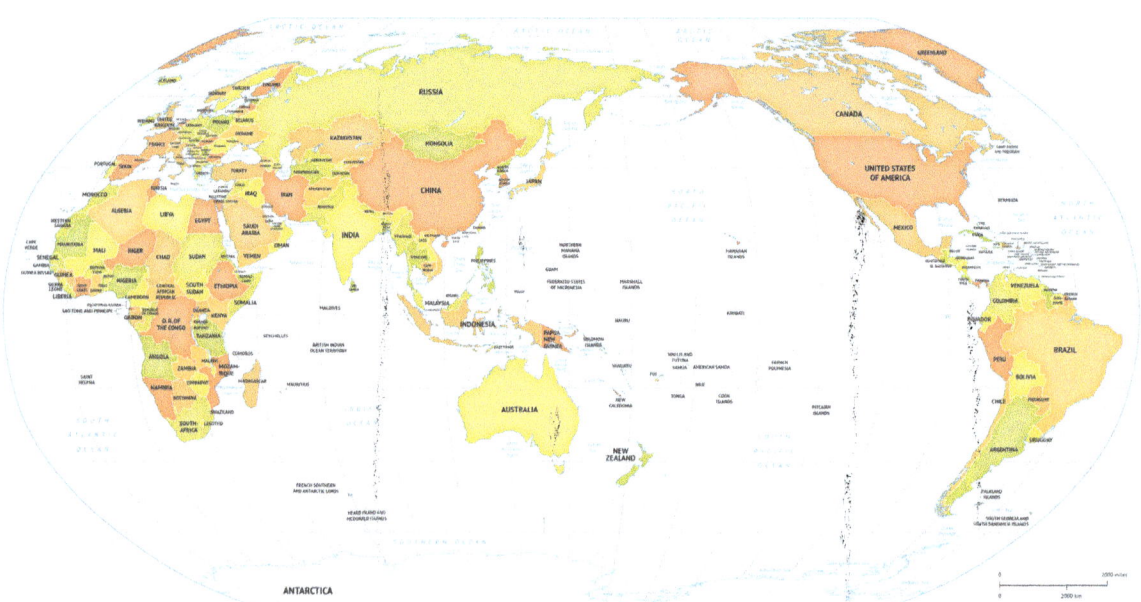

Map of World political Robinson Asia-Australia centered. Source: One Stop Map

To the known world Australia was a topsy-turvy land of weird plants and animals and its indigenous inhabitants were beyond comprehension. The intruders found her harsh and uncompromising. The seeds of initial settlement were from the bottom, not the top; and formed what to many was a topsy-turvy society. The interlopers following after them built upon the heritage received. With their sweat, effort and determination plus luck, initiative and dastardly deeds, the sunburnt land progressed from a distant dumping ground for convicts to one much sought after by people from all around the world. It remains a land of opportunity and, if not an alien place, a little offbeat or outer to those in the world beyond its shores and an enigma to many or perhaps most within who are unsure of who they exactly are.

Some even harbour doubts about where they are. As it continues onwards to its destiny Australia drifts northwards towards Asia at geological pace. Many believe we are already there. In their eyes we are part of Asia and should attune accordingly, which must surely be a clouded view of geography. *Geography*, said Renan, *no more makes a nation than religion, race or language* but Australia is the exception. It is no more part of Asia than it is part of Europe, Africa or the Americas. As can be seen from the map above, the island continent, set solitary in the south, is unique on planet Earth in its wholeness and completeness. Geography has been central to shaping a national identity and will continue to do so into the future. Technology in the form of modern transport and communications has brought the people of the world closer together – to the extent that many refer to a global village – but the continents remain anchored to their tectonic plates and as the COVID-19 pandemic showed, Australia can be rendered isolated and as isolated from the rest of the world as it ever was. This could well be the situation if air transport were restricted or ceased altogether to counter climate change.

Over the course of time, the continent lay languid, bringing forth life distinctive in all its forms until awakened by a world beyond that was stretching its limbs, or more precisely, the part referred to as Europe (Appendix 4). And so it was that the tenets of Western civilisation took root in the *last of lands*. That it was the English variant that finally made its presence felt was largely a matter of timing as well as, in hindsight, fortuitous, because the institutions of government, administration and justice and so-called 'values' introduced have withstood the test of time. Australia may not be perfect but is no failed state, rather quite the opposite. The society begun not by free-men but men wanting to be free has blossomed and added its imprint to that from whence they came.

Whether or not she is yet a great princess reigning in the south as foreshadowed by Darwin or the mighty nation Leichhardt foresaw is open to debate. These adventurous sons of the Enlightenment would have viewed the world through a different lens from the naysayers of the mid-1900s and their counterparts of today who, disenchanted for different reasons, detect little sign of greatness; furthermore, greatness today places more emphasis on the size of the population and the economy. Australia's relatively small population may leave her 'vulnerable' militarily, but a small population must be positive for environmental sustainability and the overall quality of life of its citizens. However, regardless of how one might view her, great or otherwise, there can be no denying her bounteous wealth, the excellence displayed in all areas of human endeavour and her increasing influence on the geopolitical stage.

Geography might not uniquely define a nation but Australia could be viewed as an exception. Its borders cannot be quibbled over. It is a massive land surrounded by sea. Those who inhabit this land may well be referred to as 'Australian' just as those from Sydney are designated 'Sydneyites' but this conjures up nothing more than a cardboard cut-out of those who would comprise a 'mighty nation'. Who and what we are today as a people or a nation is an enigma. Its resolution – breathing life into the cardboard cut-out Australian – is neither clear nor certain; the cardboard could easily crumble.

If our luck holds, we will continue to evolve as we have in the past, drawing on, not enslaved by, tradition, fortified by stories of struggle and triumph, and shaped by the land itself. Her people, fashioned over time by the demands of the sunburnt land and, given a successful prosecution of vergangenheitsaufarbeitung, an all-pervading presence of its First People heritage, would be distinctly Australian – but retaining the qualities that got their forebears through the nightmare of Changi Prison and the Burma Railway, the spirit of ANZAC and sense of freedom.

Whether or not Leichhardt's 'Old Europe' is forgotten may be a moot point if not a premature question but Australia's ties with 21st century Europe are certainly not those of a century ago. As she continues to evolve and grow in stature, we can expect memories of Europe to dim and, along with memories of Asia and elsewhere, become the stuff of history books and legends. The world beyond could well include heavenly bodies.

The Australian of the future will be different from the Australian of today just as the Australian of today differs from that of yesterday. *When British scientists first laid eyes on the platypus in the late 18th century some of them thought the specimen – sent back from its native Australia – must be a hoax.* All life and the land that sustained it were, to an extent, viewed as surreal, it being quite unlike that encountered anywhere else in the world. It is unlikely that some sense of the surreal will cease to mark the nation as it continues to evolve in a sunburnt land.

Section Two
Quo vadimus

Chapter 31
How ya goin' mate?

I can give no quintessential picture of today's Australian – there is none. The tough, resilient, independent bushman – the exemplar from the 1890s for many – is so rare as to be endangered. The bush largely remains an alien place; most of us, a mix of cultures, ethnicities and races, live in cities. The archetypical easy-going, practical larrikin, who gives no one unearned respect but everyone his due, is but a mirage and always (in the wings) are the shadows and whispering of Australia's First People. The thesis that an Australian is someone defined by specific ways of thinking and behaviour listed in the Preface appears no longer valid. Many questions remain unanswered: who am I, what am I, do I belong in this land, who are we, what are we, what will we become? Are there answers?

Soothsayers

What response can we give to the prognostications of the young (27 years old), affable, gentleman naturalist Charles Darwin, who would redefine mankind, and the youngish (34 years old) driven scientist and intrepid explorer Ludwig Leichhardt from the lower strata of Prussian society without connections, capital or prospects, who vanished without trace?

On leaving Australia, Darwin entered in his journal:

> *Farewell Australia. You are a rising child and doubtless someday will reign a great princess in the south but you are too great and ambitious for affection yet not great enough for respect. I leave your shores without sorrow or regret.*

A rather negative report card but perhaps the great man's class-based sensibilities clouded his incisive mind. Darwin, as would have Leichhardt, viewed other people through the lens of his own background and education. He thought highly of the expansion and prosperity of the wool industry and the progress of Sydney town, comparing it with London and Birmingham. He felt much more had been achieved in this little place, in a 'score of years', than had been in South America over centuries.

He was less enthusiastic about the landscape, which he found unfamiliar and alien, and found the people coarse and vulgar – children learn the vilest expressions. He deplored the facts that ex-convicts could climb the social ladder and the whole population, poor and rich, was bent on acquiring wealth – money being the driving factor behind all of their motives. Among the highest orders, wool and sheep grazing formed the constant subject of conversation. Darwin lamented the absence of factors that made one cultivated, even civilised, such as bookshops and fine music. He felt this lack of moral fibre would continue to rub off in future generations.

He had some sympathy towards Australia's First People. What he saw in Van Dieman's Land saddened him but he was somewhat positive with his experience at the King George Sound settlement (Albany), his last stay in Australia. He considered them to be good-natured, hard-working and physically robust (and sensed they were possibly bucking the trend towards extinction). Having no convicts, the settlement was almost completely at the mercy of the goodwill and labour of the local Aboriginals. However, while there he watched a corroboree, which he found most rude and barbarous, and without any meaning, although he conceded the dances may have originally represented actions such as wars and victories:

> *[T]he air resounded with their wild cries. ... the group of nearly naked figures, viewed in the light of the blazing fires, all moving in hideous harmony, formed a perfect display of a festival amongst the lowest barbarians. In Tierra del Fuego, we have beheld many curious scenes in savage life, but never, I think, one where the natives were in such high spirits and so perfectly at their ease. (Voyage of the Beagle.* Chapter 19*).*

Darwin apparently sensed a vitality in this land Australia, but found its uncivilised nature undeserving of any claim to respect. He pondered whether the sophisticated society and culture of Europe would ever take root in such an alien place – one so different from Europe that Darwin thought a geologist might suggest that 'the periods of creation have been distinct … that the creator rested from his labour'.

Leichhardt was more positive:

> *Such families of free settlers who take an interest in the colony and consider it as their fatherland are the only true treasure of the country and they will be the nucleus of a mighty nation which will make us forget the old Europe.*

However, his vision for Australia included neither Australia's First People nor those with convict connections. Its focus was on the free-settlers, who he thought should set down roots and make this country their own. More problematic is the context of his reference to old Europe; was it to a society, culture, geography or what is now termed Western Civilisation? Probably aspects of each were involved. Leichhardt was a cultivated person who read the poets and admired Schiller especially.

Unlike Darwin, he connected emotionally with this land of *my wander years*, to the beautiful, to the glorious sky of Australia to which he must return after a trip to Europe despite having no delusions about life in the bush:

> *Life in the bush without that scientific understanding which enables one to sense the deep warmth of nature like the heart of a friend is very exhausting.*

But is a scientific understanding necessary to have this emotional relationship with nature? No!! Leichhardt needed to have looked no further than his Aboriginal guides. Leichhardt had an erratic personality but believed in being a truthful observer and recorder. Given his records were highly valued for their accuracy, he would not have written the above words flippantly.

How prescient were Darwin and Leichhardt? A century on their predictions had a ring of truth. During that period Australia suffered two major depressions, two world wars and constant climatic vagaries such as droughts, floods, fires and cyclones; as well, the colonies federated. With sweat and toil and spilt blood, the Newcomers had 'made a go of it' and were prospering – a far cry from the first three years of near starvation and struggle. Socially, economically and politically the nation was soundly established, although not yet willing to strut the world stage. But some amongst us were less than enthusiastic. One disparagingly attributed this achievement to little else than undeserved luck. Some pined for a distinctly Australian voice in arts and literature. D.H. Lawrence might have found an absolute equality and considered Australia the most democratic country he had been in but retorted: *the more he saw of democracy the more he disliked it*. Bertrand Russell was instilled with hope for mankind by his visit in 1950. Donald Horne considered the possibility that the world should become like Australia would profoundly alarm most cultivated people in the world. On a visit to Australia in 1939, the testy H.G. Wells inveighed against the devastation of the environment. Darwin, it appears, was close to the mark.

Naysayers – a centennial assessment

Soon after the turn of the millennium Dorothea Mackellar (1908) declared: *I love a sunburnt country*, but most still found 'their' land somewhat alien and exhausting, and huddled along the south-eastern seaboard more than ever. Several decades later poet and satirist A.D. Hope, in his enigmatic poem, *Australia* (1939), wrote:

> *... trees, drab green and desolate grey*
> *Such savage and scarlet as no green hills dare*
> *Springs in that waste ...*
> *Where second-hand Europeans pullulate*
> *Timidly on the edge of alien shores.*

A.D. Hope may have used the Australian landscape as the backdrop for his critique of society but he certainly did not reveal any love for an alien, sunburnt country. He expressed no wish to live in that waste nor did artist Sidney Nolan reside in the desert land he painted. The Australian landscape is no English countryside nor Tuscan hills. Australian artists and writers have often found their muse in the soft, gentle light of Europe as opposed to the glaring brightness of their sunburnt land. The Australian heartland remained the domain of a few stoic individuals and those First People, who had always considered it home. Darwin, I suspect, if he had lived here, would have chosen a home on Sydney Harbour. Leichhardt might have chosen the Blue Mountains and made annual forays into the outback pursuing scientific interests rather than nurturing his soul.

Australia, for Hope and others, was a cultural wasteland both physically and intellectually. They were not alone in this. Post-WWII migrants from continental Europe were dispirited by the strangeness of Australia and an unfamiliar society, which they regarded as culturally impoverished vis-à-vis that from whence they had come: the sophisticated cosmopolitan culture of Europe in which art, writing, philosophy and affairs of the world were discussed, often in a refined and cultivated way over fine food within tasteful surroundings. They found the streets empty and drained of life and wondered where the real city, the centre of its life, might be found – a physical, spiritual or social centre, where a vibrant urban life should be. The sprawling suburbs bore no organic relationship to the city. Architect Robin Boyd entitled his critique of the cities and the monotonous and repetitive nature of the surrounding suburbs *The Great Australian Ugliness*. The Australian story appeared one of material triumph and aesthetic calamity.

But it was the people, fun-loving and obsessed with sport and outdoor activities, who filled the naysayers with despair. The ordinary people were judged adaptable, a positive trait, but wallowed in a cosy provincialism and, as Hope put it:

> *Whose boast is not: 'we live' but 'we survive',*
> *A type who will inhabit the dying earth.*

They accused the intelligentsia of being mainly second-rate and letting the nation down through lack of imagination and leadership. Those aspiring to a high culture were deemed provincial and, surrendering to the assertion their culture was inferior to that of Britain, suffered from an ignominious 'cultural cringe'. An extreme anti-intellectualism existed among many educated Australians and among the general populace were some who warmed to Chairman Mao's policy of sending intellectuals, especially those inhabiting universities, into the countryside to work in the rice paddies.

Overall, the people were thought to lack imagination but could be skilful improvisors and willingly 'give it a go' if forced into action. They were charged with being lured into complacency by settling for an easy existence – a remarkable development in a land that had never before made existence easy. Lacking any particular direction and seemingly unaware of the challenges that lay ahead, they were charged with approaching the future like 'sleep walkers'.

Inferiority – a transplanted society

Why did a people, who had progressed so admirably, have such an inherent lack of faith in themselves? Why was its culture, not only at the high end but often at the popular level, held by its critics in such disdain? Why was to be Australian inferior? Certainly it lacked the richness of age and tradition but more importantly, not only had it no ancient churches, castles and ruins – the memorials of generations departed – its past from which myths and legends grow was ringed with doubt.

The Australian character has been formed in part in reaction to the put-downs of outsiders, especially the English to whom it was second rate to be a colonial; those who had promoted federation believed this would put colonial inferiority behind them. It did not!! Of all colonialists around the world, the Australians were viewed as a race apart. They had no claim to the nobility of the religiously pious, the political exile or the social dreamer – only to a penal beginning. Those whom Darwin encountered largely came from English jails, poor houses and slums. A century later Darwin would have found them, as previously, loud and wanting of refinement. Churchill condescendingly reminded them they came from bad stock. However, grace, elegance and gentility do not sprout from the travails of survival in a sunburnt land; one that calls for resilience, fortitude and stoicism, and mutual support. Patrick White reckoned the landscape he knew made monsters out of its inhabitants. That the sophisticated society and culture of Europe could be transplanted into a land as alien as Australia was unrealistic. Old ways had to be shed, not simply recycled but built anew.

These cultural monsters displayed an independence of spirit with an informality and openness of manner that appalled those who were used to social stiffness or deference and who sometimes uttered the truth with a directness that might horrify those from more devious cultures. They showed a distrust of extreme politeness and were generally free of the extreme forms of snobbery, rudeness and deference, which are the outward signs of social antagonism in older countries. They were cynical and self-denigrating towards themselves as well as towards the world they perceived around them. This deeply inlaid skepticism was a genuine philosophy of life. These successors of 'government men' viewed themselves as Australians; free-men living under the rule of law in a nation of British heritage shaped by liberal and Enlightenment principles.

Despite its perceived shortcomings, Australia had come a long way since its humble, some say dastardly, beginnings. Such progress was partly due to the efforts of men unshackled from the strictures that bound them in the countries from whence they came. But, paradoxically, it was also very much driven by the shame of the unspeakable stain, the legacy of its convict beginnings – a driven people striving for respect. In the end it needed more than the blood of war to wash away the collective shame, although that was a great salve. Complete healing came only in the second half of the 20th century after acknowledgement and then ownership with pride.

Millennium Australia

By the turn of the millennium Australia bore little relationship to that of half a century previously. Many of the naysayers' wishes had been realised. Australia had become a more interesting and exciting place, one of intellectual pursuit, yet retaining its relaxed lifestyle. Not only had its population doubled but its make-up was a kaleidoscope of ethnicities, the White Australia Policy having been abandoned.

Diversity in the population is considerable. The 2016 census showed nearly half of the total population were either born overseas or at least had one parent born overseas. Ninety-seven percent of the total population came from over 190 different countries and had 300 different ancestries. The vast majority live in or close to Australia's main cities; the rest are sprinkled unevenly elsewhere.

Three per cent of the total population are of Aboriginal or Torres Strait Islander heritage – someone who identifies as Aboriginal or Torres Strait Islander and is accepted as such by the community in which he or she lives. Amongst them there is also considerable diversity and, like the population in general, they lead diverse and varied lifestyles. Most Aboriginal and Torres Strait Islander people live in cities and towns, with 35 per cent living in major cities, and only 21 per cent living in remote areas. Living in a city does not mean being somehow 'less Aboriginal or Torres Strait Islander', although some who embrace modern life feel rejected.

Around the world, Australia is the land of promise and opportunity. More than ever, immigrants flock here. Regrettably, the erasing of the convict stain has not left an untroubled Australian psyche. In its place, gnawing at the nation's soul, is the question of the dispossession of Australia's First People and their ensuing treatment.

A troubled psyche – Aboriginal dispossession

Some say that Australia, unlike other nations that define themselves by battles and heroic death, became a nation peacefully. They would be correct in that no shot was fired in anger between the colonies in the lead-up to federation, but they would be wrong in assuming federation was our beginning and, for that matter, the arrival of the First Fleet. When Phillip landed at Sydney Cove the continent of Australia was already inhabited and had been for 60,000 years by people who had lived out their lives untouched by the rise and fall of civilisations throughout the rest of the world. This enabled them to maintain a rudimentary way of life in harmony with nature. But lack of exposure to the outside world had left them totally at the mercy of more sophisticated people: vulnerable to murder and expropriation of their land and, as a consequence, the extinction of their long-established way of life – the loss of land, language and culture.

A thick fog or mystery obscures aspects of the legal foundation of the Port Jackson colony. The British government claimed sovereign rights over the land called New South Wales without any form of coercion of or consent from the local inhabitants, nor transacting any treaty or covenant of any kind. One may raise an eyebrow at the commissioning proclamation commanding Phillip to protect the lives and livelihoods of the natives and encourage friendly relations yet claiming sovereignty on the basis the land was 'ownerless and empty'. The legitimacy of Britain's occupation of New South Wales resting on *Terra Nullius* had important implications subsequently.

The Mabo and Wik High Court decisions overturned *Terra Nullius* and recognised indigenous land rights under certain circumstances. However, this did little or nothing to rectify the mistake, oversight or wilful interpretation of the law by the British, when claiming possession of half the continent of Australia. The clock cannot be rewound. A mutual agreement of some kind, that puts to rest ongoing assertions into perpetuity that the land was stolen and the way that it was perpetrated, is sorely needed – in other words, a 'treaty'.

A further legal cloudiness surrounding taking possession was the legal status of First Australians under British law that accompanied it. Given classifying them amongst the fauna would be not only outrageously offensive but also totally untrue, they could have been only British subjects or enemies; outlaws would be inappropriate. They were not rebellious subjects of the monarch and certainly were not aliens, an alien being a foreigner, especially one who is not a naturalised citizen of the country where he or she is living. The word 'foreigner', in this sense, was brought to my attention some years ago when I had to remind Chinese students they were the foreigners, not the local people to whom they were referring.

The legal status is important because, if they were British subjects, then any killing of them not sanctioned by British law amounted to murder, whereas, if they were enemies, the hostilities between them and the colonists would be classified as war – although a protracted asymmetrical war of guerrilla-type execution – and killing by either combatant judged according to the rules of war. In hindsight, the latter appears a more acceptable interpretation. Doing so casts the colonists, historically, as invaders but that must be preferable to being considered callous murderers, although it could be said the convicts and their guards, who arrived at Sydney Cove in 1788, bore little resemblance to Spanish Conquistador Pizarro's force that subjugated the Incas. Whatever the presumed legal status of Australia's First People, the law was applied indiscriminately, if at all, for more than a century as dispossession proceeded inexorably throughout the continent. The failure to apply the law both justly and impartially overall begs some form of acknowledgement.

Whatever the reasons for the foregoing anomalies or how one may view them, the nation cannot be at peace with itself while they remain unresolved. How this might be done is a vexed question. For better or worse, the landscape today is largely unrecognisable from that prior to colonisation. The protagonists in the dispossession are gone; few if any Australian citizens today, whether or not claiming Aboriginal heritage, resemble their compatriots of two centuries ago.

Cultures and societies continually evolve. After two centuries, the supposedly original British culture is no longer truly British – changes have been inexorably wrought by survival in a sunburnt land and the influx of subsequent immigrants. The Australian-born antecedents of about half of us go no further back than the end of WWII. Neither have Australia's First People been immune to change. Many have prevailed over adversity to play a significant role in contemporary Australian society; their ranks include sportsmen and –women, dancers, musicians, actors, writers, lawyers, scientists, journalists, academics and politicians. Regrettably, many remain destitute – unable to cope with the legacy of the past and the complexities of the present day.

In a sense, the disquiet regarding the dispossession and heinous treatment of Australia's First People bears a similarity with European settlement having a convict beginning; a closeted historical blot remedied only by letting in the light. It differs in that the convict stain was carried by specific individuals and families, whereas the taint of dispossession is borne by the community at large, all of whom being beneficiaries, not only of the fruits of bygone labour, but also advantages arising from the iniquitous treatment of the country's First People. Accepting the former was an individual journey, while coming to terms with the latter is an obligation for both the individual and the nation. It will be nothing if not arduous, and pointless if not unifying.

Letting in the light

Coming to terms with our past requires not a revision of history but the addition to and alignment of history by transmogrifying the shadowy figures on the colonial stage into acknowledged players with tangible complementary parts in the colonial drama. It involves sorting out in a formal way the contentious issues alluded to above and dealing with lingering legal and ethical issues. It would also involve story-telling for the airing of past and present grievances and harmonious mutual endeavours, because history, as claimed by Holocaust chronicler Susan Neiman, is remembering the past but it needs memory in order to be meaningful. It would shine in the light of truth and kindle mutual understanding.

The process is better described by the German word vergangenheitsaufarbeitung rather than reconciliation, the currently-used terminology, which means a reuniting, bringing back together, or the restoration of friendly relations or harmony – none of which previously existed. Vergangenheitsaufarbeitung is not a return to the past but has a forward focus predicated on acknowledging and accepting the past. Such an undertaking would elicit strong responses throughout the country as can be judged by the response to the Brereton Report into alleged war crimes of Australia's defence forces in Afghanistan. For the country it would be cathartic and all going well should clarify what it is to be Australian. Initiation and conduct of the process, which would call for patience and forbearance, would be formal undertakings by representatives of the nation as a whole and those of its First People.

This bears some similarity to a proposal for a First Nations Voice and Makarrata put forward by the First Nations National Constitutional Convention 2017 in its *Uluru Statement from the Heart*; the delegates, selected from participants in regional Dialogues held around the country, were entrusted to come up with an approach to constitutional reform to recognise Aboriginal and Torres Strait Islander peoples. They differ in that convention delegates focused on empowerment and taking *a rightful place in our own country,* whereas vergangenheitsaufarbeitung includes nation building; one where indigenous people would be an integral part – the acknowledged headwaters of the river 'Australia' – the long upper reaches that remain ignored and unexplored.

Confluence of the waters

Constitutional recognition is one means for ensuring Australia's first people have a rightful place in their own country. However, constitutions are instruments not easily amended and rightly so because they need to stand the test of time. Consequently, changing the Australian constitution to cure specific maladies currently afflicting many of its indigenous population is contentious – constitutional changes for this purpose become redundant once remedial measures have taken effect; surely any changes contemplated would have in mind a vision which the First People have of the way they viewed themselves and wished to live a century from now. Also, identifying a specific group of citizens within the constitution is open to the legal risk of future interpretation beyond what was intended. As indicated earlier, a treaty between the nation and its First People is sorely needed. This would be best negotiated prior to undertaking any changes to the constitution or other matters. Furthermore, any thought and effort given to changing the constitution may be best left to the drafting of a constitution for becoming a Republic.

The naysayers of the mid-twentieth century called for a culture unashamedly Australian, one that reflected the peculiarities of the Australian environment. No better way of achieving this must surely be to do what should have begun at the start of colonisation: the incorporation of aspects of indigenous culture into the colonial mainstream. Indigenous names have seeped into the Australian lexicon but much more language-wise could be embraced: further common names of interest as well as concept words and pertinent grammar and syntax. This would be of far greater merit than *devoting urgent attention to learning about the Chinese language and Chinese ways of thinking*, which some exhort, because Chinese sounds are proliferating in Australia, especially at tourist venues. It would play a part in the mixing of the waters and thereby contribute to fostering a shared national identity; one that makes us feel and be seen as uniquely Australian.

If dispossession were deemed to have been withstood by war-like acts of resistance, how best should we commemorate the conflict? Some suggest its inclusion in the Australian War Memorial (AWM) but this would do neither it nor the current purpose of the AWM the justice each deserves: the indigenous story would be incomplete and the symbolic focus of the AWM, one of commemoration of sacrifices made in international warfare, blurred. The AWM is the place for lauding the service of those of indigenous heritage, who served in both world wars and individuals such as Kitty Hawk fighter pilot Len Waters. The story and symbolism regarding the frontier conflicts and the confluence of the headwaters of the river 'Australia' with its mainstream deserve a major shrine of its own located presumably in Canberra on an appropriate site of major symbolic significance. Its focus would be on bringing together – from acknowledging the past to looking optimistically to the future – of all peoples and promoting a sense of national identity and unity.

Chapter 32
Identity

The self and belonging – acceptance

Most, if not all, of those who now populate the continent of Australia, appear uncertain about who they actually are, both as individuals and as a people; in other words, an apparent lack of a personal and national identity, and the concomitant feeling of belonging.

Identity is a complex concept. It is who or what a person or thing is. It is how you define who you are. It is also how others define you and these definitions are often not the same. Over time a multitude of internal and external factors shape a person's identity: memories, life experiences, relationships, values, society, family, friends, ethnicity, race, culture, opportunities, media, personal characteristics, personal interests, location and surrounding environments are but some of these. Some factors may have more of an influence than others and some may not have much or any influence at all; for example, voice is a strong identifier – Stephen Hawking chose to keep using his first speech synthesizer ... *because I have identified with it*. The factor standing out may change depending on whom you are with, what you are involved in or where you are in your life.

Closely linked to a sense of identity is a sense of belonging: the psychological feeling of connectedness to a group or a community. Humans have an emotional need to be an accepted member of a group – an 'inherent' desire to belong and be a part of something greater than themselves – bikie gangs and sports fan clubs are simple examples, while a nation, Australia for example, signifies a much broader sense.

Humans can also develop an emotional connectedness with place, which can turn place into an anchor of their identity. Hence, to feel Australian would be to feel a connectedness to the geographic area Australia. Aircraft touchdown can be a barometer for a sense of belonging to place. When the wheels of the aircraft touch the tarmac on your return from overseas, do you merely feel a sense of relief you are safely down or does a deeper emotion of 'being back home' well up within you?

In summary, to be Australian would be to feel Australian, to feel accepted by fellow Australians and to feel an affinity with the geographic entity called Australia.

To feel Australian – doubts about identity

On the Mediterranean waterfront in the mid-twentieth century, George Johnson, author of the acclaimed *My Brother Jack*, could recognise from 150 yards away an Australian arriving on the noonday steamer. It is unlikely that skin colour was the defining characteristic despite passengers being uniformly 'white' – except for those with the coveted sun tan. More than likely, Johnson was guided by body language and behaviour. Johnson's Australians also shared specific beliefs and values that would have required closer proximity and examination to ascertain, for instance, when having a beer in a pub as the fictional Italian immigrant character Nino Carlotta discovered much to his surprise. They were a very homogeneous lot. It is debatable whether Johnson could repeat this with today's heterogeneous population – a heterogeneity further boosted by intermarriage across all ethnic and cultural groups – but the possibility should not be overlooked, because how we view ourselves and others, as mentioned earlier, is not straight-forward.

Those of Asian background, whom I know or come in contact with, do not identify as Australians, whom they see as being the descendants of the Australians Johnson observed over half a century ago. They define themselves primarily on physical features such as skin colour. They overlook the fact that the intangible characteristics Johnson probably used can also be part of their makeup and consequently influence how others see them. Australian-reared Chinese report that, when visiting China, the local Chinese can tell immediately they are visitors by the way they speak, look, walk and carry themselves; likewise, Australian-born Filipinos and Indians differ from visitors from their ancestral lands. This phenomenon is reflected in the epithets *coconut* and *banana* used at times by Chinese and those from the Indian subcontinent, when referring to their compatriots born and reared in Australia. These terms arise from a tendency to link a specific mix of shared tangible and intangible traits of body language, behaviour, beliefs and values to skin colour. A *coconut* refers to being brown on the outside and white on the inside. A *banana* refers to being yellow on the outside and white on the inside. In other words, skin colour belies a significant aspect of a person's identity: a 'white' core of characteristics manifested in the current version of Johnson's Australian.

A variant of this genesis of confusion about identity – linking it to physical characteristics – is exemplified by a tertiary student of Indian background, who spoke only English. She had migrated from India to New Zealand when a baby of seven months and came to Australia at the age of eleven years. *I do not know who I am*, she exclaimed to a classmate. I was left in no doubt about this notion of who an Aussie is when enquiring about a little girl being dropped off next door for a guzheng lesson. *She is mixed. Her mother is Chinese, her father is Aussie*, said my Chinese neighbour, whose Chinese wife was the guzheng teacher. I asked how he regarded the little girl: Chinese, Aussie or what? This was a significant question given the increasing number of children of mixed heritage. The answer could only be Aussie but *no, she was mixed*, he said. How the child identified or how her classmates saw her was not explored. The term Eurasian, which some favour, is unsatisfactory given the possibility of many other combinations of ethnic background, which would render such terminology meaningless or of limited use. In today's global village, the issue of national descriptor is muddied further by the size and variety of a country's resident expatriate and transient population.

Emphasis on biological markers of identity can be revealing in some situations. A case in point was an Australian Chinese who realised when visiting China that what made him different in Australia made him the same there. To his surprise he took some time getting used to being a member of the majority – where he did not stand out; describing himself as Chinese was inadequate for self-identification. Furthermore, when surrounded by Chineseness he never felt more Australian. Identity can be problematic in the absence of a majority. The belief in 'looks' being the indicator of group identity resulted in the following response from a Filipino student, when asked about the background of a classmate. *It is easy*, he said, *to identify a 'local' in the Philippines where all look the same, but not here where there are so many different people.*

To be surrounded by people who do not look like you can be a sobering experience. But not only those, who view the descendants of Johnson's Australians as being exclusively Australian, are unsure who they are. Many of these 'Aussies', especially those who live in suburbs with a high density of immigrants, harbour doubts about who they are. That, by default, they are considered 'Aussie' provides little reassurance.

Doubts about identity also occur within Australia's First Nations people. Many young indigenous people with mixed lineage feel confused about their identity, who they are and where they belong. According to a prominent young indigenous person: *It's hard to feel accepted or secure when you're constantly being questioned about who you are.* Skin colour is questioned. At times they feel either 'too white' or 'too black' for non-indigenous people and often just not 'black enough' for their compatriots of indigenous heritage. Sometimes their legitimacy and authenticity is challenged, no matter what their skin colour is. Epithets such as 'Uncle Tom' or 'Jackey Jackey' are used to imply assimilation, which is frowned upon by some members of the indigenous community. The latter fail to realise they are not an authentic imitation of their indigenous forebears of two centuries ago, just as those with convict ancestry have little in common with their convict predecessors.

A young person of Aboriginal heritage pointed out that having one's sense of identity challenged can be hurtful:

> *Unfortunately, I have not had the privilege of living on my country, learning my language or practising cultural tradition. Does this mean I am not Aboriginal? That I do not have a right to identify? The answer is simple. This is not a question for others to decide. I am me.*

We may, to a lesser or greater degree, define ourselves internally, with limited reference to others. But we often categorize ourselves, as the above young woman desires, in terms of other people and groups; hence the pain, elicited by the discounting of her identity, she feels when disowned by her perceived immediate compatriots. But not only does she feel an outcast; their rejection also threatens the roots of her being – her connection to ancestors and all that has gone before and makes her who she is. Our sense of self threads its way back through not only our lifetime but also the lives of those who preceded us. The popular TV program *Who do you think you are?* shows our interest in ancestral history. Tracing ancestral connections anchors a sense of self. It is not surprising that adopted children are driven to seek out their biological parents. Another instance of the significance of the past in regards to who we are is that few, who have suffered a serious traumatic injury, would want that it had never occurred; it is part of who and what we are. In his autobiography quadriplegic doctor, Dinesh Palipana, writes:

> *I feel very fortunate to be living here and to have had access to all the things that I do. I'm very grateful for life and for the journey I've had so far. It's made me who I am. I previously thought that the spinal cord injury meant that I was going to miss out on life.*

This is a very personal matter. It would be somewhat hasty to apply it to a nation but this should not be overlooked.

An Australian character

Our identity is indeed far from simple and straightforward. Its very notion means no two people are the same although, as seen in Johnson's Australians, a set of shared characteristics can contribute to shaping a collective identity. Some pundits, however, attack the 'old Australian character' and the concept of a national character, arguing that:

> *A diverse nation has no need to discover, define or celebrate a distinctive character; it should be committed solely to the civic values of democracy, the rule of law and toleration – or better the welcoming of difference.*

Civic values such as these are certainly important but they are values that a liberal nation anywhere needs to cultivate and so, by their very nature, are unlikely to define a nation for which one would live or die. Far be it that diversity is central to our national identity, as is so often claimed; diversity is a characteristic of many countries in the global village today. It is doubtful that anyone would lay down his or her life for diversity. All we have at present is the set of characteristics in what might be termed the host culture, the remnants of those seen in Johnson's Australians.

Johnson's Australians had been evolving since a national identity first began to emerge in the Currency Lads and Lasses and the subsequent exposure to the rigors of global wars and survival in a sunburnt land. The contributing characteristics have served us well personally, nationally and internationally, examples being when prisoners of the Japanese (Changi, Burma railway) and even today when coping with the ravages of bushfires, floods or cyclones from which no one, whether city or country dweller, is immune. To discount them, or worse forego them, would be foolhardy. Far better to foster them at every opportunity, that they may imbue all who call Australia home, well-knowing when doing so, the 'Australian character', as it has in the past, will continue to evolve as we adapt to ongoing change and challenges of a sunburnt country. But given the diversity of the Australian population of today, it is doubtful that having some characteristics in common, no matter how laudable this may be, is enough to form an over-arching collective identity that sustains a united people – to underpin a 'sense of belonging' and nationhood. The list of qualities as given in the Preface is no longer valid. Something, more meaningful to each and everyone and more embracing, is required. With this in mind, vergangenheitsaufarbeitung is not only a matter of coming to terms with the past but also an opportunity to redefine who and what we are as we progress into the future.

Chapter 33
Nationhood

A spiritual entity

Australians are an irreligious lot, a well-to-do Afro-American woman once remarked to me. More recently they have been referred to as *neo-pagan*. They have certainly regarded overt religiosity, like matters of money, as a form of bad manners. Historian Manning Clark pondered whether a society, that kept religion a private matter, could sustain itself. The French historian-philosopher Ernest Renan believed so. He also refuted having factors in common such as race, language and territory as being necessary ingredients. What makes up a people – a nation, he argued, was in essence, a spiritual principle; the outcome of the profound complications of history; it is a spiritual family not a group determined by mountains and rivers. *Two things, which in truth are but one, constitute this soul or spiritual principle. One lies in the past, one in the present. One is the possession in common of a rich legacy of memories; the other is the desire to live together, the desire to continue to invest in the heritage ... jointly received.* A notion of the spiritual is evident in the federation of Australia. When push came to shove, it was the sacred ideal of nationhood that got it over the line, not borders, defence or immigration:

> *Australia was to federate to meet its destiny to be a great nation proud and independent, respected around the world.*

A sense of spirituality is expressed in the myriads of war memorials scattered throughout the land: but no more so than the Hall of Memory in the Australian War Memorial. A sense of the spiritual is also there in ANZAC. The spiritual was present when a lone bushman of no formal religion interred a workmate or a stranger. It can be felt in the earthy droning of the didgeridoo calling forth the spirits of the land. It will be what closes the ring of vergangenheitsaufarbeitung.

Shared experience

A nation, like an individual, Renan asserted, is the culmination of a long past of endeavours, sacrifice and devotion. Its essence, he emphasized, is that: *all individuals have many things in common....* He contended that the sharing, in the past, of a glorious heritage and regrets, and of having, in the future, a [shared] programme to put into effect, and the fact of having suffered, enjoyed and hoped together, are the kinds of things that can be understood in spite of differences of race, language and religion.

Suffering in common, he believed, unifies more than joy does and where national memories are concerned, griefs are of more value than triumphs, for they impose duties, and require a common effort; the response to recent natural disasters verifies that. It explains that which so puzzles foreigners, the significance we place on ANZAC which, militarily, was a disastrous defeat. People, Renan added, unite in their memories of suffering because alleviating grief requires a 'common effort', which serves as a foundation for unity. Members of a community feel as though they have accomplished something great, when they are able to survive in adverse conditions.

Australia may be a lucky country but is no stranger to suffering. Whatever interpretation is placed upon the events of 1788, no one can deny that sacrifice and suffering were an integral part of life as the foundations of modern Australia were laid. It was the lot of both Newcomers and the First People they so callously dispossessed. The convicts, emancipists and free-settlers toiled to establish a civilised society in a land, both alien in nature and hostile in the resistance their presence provoked. For the indigenous people sacrifice was ultimate and their suffering (seemingly) endless. This was not the mutual suffering that Renan referred to when nation building. However, much mutual endeavour took place. From the very beginning the First People aided and worked, at times willingly, with the Newcomers who sought to occupy their land – as Darwin observed during his stay at King George Sound.

Renan followed his thoughts about suffering and unity by pointing out that nationhood failed to materialise in countries with rigid stratification, or where different communities were played off against one another, and where the integration of different groups could not take place. Unity cannot be taken for granted, hence the urgency of vergangenheitsaufarbeitung for the coming together of Australia's First People with those who now share the country with them. Furthermore, building a sense of togetherness and belonging is also an issue in the non-Aboriginal population, whose makeup is now quite diverse, much of it due to relatively recent immigration. An Australia consisting of a loose collection of communities that occasionally offer little more than a passing nod to each other is a fainthearted vision indeed.

Remembering and forgetting

The Australia of today, however, is not the upshot of a long past as prescribed by Renan. It is a young country *without songs, architecture and history* found in countries elsewhere. It had no glorious heritage. The poet's disparaging assessment of the Newcomers *whose boast is not: 'we live' but 'we survive'*, ignores the fact that his Australia, *the last of lands,* was never like countries elsewhere. To have survived was no mean feat for the Newcomers. That the First Australians had maintained their traditional way of life for 60 millennia in the face of geological and climatic changes verges on miraculous. Australians can be justly proud of their achievements both before and after 1788.

Furthermore, a nation, Renan pointed out, is bound not by its real past but by the stories its people tell themselves; by what they remember and what they forget. He placed considerable emphasis on forgetting: *Forgetfulness, and I would even go so far as to say historical error, is a crucial factor in the creation of a nation.* Australia is an immigrant nation. Within the body politic, as for the individual, some memories are best allowed to fade and eventually forgotten, for instance former Catholic-Protestant discord. It is imperative that all who would call this country home forget conflicts and feelings in their original homelands and forge friendships in their new situation. The recent flare-up of animosity and violence over the Palestine-Israel conflict underscores the need to forget the past and focus on the future in this new land. Much forgetting with a different orientation best befalls new arrivals as, over time, memories harking back to their native land are replaced by those of establishing a new life in a sunburnt land.

Moreover, Renan considered: *all nations, even the most benevolent in later practice, are founded on acts of violence, which are then forgotten.* However, some enormities can be so great, the Jewish Holocaust being an example, they need confronting for healing of the national soul. Letting in the light is the wise course of action. Such is the case with the dispossession and treatment of Australia's First People. Forgetting is not an option. Truth-telling is at the core of vergangenheitsaufarbeitung, their story told and the enormities suffered post-1788 conceded and amended, but when doing so, ensuring truth shackles neither original inhabitants nor Newcomers to a past that cannot be changed.

In whatever way we portray the past, we engage in remembering and forgetting. In a curious way we choose, consciously or unconsciously, what to remember and what to forget. Remembering is of a more substantive nature; celebrations, for example, whether public or private, require forethought and planning, whereas forgetting, more often, is a failure to remember. In this way we create the stories we tell ourselves about who and what we believe we are. Stories added to, altered, trimmed and retold; stories that over time can subsume into an Australian narrative; a grand narrative composed of stories, myths and legends, beginning at the beginning of time and evolving inexorably with each passing year, generation and migration; like Christmas celebrations, forever changing but for each and everyone always remaining Christmas.

Chapter 34
Weaving a Grand Narrative

People were telling stories long before they invented writing. Story-telling forges connections among people, and between people and ideas. A story can be told in different ways and it is not the story itself but the meaning we give it that counts. Scholar of comparative mythology, Joseph Campbell, said: *if you're going to have a story, have a big story, or none at all*. Both Newcomers and First People have stories to tell: stories both ancient and modern; stories of toil, struggle, failure and achievement, even heroism; stories that may not bear close examination but if woven together would form a potential flux for uniting a people. A story beginning in the Dreamtime, gathering threads as it goes, would be a big story; one that could define us as individuals and as a people. But to do so, the progressing threads must weave a singular cloth, which would need a leap of faith by Australia's First People in that it requires a change in how 26 January 1788 is viewed.

Manning Clark begins his history of Australia: *Civilization did not begin in Australia until the last quarter of the eighteenth century* (see Appendix 5). The alternative, 'Aboriginal life in Australia ended in the last quarter of the eighteenth century' would have been, at its best, little more than a panegyric and a dubious one at that. Against all odds, Australia's First People have survived. Despite the ravages of dispossession – which still plagues many – civilisation in all its meanings is now also a cornerstone of Aboriginal life. Men and women of Aboriginal lineage feature prominently from sport to academia, in writing and the visual and performing arts. Journalist Stan Grant and public figure Warren Mundine are examples. The wonders of technology serve those of Aboriginal heritage just as they serve all the rest of us.

In many ways ancient and less ancient have coalesced but the descendants of Australia's First People generally view the arrival of the First Fleet as a 'kiss of death'; but in the grand scheme of things perhaps it brought a breath of life. A people and their culture can be left frozen in time as are the Sentinelese, the indigenous inhabitants of North Sentinel Island, to which travel and even close approach is prohibited; or they can be allowed to evolve, often doing so by incorporating features from other cultures. The alleged charm of a simpler, more primitive existence is more or less illusory and, however viewed, such an existence is incongruent with contemporary Australian society. Preserving, consolidating and building on the learning, wisdom and customs garnered over a thousand lifetimes may be better served by harnessing the opportunities offered by civilisation.

This linking can be thought of as a non-zero-sum situation – somewhat akin to the adoption of many aspects of Greek culture by the Romans – despite having, in the eyes of some, aspects of cultural appropriation. Such melding could be considered a way of keeping alive and evolving much that Aboriginal people hold dear and even sacred in a rapidly-changing world where outer space is the new frontier. The colourful, variegated, textured tapestry that is Australia, the threads of which range from short to very long, would be an antidote for the doubts that afflict all who live here – no matter how shallow or deep their roots, no matter what their heritage – by eliciting a feeling of connection and thereby a sense of identity and belonging. With the passage of time, the pattern of the Australian story would become increasingly intricate as intermarriage and each wave of migration add their threads.

The past – having done great deeds together

Man does not improvise, Renan professed. He has a purpose in his pursuits and so the nation at any point, like the individual, is the product of its past. Thousands of years of husbandry produced *the Biggest Estate on Earth* – the Australian landscape as it was at the time of the arrival of Europeans. A more recent endeavour was the technically challenging Snowy Hydro Scheme, the construction of which involved immigrants of many nationalities and was very much a unifying [nation-building] enterprise. Australia's colonial past is somewhat chequered. Nonetheless, the Australia of today is the legacy of all the ancestors, both Aboriginal and non-Aboriginal who, accordingly, warrant our acknowledgement and some even our veneration. To foreswear their exploits, as some would have us do, would repudiate much of what we are today because, as Renan says, *they made us what we are*. Their stories would make up much of the canon of stories, myths and legends forming a grand narrative giving rise to a sense of commonality and belonging.

But the essential condition for being a people, as espoused by Renan, is not only rooted in the past – in having performed great deeds together – *the social capital upon which one bases a national idea*; it also lies very much in the present in having *a common will to wish to perform still more – the desire to live together and the desire to continue to invest in the heritage ... jointly received.*

The present – harmony

Thomas Jefferson, a Founding Father of the United States of America, stated: *I like the dreams of the future better than the history of the past*. Renan more reflectingly opined: *One loves the house that one has built and that one passes on*. Before we dream, however, we need to put in order our house, the house we have inherited, the house we shall pass on – that it may be at peace with itself.

There can be no harmony while Australia's First People remain aggrieved. An Elder of the Yolngu people of north-east Arnhem Land stated passionately: *We can build Australia together if our right is recognised; if we are put on the same level, not as second-class citizens of this country*. The course of action referred to above as vergangenheitsaufarbeitung must begin with addressing these grievances, in particular the central issues of dispossession and racism (see Appendix 6); to have the negative feelings of oppression and disinheritance replaced by those of acknowledgement, belonging and acceptance. Very little towards this end has been achieved to date, for which the reasons are many and varied. Not the least is the ongoing picking at the festering wound of past inequities. Another is the lack of a vision of the future. Aboriginal leaders mostly speak about the present-day plight of their people. Occasionally what might be termed their dreams are mentioned but these are set in a distant past; they are not dreams to inspire. A vision that inspires would look to the future; one where they view themselves as being an integral part of a harmonious society in which they participate fully in a productive and personally fulfilling way; one where they, Australia's First People, no longer feel as strangers in their own land. Neville Bonner put it eloquently: *A piano like a society sounds best when the black-and-white keys are played together.* To move from vision to reality, that is vergangenheitsaufarbeitung, is a pressing necessity, not only for unity and harmony but also for defining who we are.

There can be no harmony while the cry of Australia's First People is echoed in the broader population by those who have come here in recent decades, ostensibly to make it their new home, and who feel unwelcomed, unaccepted or not belonging; in other words, alienated from everyday life. That they, or more importantly their children, should have doubts about who they are or whether they belong is disturbing because they are the future of the nation. Feelings such as these belie the oft-repeated assertion that diversity is a source of strength;

it is not a strength in itself. It is a potential strength that requires unison and harmony to be realised. The essence of a nation, according to Renan, is that: *all of its individual members have a great deal in common*. Commonality not difference surely is the focus for fostering unison and harmony. A nation, as defined by Renan, is more than a collection of communities of interest; it is: *a body and soul at the same time* – the European Economic Community is not a motherland.

The present – the desire to live together

Renan stated a nation is a: *… great solidarity … . It presupposes a past but is reiterated in the present by a tangible fact; consent, the clearly expressed desire to continue a common life.* This is more than a case of people simply co-existing, merely tolerating each other and having minimal interaction with each other. Rather it is one where people meet and mix as they go about their daily activities within the broader community, and in doing so develop relationships that are able to surmount tribal animosities and differences. An example from our colonial past is the Irish-English story. The Catholic Irish had been in the thrall of the Protestant English for centuries and their resentment bordered on hatred. In Australia Irish immigrants were distributed throughout the general population – rather than settling in ghettos as they did in North America – thereby ensuring opportunities for interaction prevailed; as a result, an Irish component contributed to much of the make-up of Johnson's Australian. A somewhat similar example could be drawn from post-WWII immigrants from the Balkan states.

The day-to-day coming together of the people in the broader community for work, pleasure and other activities facilitates mutual understanding and fosters ties, from which feelings of acceptance, belonging and identity can grow. The sense of being part of a wider community fills a universal desire to belong somewhere, to something or to someone. This was made clear by COVID-19 virus lockdowns – not being able to gather together – when many felt they had lost a sense of belonging. Only time will tell whether or not COVID-19 pandemic tribulations were positive or negative apropos Renan's criterion of suffering together being unifying.

It is said: *bonds that bind best are made in bed.* These bonds helped dampen the rancour between the Irish and English and overcome the prejudices of the latter towards the former; they bridged the divide between Johnson's Australians and post-WWII European immigrants. They remain the surest means for knitting together east and west and north and south – the great diversity of people who reside in Australia today – into a harmonious unison of people or more specifically a nation. Despite differences in skin colour, which was not an issue in the Irish-English divide, Cupid continues to cast bonding spells, a state of affairs to be encouraged and facilitated, but one where identity issues lurk when ethnicity is used as a qualifier to being 'Australian' (see Appendix 7).

How much is the desire to 'live together' reflected in the stories we tell ourselves? What stories do we tell our children? What stories grab the attention of the very recent arrivals to this ancient land; those who have come purportedly to put down roots; those who wish to feel and be seen as Australian? Do we, in our stories, pay homage to those who preceded us; those responsible for establishing all we have inherited: lifestyle, landscape and built environment, and political, cultural and educational institutions? Story-telling, as mentioned earlier, builds connections among people, and between people and ideas. Stories – manifested in films, paintings, speeches, yarns exchanged at the pub – under-write much of our identity, who and what we think we are, not just as individuals but also as a people. In telling these stories, do we draw all the threads together so that they may engender a sense of nation and national belonging?

The present – invest in the heritage jointly received

Renan contends an ongoing willingness to come together and do things together is a daily affirmation or consent to their continuing to exist as a nation; in other words, a preparedness to suffer, toil and dream together – *to invest in the heritage received* or, as Leichhardt put it: *take an interest in the colony and consider it as their fatherland.* Unlike their convict and early immigrant forebears, new arrivals to Australia today no longer have to hew an existence out of a native forest and their farewells need no longer end in 'forever'. They are no more than a relatively cheap 24-hour aircraft flight from their native land in contrast to an unpleasant 9-month voyage on a sailing ship in earlier days; consequently, putting down roots is no longer a necessity but a choice. Nevertheless, foresaking the familiarities of one's native soil for the chance of a new life in a foreign land fraught with hardship and challenges remains a formidable undertaking. Roughly 15% of British migrants to Australia after WWII returned to the UK.

Putting down roots is no easy undertaking. Unsurprisingly, not all who come here wish to. For instance, some take on Australian Citizenship for very pragmatic reasons, such as possessing a passport that has minimal restrictions on the holder's scope to travel, giving little thought, if any, to associated identity and allegiance consequences. Pragmatism very much underlies the presence of holders of Permanent Resident visas (see Appendix 8) and Temporary visas of various sorts and who, in 2016, made up about 15% of the total resident population. For the above 'pragmatic' residents, as with tourists and expatriates, the point at issue is not 'belonging', in a 'sentimental' sense, to people and place but simply one of 'being tolerated' or 'welcome'. Not unexpectedly, the issue for those committed to building a 'new life' (see Appendix 9), often for the sake of their children and their children's children, is more one of sentiment: forming an emotional connection with a sunburnt land and its people and all that entails – a desire to be and feel 'Australian'. Putting down roots, therefore, is not simply a matter of taking on Australian citizenship or just working and paying taxes due. At its core is commitment; commitment to a new life and the wellspring for that life, the sunburnt land upon which all tread.

Relationships with the land

Ever since the Dreamtime, the Land has been shaping all who have walked upon it; the First Australians were shaped in a deeply spiritual way. Developing deep, sustaining roots in the Land is the only way we can become a 'true people' propounded ecologist Tim Flannery in his 2002 Australia Day speech: *it is the only thing that we all, uniquely, share in common. It is at once our inheritance, our sustenance, and the only force ubiquitous and powerful enough to craft a truly Australian people.* In a similar vein, some believe to become a 'true people', i.e. to shape an 'Australian' identity, is bound up with developing a true understanding of our country. Leichhardt, the explorer and naturalist, prescribed a scientific understanding. He reckoned life in the bush to be very exhausting, if one were unable to sense the deep warmth of nature.

Without a doubt, the rigours of the bush helped sculpt the tough independent bushman image of over a century ago but even then, and even more so now, most of us *pullulate timidly on the edge of alien shores,* a situation generally ascribed to the quality of, or lack of, facilities and opportunities of all kinds outside the metropolis. This may be so but the fact that few of us wish to settle permanently in regional areas, let alone 'the bush', suggests a dissonance between us Newcomers and 'the bush'; a dissonance resulting not only from its harshness and unfamiliarity but also a concomitant uncanny strangeness not existent in the forests of fairy tales – a mysteriousness emanating from the very ancientness of the Land. From the First Fleet onwards, the Australian countryside has challenged the Newcomers as they set about extracting its bounty. They have ameliorated an existential unease by keeping the bush at bay with gardens reminiscent of their native land.

A garden is a planned space … for which designs may draw on philosophical and aesthetic principles and often features have symbolic significance. Overall, the single identifying feature of a garden is 'control', whether in the simplicity of a Japanese garden or the elaborate ornateness of gardens such as at Versailles. The apparent absence of control singles out the Australian bush from the poppied fields of Flanders and the English countryside abloom with daffodils. Order is wanting from its myriad of landscapes but not so tranquillity. However, the

Ju Raku En Japanese garden, Toowoomba, 2022. Source: Peter Hasker

Versailles, June 2013. Source: jm jmgbjm, Flickr

Nindooinbah homestead, Beaudesert district, Queensland, 2012. Source: Gary Corbett, Nindooinbah Homestead

Camped out in brigalow country, *New Twin Hills* outstation, Clermont District, 1962. The author is sitting in the distance on the right. Source: Peter Hasker

Holding cattle by a billabong, *New Twin Hills* outstation, Clermont District. Source: Peter Hasker

tranquillity of the bush – a billabong amidst a eucalypt woodland or the erstwhile brigalow scrub – is not the peacefulness and serenity of a Japanese garden. Newcomers find the quietness of its wildness [sic] unnerving or even scary, but order was not lacking in the Australian landscape when the First Fleet entered Port Jackson. Over millennia Australia's First People had created a park-like landscape with the judicious use of fire. A recent historian has dubbed it *The Biggest Estate on Earth* but considers it has since *fallen into disorder* and, in the eyes of Australia's First People would be viewed as a *garden left wild*. For them, the land was not a source of fear but the source of their being. For those who obey the lore, *no land can be hostile*.

The relationship of Australia's First People with the Land, or 'Country' as they call it, is profound. Their spiritual beliefs are intimately associated with it. It is imbued with the power of Ancestor Spirits. They have a connection and sense of belonging to Country and it is a major part of their identity:

> *... knowledge [of country] ... enables me to identify who I am, who my family is, who my ancestors were and what my stories are.*

No ancient ruins lie buried in this primeval land. No terracotta army lies beneath its soil. No Ozymandias stands in its desert dunes. No archaeological dig will unearth its story. Its story is written in the landscape as imprints left by Ancestral and Creator Spirits as they lived out their lives. The Land is central to the psyche of the First People. For Newcomers to develop a deep understanding of and connection with the Land seems far from simple and straightforward – presuming it is possible.

It may be that an identity of sorts will emerge from the life in our burgeoning coastal regions, even sophisticated forms of cultural activity as occurs in metropolises around the world, but would it have any semblance of Australianness? Hopefully, our historical affair with sport so scorned by the naysayers may continue, but sport is not peculiar to Australia. Perhaps our frolicking at the seaside might mark us apart and so warrant the stamp of Australianness; but it could hardly be regarded as signifying a deep understanding of, and connection with, the Land.

The reality of Australia's First People's connection with the Land suggests the quest for authentic Australianness and an accompanying ingrained feeling of belonging ought not only incorporate them but also begin with them. In recent years, people of Aboriginal heritage have been making significant footprints in the field of artistic endeavour – the arena of image, symbolism and change. Much of it has expressed the hurt of dispossession but some of it also conveys a spirituality integral to which are song-lines tracing the journeys of ancestral spirits as they created the land, animals and lore. Here lies an opportunity like no other for Newcomers to understand the oldest culture in the world and conjointly begin piecing together a unifying vision, a grand narrative, the variegated, textured tapestry that is the story of Australia. Hence the necessity of a successful prosecution of vergangenheitsaufarbeitung, not only for coming to terms with the past but also for laying a foundation for the future.

We are at an inflection point. We either continue as a diversity of tribes 'pullulating timidly' on the edge of 'alien shores' living out our lives as if on an extensive tourist resort, or we put down deep permanent roots for a future that embraces all who would call this continent home: *the one place where no one can tell you that you do not belong, and that you are an integral part of the national story.*

We cannot foretell the Australia of the future and those who would inhabit her; like waves breaking on the seashore, only the passing years will expose the reality. But we can dream and it is from dreams that reality emerges; and when doing so, we should reflect carefully on what we have inherited lest we fritter it away. Furthermore, any thoughts of the future should keep well in mind the topsy-turvy nature of our sunburnt land.

Chapter 35
Reflections

Inheritance

We may or may not pass muster with Darwin or Leichhardt – they measured with a different tape. We may still be the 'Lucky Country' of the naysayers. We may fail to meet the criteria of current critics but none can dispute we are the land of *great expectations*, a wealthy country, politically stable and free of internecine strife and entrenched corruption; a country where the government has the capacity to deliver services reliably; a country where one is safe and free, and can grow rich. Our quality of life is one of the highest in the world, a fact borne out by our being a prime migrant destination; almost 30% of us were foreign-born according to the 2021 census. How we achieved this should be foremost in the minds of all when giving thought to our hopes and aspirations as individuals and as a people.

Freedom, honesty, trust and the law

Central to the notion of Australia is the concept of freedom, a concept so viscerally portrayed in Sidney Nolan's Ned Kelly paintings. Freedom, which takes many forms, is a bit like one's stomach. You are conscious of it only when something goes wrong. The convict settlement of Australia is paradoxical in that men and women banished to the end of the earth found freedom: socially, economically and politically. Those sentenced to the brutalities at Port Arthur or Norfolk Island would disagree and freedom is the last thing Australia's First People would associate with the arrival of the First Fleet (*Terra Nullius*). However, no one can repudiate that Australia rates highly among countries of the world in this matter. When asked why they came here, many immigrant friends and others have ended their answer: *and there's the freedom*. The freedom in question is the capacity to live one's life unfettered by authority or society at large.

How did we come to this situation? Its place in the timeline of discovery and settlement can be discounted. The clean political palette of a new land may have beckoned. The rigours of the sunburnt land may have played a part. Our convict forebears may deserve some thanks. More than likely it was the fact the colonists were British. For over half a millennium the British people had been curbing the powers of authority in an experiment with democracy, the handmaiden of freedom, and so it was their political and legal institutions that took root in Australia. In the end, however, freedom emanates from a state of mind which manifests itself in habits, ways, mores and values of a people, the pre-cursors of behaviour and action. Likewise, democracy is a mindset and its practice cannot be conjured up with a stroke of a pen and like most aspects of culture has a long incubation period.

The freedom in question is not absolute but moderated by the rule of law. We might expect that people having convict origins and Ned Kelly as a hero would be an unruly lot but not so according to the historian John Hirst, when writing about the second half of the 20th century. He considered us a law-abiding lot. We willingly comply with laws and regulations and so buckle up our seat belts and adhere to the rules of the road. We are, I have been told, very trusting, which suggests an innate honesty present throughout the body politic. It would be stretching credulity to suggest that this had anything to do with our convict ancestors or their offspring, the Currency Lads and Lasses. Trust, like mateship, was more likely a characteristic essential to survival in an isolated harsh environment. Unquestionably, trust is essential for freedom.

A polity short on trust and its counterpart honesty and having a cavalier disregard for compliance with the law is predisposed to corruption. A case in point would be the apparent decline in standards in the accounting and legal profession in recent decades. Corruption of any kind 'white ants' the core of society and a casualty is surely freedom.

Spirit of ANZAC

ANZAC Day could be considered a *de facto* national day. Unlike the controversial Australia Day (26 January) it has spiritual undertones and any meaningful thoughts about Australia would, therefore, be lacking were ANZAC disregarded. It has critics. Some suggest it militarises our history; others question its historicity, accusing it of replacing historical fact with mythology. Some even demand that the Spirit of Anzac be 'dismantled'. But the ANZAC legend is neither mythology nor history. It is a national story in the true sense of Renan's meaning that can be summarised in about 100 words.

> *The archetypical image of an Australian, a tough, resilient, independent bushman, may best hang on the wall of mythology; ever since the First Fleet sailed into Port Jackson we have been a very urbanised society. Nonetheless, the ordeals of convict and pioneer-settler life tempered a spirit that finally blossomed on the battlefields of Europe as the Spirit of ANZAC, which was reaffirmed two decades later in the Second World War. The men of ANZAC were no mythological superbeings but ordinary men from the city and bush who did extraordinary things. The qualities attributed to them give substance to a living legend from which all can draw inspiration.*

To thrive

American poet, author and scholar, Maya Angelou, suggested that: *our mission in life should be not merely to survive, but to thrive; and to do so with some passion, some compassion, some humour and some style.* She wrote about the individual but her words could refer to a nation. Hope and his mid-20th century naysayer contemporaries castigated their fellow Australians for merely 'surviving'. We have progressed since then but are we thriving? The answer, like beauty, is in the eye of the beholder.

Our population increases at a greater rate than the post-WWII instigators intended but is this indicative of thriving or simply needless increase to the detriment of the environments of both the city and countryside – its ecosystems? Are large cities a prerequisite for thriving social, intellectual and artistic activity – commercial activity may thrive with an increasing population but at a cost that may eventually sour the grapes. The fermentation of creativity and ideas is not a function of population size but of salons, coffee houses and public spaces, where people with the time and inclination can meet and talk freely. Populations of Dr Johnstone's London and Marco Polo's Beijing were under one million. The population of classical Athens was about 150,000, a large percentage of whom were slaves. In the future slaves, in the form of robots with artificial intelligence, will decrease the need for human labour and surely expunge drudgery from daily life, thereby releasing time for more meaningful living, which must surely involve the mind, the body and the spirit.

The nation's coffers overflow with the proceeds from mining of iron ore, coal and other valuable minerals. The wealth generated from these resources may rival or exceed that of the gold-rush era which stimulated diverse economic activities. Our material prosperity is evident

Chapter 35: Reflections

Bulk carrier at Port Hedland, 2019. Source: Sam Brown

Map of Australia's coal terminals, 2012. Source: Zouillon, Wikimedia Commons

Day and night at Port Hedland, Western Australia, trains 3 km long unload cargo into massive bulk carriers. Likewise in the east, fleets of ships are loaded with coal for export to foreign countries. Newcastle is the largest coal port in the world.

in the abundance and diversity of goods available to us but can our current achievements match the legacy of the gold-rush era (see Gold, page 73)? Are we building the infrastructure and communication systems needed to foster national unity? Is our architecture distinctly Australian? Does it reflect our open way of life – our friendliness, welcoming attitude and love of the outdoors? Houses should be designed to encourage social interaction rather than social isolation. However, regardless of one's opinions on the built environment, a nation that cannot adequately house its people cannot be considered 'thriving'.

Little importance is placed on dress despite a thriving fashion industry. The man on the street might even be considered sloppy, if not impoverished. The men of the First AIF were a scruffy lot. Comfort is what matters, generally reflecting an informal approach to life, although dress could be a function of climate. A climatically appropriate dress, that fits our informal way of life and yet is stylish, would add to the image of who we are.

Our thriving as a nation may be assessed by our ability to live and work together towards a common goal, despite our diverse backgrounds. Our current uncertainty about our sense of identity and belonging must have significant implications on our capacity to thrive.

Chapter 36
Where Are We Going?

A unifying agency

The question is not who we are; it appears we know not, but where are we going? We are a highly diverse people who have no binding scaffolding of ideology or religion to give a strong collective identity. We may coexist harmoniously provided our expectations are fulfilled but it is unrealistic to presume we could weather the economic, political or social storms that will surely befall us in the future. Cracks in the social fabric are already evident, as highlighted by rising animosities and recent violent rallies over the conflicts in the Middle East. A unifying agency is sorely needed.

French philosopher Ernest Renan's concept of a nation as a spiritual principle is put forward as a unifying agency. A nation, he said, *is bound not by its real past but by the stories it tells itself...* . The task before us, both Newcomers and First People, is to set about telling stories – individual and community – in such a way that they become 'our' story.

Renan believed that people unite in their memories of suffering. The terror and suffering of those seeking our shores on leaky boats in the 1990s would have much in common with that experienced by their convict counterparts two centuries ago. The tongue's sting and the lash bite are both painful. The shock of beginning in a new land – the loneliness of the city and the loneliness of the bush – have much in common. Stories told with imagination and symbolism will engender a sense of national identity and belonging.

Building a sense of identity will become increasingly difficult as the percentage of people born overseas grows in comparison with the 'host' population, i.e. the descendants of Johnson's Australians, who carry the values and public attitudes that have stood the test of time. Furthermore, it would be unfortunate if certain communities were to become so large they became more self-sufficient and had a lesser need to connect with groups outside of themselves and thereby Balkanise the country.

Belonging

Renan stated that a nation is a spiritual family; that geography makes a nation no more than race, language or religion. In Australia's case, however, a certain degree of national integrity would be engendered by it being an island continent. The sea is an unquestionable delineator; there is no fluidity about where one lives. It not only keeps us in, but also keeps others out. In this way, geography has influenced us and probably will continue to do so.

A further dimension of the land Australia is the relationship between it and the people who tread upon it. The profound connection of Australia's First People with 'the Land' contrasts with the ambivalence of the Newcomers as mentioned above. The latter, who largely cling to coastal shores, will develop a heartfelt feeling of belonging and attachment to it only by recognising the ethos and character in all its beauty and strength without the filter of foreign eyes. In other words, not always looking for well-kept green fields and gardens, and not always seeing our rocks, deserts and vast spaces as harsh and unwelcoming. Australia's

First People have much to teach us Newcomers, including how to embrace this driest of continents; for embrace it we must if we are ever to truly feel a sense of belonging, cultivate Australianness and establish deep roots – to *love a sunburnt country*. Whether viewing our *savage and scarlet* inland landscape through new eyes would trigger a migration away from the coastal fringe is questionable. The human affinity with water is deep. Only vast volumes of permanent water may lure us to the lands *where the dead men lie*.

To the First People, their traditional 'Country' – their ancestral Land – represents intricate social systems and identity; *disconnection from it is considered a form of homelessness*. Connecting with 'Country' when residing in urban areas can be challenging for them: *For many ... it's a visceral connection; you look beyond the buildings and concrete and feel a sense of belonging*. On the other hand, Newcomers see the Land around them only as a physical place, perhaps with some emotional and aesthetic connotations. Most Newcomers find life in the bush or even in the rural areas, incredibly draining, exhausting or boring and therefore opt for residing in a city. But when entombed by glass, concrete and bitumen, is it possible to form an attachment to:

> *... ... a sunburnt country, a land of sweeping plains,*
> *Of ragged mountain ranges, of droughts and flooding rains.*
>
> *...*
>
> *The sapphire-misted mountains, the hot gold hush of noon,*
> *Green tangle of the brushes where lithe lianas coil,*
> *And orchids deck the tree-tops, and ferns the warm dark soil.*
>
> *...*
>
> *An opal-hearted country, a wilful, lavish land –?*

Australia is a land with many landscapes ranging from deserts and rainforests to snowy mountains, the interaction with which had a defining influence on those who settled here. A century ago, the inland or more colloquially the 'outback' symbolised the true essence of the country. However, the 'outback' has largely disappeared from the national psyche and so where now might the Newcomer get a sense of belonging or Australianness? Whatever the answer, it surely must include a form of communion with the Land. It might still possibly be that the heart of this great land is still to be found, as it was a century ago, somewhere out there in the centre. Widely travelled friends of mine recently flew over Lake Eyre (July 2023), an experience that aroused feelings of awe and specifically, becoming cognisant of the very vastness of our great land which no picture can truly capture. Accordingly, wherever we are, a measure of a sense of Australianness must surely be:

> *Though earth holds many splendours, wherever I may die,*
> *I know to what brown country my homing thoughts will fly.*

A blank sheet

Compared with Europe and Asia, Australia appears a young country, yet it is old. But it has no ancient ruins, the detritus of past civilisations that tells a story. Its First People were nurturers of the land, not tillers or builders. Their story is not found in crumbling edifices but in rock art, a progenitor of civilisation, of songs and dance. Modernity came late to its shores. The people who brought it, as stated in this writing, left much of their past behind. Having few ties with tradition gives the opportunity to release full-blown creativity – a chance to be pioneers and create something new. Apart from the values and public attitudes that have served us so well and therefore must be considered the cornerstone of our way of life, Australia is virtually a blank sheet upon which to write what we will.

The inexorable advance in technology will change the nature of human beings. Whether or not such changes are considered 'accelerated evolution', in the Darwinian sense, matters little, for the outcome is inevitable. The products of gene manipulation and reproductive biology cannot even be guessed. The use of robots and AI could provide humans with more free time and energy to focus on intellectual and more advanced activities.

Those who dwell in the land of *Terra Australis* will be changed in many ways; for instance, it is possible that robots and AI will eventually replace the need for immigration as a source of skills and labour, which would influence national identity. It is anyone's guess what changes may eventuate, but a certainty is that our sunburnt land will play a part.

The realisation of a great nation in the south, as Darwin and Leichhardt envisioned, depends on many factors. At its core, it requires the diverse population of the continent – including our First People, long-standing Newcomers, as well as the various recently arrived ethnicities and those with mixed heritage through intermarriage – to be instilled with a strong sense of being Australian and a shared commitment to a common national purpose. Over time, this undertaking will entail remembering and forgetting certain aspects of former life and history. Furthermore, it presupposes that every individual develops a genuine emotional connection to the Land, even if it may not mirror the depth and nature of that felt by the First People.

A pivotal factor in achieving the above outcome is vergangenheitsaufarbeitung, a term recurrently cited in this discourse. This process entails Australia's First People and Newcomers addressing historical injustices and ensuring that the former become an integral and respected part of society. Simultaneously, pertinent elements of Aboriginal heritage would be woven into the fundamental fabric that binds the diverse population living in this sunburnt land. This would help create a shared Australian identity, where all individuals harbour mutual respect for one another. It would acknowledge the past while setting a firm gaze towards the future, demanding a pioneering spirit and a readiness to forge a new collective identity and become a new people.

How one might recognise this Australian of the future is anybody's guess. It certainly will not be by physical features as captured in a photograph, although there may be a certain glint in the eye. Whatever makes up the future Australian, I hope it includes some of the qualities mentioned in this discussion such as the resilience of the Australian POWs who were forced to work on Burma's Death Railway and our unique quirky sense of humour. These attributes have evolved from building a country that has become a popular destination for migrants worldwide. I hope the values and customs of these Australians will continue to include those that have served the test of time such as commitment to democracy, fair elections and the rule of law. Overall, I hope this sunburnt country remains a place of social and economic mobility, offering opportunities to those willing to work hard, and unequivocally a land of freedom.

> *Two roads diverged in a wood, and I –*
> *I took the one less traveled by,*
> *and that has made all the difference*
>
> Robert Frost

Appendix 1
Asian Immigration to USA and Canada

In the latter part of the 19th century laws restricting Asian immigration were enacted in North America. Chinese had joined in the North American gold-rushes of the 1850s and later worked on their respective transcontinental railways. As gold became harder to find and competition increased, animosity toward the Chinese and other foreigners increased. In 1885 the Canadian Government levied a 'head tax on Chinese immigrants', which was later increased. In addition, municipal ordinances restricted employment opportunities even in industries not attractive to white Canadians, such as laundries. In 1923 these prohibitive fees were replaced with an outright ban on Chinese immigration to Canada with the exceptions of merchants, diplomats, students and 'special circumstances' cases. The Chinese who entered Canada before 1924 had to register with the local authorities and could leave Canada for a maximum of only two years. Independent Chinese immigration in Canada came after Canada eliminated race and the 'place of origin' section from its immigration policy in 1967.

In 1875, Chinese women were banned from immigrating to the United States. The Chinese Exclusion Act of 1882, which prohibited all immigration of Chinese labourers, was renewed in 1902 and repealed in 1943. The Immigration Act of 1924 excluded Japanese and other Asians and further restricted immigration of southern and eastern Europeans, Jews and Arabs. The purpose of the act was 'to preserve the ideal of U.S. homogeneity'. In 1952 and 1965 direct ethnic barriers and quotas on national origin, respectively, were abolished.

Appendix 2
Montesquieu

Montesquieu (Charles Louis de Secondat, baron de La Brède et de Montesquieu, 1689–1755) was an 18th-century French jurist and political philosopher. He proposed three fundamental forms of government: republics, monarchies and despotisms, each sustained by a distinct 'spirit' that reflects the shared beliefs and values of both the governed and the governing.

- Republics are guided by virtue, where free governments are led by popularly elected officials. Different types of republics exist, ranging from more democratic to more aristocratic, depending on the levels of public participation. The virtue Montesquieu attributed to republics was not a moral or Christian one, but rather a political virtue, characterised by a 'love of the homeland', respect for 'laws and country' and values of 'equality' and 'frugality'.

- Monarchies are driven by honour, characterised by hereditary leadership and established rules of succession. In this system, people recognise their place in the hierarchy and accept the authority of the monarch, contributing to the order and stability of the government.

- Despotisms operate on fear, where arbitrary power is exercised over a population that is coerced, manipulated or seduced (e.g. by luxury). Despotism is a form of absolute rule that, although oppressive, can still foster willing obedience. It is distinct from tyranny, autocracy or dictatorship in that it can produce compliance.

Montesquieu also introduced the concept of the 'separation of powers' of government. He warned of the dangers of concentrating power and emphasised the need for legislative, executive and judicial functions to be held by different bodies, each bound by the rule of law. He believed that free governments depend on constitutional arrangements with checks and balances to prevent the abuse of power.

Appendix 3
Territorial Imperative

No one should find it strange that indigenous people would harbour resentment towards or defend their land against anyone who lands uninvited on its shores. Words emblazoned on a painting hanging at the Gold Coast HOTA art gallery read: *first one, then four, then more, and more, they came and came, and they came.* Significantly, it does not take generations to develop such feelings.

The Currency Lads and Lasses, those early native-born colonials, did not take kindly to new arrivals and neither have subsequent waves of migrants been welcomed with open arms by those already rooted here, even if of recent arrival.

> *One of the ongoing strengths of the Australian immigration system was that, whilst we tended to demonise each new group for awhile, we ultimately welcomed them, adding and absorbing their ways to ours, their food, their dress, their music, their customs and their scholarship, to enrich and expand our culture; but we expected them to fit in.*

Humans are instinctively territorial. New arrivals may bring much benefit but are perceived as a threat; a threat, seemingly rather nebulous but with identity being the basis of concern and, in many cases, probably a root cause of racism.

Appendix 4
A Matter of Geography

The island continent, Australia, was launched at the end of the last ice age, when the land masses and seas forming the global map we know today were configured by the melting of the ice sheets and the accompanying rise in the levels of the ocean. Isolated by a moat of water, the plant, animal and human life it carried remained undisturbed by the world at large until the coming of the Europeans from the other side of the globe. It could well have been settled by those from adjacent South-east Asian lands to the north which, from the first century of the Christian era until the 1600s, were subjected to three consecutive colonising movements: the Hindu-Buddhist, the Chinese and Islam.

All these movements were driven by trade and finding wondrous treasure; the Hindu-Buddhists and Islam sought religious converts as well. However, none advanced beyond Timor and Macassar because an imaginary line running from Timor through Banda to Macassar separated the civilised world from the unknown. Venturing further was deterred by qualms about what lay beyond or even fear stoked by terrifying stories of monsters and geological impossibilities. By the time any inducement and capability to search the seas beyond eventuated, the Asian states were rendered powerless by material weakness, lack of sea power and bloody internal conflict and had succumbed to the presence of European influence. The Portuguese had arrived at the beginning of the 16th century and were followed by the Dutch at the end of the century.

The Europeans had been lured by seeking direct access to spices and visions of gold but were also interested in exploring the world beyond its known limits. Their improvements in ship-building, aids to navigation and map-making had made it possible for their ships to cross the oceans. They speculated about the lands to the south and south-east of Java. Also, the idea of a south land had been on European minds since antiquity to the extent that it appeared as words, *Terra Australis Incognita*, on early maps of the world. Thus it was the European, not the Asian, who eventually mapped and settled Australia.

Appendix 5
Civilisation

Civilisation, civilised and culture are words with broad ranges in meaning. To give some context to the word 'civilisation', the following reproduces Manning Clark's footnote qualifying his use of the word, a definition given by the economist Wolfgang Kasper and a summary of the thoughts of art historian Kenneth Clark on its meaning.

Manning Clark

In a footnote Manning Clark states: *A distinction is made between 'civilisation' in the sense described in the Oxford English Dictionary, of a people brought out of a state of barbarism, and 'culture' in the sense defined in the* Grosse Brockbaus *as the sum of the efforts made by a community to satisfy and reconcile the basic human requirements of food, clothing, shelter, security, care of the weak and social cohesion by controlling its natural environment. The word 'culture' is not used in its other sense of 'the efforts made to ennoble, refine and cultivate the human personality by sublimating its instinctual nature'.*

Wolfgang Kasper

In a Policy Paper discussing the future of western civilisation Kasper states: *As so often in the social sciences, it is the invisible that matters most. A civilisation is built on shared values and beliefs, on habits, manners, customs, attitudes and laws, which form the 'cultural DNA', define the civilisation, shape social relations and governance structures and give the community a degree of cohesion. These qualities constitute the 'cultural software' that shapes the hardware — the architecture, the arts, the industries, the infrastructures and the implements, and how these are used. Historians all too often focus only on the visible.*

Kenneth Clark

In *By the Skin of our Teeth*, the first chapter of the book on his celebrated TV series *Civilisation*, Clark mused on 'what is civilisation?'. He professed he had no clear idea what the word meant except that civilisation was preferable to barbarism. He could not define it but thought he could recognise it when he saw it.

He believed deeds, words and art define great nations but not one of these alone can be understood without knowing the other two. Of the three, he considered only art was trustworthy but this did not mean the history of civilisation is the history of art. *Great works of art can be produced in barbarous societies – in fact the very narrowness of primitive society gives their ornamental art a particular vitality.*

He compared an African mask to a head of Apollo, which he had no doubt embodied a higher state of civilisation than the mask. Both represent spirits, messengers from a world of our own imagining. The mask depicts a world of fear and darkness ready to inflict horrible punishment for the smallest infringement of a taboo. The Apollo depicts a world of light and confidence in which the gods descend to earth in order to teach us reason and the laws of harmony.

He pointed out that, even though there was plenty of superstition and cruelty in the Greco-Roman world, the contrast between these images meant something. *It meant that at certain epochs mankind has felt conscious of something about himself – body and spirit – which was outside the daily struggle for existence and the night to night struggle with fear; and has felt the need to develop these qualities of thought and feeling so that they might approach as nearly as possible to an idea of perfection – reason, justice, physical beauty, all of them in equilibrium. He has managed to satisfy this need in various ways – through myths, through dance and song, through systems of philosophy and through the order that he has imposed on the visible world.*

Clark considered civilisation, however complex and solid, is actually quite fragile and can be destroyed, its enemies being:

> *Fear of war, of invasion, of plague, of famine, which makes it simply not worthwhile constructing things or planting trees or even planning next year's crops;*

> *Fear of the supernatural, which means that you dare not question anything or change anything;*

> *Loss of self-confidence – Civilisation requires a little prosperity, enough to provide some leisure, but far more it requires confidence in the society in which one lives and in one's own mental powers, and belief in its philosophy and its laws;* and

> *Exhaustion – that feeling of hopelessness which can overtake people even blessed with a high degree of prosperity. Clark maintains all great civilisations have exhibited energy, vitality and discipline. He accepted fine sensibilities, good conversation and all that can be among the agreeable results of civilisation but they are not what make a civilisation. A society can have these amenities and yet be dead and rigid.*

Civilisation, Clark feels, means something more than energy and will and creative power. That something is a sense of permanence. Civilised man, he conjectured, must feel that he belongs somewhere in space and time; that he consciously looks forward and looks back; and for this purpose it is a great convenience to be able to read and write.

Clark ends his musing pointing out that for over 500 years in Western Europe practically no lay person from kings and emperors downwards could read or write. During that time the monasteries became the guardians of civilisation because they provided a minimum of stability. Civilisation, he considered, needed stability. The monks were able to preserve and copy ancient manuscripts. With the onset of the Renaissance, European civilisation got a new lease of life. As Clark puts it, we got through *By the skin of our teeth.*

Clark believed one should not try to assess a culture without knowing its language because so much of its character is connected with the actual use of words and so focussed specifically on European civilisation, the civilisation arising from the ancient Greeks and Romans and which, in its current form, is referred to as 'The West'.

There can be no doubt that the civilisation Kenneth Clark examined is ailing, largely afflicted by a loss in confidence arising from not only challenges from 'The East' but also challenges from within – from doubts about itself, its values and its more recent history. This must have a profound influence on Australia, given it was 'European' civilisation that came to it in the last quarter of the 18th century.

Appendix 6
Racism

None can doubt the significant part that race, more specifically attitudes towards non-European races, has played in post-1788 Australia. In the lead-up to federation, the already dispossessed First People of Australia were given no role in drafting a constitution, which virtually ignored their existence in the land of their ancestors. However, the constitution as drafted did contain references to race, reflecting attitudes widely held at the time, which can be gleaned from sentiments expressed by Edmund Barton, the Champion of Federation. As a constitutional convention delegate he suggested that a power was needed to enable the Commonwealth to *regulate the affairs of the people of coloured or inferior races who are in the Commonwealth*. On becoming Australia's first Prime Minister he introduced the Bill that, in effect, set up the White Australia Policy:

> *I do not think that the doctrine of the equality of man was really ever intended to include racial equality. There is no racial equality. There is that basic inequality. These races are, in comparison with white races – I think no one wants convincing of this fact – unequal and inferior.*

The zeitgeist regarding race today is a far cry from that at the time of federation but race remains an issue of discontent; one of particular significance to Australia's First People and therefore a vital task for vergangenheitsaufarbeitung. Race is also an issue throughout the body politic more generally but not to the extent experienced by the First People.

In his stinging critique of mid-20th century Australia, Donald Horne wrote:

> *Australia is the most egalitarian of countries, untroubled by obvious class distinctions, cast or communal domination, the tensions of racialism or the horrors of autocracy.*

He acknowledged Australia might have a reputation of being racist but this was because of its White Australia Policy. With his focus mainly on Asia he added, and from my experience I concur:

> *Asians do not worry much about the Aborigines. Their treatment of their own Aborigines is often worse than Australia's. Besides the Aborigines are 'blacks' and there's probably more prejudice against 'blacks' in Asia than in Europe or in Australia. ... The treatment given to the Aborigines was like that of other migrating races when confronted with an extremely weak and disorganised Aboriginal society. Most of the dominant races in Asia treated their Aborigines similarly. They pushed them out of the way. To make this comparison is not to excuse present attitudes, but to place Australian settlement in the context of the whole world's savage history of settlement. There was nothing peculiarly Australian in past treatment of the Aborigines ...*

Horne rightly believed the plight of the Aboriginals should remain on the consciences of present Australians, including those born elsewhere, because:

> *What matters is the position now. ... modern Australians have made a mess of restoring the Aborigines to the human race.*

The term racism and its derivatives are used so broadly, often as epithets mouthed in response to perceived slights of any kind or in gratuitous comments, they are rendered very much meaningless. The term encompasses physical features, skin colour, clothes worn, language, speech accent, body ornamentation, behaviour, cultural mores, ethnicity, nationality, religion, class and caste, in fact virtually any aspect of life, which is nonsensical and mischievous. The self-imposed blandness of language required to avoid mention of anything with a potential 'racial' connotation shackles communication and can at times result in it being virtually worthless. The probability of this occurring is more likely in a country with a very diverse population, such as Australia.

The Runnymede Trust, the UK's leading independent equality think tank, felt the words 'race' and 'racial' were not at all satisfactory. Despite this, the terminology continues to be used, no matter how inappropriate it may be for a specific instance. However, in the absence of more precise terminology, I use it. Rather than join in what is a fruitless discourse I shall simply state that, in my experience, all humans are racist. Only a person in a comatose-like state, totally disinterested in and mindless regarding surrounding life, would be oblivious to differences between people. But that does not presuppose prejudice, discrimination, dislike or urge to offend, insult, humiliate or intimidate, but simply designates awareness. Many people, Chinese and Indian for example, identify strongly in what might be termed a 'racial' way: I am Chinese or she is Indian. It is also the case that how we see ourselves can condition how we perceive certain situations, which may result in our responding to the views of others as being a 'racist', when they are well-meaning people.

The world is awash with claims and counter claims about racism. Wherever and whatever form this takes is transcended by the 'racism' that has been directed towards the Aboriginals, Australia's First People. They were considered hardly worthy of awareness – of being human beings. Horne notes that: *in the early years of settlement they were treated, at worst, as 'treacherous animals' or with indifference*. There still exists a segment of the non-Aboriginal population who look upon anyone of Aboriginal descent in this puzzling, irrational and unedifying way – that they are non-human. Above all else, it is this particular form of racism that must be expunged from the face of this land. Regrettably, vergangenheitsaufarbeitung cannot be expected to weave miracles. Those with a diehard attitude will just have to die off. Also, tackling the racism which allegedly permeates the world in general would be wisely left for another occasion. To do otherwise would blur the focus on the very specific form of 'racism' in question – which is not only a far more pressing need but would also be more readily achievable.

The issue of racism in the broader sense is clouded by complexity and its elimination presents a greater challenge because of the lack of a clear definition (perception) of what the issue exactly is. This statement needs explanation and in doing so some comments about the terms 'race' and 'racism' as currently used are necessary. The term 'race' is said by some to be: *an artificial construct used to classify people on the basis of supposed physical and cultural similarities deriving from their common descent*. The issue, therefore, may be either of a biological nature or of a cultural behaviour or practice, or a combination of both. Given 'cultural' may refer to virtually any aspect of life at the family, community or national level, any endeavour towards overcoming racism Australia-wide would be fraught with difficulty – 'What is one man's meat is another man's poison'. A catch-cry of 'acceptance of difference' would be nothing more than a motherhood statement and a bad one at that; some differences are unworthy of even toleration – for example 'caste' or a notorious biker gang. Furthermore, the nexus between physical and cultural can obscure the nature of the difference responsible for gratuitous discrimination; for example, is it the head, the hat or the tipping?

Undoubtedly, difference, or more specifically a negative response to it, is at the core of racism. Environment and learning, however, are only partly responsible for the prejudices that induce these responses. Unsurprisingly, they also have an evolutionary aspect. Whereas recognising and favouring people who looked and sounded similar facilitated living and working together in the small close-knit communities of the far distant past, it is a hindrance in the large, diverse, more-complex society of today, where difference is encountered all the time. We are all, through no fault of our own, predisposed to have racist biases. However, we have the power to recognise prejudice in ourselves and challenge it, and, over time, change ourselves.

It is probably true to say the marker most associated with racial difference and *ipso facto* racial sensitivities is skin pigmentation. Skin colour is intrinsic to how we view ourselves and how others view us and has racial implications because of it allegedly being a proxy for power. Thus some subscribe to a non-taxonomical definition of race: *the technology of power and control for the management of human difference*; in other words, the means by which the dominant group maintains its position of superiority. A reference to skin colour can cause considerable offence and, in response, the accusation of racism. This is no better illustrated than the racist charge imbroglio engulfing the British royal family regarding the skin colour of Prince Harry and Meaghan's baby. The inference is that white skin embodies superiority because power structures, etc. favour people of European heritage. Presumably, changes in 'those in power' would be mirrored in how skin colour is perceived. This, however, would be confuted by proponents of critical racial theory, who espouse that white people have inherent 'white privilege' from their 'whiteness' and black people are inherently disadvantaged by having dark skin. What is exactly meant by this is unclear; does it mean colour has an intrinsic value in a Darwinian sense other than a response to sunlight? Interestingly, over the years many university students, mostly from China, have asked me about the whiteness of their skin; Indian students have told me fairer-skinned girls can be more sought after for marriage. The focus on skin in regards to race, as well as it being a canvas for adornment and the care and attention it receives cosmetically, suggests deep subconscious psychological processes are at play and hence the complex nature of skin in human interaction and its place in the racism debate.

Given the foregoing plus the call by some to erase the concept of race and others who advocate the opposite – that we should feel comfortable talking about it – it would be a bold person who professed a way of addressing it. The aphorism *Give me the child until he is seven and I'll give you the man* would be central to any course of action. It could be said that, despite racism lacking in definition, it is clearly recognisable (felt) by those on the receiving end; it may be less clear to the perpetrator. Designing, let alone executing, a public campaign to counteract 'racism' would be far from simple. Having said this, the aim of any anti-racist campaign could be summed up in one word: respect, respect for one another. This is aptly put in the following words:

> *Oh, East is East, and West is West, and never the twain shall meet,*
> *Till Earth and Sky stand presently at God's great Judgment Seat;*
> *But there is neither East nor West, Border, nor Breed, nor Birth,*
> *When two strong men stand face to face, though they come from the ends of the earth!*

The poet points out that it is mutual respect that matters, not border, breed [race] or birth. The character, prowess and integrity of the other are their only criteria for judging and accepting one another. This kind of respect has to be earned, freely given; it cannot be demanded or cajoled. In the end, everything else becomes a technicality the minute you are able to respect the other exactly as you want to be respected; but this comes with a caveat: *self-respect and acceptance of oneself*. This is the challenge before us.

Appendix 7
Qualifiers of Australianness

We no longer refer to ourselves as Irish-Australian, nor as German-, Russian- or Italian-Australian, or assign any European country of origin as a descriptor for qualifying one's Australianness. Yet a qualifier of Australianness is commonly used by many who seek a new life in this sunburnt land: for example, Indian-, Chinese- or African-Australian. This may suggest a commonality of physical features within the geographic entity 'Europe' that is not found elsewhere, which would be misleading given that people from China, Korea, and Japan, for instance, could be similarly grouped. Alternatively, and again misleadingly as reflecting on two world wars would bear out, it may be based on the assumption of European 'cultural' uniformity and East Asian 'cultural' diversity. By the very nature of being first, Australia's First People could claim no need for a qualifier although 'Indigenous' commonly precedes 'Australian' as an identity descriptor. The reference to 'mixed' Australian – the fruits of Cupid's labours – highlights the limitations or narrowness of this terminology or even it being detrimental from the point of view of promoting togetherness. 'Mixed', for instance, can imply an identity crisis as the antithesis of 'pure'. The use of these qualifiers begs the question: What is 'Australian'? One thing is certain: a fixation on 'whiteness' would not be a defining characteristic.

Appendix 8
The Holy Grail of Permanent Residency

It would be little short of exaggeration to claim that many who set foot on our shores seek the holy grail of a Permanent Residence Visa (PR). The key benefit about holding a PR is the right to stay in Australia indefinitely although conditions do apply. The following observations are made with the understanding that Australian migration laws and regulations are complex and very fluid.

In addition to the legal right to remain in Australia indefinitely, permanent residents enjoy a range of rights, such as being able to: work and study in Australia; enrol in Medicare; apply for bank loans to buy property; travel to and from Australia (although restrictions may apply as right of re-entry is not automatic); and apply for Australian citizenship, if eligible.

Unlike Australian citizens, permanent residents generally cannot: hold an Australian passport; vote in Australian Government elections unless enrolled as a British subject before 26 January 1984; access student loans; join the Australian Defence Force; secure ongoing work in the Australian Government; or return to Australia from overseas without a valid travel facility.

A PR may be obtained through various pathways, the most common being: skilled migration; family migration; and business migration. Each involves different types of visas. The primary motivation for seeking permanent residency is generally the virtually unrestricted right to work, as wages and salaries in Australia are significantly higher than in many other countries, particularly in Asia. As I have been told, *It is all about money.*

The process of applying for a PR can be challenging/difficult, time-consuming and overwhelming. It demands considerable patience and sacrifice, an example being the time, effort and expenses that many overseas students invest in the hope of eventually gaining their PR. Many who pursue permanent residency turn to unethical practices, often assisted by compromised lawyers and accountants. Entering into a 'fake' marriage is an example. To do so often involves a payment exceeding one hundred thousand dollars plus accepting several years of servitude.

Money, of course, is merely a means to a 'better life'. Many individuals from poorer countries, such as Filipinos, send remittances to support their families back home. Beyond the chance to earn substantial income, those holding PRs benefit from Australia's relaxed lifestyle, along with the various perks and attractions highlighted in this thesis.

It is important to acknowledge the significant contributions PR holders make to Australia. They play a crucial role in sustaining key sectors like hospitals, aged care and other essential services.

Appendix 9

A New Life

An inkling of the concept of a 'new life' and associated cultural transformation can be gleaned from Charles Dickens' evergreen novel *Great Expectations*, major characters being the convict Magwitch and orphan boy Pip.

Magwitch is transported to New South Wales for life for felony, where he amasses a considerable fortune from sheep farming. With this wealth he attempts to turn Pip, destined to the life of a lowly blacksmith, into an English gentleman, in return for a small favour Pip did for him, when the convict was fleeing the police. However, the reality of life in England so starkly depicted by Dickens indicated this project could never have succeeded; and maybe still cannot.

The tragedy of the tale is three-fold: Firstly, Magwitch could not see this; secondly, he mistakenly bestowed a high value on being an English gentleman; and finally, because of his blind attachment to the English culture, he failed to grasp there was a 'new life' and a 'new culture' in New South Wales, that had given him both wealth and freedom.

Rather than seeking to turn Pip into an English fop, Magwitch should have discarded all his cultural baggage and had Pip join him in Australia, where he could become a new man and lead a new life. This surely is Australia's story with its message that those, who come here with great expectations of a new life, must leave their old one behind.

Readings

Chapter 1

Campbell-Muir Angelique (1998). *Australia files – landmarks.* Heinemann.

Cooper Alastair (1989). *Atlas & Encyclopedia of the sea. The Times.* Harper & Row Publishers, Sydney.

Geddes Margaret Ed. (2001). *Australian Almanac 2001.* Hardie Grant Books.

Gould SJ Consultant Editor; Osborne R, Tarling D General Editors (1996). *The Historical Atlas of the Earth: a visual celebration of earth's physical past.* Henry Holt & Company, New York.

Martin Fred (1998). *Australia.* Heinemann Library.

Mirtschin Peter, Davis Richard (1982). *Dangerous Snakes of Australia. An Illustrated Guide to Australia's Most Venomous Snakes.* Rigby.

Parish Steve (1996). *Discover and Learn about Australia.* Steve Parish Publishing.

Parish Steve, Slater Pat (1997). *Amazing facts about Australia's heritage.* Volume 7. Award-winning series. Steve Parish Publishing.

Poirier John (1999). *Satellites Show World's Highest Mountain is Even Taller.*

White ME (1994). *The greening of Gondwana: The 400 million year story of Australia's plants.* New revised updated Edn. Reed, Chatswood, NSW.

Chapter 2

Berzins Baiba Beata (1988). *The coming of the strangers: life in Australia 1788-1822.* Collins.

Blainey Geoffery (1982). *The Blainey View.* ABC and Macmillan Publishing.

Blainey Geoffery (1994). *A Shorter History of Australia.* William Heinemann, Australia.

Day MF (1969). *The ecology of conservation.* In: *The Last of Lands.* Webb LJ, Whitelock D, Brereton J Le Gay Eds. Jacaranda Press.

Geddes Margaret Ed. (2001). *Australian Almanac 2001.* Hardie Grant Books.

Gilroy Rex (2000). *Pyramids in the Pacific.* URU Publications, PO BOX 202, Katoomba, New South Wales, Australia.

Grimshaw Patricia, Lake Marilyn, McGrath Ann, Quartly Marian (1994). *Creating a Nation.* McPhee Gribble Publishers.

Hill David (2012). *The Great Race: the race between the English and the French to complete the map of Australia.* William Heinemann, Australia.

Macintyre Stuart (2004). *A Concise History of Australia.* 2nd Edn. Cambridge University Press.

Martin Fred (1998). *Australia.* Heinemann Library.

McIntyre KG (1982). *The Secret Discovery of Australia.* Picador, Sydney.

Menzies Gavin (2003). *The Year the Chinese Discovered the World.* William Morrow.

Parish Steve, Slater Pat (1997). *Amazing Facts about Australia's Heritage.* Volume 7. Award-winning series. Steve Parish Publishing.

Perr TM (1982). *The discovery of Australia: the charts and maps of the navigators and explorers.* Nelson Publishing.

Poirier John (1999). *Satellites Show World's Highest Mountain is Even Taller.*

Wright EH, Wright MH Eds (1945). Richards Topical Encyclopedia. Volume 5. *History of Australia.* p. 542 & *The History of India.* p. 377. JA Richards Publishing Co., New York.

Chapter 3

Anon (2014). *Beating the Bigots.* In: *Insight, The Courier Mail,* Saturday 15 March 2014.

Australian English and Culture with the Lonely Planet Australian Phrasebook.

Berzins Baiba Beata (1988). *The coming of the strangers: life in Australia 1788-1822.* Collins Australia/State Library of New South Wales.

Blainey Geoffery (1982). *The Blainey View.* ABC and Macmillan Publishers.

Blainey Geoffery (1994). *A Shorter History of Australia.* William Heinemann Publishers.

Cole Tom (1988). *Hell West and Crooked.* Angus and Robertson.

Elder Bruce (1998). *Blood on the Wattle: Massacres and Maltreatment of Aboriginal Australians since 1788.* Revised Edn. New Holland Publishers.

Ellis Jean (1995). *From the Dreaming.* Harper Collins Publishing.

Ellis Jean (1995). *This is the Dreaming.* Harper Collins Publishing.

Gammage Bill (2011). *The Biggest Estate on Earth: How Aborigines Made Australia.* Allen & Unwin.

Geddes Margaret Ed. (2001). *Australian Almanac 2001.* Hardie Grant Books.

Glendinnen Inga (2005). In: *Dancing with Strangers: Europeans and Australians at first contact.* Cambridge University Press.

Grantler Kieza (2012). *Pilot only wanted for war.* The Courier Mail, 23-24 September 2012. p. 58.

Grimshaw Patricia, Lake Marilyn, McGrath Ann, Quartly Marian (1994). *Creating a Nation.* McPhee Gribble Publishers.

Huntsman Leone (2003). *Sand in our Souls. The Comfort Zone*, Radio National, 1 April 2003.

Isaacs Jennifer (1980). *Australian Dreaming: 40,000 years of Aboriginal history.*

Johnson Susan (2013). *Black Russian.* QWeekend, The Courier Mail, 23-24 February 2013.

Macintyre Stuart (2004). *A Concise History of Australia.* Cambridge University Press.

Miranda Charles (2022). *Guardians of the north.* QWeekend, 2-3 July 2022.

Oodgeroo Nunukul (1991). *The Beginning of Life, Stradbroke Dreamtime.* Angus & Robertson, Sydney.

Parish Steve (1996). *Discover and Learn about Australia.* Steve Parish Publishing.

Parish Steve, Slater Pat (1997). *Amazing Facts about Australia's Heritage.* Volume 7. Award-winning series. Steve Parish Publishing.

Pixley Norman (1950). *An outline of the history of the Queensland police force 1860–1949.* Journal of the Royal Historical Society of Queensland 4(3):340-360.

Reynolds Henry (1996). *Aboriginal Sovereignty.* Allen & Unwin.

Reynolds Henry (2000). *Why weren't we told?* Penguin Books.

Reynolds Henry (2018). *Whispering in our hearts revisited.* New South Publishing.

Richards Johnathon (2005). *A question of necessity: The Native Police in Queensland.* PhD Thesis. Griffith University, Queensland.

Sutton Peter, Walshe Keryn (2021). *Farmers or Hunter-gatherers? The Dark Emu Debate.* Melbourne University Press.

Chapter 4

Berzins Baiba Beata (1988). *The coming of the strangers: life in Australia 1788-1822.* Collins Australia/State Library of New South Wales.

Blainey Geoffery (1994). *A Shorter History of Australia.* William Heinemann.

Clark Manning (1993). *A History of Australia.* Melbourne University Press.

Clarke Peter (2001). *The Essential Guide to Norfolk Island.* Updated edition. Shearwater Press.

Cosgrove Betty (1994). *Peter Fitzallan MacDonald: a life apart.* A dissertation submitted to the History Department, Faculty of Arts, University of Central Queensland for Degree of Master of Arts.

Evans Raymond (2003). *Misery at Moreton Bay. Bite the Blue Sky. Brisbane Beginnings.* Museum of Brisbane.

Grimshaw Patricia, Lake Marilyn, McGrath Ann, Quartly Marian (1994). *Creating a Nation.* McPhee Gribble Publishers.

Hughes Robert (1987). *The Fatal Shore.* Kopf, New York.

Keneally Thomas (2005). *The Commonwealth of Thieves.* Random House.

Macintyre Stuart (2004). *A Concise History of Australia.* 2nd Edn. Cambridge University Press.

Parish Steve (1996). *Discover and Learn about Australia.* Steve Parish Publishing.

Parish Steve, Slater Pat (1997). *Amazing facts about Australia's heritage.* Volume 7. Award-winning series. Steve Parish Publishing.

Vale Michelle (1994). *Warby: My Excellent Guide.* Compiled and published by Michelle Vale. ISBN 0646 223569

Chapter 5

Berzins Baiba Beata (1988). *The coming of the strangers: life in Australia 1788-1822.* Collins Australia/State Library of New South Wales.

Blainey Geoffery (1994). *A shorter history of Australia.* William Heinemann.

Cosgrove Betty (1994). *Peter Fitzallan MacDonald: a life apart.* A dissertation submitted to the History Department, Faculty of Arts, University of Central Queensland for Degree of Master of Arts.

Cunningham P (1828). *Two Years in New South Wales.* 3rd Edn. Volume 2. p. 46-52. Henry Colburn, London.

Keneally Thomas (2005). *The Commonwealth of Thieves.* Random House.

Moore Bruce (2008). *Speaking our Language. The Story of Australian English.* Oxford University Press.

Moore Greg de (2008). *Tom Wills. His spectacular rise and fall.* Allen & Unwin. UQFL204

Ward Russell, Robertson John (1969). *Such Was Life: Select Documents in Australian Social History 1788-1850.* Ure Smith.

Wilkes GA (1986). *Exploring Australian English.* ABC Enterprises.

Chapter 6

Blackwell Doris, Lockwood Douglas (1965). *Alice on the Line.* Rigby.

Cosgrove Betty (1994). *Peter Fitzallan MacDonald: a life apart.* A dissertation submitted to the History Department, Faculty of Arts, University of Central Queensland for Degree of Master of Arts.

Macintyre Stuart (2004). *A Concise History of Australia.* Cambridge University Press.

Parish Steve (1996). *Discover and Learn about Australia.* Steve Parish Publishing.

Parish Steve, Slater Pat (1997). *Amazing Facts about Australia's Heritage.* Volume 7. Award-winning series. Steve Parish Publishing.

Vale Michelle (1994). *Warby: my excellent guide.* Compiled and published by Michelle Vale. ISBN 0646 223569

Chapter 7

Berzins Baiba Beata (1988). *The coming of the strangers: life in Australia 1788-1822.* Collins Australia/State Library of New South Wales.

Cathcart Michael (2009). *The Water Dreamers. The remarkable history of our dry continent.* Text Publishing.

Macintyre Stuart (2004). *A Concise History of Australia.* Cambridge University Press.

Moore Bruce (2008). *Speaking our Language. The Story of Australian English.* Oxford University Press.

Parish Steve (1996). *Discover and Learn about Australia.* Steve Parish Publishing.

Parish Steve, Slater Pat (1997). *Amazing Facts about Australia's Heritage.* Volume 7. Award-winning series. Steve Parish Publishing.

Tracey JG, Webb LJ, Williams WT. *The Australian Flora.* In: *Last of Lands.*

Chapter 8

Blainey Geoffery (1994). *A Shorter History of Australia.* William Heinemann.

Clarke Frank G (2002). *History of Australia. The Greenwood Histories of the Modern Nations.* Greenwood Publishing Group.

Cosgrove Betty (1994). *Peter Fitzallan MacDonald: a life apart.* A dissertation submitted to the History Department, Faculty of Arts, University of Central Queensland for Degree of Master of Arts.

FitzSimons Peter (2012). *Eureka: the unfinished revolution.* William Heinemann, Australia.

Hill David (2010). *Gold: The Fever that Forever Changed Australia.* Random House Publishing.

Hodges Eleanor (1992). *The Bushman Legend. Intruders in the Bush: The Australian Quest for Identity.* John Carroll Ed. Oxford University Press, Melbourne.

Molony John (2004). *Eureka and the Prerogative of the People.* Papers on Parliament No. 42.

Moore Bruce (2000). *Gold! Gold! Gold!: a dictionary of the nineteenth-century Australian gold rushes.* Oxford University Press.

Moore Bruce (2008). *Speaking our Language. The Story of Australian English.* Oxford University Press.

Parish Steve, Slater Pat (1997). *Amazing facts about Australia's heritage.* Volume 7. Award-winning Series. Steve Parish Publishing.

The Rockhampton Morning Bulletin (1917). Alexander MacDonald obituary. 21 June 1917.

Chapter 9

Adam-Smith Patsy (1981). *Outback Heroes.* Lansdowne Press, Sydney. p. 102.

Boxall GE (1908). *History of the Australian Bushrangers.* 3rd Edn.

Brown Max (1956). *Australian Son: a Life of Ned Kelly.* Georgian House.

Clark Manning (1978). *A History of Australia.* IV. *The earth abideth forever, 1851-1888.* Chap. 13. *Uproar in the bush.* Melbourne University Press.

Education Australia (2003). *Early Australia and Australia's First Century – 50,000bp–1869*. Moondrake Harcourt. Woollahra Sales and Imports.

Hughes Robert (2003). *The Fatal Shore: Bolters and Bushrangers*. Vintage.

McArthur George (2011). *Shrine for Kelly*. The Courier Mail, 2 September 2011, page 7.

Melville Robert (1964). *Ned Kelly. 27 paintings by Sidney Nolan*. Thames and Hudson, London.

Ronan Tom (1982). *Moleskin Midas*. Reprint, Curry O'Neil.

Chapter 10

Berzins Baiba Beata (1988). *The coming of the strangers: life in Australia 1788-1822.* Collins Australia/State Library of New South Wales.

Wright EH, Wright MH Eds (1945). Richards Topical Encyclopedia. Volume 5. *History of Australia*. p. 542 & *The History of India*. p. 377. JA Richards Publishing Co., NY.

Chapter 11

Barwick John, Barwick Jennifer (2004). *Settlement and Exploration, 2004*. Australian Library Series. William Heinemann Publishing.

Blainey Geoffery (1994). *A Shorter History of Australia*. William Heinemann Publishing.

Cosgrove Betty. (1994). *Peter Fitzallan MacDonald: a life apart*. A dissertation submitted to the History Department, Faculty of Arts, University of Central Queensland for Degree of Master of Arts.

Education Australia (2003). *Early Australia and Australia's First Century – 50,000bp–1869*. Moondrake Harcourt. Woollahra Sales and Imports.

Kuhnen Frithjof (1982). *Man and Land: An introduction into the problems of agrarian structure and agrarian reform*. Breitenbach Publishing.

Macintyre Stuart (2004). *A Concise History of Australia*. 2nd Edn. Cambridge University Press.

Parish Steve (1996). *Discover and Learn about Australia*. Steve Parish Publishing.

Parish Steve, Slater Pat (1997). *Amazing facts about Australia's heritage*. Volume 7. Award-winning series. Steve Parish Publishing.

Pascoe Bruce (2018). *Dark Emu: Aboriginal Australia and the Birth of Agriculture*. Magabala Books.

Zachariah Richard (2017). *The Vanished Land: Disappearing dynasties of Victoria's Western District*. Wakefield Press.

Chapters 12 - 14

Atkinson Sally-Anne (2019). *Arise, Sir Brisbane*. In: *Insight*. p. 41, 44, 45. The Courier Mail, 19 January 2019.

Australia through Time (1883). *Australia Irish animosity erupts*. Random House Australia, 2005 Edn.

Blainey Geoffery (1994). *A Shorter History of Australia*. William Heinemann.

Clark Manning (1979). *A history of Australia*. Volume 3: *The Beginning of Australian Civilization*. Chapter 10. *A place for a belly full but not a full-blown civilisation*.

Cosgrove Betty. (1994). *Peter Fitzallan MacDonald: a life apart*. A dissertation submitted to the History Department, Faculty of Arts, University of Central Queensland for Degree of Master of Arts.

Coupe Sheena, Coupe Robert, Andrews May (1994). *Their ghost may be heard: Australia to1900*. 2nd Edn. Longman Cheshire, Melbourne.

Diamond Jarrod (1998). *Guns, germs and steel*. WW Norton & Co.

Esposto Alexis (2019). ABC RN *Saturday Extra,* 7 September 2019.

Fitzpatrick Brian (1965). *Labour History.* No. 9 (November 1965). In: *Indentured labour in Australia.* p. 3-5. Liverpool University Press.

Grimshaw Patricia, Lake Marilyn, McGrath Ann, Quartly Marian (1994). *Creating a Nation.* McPhee Gribble Publishers.

Hirst John (2007). *The Australians, Insiders and Outsiders on the National Character since 1770.* Black Inc.

Hirst John (2010). *Looking for Australia. Historical essays. A nation of immigrants.* Black Inc. p. 201-206.

Hurmuz Hatice, Basarin Vecihi (1993). *The Turks in Australia: celebrating 25 years in Australia.* Turquoise Publications.

Jackson RV (1977). *Australian economic development in the nineteenth century.* ANU Press.

MacDougall AK (2008). *The illustrated history of Australia.* Five Mile Press.

Macintyre Stuart (1999). *A concise history of Australia.* Cambridge University Press.

Nicholas Stephen Ed. (1988). *Convict workers: re-interpreting Australia's past.* School of Economics UNSW. Cambridge University Press.

Smith Babette (2008). *Australia's birth stain; the startling legacy of the convict era.* Allen & Unwin.

Chapter 15 - 16

Andersen Reg (2005). *Spirit of ANZAC. Headstart, The Courier Mail,* 19 April 2005.

Article – School Speech. *Morning Bulletin,* Rockhampton, 12 December 1912.

Article – Trooper L. Lyons. *Morning Bulletin,* Rockhampton, 16 August 1915.

Article – Death of Peter Stuart. *Morning Bulletin,* Rockhampton, 21 September 1916.

Article – An officer's letter. *Morning Bulletin,* Rockhampton, 30 November 1916.

Australian Imperial Force Base Records Office, Victoria Barracks, Melbourne. Letter to Dr S. Stuart. 2 October 1919.

Blainey Geoffery (1994). *A Shorter History of Australia.* William Heinemann.

Cranston F (1983). *Always Faithful: a history of the 49th Australian Infantry Battalion, 1916-1982.* Boolarong Publications, Brisbane.

Duffy Michael (2003). *How one Australian refined the art of war. Note Book, The Courier Mail,* 8 July 2003.

Freudenberg Graham (2006). *ANZAC story still evolving. Perspectives, The Courier Mail,* 26 April 2006.

Gallipoli. *Headstart 2, The Courier Mail,* 16 April 2002.

Geddes Margaret Ed. (2001). *Australian Almanac 2001.* Hardie Grant Books.

Harvey Norman K (1941). *From ANZAC to the Hindenburg Line: the history of the 9th Battalion, A.I.F.* 9th Battalion, A.I.F. Association, Brisbane.

Stuart Gerald EM (1919). *3rd Australian Light Horse Field Ambulance – From formation to March 1919.* Series Number: AWM224, Control Symbol: MSS274. Transcribed by: Geoff Lewis, Revision: 1.0, Date: 5/1/2004. Copyright: Lieutenant Colonel Gerald E.M. Stuart.

Wrench CM (1985). *Campaigning with the fighting 9th (in and out of the line with the 9th A.I.F.) 1914-1919.* Boolarong Publications, Brisbane.

Chapters 17 - 19

Butler AG (1930). *Official History of the Australian Army Medical Service 1914-1918.* Volume 1. *Gallipoli, Sinai and Palestine*. New Guinea, Australian War Memorial.

Hamilton Jill (2002). *First to Damascus: The Story of the Australian Light Horse and Lawrence of Arabia.* Kangaroo Press.

Hamilton Patrick (1996). *Riders of Destiny: The 4th Australian Light Horse Field Ambulance, 1917-1918: An Autobiography and History.*

Stuart Gerald EM (1919). *3rd Australian Light Horse Field Ambulance – From formation to March 1919.* Series Number: AWM224, Control Symbol: MSS274. Transcribed by: Geoff Lewis, Revision: 1.0, Date: 5/1/2004. Copyright: Lieutenant Colonel Gerald E.M. Stuart.

Chapter 20

Laffin John (1993). *We're on a Great Enterprise. Our Finest Hour. Australia on the Western Front 1916-1918.* The Australian Magazine, Special 75th Anniversary Edition, 7-8 August 1993.

McMullin Ross (2008). *Remembering Fromelles.* ABC Radio National, *Perspectives*, 24 April 2008.

Pinkney Matthew (1998). *Foreign Fields. Features*, The Courier Mail, 24 April 1998.

Chapter 21

Charlton Peter (2002). *Mourning Glory.* The Courier Mail, 18 May 2002.

Cranston F (Frederick) (1983). *Always Faithful: a history of the 49th Australian Infantry Battalion, 1916-1982.* Boolarong Publications, Brisbane.

Daley Paul (2009). *Beersheba: A Journey Through Australia's Forgotten War.* Melbourne University Press.

Fewster Kevin Ed. (2006). *Bean's Gallipoli: The Diaries of Australia's Official War Correspondent.* 3rd Edn.

Gibbs Philip (2005). *Now it can be told.* Kessinger Publishing.

Jill, Duchess of Hamilton (2002). *First to Damascus. The story of the Australian Light Horse and Lawrence of Arabia.* Kangaroo Press.

Kitching Kimberley (2020). *These great Australians deserve our respect.* The Courier Mail, 19 June 2020.

Laffin John (1993). *We're on a Great Enterprise. Our Finest Hour. Australia on the Western Front 1916-1918.* The Australian Magazine, Special 75th Anniversary Edition, 7-8 August 1993.

Chapter 22

Dornan Peter (2006). *The Last Man Standing – Herb Ashley and the Battle of El Alamein.* Allen & Unwin.

FitzSimons Peter (2006). *Tobruk.* Harper Collins.

Geddes Margaret Ed. (2001). *Australian Almanac 2001.* Hardie Grant Books.

Parish Steve, Slater Pat (1997). *Amazing Facts about Australia's Heritage.* Award-winning series. Steve Parish Publishing.

Chapter 23

Dornan Peter (2006). *The Last Man Standing – Herb Ashley and the Battle of El Alamein.* Allen & Unwin.

FitzSimons Peter (2006). *Tobruk.* Harper Collins.

Chapter 24

Beaumont Joan Ed. (1996). *Australia's War 1939-45*. Allen & Unwin.

Dean Penrod (1998). *Singapore Samurai*. Kangaroo Press.

Uhr Janet (1998). *Against the Sun – The AIF in Malaya, 1941-42*. Allen & Unwin.

Uren Tom (1998). *Hellfire Revisited. Features, The Courier Mail*, 24 April 1998.

Chapter 25

Beaumont Joan Ed. (1996). *Australia's War 1939-45*. Allen & Unwin.

FitzSimons Peter (2004). *Kokoda.* Hodder.

Ham Paul (2004). *Kokoda.* Harper Collins.

Schnell S, Gibbons S (2008). *Beyond Kokoda*. The History Channel.

Sublet Frank (2000). *Kokoda to the Sea.* Slouch Hat Publications.

Chapter 26

Catanzaro Francis B (2002). *With the 41st Division in the Southwest Pacific: A Foot Soldier's Story.* Indiana University Press.

McCartney William F (2007). *The Jungleers: a History of the 41st Infantry Division.* Kessinger Publishing.

Chapter 27

Andersen Reg (2005). *Spirit of ANZAC. Headstart, The Courier Mail*, 19 April 2005.

Blainey Geoffery (1994). *A Shorter History of Australia.* William Heinemann.

Cameron David W (2007). *25 April 1915: The Day the ANZAC Legend was Born*. Allen & Unwin.

Freudenberg Graham (2006). *The Courier Mail*, April 2006.

Chapter 28

Adams Nancy (1961). *Saxon sheep.* Cheshire, Melbourne.

Arthur Bowes Journal. *The women come ashore.* firstfleet.uow.edu.au/stories.html

Berzins Baiba Beata (1988). *The coming of the strangers: life in Australia 1788-1822.* Collins Australia/State Library of New South Wales.

Bird Delys. *Born for the Bush: An Australian Women's Frontier.*

Blainey Geoffery (1994). *A Shorter History of Australia.* William Heinemann.

Clark Manning (1979). *A history of Australia.* Volume 3: *The Beginning of Australian Civilization*. Chapter 10. *A place for a belly full but not a full-blown civilisation*.

Conway Jill Kerr (1989). *The Road from Coorain.* Vintage Books.

Cosgrove Betty (1994). *Peter Fitzallan MacDonald: a life apart*. A dissertation submitted to the History Department, Faculty of Arts, University of Central Queensland for Degree of Master of Arts.

Coupe Sheena Ed. (1989). *Frontier Country – Australia's outback heritage*. Volume 1. Weldon Russell Publishing.

Durack Mary (1997). *Kings in Grass Castles.* Bantam Books, Sydney.

Grimshaw Patricia, Lake Marilyn, McGrath Ann, Quartly Marian (1994). *Creating a Nation.* McPhee Gribble Publishers.

Hill Ernistine (1945). *The great Australian loneliness.* Robertson and Mullins, Melbourne.

Isaacs Jennifer (1998). *Pioneer women of the bush and outback*. Lansdowne Press.

Oxley Deborah (1996). *Convict maids – the forced migration of women to Australia.* Cambridge University Press.

Shepherd Barrie (2006). *Early settlers: life in a harsh land.* In: *Australia changing times.* Echidna Books.

Storey Robyn (2005). *Valley Belles: gutsy girls and feisty females.* University Publishing Unit, Central Queensland University.

Vale Michelle (1994). *Warby: My Excellent Guide*. Compiled and published by Michelle Vale. ISBN 0646 223569

Veitch Alan (2006). *A century of one-piece swimsuits. The Courier Mail*, 24 August 2006.

Chapter 29

Adam-Smith Patsy (1981). *Outback Heroes.* Lansdown Press, Sydney.

Australian Afghan Cameleer History. https://www.camltreksaustralia.com.au/camel-history

Blainey Geoffery (1967). *The Tyranny of Distance: How distance shaped Australia's history.* Pan Macmillan Australia.

Blainey Geoffery (1994). A *Shorter History of Australia.* William Heinemann.

Cathcart Michael (2009). *The Water Dreamers. The remarkable history of our dry continent.* Text Publishing.

Cooper Bob (2012). *Outback Survival.* Hachette Australia.

Coupe Sheena (1989). *Frontier Country: Australia's Outback Heritage.* Weldon Russell, Willoughby, New South Wales.

Chapters 30 - 36

Armstrong Patrick (2009). *Charles Darwin in Australia. Journal of the Royal Society of Western Australia* 92:385–388.

Avins Jenni (2015). *The Dos and Don'ts of Cultural Appropriation. Borrowing from other cultures isn't just inevitable; it's potentially positive.* Jenni Avins, 21 October 2015.

Bradford Vivian (2010). *Public forgetting: the rhetoric and politics of beginning again.* Pennsylvania State University Press.

Clark Kenneth (1969). *Civilisation.* British Broadcasting Corporation.

Clark Manning (1962). *A History of Australia 1. From the earliest times to the age of Macquarie.* Melbourne University Press.

Country Life (13 November 2013). HRH Prince of Wales guest editor.

Davis Megan, Williams George (2021). *Everything You Need to Know About the Uluru Statement from the Heart.* University of New South Wales.

Flannery Tim (2002). Australia Day address. https://www.australiaday.com.au/events/australia-day-address/dr-tim-flannery/

Gammage Bill (2012). *The biggest estate on earth.* Allen & Unwin.

Goodman Robert B, Johnson George (1966). *The Australians.* Rigby, Adelaide.

Hesketh Rollo (2013). *A.A. Phillips and the 'Cultural Cringe': Creating an 'Australian Tradition'. Meanjin Quarterly*, Volume 72, Number 3, 2013.

Hirst John (2000). *The sentimental nation: the making of the Australian Commonwealth.* Oxford University Press.

Hirst John (2008). *Freedom on the fatal shore. Australia's first colony.* Black Inc.

Hirst John (2009). *Sense and nonsense in Australian history.* Black Inc.

Hirst John (2009). *Looking for Australia: historical essays.* Black Inc.

Hirst John (2010). *The Australians: insiders and outsiders on the national character since 1770*. Black Inc.

Horne Donald (1964). *The Lucky Country*. Penguin Books.

Johnson Susan (2017). *Where apples fall. QWeekend, The Courier Mail*, 21-22 October 2017.

Kipling Rudyard. *Poems Summary and Analysis of "The Ballad of East and West".*

https://www.gradesaver.com/rudyard-kipling-poems/study-guide/summary-the-ballad-of-east-and-west

Larkins John, Howard Bruce (1981). *The young Australians: Australian children since 1788*. Rigby.

Lentin Alana (2020). *Why race matters.* Wiley.

Li Jason Yat-sen (2021). *The five personalities of China. Conversations with Richard Fidler.* ABC Regional News.

Maddison Sarah (5 April 2019). *The Conversation. It's time for indigenous nationhood to replace a failing colonial authority.*

Marshall Paul (2018). *Kipling's "The Ballad of East and West" is Hardly Racist.*

https://providencemag.com/2018/08/rudyard-kipling-ballad-east-west-hardly-racist/

https://en.wikipedia.org/wiki/The_Ballad_of_East_and_West

Morrow James (2021). *Indigenous history 'romanticised'. The Courier Mail*, 4 May 2021.

Neiman Susan, Director, Einstein Forum in conversation with interviewer and moderator, Michaela Kalowski. ABC Regional News Conversations.

Palipana Dinesh (2022). *Stronger.* Pan Macmillan, Australia.

Peanut Butter, Jelly & Racism (2016). *New York Times* series Who Me, Biased?

Portrait of Leichhardt (1945). *The Bulletin*, Volume 66, No. 3399, 4 April 1945 (Trove).

Reynolds Henry (1996). *Aboriginal Sovereignty*. Allen & Unwin.

Reynolds Henry (2000). *Why weren't we told?* Penguin Books.

Reynolds Henry (2018). *Whispering in our hearts revisited*. New South Publishing.

Steinberg David I (2019). *Misunderstood and misquoted, Kipling bridges East-West divide.*

https://asia.nikkei.com/Editor-s-Picks/Tea-Leaves/Misunderstood-and-misquoted-Kipling-bridges-East-West-divide

Sussex Roly (2019). *Language that's made in China. Qweekend*, P25, *The Courier Mail*, 2-3 February 2019.

Sutton Peter, Walshe Keryn (2021). *Farmers or Hunter-gatherers? The Dark Emu Debate*. Melbourne University Press.

The Leichhardt diaries: Early travels in Australia during 1842–1844 (2013). *Memoirs of the Queensland Museum: Culture*, Volume 7, Part 1.

ter Kuile Casper (2021). *How everyday practices build joyful belonging.* ABC Radio National, 31 January 2021.

Widdicome Lizzie (21 October 2019). *The New Yorker, Cultural Comment. What can we learn from Germans about confronting our history?*

Appendix 2

Bok Hilary (2018). *Baron de Montesquieu, Charles-Louis de Secondat*. The Stanford Encyclopedia of Philosophy. Winter 2018 Edition. Zalta Edward N. Ed. [https://plato.stanford.edu/archives/win2018/entries/montesquieu/]

Charles de Secondat, Baron de Montesquieu (1748). *The Spirit of Laws*. Translated by Thomas Nugent 1752. Batoche Books. Kitchener 2001. McMaster University. [https://historyofeconomicthought.mcmaster.ca/montesquieu/spiritoflaws.pdf]

Cobby JA and Abraham Henry J (1958). *Elements of Democratic Government*. 3rd Revised and enlarged Edition. Oxford University Press, New York.

Rutledge David (2020). *Montesquieu and Despotism. ABC RN, The Philosopher's Zone*, Sunday 12 July 2020. [https://www.abc.net.au/radionational/programs/philosopherszone/montesquieu-and-despotism/12438306]

Appendix 4

Clark Manning (1999). *History of Australia.* Volumes 1 & 2. *From the Earliest Times to 1838.* Melbourne University Press.

Appendix 5

Clark Kenneth (1969). *Civilisation – A Personal View*. BBC and John Murray.

Clark Manning (1962). *A History of Australia*. Volume 1. *From the earliest times to the age of Macquarie*. Melbourne University Press.

Kasper Wolfgang (2019). *Does western civilisation have a future?* C.I.S. Policy Paper No. 17. February 2019.

Appendix 6

Australian Broadcasting Corporation (2021-22). *The school that tried to end racism*. Episodes 1, 2, 3.

Moses Yolanda (2017). *Why Do We Keep Using the Word "Caucasian"?* SAPIENS – *Anthropology Magazine*.

Wyatt Caroline (2020). *The Science Behind Racism: A Psychological Approach.* The Oxford Scientist.

Appendix 8

Comprehensive information about Permanent Resident Visas may be sourced at the Australian Federal Government website: https://immi.homeaffairs.gov.au/visas/permanent-resident/visa-options.

Image and Illustration Credits

Page	Title	Source / Credit
2	Gondwana	Diaz Professor J E (2014). Continental Drift Plate Theory. [https://issuu.com/javierernestodiazmontilla/docs/teor__a_de_placas__deriva_continent]. Accessed March 2024.
3	Pangea	Daigle S (2022). *Puzzle Me Pangaea and the Seven Continents.* [https://www.blurb.com/b/11230667-puzzle-me-pangaea-and-the-seven-continents]
3	Laurasia-Gondwana 200 million years ago	Kudling L (2008). Wikimedia Commons. [https://en.wikipedia.org/wiki/Tethys_Ocean]. Licensed under Creative Commons Attribution 3.0 Unported. [https://creativecommons.org/licenses/by/3.0/deed.en]
3	Gondwana splits	Australian Antarctic Division. [https://www.antarctica.gov.au]
4	Elevation	Bureau of Meteorology, Australian Government Directory. Licensed under Creative Commons CC-BY-3.0-AU-Deed. [https://creativecommons.org/licenses/by/3.0/au/deed.en]
4	Uluru	Photo by Antoine Fabre (2019) on Unsplash.
4	Wolfe Creek crater	Tourism WA.
5	Wilpena Pound	Vaughton J. Words on Wheels. [https://wordsonwheels.com.au/shop/3-day-2-nights-flinders-ranges-adventure-tour/]
5	Twelve Apostles	Photo by Trevor Kay (2020) on Unsplash.
5	The Three Sisters	Jürgensen S (2010). Flickr. [https://www.flickr.com/photos/94039982@N00/4941503332]. Licensed under CC BY-NC-ND 2.0 DEED. [https://creativecommons.org/licenses/by-nc-nd/2.0/]
6	Iron ore – haematite	Learning Geology (2015). [http://geologylearn.blogspot.com/2015/03/iron-ore.html]
6	Australian bauxite, Weipa	The Australian Aluminium Council. [https://aluminium.org.au/australian-industry/australian-bauxite/]. Accessed April 2024
6	Newland Coal Mine dragline	McGrath C. Environmental Law Australia. [http://envlaw.com.au/newlands-coal-mine-case/]. Image source Leighton Holdings.
6	Welcome Stranger nugget replica at Rural Transaction Center	Dunolly Museum, Victoria, Australia. [https://dunollymuseumsite.wordpress.com/welcome-stranger-nugget/]
6	Opals	Brisbane Opal Museum. [https://www.brisbaneopalmuseum.com.au]
6	Australian pink diamonds, sourced from Argyle mine	*Jewellery World Magazine.* [https://jewelleryworld.net.au/news/local-news/sydney-start-up-launches-australian-diamond-project-on-the-international-stage/]

Image and Illustration Credits

Page	Title	Source / Credit
7	Average annual rainfall (1961 to 1990)	Bureau of Meteorology, Australian Government Directory. Licensed under Creative Commons CC-BY-3.0-AU-Deed. [https://creativecommons.org/licenses/by/3.0/au/deed.en]
7	Average annual maximum temperature (1961 to 1990)	Bureau of Meteorology, Australian Government Directory. Licensed under Creative Commons CC-BY-3.0-AU-Deed. [https://creativecommons.org/licenses/by/3.0/au/deed.en]
8	Deserts	Bureau of Meteorology, Australian Government Directory. Licensed under Creative Commons CC-BY-3.0-AU-Deed. [https://creativecommons.org/licenses/by/3.0/au/deed.en]
8	Climate zones (arid and semi-arid)	Bureau of Meteorology, Australian Government Directory. Licensed under Creative Commons CC-BY-3.0-AU-Deed. [https://creativecommons.org/licenses/by/3.0/au/deed.en]
8	Climate variability (1900 to 1996)	Bureau of Meteorology, Australian Government Directory. Licensed under Creative Commons CC-BY-3.0-AU-Deed. [https://creativecommons.org/licenses/by/3.0/au/deed.en]
8	National, state and territory population, June 2023	Australian Bureau of Statistics. [https://www.abs.gov.au/statistics/people/population/national-state-and-territory-population/latest-release]. Accessed March 2024. Licensed under CC BY 4.0 licence. [https://creativecommons.org/licenses/by/4.0/]
9	Coopers Creek in flood	Source unknown.
9	Murray-Darling Basin	Crawford J (20-07-2021). *How capitalism is killing the Murray-Darling Basin*. [https://redflag.org.au/article/how-capitalism-killing-murray-darling-basin]. Accessed April 2024. Licensed under CC BY 4.0 licence. [https://creativecommons.org/licenses/by-nc-nd/4.0/]
9	Snowy River Scheme – *Snowy! Power of a Nation*	Powerhouse Museum (SMA 1993: 8). [http://archive.maas.museum/hsc/snowy/civil.html]. Accessed March 2024.
10	Dingo (*Canis lupus*)	Photo by David Clode (2019) on Unsplash.
10	Kangaroo (*Macropus* spp.)	Photo by James Wainscoat (2024) on Unsplash.
11	Koala (*Phascolarctos cinereus*)	Photo by Di Weng (2024) on Unsplash.
11	Wombat (*Vombatidae*)	Photo by Betty Chen (2022) on Unsplash.
11	Marsupial lion (*Thylacoleo carnifex*)	Schouten P. University of New South Wales, Sydney. [https://www.unsw.edu.au/newsroom/news/2018/10/climate-change-the-likely-killer-of-australian-marsupial-lion]. Accessed March 2024.
11	*Diprotodon optatum*	Musser Anne (23-08-2021). Australian Museum. [https://australian.museum/learn/australia-over-time/extinct-animals/diprotodon-optatum/]. Accessed March 2024.
11	Platypus (*Ornithorhynchus anatinus*)	Photo by Ronald Bradford (2022) on Unsplash.
11	Giant kangaroo (*Procoptodon goliah*)	Musser Anne (04-12-2018). Australian Museum. [https://australian.museum/learn/australia-over-time/extinct-animals/procoptodon-goliah/]. Accessed March 2024.
12	Carpet snake (*Morelia spilota*), Australia Zoo.	Yang Shuai (Nixie) (2009).

Page	Title	Source / Credit
12	Kookaburra (*Dacelo* spp.)	Illustration by Gould J (1804-1881). National Library of Australia (2012). *Little Book of Birds*, National Library of Australia. [https://collinsbooksballaratonlydiard.com.au/p/animals-little-book-of-birds--3]
12	Emu (*Dromaius novaehollandiae*)	Photo by Christian Bass (2021) on Unsplash.
12	Coastal taipan (*Oxyuranus scutellatus*)	Photo by David Clode (2021) on Unsplash.
13	Redback spider (*Latrodectus hasselti*)	Firus P (2004). Wikimedia Commons. [https://commons.wikimedia.org/wiki/File:Redback_frontal_view.jpg]. Licensed under Creative Commons Attribution 3.0 Unported. [https://creativecommons.org/licenses/by/3.0/deed.en]
13	Witchetty grub (*Endoxyla leucomochla*), Alice Springs, Central Australia	Barritt Michael J (02-06-2010). Flickr. [https://www.flickr.com/photos/centralaustralia/4681959010/sizes/n/]
13	Cathedral termite mound, 2.5 m, Litchfield National Park, NT	Whalan Geoff (2022). Flickr. [https://www.flickr.com/photos/geoffwhalan/51849512464]. Licensed under CC BY-NC-ND 2.0 DEED. [https://creativecommons.org/licenses/by-nc-nd/2.0/]
13	Magnetic termite mounds, Litchfield National Park, NT	Australian 4 Wheel Drive Rentals. [http://www.darwintoalicesprings.com/Litchfield-national-park.htm]. Accessed March 2024.
14	Golden wattle (*Acacia pycnantha*)	Australian National Botanic Gardens and Centre for Australian National Biodiversity Research (2015). Accessed April 2024. [https://www.anbg.gov.au/acacia/species/A-pycnantha.html] An Australian Government Initiative.
14	Double trunk boab tree (*Adansonia gregorii*)	Bradtke B. Outback Australia Travel Secrets. [https://www.outback-australia-travel-secrets.com/boab.html]. Accessed April 2024.
14	Manna gum (*Eucalyptus viminalis*)	Couch Alan (2012). Flickr. [https://www.flickr.com/photos/couchy/7059602063]. Licensed under CC BY 2.0 DEED Attribution 2.0 Generic. [https://creativecommons.org/licenses/by/2.0/]
14	Waratah (*Telopea speciosissima*)	Australian National Botanic Gardens and Centre for Australian National Biodiversity Research (2015). Accessed April 2024. [https://www.anbg.gov.au/emblems/nsw.emblem.html]. An Australian Government Initiative.
14	Golden wattle flower (*Acacia pycnantha*)	Australian National Botanic Gardens and Centre for Australian National Biodiversity Research (2015). Accessed April 2024. [https://www.anbg.gov.au/acacia/species/A-pycnantha.html] An Australian Government Initiative.
17	World map from Ptolemy, Geographia	James Ford Bell Library, University of Minnesota, edited by Sebastian Münster. Basel:P Heinricum Petrum, 1545. [https://apps.lib.umn.edu/bell/map/PTO/TOUR/1540s.html] [http://bell.lib.umn.edu/index.html]
17	Map of the world showing the name *Terra Australis*	Fine Oronce (1531). Wikimedia Commons. [https://commons.wikimedia.org/wiki/File:World_map_from_1532.jpg]. Licensed under CC BY 2.0 DEED Attribution 2.0 Generic. [https://creativecommons.org/licenses/by/2.0/]

Image and Illustration Credits

Page	Title	Source / Credit
18	The Brouwer Route was discovered by Dutch explorer Hendrik Brouwer (ca. 1581-1643) in 1611	Redgeographics (28-05-2020). Wikimedia Commons. [https://commons.wikimedia.org/wiki/File:The-Brouwer-Route.jpg]. Licensed under CC BY-SA 4.0 DEED Attribution-ShareAlike 4.0 International. [https://creativecommons.org/licenses/by-sa/4.0/deed.en]
18	The 1999 replica of *Duyfken* under sail in ca. 2006	Gerritsen Rupert (2006). Wikimedia Commons. [https://en.m.wikipedia.org/wiki/File:Duyfken_Replica_Under_Sail.jpg]. Licensed under CC BY-SA 3.0 DEED Attribution-ShareAlike 3.0 Unported. [https://creativecommons.org/licenses/by-sa/3.0/deed.en]
19	Tasman Bonaparte map	Bellin Jacques Nicolas (1703-1772) & Prevost (abbe 1697-1763) (1753). *Carte reduite des terres Australes [cartographic material] : pour servir a l'Histoire des voyages / par Le Sr. Bellin Ing, de la Marine de la Societe Royale de Londres & ca. 1753.* [https://nla.gov.au/nla.obj-230625933]
20	The Bark, *Earl of Pembroke*, later *Endeavour*, leaving Whitby Harbour in 1768	Luny Thomas (1759-1837) (1790). *The Bark,* Earl of Pembroke, *later* Endeavour, *leaving Whitby Harbour in 1768 [picture] / Thomas Luny.* [http://nla.gov.au/nla.obj-134301494]
20	Chart of part of the South Sea showing the tracts and discoveries made by His Majesty's ships, 1773	Whitchurch W (William) and Hawkesworth John (1715?-1773). Account of the voyages undertaken by the order of His present Majesty, for making discoveries in the Southern Hemisphere, 1773. *Chart of part of the South Sea shewing the tracts & discoveries made by His Majesty's ships Dolphin ... [cartographic material] / engrav'd by W. Whitchurch, Pleasant Row Islington.* [https://nla.gov.au/nla.obj-230731491]
21	General chart of *Terra Australis* or Australia, showing parts explored between 1798 and 1803 by M. Flinders, Commr. of HMS *Investigator*, 1814	Flinders Matthew (1774-1814). Voyage to *Terra Australis* & G. & W. Nicol (Firm) (1814). *General chart of* Terra Australis *or Australia [cartographic material]: showing the parts explored between 1798 and 1803 by M. Flinders Commr. of H.M.S. Investigator.* [https://nla.gov.au/nla.obj-232588549]
22	Cook takes possession	Dutch Australia Cultural Centre (DACC). *New Holland, the name for Australia from 1644 to 1824.* Published 26 July 2023. [https://dutchaustraliancultralcentre.com.au/archive/dutch-australian-history/new-holland-the-name-for-australia-from1644-1824/]
25	Aboriginals using fire to hunt kangaroos, watercolour painting by Joseph Lycett (ca. 1775-1828)	Lycett Joseph (approximately 1775-1828). Drawings of Aboriginals and scenery, New South Wales, ca. 1820. [https://nla.gov.au/nla.obj-138501179]
26	Retrieving a runaway. *Stockmen rounding up cattle on horseback at Doomadgee in the 1960s*	Knowles PC (2021). *Stockmen rounding up cattle on horseback at Doomadgee in the 1960s.* John Oxley Library, State Library of Queensland.
26	Hector Rutherford and Joyce Stuart, *The Oaks*, Glen Geddes, ca. 1951	Sheldon Mary (ca. 1951).

Page	Title	Source / Credit
26	Mary Sheldon and Alfie, *The Oaks*, ca. 1951	Sheldon Mary (ca. 1951).
28	The Aboriginal 'Emu in the Sky'. The Southern Cross is on the right	Norris Barnaby and Norris Ray (2007). Wikimedia Commons. [https://en.m.wikipedia.org/wiki/File:Emu_public.jpg]. Licensed under CC BY-SA 3.0 DEED Attribution-ShareAlike 3.0 Unported. [https://creativecommons.org/licenses/by-sa/3.0/deed.en]
29	Wandjina figures, Mount Elizabeth Station, Kimberley, 2012	Samantha Wood (2012). Flickr.
29	X-ray figure, Kakadu National Park, Australia	Schoch Thomas (2005). Wikimedia Commons. [https://commons.wikimedia.org/wiki/File:Aboriginal_Art_Australia(3).jpg]. Licensed under CC BY-SA 3.0 DEED Attribution-ShareAlike 3.0 Unported. [https://creativecommons.org/licenses/by-sa/3.0/deed.en]
29	*Gwion figures*	Courtesy of the Wunambal Gaambera Aboriginal Corporation. *New study sheds light on the disappearance of a prehistoric culture*, UQ News. [https://www.uq.edu.au/news/article/2012/12/new-study-sheds-light-disappearance-of-pre-historic-culture]
30	40,000-year-old rock painting of the Genyornis	Wolly Brian (2010). *Extinct Bird Key to Dating Australia's Oldest Cave Art* by Brendan Borrell, *Smithsonian Magazine*. [https://www.smithsonianmag.com/science-nature/extinct-bird-key-to-dating-australias-oldest-cave-art-29394729/]. Accessed April 2024.
30	*Portrait of Albert Namatjira*, 1956	Dargie William (1956). *Portrait of Albert Namatjira*. ©William Dargie/Copyright Agency, 2024
30	*Ghost gum*, Mt Sonder, McDonnell ranges, ca. 1957.	Namatjira Albert (ca. 1957). *Ghost gum*. © Namatjira Legacy Trust/Copyright Agency, 2024
30	*Glenn Helen country*	Namatjira Albert. *Glenn Helen country*. © Namatjira Legacy Trust/Copyright Agency, 2024
31	*Kurdukadji* (Emu)	Kelly Ezariah. *Kurdukadji* (Emu). © Ezariah Kelly/Copyright Agency, 2024
31	*Mayh Kuwarddewaken* (Stone Country Animals)	Badari Graham. *Mayh Kuwarddewaken* (Stone Country Animals). © Graham Badari/Copyright Agency, 2024
31	*Aboriginal landscape*, 1940	Preston Margaret (1940). *Aboriginal landscape*. © Margaret Preston/Copyright Agency, 2024
31	*Still life*, 1941	Preston Margaret (1941). *Still Life*. © Margaret Preston/Copyright Agency, 2024
35	Page from J. Stuart's bible	Photo by Tom Hasker.
37	Non-commissioned Officers (NCOs) and Gunners who served at Gallipoli; France ca. 1916. Front Centre is Indigenous soldier, 2141 Private Alfred Jackson Coombs	Australian War Memorial. Accession Number P01242.002. [https://www.awm.gov.au/collection/C204240]. Licensed under PDM 1.0 DEED Public Domain Mark 1.0 Universal. [https://creativecommons.org/publicdomain/mark/1.0/]

Image and Illustration Credits

Page	Title	Source / Credit
37	Group portrait of the 'Special Platoon' of Aboriginal Australians, who volunteered for service during the Second World War, 1940	Australian War Memorial. Accession Number P02140.002. [https://www.awm.gov.au/collection/C295499]. Licensed under PDM 1.0 DEED Public Domain Mark 1.0 Universal. [https://creativecommons.org/publicdomain/mark/1.0/]
37	Arthur Murdoch	Anon (2014). *A. Murdoch 16 - 11, one of the soldiers photographed in The Queenslander Pictorial, supplement to The Queenslander, 1917*. John Oxley Library, State Library of Queensland, Brisbane.
38	Reg Saunders, 1940	Australian War Memorial. Accession Number 003967. [https://www.awm.gov.au/collection/C25893]. Licensed under PDM 1.0 DEED Public Domain Mark 1.0 Universal. [https://creativecommons.org/publicdomain/mark/1.0/]
38	Lt Reginald Walter Saunders shaking hands with Lt Thomas Currie Derrick, 1944	Australian War Memorial. Accession Number 083166. [https://www.awm.gov.au/collection/C20546]. Licensed under PDM 1.0 DEED Public Domain Mark 1.0 Universal. [https://creativecommons.org/publicdomain/mark/1.0/]
38	Sgt Leonard Victor (Len) Waters, ca. 1944-1945	Wikimedia Commons, image credited to: Waters Patrick (08-07-2005). A Tough Landing. *The Courier Mail*. [https://commons.wikimedia.org/wiki/File:LenWaters.jpg]
38	Waters' P-40 N-15 Kittyhawk aircraft, *Black Magic*	Australian War Memorial. Accession Number P02808.001. [https://www.awm.gov.au/collection/C364993]. Licensed under PDM 1.0 DEED Public Domain Mark 1.0 Universal. [https://creativecommons.org/publicdomain/mark/1.0/]
39	Badge of the North-West Mobile Force	Wikimedia Commons. [https://en.wikipedia.org/wiki/NORFORCE]. Image credited to: Digger History. [http://www.diggerhistory.info/images/badges-regt/badge-regiment-norforce.gif]. Accessed April 2024.
39	Australian Defence Force soldiers from Regional Force Surveillance Unit on deployed Operation Resolute	McAneny Sgt Jarrod (19-10-2022). Department of Defence. [http://images.defence.gov.au/20221019adf8595729_0036.jpg]. © Department of Defence – All rights reserved.
42	Captain Arthur Phillip	Macbeth-Raeburn H (Henry) (1860-1947) and Wheatley Francis (1747-1801) (1936). *The pioneer, in 1788 Captain Arthur Phillip R.N. proceeded from Botany Bay to Port Jackson ... [picture] / H. Macbeth-Raeburn*. [http://nla.gov.au/nla.obj-136096089]
42	HMSS *Sirius*	Timbury Cheryl (15-10-2011). HMSS *Sirius*. First Fleet Fellowship Victoria Incorporated. [https://firstfleetfellowship.org.au/ships/hms-sirius/]. Image credited to Marine artist Frank Allen.
42	Route of the First Fleet	Wills Sandra (2006). *Interactive Map of the Route of the First Fleet*. First Fleet Online, University of Wollongong: Learning, Teaching and Curriculum Unit. [http://firstfleet.uow.edu.au/s_map.html]. Accessed April 2024.
43	*The First Fleet in Sydney Cove, 27 January 1788*, painting by John Allcot, 1937	Allcot John (1888-1973) (1937). *The First Fleet in Sydney Cove, January 27, 1788 [picture] / John Allcot, 1937*. [http://nla.gov.au/nla.obj-135776002]

Page	Title	Source / Credit
43	*View of the settlement on Sydney Cove, Port Jackson, 20 August 1788*	Hunter J, Dayes E, Hunter J and Stockdale JJ (1793). *View of the settlement on Sydney Cove, Port Jackson, 20 August 1788. [picture]*. Piccadilly England: Publish'd ... by I. Stockdale.. [https://find.slv.vic.gov.au/permalink/61SLV_INST/1sev8ar/alma9916829923607636]
43	Circular Quay (Sydney Cove), 1994	Helyar J (1994). Wikimedia Commons. [https://commons.wikimedia.org/wiki/File:Sydney_1994_(4).jpg]. Licensed under CC BY-SA 4.0 DEED Attribution-ShareAlike 4.0 International. [https://creativecommons.org/licenses/by-sa/4.0/deed.en]
44	Bennelong, native interpreter (copy of etching), 1937	Mitchell Library, State Library of New South Wales. Reference code 9628743. [https://collection.sl.nsw.gov.au/record/n88XbMLn]
44	Sydney Opera House, Bennelong Point	Read Peter (2023). University of Sydney. *A History of Aboriginal Sydney.* [https://www.historyofaboriginalsydney.edu.au/central/1800s]. Accessed April 2024.
47	*Flogging prisoners, Tasmania*, drawing by James Reid Scott, 1859	Scott James Reid (1839-1877) (1850). *[Flogging prisoners, Tasmania] [picture] / [James Reid Scott]*. [http://nla.gov.au/nla.obj-135505322]
47	Relics of convict discipline, Beattie Museum, Hobart	Searle EW (Edward William) (1887-1955) and Beatties Studio (1911). *Relics of convict discipline [Beattie Museum, Hobart] [picture]*. [http://nla.gov.au/nla.obj-142164079]
48	Australia's first postmaster, Isaac Nichols, 1809	*Defining Moments: First post office, 1809: Convict Isaac Nichols appointed as Australia's first postmaster* (2023). National Museum of Australia. [https://www.nma.gov.au/defining-moments/resources/first-post-office]. Image credit: Stamp designer and engraver: Frank Manley, The Australian Postal Corporation. Used with permission.
50	*Flogging a prisoner at Port Arthur*	Victorian Collections. [https://victoriancollections.net.au/items/609d18c5ce20e27f83676844]. Accessed April 2024
51	The *Pitt* off Dover, 1787	Artist: Dominic Serres (1719–1793); Engraver: John William Edy (1760 or 1762–1820); Publisher: John Harris (1756–1846). National Maritime Museum, Greenwich via Wikimedia Commons. [https://commons.wikimedia.org/wiki/File:Pitt_(1780).jpg]
52	John Warby's cottage, later known as *Leumeah House*, built between 1816 and 1826	Photo supplied by Michelle Vale.
52	John Warby's barn, later known as *Leumeah Barn*, built between 1816 and 1828	Photo supplied by Michelle Vale.
53	Conditional Pardon paperwork for Alexander MacDonald	Images supplied by David MacDonald.
54	St Luke's Anglican Church, Liverpool, NSW	Maggie To, St Luke's Parish, Liverpool. [www.stlukesliverpool.org.au]

Image and Illustration Credits

Page	Title	Source / Credit
58	A relaxed Currency Lad and stiff-backed English couple at Lady Macquarie's Chair, Sydney, 1830	Australian Prints and Printmaking. [https://www.printsandprintmaking.gov.au/works/28098/images/10200/]. An initiative of National Gallery of Australia. Accessed April 2024.
59	Mount Hay, Blue Mountains National Park	Photo by Bob Mendelsohn, Flickr.
59	Looking north along the Nepean River, 2006	Brian Voon Yee Yap (2006). Wikimedia Commons. [https://commons.wikimedia.org/wiki/File:Aus_nsw_nepean_river_dsc05078.jpg]. Licensed under CC BY-SA 3.0 DEED Attribution-ShareAlike 3.0 Unported. [https://creativecommons.org/licenses/by-sa/3.0/deed.en]
59	Kanangra Walls and Valley	Photo by Chris Couvret, Flickr.
59	Mount Banks, Blue Mountains, NSW	Adam JWC (2009). Wikimedia Commons. [https://commons.wikimedia.org/wiki/File:Mount_banks,.jpg]. Licensed under CC BY-SA 2.5 DEED Attribution-ShareAlike 2.5 Generic. [https://creativecommons.org/licenses/by-sa/2.5/]
60	*Convicts building a road over the Blue Mountains, NSW*, by Charles Rodius (1802-1860), 1833	Rodius Charles (1802-1860) (1833). *[Convicts building road over the Blue Mountains, New South Wales, 1833] [picture] / Chs. Rodius*. [http://nla.gov.au/nla.obj-135505644]
61	The Murray-Darling Basin, Lake Eyre Basin and Great Artesian Basin	Australian Government, Department of the Environment and Heritage (2006). Licensed under CC BY 4.0 DEED Attribution 4.0 International. [https://creativecommons.org/licenses/by/4.0/]
61	Eyre's expeditions	Project Gutenberg Australia (2007). Wikimedia Commons. [https://commons.wikimedia.org/wiki/File:Eyre-map.jpg]
61	The first expedition of Leichhardt	Project Gutenberg Australia (2007). Wikimedia Commons. [https://commons.wikimedia.org/wiki/File:Leichhardt-map.jpg]
63	Map of the explorer Augustus Charles Gregory's route in Australia	Project Gutenberg Australia (2007). Wikimedia Commons. [https://en.wikipedia.org/wiki/File:Gregory-map.jpg]
63	*Return of Burke and Wills to Coopers Creek* (1873-1876)	Armytage JC & Chevalier Nicholas (1874). *Return of Burke & Wills to Coopers Creek*. Virtue & Co, [London]. Accessed April 2024. [http://nla.gov.au/nla.obj-138430884]
63	Burke and Wills track	Wilkins Peter W. *The Burke and Wills Expedition of 1860*. Wilkins Tourist Maps [https://www.wilmap.com.au/explorers/burkwill.html]. Accessed April 2024.
64	John McDowell Stuart's route, 1862	Project Gutenberg Australia (2007). Wikimedia Commons. [https://en.m.wikipedia.org/wiki/File:Stuart-map.jpg]
64	Central Mount Stuart, 2003	Tannin (2003). Wikimedia Commons. [https://commons.wikimedia.org/wiki/File:Central_Mt_Stuart.jpg]. Licensed under CC BY-SA 3.0 DEED Attribution-ShareAlike 3.0 Unported. [https://creativecommons.org/licenses/by-sa/3.0/deed.en]

Page	Title	Source / Credit
64	Map showing the routes travelled and discoveries made by the exploring expeditions equipped by Thomas Elder and under the command of Ernest Giles, during the period 1872-76	Giles Ernest (1835-1897), Berry Edwin S, Crawford Frazer S (Frazer Smith) (-1890), Elder Sir Thomas (1818-) and Goyder GW (George Woodroffe) (1826-1898) (1876). *Map showing the routes travelled and discoveries made by the exploring expeditions equipped by Thomas Elder and under the command of Ernest Giles [cartographic material]: between the years 1872-6 / compiled by order of the Surveyor General from Mr. Giles original plans; drawn by Edwin S. Berry.* [http://nla.gov.au/nla.obj-232133673]
67	*Hobart Town, taken from the garden where I lived, 1832* by John Glover	Dixson Galleries, State Library of New South Wales. Reference code 404681. [https://collection.sl.nsw.gov.au/record/YEGmp0bn]
68	*A direct north general view of Sydney Cove, ... 1794* by T. Watling	Dixson Galleries, State Library of New South Wales. Reference code 433037. [https://collection.sl.nsw.gov.au/record/9gkdJ5v9]
68	*Near Heidelberg* by Arthur Streeton, 1890	Streeton Arthur (1890). *Near Heidelberg.* National Gallery of Victoria, Melbourne. Felton Bequest, 1943. [https://www.ngv.vic.gov.au/explore/collection/work/3055/]
68	*Sunlight Sweet*, Coogee by Arthur Streeton, 1890	Wikimedia Commons (2005). [https://en.m.wikipedia.org/wiki/File:Sunlight_Sweet_Coogee_Arthur_Streeton.jpg]
69	*Lost* by Frederick McCubbin, 1886	McCubbin Frederick (1886). *Lost.* National Gallery of Victoria, Melbourne. Felton Bequest, 1940. [https://www.ngv.vic.gov.au/explore/collection/work/5975/]
70	*Central Australia,* 1949	Nolan Sir Sidney (1949). *Central Australia.* © The Sidney Nolan Trust. All rights reserved. DACS/Copyright Agency, 2024.
71	*North ranges looking south,* 1950s	Namatjira Albert (1950s). *North ranges looking south.* © Namatjira Legacy Trust/Copyright Agency, 2024
71	Blythewood Grange, Ballarat, built by a successful goldminer in 1878	Club Wyndham, Ballarat. Trademark Collection by Wyndham. [https://www.wyndhamhotels.com/trademark/ballarat-australia/club-wyndham-ballarat-trademark-collection/overview]. Accessed April 2024.
72	Highset Queenslander with front verandah, 2016	Coghlan Michael (2016). Flickr. [https://www.flickr.com/photos/mikecogh/31139768556]. Licensed under CC BY-SA 2.0 DEED Attribution-ShareAlike 2.0 Generic. [https://creativecommons.org/licenses/by-sa/2.0/]
72	Sydney Opera House	Photo by Alexander Bickov (2020) on Unsplash.
72	Australian Parliament House, Canberra	Biggs Christoper (2016). Flickr. [https://www.flickr.com/photos/c-j-b/31482610945/in/faves-200164796@N08/]
74	*Australian gold diggings,* ca. 1855 by Edwin Stocqueler (1829-1895)	Stocqueler Edwin (1829-1895) (1855). *Australian gold diggings, ca.1855 [picture] / [Edwin Stocqueler].* [http://nla.gov.au/nla.obj-134299327]
75	*The Gold Diggers* by Emil Todt, 1854	Todt Emil (1854). *The Gold Diggers.* National Gallery of Victoria, Melbourne. Gift of Mrs Leonard Terry, 1884. [https://www.ngv.vic.gov.au/explore/collection/work/3628/]
77	*Swearing Allegiance to the Southern Cross* by Charles A. Doudiet, 1854	Doudiet Charles A (1854). *Defining Moments: Eureka Stockade* (2023). National Museum of Australia. [https://www.nma.gov.au/defining-moments/resources/eureka-stockade]. Image credit: *Swearing Allegiance to the Southern Cross,* 1854, Charles A Doudiet, watercolour. Art Gallery of Ballarat.

Image and Illustration Credits

Page	Title	Source / Credit
78	The Eureka flag	Martyman. Wikimedia Commons. [https://commons.wikimedia.org/wiki/File:Eureka_Flag.svg]
83	Yang Shuai (Nixie) at Monument to Canoona gold discovery, Pacific Highway, just south of *Glen Geddes*, 2011	Peter Hasker
84	Mater Hospital, Rockhampton in 1919	Pearce Frazer (25-06-2023). *Homeowners in historic Rockhampton uncover fascinating histories with new research service.* ABC Capricornia. [https://www.abc.net.au/news/2023-06-25/house-history-search-uncovers-story-riches-in-rockhampton/102510170]. Image credit: Rockhampton Historical Society.
86	*Bailed up* by Tom Roberts, 1895, Inverell district where Captain Thunderbolt had operated	Roberts Tom (1895). *Bailed up.* Located at Art Gallery of New South Wales. Source: Wikimedia Commons. [https://commons.wikimedia.org/wiki/File:Tom_Roberts_-_Bailed_up_-_Google_Art_Project.jpg]
87	Statue of Captain Thunderbolt, Uralla, NSW	McGoodwin (2008). Wikimedia Commons. [https://commons.wikimedia.org/wiki/File:Thunderbolt.JPG]. Licensed under CC BY-SA 4.0 DEED Attribution-ShareAlike 4.0 International. [https://creativecommons.org/licenses/by-sa/4.0/]
88	Ned Kelly's armour at State Library of Victoria	Chensiyuan (2018). Wikimedia Commons. [https://commons.wikimedia.org/wiki/File:Ned_kelly_armour_library.JPG], Licensed under CC BY-SA 4.0 DEED Attribution-ShareAlike 4.0 International. [https://creativecommons.org/licenses/by-sa/4.0/]
89	Ned Kelly, taken day before execution, 1880	*The life and adventures of the Kelly outlaws: the daring Australian bushrangers.* Frearson and Brother, Adelaide, 1881. [http://nla.gov.au/nla.obj-1181397]
90	New South Wales as proclaimed by Cook	Dutch Australia Cultural Centre (DACC). *New Holland, the name for Australia from 1644 to 1824.* Published 26 July 2023. [https://dutchaustraliancultural centre.com.au/archive/dutch-australian-history/new-holland-the-name-for-australia-from1644-1824/]
91 - 92	Maps showing progressive establishment of States	Source unknown.
96	Australian flag	Department of the Prime Minister and Cabinet. [https://www.pmc.gov.au/honours-and-symbols/australian-national-symbols/australian-national-flag]. Accessed April 2024.
96	Australian Coat of Arms	Department of the Prime Minister and Cabinet. [https://www.pmc.gov.au/honours-and-symbols/commonwealth-coat-arms]. Accessed April 2024.
96	Golden wattle flower (*Acacia pycnantha*)	Australian National Botanic Gardens and Centre for Australian National Biodiversity Research (2015). Accessed April 2024. [https://www.anbg.gov.au/acacia/species/A-pycnantha.html] An Australian Government Initiative.
96	Black opal from Lightning Ridge, NSW	© Commonwealth of Australia (Geoscience Australia) (2021). [https://www.ga.gov.au/education/minerals-energy/australian-mineral-facts/opal]. Licensed under CC BY 4.0 LEGAL CODE Attribution 4.0 International. [https://creativecommons.org/licenses/by/4.0/legalcode]. Accessed April 2024.

Page	Title	Source / Credit
102	The south-eastern portion of Australia compiled from the colonial surveys, and from details furnished by exploratory expeditions, by John Arrowsmith.	Arrowsmith John (1842). Wikimedia Commons. [https://commons.wikimedia.org/wiki/File:1842NSWArrowsmith.jpg]. Source credited: Lee Jackson Maps. [http://www.leejacksonmaps.com/aust.htm#ARRO0011]
104	Squatters House, post 1847, Delegate, NSW	© New South Wales Government. [https://www.nsw.gov.au/visiting-and-exploring-nsw/locations-and-attractions/early-settlers-hut]. Licensed under CC BY 4.0 DEED Attribution 4.0 International. [https://creativecommons.org/licenses/by/4.0/deed.en]
104	Purrumbete House, Weerite, Vic.	Ruwolt Jon (2023). *The Architects of our Arts and Crafts style Houses in Australia*. Image credit: Purrumbete homestead. [https://www.federation-house.com/arts-and-crafts-architects]. Accessed April 2024.
105	Selector's hut in Camp Mountain, Samford Valley	Heritage branch staff, State of Queensland: Queensland Heritage Register (2009). Wikimedia Commons. [https://en.m.wikipedia.org/wiki/File:Selector's_Hut_(former)_from_NW_(2009).jpg]. Licensed under CC BY 4.0 DEED Attribution 4.0 International. [https://creativecommons.org/licenses/by/4.0/]
106	Soldier-settlers clearing land at Beerburrum, north of Brisbane, to make way for pineapples	Wood Margaret (2015). *From Gallipoli to Australian Farms: Soldier settler success and failure and contribution to the future of agriculture*. ABC Rural. [https://www.abc.net.au/news/rural/2015-04-23/remembering-soldier-settlers-a-window-to-agricultural-past/6408988]. Accessed April 2024.
127	Components of annual population growth ('000s), Australia, 1982-2015	Australian Bureau of Statistics (2016). *Components of Annual Population Growth (a)(b), Australia,* 3101.0 - Australian Demographic Statistics, Dec 2015. [https://www.abs.gov.au/ausstats/abs@.nsf/Previousproducts/3101.0Main%20Features2Dec%202015?opendocument&tabname=Summary&prodno=3101.0&issue=Dec%202015&num=&view=]. Accessed April 2024.
128	Change in ethnic makeup of Australian population born overseas.	Parliamentary Library Research Papers 2018-19. *Population and migration statistics in Australia,* 7 December 2018. Joanne Simon-Davies, Statistics and Mapping Section. [https://www.aph.gov.au/About_Parliament/Parliamentary_Departments/Parliamentary_Library/pubs/rp/rp1819/Quick_Guides/PopulationStatistics]
129	Ten most-commonly-nominated ancestries in the 2016 census	Australian Bureau of Statistics (2017). *The Ancestries of Australians.* [Ancestry is not always connected to a person's place of birth; it is the cultural or ethnic group with which the person most closely identifies. Over 300 ancestries were separately identified in the 2016 Census. The ten most commonly reported ancestries were:]. 2071.0 - Census of Population and Housing: Reflecting Australia - Stories from the Census, 2016. [https://www.abs.gov.au/ausstats/abs@.nsf/Lookup/by%20Subject/2071.0~2016~Main%20Features~Cultural%20Diversity%20Article~60]. Accessed April 2024.

Image and Illustration Credits

Page	Title	Source / Credit
130	The Population Density of Australia, 2016	@NaytaData (2018). Demography – the study of human population and society. [https://www.facebook.com/photo/?fbid=1313718935424879&set=a.473069252823189]. Data source: Australian Bureau of Statistics. Accessed April 2024.
133	Main geographical regions of World War I	ANZAC Day Commemoration Committee. *World War I – Overview*. [https://anzacday.org.au/ww1-overview]. Accessed April 2024.
134	P. F. Stuart	Peter Hasker
135	Rockhampton Grammar School tennis fours, 1913	Peter Hasker
135	Eureka Football Club – Premiers 1912-13, Charity Cup winners 1912-13-14	Peter Hasker
136	Silver medal	Peter Hasker
138	An overview of the Gallipoli Peninsula. The dotted lines approximately mark the furthest advance of Allied Forces	Scott Simeon (2005). Wikimedia Commons. [https://commons.wikimedia.org/wiki/File:Gallipolimap2.png]. Licensed under CC BY-SA 3.0 DEED Attribution-ShareAlike 3.0 Unported. [https://creativecommons.org/licenses/by-sa/3.0/]
138	The Gallipoli Peninsula Map	ANZAC Day Commemoration Committee. *Maps of World War I*. [https://anzacday.org.au/maps-of-world-war-1]. Map courtesy of Department of Public Information – Army. Accessed April 2024.
139	Anzac Cove	Google images
140	Map of the planned landing of the 2nd and 3rd Brigades of the Australian 1st Division	Gsl (2004). Wikimedia Commons. [https://en.m.wikipedia.org/wiki/File:Anzac_landing_plan_April_25_1915.jpg]. Licensed under CC BY-SA 4.0 DEED Attribution-ShareAlike 4.0 International. [https://creativecommons.org/licenses/by-sa/4.0/deed.en]
140	The Landing at ANZAC, 25 April 1915	ANZAC Day Commemoration Committee. *The Landing*. [https://anzacday.org.au/the-landing]. Map courtesy of *The Courier Mail*. Accessed April 2024.
141	Australian troops charge a Turkish trench at The Nek, 7 August 1915	Unknown (2018). Wikimedia Commons. [https://en.m.wikipedia.org/wiki/File:Scene_just_before_the_evacuation_at_Anzac._Australian_troops_charging_near_a_Turkish_trench._When_they_got_there_the..._-_NARA_-_533108.jpg]. Source: U.S. National Archives and Records Administration. National Archives Identifier: 533108.
142	Mudros Harbour, Lemnos Island, April 1915	Australian War Memorial. Accession Number H16825. [https://www.awm.gov.au/collection/C384086]. Donor Major FJ McAdam. Licensed under PDM 1.0 DEED Public Domain Mark 1.0 Universal. [https://creativecommons.org/publicdomain/mark/1.0/]
149	Ottoman Empire, 1914	The National Archives. [https://www.nationalarchives.gov.uk]
150	Western Desert campaign against the Senussi	Serag Yehya M (2018). ResearchGate. [https://www.researchgate.net/figure/An-old-map-showing-the-borders-between-Egypt-and-Libya-in-1915-with-Ghaboub-within-the_fig7_328556520]. Accessed April 2024.

Page	Title	Source / Credit
151	The 1st Australian Light Horse Brigade passing over the steep sandhills at Esdud, January 1918	Australian War Memorial. Accession Number B01510. [https://www.awm.gov.au/collection/C53712]. Licensed under PDM 1.0 DEED Public Domain Mark 1.0 Universal. [https://creativecommons.org/publicdomain/mark/1.0/]
151	Belah. An Australian Light Horse camp in the desert	Australian War Memorial. Accession Number B01615. [https://www.awm.gov.au/collection/C989390]. Licensed under PDM 1.0 DEED Public Domain Mark 1.0 Universal. [https://creativecommons.org/publicdomain/mark/1.0/]
151	Egypt and Palestine map	Hamilton Patrick M (1892-1977) (1996). *Riders of destiny: the 4th Australian Light Horse Field Ambulance 1917-1918: an autobiography and history*. Mostly Unsung Military History Research and Publications, Gardenvale, Vic. [page 8, map 1]
152	Gaza-Beersheba line	Hamilton Patrick M (1892-1977) (1996). *Riders of destiny: the 4th Australian Light Horse Field Ambulance 1917-1918: an autobiography and history*. Mostly Unsung Military History Research and Publications, Gardenvale, Vic. [page 87, map 5]
153	This photograph possibly represents a re-enactment of a charge for a cinematographer when a brigade was staged near Belah in February 1918	Australian War Memorial. Accession Number P12049.007. [https://www.awm.gov.au/collection/C2100804]. Licensed under PDM 1.0 DEED Public Domain Mark 1.0 Universal. [https://creativecommons.org/publicdomain/mark/1.0/]
153	Beersheba, Palestine, November 1917. Ambulances waiting in front of the town mosque to collect battle casualties from the local Turkish hospital which is out of sight	Australian War Memorial. Accession Number P01668.004. [https://www.awm.gov.au/collection/C254306]. Licensed under PDM 1.0 DEED Public Domain Mark 1.0 Universal. [https://creativecommons.org/publicdomain/mark/1.0/]
155	Palestine map	Hamilton Patrick M (1892-1977) (1996). *Riders of destiny: the 4th Australian Light Horse Field Ambulance 1917-1918: an autobiography and history*. Mostly Unsung Military History Research and Publications, Gardenvale, Vic. [page 116, map 7]
156	Camp at the foot of the Judaean Hills in the Jordan Valley, near Jericho	Hurley Frank (1917-1918). *Exhibition of war photographs / taken by Capt. F. Hurley, August 1917- August 1918*. State Library of New South Wales. Reference code 423850. [https://collection.sl.nsw.gov.au/record/9gkdWXq9/ozAXGb8rwegXQ]. Image no. 117.
156	Jordan Valley, Palestine, ca. 1917. An Australian Light Horse unit raising dust on the move	Australian War Memorial. Accession Number H02984. [https://www.awm.gov.au/collection/C298998]. Donor J Campbell. Licensed under PDM 1.0 DEED Public Domain Mark 1.0 Universal. [https://creativecommons.org/publicdomain/mark/1.0/]
158	*Damascus Incident*, Power H Septimus. Depicts the 3rd Australian Light Horse Brigade advancing on Damascus	Australian War Memorial. Accession Number ART03647. [https://www.awm.gov.au/collection/C173332]. Licensed under PDM 1.0 DEED Public Domain Mark 1.0 Universal. [https://creativecommons.org/publicdomain/mark/1.0/]

Image and Illustration Credits

Page	Title	Source / Credit
159	*The Capture of Damascus*	New South Wales Lancers Memorial Museum Incorporated. *The Australian Light Horse*, adapted from *The Australian Light Horse* by RJ Hall (November 1968). [https://www.lancers.org.au/site/light_horse.php]. Accessed April 2024.
159	The Desert Mounted Corps Memorial stands near the summit of Mt Clarence, Albany, Western Australia	Grant65 (2007). Wikimedia Commons. [https://en.m.wikipedia.org/wiki/File:Desert_Mounted_Corps.jpg]. Licensed under CC BY-SA 3.0 DEED Attribution-ShareAlike 3.0 Unported. [https://creativecommons.org/licenses/by-sa/3.0/deed.en]
160	General Sir Harry Chevaulle [i.e. Chauvel] inspecting the 1st Squadron A.F.C. at the Medjdel aerodrome, January 1918	Hurley Frank (1917-1918). Mitchell Library, State Library of New South Wales. Reference code 447411. Image no. 18. [https://collection.sl.nsw.gov.au/record/9qoQ5OL1/EDb8Xew6ZOzLP]
161	Men of the original (1st) Light Horse Regiment at Roseberry Park Camp, NSW, before departure from Australia	Australian War Memorial. Accession Number J00450. [https://www.awm.gov.au/collection/C1821]. Licensed under PDM 1.0 DEED Public Domain Mark 1.0 Universal. [https://creativecommons.org/publicdomain/mark/1.0/]
161	Studio portrait of 2436 Private (Pte) Harry C. Murray, 11th Light Horse Regiment	Australian War Memorial. Accession Number P00889.004. [https://www.awm.gov.au/collection/C1068776]. Licensed under PDM 1.0 DEED Public Domain Mark 1.0 Universal. [https://creativecommons.org/publicdomain/mark/1.0/]
162	Spear pump at Zilzie	Peter Hasker
163	The 1st Australian Light Horse Brigade horses at water	Australian War Memorial. Accession Number B01490. [https://www.awm.gov.au/collection/C968746]. Licensed under PDM 1.0 DEED Public Domain Mark 1.0 Universal. [https://creativecommons.org/publicdomain/mark/1.0/]
164	Australian Mounted Division, Horse Show and Sports, Palestine. (trophy)	Photo by Bill Hasker.
165	Desert Mounted Corps memorial, Sydney	Photo by Gail Strong.
166	Middle East, ca. 1917. A camel fitted with a cacolet designed to carry wounded in a prone position	Australian War Memorial. Accession Number H02808. [https://www.awm.gov.au/collection/C251958]. Donor J. Hunter. Licensed under PDM 1.0 DEED Public Domain Mark 1.0 Universal. [https://creativecommons.org/publicdomain/mark/1.0/]
167	A horse-drawn sand sledge designed for use in the desert during the Sinai campaign, ca. 1917	Australian War Memorial. Accession Number H00789. [https://www.awm.gov.au/collection/C58346]. Licensed under PDM 1.0 DEED Public Domain Mark 1.0 Universal. [https://creativecommons.org/publicdomain/mark/1.0/]
167	*Walk (An incident at Romani)*, 1919-1922 by George W. Lambert.	Lambert George W (1919-22). *Walk (An incident at Romani)*, Oil on canvas 92 x 138 cm. Gift of the 2nd Light Horse Field Ambulance in memory of Comrades who did not return from the war, ca.1922. Collection: Queensland Art Gallery, Gallery of Modern Art. [https://blog.qagoma.qld.gov.au/george-w-lambert-an-incident-at-romani-in-memory-of-the-light-horse-field-ambulance-australia/]

Page	Title	Source / Credit
172	Officers of the 3rd Australian Light Horse Brigade Field Ambulance	Australian War Memorial. Accession Number B00801. [https://www.awm.gov.au/collection/C954689]. Licensed under PDM 1.0 DEED Public Domain Mark 1.0 Universal. [https://creativecommons.org/publicdomain/mark/1.0/]
172	Deir-El-Belah, Palestine, ca.1917. Group portrait of officers of the 3rd Australian Light Horse Field Ambulance (ALHFA) sitting in front of a tree	Australian War Memorial. Accession Number P02171.002. [https://www.awm.gov.au/collection/C296966]. Licensed under PDM 1.0 DEED Public Domain Mark 1.0 Universal. [https://creativecommons.org/publicdomain/mark/1.0/]
175	The push to Damascus	Butler AG (Arthur G) (1872-1949) (1938). *The official history of the Australian Army Medical Service in the war of 1914-18, Volume I – Gallipoli, Palestine and New Guinea (2nd edition, 1938) / [A.G. Butler]*. Australian War Memorial, Melbourne. [map 21]
176	A group comprising all ranks and transport of the 3rd Australian Light Horse Field Ambulance, ca. 1918	Australian War Memorial. Accession Number B00800. [https://www.awm.gov.au/collection/C80332]. Licensed under PDM 1.0 DEED Public Domain Mark 1.0 Universal. [https://creativecommons.org/publicdomain/mark/1.0/]
177	3rd Light Horse Field Ambulance Casualty Clearing Station at Gamil on the Wady Ghuzze during the operation of blowing up the Turkish Railway from Beersheba to El Aiya	Australian War Memorial. Accession Number J00459. [https://www.awm.gov.au/collection/C1830]. Licensed under PDM 1.0 DEED Public Domain Mark 1.0 Universal. [https://creativecommons.org/publicdomain/mark/1.0/]
178	45th memorial plaque located in the grounds of Shrine of Remembrance, St Kilda Road, Birdwood Avenue and Domain Road, Melbourne, Victoria. Jessica Bowman and Bill pictured	Photo by Bill Hasker.
179	The Western Front – early summer 1916	Weintraub Stanley (2014). *Silent Night: The Story of the World War I Christmas Truce*. Map of the Week. [https://mapoftheweek.blogspot.com/2014/12/the-christmas-truce-1914.html]. Accessed April 2024.
179	The Somme sector	Renard Craig (1996). *The Somme: graveyard of armies*. Digger History. [http://www.diggerhistory.info/pages-battles/ww1/france/somme-1916.htm]. Accessed April 2024.
182	Exterior view of Mouquet Farm, before its destruction by shellfire	Australian War Memorial. Accession Number J00181. [https://www.awm.gov.au/collection/C1717]. Licensed under PDM 1.0 DEED Public Domain Mark 1.0 Universal. [https://creativecommons.org/publicdomain/mark/1.0/]

Page	Title	Source / Credit
182	Looking south towards Pozieres, this position was the scene of severe trench warfare. Mouquet Farm, October 1916	Australian War Memorial. Accession Number E00005. [https://www.awm.gov.au/collection/C1067]. Licensed under PDM 1.0 DEED Public Domain Mark 1.0 Universal. [https://creativecommons.org/publicdomain/mark/1.0/]
182	AIF Memorial, Mouquet Farm, France, 2012	Diprose Dianne (2012). Flickr. [https://www.flickr.com/photos/spelio/7067318383]. Licensed under CC BY-NC-SA 2.0 DEED Attribution-NonCommercial-ShareAlike 2.0 Generic. [https://creativecommons.org/licenses/by-nc-sa/2.0/]
182	*Mouquet farm, Pozières* – watercolour over pencil on cardboard by Fred Leist (1878–1945), Australian official war artist	Australian War Memorial. Accession Number ART02875. [https://www.awm.gov.au/collection/C176453]. Licensed under PDM 1.0 DEED Public Domain Mark 1.0 Universal. [https://creativecommons.org/publicdomain/mark/1.0/]
184	Stretcher bearers of the 57th Battalion, passing through the cemetery near the mound in Polygon Wood in the Ypres Sector	Australian War Memorial. Accession Number E01912. [https://www.awm.gov.au/collection/C54976]. Licensed under PDM 1.0 DEED Public Domain Mark 1.0 Universal. [https://creativecommons.org/publicdomain/mark/1.0/]
184	Five Australians, members of a field artillery brigade, passing along a duckboard track over mud and water among gaunt bare tree trunks in the devastated Chateau Wood, a portion of one of the battlegrounds in the Ypres salient. Hurley James Francis (Frank), 1917	Australian War Memorial. Accession Number E01220. [https://www.awm.gov.au/collection/C1119]. Licensed under PDM 1.0 DEED Public Domain Mark 1.0 Universal. [https://creativecommons.org/publicdomain/mark/1.0/]
185	Aerial view of the village of Passchendaele before and after the Third Battle of Ypres, 1917	Unknown (1917). Wikimedia Commons. [https://en.wikipedia.org/wiki/File:Passchendaele_aerial_view.jpg]. Source: United Kingdom Government. Photograph Q 42918A from the collections of the Imperial War Museums.
186	Portrait of Sir John Monash taken outside the General's headquarters near Villers-Bretonneux in May, 1918	Mitchell Library, State Library of New South Wales. Reference code 897276. [https://collection.sl.nsw.gov.au/record/9Bv7EOZ9]
186	The Australian Corps Memorial Park at Le Hamel, France	Tasker Belinda (06-11-2008). Anzac memorial at Le Hamel, France, in $8M restoration. *The Courier Mail*. [https://www.couriermail.com.au/news/special-features/timely-honour-for-anzacs/news-story/662dd02500d25ea2383e277529bfa8da]. Accessed April 2024.
187	Villers-Bretonneux Military Cemetery and The Australian War Memorial – Villers-Bretonneux	Villers-Bretonneux Memorial. Commonwealth War Graves Commission. [https://www.cwgc.org/visit-us/find-cemeteries-memorials/cemetery-details/93000/villers-bretonneux-memorial/]. Accessed April 2024.

Page	Title	Source / Credit
188	Etaples Military Cemetery	Etaples Military Cemetery. Commonwealth War Graves Commission. [https://www.cwgc.org/visit-us/find-cemeteries-memorials/cemetery-details/56500/etaples-military-cemetery/]. Accessed April 2024.
189	*Cobbers*, bronze statue depicting the rescue of a wounded soldier – Australian Memorial Park, Fromelles	Crane Robert (2001). *Australian Battlefields of World War 1 – France*. Anzacs in France. [http://www.anzacsinfrance.com/2001/]. Accessed April 2024.
189	Cheng Ling kneels along with her husband and daughter at her grandfather's grave in France, 2009	*South China Morning Post*. China's WWI SCMP Chronicles.
191	Private William Edward (Billy) Sing DCM, ca. 1918	Australian War Memorial. Accession Number P02140.002. [https://www.awm.gov.au/collection/C972045]. Licensed under PDM 1.0 DEED Public Domain Mark 1.0 Universal. [https://creativecommons.org/publicdomain/mark/1.0/]
191	Private Caleb James Shang, DCM and Bar, MM	Australian War Memorial (2020). *Caleb Shang*. [https://www.awm.gov.au/collection/C972045]. Image credit: Cairns Historical Society. Licensed under CC BY-NC 3.0 AU DEED Attribution-NonCommercial 3.0 Australia. [https://creativecommons.org/licenses/by-nc/3.0/au/]
191	Wellington Lee, P00899 SH030 DJG20	Museum of Chinese Australian History. [https://www.chinesemuseum.com.au]. Accessed January 2024.
192	Men bathing, enjoying a swim in the sea after returning from the trenches. Gallipoli Peninsula, Turkey, ca. 1915	Australian War Memorial. Accession Number G00269. [https://www.awm.gov.au/collection/C57095]. Licensed under PDM 1.0 DEED Public Domain Mark 1.0 Universal. [https://creativecommons.org/publicdomain/mark/1.0/]
193	A group of the 46th Australian Infantry Battalion just after coming out of the line in front of Monument Wood, May 1918	Australian War Memorial. Accession Number E02307. [https://www.awm.gov.au/collection/C363901]. Licensed under PDM 1.0 DEED Public Domain Mark 1.0 Universal. [https://creativecommons.org/publicdomain/mark/1.0/]
193	Brigadier General H. E. 'Pompey' Elliott, standing at the door of a captured German Divisional Headquarters near Harbonnieres	Australian War Memorial. Accession Number E02855. [https://www.awm.gov.au/collection/C55009]. Licensed under PDM 1.0 DEED Public Domain Mark 1.0 Universal. [https://creativecommons.org/publicdomain/mark/1.0/]
195	Illustration of method of attachment to fixed object as required in Field Punishment no 1	Australian War Memorial (2021). *Field Punishment*. [https://www.awm.gov.au/articles/encyclopedia/field_punishment]. Licensed under CC BY-NC 3.0 AU DEED Attribution-NonCommercial 3.0 Australia. [https://creativecommons.org/licenses/by-nc/3.0/au/]

Image and Illustration Credits

Page	Title	Source / Credit
196	Australian troops resting during World War I, ca. 1918, by Frank Hurley (1885-1962)	Hurley Frank (1885-1962) (1918). *Australian troops resting during World War I / Frank Hurley*. [https://nla.gov.au/nla.obj-147393480]
200	Laverton, Vic., 14 November 1944. Avro Lancaster bomber aircraft 'G for George' on the airfield at RAAF Station, Laverton	Australian War Memorial. Accession Number VIC1747A. [https://www.awm.gov.au/collection/C293100]. Licensed under PDM 1.0 DEED Public Domain Mark 1.0 Universal. [https://creativecommons.org/publicdomain/mark/1.0/]
204	North African campaigns	Ashley WP (January 1942). *How a Gallant Garrison Held a Mighty Foe at Bay*. ANZAC Day Commemoration Committee. [https://anzacday.org.au/ww2-tobruk]. Accessed April 2024.
206	VX47906 Corporal Frank Joseph Littlejohn (left) and another member of 2/32nd Battalion with a painted bren gun carrier	Australian War Memorial. Accession Number P02522.002. [https://www.awm.gov.au/collection/C331912]. Licensed under PDM 1.0 DEED Public Domain Mark 1.0 Universal. [https://creativecommons.org/publicdomain/mark/1.0/]
207	2/32nd Australian Infantry Battalion holding German counter-attack at El Alamein, Western Desert, Egypt, on 31 October 1942	Australian War Memorial. Accession Number ART22251. [https://www.awm.gov.au/collection/C175326]. Licensed under PDM 1.0 DEED Public Domain Mark 1.0 Universal. [https://creativecommons.org/publicdomain/mark/1.0/].
208	25-pounder guns of the 2/8th Field Regiment at Royal Australian Artillery in action on the coastal sector near El Alamein	Australian War Memorial. Accession Number 024515. [https://www.awm.gov.au/collection/C8311]. Licensed under PDM 1.0 DEED Public Domain Mark 1.0 Universal. [https://creativecommons.org/publicdomain/mark/1.0/]
210	Map of Imperial Japanese advances in the South-west Pacific and South-east Asia areas during the first five months of the Pacific Campaign of the Second World War	*Map of Japanese advances in the Pacific, 1941–1942*. National Museum of Australia. [https://digital-classroom.nma.gov.au/images/map-japanese-advances-pacific-1941-1942]. Image source: United States Army Center of Military History. *The Campaigns of MacArthur in the Pacific, Volume I*.
211	Map of New Guinea showing Kokoda track position	ANZAC Day Commemoration Committee. *The War in Asia and the Pacific*. [https://anzacday.org.au/ww2-the-war-in-asia-and-the-pacific]. Accessed April 2024.
213	*Working party returning to Changi camp*, 1944	Griffin Murray (1944). Australian War Memorial. Accession Number ART25108. [https://www.awm.gov.au/collection/C170563]. Licensed under PDM 1.0 DEED Public Domain Mark 1.0 Universal. [https://creativecommons.org/publicdomain/mark/1.0/]
213	*Changi prison camp, early days*, 1942	Griffin Murray (1942). Australian War Memorial. Accession Number ART24480. [https://www.awm.gov.au/collection/C175795]. Licensed under PDM 1.0 DEED Public Domain Mark 1.0 Universal. [https://creativecommons.org/publicdomain/mark/1.0/]

Page	Title	Source / Credit
214	Thai-Burma Railway, Death Railway	Wolny W (2005). Wikimedia Commons. [https://en.m.wikipedia.org/wiki/File:Death_Railway.png]. Licensed under CC BY-SA 3.0 DEED Attribution-ShareAlike 3.0 Unported. [https://creativecommons.org/licenses/by-sa/3.0/deed.en]
214	Hellfire Pass	Iliff David (2004). Wikimedia Commons. [https://en.m.wikipedia.org/wiki/File:Hellfire_Pass_-_June_2004.jpg]. Licensed under CC BY-SA 2.5 DEED Attribution-ShareAlike 2.5 Generic. [https://creativecommons.org/licenses/by-sa/2.5/deed.en]
215	Burma or Thailand, 1945. An emaciated Australian prisoner of war (POW) showing the effects of beriberi, typical of the condition of many of the Allied prisoners of the Japanese at the end of the war	Australian War Memorial. Accession Number P01433.020. [https://www.awm.gov.au/collection/C195456]. Donor B. Theobald. Licensed under PDM 1.0 DEED Public Domain Mark 1.0 Universal. [https://creativecommons.org/publicdomain/mark/1.0/]
215	Three 'fit' workers at Shimo Songkurai No 1 Camp, standing outside the camp hospital. Burma Thailand Railway: Songkurai, ca. 1943	Australian War Memorial. Accession Number P02569.192, [https://www.awm.gov.au/collection/C340339]. Licensed under PDM 1.0 DEED Public Domain Mark 1.0 Universal [https://creativecommons.org/publicdomain/mark/1.0/]
217	Darwin, NT, 19 February 1942. Scene during the first Japanese air raid on the harbour	Australian War Memorial. Accession Number 134955. [https://www.awm.gov.au/collection/C58182]. Licensed under PDM 1.0 DEED Public Domain Mark 1.0 Universal. [https://creativecommons.org/publicdomain/mark/1.0/]
217	Darwin, NT, 19 February 1942. Bomb damage to the Darwin Post Office and surrounding buildings as a result of the first Japanese air raid	Australian War Memorial. Accession Number P00480.001. [https://www.awm.gov.au/collection/C256477]. Donor W Harvey. Licensed under PDM 1.0 DEED Public Domain Mark 1.0 Universal. [https://creativecommons.org/publicdomain/mark/1.0/]
217	Corrugated iron from air-raid shelter used as a cubby-house in our backyard	Peter Hasker
218	Several men watch as a Japanese midget two-man submarine is raised from the harbour bed	Australian War Memorial. Accession Number 060696. [https://www.awm.gov.au/collection/C48694]. Licensed under PDM 1.0 DEED Public Domain Mark 1.0 Universal. [https://creativecommons.org/publicdomain/mark/1.0/]
220	Map of Kokoda track, Territory of Papua	Touma Elaine (2023). *Map of the Kokoda Trail, Territory of Papua*. National Museum of Australia. [https://digital-classroom.nma.gov.au/images/map-kokoda-trail-territory-papua]. Accessed April 2024.
221	Native bearers (popularly known as 'Fuzzy Wuzzy Angels') carry a wounded Australian soldier on a stretcher	Australian War Memorial. Accession Number 013286. [https://www.awm.gov.au/collection/C32742]. Licensed under PDM 1.0 DEED Public Domain Mark 1.0 Universal. [https://creativecommons.org/publicdomain/mark/1.0/]

Image and Illustration Credits

Page	Title	Source / Credit
222	Native porters are carrying wounded Australian soldiers on stretchers from the jungle battlefield through a mountain stream to the hospital behind the lines, following a sharp clash with Japanese forces	Australian War Memorial. Accession Number 013256. [https://www.awm.gov.au/collection/C32714]. Licensed under PDM 1.0 DEED Public Domain Mark 1.0 Universal. [https://creativecommons.org/publicdomain/mark/1.0/]
223	Papua, 14 July 1942. Kokoda Village and airfield	Australian War Memorial. Accession Number 128400. [https://www.awm.gov.au/collection/C48363]. Licensed under PDM 1.0 DEED Public Domain Mark 1.0 Universal. [https://creativecommons.org/publicdomain/mark/1.0/]
226	Courage, Endurance, Mateship and Sacrifice are the words placed on the pillars at a memorial in Isurava	Melocco Stone. [http://www.melocco.com.au/projects]. Accessed April 2024.
226	The Isurava Memorial honours the Australians and Papua New Guineans who fought and died on the Kokoda Track in World War II	Swanston Tim and Gunga Theckla (01-05-2023). *Major route into the Kokoda track appears to have been blockaded amid tour operator feud*. ABC News. [https://www.abc.net.au/news/2023-05-01/major-route-into-the-kokoda-track-appears-to-have-been-blockaded/102285692]. Accessed April 2024.
227	Members of the 39th Battalion, AMF, parade after weeks of fighting in dense jungle during the Kokoda campaign	Australian War Memorial. Accession Number 013289. [https://www.awm.gov.au/collection/C37797]. Licensed under PDM 1.0 DEED Public Domain Mark 1.0 Universal. [https://creativecommons.org/publicdomain/mark/1.0/]
230	The 'Golden Stairs' on the Kokoda Track between Uberi and Imita Ridge	Australian War Memorial. Accession Number 026821. [https://www.awm.gov.au/collection/C10419]. Licensed under PDM 1.0 DEED Public Domain Mark 1.0 Universal. [https://creativecommons.org/publicdomain/mark/1.0/]
230	Allies retake Kokoda. Australian flag is raised as troops enter Kokoda, watched by a group of Australian troops. John Earl (Earl) McNeil, Kokoda Track, 14 November 1942	Australian War Memorial. Accession Number 013572. [https://www.awm.gov.au/collection/C33002]. Licensed under PDM 1.0 DEED Public Domain Mark 1.0 Universal. [https://creativecommons.org/publicdomain/mark/1.0/]
234	MacArthur Chambers, Brisbane, Queensland	Kgbo (2018). Wikimedia Commons. [https://commons.wikimedia.org/wiki/File:MacArthur_Chambers,_Brisbane,_Queensland_01.jpg]. Licensed under CC BY-SA 4.0 DEED Attribution-ShareAlike 4.0 International. [https://creativecommons.org/licenses/by-sa/4.0/deed.en]
236	Letter from one of the tennis players	Hasker family.

Page	Title	Source / Credit
236	Buna, Papua New Guinea. General Sir Thomas Blamey and Lieutenant General RL Eichelberger at the entrance to a Japanese pillbox near the Buna airstrip, 1943	Australian War Memorial. Accession Number 014091. [https://www.awm.gov.au/collection/C194789]. Licensed under PDM 1.0 DEED Public Domain Mark 1.0 Universal. [https://creativecommons.org/publicdomain/mark/1.0/]
236	Rockhampton, Queensland, Australia, April 1943. General Douglas MacArthur and Lieutenant General Eichelberger inspect the 542nd Regimental Area. Colonel Fowlkes and Lieutenant Colonel Simpson escort our distinguished visitors	Dunn Peter (2003). *542nd Engineer Amphibian Regiment, 2nd Engineer Amphibian Brigade in Australia During WWII*. Australia @ War. [https://www.ozatwar.com/usarmy/542ndengineeramphibianregiment.htm] Image credit: Steve Schaffer. Accessed April 2024.
237	The Sergeants' Mess, Zilzie Beach	Peter Hasker
238	ANZAC Day 1916 dinner menu and seating arrangements	Peter Hasker
241	ANZAC Day parade, Brisbane, 2007	*The Courier Mail*
242	Lone Pine Memorial, Gallipoli, 2012	Lascar Jorge (2012). Flickr. [https://www.flickr.com/photos/jlascar/8708815317]. Licensed under CC BY 2.0 DEED Attribution 2.0 Generic. [https://creativecommons.org/licenses/by/2.0/]
242	Mustafa Kemal Ataturk Memorial, Canberra unveiled in 1985 honours the heroism and sacrifice of both the ANZAC and Turkish troops who took part in the Gallipoli campaign	Ellis Peter (2005). Wikimedia Commons. [https://en.m.wikipedia.org/wiki/File:AS_Kemal_Ataturk_1.jpg]. Licensed under CC BY-SA 3.0 DEED Attribution-ShareAlike 3.0 Unported. [https://creativecommons.org/licenses/by-sa/3.0/deed.en]
243	Rockhampton cenotaph, Diggers Park, Botanical Gardens	Photo by Ricki Palmer.
245	Anzac Day 2019	Peter Hasker
247	St John's Anglican Church, Parramatta	*St John's Anglican Cathedral*. Hope Media Ltd. [https://hope1032.com.au/church/anglican-diocese-of-sydney/st-johns-anglican-cathedral/]. Accessed April 2024.
250	Woman in front of a wattle and daub hut with bark roof, Hill End, New South Wales, ca.1872	Bayliss Charles (1850-1897), Merlin Beaufoy (approximately 1830-1873) and American & Australasian Photographic Company (Sydney, NSW) (1872). *Woman in front of a wattle and daub hut with bark roof, Hill End, New South Wales, ca.1872 [picture]*. [http://nla.gov.au/nla.obj-148052052]

Image and Illustration Credits

Page	Title	Source / Credit
250	Standing woman outside a selector's bark hut, Australia, ca. 1895	Kerry & Co. (1895). *Standing woman outside a selector's bark hut, Australia, ca. 1895 [transparency] / Kerry & Co.* [https://nla.gov.au/nla.obj-149700798]
252	*The drover's wife*, ca. 1945. Artist Russell Drysdale	Drysdale Russell (ca. 1945). *The drover's wife*. irn: 76616. Oil on canvas 51.5 (h) x 61.5 (w) cm, framed (overall) 702 (h) x 796 (w) x 87 (d) mm. National Gallery of Australia, Canberra. Gift of American Friends of the National Gallery of Australia, Inc., New York, NY, USA, made possible with the generous support of Mr and Mrs Benno Schmidt of New York and Esperance, Western Australia, 1987. © Estate of Russell Drysdale. 87.1612
255	Annette Kellerman in her famous custom swimsuit, ca. 1900	Bain News Service, publisher (ca. 1900). Wikimedia Commons. [https://commons.wikimedia.org/wiki/File:Annette_Kellerman1.jpg]. Source: This image is available from the United States Library of Congress's Prints and Photographs division under the digital ID ggbain.03569.
255	Palm Beach police measuring swimsuit length, 1925	Ferris Vintage Photos (1920s). Etsy. [https://www.etsy.com/au/listing/1009113865/measuring-swimsuits-photo-beach-police]. Accessed April 2024.
256	Women's College, Sydney University	Peter Hasker
256	Adah Stuart photos	Peter Hasker
257	*Kooltandra* sketch by Ben Wickham, 1973	Peter Hasker
260	Simpson Desert, aerial view of parallel dunes	Charlie Atherton
261	Tom Kruse on the Birdsville Track. Photo is a still from the film *The Back of Beyond*, John Heyer, 1954	Lennon T (14-09-2016). Filmmaker John Heyer went to the back of beyond to put real Australia on the world screen. *The Daily Telegraph*. [https://www.dailytelegraph.com.au/news/filmmaker-john-heyer-went-to-the-back-of-beyond-to-put-real-australia-on-the-world-screen/news-story/5a08aece8a11d33ea300cecb455d1450]
261	Camel train on its way from Oodnadatta in South Australia to Alice Springs in the Northern Territory in 1872, a distance of over 500 km	Department of Information (1872). Commonwealth of Australia (National Archives of Australia). Citation: NAA: A1200, L26071. [https://www.naa.gov.au/students-and-teachers/learning-resources/learning-resource-themes/science-and-technology/communication/last-camel-train-used-deliver-mail-outback-australia]. Licensed under CC BY 4.0 DEED Attribution 4.0 International. [https://creativecommons.org/licenses/by/4.0/deed.en]
262	Refuelling at QANTAS hangar, Longreach	Morse Teel Caroline (09-05-2014). *9 Things You Didn't Know About Flying QANTAS*. SmarterTravel Media. [https://www.smartertravel.com/9-things-you-didnt-know-about-flying-qantas/?photo=64958]. Source: QANTAS Founders Museum. Accessed April 2024.
262	Early premises of QANTAS, in Longreach, Queensland	Anon (n.d.). *Early premises of QANTAS, in Longreach, Queensland*. Brisbane: John Oxley Library, State Library of Queensland. Record number 99183506559302061.
262	QANTAS hangar, Cloncurry	Anon (2004). *Air hangar for Qantas Empire Airways Ltd*. Brisbane: John Oxley Library, State Library of Queensland. Record number 99183513715802061.

Page	Title	Source / Credit
264	*The bush burial*, Frederick McCubbin, 1890	McCubbin Frederick (1890). *The bush burial*. Geelong Gallery. Purchased by public subscription, 1900. [https://www.geelonggallery.org.au/collection/explore-the-collection/frederick-mccubbin]
264	*The pioneer*, Frederick McCubbin, 1904	McCubbin Frederick (1904). *The pioneer*. Located at National Gallery of Victoria. Source: Wikimedia Commons. [https://commons.wikimedia.org/wiki/File:Frederick_McCubbin_-_The_pioneer_-_Google_Art_Project.jpg]
264	*The selector's hut (Whelan on the log)*, 1890, Arthur Streeton (1867 – 1943)	Streeton Arthur (1890). *The selector's hut (Whelan on the log)*. National Gallery of Australia. Accession Number 61.15. [https://searchthecollection.nga.gov.au/object/46752]
265	Highways, roads and rail lines map	Sieuwert Oost. IA Connections. Publishers of the Australia Tourist Guide. [https://www.sydney-australia.biz/maps/australia/australia-rail-map.php]
266	Map of World political Robinson Asia-Australia centered	One Stop Map. License purchased April 2024.
289	Ju Raku En Japanese garden, Toowoomba, 2022	Peter Hasker
289	Versailles, June 2013	jm jmgbjm (2013). Flickr. [https://www.flickr.com/photos/jmgbjm/17989947075].
289	Nindooinbah homestead, Beaudesert district, Queensland, 2012	Corbett Gary (2012). *Restoration a labour of love. Nindooinbah Homestead. Our Lifestyle*, Nov/Dec 2012. [https://www.nindooinbah.com.au/wp-content/uploads/2017/08/NindooinbahHomestead-2012.pdf]
289	Camped out in brigalow country, *New Twin Hills* outstation, Clermont district, 1962. The author sitting in the distance on the right.	Peter Hasker
289	Holding cattle by a billabong, *New Twin Hills* outstation, Clermont district, 1962	Peter Hasker
293	Bulk carrier at Port Hedland, 2019	Sam Brown
293	Map of Australia's coal terminals, 2012	Zouillon (03-12-2012). Wikimedia Commons. [https://commons.wikimedia.org/wiki/File:Map_australian%27s_coal_terminales.PNG]. Licensed under CC BY-SA 3.0 DEED Attribution-ShareAlike 3.0 Unported. [https://creativecommons.org/licenses/by-sa/3.0/deed.en]

Glossary

Term	Meaning
8-hour day	8-hour working day
About time	Something now happening or about to happen should have happened earlier
At home	You feel comfortable in the place or situation that you are in
Backbone	Symbol of strength and character
Belly filled with fire	Determination to succeed
Brown nosers	Those who try too hard to please someone, especially someone in a position of authority, in a way that other people find unpleasant
Bushranger	An outlaw living in the bush
Campfire oven	A metal pot or box with a heavy lid, used for baking over an open fire
Clap sticks	Traditional Aboriginal twin sticks tapped together to create sounds to accompany dancing or songs and usually made out of wood of eucalyptus
Come to terms with	Come to accept (a new and painful or difficult event or situation)
Cow cockies	Small-scale farmers
Didgeridoo	An Aboriginal wind instrument (hollow branches or stems of trees) played with vibrating lips using circular breathing to produce a continuous drone to accompany dancing or singing
Dig in	To establish defensive position especially by digging trenches
Emancipists	Convicts who have served out their sentence or have been pardoned
Fair go	To give somebody a reasonable chance at something; to treat them fairly
Free-settlers	People who chose to go to New Holland (now Australia)
Glory box	A piece of furniture commonly used by unmarried young women to collect items, e.g. clothing and household linen, in anticipation of married life
Goyder Line	A boundary line across South Australia corresponding to a rainfall boundary believed to indicate the edge of the area suitable for agriculture
Have a go	Attempt to do something

Term	Meaning
Hopeless with money	Wasteful with money
Kiss of death	An action or event that causes certain failure
Kowtow	To act in an excessively subservient manner
Looked down on	To think of or treat (someone or something) as unimportant or not worthy of respect
Making do	Managing with the limited or inadequate means available
Mate and mateship	An Australian cultural idiom that embodies equality, loyalty and friendship
Nail in the coffin	Something that makes it more likely that someone or something will fail, be destroyed, etc.
Navvy	A labourer employed in the excavation and construction of a road, railway or canal
No-man's land	The space between opposing trenches or lines of troops in war.
Ponzi scheme	An investment fraud that pays existing investors with funds collected from new investors
Pricking the pompous	Bringing down those who think they are more important than they really are
Push came to shove	Critical time when a decision or action must be made
Rattle of convict bones	Having a convict ancestor
Read the Riot Act	To chastise loudly, or to issue a severe warning
Run riot	Behave in a violent and unrestrained way
Shoot through	To leave, especially in order to avoid somebody/something
Skeletons in the cupboard	Keeping secret a bad or embarrassing fact about oneself
Squatter	Person who unlawfully occupies an uninhabited building or unused land/large-scale sheep or cattle farmer
Steel oneself	To make (oneself) ready for something difficult or unpleasant
Tall poppies	People who are conspicuously successful and whose success frequently attracts envious hostility
Times got hard	A period of great difficulty, especially financially
White ants something	Tells stories to undermine others like termites eat away buildings

About the Author

The author was born in September 1938 in Rockhampton, Queensland where he attended primary school. He went to secondary school in Victoria, after which he studied for a Bachelor of Agricultural Science at Melbourne University.

Many school holidays were spent on a cattle property near Rockhampton owned by an aunt, a medical practitioner. An aboriginal family residing there carried out daily operations and stock work. While in Victoria, he also spent holidays on a sheep property in the Western District. On graduating from university, the author worked for two years on a large cattle property, *Elgin Downs*, in Central Queensland. At that time the technological advances and changes that began to define the 1960s were only just emerging. The stockmen (ringers) were hardened, skilled men who took immense pride in their work ethic and horsemanship, with horses still playing a central role in cattle operations. Roads remained unsealed and telephone communication was conducted over a 'party line'.

A horse-riding accident abruptly ended the author's life in the bush, opening an unexpected new chapter. He spent two years in hospital, which provided ample time for reading. Many of the staff were immigrants from Northern Europe and Russia. After his discharge, he embarked on house construction with a Slovenian friend he had met in hospital. When that proved unsuccessful, he completed a Diploma in Information Processing, which led to a twenty-year career with the Queensland Department of Primary Industries (DPI).

Upon retiring from The DPI the author obtained a Certificate in TESOL (Teaching English to Speakers of Other Languages) from Trinity College, London. He then worked part-time for five years at a small English language college in Brisbane's CBD, before volunteering for nine years as a teacher's aide in migrant English classes at South Brisbane TAFE.

After leaving hospital in 1964, he settled in Sunnybank, Brisbane, relying heavily on personal assistance from others for daily living. In the first 20 years, his caregivers were Australian-born, but since then, they have come from 22 different countries, spanning every continent.

The genesis of this book was a simple question from a Chinese primary school student: 'What is an Australian?' When he visited China, the author spent two afternoons with senior classes at the Xiaogan City Normal High School telling them about Australia and answering their questions. The project gained further momentum when the author learned he could possibly deliver a series of lectures about Australia at a Chinese university.

Further inspiration came from the many questions about Australia posed by caregivers and their friends, plus the striking ignorance of Australia and its history he observed in his nieces and nephews, their children and fellow native-born Australians. The author's struggle to fully answer the Chinese school student's question, coupled with the widespread lack of awareness among native-born Australians about their country's demographic changes, led him to reflect deeply on the concept of nationhood – an exploration undertaken in Section 2 of the book: "Where are we going?"

www.ingramcontent.com/pod-product-compliance
Lightning Source LLC
Chambersburg PA
CBHW081418300426
44109CB00019BA/2335